LIVES AND TIMES

A WORLD HISTORY READER

VOLUME II

EDITED BY

JAMES P. HOLOKA
EASTERN MICHIGAN UNIVERSITY

JIU-HWA L. UPSHUR
EASTERN MICHIGAN UNIVERSITY

WEST PUBLISHING COMPANY
MINNEAPOLIS/ST. PAUL   NEW YORK   LOS ANGELES   SAN FRANCISCO

WEST'S COMMITMENT TO THE ENVIRONMENT

In 1906, West Publishing Company began recycling materials left over from the production of books. This began a tradition of efficient and responsible use of resources. Today, up to 95% of our legal books and 70% of our college texts and school texts are printed on recycled, acid-free stock. West also recycles nearly 22 million pounds of scrap paper annually—the equivalent of 181,717 trees. Since the 1960s, West has devised ways to capture and recycle waste inks, solvents, oils, and vapors created in the printing process. We also recycle plastics of all kinds, wood, glass, corrugated cardboard, and batteries, and have eliminated the use of Styrofoam book packaging. We at West are proud of the longevity and the scope of our commitment to the environment.

Production, Prepress, Printing and Binding by West Publishing Company.

Artwork by Christian Holoka.

 TEXT IS PRINTED ON 10% POST CONSUMER RECYCLED PAPER    PRINTED WITH SOY INK™

CONTENTS

PREFACE

Lives and Times is intended to introduce undergraduate history students to original source materials that are both intrinsically interesting and useful for the development of a deeper understanding of history. In considering the vast array of available sources, we decided wherever possible to select autobiographical and biographical accounts, in the latter case, preferring items written by authors contemporary with their subjects rather than works by modern scholars. Such accounts tell us what the people thought about themselves, the world they lived in, and the problems they faced living together.

Biographies and autobiographies have always held a special attraction for students of history. Our discipline is multi-faceted. To gain a detailed knowledge of any era or person, the historian must consult various types of sources of information, including statistical data, legal documents, government files, and diaries and personal letters, among others. No single collection of readings on world history can embrace all these types sources; nor can beginning history students be expected to deal with some of the more complex documents. We have chosen to limit ourselves primarily to biographical and autobiographical sources because of their human interest and the light they shed on their subjects' motivations, emotions, ambitions, and conflicts. Moreover, the study of people of different eras and cultures lends immediacy to history and bridges the gap between centuries and continents through our common humanity. When suitable contemporary biographical or autobiographical information was lacking, we have drawn on other sources such as poetry, inscriptions, archaeological reports, and newspaper accounts to help form an accurate picture of life in other eras.

The selections in this anthology tell the stories of people from the earliest times to the present around the world; they reflect a wide range of perspectives and experiences, featuring men, women, and children from many different walks of life and social classes. Kings, queens, generals, statesmen and government leaders, great religious leaders and philosophers are represented because their lives and deeds shaped history. Accounts of major battles and political affairs are featured for the same reason. However, we have sought to put the spotlight on individuals from many other walks of life, including explorers, inventors, scientists, recluses, merchants, farmers, factory workers, priests, nuns, and even slaves. Throughout, we have aimed to lead readers to a wider, global view of history by exploring the lives and thoughts of ordinary and extraordinary men and women, with all their human idiosyncrasies, strengths, and frailties.

Although we have relied mostly on sources originally written in English or already translated into English, we have also translated from a number Greek, Latin, French, and Chinese sources. We hope the result is a truly ecumenical collection that illuminates the lives and times of many people from antiquity to the present.

The readings in the two volumes of *Lives and Times* are grouped in eleven sections, by chronology and subject matter. A short essay introduces each section and explains the mutual relationship of the readings grouped therein.

This anthology is not intended for use in association with any one textbook; rather, it is designed to accompany any textbook in a variety of courses. Instructors may choose from the anthology to suit their own purposes. Each reading is equipped with an introduction providing essential background. Introductions are followed by questions meant to assist the reader in identifying important points in the selection.

For their encouragement in our endeavor and for specific suggestions, we are thankful to many colleagues, especially professors George Cassar, Richard Goff, Michael Homel, and Janice Terry, and to Mr. Charles Zwinak. We are grateful also to Professor Kuei-sheng Chang of the Geography Department of the University of Washington for graciously letting us use a chapter of his Ph.D. dissertation on the Ming Chinese explorer Cheng Ho (Reading 6.12), to Mrs. Helen Hsiung (Mao Yen-wen) for allowing us to translate a passage from her privately published memoirs, *Wan Shih* (Reading 11.10), to Professor Benjamin Stolz of the Department of Slavic Languages and Literature of the University of Michigan for his kind permission to quote from his translation of Konstantin Mihailovic's *Memoirs of a Janissary* (Reading 6.6), and to Professor Paul Kahn for permitting us to excerpt from his translation of *The Secret History of the Mongols* (Reading 6.1). A number of public institutions in several countries allowed us to quote from their publications without fee. We are indebted to the University of Michigan's Harlan Hatcher Library for privileges and the guidance of its staff. We are much beholden to Ms. Nancy Snyder, head secretary of the Department of History, Eastern Michigan University, for her administrative assistance. Mr. Daniel Sprung of the Eastman Kodak Company in Rochester, New York was instrumental to our production of camera-ready pages. At West Educational Publishing, Mr. Clark Baxter, Ms. Patricia MacDonald, and their staff were consistently helpful and supportive. Finally, we thank Christian Holoka for the extraordinary talent and efficiency he brought to the creation of the art that graces our collection.

J.P.H.
J-H.L.U.

SECTION 6

GREAT LAND EMPIRES

The readings in this section describe the great land empires that arose across Asia and Europe beginning in the early second millennium and lasting into the early modern era. The first was also the largest of any empire the world had seen: the Mongol Empire was founded by Genghis Khan, one of the world's most terrifying conquerors, and enlarged by his sons and grandsons. Several readings offer views of the Mongol empire from different perspectives, through the eyes of proud Mongol chroniclers, through those of terrified Russian monks in a city besieged by Mongol armies, and through the awestruck eyes of the Venetian traveler Marco Polo who served Genghis Khan's grandson Kubilai Khan, who described China under Mongol rule. Timurlane was descended from Genghis Khan, and his ruthless conquest formed the final chapter of several centuries of Mongol ravages.

Although not nearly as extensive as the Mongol realm, several great and enduring empires arose out of the ashes of Mongol imperialism. They ranged from the Mamluk dynasty of Turkic slaves who ruled Egypt to the Ottoman Turks who finally extinguished the Byzantine Empire and built an empire that embraced West Asia, southern Russia and the Balkan Peninsula in Europe, and all North Africa. They included also the Moghul Empire in India and the Ming Empire in China. The accounts selected here range from autobiographical tales of wars and conquest to accounts of life in the empires as recorded by visiting ambassadors and private travelers to a recounting of the naval expeditions of China's greatest admiral around Asia and East Africa.

The Russian chronicle of Mongol barbarity and oppression explain Russian fear of the "Yellow Peril" even in the twentieth century; Marco Polo's tales of the fabulous East inspired later European voyages of explorations; the horrific impression that Timurlane's army made across northern India led Indians to call all later central Asian conquerors Mongols (or Moghuls). Similarly Serbian nationalism originated in the crucible of the Ottoman conquest and dominion of their country for six hundred years, while Hindu resistance to Muslim conquerors was epitomized in the desperate but ineffective sacrifice of the Rajputs. In a somewhat different vein, China's Ming emperor sent grand naval expeditions to show the flag across the Asian continent to signify China's expulsion of the hated Mongols and recovery of national pride. These readings are thus instructive in their own right and for their depiction of the lasting effects of historical events on peoples and nations.

▶ **Chingis Khan**

CHINGIS KHAN AND HIS SON

Since earliest times various nomadic groups have lived and wandered in Mongolia, a landlocked region between present-day China and Russia. The Mongols, who claimed descent from the feared Hsiung-nu of a thousand years earlier, became an identifiable people in the early 1100s. They were organized into clans; related clans formed tribes. Tribal chieftains were elected by clan nobles for their military prowess, and retained power by success in war. War captives became slaves, which motivated the strong to go to war. Mongols learned to ride as others learned to walk; they and their horses were equally renowned for their stamina and toughness. In war all men were soldiers.

Like other nomads in the region, Mongols practiced unlimited polygyny [one husband, many wives], a man's power and status being defined by the number of his wives. The first wife, however, enjoyed unique privileges--her sons had first claim to succeed their father, and she could act as regent for sons.

Temujin (1155-1227) was born in a time of conflict both among Mongol tribes and against neighboring Turkish peoples. Tribes feuded and fought for grazing land, animals, and women. Temujin was a great military genius. Inured in youth to hardship caused by his father's early death, he capitalized on prevailing conditions and trends in his rise to power. For example, when a sharp drop in temperatures in the region reduced the grass available for the nomads' animals, the Mongols sought access to outside resources through raids and war. Conflicts with non Mongols fostered a growing sense of ethnic identity and unity. Initially relying on family and friends, Temujin organized a disciplined army with an effective command structure and intelligence network. He ruthlessly used massacres and enslavement to terrorize victims into submission. On the other hand, he liberally rewarded his supporters for loyalty and success.

In 1206, after subduing all other tribal groups in Mongolia, Temujin was acclaimed Chingis (or Genghis) Khan ("universal ruler"). In his remaining twenty-one years, Chingis led his Mongols to conquer all north and northwest China, Afghanistan, Persia, and Central Asia. He also paved the way for his sons and grandsons to expand the Mongol realm across much of Eurasia till it became the biggest land empire in history.

The Secret History of the Mongols was written in the thirteenth century in the newly invented Mongolian script by compilers from oral traditions. Although the original Mongolian texts have perished, a later Chinese translation called *Yuan Ch'ao Pi Shih (The Secret History of the Mongols)* provides the basis for all modern translations.

The Secret History of the Mongols begins with the mythical origins of the Mongols, continues with Temujin's family and early struggles, his election as Chingis Khan, his military organization, and his campaigns in north China against the Chin Empire (Cathay, in present-day northwest China), and the Middle East. Its final section deals Chingis's death, the election of his third son Ogotai as successor in 1228/9, Ogotai's campaign in the Middle East and eastern Europe, and an assessment of his reign.

This selection is from *The Secret History of the Mongols*. It deals with Temujin's election as Chingis Khan, his campaigns, and the election of his successor.

QUESTIONS:

1) What did Temuchin's supporters promise when they elected him Chingis Khan? What does the promise reflect of their values?

2) Show an example of an effective Mongol military tactic.

3) How did Chingis Khan arrange his succession and how did his followers ratify it?

Altan, Khuchar, and Sacha Beki conferred with each other there [at Temujin's camp at Kingurcha Stream], and then said to Temujin:

"We want you to be khan. Temujin, if you'll be our khan we'll search through the spoils for the beautiful women and virgins, for the great palace tents, for the young virgins and loveliest women, for the finest geldings and mares. We'll gather all these and bring them to you. When we go off to hunt for wild game we'll go out first to drive them together for you to kill. We'll drive the wild animals of the steppe together so that their bellies are touching. We'll drive the wild game of the mountains together so that they stand leg to leg. If we disobey your command during battle take away our possessions, our children, and wives. Leave us behind in the dust, cutting off our heads where we stand and letting them fall to the ground. If we disobey your counsel in peacetime take away our tents and our goods, our wives, and our children. Leave us behind when you move, abandoned in the desert without a protector."

Having given their word, having taken this oath, they proclaimed Temujin khan of the Mongol and gave him the name Chingis Khan....

And so in the Year of the Tiger, having set in order the lives of all the people whose tents are protected by the skirts of felt, the Mongol clans assembled at the head of the Onan. They raised a white standard of nine tails and proclaimed Chingis Khan the Great Khan....

After this in the Year of the Sheep Chingis Khan set out to fight the people of Cathay [the Chin Empire in north China]. First he took the city of Fu-chou then marching through the Wild Fox Pass he took Hsuan-te-fu. From here he

sent out an army under Jebe's command to take the fortress at the Chu-yung Kuan. When Jebe arrived he saw the Chu-yung Kuan was well defended, so he said:

"I'll trick them and make them come out in the open. I'll pretend to retreat and when they come out I'll attack them."

So Jebe retreated and the Cathayan army cried:

"Let's go after them!"

They poured out of their fortifications until the valleys and mountainsides were full of their soldiers. Jebe retreated to Sondi-i-wu Ridge and there he turned his army around to attack as the enemy rushed towards him in waves. The Cathayan army was beaten and close behind Jebe's forces Chingis Khan commanding the great Middle Army attacked as well, forcing the Cathayan army to retreat, killing the finest and most courageous soldiers of Cathay, the Jurchin and Khara Khitan fighters, slaughtering them along the sides of Chu-yung Kuan so that their bodies lay piled up like rotting trees. Jebe charged on through the gates of Chu-yung Kuan, capturing all the forts in the pass, and Chingis Khan led his army through to pitch camp at Lung-hu-tai. He sent an army to attack the capital at Chung-tu and sent others out to take all the cities and towns nearby. He sent Jebe off with an army to attack the city of Tung-ching. When Jebe arrived at the walls of the city, he attacked, but he saw that it couldn't be taken this way. So he hastily abandoned his encampment outside Tung-ching, leaving a great deal behind just outside the city walls, and retreated to a place six days march from the city. This caused the people of Tung-ching to drop their defenses and open their gates to loot the camp our army had left. Then Jebe turned his army around, and having each of his men take a spare horse, they rode back across the six days march in one night, surprising the enemy outside their walls and taking the city of Tung-ching. After he'd taken the city Jebe rejoined Chingis Khan....

[The king of Chin or Cathay decided to surrender as a result of his defeats.] He sent a message offering tribute to Chingis Khan and gave him one of his daughters as a wife. The gates of Chung-tu [capital of the Chin empire] were opened and they set out great quantities of gold, silver, satins, and other goods, letting the men of the Mongol army divide it themselves depending on how many beasts each had to carry the load....

During the same campaign Chingis Khan went off to fight the Tanghut. When he arrived at their cities the Tanghut leader, Burkhan Khan said to him:

"I'll surrender to you and be like your right hand, giving all my strength to you."

He gave Chingis Khan one of his daughters, Chakha, as a wife....

[Subsequently the Tanghut king attempted to reassert his independence, was badly defeated, and again offered to surrender.] He brought out images of the Buddha made from gold. Then followed bowls and vessels made of silver and gold, nine and nine, young boys and young maidens, nine and nine, fine geldings and fine camels, nine and nine, and every other thing in his realm, each arranged according to its color and form, nine and nine.

Chingis Khan ordered Burkhan to present himself outside the closed door of his tent. Burkhan was told to wait there three days, and on the third day Chingis Khan decided what to do....

Chingis Khan said:

"See that he is executed."...

Chingis Khan took everything from the Tanghut people.... He ordered that the men and women of their cities be killed, their children and grandchildren, saying:

"As long as I can eat food and still say, 'Make everyone who live in their cities vanish,' kill them all and destroy their homes. As long as I am still alive keep up the slaughter."

This is because the Tanghut people made a promise they didn't keep. Chingis Khan had gone to war with the Tanghut people a second time. He had destroyed them, and coming back to Mongolia, in the Year of the Pig, Chingis Khan ascended to Heaven. After he had ascended [his wife] Yesui Khatum was given most of the Tanghut people who remained....

In the Year of the Rat a Great Assembly was called. All the people of the Right Wing led by [his second son] Chagadai and [his grandson] Jochi's son Batu came. All the people of the Left Wing arrived, led by Prince Odchigin and Khasar's sons, Yegu and Yesunge [Chingis's sons by his secondary wives]. The people of the Middle Wing were led by [Chingis's fourth son] Tolui, and with him were all the royal daughters and their husbands. This huge assembly met at Kodegu Aral on the Keluren River, and according to the wishes of Chingis Khan they raised up Ogodei [Chingis's third son] as the Great Khan. Chagadai raised up his younger brother as the Khan and both Elder Brother Chagadai and Tolui delivered the nightguard, the archers, and the eight thousand dayguards to Ogodei, the same men who had guarded the golden life of their father Chingis Khan, along with his private slaves and the ten thousand men who had served him. They also gave him command of all the people of the Middle Wing.

Once Ogodei Khan had allowed himself to be named Khan...he took the advice of Elder Brother Chagadai and sent Okhotur and Mungetu to relieve Chormakhan, who was still at war with the Caliphate Sultan of Baghdad, a war his father Chingis Khan had left unfinished. Subetei the Brave had already crossed the Volga and Ural rivers into the lands of the Kanghli, Kipchakh, Russian, Magyar, and Bulghar peoples. He had gone to war against the city of Kiev and had run into great resistance there. So Ogodei sent off an army to relieve him, led by Jochi's eldest son Batu....."

Kahn, Paul. *The Secret History of the Mongols: The Origins of Chingis Khan.* [Based on *Yuan Ch'ao Pi Shih*. Trans. Francis W. Cleaves.] San Francisco: North Point Press, 1984. Pp. 48-49, 125, 160-162, 180-182.

MONGOLS SEEN THROUGH RUSSIAN EYES

► Mongol Horseman

Between Temuchin's election as Genghis Khan or Universal Ruler in 1206 and Timurlane's death while marching towards China in 1405, Mongol hordes terrified and terrorized much of Asia and Europe. Genghis and his descendants conquered and plundered Korea, China, Persia, Central Asia, the Middle East, Russia to the Baltic and Caspian seas and Caucasus mountains, and Europe to the gates of Vienna and Adriatic Sea. With their unmatched cavalry and uncanny ability to master new military techniques, they dominated the largest empire the world had seen. They ruled conquered lands ruthlessly as an occupation force until, divided and weakened, they were overthrown by their resurgent victims. Mongol conquests altered the course of history in most of the lands of their victims, generally for the worse.

Genghis Khan's armies first invaded southern Russia in 1224 and plundered the Grand Duchy of Kiev. After his death the sons of his oldest son received southern Russia as their patrimony. Mongols who settled in southern Russia were called the Golden Horde. To consolidate and extend the Golden Horde's territory, Genghis's sons and grandsons later extended their conquests through northern Russia, taking Moscow and other cities, then proceeding to Poland and Hungary. Mongol rule was short-lived in the rest of Europe, but during the next two centuries most of Russia submitted to Mongol overlordship, paying heavy tribute, which was often collected by force. Mongol domination also isolated Russia from Europe and European political and cultural developments.

Novgorod was a Russian principality: its capital was about a hundred miles southeast of St. Petersburg. It was a prosperous trading city in the Middle Ages, comparable to Florence and Bruges, and enjoyed great wealth. It was unique in Russia because its citizens had republican freedoms and elected their princes. Located in the northern frontier of Russia, Novgorod was moreover a bastion of Russian culture, which it upheld in numerous battles against neighboring Swedes, Germans, and Lithuanians.

Novgorod was also unique because it escaped Mongol conquest. At the time of the Mongol invasion Novgorod was ruled by Prince Alexander (1218-1263), who received the surname Nevsky for his epochal defeat of the Swedes on the Neva River near present-day city St. Petersburg. His feats made him a hero to Russians, and a saint of the Russian Orthodox church. Although cold, wet weather and swampy terrain compelled the Mongols to lift their siege of Novgorod, Alexander Nevsky submitted to the Mongols so that his city could be spared the devastation inflicted on other Russian cities. Thus he obeyed the "Tartar Tsar," paid the tribute Mongols assessed (even protecting the hated Mongol assessors against harm from Novgorod's outraged citizens), and rendered personal homage (in 1247) at Sarai, capital of the Golden Horde. Novgorod and the rest of Russia were liberated from Mongol rule at the end of the fourteenth century.

The Chronicles of Novgorod, 1016-1471, written by anonymous monks, record events that affected the principality. The selection that follows deals with the Mongol invasions and rule, in Novgorod and Russia generally. Russians, like many other Christians, believed the Mongols, or Tartars, had been sent by God to punish them for their sins.

QUESTIONS:

1) How did the Mongol invaders appear to the Russian chroniclers?
2) What did the Mongols do to instill fear among Russians?
3) By what means and at what price did Prince Alexander save Novgorod from Mongol rule?

[In 1224] unknown tribes came, whom no one exactly knows, who they are, nor whence they came out, nor what their language is, nor what race they are, nor what their faith is; but they call them Tartars.... God alone knows who they are and whence they came out.... For we have heard that they have captured many countries, slaughtered a quantity of the godless Yas, Obez, Kasog and Polovets people and wrought much evil to the Russian Land.... And the cursed Polovets people, the survivors of those who were killed, escaped [to Russia] ... and brought many gifts: horses and camels, buffaloes and girls; and they gave gifts [of these] to the Russian *Knyazes* [princes], saying thus: "Our land they have taken away to-day; and yours will be taken to-morrow."....

[The Russians decided to give help. One of their princes] Mstislav having forded the Dnieper went across with 1,000 men, against the Tartar outposts, and defeated them and the remainder of them fled ... to the Polovets *kurgan* [fort].... And the Tartars turned back from the river Dnieper, and we know not whence they came, nor where they hid themselves again; God knows whence he fetched them against us for our sins....

[In 1236] the godless Tartars having come, they captured all the Bolgar Land [Bulgaria on the Volga, the present-day Kazan, etc.] and took their great city, and they slew all, both wives and children....

[In 1238] foreigners called Tartars came in countless numbers, like locusts, into the land of Ryazan, and on first coming they halted at the river Nukhla, and took it, and halted in camp there. And thence they sent their emissaries to the Knyazes of Ryasan, a sorceress and two men with her, demanding from them one-tenth of

everything: of men and Knyazes and horses--of everything one tenth. And the Knyazes of Ryazan, Gyurgi, Ingvor's brother, Oleg, Roman Ingorevich, and those of Murom and Pronsk, without letting them into their towns, went out to meet them to Voronszh. And the Knyazes said to them: "Only when none of us remain then all will be yours." And then they let them go to Yuri in Volodimir, and then they let the Tartars at Voronazh go back to the Nukhla. And the Knyazes of Ryazan sent to Yuri of Volodimir asking for help, or himself to come. But Yuri neither went himself nor listened to the request of the Knyazes of Ryasan, but himself wished to make war separately. But it was too late to oppose the wrath of God.... And then the pagan foreigners surrounded Ryazan and fenced it in with a stockade. And Knyaz Yuri of Ryazan, shut himself in the town with his people, but Knyaz Roman Ingorovich began to fight against them with his own men ... and the Tartars surrounded them at Kolomno, and they fought hard and drove them to the ramparts. And there they killed Roman ... and many fell here with the Knyaz.... And the men of Moscow ran away having seen nothing. And the Tartars took the town on December 21, and they had advanced against it on the 16th of the same month. They likewise killed the Knyaz and Knyaginya, and men, women, and children, monks, nuns and priests, some by fire, some by the sword, and violated nuns, priests' wives, good women and girls in the presence of their mothers and sisters.... And who, brethren, would not lament over this, among those of us left alive when they suffered this bitter and violent death? And we, indeed, having seen it, were terrified and wept with sighing day and night over our sins....

But let us return to what lies before us. The pagan and godless Tartars, then, having taken Ryazan, went to Volodimir.... And it was in the morning Knyaz Vsevolod ... saw that the town must be taken, and entered the Church of the Holy Mother of God and were all shorn into the monastic order.... And when the lawless ones had already come near and set up battering rams, and took the town and fired it on Friday ... Knyaz and Knyaginya ... seeing that the town was on fire and that the people were already perishing, some by fire and others by the sword, took refuge in the Sacristy. The pagans breaking down the doors, piled up wood and set fire to the sacred church; and slew all, thus they perished.... And the accursed ones having come then took Moscow, Pereyaslavl, Yurek, Dmitrov, Volok, and Tver; there they also killed the son of Yaroslav. And then the lawless ones came and invested Torzhok on the festival of the first Sunday in Lent. They fenced it all round with a fence as they had taken other towns, and here the accursed ones fought with battering rams for two weeks. And the people in the towns were exhausted and from Novgorod there was no help for them; but already every man began to be in perplexity and terror. And so the pagans took the town, and slew all from the male sex even to the female, all the priests and the monks, and all stripped and reviled gave up their souls to the Lord in a bitter and wretched death.... And the accursed and godless ones then pushed on from Torzhok by the road of Seregeri up to Ignati's cross, cutting down everyone like grass, to within 100 versts [about 60 miles] of Novgorod. God, however, and the great and sacred apostolic cathedral Church of St. Sophia, and St Kyuril, and the prayers of the holy and orthodox Vladyka, of the faithful Knyazes, and of the very reverend monks of the hierarchical Veche, protected Novgorod....

[In 1245] There was an invasion of pagan Tartars into the Russian Land; and these [Mikhail and Fedor, Russian princes] shut themselves in the towns. And envoys came from *Tsar* Baty [Batu Khan, a grandson of Genghis, and leader of the Golden Horde] to Mikhail, who then held Kiev; and he seeing their words of deceit, ordered them to be killed and himself fled with his family to Hungary; and some fled to distant parts; and others hid in caves and forests, and few of them stayed behind; and these after some time settled in the towns; and they [Tartars] counted their number and began to levy tribute upon them. And Knyas Mikhail having heard this, he brought back the people who had fled on all sides to strange lands, and they came to their own land. And the Tartars began to summon them with insistence to go to Baty, saying to them: "It is not meet for you to live in the land of the Khan and of Baty without doing homage to them." And many having gone bowed. And Baty had this custom of the Khan's: If any one came to do obeisance, he would not order him to be brought before him, but wizards used to be ordered to bring them through fire and make them bow to a bush and to fire; and whatever anyone brought with him for the Tsar, the wizards used to take some of everything and throw it into the fire, and then they used to let them go before the Tsar with their gifts. And many Knyazes and their Boyars [nobles] passed through the fire, and bowed to the bush, their idols, for the glory of this world....

[When ordered to perform the ritual] Mikhail and Fedor answered as with one mouth: "We will not bow, and will not listen to you, for the sake of the glory of this world," and began to sing "Thy martyrs, O Lord, did not deny Thee, nor did they turn away from Thy commandments, but rather suffered for Thy sake, O Christ, and endured many tortures and received perfect crowns in heaven," and so forth. And the executioners having arrived, and having jumped off their horses, they seized Mikhail, they stretched him out and holding his arms, began to strike him with their hands over the heart, and threw him prone on the ground and struck him with their heels ... [then] cut off the head of the holy ... Mikhail, and hurled it away.... [When Fedor also refused] they began to torture Fedor as before they had Mikhail, and then they cut off his honoured head too....

[In 1257] Evil news came from Russia, that the Tartars desired the tamga [a customs tax] and tithe on Novgorod; and the people were agitated the whole year....

The same winter Tartar envoys came with Alexander, and ... began to ask the tithe and *tamga* and the men of Novgorod did not agree to this, and gave presents to the Tsar, and let the envoys go with peace....

[In 1259] The same winter the accursed raw-eating Tartars, Berkai and Kasachik, came with their wives, and many others, and there was a great tumult in Novgorod, and they did much evil in the province, taking contribution for the accursed Tartars. And the accursed ones began to fear death; they said to Alexander: "Give us guards, lest they kill us." And the Knyaz ordered the son of the Posadnik and all the sons of the Boyars to protect them by night. The Tartars said: "Give us your numbers for tribute or we will run away [and return in greater strength]." And the common people would not give their numbers for tribute but said: "Let us die honourably for St. Sophia and for the angelic houses." Then the people were divided: who was good stood by St. Sophia and by the True Faith; and they made opposition; the greater men bade the lesser be counted for tribute. And the accursed ones wanted to escape, driven by the Holy Spirit, and they devised an evil counsel how to strike at the town at the other side, and the others at this side by the lake, and Christ's power evidently forbade them and they durst not. And becoming frightened they began to crowd to one point to St. Sophia, saying: "Let us lay our heads by St Sophia." And it was on the morrow, the Knyaz rode down from the *Gorodishche* and the accursed Tartars with him, and by the counsel of the evil they numbered themselves for tribute; for the Boyars thought it would be easy for themselves, but fall hard on the lesser men. And the accursed ones began to ride through the streets, writing down the Christian houses; because for our sins God has brought wild beasts out of the desert to eat the flesh of the strong, and to drink the blood of the Boyars. And having numbered them for tribute and taken it, the accursed ones went away, and Knyaz Alexander followed them, having set his son Dmitri on the throne....

[In 1325] Knyaz Alexander Mikhailovich came back from the Horde and with him came Tartar collectors, and there was much hardship in the Low Country [Novgorod]....

The same winter [1327] a very great force of Tartars came, and they took Tver and Kashin and the Novi-torg district, and to put it simply, laid waste all the Russian Land, God and St. Sophia preserved Novgorod alone, and Knyaz Alexander fled to Pleskov, and his brothers Kostyantin and Vasili to Ladoga. And the Tartars sent envoys to Novgorod, and the men of Novgorod gave them 2,000 in silver, and they sent their own envoys with them, with numerous presents....

And then, too, the Tartars killed Knyas Ivan of Ryazan.

Michell, Robert and Nevil Forbes, trans. *The Chronicle of Novgorod, 1016-1471.* Vol. 25. London 1914. Pp. 64-66, 81-84, 88, 91, 96-97, 123, 125.

► Marco Polo

MARCO POLO'S AWESTRUCK DESCRIPTION OF MONGOL RULE

Marco Polo's *Travels* describe his journey from Europe to Asia and his stay in China between 1274 and 1290. Dictated to Polo's cell-mate in prison in Genoa in 1298, his book soon appeared in many languages.

Marco Polo described Yuan dynasty China under his host and patron, Kubilai Khan, the last great Mongol conqueror. Because Kubilai Khan distrusted Chinese, and few Mongols had the training or liking for administration, he appointed non-Chinese to important positions in his government. He trusted them because they were entirely dependent on him, had no roots in the country where they governed. Marco Polo was one of the Khan's appointees and ruled a large city in southern China, though he never learned Chinese. Thus his book described China from the Mongol's point of view. The many wonders he described so amazed contemporary Europeans that for centuries the book was ridiculed as fanciful. Tradition has it that up to his last days in 1324, his friends begged him to confess to having lied about his experiences. The phrase "its a Marco Polo" meant a tall tale.

Even during Kubilai Khan's rule and while the last conquests were still fresh in memory, the legendary prowess of the Mongol warriors was becoming a thing of the past. Incredibly successful in war, they settled down to enjoy fabulous wealth and power, soon degenerating to useless drones. In the first excerpt, Polo describes the hardy life and the military organization that made the intrepid Mongol warrior a world conquerors. Next he describes the riches and splendor of Kubilai's life, imitated in lesser degrees by his followers. Finally he describes with awe such things as coal for fuel, paper money, and porcelain or chinaware utensils, which had long been common in China but seemed fantastic to Europeans.

QUESTIONS:

1) What Mongol military organization and practices made them invincible?
2) What pursuits of Kubilai Khan suggested his nomadic origins?
3) What practices in Kubilai Khan's China amazed Marco Polo?

Their arms are bows, iron maces, and in some instances, spears; but the first is the weapon at which they are the most expert, being accustomed, from children, to employ it in their sports. They wear defensive armour made from buffalo and hides of other beasts, dried by the fire, and thus rendered extremely hard and strong. They are brave in battle, almost to desperation, setting little value upon their lives, and exposing themselves without hesitation to all manner of danger. Their disposition is cruel.

They are capable of supporting every kind of privation, and when there is a necessity for it, can live for a month on the milk of their mares, and upon such wild animals as they may chance to catch. Their horses are fed upon grass alone, and do not require barley or other grain. The men are trained to remain on horseback during two days and two nights, without dismounting; sleeping in that situation whilst their horses graze. No people on earth can surpass them in fortitude under difficulties, nor show greater patience under wants of every kind. They are most obedient to their chiefs, and are maintained at small expense. From these qualities, so essential to the formation of soldiers, it is, that they are fitted to subdue the world, as in fact they have done in regard to a considerable portion of it.

When one of the great Tartar chiefs proceeds on an expedition, he puts himself at the head of an army of an hundred thousand horse, and organizes them in the following manner. He appoints an officer to the command of every ten men, and others to command an hundred, a thousand, and ten thousand men, respectively. Thus ten of the officers commanding ten men take their orders from him who commands a hundred; of these, each ten, from him who commands a thousand; and each ten of these latter, from him who commands ten thousand.

By this arrangement each officer has only to attend to the management of ten men or ten bodies of men....When the army proceeds on service, a body of two hundred men is sent two days' march in advance, and parties are stationed upon each flank and in the rear, in order to prevent its being attacked by surprise.

When the service is distant they carry but little with them, and that, chiefly what is requisite for their encampment, and utensils for cooking. They subsist for the most part upon milk, as has been said. They are provided with small tents made of felt, under which they shelter themselves against rain. Should circumstances render it necessary, in the execution of a duty that requires despatch, they can march for ten days without lighting a fire or taking a meal. During this time they subsist upon the blood drawn from their horses, each man opening a vein, and drinking from his won cattle.

They make provision also of milk, thickened and dried to the state of a paste....Upon going on service they carry with them about ten pounds for each man, and of this, half a pound is put, every morning, into a leathern bottle, with as much water as is thought necessary. By their motion in riding the contents are violently shaken, and a thin porridge is produced, upon which they make their dinner.

When these Tartars come to engage in battle, they never mix with the enemy, but keep hovering about him, discharging their arrows first from one side and then from the other, occasionally pretending to fly, and during their flight shooting arrows backwards at their pursuers, killing men and horses, as if they were combating face to face. In this sort of warfare the adversary imagines he has gained a victory, when in fact he has lost the battle; for the Tartars, observing the mischief they have done him, wheel about, and renewing the fight, overpower his remaining troops, and make them prisoners in spite of their utmost exertions. Their horses are so well broken-in to quick changes of movement, that upon the signal given, they instantly turn in any direction; and by these rapid manoeuvres many victories have been obtained.

All that has been here related is spoken of the original manner of the Tartar chiefs; but at the present day they are much degenerated. Those who dwell in Cathay, forsaking their own laws, have adopted the customs of the people who worship idols, and those who inhabit the eastern provinces have adopted the manners of the Saracens [Muslims].

* * * * *

In this [capital city, Shangtu, Kubilai Khan] caused a palace to be erected, of marble and other handsome stones, admirable as well for the elegance of its design as for the skill displayed in its execution. The halls and chambers are all gilt, and very handsome. It presents one front towards the interior of the city, and the other towards the wall; and from each extremity of the building runs another wall to such an extent as to enclose sixteen miles in circuit of the adjoining plain, to which is no access but through the palace. Within the bounds of this royal Park there are rich and beautiful meadows, watered by many rivulets, where a variety of animals of the deer and goat kind are pastured, to serve as food for the hawks and other birds employed in the chase, whose pens are also in the grounds. The number of these birds is upwards of two hundred, without counting the hawks; and the Great Khan goes in person, once every week, to inspect them. Frequently, when he rides about this enclosed forest, he has one or more small leopards carried on horseback, behind their keepers; and when he pleases to give direction for their being slipped, they instantly seize a stag, goat, or fallow deer, which he gives to his hawks, and in this manner he amuses himself.

In the centre of these grounds, where there is a beautiful grove of trees, he has built a Royal Pavilion, supported upon a colonnade of handsome pillars, gilt and varnished. Round each pillar a dragon, likewise gilt, entwines its tail, whilst its head sustains the projection of the roof, and its talons or claws are extended to the right and left....The building is supported on every side like a tent by more than two hundred very strong silken cords, and otherwise, from the lightness of the materials, it would be liable to oversetting by the force of high winds. The whole is constructed with so much ingenuity of contrivance that all the parts may be taken apart, removed, and again set up, at his Majesty's pleasure....

It is to be understood that the Khan keeps up a stud of about ten thousand horses and mares, which are white as snow. Of the milk of these mares no person can presume to drink who is not of the family descended from Chinghis Khan....

So great, indeed, is the respect shown to these horses that, even when they are at pasture in the royal meadow or forest, no one dares to place himself before them, or otherwise to check their movements. The astrologers whom he entertains in his service, and who are deeply versed in the art of magic have pronounced it to be his duty, annually, on the twenty-eighth day of the moon in August, to scatter in the wind the milk taken from these mares, as an honour to all the spirits and idols whom they adore.

* * * * *

In this city of Kanbalu is the mint of the Great Khan, who may truly be said to possess the secret of the alchemists, as he has the art of producing money by the following process.

He causes the bark to be stripped from those mulberry-trees the leaves of which are used for feeding silk-worms, and takes from it that thin inner rind which lies between the coarser bark and the wood of the tree. This being steeped, and afterwards pounded in a mortar, until reduced to a pulp, is made into paper, resembling, in substance, that which is manufactured from cotton, but quite black. When ready for use, he has it cut into pieces of money of different sizes, nearly square, but somewhat longer than they are wide. Of these, the smallest pass for half a tournois; the next size for a Venetian silver groat; others for two, five, and ten groats; others for one, two, three and as far as ten bezants of gold. The coinage of this paper money is authenticated with as much form and ceremony as if it were actually of pure gold or silver; for to each note an number of officers, specially appointed, not only subscribe their names, but affix their seals also. When this has been regularly done by the whole of them, the principal officer, appointed by his Majesty, having dipped into vermilion the royal seal committed to his custody, stamps with it the piece of paper, so that the form of the seal tinged with the vermilion remains impressed upon it. In this way it receives full authenticity as current money, and the act of counterfeiting it is punished as a capital offence.

When thus coined in large quantities, this paper currency is circulated in every part of the Great Khan's dominions; nor dares any person, at the peril of his life, refuse to accept it in payment. All his subjects receive it without hesitation, because, wherever their business may call them, they can dispose of it again in the purchase of merchandise they may require, such as pearls, jewels, gold, or silver. With it, in short, every article may be procured....

When any person happens to be possessed of paper money which from long use has become damaged, they carry it to the mint, where, upon the payment of only three per cent, they receive fresh notes in exchange. Should any be desirous of procuring gold or silver for the purpose of manufacture, such as of drinking-cups, girdles, or other articles wrought of these metals, they in like manner apply to the mint, and for their paper obtain the bullion thy require.

All his Majesty's armies are paid with this currency, which is to them of the same value as if it were gold or silver. Upon these grounds, it may certainly be affirmed that the Great Khan has more extensive command of treasure than any other sovereign in the universe....

Throughout this province [Cathay] there is found a sort of black stone, which they dig out of the mountains, where it runs in veins. When lighted, it burns like charcoal, and retains the fire much better than wood; insomuch that it may be preserved during the night, and in the morning be found still burning. These stones do not flame, excepting a little when first lighted, but during their ignition give out a considerable heat.

It is true there is no scarcity of wood in the country, but the multitude of inhabitants is so immense, and their stoves and baths, which they are continually heating, so numerous, that the quantity could not supply the demand. There is no person who does not frequent a warm bath at least three times in the week, and during the winter daily, if it is in their power. Every man of rank or wealth has one in his house for his own use; and the stock of wood must soon prove inadequate to such consumption; whereas these stones may be had in the greatest abundance, and at a cheap rate....

The noble and handsome city of Zai-tun [from which the English word "satin" derives], which has a port on the seacoast celebrated for the resort of shipping, [is] loaded with merchandise, that is afterwards distributed through every part of the province of Manji. The quantity of pepper imported there is so considerable, that what is carried to Alexandria, to supply the demand of the western parts of the world, is trifling in comparison, perhaps not more than the hundredth part. It is indeed impossible to convey an idea of the number of merchants and the accumulation of goods in this place, which is held to be one of the largest ports of the world. The Great Khan derives a vast revenue from this place, as every merchant is obliged to pay ten per cent upon the amount of his investment....

Many persons arrive in this city from the interior parts of India for the purpose of having their persons ornamented by puncturing with needles in the manner before described, as it is celebrated for the number of its artists skilled in that practice.

The river that flows by the port of Zai-tun is large and rapid....At the place where it separates from the principal channel stands the city of Tin-gui. Of this place there is nothing further to be observed, than that cups or bowls and dishes of porcelainware are there manufactured. The process was explained to be as follows. They collect a certain kind of earth, as it were, from a mine, and laying it in a great heap, suffer it to be exposed to the wind, the rain, and the sun, for thirty or forty years, during which time it is never disturbed. By this it becomes refined and fit for being wrought into the vessels above mentioned. Such colours as may be thought proper are then laid on, and the ware is afterwards baked in ovens or furnaces. Those persons, therefore, who cause the earth to be dug, collect for their children and grandchildren. Great quantities of manufacture are sold in the city, and for a Venetian groat you may purchase eight porcelain cups.

Konroff, Manuel, ed. *The Travels of Marco Polo*. [Based on Marsden's Translation.] New York: H. Liveright, 1926. Pp. 93-95, 105-107, 159-161, 171-172, 254-256.

TIMURLANE, THE LAST MONGOL CONQUEROR

▶ **Timurlane**

Timur the Lame or Timurlane was the last great, terrifying Mongol conqueror. His rule and that of his successors were a continuation both politically and culturally of the Mongols of the Chagatai Khanate. All Turkic and Mongol peoples who competed for power in central and western Asia in the fourteenth century were Muslims. But Timur's conquests wrought so much terror and destruction to all his victims that Christians and Muslims alike called him the Scourge of God.

Timur, who claimed descent from Genghis Khan, was born in 1336, the son of a petty chief in central Asia, when the Chagatai khanate was breaking up. Ascending the throne of a minor state based in Samarkand in 1369, he took advantage of the fragmented political conditions in western and central Asia and northern India to conquer huge territories. His first victims were the Persians in the time of the last weak rulers of the il-khanate. Massacring those who resisted him by the tens of thousands, he gained a reputation as fearsome as that of Genghis Khan. After mastering the Persian world, he extended his conquests to Mesopotamia, Armenia, and Anatolia. Next his troops subjugated the Golden Horde in southern Russia. His forces went as far north as Moscow, which they held for a year.

In 1398 Timur invaded India. He ordered 100,000 male captives slaughtered after taking Delhi, and enslaved most of the remaining population of the city. After staying for fifteen days Timur moved on, leaving behind such desolation that according to one account, "for two months not a bird moved a wing in Delhi." He was planning to attack China when he died in 1405, at age seventy.

Whereas Genghis Khan and his successors superimposed their rule over subjugated areas, Timur devastated and then retreated from many of his conquered lands, leaving them in political chaos. Since he left no capable successors, Timur's empire fell apart soon after his death. However, Timur did enrich his capital Samarkand with loot from every conquered land. He also settled captured artisans there to build and decorate his palaces, mosques and other public buildings. These monuments consequently show many cultural influences.

The reading below is from the *Decline and Fall of Byzantium to the Ottoman Turks* by Doukas, a famous historians of the late Byzantine Empire. His work chronicled the rise of the Ottoman Turks and also their set back at the hands of Timur, who soundly defeated and captured Sultan Bayazid in 1402. Timur's forces controlled Anatolia, Asia Minor, and Mesopotamia until his death in 1405. The excerpt shows something of Timur's ability both as a military commander and as a savagely brutal destroyer of defeated peoples.

QUESTIONS:

1) Describe some of Timur's actions that gave him the name the Scourge of God.
2) How did Timur defeat the Ottoman sultan?

3) Give some examples of Timur's military genius.

With the coming of Spring [1402], lo, Temir-khan went from Persia to the regions of the Don and gathered the Tauro-Scythians and Zykhians and Abasgians. He demolished the fortresses of the Bosporos and then crossed to the region of Armenia. He passed through Cappadocia with a large army, conscripting many Armenians, until he came to the region of Galatia, by which time he had as large an army as did Xerxes of old.

With all his Thracian and Eastern troops and newly conscripted forces assembled, and with the Serb Stefan, Lazar's son, and a host of lancers, Bayazid set out to meet Temir....

That evening, the Scythian [Timur] issued orders throughout the whole camp that all were to be ready in the morning, mounted and fully armed. Rising at early dawn, he deployed all his commanders. He placed his eldest son commander over the right wing and his grandson (for Temir was more than sixty years old) over the left. Temir took up his position in the rear. He addressed his troops as follows:

"O my assembled troops and invincible army, adamantine in nature, and stalwart wall, and of an indomitable breed. You have heard of the heroic exploits performed from the beginning by our fathers, not only in the East but also in Europe and Libya and, in a word, throughout the world. You know full well the expedition undertaken by Xerxes and Artaxerxes against the Greeks--the Greeks, I say--those heroic men and demigods. Compared to them these half-Greek and half-Turkish barbarians are like the locust to lions. It is not to give you courage that I recall these feats for the prey is already in our hands. Let not this bugbear escape from our hands. Capture it whole and uninjured so that we may take it back to Persia where we will exhibit it to our children and teach it not to demand that we abjure our wives. Now I wish this great field which lies before us to be surrounded. Let the right wing be led forward in a circling maneuver and also the left wing. Encircle the whole plain and let the enemy be enclosed in the middle like the center of the polar axis...."

At sunrise Bayazid deployed his legions. Sounding the call to battle, he stood there waiting for the initial charge of the Scythians. The Scythians, on the other hand, carried out their orders without sound or clamor or noise of any kind, working like indefatigable ants. Bayazid began to jabber and to curse his nobles. He berated the commanders and flogged them for not deploying themselves properly for battle. One commander fighting under Aydin's standard, hearing that his lord Aydin had joined his brother, abandoned his position, and taking up the standard, defected to the enemy with five hundred heavily armed troops. The forces of Saruchan did the same. The troops of Menteshe and Germiyan, when they saw their rulers shouting and signaling, also deserted and went over to their adversaries. Bayazid, like the jackdaw, was gradually shorn of his feathers. The Scythian troops enfolded him until the circle was finally closed....

When Bayazid [who had been captured] was conducted to the door of the tent, Temir's followers raised their voices acclaiming Temir-khan, and along with the acclamation they referred to Bayazid, saying, "Lo, the leader of the Turks has come to you a captive."...Glancing up and beholding the guards with Bayazid standing in the middle like a criminal, he inquired, "Is this he who a short while ago insisted on our divorcing our wives unless we opposed him in battle?" Bayazid answered, "I am the one, but it is not fitting that you should despise those who have fallen. Since you are also a ruler, you must know that it is your duty to defend the borders of your dominion."... After Bayazid had entered the tents which Temir had provided, Temir issued orders for a trench to be dug around the tents. One thousand heavily armed Persian troops were to keep watch in a ring around the tents. Outside the trench five thousand lightly armed household troops were to stand guard in rotation day and night.... [After a failed attempt to rescue Bayazid led by his son] a careful watch was set over Bayazid. During the night he was bound by iron collars and manacles while during the day many soldiers kept watch over him.

Temir remained eight days in that field where the battle had taken place. During that time the Persian army was dispersed from Galatia to Phrygia, Bithynia, Paphlagonia, Asia Minor, Caria, Lycia, and Pamphylia, so that it seemed that the entire army of Temir, as well as Temir himself, was in every province and city. In those eight days the army spread out and inundated everything. Temir took many captives and, seizing the riches of Ankara, burned and destroyed all those who resisted him....

Departing from Kutahiya, Temir came to Prusa, wreaking destruction, taking captives, and seizing every treasure whose existence was revealed through torture and diverse punishments. He burned, lynched, buried men alive, and inflicted every conceivable kind of torment. Opening up the coffers, he emptied out the gold and silver treasures which had been won from the Romans; precious stones and pearls were counted by the bushels like grains of wheat. In Prusa he also found Bayazid's wives and concubines.... He took captive the youths and maidens. He chastised and punished everyone, both Turks and Romans, by burning them alive or leaving them to die in prison from starvation in order to amass gold and silver....

Temir pitched his tents before the fortress of the Knights Hospitalers, rebuilt in the days of Umer, and demanded its surrender. The Knights Hospitalers, however, refused because there were many men and women ... from other cities as well who had taken refuge in the fortress. They were confident that the fortress would not fall to anyone. Bayazid had annually attacked the fortress and had, moreover, set a secure watch over the exits in order to compel its surrender because of famine, but he achieved nothing by warfare. Temir conceived the idea of blockading the mouth of the harbor. He issued orders in the evening that at daybreak every soldier was to pick up one stone and cast it into the mouth of the harbor, and it was done. When the defenders of the fortress saw this, they lost heart.... Temir's troops had transformed the sea into dry land by the first hour of the morning....

The Scythians succeeded in crossing the mouth of the harbor, and appeared before the moat. The Knights Hospitalers fought bravely from the battlements, and their arrows cut down the Scythians who fell into the moat like locusts swallowed up by swallows. Their corpses filled up the moat, but the Scythians multiplied like the heads of Hydra. When the moat, therefore, became full of bodies, the remaining Scythians, countless numbers of them, crossed the moat by treading on the corpses. They set up scaling ladders and some ascended to the top while others took the descent to Hades. The living had no concern for the dead whether he was father or son. There was only one objective in everyone's mind: Who should be the first to reach the top and raise the standard on the tower? Climbing up on all sides, they pursued the Friars who fled inside to save themselves. The triremes [boats] were drawn up to the citadel, and the Knights Hospitalers boarded in utter confusion and disorder, taking with them the *baiulus* and the remaining members of their order.... The Scythians then took possession of the acropolis, and, herding the captives into one place (for together, with wives and children, there were more than a thousand), led them before Temir, who commanded that all should be beheaded by the sword. He erected a tower by laying rows of stones and heads in alternating sequence. Where there was a stone, on one level, a head was placed above it on the next level, and where there was a head, a stone was set above it, and all the faces looked outwards. It was indeed a strange sight to behold and an inhuman contrivance!...

The troops moved from city to city, leaving each in such a state of desolation that not even the bark of a dog nor the cackle of a hen nor the cry of a child was any longer heard. Like the fisherman who casts his net and pulls it to land, bringing from the sea whatever his catch might be, large fish or small, even the paltriest little fish and tiny crab, so did they plunder all of Asia before riding away.

From Mylasa they went to Kaptiane of upper Phrygia and perpetrated the same crimes. From Laodicia they moved to Phrygia Salutaria which the Turks call Qara Hisar in their tongue. It was here that after much suffering Yildirin Bayazid died. It is rumored that he took his own life by poison. Temir, however, wanted to take him alive to Persia to show the Persians what sort of beast he had captured: first, to exhibit him as a spectacle and to parade him about, and then after he had suffered much torment, to take his life....

After he had spent a full year outside Persia, Temir returned as conqueror and trophy-bearer, bringing back more spoils and booty than any Persian tyrant who had preceded him.

Doukas. *Decline and Fall of Byzantium to the Ottoman Turks* [Historia-Byzantina].   Ed. and trans. Harry J. Magoulias. Detroit: Wayne State Univ. Press, 1975. Pp. 90, 92-93, 95-96, 99-100.

MAMLUK RULE IN EGYPT

▶ **Egyptian Lusterware of Mamluk Era**

"Mamluk" in Arabic means slave and applies mainly to ex-slave soldiers of Turkish origin. Beginning as the former slave professional soldiers of early Muslim caliphates, Mamluks had become masters in the thirteenth century upon the collapse of the Ayyubid dynasty, founded by Salah ed-Din (victor against Christian forces during the Third Crusade). Mamluk sultans ruled Egypt and Syria between 1250 and 1517. They successfully resisted Mongol attempts to conquer Egypt.

Although the institution of recruiting slave soldiers in Muslim empires was a cohesive and long lived one, it however was often full of strife, and Mamluk rule in Egypt was anything but stable. The average reign of a Mamluk sultan was six years; there were often bloody power struggles. Mamluks controlled the local inhabitants and excluded them from power through a feudal land tenure system, and scorned local ways. Even though Ottoman conquest ended the Mamluk dynasty in 1517, Mamluks continued to rule Egypt until early nineteenth century as vassals of the Ottoman dynasty.

This reading, by a leading expert on the subject, explains the unique features of the Mamluk recruitment system and governing institution.

QUESTIONS:

1) Who were the Mamluks, how were they recruited, trained and maintained as a military elite?
2) What was the relationship between the Mamluks and the Arabs?
3) How did the Mamluks rule Egypt and perpetuate themselves?

The *mamluk* military-slave institution is, generally speaking, an exclusively Muslim phenomenon. In any case, it has no parallel worthy of the name outside the Muslim world.

The basic reason for the adoption of the *mamluk* system is to be sought in the very character of Islam and in its achievements: the Muslim religion had set itself from the outset the target of islamizing the whole world, with force of arms as the main instrument for attaining that objective.... The swift expansion of Islam in the early years of its existence, on the one hand, and the adherence of the Muslims to their basic idea of conquest, on the other, created immediately a very wide gap between the growing need of suitable military manpower and the quite limited human resources available in the Arabian peninsula. At a somewhat later stage the need for non-Arab manpower was accentuated by the inevitable decline of the military qualities of the Arabs, in general, and of those of the Arab tribesmen in particular, as a result of their constant contact with a higher civilization and its luxuries, [and] the waning of their religious fervour....

The beginnings of the Mamluk institution are shrouded in obscurity. What is certain, however, is that there are clear indications to its existence already under the Umayyads ... in the eighties of the seventh century.... The turning point [came] in the first half of the ninth century. Henceforward Mamluk regiments, constituting the core of the Muslim rulers' armies, spread quickly over most of the important military centers of Islam, where they stayed for many generations. The only interpretation for this astounding success is the superiority and relative reliability of the Mamluk system on the one hand, and the far better military qualities of the human material from which the Mamluk recruits had been selected on the other....

The appearance of the Mamluks in such a great force did not bring about the elimination of the other kinds of armies.... It did reduce them, however, to a much lower status. This created tensions between the Mamluks and those armies. In addition, there were splits and strife inside Mamluk aristocracy, based mainly on the allegiance to different patrons.... It was a system with its grave defects.... Yet any other Muslim army would have had most of its defects with little of its great merits....

One basic trait of [this] Muslim military aristocracy is that, throughout its history ... it is of a specifically urban character....

The Muslim warriors who settled in the towns, in the old ones or in the new ones which they themselves built, used to establish their own separate quarters. Arabs of a certain tribe lived separately from those of a different one, and woe betide a tribesman who chanced to enter an 'alien' quarter! Moreover, the Arabs lived apart from the non-Arab citizens, the aim being to fortify the Arab military power by retaining the tribal organization. Although this urban concentration of the tribes helped to achieve this end and facilitated their employment in battle, at the same time it deepened and sharpened the ancient inter-tribal conflicts and provoked new ones on a scale unknown in the Arabian Peninsula.... But, even without inter-tribal enmity, there is no doubt that the Arabs would have been displaced within a short interval of time; for a nomad body which erupts into an area of civilization inevitably loses its original character, and its military strength decays sooner or later....

The fate that befell the Arab nomads was bound also to overtake other nomads who invaded the Muslim world while retaining their tribal organization, such as the Turks and the Mongols. The only way in which nomad vitality could be preserved in an area of civilization, and particularly as part of an urban society, was that provided by the mamluk system. In no other civilization did this system reach such a peak of perfection and endurance, or encompass as many splendid achievements as it did in the Muslim world. The essence of it was this. Young children from nomad tribes were brought as slaves from the non-Muslim areas into the Muslim world; they were converted to Islam, given a fanatical orthodox education and trained in the finest methods of combat. On the completion of their Muslim education and military training they were set free. Thus there grew up a soldier of nomad origin with an excellent military training and a strong Muslim conscience, faithful to the masters who had bought him and then set him free, and to his companions in slavery and manumission. The descendants of these soldiers were not allowed to join the military aristocracy to which their fathers belonged, since they had been born free and had grown up in an area of civilization and were Muslim by birth. The Mamluk aristocracy was, therefore, a one-generation nobility only, all its members having been born in the steppe and being Muslims of the first generation. To assure continuity of this aristocracy, it was necessary constantly to bring in new nomad children from the non-Muslim areas. In theory it was possible to safeguard both the nomad vitality and the Muslim freshness *ad infinitum*. In practice, things did not work out like that, primarily because of the conflict which arose between the theory behind the system and human nature itself.... Nonetheless, no other Muslim military aristocracy succeeded in surviving for so long--a thousand years at least--and with so much power as the Mamluk aristocracy wielded, in all its ramifications. Without the Mamluk military and social system, there is no doubt that the destiny of Islam would have been very different from what it actually was.

The Mamluk system was based on a clear racial preference, since the Mamluks were not taken from just any nomad or non-Muslim area, but chiefly from the area stretching from Central Asia to the Balkans and the Adriatic Sea, which constitutes a large part of what is usually called the European-Asiatic or Eurasian steppe. For this, there were three main reasons: (a) The Eurasian steppe was a huge reservoir of nomad man-power, second to none in the world and far larger than the corresponding resources of the Arabian peninsula. (b) The majority of the steppe-peoples had superior military qualities, to a degree found hardly anywhere else. (c) The areas of civilization where Islam established itself, there was a very marked preference for the fair-skinned races of the North over the darker ones of the South; this no doubt originated in the pre-Islamic period, but Islam did not bring about its supersession. These three elements were the cause that no other group--either within the Muslim world, or in the areas beyond it whence slaves were brought--could effectively challenge the Mamluks or counterbalance them.

The Mamluk military aristocracy acquired a thoroughly exclusive character at a very early state. It was entirely closed to those who did not fulfil the conditions enumerated, and its members looked down on those who did not belong to it....

The military aristocracy of Cairo during the Mamluk Sultanate, which lasted from 1250 to 1517 ... included Egypt and Syria in its territory.... Few military aristocracies in Islamic history were as bound to the capital and as closely identified with it, in almost total disregard of the other towns, as were the Mamluks in relation to Cairo during the years 1250-1517. The physical structure of the Nile country, which creates almost ideal conditions for a centralized system of government, enabled the vast majority of Mamluks stationed in Egypt to live in the capital.... The fact that there were no important inland towns in Egypt except Cairo and the growing inclination of the holders of feudal fiefs to be absentee landlords--combined to strengthen and hasten the process of concentration of military society in the capital.... The history of the Mamluk military aristocracy, was, therefore, first and foremost, the history of the aristocracy within the narrow confines of Cairo....

During the epidemics which afflicted Egypt again and again, the Mamluks, as foreigners, were stricken more severely than the natives, and the Mamluks of the reigning Sultan suffered more fatalities than those of his predecessors, who had lived in Egypt for a longer period. Entire barracks were emptied during the epidemics, yet the Mamluks did not leave Cairo even once. They would not abandon the capital even during the Black Death in 1348/9, for to have done so would have meant relinquishing their power to an opponent Mamluk faction besides losing their feudal estates and other kinds of property which changed hands frequently during an epidemic when the owners died....

Throughout the long period of their rule, there was no challenge whatsoever to the social and military predominance of the Mamluks....

The exclusive character of the Mamluk military aristocracy was expressed in several ways, chiefly these:
1. The first names of the Mamluks were Turkish; Mamluks of races other than Turkish were also given Turkish names. This was the immediate distinguishing mark of the military aristocracy, and whoever did not belong to it was not permitted to be called by a Turkish first name. This embargo was particularly strict for the urban population throughout the Mamluk Sultanate, and especially so for that of the capital.... Still more important, even the sons of Mamluks were, with rare exceptions, given not Turkish but Arab-Muslim names. This facilitated their exclusion from the Mamluk aristocracy, the one-generation nobility, on the one hand, and their integration with the local urban population on the other. The sons of the Mamluks, who were called *Awlad al-nas*, and of whom the vast majority lived in Cairo, belonged to a military unit, or class, of free people ... [and] formed a kind of intermediate link between the Mamluk aristocracy and the civil population of the capital, and their sons were already completely assimilated to that population. One may infer the crucial importance of Turkish names in the Mamluk Sultanate from the following episode. The Sultan Jaqmaq (1438-1453), who was very pious, wanted to alter his name to Muhammad, but changed his mind and decided to be called by

the two names Jaqmaq and Muhammad, because he feared that the rulers who were neighbours of the Mamluk Sultanate might think that he was not a Mamluk, and be tempted to covet his throne....

2. the Mamluks spoke a Turkish dialect. They did not want the local population to understand or speak it. The few local officials who learned Turkish, and were used by the Mamluks as interpreters, enjoyed a special status; the Mamluks usually despised the Arab language; many among them did not know it, and those who studied it knew it only superficially....

3. The Mamluks usually married either slave-girls of their own provenance, or married the daughters of other Mamluks.... It follows, therefore, that most descendents of Mamluks were of pure Mamluk blood, yet they were excluded from the upper class because they were not themselves born in the countries of origin of the Mamluks and had not been slaves.

4. Only Mamluks were allowed to purchase Mamluk slaves. The rest of the population, with few exceptions, could own only negro slaves.

5. The dress of the Mamluk aristocracy was very different from that of the rest of the inhabitants.

6. Only Mamluks, again with rare exceptions, were allowed to ride horses,

7. Although the Mamluks were successfully educated to Muslim orthodoxy, law cases in which both parties were Mamluk were often judged not according to the laws of the Muslim *Shari'a* but according to the laws of the Mongol *Yasa* [code created by Genghis Khan]....

The population of Cairo never seriously troubled the Mamluks, and even less did it ever become a threat to them as did the population of Baghdad at certain stages. Sporadic outbursts of unrest caused by the harshness of Mamluk domination, outbursts seldom accompanied by violence, were extinguished almost before they started....

That the Mamluk aristocracy formed a one-generation nobility of Islamized unbelievers had far-reaching repercussions on the social and religio-cultural character of Cairo as well as on its physical character. The Mamluks, under whom the city reached its zenith of greatness and wealth, erected religious and public buildings in it on a scale unknown till then. Their monuments there, especially the religious ones, are even today one of Cairo's outstanding features. In point of fact many sons of Mamluks became men of religion and letters, and a large part of the history of the Mamluk Sultanate was written by Mamluk descendants.... [This is because] the Mamluks are concerned for the fate of their descendants because they cannot introduce them into the upper class, they try to assure their future in the following ways: They build many mosques, *madrasahs*, *zawiyas* [religious schools] and the like and assign to them *waqfs* [charities endowed with religious funds] with high incomes. They appoint their sons as administrators or superintendents of the *waqfs* or else guarantee them part of the *waqf* income by other means.... For this reason, the *waqfs* have become very numerous and the incomes and profits from them enormous.... People have travelled from Iraq and the Maghreb [North Africa] to Egypt seeking knowledge. There has been a great demand for religious sciences and these have been very much cultivated there....

But the expansion of endowments could not go on for ever; it was, after all, detrimental to the vital interests of the military aristocracy, whose own revenues it reduced. As long as the Mamluk sultanate flourished and prospered, as long as the expansion of the *waqfs* property was in its early stages, the rival interests did not clash sharply. The economic decline of Egypt, however, which was hastened by the special structure of Mamluk society, was, sooner or later, bound to bring about a confrontation....

The peculiar fabric of Mamluk society gave rise to a paradoxical situation. Whilst a Mamluk, as an individual, had every interest in promoting the well-being of his descendants, the interests of the Mamluk aristocracy, as a body, were exactly the reverse. The contrast was particularly marked between the young and aspiring Mamluks, who wished to secure their income, and the sons of veteran Mamluks, whose power and influence were contracting.

Cairo, in this way, was the scene of an extraordinary phenomenon. The principle of a one-generation nobility, on which every Mamluk aristocracy rested, worked in two contrary directions: in the beginning it encouraged the study of religion and the foundation of religious institutions, while at a later stage its

responsibility for the enfeeblement of both was
pronounced.

Ayalon, David.   "Aspects of the Mamluk Phenomenon"
and "Preliminary Remarks on the Mamluk   Military
Institution in Islam."   In *The Mamluk Military Society:
Collected Studies*. London: Variorum Reprints, 1979. Pp.
44, 205-207. Ayalon, David.   "The Muslim City and the
Mamluk Military Aristocracy." *Studies on the Mamluks of
Egypt (1250-1517)*.   London: Variorum Reprints, 1977.
Pp. 311-314, 319-325, 327-328.

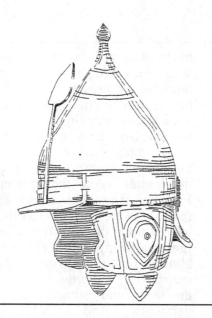

► Ottoman Helmet

A SERBIAN ACCOUNT OF OTTOMAN CONQUESTS

Just as Mamluks (Islamized former slave soldiers) played a key role in early Arab conquests, the Ottoman Turks' elite fighting force, the Janissary Corps, similarly played a crucial role in their Empire's rise to power. At its height the Ottoman Empire ruled Hungary and the Balkan peninsula, Anatolia, the Middle East, and all north Africa to the Atlantic.

Memoirs play an important part in reconstructing history. *The Memoirs of a Janissary* by Konstantin Mihailovic is a crucial first hand document of the Ottoman Empire's conquests. This unique fifteenth-century account of a Slav's experiences among the Ottomans is invaluable to understanding Balkan, especially Serbian, and Turkish history.

Konstantin Mihailovic was a Serb, born in an obscure village near Belgrade in the 1430s. Nothing is known about his parents. He and his two brothers were captured by the Turks; their attempted escape failed, they were tortured, and "taken across the sea." Probably he himself did not become a Janissary, because he was too old to go through the lengthy training and education that Janissaries received. He did, however, have some function in the Janissary corps.

Konstantin Mihailovic took part sieges at Constantinople in 1453, as part of a Serbian contingent, and at Belgrade. He also served in campaigns in Bosnia and against Vlad Drakul (Dracula) in Wallachia. Stationed with a Janissary garrison in the fortress of Zvejac in Bosnia, he was freed by Hungarian troops who captured Zvejac in 1463. Nothing is known of his life thereafter, but he did leave an important memoir that recorded some previous encounters between Ottomans and Slavs. The following details of his experiences with the Turks explain the Ottoman recruitment and training of the Janissary corps, the critical role of the Janissaries in war and in Ottoman power struggles, and Ottoman battle strategy.

QUESTIONS:

1) Who were the Janissaries, how were they recruited and trained, and what were they used for?
2) How did the Ottomans destroy the Serbian nation?
3) By what effective military strategy did the Ottomans capture Constantinople?

Whenever the Turks invade foreign lands and capture their people an imperial scribe follows immediately behind them, and whatever boys there are, he takes them all into the janissaries and gives five gold pieces for each one and sends them across the sea. There are about two thousand of these boys. If, however, the number of them from enemy peoples does not suffice, then he takes from the Christians in every village in his land who have boys, having established what is the most every village can give so that the quota will always be full. And the boys whom he takes in his own land are called *cilik*. Each one of them can leave his property to whom ever he wants after his death. And those whom he takes among the enemies are called *pendik*. These latter after their deaths can leave nothing; rather, it goes to the emperor, except that if someone comports himself well and is so deserving that he be freed, he may leave it to whomever he wants. And on the boys who are across the sea the emperor spends nothing; rather, those to whom they are entrusted must maintain them and send them where he orders. Then they take those who are suited for it on ships and there they study and train to skirmish in battle. There the emperor already provides for them and gives them a wage. From there he chooses for his own court those who are trained and then raises their wages. The younger must serve the older, and those who come of age and attain manhood he assigns to the fortress so that they will look after them, as mentioned earlier.

And at the court there are about four thousand Janissaries, and among them there is the following organization. They have over them a senior hetman called an *aga*, a great lord. He receives ten gold pieces a day, and his steward, one gold piece a day. To each centurion they give a gold piece every two days, and to their stewards, a gold piece every four days. And all their sons who grow out of boyhood have a wage from the emperor.... And no Janissary nor any decurion of theirs dare ride a horse, save the hetman himself and the steward. And among them it is so arranged that some are archers who shoot bows, some are gunners who shoot mortars, others muskets, and still others, crossbows. And every day they must appear with their weapons before their hetmans. And he gives each one a gold piece per year for a bow, and in addition a tunic, a shirt, and large trousers made, as is their fashion, of three ells of cloth, and a shirt of eight ells. And this I myself distributed to them for two years from the imperial court....

The Turkish emperor storms and captures cities and also fortresses at great expense in order not to remain there long with the army. First having battered the city or fortress walls until it seems sufficient to him, and seeing that it is the moment to launch a general assault, he then orders it to be cried throughout the army first that horses and camels and all kinds of stock be brought from pastures to the army; and when that is accomplished, he then orders it to be cried throughout the army second specifying the day of the assault. And they prefer to set the day of Friday. And they crying this, they name the rewards in this fashion: to the one who carries a banner upon the wall they promise a voivodeship [governorship]; and to the one who goes out after him the rank of *subasa*; to the third, the rank of *czeribassa*; and thus to others, money, naming the sum; and in addition, distributing various garments. And whatever is mentioned then, without fail all of this if fulfilled and carried out whether the city is taken or not taken.

Then they cry in the evening throughout the army that lighted tallow candles be raised profusely above the clouds. And that night and early in the morning the next day they prepare themselves for the assault, right up to evening.

And then they go toward the city from all sides silently, slowly approaching the fosse, carrying before them barricades woven of branches and also strongly-built ladders so that they can climb up and down both sides of the ladder. The Janissaries then in this fashion go to the place where the wall is breached, and having approached the breached place, they wait until day begins to appear. Then first the gunners fire from all the cannon and when they have fired off the cannon, the Janissaries quickly scale the walls, for at this moment the Christians are retreating before the cannon, and when they see that the Janissaries are on the walls, having turned about suddenly, they begin to fight bravely on both sides. And here the Janissaries, urging one another on, climb up. And in addition the shot from bows come very thick, for they continually bring and replenish their shot, and besides [there is] a great tumult from drums and human outcry....

Turkish or heathen expansion is like the sea, which never increases or decreases, and it is such nature: it never has peace but always rolls. If it falls calm in one region, in another it crashes against the shores.... The Turks are also of such a nature as the sea: they never have peace, but always carry on a struggle from year to year from some lands to others. If they make a truce somewhere, it is better for them, and in other regions they perpetrate evils; they take people into bondage, and whoever cannot walk they kill. And this happens many times every year: they round up and bring several thousand good Christians amongst the heathens.... Having forgotten their good Christian faith they accept and extol the heathen faith. And such heathenized Christians are much worse than true-born heathens. This then adds to the expansion of the Turks....

And thus the heathens expand, as was said of the above-mentioned sea. And this you can know yourselves, that the Turks capture people and not livestock. Who can then prevent them? Having taken [captives] they swiftly ride them away with them, and before the Christians are ready they are already where they ought to be. And the more men you maintain, wanting to prevent this, the greater the expense and torment you will bear ... [even] if you defeat them sometime on a foray they will do just the same damage as before....

The Serbian kingdom after King Uros, became a principality. They chose for themselves as ruler Prince Lazar ... some were for Prince Lazar and others were against him.... And whenever there is no unity, it cannot be good for anything in this world; as faith without deed is dead. Emperor Morat, having heard that Prince Lazar was the successor of his ruler in the Sherpa kingdom; having assembled an army, Emperor Morat marched to the Sherpa land, to the Plain of Kosovo. And Prince Lazar, without delaying, also having assembled an army, marched to the Plain of Kosovo and took up a position opposite the Emperor on the other side, at Smagovo beside a stream called the Laba.

And it was on Wednesday; on St Vitus' Day [1389] a pitched battle began, and lasted until Friday. The nobles who favored Prince Lazar fought alongside him bravely, loyally and truly; but the others, looking through their fingers, watched. And through such disloyalty and envy and the discord of evil and disloyal men this battle was lost....

Here they had brought Prince Lazar and Voivode Krajmir before Emperor Baiazit. Morat

his father and also his brother both lay on biers. And Emperor Baiazit said to Prince Lazar: "Now you see lying on biers my father and brother; how did you dare try this and oppose my father?" Prince Lazar was silent, and Voivode Krajmir said, "Dear Prince, answer the Emperor. A head is not like a willow stump that it will grow a second time." And Prince Lazar said, "Emperor, it is an even greater wonder that your father dared attack the Sherpa kingdom." And he said, "Emperor Baiazit, had I known earlier what I now see with my eyes, you would lie on a third bier. But perhaps the Lord God has deigned to have it so for our transgressions. May God's will be done this day." And with that the Emperor ordered that Prince Lazar be decapitated. And Krajmir, having asked permission of the Emperor, kneeling, held the skirt of his tunic under the head of Prince Lazar so that it would not fall to the earth; and when the head had fallen into the skirt, then Voivode Krajmir, having placed his head next to the head of Prince Lazar, said, "I have sworn to the Lord God, 'Where Prince Lazar's, there mine also.'" Both heads fell to the ground. And a Janissary brought the head of Milos Obilic and threw it before the Emperor together with those two heads, saying "Emperor, here now are the three heads of your fiercest enemies."

Later the Serbs or Raskans who were with Emperor Baiazit asked for the body of Prince Lazar and carried it to a monastery called Ravanica and there he was buried and was elevated to sainthood....

[Before the final attack on Constantinople, while a truce existed between the two sides, Emperor Mahomet] encamped on the seashore beside the Arm of St. George five Italian miles above Constantinople. He ordered his master craftsmen to take measurements, wanting to build a good fortress here; and he immediately began to carry stones himself.... And he did not move anywhere from that spot for two whole years until that fortress was finished....

At that time the Turkish emperor did not have any ships with him on the sea, and he ordered thirty-five fine ships to be made in the forest four Italian miles from the seashore. And some who knew about those ships considered it to be madness on the part of the Emperor....

And so the Turkish emperor sent to the Despot [his Sherpa vassal] asking that he dispatch fifteen hundred horses according to the earlier agreement.... The Despot dispatched a certain voivode ... and sent with him the fifteen hundred horses--for the Despot did not know his intentions.

Having finished the fortress the Emperor without giving any warning to his own men or to foreigners, and without denouncing the truce, released raiders toward Constantinople, in order to murder and beat whomever they might come upon anywhere right up to the very walls.... The Emperor, having arrived with all his might, surrounded Constantinople....

And when we had been there a week, then the Emperor wondrously and at great expense made preparations for those same ships, so that the whole army and the city looked on, and thus: The army, having made a trench up and down hill, having lined it with planks and having greased it heavily with tallow (and besides, fine runners were attached to each ship); having raised specially [prepared] sails on high, as if upon water they went, with banners, with the beating of drums and the firing of cannon, all thirty ships, one after the other. And at that moment the battle was stopped because of the great wonder: ships which were drawn on dry land by footsoldiers and buffaloes, right down to the sea. The Greeks, seeing the ships prepared thus, wanted to prevent them from reaching the sea, but they could do nothing about that. And so Constantinople was besieged by land and sea....

And the heathens lay eight weeks outside the city, firing great siege cannons so that they smashed the wall for a half furlong.... Therefore, in that place where the wall had been breached, the Emperor's Janissaries, by storming, killed the Greek officer to whom it had been entrusted. And when the leader was lost, then the others, being frightened, had to yield; and the Janissaries, having been reinforced, running along the walls, killed them. And all the Emperor's forces was turned upon the city, and there killed them in the streets, in houses, in churches.

And the Greek emperor had in readiness in the city one thousand infantry. Not being able so quickly to reach the place where the walls were breached because the Turks had greatly reinforced themselves, he fought with them bravely, holding back the heathens until he too was overpowered, and he was killed there on that spot. Having severed his already lifeless head, a Janissary brought it and cast it before the Emperor, saying, "Fortunate Lord, there you have the head of your cruelest enemy."... Thus was Constantinople conquered through ignoble falsehood and their heathen truce....

And there is among the Turks the following custom: when two brothers are left after an emperor and carry on a struggle between them, the one who first takes refuge at the court of the Janissaries will gain the imperial throne. And therefore, since one of the standing treasures is five Italian miles above Constantinople at that fortress which is called Geniassar--in our language "New Castle"--whichever of these brothers comes wanting to have some of the treasure, they will not give anything to anyone, for the fortress is securely enclosed and guarded in all things as if against enemies, and they will give them the following answer if one of them should come: "Fortunate Lord, as long as the two of you are carrying on a struggle, nothing will be given to anyone." But when one already sits securely on the throne without hindrance of the other, then the man to whom the fortress is entrusted, having taken the keys, will bring them to the emperor, submitting the fortress and all the treasures. The emperor, having rewarded him, entrusts the keys to him again so that he can administer as before as it was of old.

First it must be known that the Turkish emperor holds securely all the fortresses in all his lands, having garrisoned them with his Janissaries or protégés, not giving a single fortress to any lord; and moreover the emperor holds any fortified city and the fortress within it, having garrisoned it with his own men. And those Janissaries who are in a fortress the emperor himself supplies so that if they are besieged they will have the necessities. They have no wine or *kvas* in the fortress. But at other times [i.e. unless besieged] each must live on his wages. Wages are paid them by the imperial court every quarter year in full and without fail, and it also gives them clothing once a year.... And you must live on that and not touch the emperor's provisions unless besieged. And you yourselves must stand the night watch diligently and two guards must always be at the gate. The gate must always be closed except for the small gate....

And thus are the emperor's fortresses supplied, and also all of heathendom even to the lowliest: be he rich or poor, each looks to the emperor's hands, and the emperor further provides for each and every one according to his distinction and merit. And so no one has an inheritance, nothing from his estate that he could make a living on....

Mihailovic, Konstantin. *Memoirs of a Janissary*. Trans. Benjamin Stolz. Ed. Svat Soucek. Ann Arbor: Univ. of Michigan, 1975. Pp. 47-49, 89-93, 149-153, 157-159, 185-187, 191-193.

THE OTTOMAN EMPIRE AT ITS HEIGHT

▶ **Roxelana, Suleiman's Favorite Wife**

The Ottoman Empire reached its zenith under Sultan Suleiman the Magnificent (r. 1520-1566), one of the greatest monarchs of history. Suleiman's wars added Hungary, parts of the Balkan peninsula and north Africa, Rhodes, and Crete to an already huge empire that stretched from Baghdad to the Atlantic, and from Mecca almost to the walls of Vienna. Suleiman was an able diplomat, conscientious administrator, and a chivalrous foe. Although a devout Muslim, he was tolerant of other religions. Commerce flourished and culture prospered under his able and enlightened rule.

Unfortunately the Ottoman dynasty had no firm tradition of primogeniture in succession. Thus intrigues between members of the imperial family complicated court politics. Favorite wives often influenced the succession, and the ascent of a new sultan to the throne was frequently followed by the killing or blinding of his half-brothers. Suleiman's favorite wife reputedly induced him to kill his able son by another wife, and appoint her unworthy son his successor. This was Selim II, nicknamed "The Sot." The long decline of the Ottoman Empire began with this reign.

Ogier Ghiselin de Busbecq (1522-1592) was born in present-day Belgium, then part of the Holy Roman Empire. After receiving an excellent classical education he entered government service. In 1554 he was appointed Imperial Ambassador to the Ottoman Empire. His predecessor, who had been flung into prison when hostilities broke out between the Holy Roman and Ottoman Empires, languished for two years and died soon after being freed. De Busbecq's diplomacy helped to maintain peace between the two empires. A keen collector, in 1562 he brought back to Vienna precious manuscripts, rare ancient coins and specimens of two flowers, the lilac and tulip, previously unknown in Europe. In the letters to a friend and colleague quoted below, de Besbecq gives a unique insight into the Ottoman Empire at its height, about the life of a diplomat and the succession struggle between Suleiman and one of his sons.

QUESTIONS:

1) What were Suleiman's strong points as ruler?
2) How did the Ottoman rulers pick their successors, with what resulting problems?
3) What rules and practices made the Ottoman army strong and effective?

You will probably wish me to describe the impression which Soleiman made upon me. He is beginning to feel the weight of years, but his dignity of demeanour and his general physical appearance are worthy of the ruler of so vast an empire. He has always been frugal and temperate, and was so even in his youth, when he might have erred without incurring blame in the eyes of the Turks.   Even in his earlier years he did not indulge in wine or in those unnatural vices to which the Turks are often addicted. Even his bitterest critics can find nothing more serious to allege against him than his undue submission to his wife and its result in his somewhat precipitate action in putting Mustapha [his son by another wife] to death, which is generally imputed to her employment of love-potions and incantations....He is a strict guardian of his religion and its ceremonies, being not less desirous of upholding his faith than of extending his dominions.   For his age--he has almost reached his sixtieth year--he enjoys quite good health, though his bad complexion may be due to some hidden malady; and indeed it is generally believed that he has an incurable ulcer or gangrene of his leg.   This defect of complexion he remedies by painting his face with a coating of red   powder,   when   he   wishes   departing ambassadors   to   take   with   them   a   strong impression of his good health; for he fancies that it contributes to inspire greater fear in foreign potentates if they think that he is well and strong....

Soleiman had had a son by a concubine, who, if I mistake not, came from the Crimea. His name was Mustapha, and he was then in the prime of life and enjoyed a high repute as a soldier.   Soleiman, however, had several other children by Roxolana, to whom he was so much attached that he gave her the position of a legal wife....

Mustapha, on account of his remarkable natural gifts and the suitability of his age, was marked out by the affection of the soldiers and the wishes of the people as the certain successor of his father, who was already verging on old age.   His stepmother, on the other hand, was doing her best to secure the throne for her own children, and was eager to counteract Mustapha's merits and his rights as the eldest son by asserting her authority as a wife....

The position of the sons of the Turkish Sultan is a most unhappy one; for as soon as one of them succeeds his father, the rest are inevitably doomed to die.   The Turks tolerate no rival to the throne....Whether Mustapha was afraid of this fate or Roxolana wished to save her own children by sacrificing him, it is certain that the action of the one or the other of them suggested to Soleiman the advisability of slaying his   son....[On   campaign,   he   summoned Mustapha to his camp.]

On the arrival of Mustapha in camp there was considerable excitement among the soldiers. He was introduced into his father's tent, where everything appeared peaceful; there were no soldiers, no body-servants or attendants, and nothing   to   inspire   any   fear   of   treachery. However, several mutes (a class of servants highly valued by the Turks), strong, sturdy men, were there--his destined murderers.   As soon as he entered the inner tent, they made a determined attack upon him and did their best to throw a noose round him.   Being a man of powerful build, he defended himself stoutly and fought not only for his life but for the throne; for there was no doubt that, if he could escape and throw himself among the Janissaries, they would be so moved with indignation and with pity for their favourite, that they would not only protect him but also proclaim him as Sultan.   Soleiman, fearing this, and being only separated by the linen tent-hangings from the scene upon which there was a delay in the execution of his plan, thrust his head out of the part of the tent in which he   was   and   directed   fierce   and   threatening glances   upon   the   mutes,   and   by   menacing gestures   sternly   rebuked   their   hesitation. Thereupon the mutes in their alarm, redoubling their efforts, hurled the unhappy Mustapha to the ground and, throwing the bowstring round his neck, strangled him.   Then, laying his corpse on a rug, they exposed it in front of the tent, so that the Janissaries might look upon the man whom they had wished to make their Sultan....

I do not generally [leave my house] unless I have   dispatches   from   the   Emperor   for presentation to the Sultan, or instructions to protest against the ravages and malpractices of the Turkish garrison.   These occasions occur only twice or three times a year.   If I wished from time to time to take a ride through the city with my custodian, permission would probably not be refused; but I do not wish to put myself under an obligation, and I prefer that they should imagine that I think nothing of my close confinement. Indeed what pleasure could it give me to parade before the eyes of the Turks, who would rail at me or even hurl insults at me?...

The Turks are prone to suspicion and have conceived an idea that the ambassadors of Christian princes bring different sets of instructions, which they produce in turn to suit the circumstances and the needs of the moment, trying at first, if possible, to come to an agreement on the most favourable terms, and then, if they are unsuccessful, gradually agreeing to more onerous conditions. For this reason the Turks think it necessary to intimidate them, threatening them with war or else treating them practically as prisoners and annoying them in every possible way, so that their sufferings may make them produce sooner the instructions which they have been ordered to reserve till the last possible moment....

When it became known that Soleiman was on the point of crossing over into Asia and the day of his journey was fixed, I announced to my cavasse that I wished to witness the Sultan's departure, and bade him come early that morning and open the gates for me, as he took the keys away with him each evening....

A window was allotted to me at the back of the house, looking out upon the street by which the Sultan was to leave the city. I was delighted with the view of the departure of this splendid army. The Ghourebas and Ouloufedjis rode in pairs, the Silihdars and Spahis in single file. These are the names given to the household cavalry, each forming a separate body and having its own quarters. Their total number is said to be about 6,000 men. There was also a vast number of the household slaves of the Sultan himself and of the Pashas and the other high officials.

The Turkish horseman presents a very elegant spectacle, mounted on a horse of Cappadocian or Syrian or some other good breed, with trappings and horsecloths of silver spangled with gold and precious stones. He is resplendent in raiment of cloth of gold and silver, or else of silk or satin, or at any rate of the finest scarlet, or violet, or dark green cloth. At either side is a fine sheath, one to hold the bow, the other full of bright-coloured arrows, both of wonderful Babylonian workmanship, as also is the ornamental shield which is attached to the left arm and which is only suited to ward off arrows and the blows dealt by a club or sword. His

right hand is encumbered by a light spear, usually painted green, unless he prefers to keep that hand free; and he is girt with a scimitar studded with gems, while a steel club hangs from his horsecloth or saddle....

After the cavalry had passed, there followed a long column of Janissaries, scarcely any of whom carried any other arms except their muskets. Almost all wore uniforms of the same shape and colour, so that you could recognize them as the slaves or household of the same master....Behind them followed their captains and colonels, each with their distinguishing marks of rank. Last came their commander-in-chief, riding by himself....Next came the Sultan's own chargers, remarkable for their fine appearance and trappings, led by grooms. The Sultan himself was mounted on a splendid horse. His expression was severe and frowning, and he was obviously in an angry mood....

A few days later I was myself summoned to cross the sea. The Turks thought it advisable in their own interests that I should put in an appearance in their camp and be courteously treated as the representative of a friendly sovereign. An abode was, therefore, assigned to me in a village near the camp, and I was very comfortably lodged. The Turks were in tents in the plains hard by. Here I lived for three months and had a good opportunity of visiting their camp and acquainting myself pretty well with their system of discipline....Putting on a dress of the kind usually worn by Christians in that district, I used to wander about everywhere, unrecognized, with one or two companions. The first thing that I noticed was that the soldiers of each unit were strictly confined to their own quarters. Any one who knows the conditions which obtain in our own camps will find difficulty in believing it, but the fact remains that everywhere there was complete silence and tranquility, and an entire absence of quarrelling or act of violence of any kind, and not even any shouting or merrymaking due to high spirits or drunkenness. Moreover, there was the utmost cleanliness, no dungheaps or rubbish, nothing to offend the eyes or nose, everything of this kind being buried by the Turks or else removed from sight. The men themselves dig a pit in the ground with their mattocks and bury all excrement, and so keep the whole camp scrupulously clean. Moreover, you never see any drinking or revelry or any kind of gambling, which is such a serious vice amongst our soldiers, and so the Turks know nothing of the losses caused by cards and dice....

When I asked what [their] rations consisted, a Janissary was pointed out to me who was seated there devouring off an earthenware or wooden trencher of mixture of turnip, onion, garlic, parsnip, and cucumber, seasoned with salt and vinegar, though it would perhaps be truer to say that it was hunger that was his chief sauce, for he could not have enjoyed his meal more if it had consisted of pheasants and partridges. They drink nothing but water, the common beverage of all living creatures; and their frugal diet suits their health as well as it suits their purse....

Thus all is quiet, and silence reigns in their camp, especially at the season of their Lent, if I may so call it. Such is the powerful effect of their military discipline and the severe traditions handed down from their forefathers. There is no crime and no offense which the Turks leave unpunished. Their penalties are deprivation of office and rank, confiscation of property, flogging, and death. Flogging is the most frequent punishment, and from this not even the Janissaries are exempt, although they are not liable to the extreme penalty. Their lighter offences are punished by flogging, their more serious crimes by dismissal from the army or removal to another unit, a punishment which they regard as more serious than death itself, which is indeed the usual result of this sentence; for being deprived of the badges of their corps, they are banished to distant garrisons on the farthest frontiers, where they live in contempt and ignominy; or if the crime is so atrocious that a more impressive example must be made of the offender, an excuse is found for making away with him in the place of his exile. Such a man, however, dies not as a Janissary but as an ordinary soldier.

Busbecq, Ogier Ghislain de. *The Turkish Letters of Ogier Ghiselin de Busbecq, Imperial Ambassador at Constantinople, 1554-1562.* Trans. Edward S. Forster. Oxford: Clarendon Press, 1927. Pp. 28-32, 65-66, 132, 141-143, 146-147, 149-151, 155.

► **Persian Miniature Painting**

LIFE IN SAFAVID PERSIA

The Safavid Empire in Persia was founded by Shah Ismail in 1500 and reached its zenith under the iron hand of an able autocrat named Shah Abbas the Great, 1587-1629. The capital city Isfahan was noted for its architecture under the early Safavids. It was also known for its luxuries, culture, and learning. Many of the great mosques and palaces from that golden era still survive.

Early Safavid rulers encouraged economic development, searched for new markets, and welcomed foreign merchants. Thus a northern trade flourished with Russia, while in the south Bandar Abbas on the Persian Gulf became a thriving port for trade with Europe. English trade was conducted through the English East India Company, which had by the late seventeenth century captured the strategically important port of Hormuz from Portugal and supplanted the Portuguese as the dominant European traders. Persian silk fabrics and finely knotted carpets became famous throughout Europe. Renaissance paintings often showed Persian rugs and carpets as either floor or table coverings in their depictions of domestic scenes.

John Fryer, an Englishman connected with the English East India Company, traveled through India and Persia between 1672 and 1681. An experienced traveler with a keenly observant eye, he wrote lengthy letters to report on his travels and to help the company identify and develop its interests in the region. The excerpts below report on some of the recreational pursuits of Persians, their clothing and manners. Fryer describes only men's clothing, and mainly male entertainments, because of Islam's strict segregation of the sexes and seclusion of women.

QUESTIONS:

1) Why was Isphahan considered one of the most beautiful cities in the world?
2) Why did rich Persians hide their wealth?
3) What was a lavish Persian party like and how does it differ from ours?

The air is very rare at Isphahan, and the wind drying. The city has no need of walls, where so many marble mountains stand as a guard, or bulwark of defence. It has indeed a tower, but it is a mud one, rather serving as an armory, than to be relied on as a place of strength. The circumference of the body of the city I guess may measure seven miles....

The magnificently-arched bazaars, which form the Noble Square to the Palace, the several public inns, which are so many seraglios, the stately rows of sycamores, which the world cannot parallel, the glorious summer-houses, the pleasant gardens, the stupendous bridges, sumptuous temples, the religious convents, the College for the professors of Astronomy, are so many lasting pyramids and monuments of his [Shah Abbas'] fame; though many of them begin to sink in their own ruin, for want of timely repair....

The public bazaars are kept in better repair than less-frequented buildings.... Few cities in the world surpass it [Isphahan] for wealth, and none come near it for those stately buildings, which for that reason are kept entire, while others made of lime and slate, belonging to private persons, hardly last their founders lives, for want of timely care.

For the citizens rather choose to dwell in a tottering house, than appear lavish in costly building or apparel, for fear their governors should suspect they have too much riches, when they are sure never to be at rest till they have dived into the bottom of their treasuries ... whereby the Emperor's treasure grows exuberantly great. Which is the cause the citizens so often lay up their talents in napkins [keep under wraps], since it is a crime to expose their wealth by specious or luxurious shows....

In all their bazaars which are locked up in the dead of the night, there are watches to prevent thieves, at the common expense of every shopkeeper....

Their *Balneas* [bath houses] ... are the most sumptuous, which are in all their cities, always hot; and it is lawful for every one of both sexes, on stated times of the day to bath for a small price. The proprietor of each house gives notice to all comers by blowing a horn, when the houses are ready to attend to them ... each trying to outshine the other; insomuch that no time either of day or night passes, but you shall hear perpetual noise of horns to invite you to them. For no sooner is the fire kindled under them, but they let every one know by those loud instruments....

Their coffee-houses, where they sell *coho*, [are] better than any among us, which being boiled, has a black oil or cream swimming at top, and when it has not, they refuse to drink it. Hither repair all those that are covetous of news, as well as barterers of goods; where not only fame and common rumour is promulgated, but poetry too, for some of that tribe are always present to rehearse their poems, and disperse their fables to the company....

They are modelled after the nature of our theatres, that every one may sit around, and suck choice tobacco out of long Malabar canes ... fastened to crystal bottles [filled] with fragrant and delightful flowers into the water. Upon every attempt to draw tobacco, the water bubbles, and makes them dance in various figures, which both qualifies the heat of the smoke, and creates together a pretty sight.

All night here are abundance of lamps lighted, and let down in glasses from the concave part of the roof, by wires or ropes, hanging in a circle....

But the set dress of the Persian [city gentleman] is after this manner: His head being shaved, a large turban is placed upon his crown, of diverse colours, either silk or cotton, the figure of an over-grown cabbage, with a great broad leaf a top, which is wrought of gold or silver, and spread to make a show. His beard is cut neatly. and the whiskers kept in cases, and encouraged from one ear to the other, in fashion of an half-moon on the upper lip, with only a decent peak on the under.... Next, upon his body is a shirt, which he covers with a vest, tied double on his breast, and strait to his body as far as the waist, from whence it hangs in pleats to his ankles, sometimes quilted, sometimes not. His loins are girt with Phrigian girdles or rich sashes, above which his belt carries a falched sword or scimitar. From his hips long close breeches of linen come down to his hose, of London sackcloth of any colour, which are cut loose, not respecting the shape of the leg. Over all a loose coat of the same, without sleeves, lined with furs, or sables, or else silk, the outside either scarlet, or the finest wool of Europe, or cloth of silver or gold of their own manufacture. His shoes [are] of the best shagreen [granular surfaced] leather, mostly green, with narrow toes, high narrow heels, shod with neat iron half-moons, without shoe-ties or quarters to pull up about their heels, being the readier to slip off and on as occasion requires. Instead of gloves they tincture not only their hands, but feet, with a dark red colour ... They dye their hair yellow, or of a sandy red....

Those that breed cattle and wandering shepherds ... have no stated habitation; but where they find the best pasture they pitch their tents, together with their wives, children, and families, with all their troops, in the fattest valleys, living abroad far from great towns, like the wild Arabs, whose chief, or Father of the Tribe, is owned by them, and no other, he giving account to the Emperor for the number of their flocks, and the annual increase. For they are morose and untamed, and are apt enough to worry any who fall unadvisedly among them. Their dogs, with which they guard the folds, are like wolves, as fierce and stronger than their wolves are here....

These go clad in coarse cloths underneath, above which felts, kneaded into the form of a coat, and are covered with hats of the same, but their hats are grey, bound about with a linen cloth either of white, green or blue. Their coats are of what colour they please, but mostly blue; their hats are high-crowned, and brim slit before and behind, which if it be cold, they pull down and bind with their cloth; if the sun offend their eyes, they draw it over their faces, or cock up when it is shady. When they rest, their upper garment is put on with sleeves, armed with an undressed sheep's-skin against the injury of the weather. Their shirt next their skin is rugged enough; over it a plain jerkin is tied with a hard linen girdle of the same woof with the shirt. About the calves of their legs they bind rowlers [like modern puttie] for want of stockings, and their shoes are soled with wood, and the upper part wrought over with packthread.

The *Dervishes* professing poverty, assume this garb here ... being without beasts of burden, without wallets full of provisions, which the others seize by force, without attendance, without other ensigns or weapons more than a staff and horn, travelling without company, or indeed any safe-pass; and if they fix up their standard, it is among the tombs, none giving them harbour, or encouraging this sort of madness, as well as for the natural antipathy to beggary, as for that under this cloak many intrigues and ill designs have been carried on....

[At parties or banquets of important people] Alighting they are introduced [into] the guest-chamber, all bestrewed with flowers and sweet herbs, besides perfumed with odoriferous gums, or the aloes wood alone, or other resiny matters made into candles, and in massive silver fuming-pots very costly and delicate. Leaving their slippers where they begin to tread on carpets, they take their seats on *susannes*, a rich tapestry of needle-work that borders the carpets, behind which are placed huge velvet bolsters, before them spitting pots to void their spittle in when they smoke tobacco, or eat *pawn*. These rooms are large and airy, and open folding windows on every side, where being placed they bring their *coloons*; after which they welcome you by a flood of rose-water, or other compound water poured on your head and beard. Then they bring in, in voiders [baskets or trays], china plates of fruit, as pistachios, walnuts, almonds, hazelnuts, grapes, prunes, prunellos, apricots dried, and sweetmeats wet and dry of all sorts, amidst whereof they fill out coffee, tea, and hot rose-water, and all the while have mimicks, stage-players, and dancers to divert, between whose interludes is mixed the custom, as ancient as Nebuchadnezzar, of certain wise men repeating verses in their praise, or reading monuments of antiquity, which continues till victuals are brought in, and the cloth spread on the carpets, everyone keeping their places. First water being brought in great silver basins and ewers to wash, the courses are ushered in with loud music, and the table being filled, the servitors are placed so as to furnish every one with plates of several varieties, which they place before each, and give them long wheaten cakes, both for napkins, trencher, and bread, and sometimes thin pancakes made of rice; though boiled rice serves usually for bread, which they mix with their soups and pottage.

The usual drink is *sherbet*, made of water, juice of lemons and ambergreece, which they drink out of long thin wooden spoons, wherewith they ladle it out of their bowls.

The most admired dainty, wherewith they stuff themselves is *pullow* [a rice dish], whereof they will fill themselves up to the throat and receive no hurt, it being so well prepared for the stomach. After they have eaten well, and the cloth is removed, they wash again....

When they have tired themselves of feasting (which is not suddenly) as they depart, they return thanks, by inviting every one in course to an entertainment of the like nature, where they strive to outdo each other. Thus extravagantly luxurious and immoderately profuse are they in their great feasts, stately dining-rooms, magnificent gardens, and water-courses, exceeding the Roman voluptuousness.

Fryer, John. *A New Account of East India and Persia, Being Nine Years' Travels, 1672-1681*. Ed. William Crooke. Vol. 3. London: Hakluyt Society, 1911. Pp. 19, 21, 23, 25, 32, 34-35, 121-125, 135-138.

READING 6.9

CODE OF THE RAJPUTS

► Dancing Rajput Prince and Princess

Rajputs means "sons of kings" and *Rajasthan*, the land of the Rajputs, means "land of kings." Situated in north central India, Rajasthan sat astride the ancient invasion route to the subcontinent. During the era of disunity after the fall of the Gupta dynasty and the rule of Harsha, there rose in Rajasthan numerous states such as Chitor, Amber, and Mewar, headed by aristocratic Rajput clans that warred among themselves and defended India heroically against Muslim invaders from the northwest. These proud warrior clans claimed descent from the sun and moon and cited ancient Hindu texts, the *Puranas*, to prove their exalted genealogy. In fact their ancestors were ancient indigenous peoples, and early invading Scythians and Huns who were assimilated into the Hindu culture and given the status of kshatriyas or warriors. A Rajput rite, the *johar*, or mass immolation of women and children at the imminent fall of a fortress while the men rush to death in a last charge, came from outside of India.

The feudal civilization of Rajasthan was built according to strict code that emphasized war, loyalty, bravery, blood feuds, and honor. Rajput men disdained manual labor and farming. They hunted when not at war, but also patronized poetry, painting, and the arts. Their code of chivalry demanded defense of women, but Rajput women were no mere passive objects; they led armies into battle, mothers ruled on behalf of young sons, and rather than suffer dishonor, they died by leaping into flaming pyres. Many also committed suicide or *suttee* [it literally means a virtuous woman, one who immolates herself on her husband's funeral pyre] upon hearing news of their husbands' death in battle.

Glorifying war as the highest art of life, the Rajputs cultivated a military spirit that enabled them to resist formidable Muslim invaders. Tragically, incessant internal wars and feuds undermined their own cause.

Rajput warriors resembled the knights of medieval Europe and the samurai of feudal Japan. As in medieval Europe, bards composed heroic songs that celebrated the deeds of Rajput lords and ladies. The most famous example is the *Annals of Rajasthan*, which is comparable to the tales of King Arthur, or the *Song of Roland* which glorified Charlemagne's knights. Like the medieval European tales, the *Annals of Rajasthan* embroidered facts with much fiction.

Colonel James Tod spent seventeen years in Rajasthan when he served the British East India Company. He became an enthusiastic student of Indian history, ethnology and antiquities, collecting the materials for a ground breaking work titled *Annals and Antiquities of Rajasthan*, which he wrote after his retirement in England, and published between 1829 and 1832. Weaving together stories of the many Rajput clans, he depicted the deeds of a heroic people and their awful fate. The following selections show the Rajputs decimating each others' forces, and the fatal consequences for India, their heroic defense of Chitor against Muslim invaders, and how the last doomed Rajput men and women died.

QUESTIONS:

1) Who were the invaders the Rajputs were defending against, with what success?
2) What was expected of Rajput women?

Samarsi, prince of Chitor [13th century], had married the sister of Prithiraj, and their personal characters, as well as this tie, bound them to each other throughout all these commotions [wars between Indian rulers], until the last fatal battle on the Ghaggar. From these feuds Hindustan never was free.... From time immemorial such has been the political state of India, as represented by their own epics, or in Arabian or Persian histories: thus always the prey of foreigners, and destined to remain so....

[Samarsi was called on to defend Delhi by his brother-in-law.] The bard gives a good description of the preparation for his departure from Chitor, which he was destined never to see again. The charge of the city was entrusted to a favourite and younger son, Karna: which disgusted the elder brother, who went to the Deccan to Bidar.... Another son, either on this occasion or on the subsequent fall of Chitor, fled to the mountains of Nepal.... His arrival at Delhi is hailed with songs of joy as a day of deliverance. Prithiraj and his court advance seven miles to meet him....

In the planning of the campaign Samsarsi is consulted, and his opinions are recorded. The bard represents him as the Ulysses of the host: brave, cool, and skilful in the fight; prudent, wise, and eloquent in council; pious and decorous on all occasions; beloved by his own chiefs, and reverenced by the vassals of the Chauban.... His tent is the principal resort of the leaders after the march or in the intervals of battle, who were delighted by his eloquence or instructed by his knowledge....

On the last of three days' desperate fighting Samarsi was slain, together with his son Kalyan, and thirteen thousand of his household troops and most renowned chieftains. His beloved Pirtha, on hearing the fatal issue, her husband slain, her brother captive, the heroes of Delhi and Chitor "asleep on the banks of the Ghaggar, in the wave of the steel," joined her lord through the flame, or waited the advance of the Tatar king, when Delhi was carried by storm, and the last stay of the Chaubans, Prince Rainsi, met death in the assault. The capture of Delhi and its monarch, the death of his ally of Chitor, with the bravest and best of their troops, speedily ensured the further and final success of the Tatar [Muslims from Afghanistan] arms.... Scenes of devastation, plunder, and massacre commenced, which lasted through ages; during which nearly all that was sacred in religion or celebrated in art was destroyed by these ruthless and barbarous invaders. The noble Rajput, with a spirit of constancy and enduring courage, seized every opportunity to turn upon his oppressor. By his perseverance and valour he wore out entire dynasties of foes, alternately yielding 'to his fate,' or restricting the circle of conquest. Every road in Rajasthan was moistened with torrents of blood of the spoiled and the spoiler. But all was of no avail; fresh supplies were ever pouring in, and dynasty succeeded dynasty, heir to the same remorseless feeling which sanctified murder, legalized spoilation, and deified destruction. In these conflicts entire tribes were swept away whose names are the only memento of their former existence and celebrity.

What nation on earth would have maintained the semblance of civilization, the spirit or the customs of their forefathers, during so many centuries of overwhelming depression but one of such singular character as the Rajputs? Though ardent and reckless, he can, when required, subside into forbearance and apparent apathy, and reserve himself for the opportunity of revenge. Rajasthan exhibits the sole example in the history of mankind of a people withstanding every outrage barbarity can inflict, or human nature sustain, from a foe whose religion commands annihilation, and bent to the earth, yet rising buoyant from the pressure, and making calamity a whetstone to courage.... [Some states surrendered or made humiliating peace] Mewar alone, the sacred bulwark of religion, never compromised her honour for her safety, and still survives her ancient limits; and since the brave Samsarsi gave up his life, the blood of her princes has flowed in copious streams for the maintenance of this honour, religion, and independence.

Samarsi had several sons; but Karna was his heir, and during his minority his mother, Kuramdevi, a princess of Patan, nobly maintained what his father left. She headed her Rajputs and gave battle in person to Kutbu-d-din, near Amber, when the viceroy was defeated and wounded. Many Rajas, and eleven chiefs of inferior dignity with the title of Rawat, followed the mother of their prince.

[A later siege of Chitor] is described with great animation in [an epic] the Khuman Raesa. Badal was but a stripling of twelve, but the Rajput expects wonders from this early age. He escaped, though wounded, and a dialogue ensues between him and his uncle's wife, who desires him to relate how her lord conducted himself ere she joins him. The stripling replies: "He was the reaper of the harvest of battle; I followed his steps as the humble gleaner of his sword. On the gory bed of honour he spread a carpet of the slain; a barbarian prince his pillow, he laid him down, and sleeps surrounded by the foe." Again she said: "Tell me, Badal, how did my love behave?" "Oh! mother, how further describe his deeds when he left no foe to dread or admire him?" She smiled farewell to the boy, and adding, "My lord will chide my delay," sprung into the flame.

Alau-d-din, having recruited his strength, returned to his object, Chitor.... They had not yet recovered the loss of so many valiant men who had sacrificed themselves for their prince's safety.... [After a prolonged defense and when all hope had gone] the Rana [prince], calling his chiefs around him, said, "Now I devote myself for Chitor."

But another awful sacrifice was to precede this act of self-devotion in that horrible rite, the *Johar*, where the females are immolated to preserve them from pollution or captivity. The funeral pyre was lighted within the "great subterranean retreat," in chambers impervious to the light of day, and the defenders of Chitor beheld in procession the queens, their own wives and daughters, to the number of several thousands. The fair Padmini [a beautiful princess, the surrender of whose person was one of the invading Tatar ruler's demand] closed the throng, which was augmented by whatever of female beauty or youth could be tainted by Tatar lust. They were conveyed to the cavern, and the opening closed upon them, leaving them to find security from dishonour in the devouring element.

A contest now arose between the Rana and his surviving son; but the father prevailed, and Ajaisi, in obedience to his commands, with a small band passed through the enemy lines, and reached Kelwara in safety. The Rana, satisfied that his line was not extinct, now prepared to follow his brave sons; and calling around him his devoted clans, for whom life had no longer any charms, they threw open the portals and descended to the plains, and with a reckless despair carried death, or met it, in the crowded ranks of Ala. The Tatar conqueror took possession of an inanimate capital, strewed with brave defenders, the smoke yet issuing from the recesses where lay consumed the once fair object of his desire; and since this devoted day the cavern has been sacred: no eye has penetrated its gloom, and superstition has placed as its guardian a huge serpent, whose 'venomous breath' extinguishes the light which might guide intruders to 'the place of sacrifice.'

Thus fell, in A.D. 1303, this celebrated capital, in the round of conquest of Alau-d-din, one of the most vigorous and warlike sovereigns who have occupied the throne of India.

Tod, James. *Annals and Antiquities of Rajasthan, or the Central and Western Rajput States of India.* Vol. 1. London: Oxford Univ. Press, 1920. Pp. 297-298, 302-304, 309-312.

► Moghul Relief

BABUR, FOUNDER OF THE MOGHUL EMPIRE

Babur (1483-1530), was a descendant of Timurlane. At age twelve and after his father died, he became king of a petty and unstable Turkish state called Ferghana in Central Asia. Driven out of his ancestral land, he conquered Afghanistan. In 1524 he set out for India with twelve thousand followers. Two years later at the battle of Panipat Babur's forces routed the much larger army of the Muslim Sultan of Delhi, whose dynasty had originally come from Afghanistan. Agra and other north Indian cities followed.

While many of his followers only coveted the rich booty of northern India, Babur dreamed of building a lasting empire there. In his remaining years, he laid the foundations of the Moghul Empire that later included most of the subcontinent, and established twin capitals at Delhi and Agra. Under the Moghuls, India enjoyed unity not seen since the Guptas and Harsha. This dynasty ruled India in fact until the eighteenth century, and in name until 1857.

Babur was also a builder and patron of the arts, traits shared by many of his successors, who left a rich cultural legacy throughout India. Europeans who visited the court of the Moghuls were dazzled by its splendor; they called the emperors Great Moghuls, adding the word "Mogul" or great magnate, to the English language.

Babur wrote an autobiography called *Babur-nama* (Memoirs of Babur) in his native language, Turki; much of it is in diary form, recounting his battles and plans, dealings with friends and foes, and much more. He freely admitted his love for alcoholic drinks, and described his efforts to stop drinking to obey the dictates of Islam. In the following excerpts from the *Babur-nama*, a remarkable man and his career comes alive in the author's own words.

QUESTIONS:

1) By what means did Babur inspire and retain the loyalty of his followers?
2) What were the attractions of India for Babur, and what repelled him?
3) What was Babur's personal vice and how did he combat it?

[In 1526, Babur's army was about to fight the crucial Battle of Panipat which was the key to gaining entrance to the Ganges valley.] People estimate the army opposing us at 100,000 men; Ibrahim's elephants and those of his amirs were said to be about 1000. In his hands was the treasure of two forebears. In Hindustan, when work such as this has to be done, it is customary to pay out money to hired retainers....If it had occurred to Ibrahim to do this, he might have had another *lak* [100,000] or two of troops. God brought it right! Ibrahim could neither content his braves, nor share out his treasures. How should he content his braves when he was ruled by avarice and had a craving insatiable to pile coin on coin? He was an unproved brave; he provided nothing for his military operations, he perfected nothing, neither stand, nor move, nor fight....

When the incitement to battle had come, the Sun was spear-high; till mid-day fighting had been in full force; noon passes, the foe was crushed in defeat, our friends rejoicing and gay. By God's mercy and kindness, this difficult affair was made easy for us! In one half-day, that armed mass was laid upon the earth. Five or six thousand men were killed in one place close to Ibrahim. Our estimate of the other dead, lying all over the field, was 15 to 16,000, but it came to be known, later in Agra from the statements of Hindustani, that 40 or 50,000 may have died in that battle.

The foe defeated, pursuit and unhorsing of fugitives began. Our men brought in amirs of all ranks and the chiefs they captured; *mahouts* [elephant keepers] made offering of herd after herd of elephants.

Ibrahim was thought to have fled; therefore while pursuing the enemy, we told [several officers]...to lead swift pursuit to Agra and try to take him. We passed through his camp, looked into his own enclosure and quarters, and dismounted on the bank of standing water.

It was the Afternoon Prayer when Khalifa's younger brother-in-law Tahir Tibri who had found Ibrahim's body in a heap of dead, brought in his head....

In Sultan Ibrahim's defeat [his vassal] the Raja of Gualiar Bihramajit the Hindu had gone to hell [Babur's way of describing what happened to Hindus when they died].

Bikramajit's children and family were in Agra at the time of Ibrahim's defeat. When Himayun [Babur's son and heir] reached Agra, they must have been planning to flee, but his postings of men (to watch the roads) prevented this and guard was kept over them. Himayun himself did not let them go. They made him a voluntary offering of a mass of jewels and valuables amongst which was the famous diamond [later known as the Kohinor Diamond,

now part of Great Britain's Crown Jewels] which 'Alau'u'd-din must have brought. Its reputation is that every appraiser has estimated its value at two and half days' food for the whole world....Himayun offered it to me when I arrived at Agra; I just gave it him back....

[Babur distributed loot to reward his followers after the famous victory.] On Saturday the 29th of Rajab the examination and distribution of the treasure were begun. To Himayun were given 70 laks from the Treasury, and other and above this, a treasure house was bestowed on him just as it was, without ascertaining and writing down its contents. To some begs [lords] 10 laks were given, 8, 7, or 6 to others. Suitable money-gifts were bestowed from the Treasury on the whole army, to every tribe there was, Afghan, Hazara, 'Arab, Biluch etc. to each according to its position. Every trader and student, indeed every man who had come with the army, took ample portion and share of bounteous gifts and largess. To those not with the army went a mass of treasure in gift and largess...to the whole various train of relations and younger children went masses of red and white (gold and silver), of plenishing, jewels and slaves....

[Little wonder then] On our first coming to Agra, there was remarkable dislike and hostility between its people and mine, the peasantry and soldiers running away in fear of our men....

It was the hot-season when we came to Agra. All the inhabitants had run away in terror. Neither grain for ourselves nor corn for our horses was to be had. The villages, out of hostility and hatred to us had taken to thieving and highway-robbery; there was no moving on the roads. There had been no chance since the treasure was distributed to send men in strength into the parganas and elsewhere. Moreover the year was a very hot one; violent pestilential winds struck people down in heaps together; masses began to die off.

On these accounts the greater part of the begs and best braves became unwilling to stay in Hindustan, indeed set their faces for leaving it....

When I knew of this unsteadiness amongst (my) people, I summoned all the begs and took counsel. Said I. "There is no supremacy and grip on the world without means and resources; without lands and retainers sovereignty and command are impossible. By the labours of several years, by encountering hardships, by long travel, by flinging myself and the army into battle, and by deadly slaughter, we, through God's grace, beat these masses of enemies in order that we might take their broad lands. And now what force compels us, what necessity has arisen that we should, without cause, abandon countries taken at such risk of life? Was it for us to remain in Kabul, the sport of harsh poverty? Henceforth, let no well-wisher of mine speak of such things! But let not those turn back from going who, weak in strong persistence, have set their faces to depart!" By these words, which recalled just and reasonable views to their minds, I made them, willy-nilly, quit their fears.

As Khwaja Kalan had no heart to stay in Hindustan, matters were settled in this way:--As he had many retainers, he was to convoy the gifts, and, as there were few men in Kabul and Ghazni, was to keep these places guarded and victualled. I bestowed on him Ghazni, Girdiz and the Sultan Mas'udi Hazara, gave also the Hindustan *pargana* of G'huram, worth 3 or 4 *laks* [as fiefs]....

Loathing Hindustan, Khwaja Kalan, when on his way, had the following couplet inscribed on the wall of his residence in Delhi:--
If safe and sound I cross the Sind
Blacken my face ere I wish for Hind!

It was ill-mannered in him to compose and write up this partly-jesting verse while I still stayed in Hind. If his departure caused me one vexation, such a jest doubled it. I composed the following off-hand verse, wrote it down and sent it to him:--
Give a hundred thanks, Babur, that the generous Pardoner
Has given thee Sind and Hind and many a kingdom.
If thou have not the strength for their heats,
If thou say, "Let me see the cold side,"
Ghazni is there.
[Although many fierce campaigns remained to be fought, the Battle of Paniput had secured northern India for Babur. Much of the remainder of his memoirs describe India and his building plans for his new capital.]

Pleasant things of Hindustan are that it is a large country and has masses of gold and silver. Its air in the Rains is very fine. Sometimes it rains 10, 15 or 20 times a day; torrents pour down all at once and rivers flow where no water had been. While it rains and through the Rains, the air is remarkably fine, not to be surpassed for healthiness and charm. The fault is that the air becomes very soft and damp. A bow of those (Transoxanian) countries after going through the Rains in Hindustan, may not be drawn even; it is ruined. Not only the bow, everything is affected, armour, book, cloth, and utensils all; a house even does not last long. Not only in the Rains but also in the cold and the hot seasons, the airs are excellent; at these times, however, the north-west wind constantly gets up laden with dust and earth....

Another good thing in Hindustan is that it has unnumbered and endless workmen of every kind. There is a fixed caste for every sort of work and for every thing, which has done that work or that thing from father to son till now....

One of the great defects of Hindustan being its lack of running-waters, it kept coming to my mind that waters should be made to flow by means of wheels erected wherever I might settle down, also that grounds should be laid out in an orderly and symmetrical way. With this object in view, we crossed the Jun-water to look at garden-grounds a few days after entering Agra. Those grounds were so bad and unattractive that we traversed them with a hundred disgusts and repulsions. So ugly and displeasing were they, that the idea of making a Char-bagh in them passed from my mind, but needs must! as there was no other land near Agra, that same ground was taken in hand a few days later.

The beginning was made with the large well from which water comes for the Hot-bath, and also with the piece of ground where the tamarind-trees and the octagonal tank now are. After that came the large tank with its enclosure; after that the tank and *talar* [open-fronted audience hall] in front of the outer residence; after that the private-house with its garden and various dwellings; after that the Hot-bath. Then in that charmless and disorderly Hind, plots of garden were seen laid out with order and symmetry, with suitable borders and parterres [flower beds] in every corner, and in every border rose and narcissus in perfect arrangement.

Three things oppressed us in Hindustan, its heat, its violent winds, its dust. Against all

three the Bath is a protection, for in it, what is known of dust and wind? and in the heats it is so chilly that one is almost cold....
[Although Sunni Muslims, Babur and his followers were also hearty drinkers. Babur tells of his efforts to forswear drinking.]

On Monday the 23rd of the first Humada [1527], when I went out riding, I reflected, as I rode, that the wish to cease from sin had been always in my mind, and that my forbidden acts had set lasting stain upon my heart. Said I. "Oh! my soul!"

"How long wilt thou draw savour from sin?

Repentance is not without savour, taste it!"....

The fragments of the gold and silver [drinking] vessels were shared out to deserving persons and to darwishes [Muslim holy men]. The first to agree in renouncing wine was 'Asas; he had already agreed also about leaving his beard untrimmed. That night and the next day some 300 begs and persons of the household, soldiers and not soldiers, renounced wine. What wine we had with us was poured on the ground; what Baba Dost had brought was ordered salted to make vinegar. At the place where the wine was poured upon the ground, a well was ordered to be dug, built up with stone and having an almshouse beside it....

And I made public the resolution to abstain from wine, which had been hidden in the treasury of my breast. The victorious servants, in accordance with the illustrious order, dashed upon the earth of contempt and destruction the flagons and the cups, and the other utensils in gold and silver, which in their number and their brilliance were like the stars of the firmament. They dashed them in pieces, as, God willing! soon will be dashed the gods of the idolaters,-- and they distributed the fragments among the poor and needy. By the blessing of this acceptable repentance, many of the courtiers, by virtue of the saying that men follow the religion of their kings, embraced abstinence at the same assemblage, and entirely renounced the use of wine, and up till now crowds of our subjects hourly attain this auspicious happiness. I hope that in accordance with the saying "He who incites to good deeds has the same reward as he who does them" the benefit of this action will react on the royal fortune and increase it day by day by victories.

After carrying out this design an universal decree was issued that in the imperial dominions--May God protect them from every danger and calamity--no-one shall partake of strong drink, or engage in its manufacture, nor sell it, nor buy it or possess it, nor convey it or fetch it....

Beveridge, Annette S., trans. *Babur-nama (Memoirs of Babur)*. Vols. 1, 2. New Delhi: Oriental Books Reprint Corp., 1979. Pp. 470, 474-475, 477, 519-520, 522-523, 524-526, 531-532, 551-552, 554-555.

▶ **Indian View of European**

A FRENCHMAN'S ACCOUNT OF MOGHUL INDIA

François Bernier (1620-1688) was a French medical doctor who traveled widely through India between 1659 and 1668. He was a keen observer and recorded the sights and sounds of India in lengthy letters to friends and patrons in France. After his return, he published his collected letters as *Travels in the Mogol Empire A.D. 1656-1668*. Because his audience was primarily French Bernier frequently compared India with France.

Bernier arrived in India soon after the Moghul Emperor Aurengzeb's successful revolt against his father, whom he deposed and imprisoned. After more than one hundred years, the Moghul empire was past its prime. Corruption in government was rampant, offices were sold to highest bidders. The ever more opulent life style of the court and nobility, which was mostly Muslim, ground down the majority of Indians, who were Hindu. Unlike some of his predecessors, who were relatively tolerant of other religions, Aurengzeb fanatically persecuted Hinduism. The empire entered a tailspin of decline after Aurengzeb's death.

In samples reproduced below Bernier describes Moghul court life, some corrupt and oppressive government practices, Hindu and Muslim social practices, specially regarding women, and in general the sounds and smells of bustling city life in seventeenth-century Delhi.

QUESTIONS:

1) How did seventeenth-century Delhi compare with contemporary Paris?
2) Why did the emperor need so much money to run his government and household, with what results for the people?
3) Describe a practice that Bernier found strange and cruel.

Delhi, then, is an entirely new city, situated in a flat country, on the banks of the Gemna [Jumna], a river which may be compared to the Loire, and built on one bank only in such a manner that it terminates in this place very much in the form of a crescent, having but one bridge of boats to cross to the country. Excepting the side where it is defended by the river, the city is encompassed by walls of brick....

The citadel, which contains the Mahalle or Seraglio, and the other royal apartments of which I shall have occasion to speak hereafter, is round, or rather semicircular. It commands a prospect of the river, from which it is separated by a sandy space of considerable length and width.

On these sands are exhibited the combats of elephants, and there the corps ... pass in review before the Sovereign, who witnesses the spectacle from the windows of the palace....

Here [in the royal square] too is held a bazaar or market for an endless variety of things; which like the Pont-neuf at Paris, is the rendez-vous for all sorts of mountebanks and jugglers. Hither, likewise, the astrologers resort, both Mahometan and Gentile [Hindu]. These wise doctors remain seated in the sun, on a dusty piece of carpet, handling some old mathematical instruments, and having open before them a large book which represents the signs of the zodiac. In this way they attract the attention of the passengers, and impose upon the people, by whom they are considered as so many infallible oracles.... Silly women, wrapping themselves in a white cloth from head to foot, flock to the astrologers, whisper to them all the transactions of their lives, and disclose every secret with no more reserve than is practised by a scrupulous penitent in the presence of her confessor....

The most ridiculous of these pretenders to divination was a half-caste Portuguese, a fugitive from Goa. This fellow sat on his carpet as gravely as the rest, and had many customers notwithstanding he could neither read nor write. His only instrument was an old mariner's compass, and his books of astrology a couple of old Romish prayer-books in the Portuguese language, the pictures of which he pointed out as the signs of the European zodiac....

The two principal streets of the city, already mentioned as leading into the square, may be five-and-twenty or thirty ordinary paces in width. They run in a straight line nearly as far as the eye can reach.... In regard to houses the two streets are exactly alike. As in our Place Royale, there are arcades on both sides; with this difference, however, that they are only brick, and that the top serves for a terrace and has no additional building. They also differ from the Place Royale in not having an uninterrupted opening from one to the other, but are generally separated by partitions, in the spaces between which are open shops, where, during the day, artisans work, bankers sit for the despatch of their business, and merchants exhibit their wares. Within the arch is a small door, opening into a warehouse, in which these wares are deposited for the night.

The houses of the merchants are built over these warehouses, at the back of the arcades: they look handsome enough from the street, and appear tolerably commodious within; they are airy, at a distance from the dust, and communicate with the terrace-roofs over the shops, on which the inhabitants sleep at night; the houses, however, are not continued the whole length of the streets. A few, and only a few, other parts of the city have good houses raised on terraces, the buildings over the shops being often too low to be seen from the street. The rich merchants have their dwellings elsewhere, to which they retire after the hours of business.

The interior of a good house has the whole floor covered with a cotton mattress four inches in thickness, over which a fine white cloth is spread during the summer, and a silk carpet in the winter. At the most conspicuous side of the chamber are one or two mattresses, with fine coverings quilted in the form of flowers and ornamented with delicate silk embroidery, interspersed with gold and silver. These are intended for the master of the house, or any person of quality who may happen to call. Each mattress has a large cushion of brocade to lean upon, and there are other cushions placed round the room, covered with brocade, velvet, or flowered satin, for the rest of the company. Five or six feet from the floor, the sides of the room are full of niches, cut in a variety of shapes, tasteful and well proportioned, in which are seen porcelain vases and flower-pots. The ceiling is gilt and painted, but without pictures of man or beast, such representations being forbidden by the religion of the country.

This is a pretty fair description of a fine house in these parts, and as there are many in Delhi possessing all the properties above mentioned, I think it may be safely asserted, without disparagement to the towns in our quarters of the globe, that the capital of Hindoustan is not destitute of handsome buildings, although they bear no resemblance to those in Europe.

That which so much contributes to the beauty of European towns, the brilliant appearance of the shops, is wanting in Delhi. For though this city be the seat of a powerful and magnificent court, where an infinite quantity of the richest commodities is necessarily collected, yet there are no streets like ours of *S*. Denis, which has not perhaps its equal in any part of Asia. Here the costly merchandise is generally kept in warehouses, and the shops are seldom decked with rich or showy articles. For one that makes a display of beautiful and fine cloths, silk, and other stuffs striped with gold and silver, turbans embroidered with gold, and brocades, there are at least five-and-twenty where nothing is seen but pots of oil or butter, piles of baskets filled with rice, barley, chick-peas, wheat, and an endless variety of other grain and pulse....

There is, indeed, a fruit market that makes some show. It contains many shops which during the summer are well supplied with dry fruit from Persia, Balk, Bokara, and Samarkand [places in Central Asia]; such as almonds, pistachios, and walnuts, raisins, prunes, and apricots; and in winter with excellent fresh grapes, black and white, brought from the same countries, wrapped in cotton; pears and apples of three or four sorts, and those admirable melons which last the whole winter. These fruits are, however, very dear; a single melon selling for a crown and half....

There are many confectioners' shops in the town, but the sweetmeats are badly made, and full of dust and flies.

Bakers also are numerous, but the ovens are unlike our own, and very defective. The bread, therefore, is neither well made nor properly baked....

In the bazaars there are shops where meat is sold roasted and dressed in a variety of ways. But there is no trusting to their dishes, composed, for aught I know, of the flesh of camels, horses, or perhaps oxen which have died of disease. Indeed no food can be considered wholesome which is not dressed at home.

Meat is sold in every part of the city; but instead of goats' flesh that of mutton is often palmed upon the buyer....

The people of this neighbourhood are indifferent fishermen; yet good fish may sometimes be bought, particularly two sorts, called sing-ala and rau. The former resembles our pike; the latter our carp. When the weather is cold, the people will not fish at all if they can avoid it; for they have a much greater dread of cold then Europeans have of heat....

You may judge from what I have said, whether a lover of good cheer ought to quit Paris for the sake of visiting Delhi. Unquestionably the great are in the enjoyment of everything; but it is by dint of the numbers in their service, by dint of the korrah [whip?] and by dint of money. In Delhi there is no middle state. A man must either be of the highest rank or live miserably....

The heat is so intense in Hindustan, that no one, not even the King, wears stockings; the only cover for the feet being ... slippers, while the head is protected by a small turban, of the finest and most delicate materials. The other garments are proportionally light. During the summer season, it is scarcely possible to keep a hand on the wall of an apartment, or the head on a pillow. For more than six successive months, everybody lies in the open air without covering--the common people in the streets, the merchants and persons of condition sometimes in their courts or gardens, and sometimes on their terraces, which are first carefully watered....

But I have not enumerated all the expenses incurred by the Great Mogol. He keeps in Delhi and Agra from two to three thousand fine horses, always at hand in case of emergency: eight or nine hundred elephants, and a large number of baggage horses, mules, and porters, intended to carry the numerous and capacious tents, with their fittings, his wives and women, furniture, kitchen apparatus ... and all the other articles necessary for the camp, which the Mogol has always about him, as in his capital, things which are not considered necessary in our kingdoms in Europe.

Add to this, if you will, the enormous expenses of the Seraglio [ladies' quarters], where the consumption of fine cloths of gold, and brocades, silks, embroideries, pearls, musk, amber and sweet essenses, is greater than can be conceived.

Thus, although the Great Mogol be in the receipt of an immense revenue, his expenditure being much in the same proportion, he cannot possess the vast surplus of wealth that most people seem to imagine. I admit that his income exceeds probably the joint revenues of the Grand Seignior and the King of Persia; but if I were to call him a wealthy monarch, it would be in the sense that a treasurer is to be considered wealthy who pays with one hand the large sums which he receives with the other....

The country is ruined by the necessity of defraying the enormous charges required to maintain the splendour of a numerous court, and to pay a large army maintained for the purpose of keeping the people in subjection. No adequate idea can be conveyed of the sufferings of that people. The cudgel and the whip compel them to incessant labour for the benefit of others; and driven to despair by every kind of cruel treatment, their revolt or their flight is only prevented by the presence of a military force.

The misery of this ill-fated country is increased by the practice which prevails too much at all times, but especially on the breaking out of an important war, of selling the different governments for immense sums in hard cash. Hence it naturally becomes the principal object of the individual thus appointed Governor, to obtain repayment of the purchase-money, which he borrowed as he could at a ruinous rate of interest.... The Governor must also enforce the payment of the regular tribute to the King; and although he was originally a wretched slave, involved in debt, and without the smallest patrimony, he yet becomes a great and opulent lord.

Thus do ruin and desolation overspread the land. The provincial governors, as before observed, are so many petty tyrants, possessing a boundless authority; and as there is no one to whom the oppressed subject may appeal, he cannot hope for redress, let his injuries be ever so grievous or ever so frequently repeated.

[Religious law kept Muslim women in seclusion. When Bernier was called into the Seraglio or women's quarters to treat an ill court lady.] ... a Kashmir shawl covered my head, hanging like a large scarf down to my feet, and an eunuch led me by the hand, as if I had been a blind man....

The Princesses and great ladies of the Seraglio have also different modes of travelling. Some prefer *tchaudoules*, which are borne on men's shoulders.... They are gilt and painted and covered with magnificent silk nets of many colours, enriched with embroidery, fringes, and beautiful tassels. Others travel in a stately and close *paleky*, with gilt and covered, over which are also expanded similar silk nets. Some again

use capacious litters, suspended between two powerful camels, or between two small elephants....

Close to the Princess are the chief eunuchs, richly adorned and finely mounted, each with a wand of office in his hand, and surrounding her elephant, a troop of female servants.... Besides these attendants are several eunuchs on horseback, accompanied by a multitude of *Pagys*, or lackeys on foot, with large canes, who advance a great way before the Princess, both to the right and to the left, for the purpose of clearing the road and driving before them every intruder....

Truly it is with difficulty that these ladies can be approached, and they are almost inaccessible to the sight of man. Woe to the unlucky cavalier, however exalted in rank, who, meeting the procession, is found too near. Nothing can exceed the insolence of the tribes of eunuchs and footmen which he has to encounter, and they eagerly avail themselves of any such opportunity to beat a man in the most unmerciful manner. I shall not easily forget being once surprised in a similar situation, and how narrowly I escaped the cruel treatment that many cavaliers have experienced: but determined not to suffer myself to be beaten and perhaps maimed without a struggle, I drew my sword, and having fortunately a strong and spirited horse, I was enabled to open a passage, sword in hand, through a host of assailants, and to dash across the rapid stream....

Many persons whom I then consulted on the subject [of *suttee* or widow immolation] would fain have persuaded me that an excess of affection was the cause why these women burn themselves with their deceased husbands; but I soon found that this abominable practice is the effect of early and deeply rooted prejudices. Every girl is taught by her mother that it is virtuous and laudable in a wife to mingle her ashes with those of her husband, and that no woman of honour will refuse compliance with the established custom. These opinions men have always inculcated as an easy mode of keeping wives in subjection, of securing their attention in times of sickness, and of deterring them from administering poison to their husbands....

She [a woman about to commit suttee] was of middle age, and by no means uncomely. I do not expect, with my limited powers of expression, to convey a full idea of the brutish boldness, or ferocious gaiety depicted on this woman's countenance; of her undaunted step; of the freedom from all perturbation with which she conversed, and permitted herself to be washed; of the look of confidence, or rather of insensibility which she cast upon us; of her easy air, free from dejection; of her lofty carriage, void of embarrassment, when she was examining her little cabin, composed of dry and thick millet straw, with an intermixture of dry wood; when she entered into that cabin, sat down upon the funeral pile, placed her deceased husband's head in her lap, took up a torch, and with her own hand lighted the fire within, while I know not how many *Brahmens* were busily engaged in kindling it without....

It is true, however, that I have known some of these unhappy widows shrink at the sight of the piled wood; so as to leave no doubt on my mind that they would willingly have recanted, if recantation had been permitted by the merciless *Brahmens*; but those demons excite or astound the affrighted victims, and even thrust them into the fire. I was present when a poor young woman, who had fallen back five or six paces from the pit, was thus driven forward; and I saw another of these wretched beings struggling to leave the funeral pile when the fire increased around her person, but she was prevented from escaping by the long poles of the diabolical executioners.

Bernier, François. *Travels in the Mogul Empire*. Trans. Irving Brock. Rev. Archibald Constable. New Delhi: S. Chand and Co., 1891; 2nd ed. 1968. Pp. xxiii, 221-222, 230-231, 240-245, 247-252, 267, 310-311, 313, 371-374.

► **15th-Century Chinese Ship**

CHINA'S BRIEF MARITIME HEGEMONY

China dominated the seas from the western Pacific to the coast of East Africa during the first half of the fifteenth century, thanks to the efforts of the eunuch courtier- diplomat, admiral Cheng Ho. This remarkable episode in Chinese history is the topic of this reading.

In 1368, the army of Chu Yuan-chang (1368-1398) defeated the Mongols and established the Ming ("brilliant") dynasty (1368-1644). Because his eldest son the crown prince had died earlier, Chu Yuan-chang (Emperor Hung-wu) was succeeded by his teenage grandson, Hui-ti, in 1398. Prince Yen, the young emperor's ambitious uncle, revolted after the boy's accession, and in a civil war captured the capital city Nanking in 1402. He became Emperor Yung-lo (r. 1402-1425). Hui-ti, however, disappeared in the confusion. Yung-lo moved the capital city from Nanking of bad memory, to Peking, where his power base lay. His rule was successful: he subdued the nomads of inner Asia, and restored economic prosperity. Yung-lo, however, remained uneasy because he could not find his fugitive nephew in China. Had Hui-ti fled abroad?

In 1405, Yung-lo ordered a large naval expedition to head for the "Western Oceans" with a eunuch soldier-diplomat, Cheng Ho, as its commander. Yung-lo's ostensible goal was to proclaim the resurgence of Chinese power under the Ming dynasty and to cow the rulers of Southeast and South Asia into enrolling as vassals of the Ming. This display of force in local political disputes had the desired effect, and at least twenty states in South and Southeast Asia enrolled as Chinese tributary states. Cheng also brought with him Chinese luxury products, notably silks and porcelain, and made gifts of them to local rulers and held trade fairs. The result was increased Chinese trade throughout Asia, and even to East Africa. Cheng also had a secret mission: to obtain information about Hui-ti, but he found no trace of him. Hui-ti, who had become a Buddhist monk, was in fact found in China in 1441. Yung-lo had long since died and his great-grandson, then emperor, allowed the aged ex-emperor to end his days in monastic peace.

Cheng Ho headed seven naval expeditions, and brought great diplomatic prestige, increased trade, and geographic knowledge to China. However, China established no overseas naval bases and planted no colonies although many Chinese from coastal provinces settled in Southeast Asia.

Since Cheng was a eunuch and not a civil servant, the civil service opposed his expensive and seemingly impractical exploits, which ended with his death. A later emperor failed to equip a new expedition because the bureaucrats claimed that Cheng's charts were lost. Subsequent rulers lost interest and China never led the way in maritime matters again.

QUESTIONS:

1) What personal qualities did Cheng Ho possess that made him a successful commander?
2) What benefits did China derive from Cheng Ho's voyages?
3) What are the names of some of the modern countries visited by Cheng Ho's fleet?

[Cheng Ho] lived approximately from 1371 to 1435.... Different versions have been given by various scholars of his life. The one which is generally accepted [says the following:] ... At the beginning of the Ming dynasty, a number of generals who fought on the frontiers were in charge of selecting eunuchs for the Imperial Court. In 1381, Yunnan was pacified and Cheng Ho was one of the selected children who at that time must have been less than ten years old....

From other sources, we learn that he was born in a Mohammedan family by the name of Ma, at K'unyang in Yunnan.... His life [after he became a eunuch] may be divided into two stages. Before the age of thirty-five he had built a home in Peking but spent most of his time in army service. His long years of military life had made him courageous, adaptable and resolute. This had much to do later with his organizing technique, command ability and adaptability. The remaining thirty years of his life were almost entirely spent on the sea.

On January 1, 1404 ... he was [appointed] Superintendent of Eunuch Affairs and given the name of Cheng by the Emperor [Chinese emperors bestowed their own or other surnames as rewards to meritorious servants and government officials]. Shortly after he was appointed commander of the great [naval] expedition. Meanwhile local governments in some coastal regions were ordered to construct ocean vessels. By July, 1405, 1180 ships were built.

The largest ocean vessel was about 500 feet in length and 211.5 feet broad. The first expedition consisted of 27,000 men and 62 large vessels each of which carried about four or five hundred people, valuable gifts of silks, embroideries, and curiosities, as well as all the necessary provisions....

The fleet set sail from Liuchia Ho on the Yangtze estuary [on a southward course. After passing] ... through the Malacca Straits it entered ... the Indian Ocean. Its object was to reach the country of Kuli, the present Calicut on the Malabar Coast of India, which was then the focal point of all sea routes in the Indian Ocean, and held the key position between many states in Southern Asia and the Near East.... For some years Kuli had maintained very amicable relations with China. On account of its frequent delivery of tribute to the Ming Court, Cheng Ho was authorized to entitle the chief, Sami, king of Kuli. Cheng Ho handed Sami the imperial gifts and Sami in return gave a great celebration for their visit....

Two years later, the expedition sailed homeward. As the fleet passed by Chiu Kang ... present Palembang [on Sumatra in Indonesia], it encountered the fleet of a powerful [Chinese] pirate named Ch'en Tsu-i who had for years been a threat to the voyagers passing the Malacca Strait.... After a major sea battle, Ch'en's fleet was badly defeated. More than five thousand of his crew were killed, ten of his vessels were burned, seven others damaged and Ch'en ... was captured alive. The victory undoubtedly gave great prestige to the ... Ming dynasty in Southern Asia.

On their way back the whole expedition visited Java [where a civil war was raging. Cheng intervened on behalf of the rightful ruler and] ... raised the heir of the East King to regain his kingdom. In the summer of 1407, Cheng Ho returned to Peking and reported to the Emperor....

When winter [1407] came, Cheng Ho was against sent overseas. Two events were the outcome of his second voyage. First, Peking received tribute from the king of Po-ni or Borneo ... [who] with all his family and loads of tribute came to visit China.... Second, an international exhibition was conducted by Cheng Ho in Ceylon ... [where] he displayed the best Chinese products such as gold and silver candlesticks, embroideries and articles used in Buddhist ceremonies.... In 1911, an old stone ... [monument commemorating] this exhibition was discovered on [Ceylon] inscribed in Chinese, Tamil, and Persian....

[In 1409] Cheng Ho made his third voyage ... with the same number of crew but only forty-eight vessels.... More countries were visited [than during the previous voyages] and their rulers received gifts from the Imperial court of China. It ... was the first time a Chinese expedition succeeded in making an extended voyage to the Persian Gulf, the Red Sea and the east coast of Africa.... [While in Ceylon Cheng Ho fought] the second large battle in his overseas expeditions.... With a force of about 2,000 men [Cheng] cracked the blockade [imposed by the king of Ceylon], joined his main force, and pressed on with an all-out attack on the capital. The king was captured alive. Cheng Ho [then] set the king free ... and selected another [prince] from the royal house to replace him.... The increase in [China's] prestige from this battle was beyond measure....

Six years later, for the fourth time, Cheng Ho set out again. This time he took with him a number of interpreters ... and sailed along the same route as before ... in forty vessels.... Their mission on this voyage was to acquire information. Many books from the Near Eastern countries were translated [into Chinese as a result]. The climatic conditions and surface features of these countries were described in great detail, together with their important products....

In 1416, in return for the enormous quantities of tribute paid to the Ming court by nineteen countries, Cheng Ho was again sent out, to deliver gifts [on behalf of the Chinese emperor]. He ... brought home a variety of strange animals from different places ... [including] lions, panthers, "Western horses," giraffes, and ostriches....

In the spring of 1421, Cheng Ho was ordered to convoy a number of foreign envoys from sixteen countries [back to their homes], and for the sixth time he set sail, heading toward the Near East. The sixteen countries [included] Hormuz, Aden,.. Mogadishu, Calicut, Cochin, Ceylon, Maldive Islands, Sumatra, Malacca, etc. ....

His last voyage was begun in July, 1430.... They spent three years abroad. Everything was recorded in great detail and in chronological order. Dates of departure and anchorage and the distances from one place to another were measured by time....

It is still hard to ascertain the number of states the great voyager officially visited.... [However it is clear that Cheng went to places] which had never been visited by any Chinese before, such as the Flores group, southern Sumatra, Sembilon, Andaman Islands, Maldive Islands, Hormuz, La-sha, Juwar, Mogadishu, Brawa, Jubaland etc. .... What deserves special mention are the two voyages to East Africa ... [because before this] there is no indication that the Chinese had ever reached the shores of East Africa.... [As a result] not only were the geographical features of these countries brought to light, but many myths of the African coast told by the Arabs were converted into real knowledge.

The great extent of treeless country in present Somaliland was impressive to the Chinese. Of the interior of Mogadishu, Fei Hsin [a member of the expedition] wrote, "The land is composed of chains of hills and extensive waste. As far as the eye can reach, one fails to grasp anything but the yellow dust and barren rocks. The soil is poor and the crops sparse. It may not rain for a number of years. People make very deep wells and draw up the water in sheep-skin bags by means of cog-wheels.

[The quarter century of Cheng's voyages] was indeed the most fascinating era in China's history of ocean navigation.... Cheng Ho's expeditions succeeded in making a thorough survey of every possible sea route to nearly all insular countries in southern Asia, the Arab countries in the Near East and around the whole Indian Ocean.... What seems [especially] important are that the major sea lanes they used have been little altered by modern maritime navigation.... By reading some of the legends on the nautical charts, we find that the navigators of this period counted very little on the location of the stars in seeking their sailing directions but depended upon very delicate compasses and instruments. By looking at the stars they simply checked their general direction and thus the cartographers could ascertain the approximate location of each place they visited. As to the size of the vessels, we are surprised to see that it represented the greatest achievement in ocean craft previous to the Industrial Revolution. The last voyage was composed of 27,750 men but with only forty ships. Each ship carried about 700 men, not counting the load of tribute and presents and necessary provisions....

No name should be written greater in the history of Chinese overseas exploration than that of Cheng Ho. The scale of his operations indeed has not only dwarfed all those of his predecessors in China but also set a record scarcely matched by any in world history prior to the Industrial Revolution.... It is true that Cheng Ho missed a great share of fame and glory because he did not sail around Africa as Vasco da Gama did seventy-six years later. But it would be false to assume that he was unable to do so.... Why [is it that] Cheng Ho did not take advantage of his great task force and sail around Africa?.... [Because, in contrast to hostility between European Christians and Muslim Arabs] there was no religious conflict nor any economic rivalry between the Chinese and the Arabs [who lived to the west of China and who dominated the trade routes to Europe].... For the Chinese,

there was no pressing need to find a long winding route around Africa while they could carry on their trade directly through the Indian Ocean and the Persian Gulf to the Mediterranean shore. In 1487, Bartholomew Dias sailed around the Cape of Good Hope to the mouth of the Great Fish River. From 1492 to 1498, Christopher Columbus made four voyages across the Atlantic to the West Indies. In 1497, Vasco da Gama succeeded in sailing around the Dark Continent and hit Calicut or Kuli as ... [the Chinese] called it. Following this was the circum-navigation of Ferdinand Magellan.... What made da Gama, Columbus, and Magellan more widely known than this great Chinese explorer is largely that the former three had the great good fortune to have many successors who carried on their task. In contrast to this is China's fading maritime interest where not a single "Cheng Ho" emerged as successor to the great Eunuch Admiral.

Chang, Kuei-sheng. *Chinese Great Explorers: Their Effect upon Chinese Geographic Knowledge prior to 1600.* Diss. Michigan 1955. Pp. 299-309, 315-316, 318-319, 324, 328-329.

SECTION 7

GROWTH OF WESTERN PREEMINENCE

Before about 1400 C.E., the great civilizations of Europe and Asia were roughly comparable in their scientific and technological achievements, and each had learned from others. However, beginning in the fourteenth century, although the Asian empires were larger, wealthier, and more powerful than contemporary European states, something was happening in Europe that would give it a position of advantage over the rest of the world in later centuries. This event was the Renaissance, a rebirth of learning about the classical civilizations of ancient Greece and Rome, and an awakening in intellectual curiosity that freed the minds of men and women from earlier strictures and outmoded habits of thought. The Renaissance began in Italy and spread to northern Europe. In the absence of a similar movement, other parts of the world remained relatively static while Europe forged ahead.

This section begins with the Renaissance, followed by a reading by Martin Luther, the father of the Protestant Reformation. These two movements paralleled the voyages of discovery that opened new continents to Europeans and established direct sea routes between Europe and Asia. Two of the readings come from the journals kept during the early epic voyages. Europeans journeyed to Asia and the Americas to trade, colonize, and proselytize. Several readings pertain to the wide range of European ventures in Asia and the Americas; they range from the role of Jesuit missionaries in China and a British diplomatic mission to China, to accounts of Spanish colonial life in the Americas and the Philippines, of the Dutch in the East Indies, and of the English in North America. Other readings deal with colonial rivalries between Great Britain and France in North America and India; still others bear on the importing of slaves from Africa to the Americas, the inhumanity of the slave trade, and British efforts to end the practice. Another describes the life of native Americans.

The common thread running through this section is the European initiative in the linking of world regions and the subsequent Western dominance around the globe. The more fragile of the non-western cultures, such as those in the Americas and in Southeast Asia, quickly fell to European domination. While the proud Chinese empire remained strong and independent on the surface, by closing its doors to innovations and modernization, it had become doomed by the eighteenth century. Thus the events that began with the Renaissance resulted in Western political and economic preeminence in the modern world.

ADVICE TO TWO RENAISSANCE PRINCES

▶ **Woodcut of Renaissance Scholar**

The Renaissance in Europe occurred between about 1350 and 1600. Renaissance scholars revered ancient Greece and Rome; they systematically sought and studied manuscripts of classical authors and absorbed the humanistic outlook they found in them. Classical texts became widely available after 1450 with the spread of printing and the establishment of libraries by rich patrons. Renaissance thinkers, writers, and artists emphasized the diverse potentials of human beings and aimed at personal distinction through the full and harmonious development of both the body and the intellect.

The Renaissance began in Italy for several reasons. One was trade, which had remained important throughout the Middle Ages; it provided the material resources for cultural development. A second reason was the existence of thriving cities, since the Crusades, for example, Florence, Milan, and Genoa. Italian cities enjoyed great autonomy and contended with one another both culturally and commercially. A third reason was the ancient Roman artistic and architectural heritage, and the persistence of Latin among educated Italians, who kept alive memories of classical antiquity. Finally, Italy's geographic location allowed it to benefit from both the Islamic and the Byzantine cultures.

During the Renaissance period, innovative thinkers known as humanists espoused a secular and individualistic attitude toward ethics. They believed that all individuals were masters of their own lives, and that success or failure depended on imagination, intelligence, ambition, and self-reliance. The ideal person was the "universal man," who excelled in many different fields.

A wider world opened up by voyages of exploration also influenced writers and artists, as did scientific advances. In addition, the growth of a capitalistic economy generated wealth to sustain the many new intellectual and artistic developments.

The following passages present two contrasting Renaissance views of how princes should develop their potentials. Both offer advice to persons in positions of power, but the resemblance ceases there. In the first selection, Lorenzo de' Medici of the powerful Medici family of Florence offers counsel to his fourteen-year-old son Giovanni, already a cardinal of the Catholic Church and later Pope Leo X (r. 1513-1521). The elevation of men within the church hierarchy based on family rather than merit during the Renaissance damaged the reputation of the Catholic Church and was a contributing reason for the Reformation.

The second selection is from Niccolò Machiavelli's (1469-1527) *The Prince*, the archetypal guide book on the practice of power politics. He recommends appropriate actions to attain and retain power. The amorality of Machiavelli's book reflects the violent and unstable politics in the city-states of Renaissance Italy.

QUESTIONS:

1) What are the essential differences in the two passages of advice?
2) What does Lorenzo de' Medici seem most concerned with in giving advice to his son?
3) Does the advice given by Machiavelli appear immoral in any way? Or is morality beside the point?

You ought to be grateful to God, and continually to recollect that it is not through your merits, your prudence, or your solicitude, that [your appointment as cardinal] has taken place, but through his favor, which you can only repay by a pious, chaste and exemplary life; and that your obligations to the performance of these duties are so much the greater, as in your early years you have given some reasonable expectations that your riper age may produce such fruits.... Endeavor therefore to alleviate the burden of your early dignity by the regularity of your life and by your perseverance in those studies which are suitable to your profession. It gave me great satisfaction to learn that, in the course of the past year, you had frequently, of your own accord, gone to communion and confession; nor do I conceive that there is any better way of obtaining the favor of heaven than by habituating yourself to a performance of these and similar duties....

I well know, that as you are now to reside at Rome, that sink of all iniquity, the difficulty of conducting yourself by these admonitions will be increased. The influence of example is itself prevalent; but you will probably meet with those who will particularly endeavor to corrupt and incite you to vice; because, as you may yourself perceive, your early attainment to so great a dignity is not observed without envy, and those who could not prevent your receiving that honor will secretly endeavor to diminish it, by inducing you to forfeit the good estimation of the public; thereby precipitating you into that gulf into which they had themselves fallen; in which attempt, the consideration of your youth will give them a confidence of success. To these difficulties you ought to oppose yourself with a greater firmness, as there is at present less virtue among your brethren of the college [of cardinals]. I acknowledge indeed that several of them are good and learned men, whose lives are exemplary, and whom I would recommend to you as patterns of your conduct. By emulating

them you will be so much the more known and esteemed, in proportion as your age and the peculiarity of your situation will distinguish you from your colleagues. Avoid ... the imputation of hypocrisy; guard against all ostentation, either in your conduct or your discourse; affect not austerity, nor even appear too serious. This advice, you will, I hope, in time understand and practice better than I can express it.

Yet you are not unacquainted with the great importance of the character which you have to sustain, for you well know that all the Christian world would prosper if the cardinals were what they ought to be; because in such a case there would always be a good pope, upon which the tranquility of Christendom so materially depends. Endeavor then to render yourself such, that if all the rest resembled you, we might expect this universal blessing.... I shall ... recommend that in your intercourse with the cardinals and other men of rank, your language be unassuming and respectful, guiding yourself, however, by your own reason, and not submitting to be impelled by the passions of others, who, actuated by improper motives, may pervert the use of their reasons. Let it satisfy your conscience that your conversation is without intentional offence; and if, through impetuosity of temper, any one should be offended, as his enmity is without just cause, so it will not be very lasting. On this your first visit to Rome, it will however be more advisable for you to listen to others than to speak much yourself.

You are now devoted to God and the church: on which account you ought to aim at being a good ecclesiastic, and to show that you prefer the honor and state of the church and of the apostolic see to every other consideration. Nor, while you keep this in view, will it be difficult for you to favor your family and your native place. On the contrary, you should be the link to bind this city closer to the church, and our family with the city; and although it be impossible to foresee what accidents may happen, yet I doubt not but this may be done with equal advantage to all; observing, however, that you are always to prefer the interests of the church.

You are not only the youngest cardinal in the college, but the youngest person that ever was raised to that rank; and you ought therefore to be the most vigilant and unassuming, not giving others occasion to wait for you, either in the chapel, the consistory [gathering of cardinals] or upon deputations. You will soon get a sufficient insight into the manners of your brethren. With those of less respectable character converse not with too much intimacy; not merely on account of the circumstance in itself, but for the sake of public opinion. Converse on general topics with all. On public occasions let your equipage and your address be rather below than above mediocrity. A handsome house and a well-ordered family will be preferable to a great retinue and a splendid residence. Endeavor to live with regularity, and gradually to bring your expenses within those bounds which in a new establishment cannot perhaps be expected. Silk and jewels are not suitable for persons in your station. Your taste will be better shown in the acquisition of a few elegant remains of antiquity, or in the collecting of handsome books, and by your attendants being learned and well-bred rather than numerous. Invite others to your house oftener than you receive invitations. Practise neither too frequently. Let your own food be plain, and take sufficient exercise, for those who wear your habit are soon liable, without great caution, to contract infirmities. The station of a cardinal is not less secure than elevated; on which account those who arrive at it too frequently become negligent; conceiving their object is attained and that they can preserve it with little trouble. This idea is often injurious to the life and character of those who entertain it. Be attentive therefore to your conduct, and confide in others too little rather than too much. There is one rule which I would recommend to your attention in preference to all others. Rise early in the morning. This will not only contribute to your health, but will enable you to arrange and expedite the business of the day; and as there are various duties incident to your station, such as the performance of divine service, studying, giving audience, and so forth,

you will find the observance of this admonition productive of the greatest utility.... Deliberate every evening on what you may have to perform the following day, that you may not be unprepared for whatever may happen. With respect to your speaking in the consistory, it will be most becoming for you at present to refer the matters in debate to the judgment of his holiness, alleging as a reason your own youth and inexperience. You will probably be desired to intercede for the favors of the pope on particular occasions. Be cautious, however, that you trouble him not too often; for his temper leads him to be most liberal to those who weary him least with their solicitations. This you must observe, lest you should give him offence, remembering also at times to converse with him on more agreeable topics; and if you should be obliged to request some kindness from him, let it be done with that modesty and humility which are so pleasing to his disposition. Farewell.

* * * * *

How honorable it is for a prince to keep his word, and act rather with integrity than collusion, I suppose everybody understands: nevertheless experience has shown in our time that those princes who have not pinned themselves up to that punctuality and preciseness have done great things, and by their cunning and subtlety not only circumvented, and darted the brains of those with whom they had to deal, but have overcome and been too hard for those who have been so superstitiously exact. For further explanation you must understand there are two ways of contending, by law and by force: the first is proper to men; the second to beasts; but because many times the first is insufficient, recourse must be had to the second. It belongs, therefore, to a prince to understand both, when to make use of the rational and when of the brutal way; and this is recommended to princes ... by ancient writers, who tell them how Achilles and several other princes were committed to the education of Chiron the Centaur, who was to keep them under his discipline, choosing them a master, half man and half beast, for no other reason but to show how necessary it is for a prince to be acquainted with both, for that one without the other will be of little duration. Seeing, therefore, it is of such importance to a prince to take upon him the nature and disposition of a beast, of all the whole flock he ought to imitate the lion and the fox; for the lion is in danger of toils and snares, and the fox of the wolf; so that he must be a fox to find out the snares, and a lion to fright away the wolves, but they who keep wholly to the lion have no true notion of themselves. A prince, therefore, who is wise and prudent, cannot or ought not to keep his parole [word of honor], when the keeping of it is to his prejudice, and the causes for which he promised removed. Were men all good this doctrine was not to be taught, but because they are wicked and not likely to be punctual with you, you are not obliged to any such strictness with them; nor was there ever any prince that lacked lawful pretence to justify his breach of promise. I might instance in many modern examples, and show how many confederations, and peaces, and promises have been broken by the infidelity of princes, and how he that best personated the fox had the better success. Nevertheless, it is of great consequence to disguise your inclination, and to play the hypocrite well; and men are so simple in their temper and so submissive to their present necessities, that he that is neat and cleanly in his collusions shall never lack people to practice them upon. I cannot forbear one example which is still fresh in our memory. [Pope] Alexander VI [r. 1492-1503] never did, nor thought of, anything but cheating, and never lacked matter to work upon; and though no man promised a thing with greater asseveration, nor confirmed it with more oaths and imprecations, and observed them less, yet understanding the world well he never miscarried.

A prince, therefore, is not obliged to have all the forementioned good qualities in reality, but it is necessary to have them in appearance; nay, I will be bold to affirm that, having them actually, and employing them upon all occasions, they are extremely prejudicial, whereas, having them only in appearance, they turn to better account; it is honorable to seem mild, and merciful, and courteous, and religious, and sincere, and indeed to be so, provided your mind be so rectified and prepared that you can act quite contrary upon occasion.... A prince, especially if come but lately to the throne, cannot observe all those things exactly which make men be esteemed virtuous, being often necessitated, for the preservation of his State, to do things inhuman, uncharitable, and irreligious; and, therefore, it is convenient his mind be at his command, and flexible to all the puffs and variations of fortune; not forbearing to be good while it is in his choice, but knowing how to be evil when there is a necessity. A prince, then, is to have particular care that nothing falls from his mouth but what is full of the five qualities aforesaid, and that to see and to hear him he appears all goodness, integrity, humanity, and religion, which last he ought to pretend to more than ordinarily, because more men do judge by the eye than by the touch; for everybody sees, but few understand; everybody sees how you appear, but few know what in reality you are, and those few dare not oppose the opinion of the multitude, who have the majesty of their prince to defend them; and in the actions of all men, especially princes, where no man has power to judge, every one looks to the end. Let a prince, therefore, do what he can to preserve his life and continue his supremacy, the means which he uses shall be thought honorable, and be commended by everybody; because the people are always taken with the appearance and event of things, and the greatest part of the world consists of the people; those few who are wise taking place when the multitude has nothing else to rely upon. There is a prince at this time in being (but his name I shall conceal) who has nothing in his mouth but fidelity and peace; and yet had he exercised either the one or the other, they had robbed him before this of both his power and reputation.

Roscoe, William. *The Life of Lorenzo de' Medici, Called the Magnificent*. 6th ed. London: Cadell, 1825. Machiavelli, Niccolò. *The Prince and Other Pieces*. Ed. Henry Morley. London: Routledge, 1883. Rpt. in Whitcomb, Merrick, ed. *A Literary Sourcebook of the Italian Renaissance*. Philadelphia: Univ. of Pennsylvania Press, 1900. Pp. 80-86.

► Renaissance Merchant

HIGH FINANCE WHEELING AND DEALING IN RENAISSANCE FRANCE

The Renaissance period was most significant for its cultural developments. The revival of Greek learning and the associated burst of literary, philosophical, and artistic activity make this era of European history especially notable and fascinating. Every educated person is familiar with the great figures of the age--Michelangelo, Leonardo da Vinci, Petrarch, Machiavelli, Erasmus, Montaigne, Cervantes, and Dürer, among many others. But there were critically important developments in other areas as well, among them the rise of great banking families and merchant houses.

The horizons of Europeans expanded vastly during the Renaissance, with sea voyages that culminated in the discovery of the western hemisphere. Other voyages opened new trade routes to the West Asia, India, and China. This resulted in dramatic changes in the economies of European states and the emergence of modern capitalism. Enterprising individuals took advantage of newly accessible markets and sources of raw materials; those who accumulated capital were now willing to risk it in new business endeavors and in novel banking ventures.

In the following passage, we read of the careers of a French father and son with shrewd money management plans. They were typical members of a new entrepreneurial class whose careers in business and banking were fantastically successful, so much so that some of the new aristocrats of finance rivaled even kings and princes in their wealth.

QUESTIONS:

1) In what ways were the father and son described in the following account good opportunists?

2) What special prospects did the profession of merchant offer?

3) What role did royalty and members of the government play in the dealings of merchants described here?

Jacques de Beaune, known to history by the name of his estate at Semblançay, was a merchant of Tours. He was the son of Jean de Beaune, who appears in 1454 as provisioner to the House of Angoulême, and who, ten years later, was one of the biggest businessmen in the kingdom. Jean de Beaune's specialty was cloth, but he dealt in other things as well. We find him, for example, taking an active part in the great commercial undertakings of Louis XI. When Louis XI had four ships built in 1464, the Saint Martin, the Saint Nicholas, the Saint Louis, and the Saint Mary, to follow the four ships that Jacques Coeur had already sent off on the Mediterranean, Jean de Beaune joined Geoffrey le Cyvrier of Montpellier, J. de Cambrai of Lyon, Nicholas Arnoul of Paris, and Jean Plat of Bruges to provide the necessary capital. It was, as can be seen, a broadly based international corporation of great merchants.

Jean de Beaune, then was among those who were charged with receiving goods brought by ship from the Levant and putting these goods into circulation. It 1470 it was he who provided the first raw silks for Italian silk-makers whom Louis XI had brought from the other side of the Alps to settle first in Lyon, then in Tours. Later, with his son-in-law, Jean Briçonnet, he sent to London at the request of the king 25,000 écus worth of spices, cloth of gold, and silk, in an attempt to recapture direct access to the English market, freeing the French from the need to trade through Bruges [in Austrian-controlled Belgium]. Deals at once commercial and political were joined by a financial element. The king drew Jean de Beaune into the seizure of the goods of Cardinal Balue and Philippe de Commines. In 1473 Jean lent the king 30,000 livres, half of which was provided by his son-in-law Briçonnet, to retake Perpignan from the king of Aragon. He was treasurer for the household of the dauphin, Charles (the future Charles VIII). Profit, riches, honors naturally followed. When the king created the position of mayor of Tours in October 1471, Jean de Beaune was the first to hold that office. He married money. He had a house, stables, gardens in Tours, farm land, vineyards, house and property in Touraine worth nearly 23,000 livres. Jean de Beaune was the sketch, the rough draft, the preparation. His son, Jacques de Semblançay, was the finished picture.

First, Jacques was also a merchant draper, but we have just seen in Jean de Beaune how broad the implication of such a profession might be. Jean had three sons. One joined the clergy and the other two, Guillaume and Jacques, were drapers. He left six daughters: six sons-in-laws were drapers or financiers. Jacques, having followed his father into the business, married Jeanne Ruzé, a caste marriage, money marrying money. The Ruzés were, along with the

Beaune's, the Briçonnets, and the Berthelots, the elite of Touraine's rich bourgeois merchant class. The intricate interlacing of alliances by marriage among these families suggests the coherence of their circle, the world of big business and high finance.

Jacques began as a salesman. He sold broadcloth, silk, wool, and linen to several princes. He was the official draper to the houses of Orléans, Angoulême, and La Tremoille. In association with Briçonnet, he sold, between October 1490 and January 1492, 41,127 livres worth of cloth the Charles VIII. At the same time, like his father, he was engaged in financial deals, lending money, keeping his capital at work.

The year 1492 marked a new stage. He was appointed treasurer general to Duchess Anne of Brittany who had become queen of France in 1491. Then, in September of 1492, he added the duties of master of the duchess' household. Jacques de Beaune was no longer a bureaucrat who followed orders. He was a royal administrator who gave them. As such, he was paid, deservedly, 24,000 livres for the treasury, and 2,000 livres for the household. He managed an ordinary budget of 100,000 livres granted the duchess by the king, to which were added annual supplements of 20,000, 40,000, 50,000 livres sometimes. And then, these sums were not paid in cash. They were rights to collect designated receipts--that is, Jacques de Beaune was supposed to do what he could to get the money which, in theory, he was intended to have. Moreover, Anne de Bretagne spent freely, and her squandering caused the treasurer a great deal of work. From January to September 1492, she spent 277,750 livres; from October 1492 to September 1493, 201,199 livres. These expenses were covered by a regular annual budget of 100,000 livres. She spent money for the arts, for luxuries, for her constant travel and that of her court: a great train of carts for baggage and carts for travelers, litters filled with maids and ladies of honor, an army of guides, ushers, boatmen to help cross rivers, horsemen for an escort, people to assure the lodging of the court, and on and on. The administrator of all these people and services was Jacques de Beaune. It was he who advanced money when funds had run out, he who bought back the jewels the queen had pawned in Lyon during the Naples war. It was he who provided dowries for the maids of honor to whom the queen gave sums she did not have. It was he who lent his mistress 20,000 livres in 1495-96. He was an administrator, not a bureaucrat, but still a merchant and a private citizen who was not forbidden to make his own money work as he saw fit. Already he had one foot in the world of the court and politics. In his person commerce acceded to state honors and public offices.

Another barrier was breached in 1496. Jacques de Beaune became one of the four generals of finance, that is, one of the four sovereign administrators of the revenue produced by the *taille* [general tax on property owned by commoners], the *aides* [a type of sales tax], and the *gabelle* [tax on salt]. These four men alone could authorize the use of such moneys by their signatures. This was the source of their importance, their power, their standing. They were neither ministers not great officers of the crown nor gentlemen. Merchants remained ordinary commoners despite their ennoblement and the estates from which they took their names. But they were much more powerful than ministers and great officers of the crown. Such men were at their service, for there was not one of them who did not need the generals of finance to assure the speedy processing of their pensions and appointments. Without them nothing could be done. Lords, cities, sovereign courts needed them to pay wages; poets and courtiers needed them to receive their grants. They were flattered, showered with gifts and offers of hospitality from all sides. Those were the honors. But there was also profit.

Semblançay, the administrator of royal finances, remained at the same time a private citizen who engaged in speculation and who made money. Most visibly he had what amounted to a private bank, at which the beneficiaries of royal generosity negotiated the letters of payment granted them by Semblançay himself. These letters were assigned to various individual tax collectors or *grenetiers* in the kingdom. So as to avoid going great distances and engaging in complicated procedures, the recipients of royal letters of payment generally requested one of the generals of finance to advance them the money. In exchange for a certain percentage, they left to the general the task of getting the money from the tax collectors. Semblançay also found loans for the sovereign at tight moments. He himself lent to the king, and sometimes large sums. For example, in 1503 under Louis XII wars were being waged everywhere, in Naples, Perpignan, Bayonne, Calabria, and Catalonia. Finances were at their lowest ebb. The queen lent 50,000 livres, Jacques de Beaune, 23,000, his father-in-law Guillaume Briçonnet, the duke of Nemours, and the Marechal de Gye 20,000 each. You need not suppose that Jacques de Beaune was in danger of losing his money. He had a thousand potential means of having it back a hundred times over. He made use of them, so much, and so well that one day he became so rich ... that the accumulated hate burst forth and the king had him thrown into prison where he was made to cough up some of his money before finally being hanged at the Montfaucon gallows for dereliction of duty. Semblançay had done nothing but play the game according to the rules.

The example of Semblançay is typical. It was characteristic of an entire large social movement. At the lowest level, the small merchant selling at a fair lent his profit at interest and made money from those poorer than he. At the top, the court merchant, become princely administrator or general of finance, implicated in the highest dealings of politics and diplomacy, moved in the same circle as kings and queens. Both were part of the same pyramid.

Because financial dealings were not at the time separate from commercial dealings, the profession of merchant held the promise of greater things. From such beginnings came enormous fortunes like those of the Ponchers, the Briçonnets, the Beaunes in Paris and Tours, the Du Peyrats in Lyon, the Pincés in Angers, the Bonalds and Vigouroux in Rodez, the Roquettes and Assezats in Toulouse. All lived like princes, lavish princes, Renaissance princes. They did not merely earn huge sums, they spent them as well. All have left their names in the history of the arts because they all filled their fine houses with collections of furniture, fabrics, jewels, works of art truly worthy of a prince. Beneath them were many lesser merchants who had taken 80,000 or 100,000 livres of capital from their business, bringing them a yearly income of 5,000 to 10,000 livres, as much as could be expected from a county or a barony, the income of [a] good bishopric or an abbey. In theory such men were as rich as the richest gentlemen of their provinces. In practice they were richer because they were not encumbered by the same obligations.

A new aristocracy was on the rise, an aristocracy of parvenus which the old aristocracy refused to recognize, which it envied and hated, yet which it was ready enough to marry into.

The aristocracy of capital, of precious metals, was mistress of gold. In a world more and more affected by the thirst for gold, in a world where economic and financial problems were coming more and more to the fore, it was thereby, in part, mistress of Europe's destiny.

Febvre, Lucien. *Life in Renaissance France*. Ed. and trans. Marian Rothstein. Cambridge: Harvard Univ. Press, 1977. Pp. 115-121.

▶ **Woodcut of Martin Luther**

MARTIN LUTHER'S TABLE TALK

▶ **Woodcut of Martin Luther**

Martin Luther (1483-1546), a German priest, theologian, and teacher at the University of Wittenberg, was the principal figure in a movement that ended the unity of western Christianity and began the Protestant Reformation. The immediate cause of Luther's breach with the Roman Catholic church in 1517 was the practice of selling indulgences. Luther also attacked other abuses of the church: clergymen, for example, were often so inadequately educated that they could not read Latin or Greek, the languages of liturgy and Holy Scripture; worse yet, many lived in great affluence and ignored their vows of chastity. There were also widespread abuses in the assigning and discharging of church offices, and the collecting of exorbitant fees for prayers and religious services. Luther responded to questions about indulgences with the publication of his ninety-five theses, which attacked Church practices on many issues. Luther became leader of a massive popular movement directed against the corruption of the papacy and the Roman Catholic church.

Luther stressed the importance of faith--rather than the performance of sacraments, rituals, or good deeds and the veneration of relics--as the true path to God. He also denounced the pope and the Roman Catholic hierarchy. He was duly excommunicated in 1521 and refused to recant his views at the Diet of Worms, held later that year. Luther was condemned for heresy but escaped punishment because of the protection and support of Elector John Frederick of Saxony.

Luther insisted that the church was comprised of all believers, and dismissed the claims of authority by church leaders and councils. He also criticized the church for neglecting the study of Holy Scripture, insisting that the Bible was the ultimate authority for all Christians. To make it more accessible to the unlearned, Luther translated the Bible into German. Luther also espoused the abolition of celibacy for the clergy, the dissolution of monasteries, greater participation in church activities by lay persons, and the reduction of the sacramental rites from seven in the Catholic church to two, baptism and the Lord's Supper.

Luther's movement forever fractured the unity of the Christian church. The Lutheran church continued to spread after his death. Other important Protestant movements, such as Calvinism in Switzerland and Anglicanism in England further splintered Christianity.

The selections that follow are from Luther's *Table Talks*, a collection of sayings, opinions, reminiscences, and conversations assembled by his friends.

QUESTIONS:

1) Why was the Bible so important to Luther?
2) What about the behavior of popes was so objectionable to Luther?

3) What were Luther's attitudes about women?

That the Bible is God's word and book I prove thus: All things that have been, and are, in the world, and the manner of their being, are described in the first books of Moses on the creation; even as God made and shaped the world, so does it stand to this day. Infinite potentates have raged against this book, and sought to destroy and uproot it--king Alexander the Great, the princes of Egypt and of Babylon, the monarchs of Persia, of Greece, and of Rome, the emperors Julius and Augustus--but they nothing prevailed; they are all gone and vanished, while the book remains, and will remain for ever and ever, perfect and entire, as it was declared at the first. Who has thus helped it--who has thus protected it against such mighty forces? No one, surely, but God himself, who is the master of all things....

While the Romish church stood, the Bible was never given to the people in such shape that they could clearly, understandingly, surely, and easily read it, as they now can in the German translation, which, thank God, we have prepared here at Wittenberg.

* * * * *

I did not learn my divinity at once, but was constrained by my temptations to search deeper and deeper; for no man, without trials and temptations, can attain a true understanding of the Holy Scriptures. St. Paul had a devil that beat him with fists, and with temptations drove him diligently to study the Holy Scripture. I had hanging on my neck the pope, the universities, all the deep-learned, and the devil; these hunted me into the Bible, wherein I sedulously read, and thereby, God be praised, at length attained a true understanding of it. Without such a devil, we are but only speculators of divinity, and according to our vain reasoning, dream that so and so it must be, as the monks and friars in monasteries do. The Holy Scripture of itself is certain and true: God grant me the grace to catch hold of its just use.

* * * * *

Twenty years is but a short time, yet in that short time the world were empty, if there was no marrying and production of children. For I believe, when a little child dies of one year old, that always one, yea, two thousand die with it, of that age or younger; but when I, Luther, die, that am sixty-three, I believe that not three-score, or one hundred at the most, will die with me of that age, or older; for people now grow not old; not many people live to my years. Mankind is nothing else but a sheep-shambles, where we are slain and slaughtered by the devil. How many sorts of deaths are in our bodies? Nothing is therein but death.

* * * * *

There are three sorts of people: the first, the common sort, who live secure without remorse of conscience, acknowledging not their corrupt manners and natures, insensible of God's wrath against their sins, and careless thereof. The second, those who through the law are scared, feel God's anger, and strive and wrestle with despair. The third, those that acknowledge their sins and God's merited wrath, feel themselves conceived and born in sin, and therefore deserving of perdition, but, notwithstanding, attentively hearken to the gospel, and believe that God, out of grace, for the sake of Jesus Christ, forgives sins, and so are justified before God, and afterwards show the fruits of their faith by all manner of good works.

* * * * *

I never work better than when I am inspired by anger; when I am angry, I can write, pray, and preach well, for then my whole temperament is quickened, my understanding sharpened, and all mundane vexations and temptations depart.

* * * * *

The anabaptists [a minor Protestant sect] cavil as to how the salvation of man is to be effected by water. The simple answer is, that all things are possible to him who believes in God Almighty. If, indeed, a baker were to say to me: "This bread is a body, and this wine is blood," I should laugh at him incredulously. But when Jesus Christ, the Almighty God, taking in his hand bread and wine, tells me: "This is my body and my blood," then we must believe, for it is God who speaks--God who with a word created all things.

* * * * *

I would not have preachers in their sermons use Hebrew, Greek, or foreign languages, for in the church we ought to speak as we use to do at home, the plain mother tongue, which every one is acquainted with. It may be allowed in courtiers, lawyers, advocates, &c., to use quaint, curious words. Doctor Staupitz is a very learned man, yet he is a very irksome preacher; and the people had rather hear a plain brother preach, that delivers his words simply to their understanding, than he. In churches no praising or extolling should be sought after. St. Paul never used such high and stately words as Demosthenes and Cicero did, but he spake, properly and plainly, words which signified and showed high and stately matters, and he did well.

* * * * *

Antichrist is the pope and the Turk together; a beast full of life must have a body and soul; the spirit or soul of antichrist, is the pope, his flesh or body the Turk. The latter wastes and assails and persecutes God's church corporally; the former spiritually and corporally too, with hanging, burning, murdering, &c. But, as in the apostle's time, the church had the victory over the Jews and Romans, so now will she keep the field firm and solid against the hypocrisy and idolatry of the pope, and the tyranny and devastations of the Turk and her other enemies.

* * * * *

Whence comes it that the popes pretend 'tis they who form the church, when, all the while, they are bitter enemies of the church, and have no knowledge, certainly no comprehension, of the holy gospel? Pope, cardinals, bishops, not a soul of them has read the Bible; 'tis a book unknown to them. They are a pack of guzzling, stuffing wretches, rich, wallowing in wealth and laziness, resting secure in their power, and never, for a moment, thinking of accomplishing God's will. The Sadducees were infinitely more pious than the papists, from whose holiness God preserve us. May he preserve us, too, from security, which engenders ingratitude, contempt of God, blasphemy, and the persecution of divine things.

* * * * *

Kings and princes coin money out of metals, but the pope coins money out of everything-- indulgences, ceremonies, dispensations, pardons; 'tis all fish comes to his net. 'Tis only baptism escapes him, for children came into the world without clothes to be stolen, or teeth to be drawn.

* * * * *

A gentleman being at the point of death, a monk from the next convent came to see what he could pick up, and said to the gentleman: Sir, will you give so and so to our monastery? The dying man, unable to speak, replied by a nod of the head, whereupon the monk, turning to the gentleman's son, said: You see, your father makes us this bequest. The son said to the father: Sir, is it your pleasure that I kick this monk down stairs? The dying man nodded as before, and the son forthwith drove the monk out of doors.

* * * * *

They once showed here, at Wittenberg, the drawers of St. Joseph and the breeches of St. Francis. The bishop of Mayence boasted he had a gleam of the flame of Moses' bush. At Compostella they exhibit the standard of the victory that Jesus Christ gained over death and the devil. The crown of thorns is shown in several places.

* * * * *

They show, at Rome, the head of St. John the Baptist, though 'tis well known that the Saracens opened his tomb, and burned his remains to ashes. These impostures of the papists cannot be too seriously reprehended.

* * * * *

If the pope were the head of the Christian church, then the church were a monster with two heads, seeing that St. Paul says that Christ is her head. The pope may well be, and is, the head of the false church.

* * * * *

There are many that think I am too fierce against Popedom; on the contrary, I complain that I am, alas! too mild; I wish I could breathe out lightning against the pope and Popedom, and that every word were a thunderbolt.

* * * * *

The pope and his crew can in nowise endure the idea of reformation; the mere word creates more alarm at Rome, than thunderbolts from heaven, or the day of judgment. A cardinal said, the other day: Let them eat, and drink, and do what they will; but as to reforming us, we think that is a vain idea; we will not endure it. Neither will we Protestants be satisfied, though they administer the sacrament in both kinds, and permit priests to marry; we will also have the doctrine of the faith pure and unfalsified, and the righteousness that justifies and saves before God, and which expels and drives away all idolatry and false-worshipping; these gone and banished, the foundation on which Popedom is built falls also.

* * * * *

It was asked: Can good Christians and God-fearing people also undergo witchcraft? Luther replied: Yes; for our bodies are always exposed to the attacks of Satan. The maladies I suffer are not natural, but devil's spells.

* * * * *

When I am assailed with heavy tribulations, I rush out among my pigs, rather than remain alone by myself. The human heart is like a millstone in a mill; when you put wheat under it, it turns and grinds and bruises the wheat to flour; if you put no wheat, it still grinds on, but then 'tis itself it grinds and wears away. So the human heart, unless it be occupied with some employment, leaves space for the devil, who wriggles himself in, and brings with him a whole host of evil thoughts, temptations, and tribulations, which grind out the heart.

* * * * *

Between husband and wife there should be no question as to *meum* [mine] and *tuum* [yours]. All things should be in common between them, without any distinction or means of distinguishing.

* * * * *

St. Augustin said, finely: A marriage without children is the world without the sun.

* * * * *

Men have broad and large chests, and small narrow hips, and more understanding than the women, who have but small and narrow breasts, and broad hips, to the end they should remain at home, sit still, keep house, and bear and bring up children.

* * * * *

Dr. Luther said one day to his wife: You make me do what you will; you have full sovereignty here, and I award you, with all my heart, the command in all household matters, reserving my rights in other points. Never any good came out of female domination. God created Adam master and lord of living creatures, but Eve spoilt all, when she persuaded him to set himself above God's will. 'Tis you women, with your tricks and artifices, that lead men into error.

* * * * *

There are two sorts of adultery; spiritual adultery, committed only in sight of God, when one desires the husband or wife of another; and bodily adultery, when the offence is actually committed, a crime most odious, but little regarded by the world, a crime at once against God, against society, and against one's family.

* * * * *

Dr. Luther said, in reference to those who write satirical attacks upon women, that such will not go unpunished. If the author be one of high rank, rest assured he is not really of noble origin, but a surreptitious intruder into the family. What defects women have, we must check them for in private, gently by word of mouth, for woman is a frail vessel. The doctor then turned round and said: let us talk of something else.

* * * * *

St. Ulrich, bishop of Augsburg, related a fearful thing that befel at Rome. Pope Gregory, who confirmed celibacy, ordered that a fish-pond at Rome, hard by a convent of nuns, to be cleared out. The water being let off, there were found, at the bottom, more than six thousand skulls of children, that had been cast into the pond and drowned. Such were the fruits of enforced celibacy, but the popes who succeeded him, re-established it.

In our own time, there was in Austria, at Nieuberg, a convent of nuns, who, by reason of their licentious doings, were removed from it, and placed elsewhere, and their convent filled with Franciscans. These monks, wishing to enlarge the building, foundations were dug, and in excavating there were found twelve great pots, in each of which was the carcass of an infant. How much better to let these people marry, than, by prohibition thereof, to cause the murder of so many innocent creatures.

* * * * *

I have oftentimes noted, when women receive the doctrine of the gospel, they are far more fervent in faith, they hold to it more stiff and fast, than men do; as we see in the loving Magdalen, who was more hearty and bold than Peter.

* * * * *

I am a great enemy to flies: *Quia sunt imagines diaboli et haereticorum* [because they are images of the devil and of heretics]. When I have a good book, they flock upon it and parade up and down upon it, and soil it. 'Tis just the same with the devil; when our hearts are purest, he comes and soils them.

Hazlitt, William, ed. & trans. *The Table Talk of Martin Luther*. London: Bell, 1878. Pp. 1-2, 27, 57, 61, 152-153, 163, 185, 193, 196-199, 206, 208-209, 252, 275, 298-300, 302-303, 307-308, 367.

VASCO DA GAMA OPENS THE ROUTE TO INDIA VIA AFRICA

Portugal and Spain initiated the great age of exploration and discovery in the fifteenth century. Under sponsorship of kings of Portugal, explorers sailed down the west coast of Africa; Bartolomeu Dias reached the Cape of Good Hope in 1488, and Vasco da Gama discovered a sea route to India between 1497 and 1499. This momentous event crowned Portugal's leadership in voyages of discovery and altered world trade patterns. Its first beneficiary, Portugal, reaped huge financial gains from the profitable spice trade that had for centuries traveled by land through the Middle East to Alexandria in Egypt, thence by sea in Venetian vessels to European ports. The losers were Venice and other Mediterranean ports, which went into decline.

Trade with Asia made Portugal wealthy in the sixteenth century; Lisbon became a thriving port. By the end of the sixteenth century, however, Portugal had been exhausted by defending the sea routes to Asia, building and garrisoning forts at strategic points in Africa and Asia to maintain its trade monopoly, and manning naval patrols against its powerful European rivals. By the seventeenth century, Spain, England, and the Netherlands had eclipsed Portugal.

The Portuguese nevertheless proudly remember their far-seeing monarchs who financed the voyages, and the great seamen who opened up the world to Europe and added to knowledge of cartography and geography. Under King Joao, Bartolomeu Dias traced the west African coast down to the Cape of Good Hope. King Manuel chose Vasco da Gama to complete the discovery of an ocean route to India, and to look for a mighty mythical Christian sovereign named Prestor John. Legend had him either in Africa (some thought he was emperor of Ethiopia) or in India. Europeans hoped to find in Prester John an ally against the Moors.

Born around 1460, Vasco da Gama came from a genteel family which had distinguished itself in Portugal's wars against the Muslim Moors. After serving in the Portuguese navy, he amply proved his ability during his difficult voyage to India, never losing the confidence of his sailors. Da Gama ranks with Christopher Columbus and Ferdinand Magellan as one of the greatest navigators of the Age of Explorations and Discoveries. Europeans were the newest comers along the east African coast, where Africans had long been familiar with *Indian*, Arab and Chinese voyagers

The following reading comes from the only surviving record of da Gama's voyage, the *Rotiero*, written by a member of the expedition.

QUESTIONS:

1) What were some of the natural hazards faced by the Portuguese sailors?

2) How did Vasco da Gama deal with local peoples he met on his voyage?

3) What help did Vasco da Gama receive on his way to help him reach India?

By Christmas Day, the 25th of December we had discovered seventy leagues of the coast [beyond Dias' furthest]. On that day, after dinner, when setting a studding-sail, we discovered that the mast had sprung a couple of yards below the top, and that the crack opened and shut. We patched it up with backstays, hoping to be able to repair it thoroughly as soon as we should reach a sheltered port.

On Thursday [28 December] we anchored near the coast, and took much fish. At sunset we again set sail and pursued our route. At that place the mooring-rope snapped and we lost an anchor.

We now went so far out to sea, without touching any port, that drinking-water began to fail us, and our food had to be cooked with salt water. Our daily ration of water was reduced to a quartilho [about a pint]. It thus became a necessity to seek a port.

On Thursday, January 11th [1498] we discovered a small river and anchored near the coast. On the following day we went close in shore in our boats, and saw a crowd of negroes, both men and women. They were tall people, and a chief was among them. The captain-major [da Gama] ordered Martin Affonso … and another man to land. They were received hospitably. The captain-major in consequence sent the chief a jacket, a pair of red pantaloons, a Moorish cap and a bracelet. The chief said that we were welcome to anything in his country of which we stood in need; at least this is how Martin Affonso understood him….

This country seemed to us to be densely peopled. There are many chiefs, and the number of women seemed to be greater than that of the men, for among those who came to see us there were forty women to every twenty men. The houses are built of straw. The arms of the people included long bows and arrows and spears with iron blades. Copper seemed to be plentiful, for the people wore [ornaments] of it on their legs and arms and in their twisted hair. Tin, likewise, is found in the country, for it is to be seen on the hilts of their daggers, the sheaths of which are made of ivory. Linen cloth is highly prized by the people, who were always willing to give large quantities of copper in exchange for shirts. They have large calabashes in which they carry sea-water inland, where they pour it into pits, to obtain salt [by evaporation].

We stayed five days at this place, taking in water, which our visitors conveyed to our boats. Our stay was not, however, sufficiently prolonged to enable us to take in as much water as we really needed, for the wind favoured a prosecution of our voyage…. We called the country *Terra da Boa Gente* (land of good people), and the river *Rio do Cobre* (copper river).

[By March 1498 the expedition had reached Mozambique.] The people of this country are of a ruddy complexion and well made. They are Mohammedans, and their language is the same as that of the Moors [i.e., Arabic].… They are merchants, and have transactions with white Moors [Arab], four of whose vessels were at the time in port, laden with gold, silver, cloves, pepper, ginger, and silver rings, as also with quantities of pearls, jewels, and rubies, all of which articles are used by the people of this country.…

These Moors, moreover, told us that along the route which we were about to follow we should meet with numerous shoals; that there were many cities along the coast, and also an island, one half of the population of which consisted of Moors and the other half of Christians, who were at war with each other. The island was said to be very wealthy.

We were told, moreover, that Prester John resided not far from this place; that he held many cities along the coast, and that the inhabitants of those cities were great merchants and owned big ships. The residence of Prester John was said to be far in the interior, and could be reached only on the back of camels. These Moors had also brought hither two Christian captives from India. This information, and many other things which we heard, rendered us so happy that we cried with joy, and prayed God to grant us health, so that we might behold what we so much desired.…

[On 14 April de Gama's party arrived at Melinde, a port on the coast of present-day Kenya.] On Easter Sunday [15 April] the Moors whom we had taken in the boat told us that there were at this city of Melinde four vessels belonging to Christians from India, and that if it pleased us to take them there, they would provide us, instead of them, Christian pilots and all we stood in need of, including water, wood and other things....

On Monday morning [16 April] the captain-major had the old Moor taken to a sandband in front of the town, where he was picked up by an *almadia* [a type of small boat]. The Moor explained to the king the wishes of the captain-major, and how much he desired to make peace with him [in an earlier altercation da Gama's men had taken several Moors captive]. After dinner the Moor came back in a *zavra* [a type of small boat], accompanied by one of the king's cavaliers and a sharif [Muslim religious teacher]: he also brought three sheep. These messengers told the captain-general that the king would rejoice to make peace with him, and to enter into friendly relations; that he would willingly grant to the captain-major all his country afforded, whether pilots or anything else. The captain-major upon this sent word that he proposed to enter the port on the following day, and forwarded by the king's messengers a present consisting of a *balandrau* [surcoat], two strings of coral, three wash-hand basins, a hat, little bells and two pieces of *lambmel* striped cotton].

Consequently, on Tuesday [17 April] we approached nearer to the town. The king sent the captain-major six sheep, besides quantities of cloves, cumin, ginger, nutmeg and pepper, as also a message, telling him that if he desired to have an interview with him he (the king) would come out in his *zavra*, when the captain-major could meet him in a boat.

On Wednesday [18 April]. after dinner, when the king came up close to the ship in a *zavra*, the captain-major at once entered one of his boats, which had been well furnished, and many friendly words were exchanged when they lay side by side....

On Thursday [19 April] the captain-major and Nicolau Coelho rowed along the front of the town, bombards [an early type of canon that fired stone balls] having been placed in the poops of their long-boats. Many people were along the shore, and among them two horsemen, who appeared to take much delight in a sham-fight. The king was carried in a palanquin [closed litter born on men's shoulders] from the stone steps of his palace to the side of the captain-major's boats. He again begged the captain to come ashore.... The captain however, excused himself.

We found here four vessels belonging to Indian Christians. When they came for the first time on board Paolo da Gama's ship, the captain-major being there at the time, they were shown an altar-piece representing Our Lady at the foot of the cross, with Jesus Christ in her arms and the apostles around her. When the Indians saw this picture they prostrated themselves, and as long as we were there they came to say their prayers in front of it, bringing offerings of cloves, pepper, and other things....

On the day on which the captain-major went up to the town in the boats, these Christian Indians fired off many bombards from their vessels, and when they saw him pass they raised their hands and shouted lustily *Christ! Christ!**

The town of Malindi lies in a bay and extends along the shore.... Its houses are lofty and well white-washed, and have many windows; on the landside are palm-groves, and all around it maize and vegetables are being cultivated.

We remained in front of this town during nine days, and all this time we had fetes, sham-fights, and musical performances.

We left Malindi on Tuesday, the 24th of the month [of April] for a city called Qualecut [Calecut], with the pilot whom the king had given us. The coast there turns north and south, and the land encloses a huge bay with a strait....

On Friday, the 18th of May, after having seen no land for twenty-three days, we sighted lofty mountains, and having all this time sailed before the wind we could not have made less than 600 leagues. The land, when first sighted, was at a distance of eight leagues, and our lead reached bottom at forty-five fathoms. That same night we took a course to the S.S.W., so as to get away from the coast. On the following day [19 May] we again approached the land, but owing to the heavy rain and a thunderstorm, which prevailed whilst we were sailing along the coast, our pilot was unable to identify the exact locality. On Sunday [20 May] we found ourselves close to some mountains, and when we were near enough for the pilot to recognize them he told us that they were above Calecut, and that this was the country we desired to go to.

---

*E. G. Ravenstein, editor of the journal, asserts that the Indians were not Christians, but thought the Christian pictures the Portuguese showed them were variants of their own religious pictures, and were in fact offering prayers to their Hindu deities when they prostrated themselves, and were calling Krishna, a popular deity, rather than Christ.

Velho, Alvaro. *A Journal of the First Voyage of Vasco Da Gama, 1497-1499*. London: Hakluyt Society, 1898. Pp. 16-18, 22-24, 28-29, 40-41, 44-48.

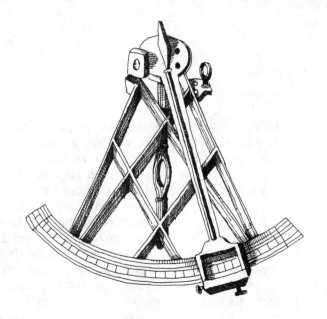

► Sextant

FERDINAND MAGELLAN: NAVIGATOR AND EXPLORER IN THE AGE OF DISCOVERY

One eminent historian, Samuel Eliot Morison, has written that "of the three greatest navigators in the age of discovery--Columbus, Magellan, and Vasco da Gama--Magellan stands supreme." The fifteenth and sixteenth centuries were a heroic era in European voyages of exploration. Portuguese navigators pioneered in sailing around Africa to find a route to Asia. They succeeded when Vasco da Gama reached India in 1498. Convinced that the earth was spherical and relatively small in circumference, Spanish explorers sought a sea route to Asia by sailing westward from Europe. In 1492, with the backing of Queen Isabella of Castile, Christopher Columbus sailed westward from the Canaries and thirty-three days later landed in the Bahamas, about where he had calculated Asia to be. Assuming that he was off the coast of Asia, he called the islands the "Indies" and their inhabitants "Indians." Columbus made three more voyages, the last in 1506. By 1507, it had become clear that the lands Columbus and others had reached were not Asia but a "New World." It was named America in honor of navigator-geographer Amerigo Vespucci, who had charted much of the New World.

Between 1506 and 1520, other Spanish expeditions continued to search for a water route across or around the American continent to Asia. In 1513, Vasco Núñez de Balboa crossed the Isthmus of Panama and discovered a "western ocean" that might lead to Asia. In 1519, the Spanish government dispatched an expedition under Ferdinand Magellan (c. 1480-1521) to search for a passage to the Pacific and Asia via the southern end of the American continent. Magellan's fleet of small ships struggled for thirty-eight days through a stormy water passage (later called the Strait of Magellan) at the tip of South America to reach the peaceful (pacific) western ocean. Magellan sailed northwest, but was killed in a skirmish in the present-day Philippines. His navigator, Juan Sebastián del Cano, and the surviving crew pushed on across the Indian Ocean, returning to Spain in 1522. In circumnavigating the earth, Magellan's expedition accomplished perhaps the greatest feat of exploration in history.

An Italian observer, Antonio Pigafetta, accompanied Magellan on this historic voyage. Pigafetta's account of the journey was published first in French in 1525, and was later translated into Italian and English. A selection of Pigafetta's description of the discovery of the Strait of Magellan and of the hardships endured by the captain-general and the crews of the expedition's four ships is reproduced below.

QUESTIONS:

1) What is opinion is Pigafetta's opinion of Magellan?
2) How exactly are the straits of Megallan discovered?

3) What sort of hardships do they encounter in the Pacific?

In this port of St. Julian there were a great quantity of long capres [oysters], called Missiglione; these had pearls in the midst. In this place they found incense, and ostriches, foxes, sparrows, and rabbits a good deal smaller than ours. We set up at the top of the highest mountain which was there a very large cross, as a sign that this country belonged to the King of Spain; and we gave to this mountain the name of Mount of Christ.

Departing thence, we found in fifty-one degrees less one-third (50° 40' S.), in the Antarctic, a river of fresh water, which was near causing us to be lost, from the great winds which it sent out; but God, of his favour, aided us. We were about two months in this river, as it supplied fresh water and a kind of fish an ell [45 inches] long, and very scaly, which is good to eat. Before going away, the captain [Magellan] chose that all should confess and receive the body of our Lord like good Christians.

After going and taking the course to the fifty-second degree of the ... Antarctic sky, on the day of the Eleven Thousand Virgins [21 October], we found, by a miracle, a strait which we called the Cape of the Eleven Thousand Virgins, this strait is a hundred and ten leagues long, which are four hundred and forty miles, and almost as wide as less than half a league, and it issues in another sea, which is called the peaceful sea; it is surrounded by very great and high mountains covered with snow. In this place it was not possible to anchor with the anchors, because no bottom was found, on which account they were forced to put the moorings of twenty-five or thirty fathoms length on shore. This strait was a round place surrounded by mountains, as I have said, and the greater number of the sailors thought that there was no place by which to go out thence to enter into the peaceful sea [Pacific Ocean]. But the captain-general [Magellan] said that there was another strait for going out .... The captain sent on before two of his ships, one named *St. Anthony* and the other the *Conception*, to seek for and discover the outlet of this strait, which was called the Cape de la Baya. And we, with the other two ships, that is to say, the flagship named *Trinitate*, and the other the

Victory, remained waiting for them within the Bay, where in the night we had a great storm, which lasted till the next day at midday, and during which we were forced to weigh the anchors and let the ships go hither and thither about the bay. The other two ships met with such a head wind that they could not weather a cape which the bay made almost at its extremity; wishing to come to us, they were near being driven to beach the ships. But, on approaching the extremity of the bay, and whilst expecting to be lost, they saw a small mouth, which did not resemble a mouth but a corner, and (like people giving up hope) they threw themselves into it, so that by force they discovered the strait. Seeing that it was not a corner, but a strait of land, they went further on and found a bay, then going still further they found another strait and another bay larger than the first two, at which, being very joyous, they suddenly returned backwards to tell it to the captain-general. Amongst us we thought that they had perished: first, because of the great storm; next, because two days had passed that we had not seen them. And being thus in doubt we saw the two ships under all sail, with ensigns spread, come towards us: these, when near us, suddenly discharged much artillery, at which we, very joyous, saluted them with artillery and shouts. Afterwards, all together, thanking God and the Virgin Mary, we went to seek further on.

After having entered inside this strait we found that there were two mouths, of which one trended to the Sirocco (S.E.), and the other to the Garbin (S.W.). On that account the captain again sent the two ships, *St. Anthony* and *Conception*, to see if the mouth which was towards Sirocco had an outlet beyond into the said peaceful sea....

At night the ship of the captain and the other ship went together the discover the other mouth to Garbin (S.W.), where, on always holding on our course, we found the same strait. But at the end we arrived at a river which we named the River of Sardines, because we found a great quantity of them. So we remained there four days to wait for the other two ships. A short time after we sent a boat well supplied with men and provisions to discover the cape of the other sea: these remained three days in going and coming. They told us that they had found the cape, and the sea great and wide. At the joy which the captain-general had at this he began to cry, and he gave the name of Cape of Desire to this cape, as a thing which had been much desired for a long time....

If we had not found this strait the captain-general had made up his mind to go as far as seventy-five degrees towards the antarctic pole; where at that height in the summer time there is no night, or very little: in a similar manner in the winter there is no day-light, or very little, and so that every one may believe this, when we were in this strait the night lasted only three hours, and this was in the month of October.

The land of this strait on the left hand side looked towards the Sirocco wind, which is the wind collateral to the Levant [east] and the South; we called this strait Pathagonico. In it we found at every half league a good port and place for anchoring, good waters, wood all of cedar, and fish like sardines, missiglioni, and a very sweet herb named appio (celery)....

Wednesday, the twenty-eighth of November, 1520, we came forth out of the said strait, and entered into the Pacific sea, where we remained three months and twenty days without taking in provisions or other refreshments, and we only ate old biscuit reduced to powder, and full of grubs, and stinking from the dirt which the rats had made on it when eating the good biscuit, and we drank water that was yellow and stinking. We also ate the ox hides which were under the main-yard, so that the yard should not break the rigging: they were very hard on account of the sun, rain, and wind, and we left them for four or five days in the sea, and then we put them a little on the embers, and so ate them; also the sawdust of wood, and rats which cost half-a-crown each, moreover enough of them were not to be got. Besides the above-named evils, this misfortune which I will mention was the worst, it was that the upper and lower gums of most of our men grew so much that they could not eat, and in this way so many suffered, that nineteen died .... Besides those who died, twenty-five or thirty fell ill of divers sicknesses, both in the arms and legs, and other places, in such manner that very few remained healthy. However, thanks be to the Lord, I had no sickness. During those three

months and twenty days we went in an open sea, while we ran fully four thousand leagues in the Pacific sea. This was well named Pacific, for during this same time we met with no storm, and saw no land except two small uninhabited, in which we found only birds and trees. We named them the Unfortunate Islands; they are two hundred leagues apart from one another, and there is no place to anchor, as there is no bottom. There we saw many sharks, which are a kind of large fish which they call Tiburoni. The first isle is in fifteen degrees of austral latitude, and the other island is in nine degrees, or more; now with the wind astern, sometimes on a wind or otherwise. And if our Lord and his Mother had not aided us in giving good weather to refresh ourselves with provisions and other things, we should all have died of hunger in this very vast sea, and I think that never man will undertake to perform such a voyage.

When we had gone out of this strait, if we had always navigated to the west we should have gone without finding any land except the Cape of the Eleven Thousand Virgins, which is the eastern head of the strait in the ocean sea, with the Cape of Desire at the west in the Pacific sea. These two capes are exactly in fifty-two degrees of latitude of the antarctic pole.

The antarctic pole is not so covered with stars as the arctic, for there are to be seen there many small stars congregated together, which are like to two clouds a little separated from one another, and a little dimmed, in the midst of which are two stars, not very large, nor very brilliant, and they move but little: these two stars are the antarctic pole. Our compass needle still pointed a little to its arctic pole; nevertheless it had not as much power as on its own side and region. Yet when we were in the open sea, the captain-general asked of all the pilots, whilst still going under sail, in what direction they were navigating and pointing the charts. They all replied, by the course he had given, punctually [pricked in]; then he answered, that they were pointing falsely (which was so), and that it was fitting to arrange the needle of navigation, because it did not receive so much force as in its own quarter. When we were in the middle of this open sea we saw a cross of five stars, very bright, straight, in the west, and they are straight one with another.

Stanley, Lord [of Alderley], ed. and trans. *The First Voyage Round the World, by Magellan, Translated from the Accounts of Pigafetta, and Other Contemporary Writers*. London: Hakluyt, 1874. Pp. 56-61, 64-67.

JESUIT MISSIONARIES: CULTURAL AMBASSADORS BETWEEN CHINA AND EUROPE

▸ **Jesuit Scientist in China**

During the seventeenth and eighteenth centuries, Jesuit missionaries brought Catholicism to China. They also introduced Western sciences to China and also brought Chinese philosophy and arts to Europe. Francis Xavier (1506-1552), co-founder of the Society of Jesus with Ignatius Loyola, pioneered the Catholic missionary movement in Asia. He established missions in India, Southeast Asia, and Japan, and died while waiting for official permission to enter China. Thirty years later another Jesuit priest, Father Matthew Ricci, was permitted to open a mission. Ricci's expositions on Christian morals and ethics won the respect of Chinese scholars; but it was his knowledge of mathematics, astronomy, and the sciences that opened the doors to government patronage.

Ricci mastered the Chinese language and translated religious and scientific works (including Euclid's *Geometry*) into Chinese, and Chinese classics into Latin. He noted that China was behind Renaissance Europe in scientific knowledge and that the Chinese calendar was inaccurate. Since the annual issuing of a calendar and the correct predicting of eclipses were important responsibilities of the Chinese emperors, errors had grave political consequences. Even though Ricci was not an astronomer, Chinese officials realized that his astronomical knowledge was superior to theirs.

Ricci recognized that if the Jesuits used their scientific knowledge to help the Chinese government, they might more easily win approval and protection for their missions:

> These globes, clocks, spheres, astrolabes, and so forth, which I have made and the use of which I teach, have gained for me the reputation of being the greatest mathematician in the world.... When I tell them that I have no books and that I do not wish to start to correct their rules, few people here believe me.... If the mathematicians of whom I spoke came here, we could readily translate our tables into Chinese characters and rectify their year. This would give us great face, would open wider the gates of China, and would enable us to live more securely and freely.

Ricci's Jesuit superiors sent scientists, mathematicians, cartographers, architects, linguists, and artists to China. Until about 1750, Jesuit fathers headed the Board of Astronomy of the Chinese government. They gained the respect of Chinese officials and scholars, advanced scientific knowledge in China, and won converts to Catholicism. They also translated the Chinese classics into Latin, and introduced Chinese arts, philosophy, and political ideals to Europe. They had no equals as cultural ambassadors.   Their translations from the Chinese made Confucius so admired among European intellectuals that he was called the patron saint of the Enlightenment.

The letter quoted here was written in 1612 from Peking to Rome by Father Sabatino De Ursis, a Jesuit astronomer who had been sent to China in response to Ricci's requests.

QUESTIONS:

1) What knowledge possessed by the Jesuits did the Chinese want to learn?
2) Why did the Jesuits want to be of service to the Chinese government?
3) Why was the prediction of heavenly events important to the Chinese government?

At the beginning of the present month of August, I received a letter from Your Reverence in which, because of the concern in this kingdom of China with correcting the calendar, and because of the king's having given us the task, you ask me to draw up a short treatise on the difficulties and uncertainties one meets.   You wished to know what the errors are for which correction is desired, and what the purpose of the Chinese is in this correction.   Accordingly, I shall put briefly in writing as much as I have read ... of the Chinese and what I have learned from our Dr. Paul Hsu Kuang-ch'i [an official and convert to Catholicism] and from the royal mathematicians on this subject....

According to the *Histories*, the Chinese have already used the calendar for 3970 years, which means that they have calculated the eclipses, have known the movements of the celestial bodies, and have made other observations....

The kings founded a bureau or special college for this science, and its members have no other duty than to calculate eclipses, to make the calendar each year, and to observe the stars, the comets, and other prodigious phenomena of the sky, daily and nightly, for the purpose of advising the king and of declaring whether these are good or evil omens....

The rules followed by this college for the computation of eclipses and compilations of the calendar had already been corrected 55 times, according to the *Histories*, that is if we assume that the same rules were used in antiquity.   The last correction was made 300 years ago ... under the Tartar [Yuan] Dynasty....   Besides this true Chinese calendar to which much importance is attached, there is also the Mohammedan calendar translated 230 years ago.... [This] is the origin of the calendar....

However, [the last of] those who had come from Persia to offer these books [on astronomy] had made their journey almost 70 years before and were no longer in China, only the practical part of their doctrine of the planets was translated.   The theoretical part and the other books on mathematics were ignored, though still kept in the royal palace.   Thus, the Chinese lacks works on mathematics, whether treating of planetary theory or of other scientific or speculative subjects in our European sense.   They lack such treatises whether of native or of Mohammedan origin.   Hence, even the members of the royal college of mathematicians do not know how to do anything except predict eclipses, tell fortunes, and point out propitious and unpropitious places for building, burying, and the like.

Therefore, when they saw so many of our books treating of things in a scientific manner, such as the first six *Books of Euclid*, translated by Dr. Paul and Father Matthew Ricci, of happy memory, they wanted them for themselves, because they are talented and love science.   This is why they insisted that we continue the translations.   Since, however, a work of such importance could not be done on private initiative because of the labor involved and the expenses incurred, arrangements were made to have it done as a work of official character, under order of the king.   This had been the case with the Mohammedan books mentioned above.

Thus affairs stood at the end of 1610, when the royal mathematicians themselves wanted to propose to the king that he give the order and state the procedure to complete the translation of these books.   For the time being there was no question of correcting the calendar.   This latter was a work of major importance for China and other inducements were necessary before it could be proposed to the king.

Since, however, the royal mathematicians made a mistake in the eclipse for December 15 of the above-mentioned year, a grave mandarin immediately memorialized [a *memorial* is the name of an official document submitted to the ruler] the king that the mathematicians should be punished. They had erred by six quarters of an hour in their prediction of the eclipse. If this mistake came from errors in their rules, the king should give the order and state the procedures to correct the rules, because the matter was of importance for the whole kingdom.

The king expedited this memorial and entrusted the affair to the Ministry of Rites, to which the college of mathematicians is subordinate. The latter then put aside temporarily the translations of our books and began to defend itself by again memorializing the king. Actually, it had erred by only a half hour. This memorial was also expedited by the king, who committed the affair to the same Ministry. The Ministry held a consultation and decided that the correction was necessary.

Informed by the royal mathematicians of our books, and of the possibility of having our aid for this correction, these ministers, therefore, memorialized the king saying that it was necessary to correct the calendar and that the command should be issued that men from all parts of the world should be sought who could accomplish the task. They said also that according to the mathematicians of the royal college the fathers from the Far West had books not possessed by the Chinese, although the college needed them. Also the fathers had various clocks and other instruments not possessed by the Chinese. For this reason the ministers desired that the order be issued to translate these books under the auspices of the college, and that permission be granted to the fathers to help correct the calendar.

The memorial was immediately expedited by the king, who said that his will was for the thing to be done. Accordingly, he commissioned the same Ministry of Rites, to which the responsibility properly belongs, to do it.

This Ministry, after it had received this commission, immediately began to discuss the method of putting it into execution. It decided finally that two grave mandarins of the kingdom, famous mathematicians, should do the work, and that Doctors Paul and Leo [both Chinese Catholics] should collaborate with the fathers in translating our books and correcting the calendar....

The chief intention of the royal mathematicians is to translate some of our books which they do not have in their college; also to have clocks, instruments for measuring stars, elevations, and so forth, and other useful instruments such as hydraulic devices, devices for lifting weights, leveling water, restoring rivers, drying up marshes and lagoons, which exist in great abundance in this kingdom and other instruments which they know exist in large numbers in the Great Occident--to use their expression.

All this prepares souls well for the goal which our Society has in this kingdom. In this way, we gain credit among the literati [intelligentsia], who are disposed to be satisfied with what they have, and to believe that nobody can teach them anything. It is good for them to be in this frame of mind. Even the common people dislike foreigners and have a special manner toward them. So these things by which we arouse their affection and benevolence toward us are necessary at the beginning of our apostolate, because of the fruit coming therefrom, until our Lord opens wider the gates for the preaching of the Gospel....

To calculate an eclipse of the sun the Chinese use three months, according to what a royal mathematician has told me. Therefore, we have not yet told the mandarins the time and hour of the [future] eclipses [which Ursis knows], although they have been asked about them. We have always replied that since it was necessary to use so much time it has not yet been possible to make the calculations. Rather, since they have established that nine years are necessary, they are persuaded that after nine years, when everything has been finished and the true longitude and altitude of places have been determined ... we shall tell them the time and the hour of the eclipses. In such a manner, praise be to Our Lord, we have time for everything for Your Reverence to arrange for what we must need for the mission.

D'Elia, Pasquale M., S.J.   *Galileo in China: Relations
through the Roman College between Galileo and the Jesuit
Scientist-Missionaries (1610-1640).*   Trans. Rufus Suter
and Matthew Sciascia.   Cambridge: Harvard Univ. Press,
1960.   Pp. 63-68, 80, 82.

GREAT BRITAIN GAINS SUPREMACY IN INDIA

▶ **British and French Royal Crests**

In the footsteps of Portugal and Spain, English entrepreneurs formed the English East India Company in 1600 for the purpose of trading in India. In 1608, the Moghul Emperor Jahangir allowed the company to establish trading stations in Madras, Surat, and Calcutta. When king Charles II married a Portuguese princess in 1661, she brought Bombay as her dowry. Calcutta, Madras, and Bombay remain the principal ports of India. Portugal and the Netherlands were England's initial competitors for India's trade. But Portugal was a declining power and after a period of conflicts the Dutch and English agreed to establishing de facto spheres of activity: the Netherlands in Ceylon and the East Indies and the English in India.

In 1664, the French government organized the French East India Company and established numerous trading stations in India, triggering acute Anglo-French rivalry. This rivalry expanded to military involvement in Indian affairs after Emperor Aurengzeb's death in 1707, and the rapid disintegration of the Moghul Empire. Wars of succession and invasions from Persia and Afghanistan brought anarchy to India. Provincial governors, now virtually independent, sought arms from Europeans and formed alliances by granting concessions to the British (England and Scotland united to form Great Britain in 1707) and French East India Companies. The War of Austrian Succession (1740-1748) and the Seven Years' War (1753-1760) in Europe pitted Britain against France; with their global imperial interests, the wars became world wars. Together with their respective local allies, they fought each other in North America, the Caribbean, and India.

Robert Clive (1725-1774), who created the British Empire in India, was the oldest of thirteen children. His lawyer father could not afford to give him an expensive education, for which he showed little aptitude anyway. His family found him a job as clerk for the British East India Company in Madras, where he arrived penniless in 1743. Life was dreary and prospects for advancement were few; twice Clive attempted suicide, but his pistol jammed.

The French capture of Madras in 1746 gave Clive his new vocation. He launched into a distinguished military career, showing strategic and tactical brilliance in the campaigns he directed against the French and their Indian allies. The crowning event in his military career was the Battle of Plassey (1757), where his small force of English and English-trained Indian soldiers overwhelmed a much larger French aided Indian force during a civil war between two Indian princes in the Bengal region. This victory secured the English candidate as ruler of Bengal. This and other victories practically destroyed French claims in India, as the Treaty of Paris in 1763 conceded. The French East India Company dissolved in 1769.

Prime Minister William Pitt hailed Clive as a "heaven-sent general" for his victories in India. He was ennobled as Lord Clive of Plassey. When Meer Jaffir, the British sponsored Indian prince proved a bad ruler, Clive returned to India to reorganize the administrations of Bengal. The principality was abolished, Meer Jaffir was given a pension, and Bengal and several neighboring provinces came under direct British rule. By these services, Clive became the pre-eminent builder of the British Empire in India.

The following passages from a biography of Clive include some of his own reports.

QUESTIONS:

1) Why was the British victory at the Battle of Plassey so amazing?
2) What was the result of the battle for Great Britain and France respectively?
3) Would you call Robert Clive a successful empire builder? Why?

[On] June 12 [1757], the troops stationed at Calcutta, accompanied by 150 sailors of the squadron, crossed the river and marched to join the force at Chandernagore. A few invalid Europeans and some native troops were left behind to protect the town and guard the French prisoners, a few artillerymen manned the guns on the ramparts. Chandernagore was reached that evening. The following morning, June 13, Clive, leaving behind him 100 seamen to garrison the place, began his hazardous march with a weak force. It consisted of 613 European infantry, 48 Bengal topasses [troops of mixed Portuguese and Indian ancestry, men who were more familiar with European ways than Indians], 171 artillery.... The Native infantry consisted of 2,100 men.... The artillery train was composed of 10 field-pieces, viz. 8 six-pounders and 2 small howitzers. The European infantry ... bears on its colours the word "plassey" and the proud motto *Primus in Indis*.... The Europeans, with all the artillery, ammunition and stores, were towed up the river in boats; the sepoys [Indian troops] moved in a parallel column along the right bank of the river by the high road which had been made by the Mogul Government from Hugli to Patna....

[On June 23, 1757, day of the Battle of Plassey] Between the village of Daudpur and the southern front of the entrenchment, and partly in the peninsula itself, the Nawab's [or "nabob," an Indian title equivalent to prince, his name was Surajah Dowla] vast force encamped. The royal tent was pitched a little behind the front line facing the grove.... He had 35,000 infantry, 15,000 cavalry, with 53 guns, chiefly of large calibre. His opponent [Clive] had no more than 3,200 men with 10 light field-pieces. But the English, though small in numbers, had before defeated him. His army was strong in numbers, but his generals were a source of anxiety and doubt. There was none upon whose steadfast loyalty he could depend. The most respectable men of his Court had in his insane fits of temper been spat upon, beaten, imprisoned, and had narrowly escaped death....

At dawn, June 23, Clive climbed to the roof of the hunting lodge and saw below him a wide green plain lit up with the broken lights from a blue sky across whose face drove dark masses of monsoon clouds as they rolled up from the Indian Ocean. When the sun rose in Easter splendour the enemy appeared marching out of their entrenchment at different points, "and what with the number of elephants all covered with scarlet cloth and embroidery; their horse with their drawn swords glittering in the sun; their horse cannon drawn by vast trains of oxen; and their standards flying, they made a most pompous and formidable appearance." They advanced in dense columns of cavalry and infantry interspersed with batteries of guns of different strength....

[During the day the battle was mainly a dual between the artillery, interrupted by heavy rains.] When the enemy retired to their entrenchments, Clive, drenched to the skin, went into Plassey House to change his clothes. He had determined to maintain his position in the grove during the day, and at night to force with his handful of men a passage through the vast camp of the enemy. He had learnt from past experience in the Carnatic campaign that the darkness, the suddenness and violence of the attack, would throw an enemy lacking drill and discipline into confusion and so make victory more certain....

[The strategy succeeded] Men and horses [of the enemy] fell rapidly. Among the slain were four of their principal commanders. Confusion now began to prevail in their ranks, and it was observed that "their elephants grew very unruly." Clive, with his usual decision and boldness in battle, took advantage of the critical moment. He ordered Eyre Coote to attack the mound and a party to storm the redoubt, "which we carried at the same instant with little or no loss; though the latter was defended (exclusively of blacks) by forty French and two pieces of cannon; and the former by a large body of blacks, both foot and horse." The redoubt was taken with little or no loss because the French had received orders from the Nawab to retire, and they soon afterwards learnt that he had fled....

By 5 o'clock the English were in possession of the whole entrenchment and camp, which they found had just been evacuated. An enormous mass of baggage, stores, camp equipment and cattle was scattered around them. Clive sent at once a detachment under Major Eyre Coote to follow the flying foe. The pursuit was continued for upwards of six miles....

So ended the battle of Plassey. The Nawab's army, according to Clive's calculation, lost 500 men; the victors lost only 4 Europeans and 14 sepoys killed and 9 European sentinels missing. But it is not wise to estimate victory by its cost. Plassey was a great victory because it was conclusive in result. For a force of 800 Europeans, 8 pieces of cannon and 2,100 sepoys, and no cavalry, to advance against an army of 20,000 horse and 40,000 foot, with a large number of guns, was the height of daring. By well-conducted operations and by perfect coolness of nerve Clive gained his last great battle, it was a rout. But it was a rout because Clive, after exercising the highest of all military virtues, patience, hurled his small force at the right moment against the entrenched lines and ended the contest by a vigorous pursuit....

On June 29 Clive, escorted by "only a party of 200 Europeans and 300 sepoys," entered Murshidabad [capital of the Indian prince], which he described in after years as "extensive, populous and rich as the city of London, with this difference, that there are individuals in the first, possessing infinitely greater property than any in the last city." Through the narrow, winding streets of the capital, radiant with living masses of colour, Clive, escorted by his troops, made his way to a palace and a garden spacious enough to accommodate all the troops which accompanied him. "Upon the Colonel's [Clive] arrival ... the great men, anxious for their fate, sent their submission, with offers of large presents, which the Colonel refused, assuring them he desired nothing but their assistance in settling the government." "The Hindu millionaires, as well as other men of property," Clive told the House of Commons, "made me the greatest offers ... and had I accepted these offers, I might have been in possession of millions, which the present Court of Directors [the British East India Company] could not have dispossessed me of: but preferring the reputation of the English nation, the interest of the Nabob, and the advantage of the Company, to all pecuniary considerations, I refused all offers that were made me, not only then, but to the last hour of my continuance in the Company's service in Bengal."...

[Clive continued in a letter to the Select Committee on the day after the event] In the afternoon I waited on Jaffir Ally Cawn [British ally in the conflict, Surajah Dawlat having been captured and deposed], being escorted to him by his son. As I found he declined taking his seat on the *musnud* [throne], I handed him to it; and saluted him as Nabob, upon which his courtiers congratulated him and paid him the usual homage. As this was a visit of ceremony, we could enter very little upon business. I only attempted to convince them, that it was not the maxims of the English to war against the Government, but that Surajah Dowlat [France's ally, now deposed] not only would not fulfil the treaty he had entered into with us, but was taking measures by calling the French to destroy us; but it had pleased God to overthrow him, and that as the present Nabob was a brave and good man, the country might expect to be quiet and happy under him,; that for our parts we should not anyways interfere in the affairs of Government, but leave that wholly to the Nabob; that as long as his affairs required it, we were ready to keep the field, after which we should return to Calcutta and attend solely to commerce, which was our proper sphere and our whole aim in these parts."

Clive obtained from the Company the right to repair and enlarge the fortifications at Calcutta, and he was insistent that the Select Committee should at once exercise the right....

Clive now discovered that by placing Meer Jaffir on the throne he had created a situation of the greatest complexity. Meer Jaffir did not long enjoy in peace the position won by treachery [against Surajah Dawlat]. He was not qualified for the task of governing a kingdom. He had while young proved himself a brave and capable soldier, but a long course of bhang [a narcotic made from hemp] and sensual indulgence had rendered him incapable of decision or exertion. The Mohammedan grandees despised him on account of his weakness and because his power in the land had been established by English traders, and they could not forgive the defeat suffered on the fatal field of Plassey. Meer Jaffir could not forget that his fellow-conspirators [against Surajah Dawlat] were infidel Hindu bankers.... Three aims guided his policy on attaining the throne: the first, to destroy the power of Rai Dulab [his prime minister and a man trusted by Clive] and his command of the State treasure; the second, to remove from their posts the Hindu governors or rajahs and replace them by his own kinsmen and dependents; the third, to lessen the power of the English and avoid fulfilling the stipulations of the treaty. Like the majority of Mohammedan princes, he had a strong desire to confiscate the property and treasure of the Hindu bankers. The policy he pursued towards the Hindu governors soon drove the Rajah of Purnia...into rebellion.

Forrest, George W. *The Life of Lord Clive*. London: Cassell, 1918. Vol. 1. Pp. 437-438, 452, 455, 457-459. Vol. 2. Pp. 4-5, 37, 41-42.

THE FIRST BRITISH EMBASSY TO CHINA

▶ **Symbol of Chinese Emperor**

China's attitude towards foreign relations was shaped by its traditional relationship with neighboring peoples. China maintained it had no need for foreign products but would trade with foreigners as a privilege. The lawless behavior of early European traders led to rigorous regulations which restricted their activities to Canton. China did not allow permanent diplomatic missions and classified all early European diplomats as ambassadors from tributary nations and required them to prostrate themselves before the emperor. Russia was the only exception. The two treaties that regulated relations between China and Russia were between equals.

Great Britain, the leading world maritime and trading power, chafed under China's restrictive and humiliating trade regulations. In 1793, the British government appointed Lord Macartney, an experienced diplomat, to negotiate a commercial treaty with China that would extend and improve trade, and possibly establish diplomatic relations and a permanent British mission in Peking. Additionally, he was to collect information regarding the political, military, social, and economic conditions of China.

The three ships carrying the splendidly equipped embassy arrived in China in the summer of 1793, in the midst of celebrations honoring emperor Ch'ien-lung's eighty-third birthday. Because many tributary missions were arriving simultaneously from many parts of Asia to offer congratulations, the Chinese government naturally assumed that Lord Macartney was doing likewise for Britain. Macartney and his staff were entertained with great courtesy and pomp, but as tribute ambassadors.

Due to China's complete misunderstanding regarding the real purpose of the British mission, and its proud ignorance of the modern world, nothing was accomplished and Macartney returned empty handed. In the extract below Lord Macartney recounts some of the ceremonials of the Chinese court, the negotiations regarding the proper form of saluting the Chinese emperor, who on this happy occasion excused the British ambassador from performing the kowtow, or prostration when he presented his credentials. He also astutely notes the technological backwardness of the Chinese military which still relied on bows and arrows. He correctly diagnoses the seeming splendor of the Chinese empire as essentially hollow, ripe for collapse once strong men like Ch'ien-lung were gone. He also predicts the ease with which Western powers like Britain could defeat the Chinese, and the international chaos that would attend the break up of strong government in China. Preoccupation with French revolutionary and Napoleonic wars postponed a clash between Britain and China until the nineteenth century. When war occurred, many of Macartney's predictions were realized.

QUESTIONS:

1) What did Great Britain, through its ambassador, wish to obtain from China?

2) What did the British think of the Chinese military and defenses?

3) How did China view the British embassy and what was China's response to Britain's requests?

They [Chinese officials] then introduced the subject of the court ceremonies with a degree of art, address, and insinuation that I could not avoid admiring. They began by turning the conversation upon the different modes of dress that prevailed among different nations, and, after pretending to examine ours particularly, seemed to prefer their own, on account of its being loose and free from ligatures [restrictions], and of its not impeding or obstructing the genuflexions and prostrations which, they said, were customary to be made by all persons whenever the Emperor appeared in public....

I told them ours was somewhat different, and that though I had the most earnest desire to do everything that might be agreeable to the Emperor, my first duty must be to do what might be agreeable to my own King....

He [the emperor, when he received Macartney during his summer hunt in Jehol northeast of Peking] was seated in an open palanquin, carried by sixteen bearers, attended by a number of officers bearing flags, standards, and umbrellas, and as he passed we paid him our compliment by kneeling on one knee, whilst all the Chinese made their usual prostrations. As soon as he had ascended his throne I came to the entrance of the tent, and, holding in both my hands a large gold box enriched with diamonds in which was enclosed the King's letter, I walked deliberately up, and ascending the side-steps of the throne, delivered it into the Emperor's own hands, who, having received it, passed it to the Minister.... He then gave me as the first present from him to His Majesty [King George III]....

[During the banquet that followed, the Emperor] sent for Sir George Staunton [British minister, and second in command to Macartney] and me to come to him, and gave to each of us, with his own hands, a cup of warm wine, which we immediately drank in his presence, and found it very pleasant and comfortable, the morning being cold and raw.

Among other things, he asked me the age of my King, and being informed of it, said he hoped he might live as many years as himself, which are eighty-three. His manner is dignified, but affable and condescending, and his reception of us has been very gracious and satisfactory. He is a very fine old gentleman, still healthy and vigorous, not having the appearance of a man of more than sixty....

I explained to him [a high Chinese official] the laws and customs of European nations with regard to their mutual intercourse, and told him that the Sovereigns of Europe usually kept Ambassadors constantly residing at each other's Courts for the purpose of cultivating reciprocal friendship, and preventing misunderstandings. He answered me that it was otherwise in China, which never sends Ambassadors *to* foreign countries; that Ambassadors *from* countries were only occasionally received, and, according to the laws of the Empire, allowed but forty days' residence, although on particular occasions it might have happened that the term was extended to eighty days. He mentioned some other niceties relative to the etiquette of the Court, and entered a good deal into the manners and customs of China, which, he said, he knew were different from ours; but they could not be broken through without inconvenience, and perhaps mischief, to the State, and therefore, foreigners should not be surprised or dissatisfied at them.

Their [Manchus'] weapons are chiefly the scimitar and the bow and arrow, in the exercise of which they are remarkably expert. They seemed a good deal surprised when I once told them, in answer to their enquiries, that we had left off the use of the bow in Europe, and fought chiefly with firearms in its place. The bow is the Emperor's favourite instrument of war; and I observe that he is always represented in the pictures as shooting at stags, wolves, and tigers with arrows, and never with a musket.

Their admiration has been also much excited by the presents and specimens of different manufactures which we have to distribute, and by the various little articles of use and convenience which Europeans are accustomed to--our dressing-tables, shaving-glasses, and pocket instruments.... The flexible sword-blades, of Mr. Gill's manufactory at Birmingham, they were particularly struck with; and Van-ta-gin, to whom as a military man distinguished by wound and long service, I gave a couple, seemed more pleased with them than if I had offered him any other present of a hundred times the value. I am persuaded that if we can introduce them [sword-blades] into China as an article of trade there will be a very great demand for them.

I know it is the policy of the East India Company to increase principally the export of coarser woollens, and I have little doubt that in a very few years China will call for more of them than we can easily supply; but I would recommend also sending out our very finest cloths (for what we call superfine in the invoices are really not the very finest), together with assortments of kerseymeres [fine woolen cloth with fancy weave] and vigonias. Those we wore ourselves I observed everybody greatly admired. The Emperor has lately permitted cloth to be worn in his presence in the spring and autumn, and satins or damask, lined with fine furs, for the winter.

But there are many other things that depend a good deal on ourselves, which, I think, would be more likely to secure us than proclamations and punishments. We, no doubt, labour under many disadvantages here [at Canton] at present, but some of them we have it in our own power to remove. Instead of acting towards the Chinese at Canton in the same manner as we do towards the natives at our factories elsewhere, we seem to have adopted a totally opposite system. We keep aloof from them as much as possible. We wear a dress as different from theirs as can be fashioned. We are quite ignorant of their language.... We, therefore, almost entirely depend on the good faith and good-nature of the few Chinese whom we employ, and by whom we can be but imperfectly understood in the broken gibberish we talk to them. I fancy that Pan-ke-qua, or Mahomet Soulem [Canton merchants], would attempt doing business of the Royal Exchange to very little purpose if they appeared there in long petticoat clothes, with bonnet and turbans, and could speak nothing but Chinese or Arabic. Now, I am very much mistaken, if by a proper management, we might not generally and in some few years be able to mould the China trade (as we seem to have done the trade everywhere else) to the shape that will best suit us. But it would certainly require in us great skill, caution,

temper, and perseverance, much greater, perhaps, than it is reasonable to expect. I dare say there are many hasty spirits disposed to go a shorter way to work, but no shorter way will do it. If, indeed, the Chinese were provoked to interdict us their commerce, or do us any material injury, we certainly have the means easy enough of revenging ourselves....

The forts of the Bocca Tigris [they guard the entrance to Canton] might be demolished by half a dozen broadsides. The river would be impassable without our permission, and the whole track of Canton and its correspondencies annihilated in a season. The millions of people who subsist by it would almost instantly be reduced to hunger and insurrection.... In such distraction, would Russia remain inactive? Would she neglect the opportunity of recovering Albazin and re-establishing her power upon the Armour? Would the ambition of the great Catherine, that has stretched beyond Onalaska to the eastward, overlook the provinces and partitions within grasp of her door?

Such might be the consequences to this Empire if we had a serious quarrel with it. On the other hand, let us see what would be the consequences to ourselves. It is possible that other nations, now trading or expecting to trade with China, would not behold our success with indifference, and thus we might be involved with much more formidable enemies than Chinese. But I leave that consideration aside, and proceed to others.

Our settlement in India would suffer most severely by any interruption of their China traffic, which is infinitely valuable to them.

To Great Britain the blow would be immediate and heavy. The demand from Canton for our woollens alone cannot now be less than from £500,000 to £600,000 per annum.... We should lose the other growing branches of export to China of tin, lead, copper, hardware, and of clocks, watches, and similar articles of ingenious mechanism. We should lose the import from China not only of its raw silk--an indispensable luxury in our silk fabrics--but of another indispensable luxury, or rather, an absolute necessity of life--tea....

These evils, it would seem, must infallibly follow from a breach with China. Whether in time other markets might not be found or created to make amends, I am not yet sufficiently acquainted with this part of the world ... to hazard a decision; but it is not impossible that, though prodigious inconvenience and mischief would certainly be felt at the moment from a rupture, means might be discovered to reverse or repair them.   But these inconveniences and mischiefs which I have stated as objects of apprehension may happen in the common course of things without any quarrel or interference on our part. The Empire of China is an old, crazy, first-rate Man of War, which a fortunate succession of able and vigilant officers have contrived to keep afloat for these hundred and fifty years past, and to overawe their neighbours merely by her bulk and appearance.   But whenever an insufficient man happens to have the command on deck, adieu to the discipline and safety of the ship. She may, perhaps, not sink outright; she may drift some time as a wreck and will then be dashed to pieces on the shore; but she can never be rebuilt on the old bottom.

The breaking-up of the power of China (no very improbable event) would occasion a complete subversion of the commerce ... of the world. The industry and the ingenuity of the Chinese would be checked and enfeebled, but they would not be annihilated. Her ports would no longer be barricaded; they would be attempted by all the adventurers of all trading nations, who would search every channel, creek, and cranny of China for a market, and for some time be the cause of much rivalry and disorder....

But to take things solely as they are now, and to bound our views by the visible horizon of our situation, without speculating upon probable events ... our present interests, our reason, and our humanity equally forbid the thought of any offensive measures with regard to the Chinese, whilst a ray of hope remains for succeeding by gentle ones. Nothing could be urged in favour of a hostile conduct, but an irresistible conviction of failure by forbearance.

Robbins, Helen H. *Our First Ambassador to China: An Account of the Life of George, Earl of Macartney*. London: J. Murray, 1908. Pp. 266, 290-291, 304-305, 313, 342, 383-386.

SPAIN IN THE PHILIPPINES

► Spanish Ship

In 1519 Ferdinand Magellan, serving Emperor Charles V of Spain and the Holy Roman Empire, set sail from San Lucar in Spain to reach the Molucca Islands in present day Indonesia via the western route around the American continent. From Patagonia his ships threaded the strait that bears his name, and reached the ocean which he named the Pacific. Magellan was killed on an island he named St Lazarus (in the present day Philippines) in 1521, but his ships arrived back in Spain, the first to circumnavigate the globe. Spanish expeditions easily conquered the islands of the archipelago, which was renamed Philippines in 1542. Missionaries, led by monks of the Augustinian order, converted most Filipinos to Roman Catholicism .

In 1637 Sebastian Manrique arrived in the Philippines, en route to Japan to begin missionary work. He stayed a year trying to gain passage to Japan, but the new shogunal government had closed Japan to Christian missionaries and European traders. Manrique returned to Europe in 1638. His two volume account of his trip to Asia, titled *Travels*, was published in 1649. Several chapters deal with the discovery of the Philippines and his observations of mid-17th century colonial life there; parts of these are quoted below.

Almost sixty years later, the Italian Giovanni Careri spent five years in a globe circling voyage that included the Philippines. Careri had a doctor of law degree, had served in government posts in Italy, and had previously traveled in the Middle East. He was a man of wealth and position, and an experienced observer. In just over a month in Manila, colonial capital of the Philippines, he talked to many important persons, including the governor and religious leaders. His observations along with earlier publications on the Philippines appear in *A Voyage to the Philippines* (excerpts are quoted below). This book was originally part of a set by Careri titled *A Voyage Round the World*. Many editions of Careri's volumes appeared in the original Italian, in French, and in English translations.

Both authors stress the Philippines' value to Spain as an entrepôt of international trade. They also mention the importance of the Chinese ships that brought commodities desired by Europeans to Manila, for local consumption and for trans-shipping to Europe and the Americas. Finally, both emphasize the dominant economic role of the local Chinese community in the retail trade in the Philippines. This dominance continues to the present day.

QUESTIONS:

1) How successful had Spain been in introducing its religion and culture to the Philippines?
2) What role did the Chinese play in the Philippines?
3) How did Spain administer the Philippines?

[The Philippines] were discovered by a Portuguese ... Fernando de Magellanes, whose skill discovered these wild straits, to which he bequeathed his name and thus left an everlasting memorial of his brave and intrepid spirit.... The apostles who first entered these islands to plant the Gospel there belonged to my own Order, and were true sons of my great father Augustin.

They were Fathers Andres de Urlaneta, a man most skilled in navigation, together with Fathers Fray Martin de Errada, Fray Diego de Errera, Fray Pedro de Gamboa, and Fray Andres de Aguirre. They reached these islands in the year 1565, they being then known as the Luzon Islands.... They changed the name later on in the time of the Catholic King Philip II of Spain. The Spaniards chartered some galleons, entered the islands, and seized several of them with little trouble or resistance on the part of the Indians, owing to internal dissensions and the fact that they were a feeble race little skilled in arms. In seizing these islands and placing them under the sway of the Catholic King Philip the Castillians renamed them the Philippines. These ministers of the Gospel and early sons of Augustin ... at once began to sow the word of the Lord, and finding the soil of those Indians hearts fertile, receptive, and docile, they immediately commenced to gather fruit in great quantity. They then visited other islands in the neighbourhood, and so many were converted that news of this had to be sent to Spain, whence more workers of the same Order were sent out. These apostles between them converted over two hundred thousand Indians on their first appearance, and during the earlier years of their sojourn, to our Catholic faith....

The most abundant local products are rice, herds of cattle and pigs, sugar, wax, saffron, the root called cachumba, and palmjuice from the Pangasinan country, forty leagues from Manila. Besides these, fowls and all kinds of fruit, many most delicious, are found here. A cotton also grows in this island from which they manufacture certain kinds of cloth called lampotes, talingas, and mantles of *Ilocos*. The country is, however, very poor in metals, except that an inferior quality of gold is found in that part called the Ilocos. The proximity of these islands to China ... provides them with an abundance of all that

human desire can wish for of all that is good, rich, valuable, or curious.

But all this is independent of the natural properties of this land, being due to the products of the American silver mines which come to Manila in the form of "reales", whose very scent attracts Sangleis or Chinese with such vehemence that if it were possible they would descend into hell in order to produce new articles for sale, so as to get possession of the coveted silver and longed-for reales-of-eight [Spanish dollars]. So excessive is this longing on their part that it is condensed in a local proverb, in bad Spanish, *Plata sa sangue* [Money is their life's blood].

If this important stimulant from New Spain were to fail there, the prodigality of Manila would come to an end and its inhabitants would have to be content with what the land produces, eating rice instead of bread, as they used to before they opened up trade with China.

* * * * *

Manila stands upon that point of land, where the river that comes out of the lake runs into the sea; and whence Ragia the Moor [last native ruler of pre-Hispanic Manila], who had fortified himself with ramparts upheld by palm trees, and furnished with small guns, was beaten out by Michael Lopez on the 19th of June 1571....

The palaces of Manila, tho' they be all of timber above the first floor, yet are beautiful to behold for their handsome galleries. The streets are broad, but the frequent earthquakes had spoiled their uniformity; several houses and palaces being overthrown, and little hope of rebuilding them; and this is the reason why the inhabitants live in wooden houses....

The women of quality in Manila go in the Spanish habit; the common sort have no need of tailors, for a piece of Indian stuff called *saras*, wrapped about their middle, and hanging down, serves for a petticoat; and another they call *chinina* from the waist upwards, for a waistcoat. The legs and feet stand in need of no hose and shoes by reason of the heat. The Spaniards are clothed after the Spanish fashion, only on their feet they wear wooden clogs, because of the rains. The Indians are forbid wearing stockings, and they must of necessity go bare legged. Those that live well have always a servant to carry an umbrella to save them from the sun.

The women have fine chairs, or hammocks, being nets hanging by a long pole carried by two men, in which they are carried at their ease.

Tho' Manila be small, if we look upon the circumference of its walls … yet it appears large if we include its suburbs, for within a musket shot of the gate of Parian [a city gate], is the habitation of the Chinese merchants called Sangley, who in several streets have rich shops of silk, porcelain, and other commodities. Here are found all arts and trades, so that all the citizens are worth, runs through their hands, through the fault of the Spaniards and Indians, who apply themselves to nothing. There are about 3,000 of them in this suburb, and as many more about the Islands; which is permitted them if not as Christians, at least in hopes they may become such, tho' many are converted for fear of being banished. There were formerly 40,000, but abundance of them were put to death in the tumult they raised at several times, and particularly that on St Francis' eve in 1603, and they were afterwards prohibited staying in the islands by his Catholic majesty. This order is very little observed, for there always remain behind hid many of those that come every year in 40, or 50 *chiampans* [Chinese sailing junks] loaded with commodities; the profit being very great at Manila, which they could not find in China, by reason of the small price manufactures bear....

Tho' the Philippine Islands are very remote from Europe, and from his Catholic majesty's court, to whom they are subject, yet they are excellently governed. For spirituals, there is an archbishop at Manila chosen by the king, who decides all matters not only within his own diocese, but all appeals from his suffragan [subordinate or assistant] bishops.... As for the Inquisition, there is a commissary appointed by that court at Mexico.

For temporal government there is a governor with the title of captain general, and president of the royal court, whose authority lasts eight years, and four oydores, or judges, and a solicitor, but these are for life.... Were not the Philippine Islands so remote, that government would be coveted by the chief grandees, because his government is unlimited, the jurisdiction large, the prerogatives not to be paralleled, the conveniences great, the profit unknown, and

honour greater than that of viceroy of the Indies. But, as I said, the distance makes the greatness of this post not to be known in Spain....

When I went thither the governor was D. Fausto Cruzat Gorgora [governor from 1690 to 1701], knight of Santiago, or St. James, descended from the ancient kings of Navarre, and one of the best captain generals the islands had since they were conquered. All the other governors before him had anticipated upon the revenue several thousands to maintain the soldiers; but he during his government, not only cleared all debts, but so improved the revenue, that when I was at Manila, there were 400,000 pieces of eight in the treasury; for by his great ability, wisdom, zeal and application had advanced the revenue 110,000 pieces of eight a year....

As for Manila, the author of nature placed it so equally between the wealthy kingdoms of the east and west, that it may be accounted one of the greatest places of trade in the world. The Spaniard coming west about, and the Portuguese east about, concluded their voyage at the Molucca Islands [formerly called the Spice Islands], which were formerly under the government of the Philippine Islands; and generally the middle participating of the extremes as being that which unites them; hence it was that the Philippines had share of the best of both the Indies. For here are found the silver of New Spain and Peru; and for the east, the diamonds of Golconda, the rubies, topazes, saphires, and precious cinnamon of Ceylon; the pepper of Sumatra and Java; the cloves, and nutmegs of the Moluccas; the pearls and rich carpets of Persia; the fine silks and stuffs of Bengal; the camphor of Borneo; the Benjamin [a resin] and ivory of Cambodia; the musk of Lequios; the silks, muslins, calicos, and quilts, with the curious porcelain, and other rarities of China. When there was a trade with Japan, there came from thence every year two or three ships, and brought pure silver, amber, silks, chests, boxes, and boards, of precious wood, delicately varnished; in exchange for hides, wax, and the fruit of the country.

It is easy to perceive how advantageously Manila is seated to gather vast riches by trade, because a vessel sailing thence to Acapulco,

returns loaded with silver, profit being four
hundred per cent....

Careri, Giovanni Francesco Gemelli. *A Voyage to the
Philippines*. Manila 1963. Pp. 8-10, 23-24, 26, 57-58,
197-198, 201-202.

DUTCH RULE IN THE EAST INDIES

► Japanese Picture of Portuguese

In 1602 the Dutch East India Company was founded and given extensive political, military, besides commercial authority in Asia. It became the chief instrument of Dutch imperialism in Asia, as the Dutch ousted the Portuguese from the Cape of Good Hope (on the southern tip of Africa and a vital refueling post for ships en route to Asia), Ceylon, Malacca, Sumatra, and Java. Batavia (modern Jakarta), center of Dutch power in the East Indies, was founded in 1619. The profit of its Asian trade made the Netherlands, or United Provinces, the commercial center of Europe, and Amsterdam the leading port. Riches gained from trade with the East Indies contributed to victory in the Dutch war of independence against Spain (1568-1648), and to the flowering of Dutch culture in the seventeenth century.

Unaccustomed to the tropical climate of the East Indies, and clinging to their northern European style of living, Dutch officers and traders suffered an enormously high mortality rate. Inadequate manpower caused by high casualties compelled the Dutch, as it had the Portuguese before them, to concentrate military and administrative power in several strategically important centers in the East Indies, and to rely on indirect rule in alliance with local kings for the collection of spices and other desired commodities. Local petty rulers willingly entered client relationships with the Dutch for protection and commercial gain.

In 1792 the British government sent its first embassy to China with the goal of negotiating diplomatic relations and a commercial treaty with the Chinese (see Reading 7.8). It was headed by Lord Macartney, a distinguished diplomat and official, and seconded by Sir George Staunton, also an experienced public servant. The British embassy arrived in Batavia in March 1793 and left the Dutch East Indies two and half months later, during which time Macartney, Staunton and their staff conferred with and were lavishly entertained by their Dutch hosts. A keen observer, Staunton wrote a two volume account of the embassy. The long chapter devoted to the Dutch East Indies gives a good description of Dutch life, commercial policy, and the symbiotic relationship between the Dutch East India Company and local petty rulers. Parts of that chapter are quoted below.

QUESTIONS:

1) Why was life in Java so unhealthy for most Dutch people?
2) How did the Dutch maintain high profits in their trade--use nutmeg as an example?
3) What were the major products of the East Indies that made the region so desirable?

97

The greatest number of the Dutch settlers in Batavia, such as were commonly seen at their doors, or met with in the streets, appeared wan, weak, and languid, and as if labouring with the "disease of death." Their place of residence, indeed, is situated in the midst of swamps and stagnated pools, from whence they are every morning saluted with "a congregation of foul and pestilential vapours," whence the sea breeze sets in, and blows over this morass. The meridian sun raises from the shallow and muddy canals, with which the town is intersected, deleterious miasmata [check dictionary for meaning] into the air; and the trees with which the quays and streets are crowded, emit noxious exhalations in the night. The sudden transition likewise from a cold northern region to the middle of the torrid zone, without the adoption of the habits requisite in the latter, must render the human frame more liable to be affected by any causes of disease.

Doctor Gillan [physician to the embassy] understood that "there were but few examples of strangers remaining in Batavia long without being attacked by fever, which is the general denomination, in that place, for illness of every kind...."

Of the fatal effects of the climate upon both sexes, however, a strong proof was given by a lady there, who mentioned, that out of eleven persons of her family who had come to Batavia only ten months before, her father, brother-in-law, and six sisters, had already paid the debt of nature....

The general reputation of the unhealthiness of Batavia for Europeans, deter most of those, who can reside at home with any comfort, from coming to it, notwithstanding the temptations of fortunes to be quickly amassed in it. From this circumstance it happens, that offices and professions are often necessarily entrusted to persons little qualified to fill them.... The United Provinces [Netherlands] furnish even few military recruits. The rest are chiefly Germans, many of whom are said to have been kidnapped into the service....

Every [European] man who comes to settle in Batavia must take up arms in its defence. One of the Counsellors of the Indies, after mentioning all the pains taken by him and his colleagues in government, for guarding the settlement against external attacks, frankly acknowledged that their chief dependence was upon the havock which the climate was likely to make amongst the enemy's forces. Captain Parish [an officer in the British embassy] thought likewise, that "the most effectual protection of that settlement from an European enemy proceeds from its climate."...

[There are many Chinese sailing ships or junks in Batavia harbor.] In these junks great numbers of Chinese come constantly to Batavia, with exactly the same views that attract the natives of Holland to it, the desire of accumulating wealth in a foreign land.... They become, in town, retailers, clerks, and agents; in the country they are farmers, and are the principal cultivators of the sugar-cane. They do, at length, acquire fortunes, which they value by the time and labour required to earn them.... The Dutch, on the contrary, who are sent out by the Company, to administer their affairs in Asia, become soon sensible that they have the power, wealth, and possessions of the country at their disposal. They who survive mount quickly into offices that are lucrative, and not, to them laborious. Their influence, likewise, enables them to speculate in trade with vast advantage. The drudgery and detail of business are readily undertaken by the Chinese ... who ... are employed as subordinate instruments, while their principals [live lives of] indolence and voluptuousness, tho often attended with the sacrifice of health, if not of life. Convivial pleasures, among others, are frequently carried to excess.

In several houses of note throughout the settlement the table is spread in the morning at an early hour: besides tea, coffee, and chocolate, fish and flesh are served for breakfast; which is no sooner over, than Madeira, claret, gin, Dutch small beer, and English porter, are laid out in the portico, before the door of the great hall; and pipes and tobacco presented to every guest.... This occupation continues sometimes, with little interruption, till near dinner time, which is about one o'clock in the afternoon. It is not very uncommon for one man to drink a bottle of wine in this manner before dinner. And those who have a predilection for the liquor of their own country, swallow several bottles of Dutch small beer, which, they are told, dilutes their blood, and affords plenty of fluids for free perspiration. Immediately before dinner, two men slaves go round with Madeira wine, of which each of the company takes a bumper, as a tonic or whetter of the appetite…. During dinner a band of music plays at a distance…. A considerable number of female slaves attend at table, which is covered with a great variety of dishes, but little is received, except liquors, into stomachs already cloyed. Coffee immediately follows dinner. [A nap follows] …. About six they rise, dress, drink tea, take an airing in the carriages, and form parties to spend the evening together to a late hour. The morning meetings consist generally of men, the ladies seldom choosing to appear till evening.

The native Javanese are in general too remote from civilization, to have any wants that are not easily satisfied in a warm and fertile climate. No attempt is made to enslave their persons; and they find the government of the Dutch less vexatious than that of others, who divide some share of the sovereignty of the island with them. The Sultan of Mataran rules to the east, the Emperor of Java in the centre, and the King of Bantam to the west; while the coast and effective power almost entirely belong to Holland. Those other sovereigns are descended from foreigners also: being Arabians, who imported Mahometan religion into Java, and acquired the dominion of the country….

[In Batavia] there are large store houses for holding the rich products of the Molucca or spice islands, to be distributed from hence to the rest of the world; besides coffee, pepper, sugar, and arrack [a strong alcoholic drink], produced upon the spot. The nutmeg, mace, and cloves, so long confined to the very small islands of Ternate, Banda, and Amboyna, are, no doubt, capable of being cultivated in other soils; but the Dutch Company, in order to preserve that trade entirely to themselves, and to prevent even their own commodities from overstocking the market, which might affect their price, fell upon a most extraordinary measure, which was the establishment of persons appointed with strict instructions, and considerable means of execution, under the name of *extirpator*, for the purpose of actually rooting out, from every place where they could penetrate, the trees which bear these grateful and valuable productions, except on such small spots, and in such few numbers, as promised to secure the exclusive property and

sale of them to the contrivers of a project thus calculated to counteract the bountiful intent of nature. The nutmeg had been accordingly destroyed by the extirpators in all the Moluccas, except Banda; and a dreadful eruption of a volcano in that island, a very few years ago, so effectually buried in its ashes, or otherwise injured the vegetable productions there, that, for some time, no slight apprehension was entertained of a great diminution in the supply of that valuable spice, and of the Dutch Company consequently becoming losers by their inordinate thirst of gain….

[After leaving Batavia the English ships sailed to northeast Java to] the bay of Bantam, famed formerly for being the principal rendezvous of the shipping from Europe in the East. Bantam was the great mart for pepper and other spices, from whence they were distributed to the rest of the world. The chief factory [trading station] of the English, as well as Dutch, East India Company was settled there. The merchants of Arabia and Hindustan resorted to it…. This place flourished for a considerable time; but the Dutch having conquered its neighbouring province of Jacatra, where they since have built Batavia, and transferred their principal business to it; and the English having removed to Hindostan and China, and trade, in other respects, having taken a new course, Bantam was reduced to a poor remnant of its former opulence and importance…. With the trade of Bantam the power of its sovereign declined. In his wars with other princes of Java he called in the assistance of the Dutch; and from that period he became, in fact, their captive. He resides in a palace, built in the European style, within a fort garrisoned by a detachment from Batavia, of which the commander takes his orders not from the King of Bantam, but from a Dutch chief or governor, who lives in another fort adjoining the town, and nearer to the sea side. His Bantamese majesty is allowed, however, to maintain a body of native troops, and has several small armed vessels, by means of which he maintains authority over some part of the south of Sumatra. His subjects are obliged to sell to him all the peppers they raise in either island, at a low price, which he is under contract with the Dutch to deliver to them at a small advance, and much under the marketable value of that commodity....

[Proceeding along the Sumatra coast the British ships next anchored] near to the southernmost of the three Nanka isles, lying close to the western shore of the island of Banka. This latter island is noted throughout Asia for the same cause, its tin mines, to which England owed its celebrity in Europe in very ancient times, before its arts and arms had spread its fame throughout the globe. Banka lies opposite to the river Palambang, in the island of Sumatra, on which the sovereign of Banka, possessor also of the territory of Palambang, keeps his constant residence. He maintains his authority over his own subjects, and his independence of the neighbouring princes, in great measure, by the assistance of the Dutch; who have a settlement and troops at Palambang; and enjoy the benefit of a contract with the King of Banka for the tin which his subjects procure from thence; and which, like the King of Bantam, in regard to pepper, he compels the miners to deliver to him at a low price, and sells it to the Dutch at a small advance, pursuant to his contract. Those miners, from long practice, have arrived at much perfection in reducing the ore into metal, employing wood as fuel in their furnaces, and not fossil coal, or coak, which is seldom so free from sulphur as not to affect the malleability of the metal. It is sometimes preferred, therefore, to European tin, at the Canton market; and the profit upon it to the Dutch company, is supposed not to be less any year than one hundred and fifty thousand pounds.

Staunton, George. *An Authentic Account of An Embassy from the King of Great Britain to the Emperor of China*. London 1798. Pp. 241-2, 245, 251-253, 256-259, 262, 268-269, 296-298, 305-306.

THE RICH AND THE SUPER-RICH IN SEVENTEENTH-CENTURY MEXICO CITY

In the sixteenth-century, Spaniards who had settled in Cuba and other Caribbean islands, heard stories of rich and powerful Amerindian empires on the mainland of the Americas in present-day Mexico and Peru. Hernán Cortés (1485-1547) persuaded the governor of Cuba to authorize a military expedition to Mexico; the Spanish conquests in Latin America under Cortés began in 1519.

Cortés captured the Aztec capital city of Tenochtitlán from Montezuma. He razed and rebuilt it as Mexico City, which became the capital city of colonial New Spain, a vast territory many times larger than Old Spain in Europe. The many Spanish colonists transformed Mexico City into a Mediterranean-style metropolis. Valuable silver mines, plantations for cash crops, and ranches for (all worked by Amerindian laborers) created vast wealth for the Spanish crown and for privileged Spanish settlers. Spanish-born or descended (Creole) aristocrats dominated the government. The Roman Catholic church, with its many missions and churches, prospered also; with the destruction of their culture, Amerindians were converted to Catholicism. The church also controlled education in New Spain. By the time Harvard College was founded in 1636, five European-style universities--staffed mostly by priests--had already been established in Spanish America.

In the passage that follows an English Dominican priest, Thomas Gage (c. 1600-1656), describes his stay in Mexico City in 1625, at the beginning of a twelve-year mission in Latin America. This account of life in Spanish America, published in 1648, is filled with acute observations and amusing anecdotes; it enjoyed a wide readership in the seventeenth century.

QUESTIONS:

1) What impressed Gage most about the civilization he witnessed in Spanish America?
2) How does Gage judge the society of Spanish America from a moral point of view?
3) What is Gage's opinion of the place of religious institutions in Spanish America?

To the Dominicans belonged this house called St. Jacinto, whither we were carried, and where we did abide near five months, having all things provided that were fit and necessary for our recreations .... The gardens belonging to this house might be of fifteen acres of ground, divided into shady walks under the orange and lemon trees; there we had the pomegranates, figs, and grapes in abundance, with the plantain, sapote, chicosapote, pine-fruit, and all other fruits that were to be found in Mexico. The herbs and salads and great number of Spanish *cardoes* which were sold out, brought in a great rent yearly; for every day there was a cart attended to be filled and sent to the market of Mexico; and this not at seasons of the year, as here in England and other parts of Europe, but at all times and seasons, both winter and summer, there being no difference of heat, cold, frosts, and snow, as with us, but the same temper all the whole year, the winter differing only from the summer by the rain that falls, and not by excessive frosts that nip. This we enjoyed without doors; but within we had all sorts and varieties both of fish and flesh....

The situation of this city [Mexico City] is much like that of Venice, but only differs in this, that Venice is built upon the sea-water, and Mexico upon a lake, which seeming one, indeed is two; one part whereof is standing water, and the other ebbs and flows according to the wind that blows. That part which stands is wholesome, good, and sweet, and yields store of small fish. That part which ebbs and flows is of saltish, bitter, and pestiferous water, yielding no kind of fish, small or great. The sweet water stands higher than the other, and falls into it, and reverts not backward, as some conceive it does. The salt lake contains fifteen miles in breadth, and fifteen in length, and more than five and forty in circuit; and the lake of sweet water contains even as much; in such sort that the whole lake contains much about a hundred miles....

This lake had formerly some fourscore towns, some say more, situated round about it; many of them containing five thousand households, and some ten thousand, yea and Texcoco ... was as big as Mexico [City]. But when I was there, there might be thirty towns and villages about it, and scarce any of above five hundred households between Spaniards and Indians; such has been the hard usage of the Spaniards towards them that they have even almost consumed that poor nation. Nay two years before I came from those parts, which were the years 1635 and 1636, I was credibly informed that a million of Indians' lives had been lost in an endeavour of the Spaniards to turn the water of the lake another way from the city, which was performed by cutting a way through the mountains, for to avoid the great inundations that Mexico was subject unto, and especially for that the year 1634 the waters grew so high that they threatened destruction to all the city, ruinating a great part, and coming into the churches that stood in the highest part of it, in so much that the people used commonly boats and canoes from house to house. And most of the Indians that lived about the lake were employed to strive against this strong element of water, which has been the undoing of many poor wretches, but especially of these thirty towns and villages that bordered near upon the lake which now by that great work is further from the houses of the city, and has a passage made another way, though it was thought it would not long continue but would find again its course towards Mexico [City] ....

At the rebuilding of this city [in the time of Cortés] there was a great difference between a [native] inhabitant of Mexico, and a Conqueror; for a Conqueror was a name of honour, and had lands and rents given him and to his posterity by the King of Spain, and the inhabitant or only dweller paid rent for his house. And this has filled all those parts of America with proud Dons and gentlemen to this day; for every one will call himself a descendant from a Conqueror, though he be as poor as Job; and ask him what is become of his estate and fortune, he will answer that fortune has taken it away, which shall never take away a Don from him. Nay, a poor cobbler, or carrier that runs about the country far and near getting his living with half-a-dozen mules, if he be called Mendoza, or Guzman, will swear that he descended from those dukes' houses in Spain, and that his grandfather came from thence to conquer, and subdued whole countries to the Crown of Spain, though now fortune have frowned upon him, and covered his rags with a threadbare cloak. When Mexico [City] was rebuilt, and judges, aldermen, attorneys, town-clerks, notaries, scavengers, and serjeants with all other officers necessary for the commonwealth of a city were appointed, the fame of Cortez and majesty of the city was blown abroad into far provinces, by means whereof it was soon replenished with Indians again, and with Spaniards from Spain, who soon conquered above four hundred leagues of land, being all governed by the princely seat of Mexico [City]. But since that first rebuilding, I may say it is now rebuilt the second time by Spaniards, who have consumed most of the Indians; so that now I will not dare to say there are a hundred thousand houses which soon after the Conquest were built up, for most of them were Indians. Now the Indians that live there, live in the suburbs of the city, and their situation is called Guadalupe. In the year 1625, when I went to those parts, this suburb was judged to contain five thousand inhabitants; but since most of them have been consumed by the Spaniards' hard usage and the work of the lake. So that now there may not be above two thousand inhabitants of mere [pureblood] Indians, and a thousand of such as they call there mestizoes, who are of mixed nature of Spaniards and Indians, for many poor Spaniards marry with Indian women, and others that marry them not but hate their husbands, find many tricks to convey away an innocent Uriah to enjoy his Bathsheba. The Spaniards daily cozen them of the small plot of ground where their houses stand, and of three or four houses of Indians build up one good and fair house after the Spanish fashion with gardens and orchards. And so is almost all Mexico new built with very fair and spacious houses with gardens of recreation.

Their buildings are with stone, and brick very strong, but not high, by reason of the many earthquakes, which would endanger their houses if they were above three storeys high. The streets are very broad, in the narrowest of them three coaches may go, and in the broader six may go in the breadth of them, which makes the city seem a great deal bigger than it is. In my time it was thought to be of between thirty and forty thousand inhabitants Spaniards, who are so proud and rich that half the city was judged to keep coaches, for it was a most credible report that in Mexico [City] in my time there were above fifteen thousand coaches. It is a by-word that at Mexico [City] there are four things fair, that is to say, the women, the apparel, the horses, and the streets. But to this I may add the beauty of some of the coaches of the gentry, which do exceed in cost the best of the Court of Madrid and other parts of Christendom; for there they spare no silver, nor gold, nor precious stones, nor cloth of gold, nor the best silks from China to enrich them. And to the gallantry of their horses the pride of some does add the cost of bridles and shoes of silver.

The streets of Christendom must not compare with those in breadth and cleanness, but especially in the riches of the shops which do adorn them. Above all, the goldsmiths' shops and works are to be admired. The Indians, and the people of China that have been made Christians and every year come thither, have perfected the Spaniards in that trade. The Viceroy that went thither the year 1625 caused a popinjay to be made of silver, gold, and precious stones with the perfect colours of the popinjay's feathers (a bird bigger than a pheasant), with such exquisite art and perfection, to present unto the King of Spain, that it was prized to be worth in riches and workmanship half a million of ducats [gold coins]. There is in the cloister of the Dominicans a lamp hanging in the church with three hundred branches wrought in silver to hold so many candles, besides a hundred little lamps for oil set in it, every one being made with several workmanship so exquisitely that it is valued to be worth four hundred thousand ducats; and with such-like curious works are many streets made more rich and beautiful from the shops of goldsmiths.

To the by-word touching the beauty of the women I must add the liberty they enjoy for gaming, which is such that the day and night is too short for them to end a primera when once it is begun; nay gaming is so common to them that they invite gentlemen to their houses for no other end. To myself it happened that passing along the streets in company with a friar that came with me that year from Spain, a gentlewoman of great birth knowing us to be *chapetons* (so they call the first year those that come from Spain), from her window called unto us, and after two or three slight questions concerning Spain asked us if we would come in and play with her a game at primera.

Both men and women are excessive in their apparel, using more silks than stuffs and cloth. Precious stones and pearls further much this their vain ostentation; a hat-band and rose made of diamonds in a gentleman's hat is common, and a hat-band of pearls is ordinary in a tradesman; nay a blackamoor or tawny young maid and slave will make hard shift but she will be in fashion with her neck-chain and bracelets of pearls, and her ear-bobs of some considerable jewels. The attire of the baser sort of people of blackamoors and mulattos (which are of a mixed nature, of Spaniards and blackamoors) is so light, and their carriage so enticing, that many Spaniards even of the better sort (who are too prone to venery [sexual indulgence]) disdain their wives for them....

Among [the] great benefactors to the churches of the city I should wrong my history if I should forget one that lived in my time, called Alonso Cuellar, who was reported to have a closet in his house laid with bars of gold instead of bricks, though indeed it was not so, but only reported for his abundant riches and store of bars of gold which he had in one chest standing in a closet distant from another, where he had a chest full of wedges of silver. This man alone built a nunnery of Franciscan nuns, which stood him in above thirty thousand ducats, and left unto it for the maintenance of the nuns two thousand ducats yearly, with obligation of some Masses to be said in the church every year for his soul after his decease. And yet this man's life was so scandalous that commonly in the night with two servants he would round the city, visiting ... scandalous persons ..., carrying his beads in his hands, and at every house letting fall a bead and tying a false knot, that when he came home in the morning towards break of the day he might number by his beads the uncivil stations [gaming houses and whorehouses] he had walked and visited that night. But these his works of darkness came to light, and were published far and near for what happened to him whilst I was in Mexico [City]; for one night, meeting at one of his stations with a gentleman that was jealous of him, swords on both sides were drawn, the concubine first was stabbed by the gentleman who was better manned and attended; and Cuellar (who was but a merchant) was mortally wounded and left for dead, though afterwards he recovered.

Great alms and liberality towards religious houses in that city commonly are coupled with great and scandalous wickedness. They wallow in the bed of riches and wealth, and make their alms the coverlet to cover their loose and lascivious lives. From hence are the churches so fairly built and adorned. There are not above fifty churches and chapels, cloisters and nunneries, and parish churches in that city; but those that are there are the fairest that ever my eyes beheld, the roofs and beams being in many altars with sundry marble pillars, and others with brazil-wood stays standing one above another with tabernacles [canopied niches or receptacles] for several saints richly wrought with golden colours, so that twenty thousand ducats is a common price of many of them. These cause admiration in the common sort of people, and admiration brings on daily adoration in them to those glorious spectacles and images of saints.

Besides these beautiful buildings, the inward riches belonging to the altars are infinite in price and value, such as copes, canopies, hangings, altar cloths, candlesticks, jewels belonging to the saints, and crowns of gold and silver, and tabernacles of gold and crystal to carry about their [eucharistic] sacrament in procession, a which would mount to the worth of a reasonable mine of silver, and would be a rich prey for any nation that could make better use of wealth and riches. I will not speak much of the lives of the friars and nuns of that city, but only that there they enjoy more liberty than in the parts of Europe (where yet they have too much) and that surely the scandals committed by them do cry up to Heaven for vengeance, judgment, and destruction....

The chief place in the city is the market-place, which though it be not as spacious as in Montezuma his time, yet is at this day very fair and wide, built all with arches on the one side where people may walk dry in time of rain, and there are shops of merchants furnished with all sorts of stuffs and silks, and before them sit women selling all manner of fruits and herbs; over against these shops and arches is the Viceroy['s] ... palace, which takes up almost the whole length of the market with the walls of the house and of the gardens belonging to it. At the end of the Viceroy['s] ... palace is the chief prison, which is strong of stone work. Next to this is the beautiful street called *La Plateria*, or Goldsmiths Street, where a man's eyes may behold in less than an hour many millions' worth of gold, silver, pearls, and jewels. The street of St. Austin is rich and comely, where live all that trade in silks; but one of the longest and broadest streets is the street called Tacuba, where almost all the shops are of ironmongers, and of such as deal in brass and steel, which is joining to those arches whereon the water is conveyed into the city, and is so called for that it is the way out of the city to a town called Tacuba; and this street is mentioned far and near, not so much for the length and breadth of it, as for a small commodity of needles which are made there, and for proof are the best of all those parts. For stately buildings the street called *del Aquila*, the Street of the Eagle, exceeds the rest, where live gentlemen, and courtiers, and judges belonging to the Chancery, and is the palace of the Marqués del Valle from the line of Ferdinando Cortez; this street is so called from an old idol an eagle of stone which from the Conquest lies in a corner of the street, and is twice as big as London stone....

Gage, Thomas. *The English-American, His Travail by Sea and Land, or: A New Survey of the West-India's* .... London: Cotes, 1648; rpt. London: Routledge, 1928. Pp. 60, 62, 64-65, 82-86, 90-91.

LIFE IN COLONIAL SPANISH AMERICA

At their height, the Spanish and Portuguese empires controlled three quarters of the land in the western hemisphere, an area some forty times larger than Spain and Portugal. European settlers were, however, a minority in the colonies. Because privileged aristocrats from Spain owned most of the land, and Amerindians and slaves imported from Africa provided most of the labor, few ordinary Spaniards immigrated. Despite government restrictions, some non-Catholics, including some Protestants and Jews, made their way to the Spanish colonies, and a few even prospered as landholders, merchants, and officials.

Since few white women migrated to Latin America, the outnumbered white men often took Amerindian women as concubines. Their offspring are called mestizos. By 1750, mestizo descendants of European-Amerindian unions were the largest racial group in some areas. White males and African slave women had also produced a numerous mulatto population throughout the Caribbean islands and in Brazil. Amerindians, however, remained the largest racial group in Latin America.

Pure Amerindians were the most disadvantaged group in Spanish America. After a brief experiment with enslavement, the Spanish government and the Catholic church recognized Amerindians as free subjects of the crown, though treating them as dependent minors. The church and colonial administration were enjoined to give them religious and vocational instruction. In reality, white masters and local village chiefs often forced their Amerindian charges to work in mines and factories, on ranches and farms, and as porters and construction laborers. Often separated from their families, they labored under harsh conditions that brought premature death. By the eighteenth century, some of the more brutal practices associated with forced labor were on the decline. Many Amerindians and mestizos had become peons, a status similar to that of serfs in medieval Europe, and were bound to the land by debts they could never pay off.

Orlando Roberts, an English businessman who traveled in Central America in the 1820s, wrote the account quoted below. Although he is primarily interested in natural resources, agricultural produce, and opportunities for trade, he makes keen observations of Spanish colonial society, the monopolization of power by Spanish aristocrats, the importance of the Catholic church, and the plight of Amerindians.

QUESTIONS:

1) What is Roberts' opinion of the city of Granada?

2) What does Roberts think of the influence exerted by the aristocratic members of the society he was observing?

3) What does he have to say about the role of the Catholic Church in this society?

According to the Historians of the Conquest of Guatemala, that country, when first invaded by the Spaniards under Don Pedro Alvarado, was flourishing and populous to a degree which, compared with the present small numbers and wretched condition of the aborigines, leads the mind to reflect with astonishment and abhorrence upon the massacres, cruelties and privations, by which their intrepid but bigoted and relentless conquerors reduced the natives to their present state; for instead of an uncultivated and not half peopled country containing, as at the present day, two or three poor cities, towns and villages, inhabited by a few thousands of Spanish *religieuse* and Creole descendants of Spanish adventurers, with groups of naked and degraded Indians scattered over the face of the country, living in filth and idleness, under the shelter of wretched huts or travelling in droves, loaded like beasts of burden, on the one hand,--and a comparatively small number of free and independent tribes, remnants of former kingdoms, speaking different languages, scattered along the sea-coast or among the mountains, on the other--we, at the time of the first invasion, read of no less than *thirty different nations* of Indians in Central America, congregated in wealthy cities in a state of prosperity and civilization, their kings and chiefs possessing sumptuous palaces and houses, great riches, and all the apparatus of regular governments.

* * * * *

I remained at the Colonel's house that evening, and at my departure in the morning, received a letter specially recommending me to his son, the acting Governor of Granada [Nicaragua]. After a very pleasant ride, the sergeant and I arrived in the suburbs of that city, where he halted to breakfast and wait to arrival of the soldiers, who travelled this last stage on foot.

The whole distance by the route we travelled to and from Leon ... may be computed at about one hundred and fourteen miles; and from Leon to the Pacific is, as I was assured, and have the best reason to state, not above six miles. I was told our route to Leon was not the most direct, but from the appearance of the country and leading direction of the road, I am confident the difference cannot be greater than a few miles. We proceeded to the Governor's house, where,

after reading his brother's letter, Don Cresantia Sacassa congratulated me on my safe return, but informed me that it was Don Miguel's instructions that I should take up my abode at one of the Cuartels [military barracks], out of which I was on no account to sleep, but that in the day time I should be at liberty to go where I chose.... I expressed myself satisfied with these arrangements, and took possession of a room at the barracks by fixing up my hammock and obtaining other accommodation necessary for my comfort.

The city of Granada is said to have been founded by Francisco Fernandez de Cordova about three hundred years ago. The population, including European Spaniards, Creoles, Mestizoes and pure Indians, cannot be estimated much lower than that of Leon. The principal public buildings, including the sumptuous parochial church, and the one dedicated to the Lady of Guadaloupe in the grand square, with others of minor importance, are the Franciscan convent, one of San Juan de Dios, with an hospital attached to it, another of La Merced, and three other convents, besides the barracks or cuartel in the parade. The situation of the city between the lakes and its central position in respect to the Atlantic and Pacific afford great facilities for making it the depôt for the greatest commerce in South America or perhaps in the world. It is well built, one side of the great square is chiefly formed by the principal church; a large monastery and a convent make up the greater part of another side; the guard-house, and soldiers barracks, a third; and the principal shops in the town, front the church, and complete the square. The streets are for the most part wide and paved with stone, and in some places the footpaths are raised two feet above the level of the streets and sheltered by the balconies and projecting roofs of the houses. Many of the houses are three stories high and, as the streets intersect each other, form squares of buildings, the longest sides of which extend from east to west. The town stands on a gently rising ground, which contributes much to its cleanliness; and the principal streets are terminated by views of the hills in the neighbourhood or mountains in the distance. The cross streets are narrower, but the houses in general are, like those of Leon, large, handsome, and convenient; the apartments lofty and better furnished than is usual in Spanish towns. Granada is said to be celebrated for its cabinet ware, the workmen possessing many beautiful kinds of wood. They are obliged, however, to work with very inferior tools,--good edge-tools being much wanted. One of the most valuable pieces of furniture in the family room is generally a crucifix, and an image of the virgin and child, in a case, richly ornamented, and illuminated at night. There is a great variety of shops for the sale of small wares, but not indications of a full supply of any thing like valuable goods. In the principal warehouses nothing was exposed in the windows or otherwise; every thing appeared private and concealed, and the depositories were not thrown open as at the Havannah, Buenos Ayres, and Lima.

I was given to understand that the principal trade was entirely in the hands of a few old Spaniards, natives for the most part of Catalonia and Biscay, who contrived to have the offer of every cargo that arrived at San Juan, and their transactions were managed with such secrecy as to preclude all chance of competition:--the native Creoles seldom or never receiving any notice of an arrival, until they saw the goods going into the warehouses, which, in appearance, almost resemble prisons, but are well stocked with the most valuable productions of the country such as indigo, cochineal [brilliant red dye], sarsaparilla [dried roots used as flavoring agent], cocoa, hides, barks, etc. The greater part of the retail trade in the place is, on market and holidays, carried on by the Creoles and other natives of the country, whose shops, as I before observed, are numerous; the commodities they vend, consist of a small assortment of dry goods and earthenware:--others, the places called pulperias, resemble the hucksters shops in England, and in these places are sold bread, cheese, agua-ardiente [whiskey], pottery, glass, sugar, sweetmeats, oil, and a variety of small wares, which are also vended by people in the public square, much in the manner of our travelling Jews and pedlars. The place seems poorly supplied with medicines, and the priest generally administers to both soul and body.

Close to the lake there is a pleasant promenade, much frequented in the evening by the principal inhabitants; it commands a delightful prospect of the lake .... In the course of my morning ablutions, I noticed a visible difference in the height of the waters of the lake. I cannot undertake to affirm that it had a *regular* ebb and flow, and believe the circumstance is owing to the influence of regular morning and evening breezes, impelling the waters of the lake in certain directions at particular periods of the day and night, and with greater force at some times than at others. The Strand is generally covered by daybreak with linen. I have often seen one or two hundred women and girls washing clothes in the morning, so that whether in the evening, or morning, a walk to the lake is a cheerful recreation. Near the Playa, or Embarcadero, some enterprising individuals had undertaken to build a vessel, which, from the appearance of the frame laying on the spot, I should suppose to have been intended to carry fifty or sixty tons. When she was nearly finished it was discovered that the ground had sunk, so as to cause a rise, between the ship and the lake. The ground had afterwards been levelled and every exertion made to launch the vessel, but so ignorant were they of the use of mechanical powers, that, after several fruitless attempts, they were obliged to take the vessel to pieces.

The markets at Granada are abundantly supplied with beef, pork, poultry, cheese, butter, and milk from the farms in the neighbourhood at a very reasonable rate, and with a great variety of excellent fish and water-fowl from the lake.

The neighbouring country and forests furnish game in abundance; wheat-flour is brought from Guatemala and the northern provinces, but the bread used in general by the poor and middling classes is made of Indian corn, which is also preferred by many of the gentry. The common method of preparing it is by making it into small cakes, called Tortillas;--the grain is first put into a large earthen vessel containing a strong lye of wood ashes, or lime and water, to soften it and take off the husk; it is then put upon a stone made concave for the purpose, and bruised with a small stone roller, held firmly with both hands and rolled backwards and forwards, until the corn is bruised to a fine paste; it is then shaped into round flat cakes, and baked on an earthen pan, or flat iron plate; the young women show great cleanliness and activity in preparing it, and when well toasted, it will keep good for many months.

The kinds of fish caught in the lake in the immediate vicinity are the carvalhoe or carvally, tarpoin, snook, sturgeon, rock-fish, carp, mullet, barbel, perch, red and yellow snapper, calapaver, pike, grooper, and various others;--one of them said to be a species of shark. Immense numbers of wild-fowl resort to its waters, amongst these are the large and small Muscovy duck, the red and black-legged widgeon, teal, and many others. Snipe and curlew in great numbers frequent the islands, and low savannahs, on the borders of the lake, and being seldom molested, will suffer even the large bongos [boats] to approach so near that they may be knocked down with a stick. Widgeon and teal are so numerous that they at times appear, when on the wing, to darken the air like a cloud. The terrapin and hiccatee or river-turtle, are also very numerous, and are to be met with near all the islands and creeks;--as also are shrimps and a very large species of cray-fish. Although the temperature of Nicaragua is too warm for wheat, it yields most bountifully all the other articles appertaining to the climate, such as cocoa, indigo, cochineal, cotton, and various medicinal drugs, barks, and gums, besides grapes and other delicious fruits:-- the forests abound in the most valuable timber, and various rare plants, birds and animals afford ample scope for the researches of the naturalist.

Granada is sometimes subject to earthquakes: a slight shock was felt during my stay there. The day on the evening of which it took place was very close and sultry, without a breath of wind. I was in one of the small shops, the master of which generally supplied the officers' mess at the Cuartel: and, resting myself at the moment in a hammock, smoking a cigar, and talking with the man's daughter; although I did not feel any motion of the earth, my attention was roused suddenly by a burst of apprehension from all present. Some threw themselves on their knees, others hastened to illuminate the image of the Virgin, and, on reaching the street, the whole population was hurrying to the churches, the greatest anxiety and alarm depicted on every countenance:--many had formed themselves into processions headed by their clergy; some bore lighted tapers, crucifixes, and other insignia of the Catholic faith; the *Miserere* ["Have Mercy"]

was chanted in every street, and "Santa Maria" and "misero mio" issued from every mouth. I pitied people hurrying to places in which, if the shocks had been violent, they must have been overwhelmed with inevitable destruction; but the shocks gradually became less, and I have frequently felt them more severe during my residence in tropical climates....

On calling next day at the Governor's, I found him and all his household assorting a large quantity of cocoa and indigo which had that morning arrived from Nicaragua, and they appeared too busy to think anything of the recent earthquake. The principal people consider it no degradation to be employed in the meanest offices of trade. The produce of a farm, for instance cheese, butter and milk, were retailed under the immediate superintendance of the Governor's lady, who also sold coarse checks and some other articles, the manufacture of the country. The Governor was superintendant of the customs and revenue; passports were requisite for persons travelling a distance of thirty miles; clearances were necessary for bongos crossing the lake; all public business was transacted at the Governor's house; every means seemed to have been devised by the Government to keep the trade of the country in its grasp and to extort money from the people by every possible method. All those in power were natives of old Spain and there seemed to be little cordiality between them and the majority of the natives.

I availed myself of the facilities afforded by the letter of recommendation from Leon to become acquainted with the nature of the trade of Granada and the province generally.

The articles in the greatest request and which find a ready sale in Guatemala, Comoyagua, Leon, Granada, Nicaragua, Cartago, and in the Central States generally ... are nearly similar to those demanded in Mexico and other parts of Spanish America. The Indians constantly require coarse linens of every kind--handkerchiefs and coarse cotton articles, chiefly showy red colours --moscheates or cutlass blades, of the best kind-- spear-pointed, large clasp and table knives-- felling axes, saws, locks and hinges,--nails, large needles, pins, and fish-hooks,--iron pots, frying pans, flat iron plates, and similar other articles of iron ware--tin ware for cooking, of all sorts-- small glass beads of lively colours--small Dutch looking glasses. Rum is indispensable for the Indian trade--also gunpowder, muskets and fowling pieces: the New States object to the introduction of the latter articles amongst the Indians, but these people can always be supplied by the free traders. Many other articles required by the chiefs will suggest themselves to a speculator, and it seems only requisite to observe further that such goods as are likely to be sent into the interior should be packed in small light cases, such as are easily moved, and not liable to be damaged by moisture....

There seems no doubt that my detention in Granada was to give the schooners Flor del Mer and Estrella time to receive their cargoes and proceed to sea before I should be able to leave the coast or be in a situation to communicate with any of the Independent cruizers. The cargoes consisted of the choicest productions of the country, collected and sent down in bongos, and these schooners, with their cargoes, would have made the fortune of any cruiser who might have captured them. Contrary to the Governor's promise, I was not allowed to proceed in the bongo which sailed on the first day of the month;--that boat was accompanied by others, having on board goods to complete the cargoes above named. About eight days afterwards I had a final interview with the Governor, who furnished me with the means of laying in provisions; and I obtained a passage in one of these bongos belonging to traders or sutlers [military provisioners] who cross the lake to San Carlos with groceries, liquors, tobacco, etc. at the time the soldiers there and on the river San Juan are receiving their pay. These people open a temporary store for the sale of their commodities, and generally realize a profit upon cocoa, coffee, etc. of one hundred to one hundred and fifty percent.

From the worthy Cura [Catholic priest] of Managua and my other friends in Granada, I had contrived to receive the kindest attentions and demonstrations of regard. After bidding them adieu, I left Granada in the boat mentioned, with two men and a woman, the joint owners, a padrone, and a crew of twelve Indians.

Roberts, Orlando W. *Narrative of Voyages and Excursions on the East Coast and in the Interior of Central America ....* Edinburgh 1827. Rpt. Gainesville: Univ. of Florida Press, 1965. Pp. 28-29, 232-242, 300-301.

THE BATTLE OF QUEBEC, 1759

▶ **French Musket**

During the seventeenth century, two new countries joined the race for world trade and empire: England and France. While England established colonies along the North American coast from Maine to Georgia, the French penetrated into the interior of North America from their foothold at Quebec in the St. Lawrence River Valley. French explorers proceeded along rivers, lakes, and portages throughout the enormous Mississippi-Missouri-Ohio basin extending from the Appalachians to the Rocky Mountains and from the Great Lakes to the Gulf coast between Florida and Mexico. They named the land between Florida and Mexico along the gulf coast Louisiana, after King Louis.

Spain and Portugal, the older colonial powers, came under attacks by the rising new nation states of England, France, and the Netherlands. Whereas Dutch power was based mainly in Asia, England and France competed around the world in North America, the Caribbean, and in Asia.

From the mid-eighteenth century to 1815, Britain and France fought in India and the western hemisphere to gain dominance; these conflicts were in part extensions of their wars in Europe. In these struggles, they not only used their own forces but also mobilized their colonial settlers and subsidized local allies, such as Amerindian tribes and Indian princes.

To block British advances into the interior of North America, the French built up their military forces in New France (Canada) during the early 1750s, and established a chain of forts from the Great Lakes to the upper Ohio Valley. In 1754 and 1755 the French and their Amerindian allies defeated two British expeditions at Fort Duquesne near present-day Pittsburgh, thus blocking the route into the Ohio Valley. By 1756, a general conflict had broken out in Europe, merging with the world war in progress for colonial supremacy. In North America and the Caribbean as in India, the British navy defeated the French fleet, thus cutting off French colonial forces from reinforcements. In 1758, the British captured Fort Duquesne and Louisbourg from the French, thus gaining access to the St. Lawrence River. On 13 September 1759, on the Plains of Abraham outside the fortress-city of Quebec in New France (Canada), the British army led by James Wolfe (1727-1759) defeated the French forces of Louis de Montcalm (1712-1759) in a landmark battle. Both commanders were fatally wounded, but Wolfe's successors captured Montreal in 1760, ending French control of Quebec. French losses in the Caribbean and India gave Great Britain control the conquest of New France gave Great Britain control of the world's largest colonial empire and most profitable overseas trade network. As a further consequence of the elimination of the French threat in North America, Britain's thirteen colonies were emboldened to seek greater autonomy from their mother country.

The following passage is from a memoir of the Battle of Quebec by a British naval officer, Captain John Knox.

QUESTIONS:

1) What is Knox's view of General Montcalm?
2) What is Knox's view of General Wolfe?
3) Does Knox's account of the Battle of Quebec seem unbiased? What does he see as the decisive factor in the battle?

Sept. 11, 1759. Great preparations are making throughout the fleet and army to surprise the enemy, and compel them to decide the fate of Quebec by a battle. All the long-boats below the town are to be filled with seamen, marines, and such detachments as can be spared ... in order to ... engross the attention of the Sieur de Montcalm, while the army are to force a descent on this side of the town....

Before daybreak this morning we made a descent upon the north shore, about half a quarter of a mile to the eastward of Sillery; and the light troops were fortunately by the rapidity of the current carried lower down between us and Cape Diamond. We had in this debarkation thirty flat-bottomed boats, containing about sixteen hundred men. This was a great surprise on the enemy, who from the natural strength of the place did not suspect, and consequently were not prepared against so bold an attempt. The chain of sentries which they had posted along the summit of the heights galled us a little, and picked off several men and some officers before our light infantry got up to dislodge them. This grand enterprise was conducted and executed with great good order and discretion. As fast as we landed, the boats put off for re-enforcements, and the troops formed with much regularity. The General [Wolfe], with Brigadiers Monckton and Murray, was ashore with the first division. We lost no time here, but clambered up one of the steepest precipices that can be conceived, being almost a perpendicular, and of an incredible height. As soon as we gained the summit, all was quiet, and not a shot was heard, owing to the excellent conduct of the light infantry under Colonel Howe. It was by this time clear daylight. Here we formed again, the river and the south country in our rear, our right extending to the town, our left to Sillery, and halted a few minutes. The General then detached the light troops to our left to rout the enemy from their battery, and to disable their guns, except they could be rendered serviceable to the party who were to remain there; and this service was soon performed. We then faced to the right, and marched toward the town by files till we came to the Plains of Abraham, an even piece of ground which Mr. Wolfe had made choice of, while we stood forming upon the hill. Weather showery. About six o'clock the enemy first made their appearance upon the heights between us and the town, whereupon we halted and wheeled to the right, thereby forming the line of battle....

The enemy had now likewise formed the line of battle, and got some cannon to play on us, with round and canister shot; but what galled us most was a body of Indians and other marksmen they had concealed in the corn opposite to the front of our right wing, and a coppice that stood opposite to our centre inclining toward our left. But the Colonel Hale, by Brigadier Monckton's orders, advanced some platoons alternately from the forty-seventh regiment, which after a few rounds obliged these sculkers to retire. We were now ordered to lie down, and remained some time in this position. About eight o'clock we had two pieces of short brass six-pounders playing on the enemy, which threw them into some confusion, and obliged them to alter their position; and Montcalm formed them into three large columns. About nine the two armies moved a little nearer each other. The light cavalry made a faint attempt upon our parties at the battery of Sillery, but were soon beat off; and Monsieur de Bougainville, with his troops from Cape Rouge, came down to attack the flank of our second line, hoping to penetrate there. But, by a masterly disposition of Brigadier Townshend, they were forced to desist; and the third battalion of Royal Americans was then detached to the first ground we had formed on after we gained the heights, to preserve the communication with the beach and our boats.

About ten o'clock the enemy began to advance briskly in three columns, with loud shouts and recovered arms, two of them inclining to the left of our army, and the third toward our right, firing obliquely at the two extremities of our line, from the distance of one hundred and thirty, until they came within forty yards, which our troops withstood with the greatest intrepidity and firmness, still reserving their fire and paying the strictest obedience to their officers. This uncommon steadiness, together with the havoc which the grape-shot from our field-pieces made among them, threw them into some disorder, and was most critically maintained by a well-timed, regular, and heavy discharge of our small arms, such as they could no longer oppose. Hereupon they gave way, and fled with precipitation, so that by the time the cloud of smoke was vanished our men were again loaded, and, profiting by the advantage we had over them, pursued them almost to the gates of the town and the bridge over the little river, redoubling our fire with great eagerness, making many officers and men prisoners. The weather cleared up, with a comfortably warm sunshine. The Highlanders chased them vigorously toward Charles River, and the fifty-eighth to the suburb close to St. John's gate, until they were checked by the cannon from the two hulks. At the same time a gun which the town had brought to bear upon us with grape-shot galled the progress of the regiments to the right, who were likewise pursuing with equal ardor, while Colonel Hunt Walsh, by a very judicious movement, wheeled the battalions of Bragg and Kennedy to the left, and flanked the coppice where a body of the enemy made a stand as if willing to renew the action; but a few platoons from these corps completed our victory. Then it was that Brigadier Townshend came up, called off the pursuers, ordered the whole line to dress and recover their former ground. Our joy at this success is inexpressibly damped by the loss we sustained of one of the greatest heroes which this or any age can boast of,--General James Wolfe,--who received his mortal wound as he was exerting himself at the head of the grenadiers of Louisberg; and Brigadier Monckton was unfortunately wounded upon the left of the forty-third and right of the forty-seventh regiment at much the same time, whereby the command devolved on Brigadier Townshend, who, with Brigadier Murray, went to the head of every regiment and returned thanks for their extraordinary good behavior, congratulating the officers on our success....

By the time that our troops had taken a little refreshment, a quantity of intrenching tools were brought ashore, and the regiments were employed in redoubting our ground and landing some cannon and ammunition. The officers who are prisoners say that Quebec will surrender in a few days. Some deserters who came to us in the evening agree in that opinion, and inform us that the Sieur de Montcalm is dying, in great agony, of a wound he received to-day in their retreat. Thus has our late renowned commander by his superior eminence in the art of war, and a most judicious *coup d'état*, made a conquest of this fertile, healthy, and hitherto formidable country, with a handful of troops only, in spite of the political schemes and most vigorous efforts of the famous Montcalm, and many other officers of rank and experience at the head of an army considerably more numerous. My pen is too feeble to draw the character of this British Achilles; but the same may, with justice, be said of him as was said of Henry IV of France: he was possessed of courage, humanity, clemency, generosity, affability, and politeness. And though the former of these happy ingredients, how essential soever it may be in the composition of the soldier, is not alone sufficient to distinguish an expert officer, yet I may with strict truth advance that Major General James Wolfe, by his great talents and martial disposition, which he discovered early in life, was greatly superior to his experience in generalship, and was by no means inferior to a Frederic, a Henry, or a Ferdinand....

The Sieur de Montcalm died late last night. When his wound was dressed and he settled in bed, the surgeons who attended him were desired to acquaint him ingenuously with their sentiments of him; and, being answered that his wound was mortal, he calmly replied, "he was glad of it." His Excellency then demanded "whether he could survive it long and how long." He was told, "About a dozen hours, perhaps more, peradventure less." "So much the better," rejoined this eminent warrior. "I am happy I shall not live to see the surrender of Quebec."...

We are drawing artillery and ammunition ashore with all expedition, in which we are much favored at present by the weather, and have found a convenient road for the purpose leading directly from the cove to the camp. This is the place that had been intended for our descent yesterday; but the morning being dark, and the tide of ebb very rapid, we were imperceptibly carried a little lower down, which proved a favorable circumstance, for there was a strong intrenchment that covered the road, lined by a detachment of one hundred and fifty men. It is still much more fortunate that the general had not deferred the execution of his project to another day; for two French regiments, with a corps of savages, were actually under orders of readiness to march at six o'clock on the morning of the 13th, and intrench themselves immediately along the heights; but, happily, our troops were in possession of that ground before the enemy had any thoughts of stirring. Several men and officers wounded to-day in camp by shots and shells from the town. The French regulars in the late engagement fired slugs of lead and iron from their small arms. Some of them were found in the shot pouches of the officers that were made prisoners, who, being challenged upon this subject, replied with a magnificent shrug, "It was their custom, without any ill design." A flag of truce came from the garrison this afternoon, requesting permission to bury their dead. All that were within our reach we had interred before. Brigadier Monckton took the opportunity in this cessation to pass the town to his tent at Point Levi, of which notice was sent to the governor and to our batteries on the south shore.

After our late worthy general of renowned memory was carried off wounded to the rear of the front line, he desired those who were about him to lay him down. Being asked if he would have a surgeon, he replied, "It is needless: it is all over with me." One of them then cried out, "They run, see how they run!" "Who runs?" demanded our hero with great earnestness, like a person roused from sleep. The officer answered: "The enemy, sir. Egad, they give way everywhere." Thereupon the general rejoined: "Go, one of you, my lads, to Colonel Burton--; tell him to march Webb's regiment with all speed down to Charles River, to cut off the retreat of the fugitives from the bridge." Then, turning on his side, he added, "Now, God be praised, I will die in peace!" and thus expired.

Knox, John. *Historical Journal of the Campaigns in North America for the Years 1757, 1758, 1759, and 1760.* Rpt. in *Old South Leaflets.* Boston, n.d. No. 73. Pp. 1-7, 9-12.

COLONIAL PENNSYLVANIA IN 1760

William Penn (1644-1718) was an important figure in colonial America. The son of a English admiral, Penn converted to the Society of Friends (Quakers) as a young man and conceived a plan to establish a colony in North America, where his ideals of egalitarianism and freedom of worship could be realized. He received a proprietary charter from the English government in 1681, named his colony Pennsylvania, and offered free or cheap land to settlers.

Penn became governor of the new colony and established a government with a small elected council. A larger elected assembly ratified or rejected the laws proposed by the governor and the council.

Pennsylvania attracted many settlers, because of religious freedom and plentiful fertile land. Philadelphia, the "city of brotherly love," became a large and prosperous town. It was also known as a cultural center. Many well-known schools, libraries, and fine public and private buildings graced the city.

The Reverend Andrew Burnaby (1734-1812), an Anglican minister, traveled widely in the colonies in 1759-1760. He wrote an account of his impressions that included fulsome admiration and praise for the colonists. However, as a loyal British subject, he also noted with foreboding the "errors in their ideas of independence." Burnaby's description of Philadelphia is quoted below.

QUESTIONS:

1) What does Burnaby find most remarkable about Philadelphia?
2) Does Burnaby's account of the character of colonial Pennsylvanians seem favorable?
3) What is Burnaby's view of the state of cultural development in colonial Philadelphia?

The next day I set out for Philadelphia ... and arrived there in the evening. The country all the way bore a different aspect from any thing I had hitherto seen in America. It was much better cultivated, and beautifully laid out into fields of clover, grain, and flax. I passed by a very pretty village called Wilmington; and rode through two others, viz. Chester and Derby. The Delaware river is in sight great part of the way, and is three miles broad. Upon the whole nothing could be more pleasing than the ride which I had this day. I ferried over the Schuylkill, about three miles below Philadelphia; from whence to the city the whole country is covered with villas, gardens, and luxuriant orchards.

Philadelphia, if we consider that not eighty years ago the place where it now stands was a wild and uncultivated desert, inhabited by nothing but ravenous beasts, and a savage people, must certainly be the object of every one's wonder and admiration. It is situated upon a tongue of land, a few miles above the confluence of the Delaware and Schuylkill; and contains about 3,000 houses, and 18 or 20,000 inhabitants. It is built north and south upon the banks of the Delaware; and is nearly two miles in length, and three quarters of one in breadth. The streets are laid out with great regularity in parallel lines, intersected by others at right angles, and are handsomely built: on each side there is a pavement of broad stones for foot passengers; and in most of them a causeway in the middle for carriages. Upon dark nights it is well lighted, and watched by a patrol: there are many fair houses, and public edifices in it. The stadt-house [town hall] is a large, handsome, though heavy building; in this are held the councils, the assemblies, and supreme courts; there are apartments in it also for the accommodation of Indian chiefs or sachems; likewise two libraries, one belonging to the province, the other to a society, which was incorporated about ten years ago, and consists of sixty members. Each member upon admission, subscribed forty shillings; and afterward annually ten.... They have a small collection of medals and medallions, and a few other curiosities, such as the skin of a rattlesnake killed at Surinam twelve feet long; and several North American Indian habits made of furs and skins. At a small distance from the stadt-house, there is another fine library, consisting of a very valuable and chosen collection of books, left by Mr. Logan; they are chiefly in the learned languages. Near this there is also a noble hospital for lunatics, and other sick persons. Besides these buildings, there are spacious barracks for 17 or 1800 men; a good assembly-room belonging to the society of Free Masons; and eight or ten places of religious worship; viz. two churches, three Quaker meeting-houses, two Presbyterian ditto, one Lutheran church, one Dutch Calvinist ditto, one Swedish ditto, one Romish chapel, one Anabaptist meeting-house, one Moravian ditto: there is also an academy or college, originally built for a tabernacle for Mr. Whitefield. At the south end of the town, upon the river, there is a battery mounting thirty guns, but it is in a state of decay. It was designed to be a check upon privateers. These, with a few alms-houses, and a school-house belonging to the Quakers, are the chief public buildings in Philadelphia. The city is in a very flourishing state, and inhabited by merchants, artists, tradesmen, and persons of all occupations. There is a public market held twice a week, upon Wednesday and Saturday, almost equal to that of Leadenhall [in London], and a tolerable one every day besides. The streets are crowded with people, and the river with vessels. Houses are so dear, that they will let for 100 [pounds sterling] currency per annum; and lots, not above thirty feet in breadth, and a hundred in length, in advantageous situations, will sell for 1000 [pounds] sterling. There are several docks upon the river, and about twenty-five vessels are built there annually. I counted upon the stocks at one time no less than seventeen, many of them three-masted vessels....

This wonderful province [Pennsylvania] is situated between the 40th and 43d degree of north latitude, and about 76 degrees west longitude from London, in a healthy and delightful climate, amidst all the advantages that nature can bestow. The soil is extremely strong and fertile, and produces spontaneously an infinite variety of trees, flowers, fruits, and plants of different sorts. The mountains are enriched with ore, and the rivers with fish: some of these are so stately as not to be beheld without admiration: the Delaware is navigable for large vessels as far as the falls, 180 miles distant from the sea, and 120 from the bay. At the mouth it is more than three miles broad, and above one at Philadelphia. The navigation is obstructed in the winter, for about six weeks, by the severity of the frost; but, at other times, its is bold and open. The Schuylkill, though not navigable for any great space, is exceedingly romantic, and affords the most delightful retirements.

Cultivation (comparatively speaking) is carried to a high degree of perfection; and Pennsylvania produces not only great plenty, but also great variety of grain; it yields likewise flax-seed, hemp, cattle of different kinds, and various other articles.

It is divided into eight counties, and contains many large and populous towns: Carlisle,

Lancaster, and Germantown, consist each of near five hundred houses; there are several others which have one or two hundred.

The number of inhabitants is supposed to be between four and five hundred thousand, a fifth of which are Quakers; there are very few negroes or slaves.

The trade of Pennsylvania is surprisingly extensive, carried on to Great Britain, the West Indies, every part of North America, the Madeiras, Lisbon, Cadiz, Holland, Africa, the Spanish Main, and several other places; exclusive of what is illicitly carried on to Cape François, and Monte Cristo. Their exports are provisions of all kinds, lumber, hemp, flax, flax-seed, iron, furs, and deer-skins. Their imports, English manufactures, with the superfluities and luxuries of life. By their flag-of-truce trade, they also get sugar, which they refine and send to Europe.

Their manufactures are very considerable. The Germantown thread-stockings are in high estimation; and the year before last, I have been credibly informed, there were manufactured in that town alone above 60,000 dozen pairs. Their common retail price is a dollar per pair.

The Irish settlers make very good linens: some woolens have also been fabricated, but not, I believe, to any amount. There are several other manufactures, viz. of beaver hats, which are superior in goodness to any in Europe, or cordage, linseed-oil, starch, myrtle-wax and spermaceti candles, soap, earthen ware, and other commodities.

The government of this province is a proprietary one. The legislature is lodged in the hands of a governor, appointed (with the king's approbation) by the proprietor; and a house of representatives elected by the people, consisting of thirty-seven members.... The crown has reserved to itself a power of repealing any law, which may interfere with the prerogative, or be contrary to the laws of Great Britain....

As to religion, there is none properly established; but Protestants of all denominations, Papists, Jews, and all other sects whatsoever, are universally tolerated. There are twelve clergymen of the Church of England, who are sent by the Society for the Propagation of the Gospel, and are allowed 50 [pounds] each, besides what they get from subscriptions and surplice fees. Some few of these are itinerant missionaries, and have no fixed residence, but travel from place to place, as occasion requires, upon the frontiers. They are under the jurisdiction of the bishop of London.

Arts and sciences are yet in their infancy. There are some few persons who have discovered a taste for music and painting; and philosophy seems not only to have made a considerable progress already, but to be daily gaining ground. The library society is an excellent institution for propagating a taste for literature; and the college well calculated to form and cultivate it. This last institution is erected upon an admirable plan, and is by far the best school for learning throughout America. It has been chiefly raised by contributions; and its present fund is about 10,000 [pounds] Pennsylvania money.... The Quakers also have an academy for instructing their youth in classical learning, and practical mathematics: there are three teachers, and about seventy boys in it. Besides these, there are several schools in the province for the Dutch and other foreign children; and a considerable one is going to be erected at Germantown.

The Pennsylvanians, as to character, are frugal and industrious people: not remarkably courteous and hospitable to strangers, unless particularly recommended to them; but rather, like the denizens of most commercial cities, the reverse. They are great republicans, and have fallen into the same errors in their ideas of independency as most of the other colonies have. There are by far the most enterprising people upon the continent. As they consist of several nations, and talk several languages, they are aliens in some respect to Great Britain: nor can it be expected that they should have the same filial affection to her which her own immediate offspring have. However, they are quiet, and concern themselves but little, except about getting money. The women are exceedingly handsome and polite; they are naturally sprightly and fond of pleasure; and, upon the whole, are much more agreeable and accomplished than the men. Since their intercourse with the English officers, they are greatly improved; and, without flattery, many of them would not make bad figures even in the first assemblies of Europe. Their amusements are chiefly, dancing in the winter; and, in the summer, forming parties of pleasure upon the Schuylkill, and in the country.

There is a society of sixteen ladies, and as many gentlemen, called the fishing company, who meet once a fortnight upon the Schuylkill. They have a very pleasant room erected in a romantic situation upon the banks of that river, where they generally dine and drink tea. There are several pretty walks about it, and some wild and rugged rocks, which, together with the water and fine groves that adorn the banks, form a most beautiful and picturesque scene. There are boats and fishing tackle of all sorts, and the company divert themselves with walking, fishing, going up the water, dancing, singing, conversing, or just as they please. The ladies wear an uniform, and appear with great ease and advantage from the neatness and simplicity of it. The first and most distinguished people of the colony are of this society; and it is very advantageous to a stranger to be introduced to it, as he hereby gets acquainted with the best and most respectable company in Philadelphia. In the winter, when there is snow upon the ground, it is usual to make what they call sleighing parties, or to go upon it in sledges; but as this is a practice well known in Europe, it is needless to describe it.

Burnaby, Andrew. *Travels through the Middle Settlements in North America in the Years 1759 and 1760.* 3rd ed. London 1798. Rpt. New York: Wessels, 1904. Pp. 88-98.

THOMAS JEFFERSON OFFERS A REASONED DEFENSE OF THE AMERICAN WAY

▶ **Jefferson's Home, Monticello**

Thomas Jefferson (1743-1826) was one of the principal leaders of the American Revolution and author of the Declaration of Independence. Jefferson's historical significance rests on his political career: he served as a diplomat in Europe, legislator and governor in the state of Virginia, U.S. congressman, and finally as president of the United States (1801-1809).

Jefferson was a truly multi-faceted genius. As a well born and educated Virginian, he cultivated a lifelong love of learning and was deeply concerned with educational theory and practice. This interest led to his work in founding the University of Virginia and in designing its very liberal curriculum. His plans for the buildings of the university, together with the design of his home (Monticello), make him a noteworthy figure in the history of architecture in the United States.

In his intellectual outlook, Jefferson was a true child of the eighteenth-century enlightenment. He was well acquainted with the thought of the French philosophes, whose influence is evident in his writings. In his *Notes on the State of Virginia* (1788), Jefferson offers an enlightened analysis of the political, social, economic, and cultural life in eighteenth-century Virginia. In the first of the following passages from the *Notes*, he rebuts the claims of an influential French naturalist, Georges Louis Leclerc, Comte de Buffon (1707-1788), who had theorized that the animal life of the western hemisphere was, for reasons of climate and environment, naturally inferior to that of the "old world." This theory was extended to embrace human beings, both indigenous and transplanted. Jefferson appeals to reason and scientific observation to disprove such speculations. In the second selection, Jefferson writes eloquently in favor of the principle of the separation of church and state.

QUESTIONS:

1) What is the European bias that Jefferson is seeking to counteract in his writing?
2) What is Jefferson's opinion about the interaction of Church and State?
3) What is Jefferson proudest of in the American political system?

The opinion advanced by the Count de Buffon, is I. That the animals common to both the old and the new world, are smaller in the latter. 2. That those peculiar to the new world are on a smaller scale. 3. That those which have been domesticated in both, have degenerated in America: and 4. That on the whole it exhibits fewer species....

Hitherto I have considered this hypothesis as applied to brute animals only, and not in its extension to the man of America, whether aboriginal or transplanted. It is the opinion of Mons. de Buffon that the former furnishes no exception to it: "Although the savage of the new world is about the same height as man in our world, this does not suffice for him to constitute and exception to the general fact that all living nature has become smaller on that continent. The savage is feeble, and has small organs of generation; he has neither hair nor beard, and no ardor whatever for his female; although swifter than the European because he is better accustomed to running, he is, on the other hand, less strong in body; he is also less sensitive, and yet more timid and cowardly; he has no vivacity, no activity of mind; the activity of his body is less an exercise, a voluntary motion, than a necessary action caused by want; relieve him of hunger and thirst, and you deprive him of the active principle of all his movements; he will rest stupidly upon his legs or lying down entire days. There is no need for seeking further the cause of the isolated mode of life of these savages and their repugnance for society: the most precious spark of the fire of nature has been refused to them; they lack ardor for their females, and consequently have no love for their fellow men: not knowing this strongest and most tender of all affections, their other feelings are also cold and languid; they love their parents and children but little; the most intimate of all ties, the family connection, binds them therefore but loosely together; between family and family there is no tie at all; hence they have no communion, no commonwealth, no state of society. Physical love constitutes their only morality; their heart is icy, their society cold, and their rule harsh. They look upon their wives only as servants for all work, or as beasts of burden, which they load without consideration with the burden of their hunting, and which they compel without mercy, without gratitude, to perform tasks which are often beyond their strength. They have only few children, and they take little care of them. Everywhere the original defect appears: they are indifferent because they have little sexual capacity, and this indifference to the other sex is the fundamental defect which weakens their nature, prevents its development, and--destroying

the very germs of life--uproots society at the same time. Man is here no exception to the general rule. Nature, by refusing him the power of love, has treated him worse and lowered him deeper than any animal."

An afflicting picture indeed, which, for the honor of human nature, I am glad to believe has no original.... This belief is founded on what I have seen of man, white, red, and black, and what has been written of him by authors, enlightened themselves, and writing amidst an enlightened people.... From these sources I am able to say, in contradiction to this representation [of Buffon's], that [the Indian of North America] is neither more defective in ardor, nor more impotent with his female, than the white reduced to the same diet and exercise: that he is brave, when an enterprise depends on bravery; education with him making the point of honor consist in the destruction of an enemy by stratagem, and in the preservation of his own person free from injury; or perhaps this is nature; while it is education which teaches us to honor force more than finesse; that he will defend himself against an host of enemies, always choosing to be killed, rather than to surrender, though it be to the whites, who he knows will treat him well: that in other situations also he meets his death with more deliberation, and endures tortures with a firmness unknown almost to religious enthusiasm with us: that he is affectionate to his children, careful of them, and indulgent in the extreme: ... that his friendships are strong and faithful to the uttermost extremity: that his sensibility is keen, even the warriors weeping most bitterly on the loss of their children, though in general they endeavor to appear superior to human events: that his vivacity and activity of mind is equal to ours in the same situation; hence his eagerness for hunting, and for games of chance. The women are submitted to unjust drudgery. This I believe is the case with every barbarous people. With such, force is law. The stronger sex therefore imposes on the weaker. It is civilization alone which replaces women in the enjoyment of their natural equality. That first teaches us to subdue the selfish passions, and to respect those rights in others which we value in ourselves. Were we in equal barbarism, our females would be equal drudges. The man with them is less strong than with us, but their woman stronger than ours; and both for the same obvious reason; because our man and their woman is habituated to labor, and formed by it. With both races the sex which is indulged with ease is least athletic....

So far the Count de Buffon has carried this new theory of the tendency of nature to belittle her productions on this side of the Atlantic. Its application to the race of whites, transplanted from Europe, remained for the Abbé [Guillaume Thomas François] Raynal [in his *Histoire Philosophique et Politique des Éstablissement et du Commerce des Européens dans les deux Indes* (Amsterdam 1770)].... "America has not yet produced one good poet." When we shall have existed as a people as long as the Greeks did before they produced a Homer, the Romans a Virgil, the French a Racine and Voltaire, the English a Shakespeare and Milton, should this reproach be still true, we will inquire from what unfriendly causes it has proceeded, that the other countries of Europe and quarters of the earth shall not have inscribed any name in the roll of poets. But neither has America produced "one able mathematician, one man of genius in a single art or a single science." In war we have produced a Washington, whose memory will be adored while liberty shall have votaries, whose name will triumph over time, and will in future ages assume its just station among the most celebrated worthies of the world, when that wretched philosophy shall be forgotten which would have arranged him among the degeneracies of nature. In physics we have produced a Franklin, than whom no one of the present age has made more important discoveries, nor has enriched philosophy with more, or more ingenious solutions to the phænomena of nature....

As in philosophy and war, so in government, in oratory, in painting, in the plastic art, we might shew that America, though but a child of yesterday, has already given hopeful proofs of genius, as well of the nobler kinds, which arouse the best feelings of man, which call him into action, which substantiate his freedom, and conduct him to happiness, as of the subordinate, which serve to amuse him only....

* * * * *

The present state of our laws on the subject of religion is this. The convention of May 1776, in their declaration of rights, declared it to be a truth, and a natural right, that the exercise of religion should be free.... The same convention ... when they met as a member of the general assembly in October 1776, repealed all acts of parliament which had rendered criminal the maintaining any opinions in matters of religion, the forebearing to repair to church, and the exercising any mode of worship .... Statutory oppressions in religion [were] thus wiped away....

The error seems not sufficiently eradicated that the operations of the mind, as well as the acts of the body, are subject to the coercion of the laws. But our rulers can have authority over such natural rights only as we have submitted to them. The rights of conscience we never submitted, we could not submit. We are answerable for them to our God. The legitimate powers of government extend to such acts only as are injurious to others. But it does me no injury for my neighbor to say there are twenty gods, or no god. It neither picks my pocket nor breaks my leg. If it be said, his testimony in a court of justice cannot be relied on, reject it then, and be the stigma on him. Constraint may make him worse by making him a hypocrite, but it will never make him a truer man. It may fix him obstinately in his errors, but will not cure them. Reason and free inquiry are the only effectual agents against error. Give a loose to them, they will support the true religion, by bringing every false one to their tribunal, to the test of their investigation. They are the natural enemies of error, and of error only. Had not the Roman government permitted free inquiry, Christianity could never have been introduced. Had not free inquiry been indulged, at the æra of the reformation, the corruptions of Christianity could not have been purged away. If it be restrained now, the present corruptions will be protected, and new ones encouraged. Was the government to prescribe to us our medicine and diet, our bodies would be in such keeping as our souls are now. Thus in France the emetic was once forbidden as a medicine, and the potato as an article of food. Government is just as infallible too when it fixes systems in physics. Galileo was sent to the inquisition for affirming that the earth was a sphere: the government had declared it to be as flat as a trencher, and Galileo was obliged to abjure his error. This error however at length prevailed, the earth became a globe, and Descartes declared it was whirled round its axis by a vortex. The government in which he lived was wise enough to see that this was no question of civil jurisdiction, or we all should have been involved by authority in vortices. In fact, the vortices have been exploded, and the Newtonian principle of gravitation is now more firmly established, on the basis of reason, than it would be were the government to step in, and to make it an article of necessary faith. Reason and experiment have been indulged, and error has fled before them. It is error alone which needs the support of government. Truth can stand by itself....

Difference of opinion is advantageous in religion. The several sects perform the office of [supervisor] over each other. Is uniformity attainable? Millions of innocent men, women, and children, since the introduction of Christianity, have been burnt, tortured, fined, imprisoned; yet we have not advanced one inch towards uniformity. What has been the effect of coercion? To make one half the world fools, and the other half hypocrites. To support roguery and error all over the earth....

Our sister states of Pennsylvania and New York, however, have long subsisted without any [official religious] establishment at all. The experiment was new and doubtful when they made it. It has answered beyond conception. They flourish infinitely. Religion is well supported; of various kinds, indeed, but all good enough; all sufficient to preserve peace and order: or if a sect arises, whose tenets would subvert morals, good sense has fair play, and reasons and laughs it out of doors, without suffering the state to be troubled with it. They do not hang more malefactors than we do. They are not more disturbed with religious dissensions. On the contrary, their harmony is unparalleled, and can be ascribed to nothing but their unbounded tolerance, because their is no other circumstance in which they differ from every nation on earth. They have made the happy discovery, that the way to silence religious disputes, is to take no notice of them. Let us too give this experiment fair play, and get rid, while we may, of those tyrannical laws.

Washington, H.A., ed. *The Writings of Thomas Jefferson* [1788]. Vol. 3. New York: Derby, 1861. Pp. 42, 55-58, 64-65, 150-154.

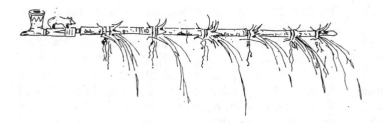

SIOUX INDIAN LIFE ALONG THE UPPER MISSOURI RIVER

As Europeans explored, invaded, and claimed the lands of the Western Hemisphere, they destroyed or displaced native populations. The thriving cultures of these indigenous peoples either vanished altogether or were profoundly altered by contact with white men.

Some Europeans were intrigued by the lives and customs of American Indians and the aura of romance that surrounded their lives. George Catlin devoted much of his life and talent to recording the lives, manners, and mores of North American Indians. A lawyer by training, he was also a skilled artist and draftsman. He satisfied his strong wanderlust and his fascination with Amerindian life by making six expeditions into regions of the North American continent previously unvisited by Europeans. During these journeys, which stretched as far north as the upper Missouri River and as far southwest as present-day Oklahoma, he lived among some fifty different Amerindian tribes.

Catlin produced numerous paintings of Amerindians, both individuals and groups, as they engaged in all sorts of activities, including dancing, buffalo-hunting, capturing wild horses, and playing a ball game similar to lacrosse. He also described and commented on these practices in voluminous notebooks, published in 1841 under the title *Letters and Notes on the Manners, Customs, and Condition of the North American Indians*.

An amateur historian and cultural anthropologist, Catlin was a sort of latter day Herodotus. He is a remarkably unbiased observer, with a sympathetic appreciation of the value and meaning of practices that his "civilized" readers might consider "primitive" or "barbaric." Catlin also foresees the dire effects of contact with Europeans on Amerindian peoples and cultures. Of particular concern to him is the fragility of the ecosystem and the destruction of resources, like the buffalo, essential to the Amerindian way of life. He is aware that he is transcribing a vulnerable and vanishing culture. In the passages below, Catlin describes some practices of the Sioux tribes he lived with; these range from pipe-smoking and dancing to buffalo-hunting and scalp-taking.

QUESTIONS:

1) Is there evidence of prejudice in Catlin's account of the Sioux?
2) What does Catlin find especially admirable about Sioux culture?
3) Does Catlin seem to think Sioux culture is something worth preserving? What threats to its existence does he seem concerned about?

During my stay among the Sioux I received many pipes from them as presents, given as assurances of their friendship. The luxury of smoking is known to all the North American Indians. They are excessive smokers, and many of them would seem to be smoking one-half of their lives. There are many weeds and leaves and barks of trees that are narcotics and of spontaneous growth, which the Indians dry and pulverize and carry in pouches and smoke to great excess--and which in several of the languages is called *k'nick-k'neck*.

They have bestowed much pain and ingenuity to the construction of their pipes. The bowls of these are generally made of red steatite, or "pipe-stone." Many of them are carved with taste and skill, with figures and groups in relief, standing or reclining upon them.

The red stone of which these pipe bowls are made is a great curiosity. I am sure it is a variety of steatite, differing from that in any known European locality, and also from any locality known in America other than the one from which all these pipes come. All are traceable, I have found, to one source. That source is a place of vast importance to the Indians--given to them by the Great Spirit for their pipes, and strictly forbidden for any other use....

The Indians shape out the bowls of these pipes from solid stone, which is not quite as hard as marble, with nothing but a knife. The stone is cherry red and takes a beautiful polish. The Indian makes the hole in the bowl of the pipe by drilling into it a hard stick with a quantity of sharp sand and water kept constantly in the hole. Drilling requires much patience.

The shafts or stems of these pipes are from two to four feet long, sometimes round but most generally flat. They are an inch or two in breadth, and wound half their length or more with braids of porcupine's quills. They are often ornamented with beaks and tufts from the wood-pecker's head, with ermine skins, and with long red hair dyed from white horse hair or the white buffalo's tail.

The *calumet*, or pipe of peace, ornamented with the war-eagle's quills, is a sacred pipe, and never allowed to be used on any other occasion then that of peace-making. The chief brings it into treaty, and unfolding the many bandages which are carefully kept around it, has it ready to be mutually smoked. After the terms of the treaty are agreed upon, it is the means of solemnizing or signing by an illiterate people who cannot draw up an instrument and sign their names to it, as is done in the civilized world....

Indian weapons are mostly manufactured by themselves, except the scalping-knives and tomahawks, which are of civilized manufacture, made expressly for Indian use, and are carried into Indian country by thousands and tens of thousands and sold at an enormous price. The scabbards of the knives and handles for the tomahawks the Indians construct themselves, according to their own taste, and often ornament very handsomely.

The Indian works not in metals. He has not been ingenious enough to design or execute anything so *savage* or destructive. In his simplicity he shapes out his rude hatchet from a piece of stone, and heads his arrows and spears with flints. His knife is a sharpened bone, or the edge of a broken silex. But his war-club is a civilized refinement, with a blade of steel eight or ten inches in length set in a club and studded around and ornamented with some hundreds of brass nails.

The scalping-knife is carried under the belt and is the knife most generally used in all parts of the Indian country. It is a common and cheap butcher knife with one edge, manufactured at Sheffield, England, perhaps for sixpence. It is sold to the poor Indian for a horse!...

As I have introduced the scalping-knife, it may be well for me to give some further account of the customs of taking the scalp, a custom practiced by all the North American Indians. When an enemy is killed in battle, the victor's left hand grasps the hair on the crown of the victim's head. The knife passes around it through the skin, tearing off a piece of the skin with the hair, as large as the palm of the hand. It is then dried, ornamented, and preserved, and highly valued as a trophy. Scalping is an operation not calculated of itself to take life. It only removes the skin, without injuring the bone of the head....

Besides taking the scalp, the victor generally cuts off and brings home the rest of the hair, which his wife will divide into a great many small locks, and with them fringe off the seams of his shirt and his leggings, which also are worn as trophies and ornaments to the dress, and then are familiarly called "scalp-locks."

The scalp, then, ... is a record of heroic deeds of the brave, who have gained their laurels in mortal combat with their enemies. It is as lawful and as glorious, after all, for an Indian to slay an enemy in battle as it is in Christian communities. But the Indian is bound to keep the record himself, for no one in the tribe will keep it for him.

As the scalp is taken as the evidence of a death, it is obvious the Indian has no inclination to take it from the head of the living. But sometimes a man falls in the heat of battle, stunned with the blow of a weapon or a gunshot, and the Indian, rushing over his body, snatches off his scalp, supposing him dead. Afterwards, the victim rises from the field of battle, and recovers from the superficial wound of the knife, wearing a bald spot on his head during the remainder of his life. There are frequent examples on our Western frontiers.

And if reading of Indian barbarities ... has ossified your heart against these people ... I will ... leave you to cherish the very beautiful, humane, and parental moral that was carried out by the United States and British governments during the Revolutionary Wars, when they mutually employed thousands of their "Red children" to aid in fighting their battles, and paid them, according to contract, so many pounds, shillings, and pence or so many dollars and cents for every "scalp" of a "red" or a "blue coat" they could bring in.

Dancing is one of the most valued amusements of the Indians, and much more frequently practiced by them than by any civilized society. It enters into their forms of worship, and is often their mode of appealing to the Great Spirit, of paying their usual devotions to their medicine, and of honoring and entertaining strangers of distinction.

Instead of the "giddy maze" of the quadrille or the country dance, the cheering smiles and graces of silkened beauty, the Indian performs with jumps and starts and yells, much to the satisfaction of his own exclusive self, and the infinite amusement of the gentler sex ....

I saw so many different varieties of dances among the Sioux that I should almost be disposed to denominate them the "dancing Indians." They had dances for everything. There was scarcely an hour, day or night, but that the beat of the drum could not be heard. The dances are almost as various and different in their character as they are numerous. Some of them are exceedingly grotesque and laughable. They can keep bystanders in an irresistible roar of laughter. Others are calculated to excite pity and forcibly appeal to sympathies. Others disgust. Still others terrify and alarm with frightful threats and contortions....

The scalp-dance is given as celebration of victory. Among the Sioux it is danced at night, by the light of their torches, and just before retiring to bed. When a war-party returns from a war excursion, bringing home with them the scalps of their enemies, they generally "dance them" for fifteen nights in succession. They make the most extravagant boasts of their prowess in war, while they brandish their war weapons. A number of young women are selected to aid ... by stepping into the center of the ring and holding up the scalps that have been recently taken. The warriors dance around in a circle, brandishing their weapons and barking and yelping in the most frightful manner, all jumping on both feet at a time, with a simultaneous stamp and blow and thrust of their weapons. It would seem as if they were actually cutting and carving each other to pieces....

Among some tribes it is the custom to bury the scalps after they have gone through this series of public exhibitions, which may be to give them public notoriety, or award public credit to the persons who obtained them and are now obliged to part with them. The great respect which seems to be paid to them while they use them, as well as the pitying and mournful song which they howl to the *manes* [departed spirits] of their unfortunate victims, and the precise solemnity with which they afterwards bury the scalps, sufficiently convince me they have a superstitious dread of the spirits of their slain enemies, and by performing many conciliatory offices, one of which is the dance, ensure their own peace....

Buffaloes ... are a subject of great importance in this vast wilderness, but they are rapidly wasting away at the approach of civilized man--and like the Indian, in a very few years they will live only in books or on canvas.

The American buffalo is the largest of the ruminating animals now living in America. The buffalo seems to have been spread over the plains by the Great Spirit for the use and subsistence of the red men, who live almost exclusively on its flesh, and clothe themselves with its skin. Its color is a dark brown, but changes as the season varies from warm to cold. Its hair or fur, long in winter and spring, turns quite light from exposure to the weather; then, when the winter coat is shed, the new growth is almost a jet black.

The buffalo bull often grows to two thousand pounds. He shakes a long and shaggy black mane that falls in great profusion over his head and shoulders, and often down quite to the ground. The horns are short but very large, and are a simple arch like those of the common ox.

The female is much smaller than the male, and always distinguishable by the peculiar shape of the horns, which are much smaller and more crooked, turning their points more in towards the center of the forehead.

One of the remarkable characteristics of the buffalo is the peculiar formation and expression of the eye. The ball is very large and white, and the iris jet black. The lids always seem to be strained open, and the ball rolling forward and down. A considerable part of the iris is hidden behind the lower lid, while the pure white of the eye-ball glares out over it in an arch, in the shape of a moon at the end of its first quarter.

These animals are, truly speaking, gregarious, but not migratory. They graze in almost incredible numbers at times, and roam about and over vast tracts of country.

Fort Pierre is at the very heart or nucleus of buffalo country. The finest animals that graze on the prairies are to be found here. I am sure I could never discover a better source for the history of the death and destruction that is being dealt to these noble animals, and hurrying their final extinction.

The Sioux are bold horsemen and great hunters. In the heart of their country is the most extensive assortment of goods, of whisky, and other saleable commodities, as well as the most indefatigable men, who constantly demand every robe that can be stripped from these animals' backs.

It is truly melancholy to anticipate the period when the last of these noble animals will fall victim to the improvident rapacity of white and red men, leaving these beautiful green fields a vast and idle waste, unstocked for ages to come, until the bones of the one and the traditions of the other will have vanished and left scarce an intelligible trace behind.

That the reader should not think me visionary in these contemplations, or romancing in making such assertions, I will cite the following item of the extravagances which are practiced in these regions.

When I first arrived at Fort Pierre the chiefs of the Sioux told me that only a few days before, an immense heard of buffalo had showed themselves on the opposite side of the river, almost blackening the plains for a great distance. A part of five or six hundred Sioux Indians on horseback forded the river about mid-day. The re-crossed the river at sun-down and came into the Fort with *fourteen hundred fresh buffalo tongues*. The tongues were thrown down in a mass, and were traded for a few gallons of whisky, which were soon demolished in a harmless carouse.

This was a profligate waste of these useful animals. Not a skin or a pound of the meat (except the tongues) was brought in. And this at a season when their skins were without fur and not worth taking off, and their camp was well stocked with fresh and dried meat. They had no occasion for using the flesh, which is a fair exhibition of the improvident character of the Indian and his recklessness in catering to his appetite, so long as inducements are held out to him for its gratification.

The Indians have no laws or regulations making it a vice or impropriety to drink to excess. They think it no harm to indulge as long as they are able to buy whisky to drink. They look to white men as wiser than themselves, and able to set them examples. They see none but sellers of whisky, who are constantly tendering it to them, and most of them setting the example by using it themselves. They easily acquire a taste for whisky sold at sixteen dollars per gallon. It soon impoverishes them, and they must soon strip the skin from the last buffalo's back to be dressed by their squaws and vended to the traders for a pint of diluted alcohol.

Nowhere has Nature presented more beautiful scenes than those of the vast prairies of the West. Of man and beast, no nobler specimens than the Indian and the buffalo--joint and original tenants of the soil, and fugitives together from the approach of civilized man. They have fled to the great plains of the West, and there, under an equal doom, they have taken up their *last abode*, where their race will expire, and their bones will bleach together....

It is not enough in this polished age that we get from the Indian his lands, and the clothes from his back, but the food from their mouths must be stopped, to add a new article to the fashionable world's luxuries. The ranks of the buffalo must be thinned, and the Indians of the great plains left without the means of supporting life, so that white men may spread buffalo robes for their pleasure and elegance over the backs of their sleighs, or trail them ostentatiously amid the busy throng.

It seems odd that we civilized people with all the comforts of the world about us should be drawing from the backs of these animals the skins for our luxuries, leaving their carcasses to be devoured by the wolves--that we should draw from that country some two thousand robes annually, the greater part of which are taken from animals killed expressly for the robe, at a season when the meat is not cured and preserved, and for each of which skins the Indian has received but a pint of whisky.

It may be answered, perhaps, that the necessities of life are given in exchange for these robes. But what, I would ask, are the necessities in Indian life, where they have buffaloes in abundance to live on? The Indian's necessities are entirely artificial--are all created. When the buffaloes have disappeared, who is to supply the Indian with the necessities of life then?

Catlin, George. *Letters and Notes on the North American Indians* [1841]. Ed. Michael M. Mooney. New York: Clarkson N. Potter, 1975. Pp. 245-255.

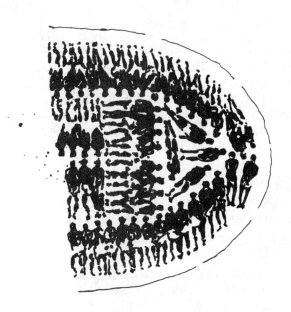

CRUSADER AGAINST THE EVILS OF THE SLAVE TRADE

▶ Slave Ship

Slavery had a long history among African peoples and societies. African slaves were also sold to the Middle East, India, and other parts of Asia by Muslim traders. The first African slaves were shipped by Spain to work in its South American possessions in 1501. Their number increased tremendously from the sixteenth century on as Spain, Portugal, and later also France, Britain and the Netherlands raced to develop colonies in the Caribbean and the Americas.

African rulers and merchants waged wars and staged raids to capture slaves to supply the demand, and some areas along the African coast prospered from the slave trade. In addition, middlemen, shipping companies, and European plantation and mine owners grew rich from this human trafficking and exploitation. Besides the degradation and misery slavery inflicted on the slaves themselves, the wars and disruptions caused by this trade also profoundly altered traditional social, economic, and political institutions throughout much of Africa.

Before 1700, most slaves were carried in Spanish ships to Spanish colonies in the Americas. In the Treaty of Utrecht, which ended the War of Spanish Succession in 1713, Great Britain won the monopoly of carrying all slaves from Africa to Spanish America in British ships. That was a great triumph for Great Britain, the rising maritime and commercial power. Many British slave traders made fortunes in the eighteenth century.

William Wilberforce (1759-1833) symbolized the conscience of Britain against the slave trade and slavery. Elected to the House of Commons (the lower house of the British parliament) in 1780, he dedicated his life to the anti-slavery crusade. A devout evangelical Christian, he believed that "God Almighty had set before him this great object" of his life. He enlisted other great men such as prime minister William Pitt and historian Edmund Burke to his cause, and lobbied to educate and awaken public interest against the entrenched economic powers that supported the continuation of slavery.

Wilberforce orchestrated a petition drive to force parliament to consider the abolition bill he had introduced. On May 12, 1789, Wilberforce made an eloquent and persuasive three hour speech before the House of Commons detailing the horrors of the slave trade as a disgrace on the British conscience. Edmund Burke, himself a famous orator, said: "the House, the nation, and Europe were under great and serious obligation to the honourable gentleman [Wilberforce] for having brought forward the subject in a manner the most masterly, impressive, and eloquent. The principles were so well laid down, and supported with so much force and order, that it equalled any thing I have heard in modern times, and was not perhaps to be surpassed in the remains of Grecian eloquence."

Largely because of Wilberforce's perseverance, the British parliament finally passed a bill that abolished the slave trade in 1807, and another that ended slavery in the British empire in 1833. Britain then exerted its influence and used the might of its navy to end of slave trade by all Western nations.

Because English shorthand was not invented until later, only a summary of Wilberforce's speech, recorded in the British parliamentary proceedings, has survived. Part of it is excerpted below.

QUESTIONS:

1) How did the slave trade affect African societies?
2) What conditions did the slaves endure during their voyage to the Americas?
3) What were the causes of a high death rate among slaves after their arrival in the Americas?

Does not every one see that a slave trade, carried on around her [Africa's] coasts, must carry violence and desolation to her very center? That in a continent just emerging from barbarism, if a trade in men is established, if her men are all converted into goods, and become commodities that can be bartered, it follows, they must be subject to ravages just as goods are; and this too at a period of civilization, when there is no protecting legislatures to defend this their only sort of property, in the same manner as the rights and property are maintained by the legislature of every civilized country.... In Europe it is the extension of commerce, the maintenance of national honour, or some great public object, that is ever the motive to war with every monarch; but, in Africa, it is the personal avarice and sensuality, the most powerful and predominant in natures thus corrupt we tempt, we stimulate in all these African princes, and we depend upon these vices for the very maintenance of the slave trade....

[Next] I must speak of the transit of the slaves in the West Indies. This I confess, in my own opinion, is the most wretched part of the whole subject. So much misery condensed in so little room is more than the human imagination had ever before conceived.... Let any one imagine to himself 6 or 700 of these wretches chained two and two, surrounded with every object that is nauseous and disgusting, diseased, and struggling under every kind of wretchedness! How can we bear to think of such a scene as this? ... The slaves ... are so wrung with misery at leaving their country, that it is the constant practice to set sail in the night, lest they should be sensible of their departure.... The surgeons tell you the slaves are stowed so close, that there

is not room to tread among them; and when you have it in evidence from sir George Yonge, that even in a ship which wanted 200 of her complement, the stench was intolerable ... that for the sake of exercise, these miserable wretches, loaded with chains, oppressed with disease and wretchedness, are forced to dance by the terror of the lash, and sometimes by the actual use of it. "I," says one of the evidence, "was employed to dance the men, while another person danced the women." ... and with respect to food, that an instrument is sometimes carried out, in order to force them to eat.... As to their singing ... we are told that their songs are songs of lamentation upon their departure which, while they sing, are always in tears, insomuch, that one captain (more humane as I should conceive him, therefore than the rest) threatened one of the women with a flogging, because the mournfulness of her song was too painful for his feelings. In order, however, not to trust too much to any sort of description, I will call the attention of the House to one species of evidence, which is absolutely infallible. Death, at least, is a sure ground of evidence, and the proportion of deaths will not only confirm, but if possible will even aggravate our suspicion of their misery in the transit. It will be found, upon an average of all the ships of which evidence has been given at the privy council, that exclusive of those who perish before they sail, not less than 12 1/2 per cent. perish in the passage. Besides these, the Jamaica report tells you, that not less than 4 1/2 per cent. die on shore before the day of sale, which is only a week or two from the time of landing. One third more die in the seasoning [acclimatizing], and this in a country exactly like their own, where they are healthy and happy as some of the evidence would pretend. The diseases, however, which they contract on shipboard, the astringent washes which are to hide their wounds, and the mischievous tricks used to make them up for sale, are, as the Jamaica report says ... one principle cause of their mortality. Upon the whole however, here is a mortality of about 50 per cent. and this among negroes who are not bought unless quite healthy at first, and unless (as the phrase is with cattle) they are sound in wind and limb.... As soon as ever I had arrived thus far in my investigation of the slave trade, I confess to you sir, so enormous so dreadful, so irremediable did its wickedness appear that my own mind was completely made up for the abolition. A trade founded in iniquity, and carried on as this was, must be abolished.... I from this time determined that I would never rest till I had effected its abolition....

[Most slaves in the British Empire went to the West Indies to work on the plantations.] Let us ask then what are the causes of the mortality in the West Indies:--In the first place the disproportion of sexes; an evil, which when the slave trade is abolished, must in the course of nature cure itself. In the second place, the disorders contracted in the middle passage; and here let me touch upon an argument for ever used by the advocates for the slave trade, the fallacy of which is no where more notorious than in this place. It is said to be the interest of the traders to use their slaves well; the astringent washes, escarotics [sic, a caustic drug], and mercurial ointments, by which they are made up for sale, is one answer to this argument. In this instance it is not their interest to use them well; and although in some respects self-interest and humanity will go together, yet unhappily through the whole progress of the slave trade, the very converse of this principle is continually occurring.

A third cause of deaths in the West Indies is excessive labour joined with improper food.... In the West Indies the whole number of slaves remains with the same master. Is the master pinched in his profits?--the slave allowance is pinched in consequence.... There is, therefore, a constant tendency to the very minimum with respect to slaves' allowance; and if in any one hard year the slaves get through upon a reduced allowance, from the very nature of man it must happen, that this becomes a precedent upon other occasions.... Here then we perceive again how the argument of interest fails also with respect to the treatment of slaves in the West Indies....

Another cause of the mortality of slaves is the dreadful dissoluteness of their manners. Here it might be said, that self interest must induce the planters to wish for some order and decency around their families; but in this case also, it is slavery itself that is the mischief. Slaves, considered as cattle, left without any instruction, depressed as to have no means almost of civilization, will undoubtedly be dissolute; and until attempts are made to raise them a little above their present situation, this source of mortality will remain....

It is now to be remarked, that all these causes of mortality among the slaves do undoubtedly admit of a remedy, and it is the abolition of the slave trade that will serve as this remedy. When the manager shall know that a fresh importation is not to be had from Africa, and that he cannot retrieve the deaths he occasions by any new purchases, humanity must be introduced; an improvement in the system of treating them will thus infallibly be effected, an assiduous care of their health and of their morals, marriage institutions, and many other things, as yet little thought of, will take place; because they will be absolutely necessary....

When we consider the vastness of the continent of Africa; when we reflect how all other countries have for some centuries past been advancing in happiness and civilization; when we think how in this same period all improvement in Africa has been defeated by her intercourse with Britain; when we reflect it is we ourselves that have degraded them to that wretched brutishness and barbarity which we now plead as the justification of our guilt; how the slave trade has enslaved their minds, blackened their character, and sunk them so low in the scale of animal beings, that some think the very apes are of a higher class....

Let us then make such amends as we can for the mischiefs we have done to that unhappy continent: let us recollect what Europe itself was no longer ago than three or four centuries. What if I should be able to show this House that in a civilized part of Europe, in the time of our Henry 7 there were people who actually sold their own children? what, if I should tell them that

England itself was that country? what, if I should point out to them that the very place where this inhuman traffic was carried on, was the city of Bristol?...

I have one word more to add upon a most material point; but it is a point so self-evident that I shall be extremely short. It will appear from every thing which I have said, that it is not regulations, it is not mere palliatives, that can cure this enormous evil; total abolition is the only possible cure for it.

Hansard Parliamentary Debates. Vol. 28 [8 May 1789 to 15 March 1791]. London 1816. Pp. 43, 45-52, 60-61.

SECTION 8

POLITICAL AND SOCIAL DEVELOPMENTS
FROM 1500 TO 1800

The intellectual and scientific advances in Europe during the Renaissance had their parallels in changes in government and politics. These developments are the topic of this section.

The first notable political change was the consolidation of strong nation states under absolute monarchs from England to Russia. Later, England led the way in limiting the power of monarchs by parliament under the rule of law. The political ideas endorsed by the Glorious Revolution in England were elaborated upon by political thinkers of the Enlightenment. The implementing of these ideas led to the revolt of British colonists in North America against Great Britain, then by French citizens against the rule of their absolutist king. The French Revolution led to decades of war and the rise of Napoleon Bonaparte, who tried to impose French domination across Europe. Napoleon's ambitions were foiled first by Great Britain at the Battle of Trafalgar, and then by Russian resistance to French conquest. Although Napoleon and French imperialism were defeated, the ideals of liberty and nationalism unleashed by the French Revolution spread throughout Europe, contributing to the triumph of nationalism in the unifications of Italy and Germany, and the creation of independent nation-states in Europe.

The readings in this section mirror political trends from the seventeenth to the nineteenth century and feature major events and leading personalities. They include accounts of such absolute monarchs as king James I of England, Louis XIV of France, and Peter the Great of Russia; others focus on the English Glorious Revolution that brought king William and queen Mary as limited monarchs to the English throne, and on the Enlightened despots Joseph II of Austria and Frederick II of Prussia. While most of the monarchs who built and strengthened their states were European, a similar trend was taking place in Japan. In sixteenth-century Japan, generals sought to centralize and consolidate a powerful state; among them was Hideyoshi, featured here. Their triumph gave Japan centuries of political stability and paved the way for its successful modernization in the late nineteenth century

Three readings deal with the French Revolution and its aftermath; one illustrates the fury of revolutionary mobs, the other two deal with the enlisting of early revolutionary zeal in imperialistic causes, which have striking parallels in present-day events. For Italians, the spreading of nationalism that came with the French Revolution culminated in the unification of Italy. Italian triumph served as a model for other oppressed nationalities and heralded the worldwide spread of nationalism in the twentieth century. The events and individuals featured here have direct influence on, and therefore are pertinent to the world we live in.

TWO ABSOLUTE MONARCHS

L'État c'est moi

▶ "The State is Myself"

Royal absolutism--the rule of a powerful monarch at the head of a highly centralized administration--emerged as the predominant form of government in major European countries in the seventeenth century. Its roots lay in the widespread desire of both rulers and peoples for political stability in the aftermath of a century of chaos following the Reformation.

Theoretical justifications for royal absolutism included the supposed scriptural teaching that God sanctified the "divine right" of kings. Many believed that some men were inherently better equipped to rule. Others argued that a single, absolute authority was needed to impose order or else natural selfishness and ambition would lead to social chaos.

Absolute monarchs depended on highly organized bureaucracies, whose members gathered information, regulated trade, collected taxes, and enforced laws and royal decrees. The revenues absolute monarchs collected funded large standing armies that they used to ensure the obedience of subjects and to wage foreign wars.

Mercantilist economic theory predominated during the seventeenth century. Its proponents preached national economic self-sufficiency and governmental intervention to stimulate production and ensure a favorable balance of trade. Some nations established colonies with the goal of forming economically self-sufficient empires. Mercantilism produced the wealth that bolstered royal absolutism.

Although France became the model of royal autocracy, England also had its powerful monarchs. Both Henry VIII (r. 1509-1547) and Elizabeth I (r. 1558-1603) of England wielded great powers, but were careful to get the support of Parliament. James I (r. 1603-1625) fancied himself a theologian and wrote treatises to justify his claim to absolute powers. When his son, Charles I (r. 1625-1649), lost his head in a struggle with Parliament over royal absolutism, Parliament's ascendancy was assured.

In France, two men, Cardinal Richelieu, who led the government from 1624 to 1643, and Cardinal Mazarin, who dominated between 1643 and 1661, laid the foundation for the royal absolutism that reached its peak under Louis XIV. Louis took direct control of his government after Mazarin's death in 1661. A firm believer in his own divine right to rule, he was very hardworking and showed great political shrewdness. Louis ruthlessly crushed all who questioned his authority. He lured the French nobility to his court at the magnificent new palace of Versailles outside Paris, and encouraged them to live extravagantly, and made them dependent solely on himself for honors, promotions, and income. Louis chose middle-class men to serve in his government because they were entirely dependent on his favor.

In the first passage below, King James I of England states his claim before the Houses of Parliament on 21 March 1609. The second selection comes from a biography of Louis XIV by a French nobleman, Louis de Rouvroy, Duc de Saint-Simon (1675-1755).

QUESTIONS:

1) How does James I try to justify his entitlement to absolute authority?
2) What is Louis de Rouvroy's opinion of the character of Louis XIV?
3) What is the significance of Versailles in Louis de Rouvroy's account of Louis XIV's lifestyle?

The state of the monarchy is the supremest thing upon earth; for kings are not only God's lieutenants upon earth, and sit upon God's throne, but even by God himself they are called gods. There be three principal similitudes that illustrate the state of monarchy: one taken out of the word of God; and the other two out of the grounds of policy and philosophy. In the Scriptures kings are called gods, and so their power after a certain relation compared to the divine power. Kings are also compared to fathers of families: for a king is truly *Parens patriae* [parent of the country], the politique father of his people. And lastly, kings are compared to the head of this microcosm of the body of man.

Kings are justly called gods, for that they exercise a manner of resemblance of divine power upon earth: for if you will consider the attributes of God, you shall see how they agree in the person of a king. God hath power to create or destroy, make or unmake at his pleasure, to give life or send death, to judge all and to be judged nor accountable to none; to raise low things and to make high things low at his pleasure, and to God are both soul and body due. And the like power have kings: they make and unmake their subjects, they have power of raising and casting down, of life and of death, judges over all their subjects and in all causes and yet accountable to none but God only. They have power to ... make of their subjects like men at the chess, a pawn to take a bishop or a knight, and to cry up or down any of their subjects, as they do their money. And to the king is due both the affection of the soul and the service of the body of his subjects.

* * * * *

At twenty-three years of age [Louis XIV] entered the great world as King, under the most favourable auspices. His ministers were the most skilful in all Europe; his generals the best; his Court was filled with illustrious and clever men ....

Louis XIV was made for a brilliant Court. In the midst of other men, his figure, his courage, his grace, his beauty, his grand mien, even the tone of his voice and the majestic and natural charm of all his person, distinguished him till his death as the King Bee, and showed that if he had only been born a simple private gentleman, he would equally have excelled in fêtes, pleasures, and gallantry, and would have had the greatest success in love. The intrigues and adventures which early in life he had been engaged in ... had exercised an unfortunate influence upon him: he received those impressions with which he could never after successfully struggle. From this time, intellect, education, nobility of sentiment, and high principle, in others, became the objects of suspicion to him, and soon of hatred. The more he advanced in years the more this sentiment was confirmed in him. He wished to reign by himself. His jealousy on this point unceasingly became weakness. He reigned, indeed, in little things; the great he could never reach: even in the former, too, he was often governed. The superior ability of his early ministers and his early generals soon wearied him. He liked nobody to be in anyway superior to him. Thus he chose his ministers, not for their knowledge, but for their ignorance; not for their capacity, but for their want of it. He liked to form them, as he said; liked to teach them even the most trifling things. It was the same with his generals. He took credit to himself for instructing them; wished it to be thought that from his cabinet he commanded and directed all his armies. Naturally fond of trifles, he unceasingly occupied himself with the most petty details of his troops, his household, his mansions; would even instruct his cooks, who received, like novices, lessons they had known by heart for years. This vanity, this unmeasured and unreasonable love of admiration, was his ruin. His ministers, his generals, his mistresses, his courtiers, soon perceived his weakness. They praised him with emulation and spoiled him. Praises, or to say truth, flattery, pleased him to such an extent, that the coarsest was well received, the vilest even better relished. It was the sole means by which you could approach him. Those whom he liked owed his affection for them to their untiring flatteries. This is what gave his ministers so much authority, and the opportunities they had for adulating him, of attributing everything to him, and of pretending to learn everything from him. Suppleness, meanness, an admiring, dependent, cringing manner--above all, an air of nothingness--were the sole means of pleasing him.

This poison spread. It spread, too, to an incredible extent in a prince who, although of intellect beneath mediocrity, was not utterly without sense, and who had had some experience. Without voice or musical knowledge, he used to sing in private the passages of the opera prologues that were fullest of his praises! He was drowned in vanity; and so deeply, that at his public suppers--all the Court present, musicians also--he would hum these self-same praises between his teeth, when the music they were set to was played!

And yet, it must be admitted, he might have done better. Though his intellect, as I have said, was beneath mediocrity, it was capable of being formed. He loved glory, was fond of order and regularity; was by disposition prudent, moderate, discreet, master of his movements and his tongue. Will it be believed? He was also by disposition good and just! God had sufficiently gifted him to enable him to be a good King; perhaps even *a tolerably great King*! All the evil came to him from elsewhere. His early education was so neglected that nobody dared approach his apartment. He has often been heard to speak of those times with bitterness, and even to relate that, one evening he was found in the basin of the Palais Royale garden fountain, into which he had fallen! He was scarcely taught how to read or write, and remained so ignorant, that the most familiar historical and other facts were utterly unknown to him! He fell, accordingly, and sometimes even in public, into the grossest absurdities....

Thus, we see this monarch grand, rich, conquering, the arbiter of Europe; feared and admired as long as the ministers and captains existed who really deserved the name. When they were no more, the machine kept moving some time by impulsion, and from their influence. But soon afterwards we saw beneath the surface; faults and errors were multiplied, and decay came on with giant strides; without, however, opening the eyes of that despotic master, so anxious to do everything and direct everything himself, and who seemed to indemnify himself for disdain abroad by increasing fear and trembling at home....

He early showed a disinclination for Paris. The troubles that had taken place there during the minority made him regard the place as dangerous ....

His love for Madame de la Vallière, which was at first kept secret, occasioned frequent excursions to Versailles, then a little card castle, which had been built by Louis XIII--annoyed, and his suite still more so, at being frequently obliged to sleep in a wretched inn there, after he had been out hunting in the forest of Saint Leger. That monarch rarely slept at Versailles more than one night, and then from necessity; the King, his son, slept there, so that he might be more in private with his mistress; pleasures unknown to the hero and just man, worthy son of Saint Louis, who built the little château.

These excursions of Louis XIV by degrees gave birth to those immense buildings he erected at Versailles; and their convenience for a numerous court, so different from the apartments at St. Germains, led him to take up his abode there entirely shortly after the death of the Queen. He built an infinite number of apartments, which were asked for by those who wished to pay their court to him; whereas at St. Germains nearly everybody was obliged to lodge in the town, and the few who found accommodation at the château were strangely inconvenienced.

The frequent fêtes, the private promenades at Versailles, the journeys, were means on which the King seized in order to distinguish or mortify the courtiers, and thus render them more assiduous in pleasing him. He felt that of real favours he had not enough to bestow; in order to keep up the spirit of devotion, he therefore unceasingly invented all sorts of ideal ones, little preferences and petty distinctions, which answered his purpose as well.

He was exceedingly jealous of the attention paid him. Not only did he notice the presence of the most distinguished courtiers, but those of inferior degree also. He looked to the right and to the left, not only upon rising but upon going to bed, at his meals, in passing though his apartments, or his gardens of Versailles, where alone the courtiers were allowed to follow him; he saw and noticed everybody; not one escaped him, not even those who hoped to remain unnoticed. He marked well all absentees from the court, found out the reason of their absence, and never lost an opportunity of acting towards them as the occasion might seem to justify...

Louis XIV took great pains to be well informed of all that passed everywhere; in the public places, in the private houses, in society and familiar intercourse. His spies and tell-tales were infinite. He had them of all species; many who were ignorant that their information reached him; others who knew it; others who wrote to him direct, sending their letters through channels he indicated; and all these letters were seen by him alone, and always before everything else; others who sometimes spoke to him secretly in his cabinet, entering by the back stairs. These unknown means ruined an infinite number of people of all classes, who never could discover the cause; often ruined them very unjustly; for the King, once prejudiced, never altered his opinion, or ... rarely ....

Never did man give with better grace than Louis XIV, or augmented so much in this way the price of his benefits. Never did man sell to better profit his words, even his smiles,--nay, his looks. Never did disobliging words escape him; and if he had to blame, to reprimand, or correct, which was very rare, it was nearly always with goodness, never, except on one occasion ... with anger or severity. Never was man so naturally polite, or of a politeness so measured, so graduated, so adapted to person, time, and place. Towards women his politeness was without parallel. Never did he pass the humblest petticoat without raising his hat; even to the chambermaids, that he knew to be such .... For ladies he took his hat off completely, but to a greater or less extent; for titled people half off, holding it in his hand or against his ear some instants, more or less marked. For the nobility he contented himself by putting his hand to his hat. He took it off for the princes of the blood, as for the ladies....

He treated his valets well, above all those of the household. It was amongst them that he was most at ease, and that he unbosomed himself the most familiarly, especially to the chiefs. Their friendship and their aversion have often had grand results. They were unceasingly in a position to render good and bad offices; thus they recalled those powerful enfranchised slaves of the Roman emperors, to whom the senate and the great people paid court and basely truckled. These valets during Louis XIV's reign were not less courted. The ministers, even the most powerful, openly studied their caprices; and the princes of the blood,--nay, the bastards,--not to mention people of lower grade, did the same. The majority were accordingly insolent enough; and if you could not avoid their insolence, you were forced to put up with it.

The King loved air and exercise very much, as long as he could make use of them. He had excelled in dancing, and at tennis .... On horseback he was admirable, even at a late age. He liked to see everything done with grace and address. To acquit yourself well or ill before him was a merit or a fault. He said that with things not necessary it was best not to meddle, unless they were done well. He was very fond of shooting, and there was not a better or more graceful shot than he. He had always in his cabinet seven or eight pointer bitches, and was fond of feeding them, to make himself known to them....

He liked splendour, magnificence, and profusion in everything: you pleased him if you shone through the brilliancy of your houses, your clothes, your table, your equipages. Thus a taste for extravagance and luxury was disseminated through all classes of society; causing infinite harm, and leading to general confusion of rank and to ruin.

As for the King himself, nobody ever approached his magnificence. His buildings, who could number them? At the same time, who was there who did not deplore the pride, the caprice, the bad taste seen in them? He built nothing useful or ornamental in Paris, except the Pont Royal, and that simply by necessity; so that despite its incomparable extent, Paris is inferior to many cities of Europe. St. Germains, a lovely spot, with a marvellous view, rich forest, terraces, gardens, and water he abandoned for Versailles; the dullest and most ungrateful of all places, without prospect, without wood, without water, without soil; for the ground is all shifting or swamp, the air accordingly bad.

The Works of the Most High and Mightie Prince, James ... King of Great Britaine. London 1616. P. 529. St. John, Bayle, trans. *The Memoirs of the Duke of Saint-Simon.* 2nd ed. London: Sonnenschein, 1888. Vol. 2. Pp. 357-359, 362-365, 367-369.

MANNERS AND MORES IN PETER THE GREAT'S RUSSIA

The reign of Czar Peter the Great (1682-1725) transformed Russia from a peripheral to a major power in Europe. Peter brought about this change both by his political and military leadership and by his unceasing efforts to modernize his backward country. He realized that Russia must emulate European science and technology to be a great power, but also catch up in cultural development. As a youth, he had received a good education from private tutors, including foreigners conversant with current intellectual trends in western Europe. In 1697-1698, Peter traveled with a diplomatic mission to many European cities, where he learned about such things as shipbuilding and persuaded various craftsmen and technical experts to come to Russia. After his return he sent the children of aristocratic Russian families to complete their education in Europe.

Peter's carried through his program of modernization with great vigor, crushing political opponents with harsh, police-state tactics. His reforms affected Russians on all levels. Peter reduced the powers of both the traditional nobility (boyars) and the church hierarchy, and streamlined the state bureaucracy. He also fostered industrial enterprises. In 1703, Peter founded a new capital city on the shores of the Baltic Sea at Saint Petersburg, which he called his "window on Europe." He founded schools, simplified the Russian alphabet, and adopted Arabic numerals. Printed material became more accessible and Russian language newspapers began to appear.

Despite Peter's strenuous efforts to revolutionize Russian society through education and the "polite arts," progress was slow and his country continued to seem somewhat backward to sophisticated Europeans. In the passage that follows, we have the observations of John Korb, an Austrian diplomat to Russia during Peter's reign. Korb offers an admiring sketch of Peter and praises his modernization crusade. He also gives a valuable account of the lives of aristocratic Russians whose circles he entered as an esteemed member of a foreign embassy; his discussion of "Female Luxury" reveals the affluence, if not the good taste, of upper-class life. Korb is less enchanted with ordinary Russians; his depiction of the Russian national reflects his own prejudices but also vividly conveys what Peter had to contend with.

QUESTIONS:

1) Can we detect notes of bias in Korb's account of Russian society?
2) Is Korb's judgment of Peter favorable?
3) What does Korb find especially admirable or especially reprehensible in the manners of Muscovites?

His Majesty the Czar.

Those brilliant gifts of nature and soul which have spread his fame throughout almost every realm of the earth, pointed him out from his infancy for kingly power and sovereign sway. A well set stature, well proportioned limbs, the vivacity of his youth, and an address beyond his years, so conciliated the affections and good will of his subjects, on account of their expectations of his natural qualifications, that he was openly preferred by the contending suffrages of numbers of people to his brother Ivan Alexiowicz, who was called to the throne of his progenitors by that pre-eminence of primogeniture which is held sacred by the nations. Ever self-reliant, he contemns death and danger, the apprehension of which terrifies others. Often he has gone quite alone to traitors and conspirators against his life, and either from their reflection on the greatness of their crime, or dread and remorse for their divulged treason alone he has made them quail by his Majestic presence; and, lest this creeping and dangerous pest should spread, he has delivered them up to chains and prison. In 1694 he sailed out of the port of Archangel, into the North Sea, beyond Cola. A storm arose and drove the ships upon the most perilous rocks. The seamen were already crying out in despair; the Boyars, who had accompanied their sovereign, had betaken themselves to their prayers and their devotion of making thousands of crossings--no doubt in terror of the contemplation of such an awful shipwreck. Alone, amidst the fury of the wild sea, the fearless Czar took the helm with a most cheerful countenance, restored courage to their despairing souls, and, until the sea subsided, found an asylum for life and limb on that very rock upon which, in rough weather, many vessels had been a prey to the foaming brine....

With what spirit, too, he laboured to introduce into Muscovy those polite arts that had for ages been proscribed there, may be easily gathered from his having sent into various countries of Europe,--into Germany, Italy, England, and Holland,--the more talented children of his principal subjects, in order that they might learn, by intercourse, the wisdom and arts of the most polished nations, and on their return be ornaments of Muscovy, and in their turn excite their juniors to the like deserts. He made known his reasons for this plan, some years

age, to his Boyars, explaining its utility to them. They all commended the monarch's prudence, but insinuated that such immense good, however desirable it might be, was unattainable. That the genius of the Muscovites was unsuited to such pursuits; that the money expended on it would be wasted in vain; and that he would fatigue himself and his subjects with profitless labour. The Czar was indignant at these sayings, which were only worthy of the profound ignorance of those that gave utterance to them. For they liked their benighted darkness, and nothing but shame at their own deformity was capable of drawing them into the light. "Are we then born less blest than other nations," the Czar continued, "that the divinity should have infused inept minds into our bodies? Have we not hands? Have we not eyes? Have we not the same habit of body that suffices foreign nations for their internal culture? Why have we alone degenerate and rude souls? Why should we alone be left out as unworthy of the glory of human science? By Hercules! we have the same minds; we can do like other folk if we only will it. For nature has given to all mankind the same groundwork and seed of virtues; we are all born to all those things; when the stimulus is applied, all those properties of the soul that have been, as it were, sleeping, shall be awakened." The greatest things may be expected from such a Prince. Let the Muscovites congratulate themselves on the treasure they possess in him, for they are now really fortunate. He chose his wife in the family of Lubochin, and she bore him a son named Alexis Petrowicz, a youth splendidly gifted and adorned with ingenuous virtues, on whom rest the hopes of his father, and the fortunes and tranquillity of Muscovy....

On the Manners of the Muscovites.

The people are rude of letters, and wanting in that virtuous discipline by which the mind is cultivated. Few study polite manners or imitate them. John Barclay, in his "Mirror of Souls," describes at length how this race, born for slavery, becomes ferocious at the least trace of liberty; placid if oppressed, and not refusing the yoke, they of their own accord confess themselves slaves of their prince. He has a right to their wealth, their bodies, and their lives. Humility more sordidly crouching the very Turks entertain not for their Ottoman sceptre. They esteem other races as well by their own character. Foreigners whom chance or choice has led into Muscovy they condemn to the same yoke, and will have them be slaves of their monarch. Should they catch and bring back any of them departing furtively, they punish them as runagates [renegades]. As for the magnates, though they be slaves themselves, towards their inferiors and the plebeians, whom they usually call, out of scorn, black men and Christians, their arrogance is intolerable, and the vulgar dread their frown extremely.

Devoid of honest education, they esteem deceit to be the height of wisdom. They have no shame of lying, no blush for a detected fraud: to such a degree are the seeds of true virtue proscribed from that region, that vice itself obtains the reputation of virtue. Yet I would not have you understand that all the inhabitants of that monarchy, without any exception, are alike ignorant and proud in their estimation of virtue. Among such a quantity of tares some wholesome plants do grow; and the rose that struggles into blossom among this rank crop of fetid leeks, blushes all the more fair, and sheds a perfume all the more grateful. Few indeed are they that just Jupiter hath loved, or shining virtue raised to the skies: but those few really stand so pre-eminent that these rare torches can remain unremarked only by the inexperienced, or such as are crushed beneath a mountain of vices. The rest are of an incult [coarse], slow, and stupid disposition, so absorbed sometimes in staring at strangers, that with their jaws and eyes wide open they quite forget themselves. Among those, however, are not to be reckoned such as are smoothed down by the transaction of affairs, or business, or that have learnt by recent travel that the sun is not shut up within the mere frontiers of Muscovy.

In their schools positively the only labour of the schoolmasters is to teach the children how to write and shape their letters. The height of learning consists in committing to memory some articles of their creed.

They despise liberal arts as useless torments of youth, they prohibit philosophy, and they have often publicly outraged astronomy with the opprobrious name of magic. It is criminal to introduce the calendar of Vogt the astronomer into Muscovy, because ... he presaged rebellion to the Muscovites. They say that evil spirits, at whose suggestion and showing astronomers may sometimes guess about the future what is beyond mortal ken, must have helped him in this black art. The Czar is endeavouring, by means of various arts and sciences, to frame a better state of things in his kingdom. If success should crown the prudent efforts of good counsel, people shall shortly be astonished at the fair edifice that will stand where there was nothing but huts before; unless some misfortune should happen or a defection of the people, or perhaps even simply the very barbarity of their inclinations should render them incapable of bearing their own good fortune, or should make them grudge to their posterity a lot so happy, and envy the labours of the present for the profit of future generations. It is but a short time ago that an enterprising Pole set up the first printing press among them, but they only print in the Russian language. The Russian characters are not very dissimilar from those of the Greeks, by whom they were taught to read and write. Their grammar and idiomatical construction too are not unlike the Greek. In the same house with the printing press, some Greek priests are maintained at the Czar's expense, who teach Italian to any that wish to learn it.

They add and subtract numbers differently from other people: they have a board, with several different descriptions of beads, by means of which they calculate accurately, with surprising quickness--just like the markers that other nations make use of: they indicate various numbers by the mode of collocation.

Though they are themselves unskilled in music, they are fond of its harmonies. They have foreign musicians, whom they pet while they are singing, but as soon as they are sated with their strains, their stinginess returns, and they are discontent to be at a yearly charge for a few hours' gratification. Nor are the exercises to which the nobility of European Courts addict themselves in use in Moscow: they take no delight in the manly exercises of horsemanship or boxing; they take no pride in dancing, nor in any other art that prevails in this age among nations that are capable of a generous ardour for praise....

The slavery laws are in vigour among the Muscovites. Some become slaves by captivity, others are so by birth, many from being sold by their fathers, or by themselves: for if they be manumitted [set free] by their dying masters, so accustomed are they to flattery, that they make themselves over as slaves to other masters, or bind themselves slaves for a sum of money. Even freemen that serve masters for regular wages cannot leave their master's service at will; for should such a one quit without his master's consent, no other will take him into his service, unless his former master or one of his friends recommend him, and answer for his being trustworthy.

Paternal authority is ample enough also, and presses very severely upon the son, for the father has the right of selling him four times over. Thus, if after being once sold, he should recover his liberty in any way, or be manumitted by his master, the paternal rights entitle his father to sell him over and over again; but after the fourth sale his father is allowed no further power over him. However, in the actual position of affairs, now that Muscovy possesses a monarch whose intellect is so highly gifted by nature, and who is urged on by the wonderful stimulus of glory, people opine that a milder statute will be substituted for this very crude authority of parents over their sons. Though, in truth, the nation itself has such a dislike of liberty, that it seems to exclaim against a happiness for which it was not created, and is so inured to its slavish condition that it will scarcely endure the prudent and kindly solicitude of the Prince for his dominions and subjects to be carried out to the full extent....

Of Female Luxury.

The women of Muscovy are graceful in figure, and fair and comely of feature: but spoil their beauty with needless shams. The shapes, unimprisoned by stays, are free to grow as nature bids, and are not of so neat and trim figure as those of other Europeans. They wear chemises interwoven with gold all through, the sleeves of which are plaited up in a marvelous way, being eight and sometimes ten ells in length, and their pretty concatenation of little plaits extends down to the hands, and is confined with handsome and costly bracelets.

Their outer garments resemble those of Eastern women: they wear a cloak over their tunic. They often dress in handsome silks and furs, and earrings and rings are in general fashion among them. Matrons and widows cover the head with furs of price: maidens only wear a rich band around their forehead and go bareheaded, with their locks floating upon their shoulders, and arranged with great elegance in artificial knots.

Those of any dignity or honorable condition are not urged to be present at banquets, nor do they even sit at the ordinary table of their husbands. They may be seen, nevertheless, at present when they go to church or drive out to visit their friends; for there has been a great relaxation of the jealous old rule which required women only to go out in carriages so closed up, that the very use of eyesight was denied to these creatures made bond-slaves to a master. Moreover, they hold it among the greatest honours that can be paid if a husband admits his guest to see his wife or daughters, who present a glass of brandy, and expect a kiss from the favoured guest; and, according to the manner of this people, duly propitiated with this, they withdraw in silence, as they came. They exercise no authority in their households. When the master is absent from home, the servants have full charge of the management of the affairs of the house, according to their honesty or caprice, without asking or acquainting the wife about anything. But the more wealthy maintain great crowds of handmaidens, who do scarcely any work, except what trifling things the wife may require of them; meantime, they are kept shut up in the house, and spin and weave linen. With such a lazy life one cannot blame the custom which condemned the poor creatures to such frequent use of the bath, so that their idleness may be at least varied from time to time with another description of sloth.

Korb, John G. *Diary of an Austrian Secretary of Legation at the Court of Czar Peter the Great.* Ed. and trans. C. MacDonnell. London: Bradbury & Evans, 1863 [orig. 1700]. Vol. 2. Pp. 125-127, 129-131, 194-202.

▶ **Samurai Ladies**

HIDEYOSHI: THE MAN WHO ALMOST UNIFIED JAPAN

Japanese emperors were figureheads who reigned but did not rule after the twelfth century. A *shogun*, or military commander, ruled in the emperor's name; between the twelfth and nineteenth century, dynasties of shoguns rose and fell from power. After the fifteenth century, a shogunal dynasty called the Ashikagas lost effective control to feudal lords and great Buddhist monasteries, who waged almost incessant civil wars. While the fifteenth and sixteenth centuries were a bleak period in Japan's political history, they were also eras of great economic growth, because needing revenues, the lords and monasteries encouraged agriculture, manufacture, and trade.

Three great men paved the way for national unification. Hideyoshi (1536-1598), the second of these men, was also the most interesting. Born a commoner and therefore without a surname, he was able to rise from foot soldier to supreme power, because of the breakdown of strict social classes during the turbulent time. (In later life Hideyoshi adopted the grand surname Toyotomi, which means "wealth of the nation.")

When Oda Nobunaga, the first paramount leader, was assassinated in 1582, Hideyoshi, a rising general in Oda's army, was appointed one of four guardians of Oda's infant grandson and heir. He acted quickly to eliminate Oda's family, defeated all rivals, and consolidated power by 1590. Hideyoshi then assigned fiefs to his supporters, ordered a land survey for tax purposes, and standardized the currency. He also ordered the confiscation of all weapons from the peasants and froze all people in their present occupations, ending social mobility.

Like many ambitious men, Hideyoshi dreamt of conquering the world. To the Japanese of the sixteenth century, the world meant China. To conquer China, he needed a passage through Korea; when the Korean government refused, Hideyoshi invaded that land in 1592 with 160,000 of his battle-hardened veterans. Korea suffered fearful destruction and was almost completely overrun, until its overlord China intervened with a large force and helped to drive off the invaders. Hideyoshi resumed his invasion in 1597, but died in the following year, whereupon the Japanese abandoned their quest.

Because Hideyoshi had no son until late in life, he had designated a nephew as heir. Then a concubine bore him a son, named Hideyori. To secure Hideyori's inheritance, he ordered his nephew, already an adult and a possible rival, to commit suicide. Because his son was a mere boy when the aging Hideyoshi became ill, he appointed a board of five regents to rule in his son's name after he died. He hoped that the boy would survive because the regents would check one another. In a repeat of what had happened after Oda's death, one of the regents, Tokugawa Ieyasu, crushed all opponents, killed all Hideyoshi's family, and established himself as the new shogun. The Tokugawa shogunate ruled Japan as a centralized feudal state until 1868.

This reading is taken from Hideyoshi's private letters, sent to his wife, mother, son, and others. They reveal his private side as well as his political hopes and plans.

QUESTIONS:

1) How did Hideyoshi deal with his enemies?
2) How did Hideyoshi attempt to secure his son's succession?
3) What sort of ambitions did Hideyoshi reveal through his letters?

[To his wife in 1587.]

Tomorrow I shall go on to Yatsushiro, from where the troops of Shimazu have retreated [back into their home province]. We have arranged matters in the following way:

Item: As regards the hostages from Shimaz Yoshihisa, this should be a daughter of about 15 [years old]....

Item: As for Yoshihisa himself, he should live in Kyoto.

Item: As regards the hostages of the Elder Councillors, about ten should be offered.

Item: As regards the hostages of Shimazu Hyogo-no-kami, he should send his eldest son, who is now 15 years old, to Osaka to stay at the headquarters there, and should offer another [son], who is now eight, as a hostage....

Yesterday we moved back to Higo province from Satsuma province. I plan to reach Hataka in Chikuzen province around the 5th day of the 6th month. We have thus already come back about halfway and we are halfway to Osaka. At Hakata, I shall give orders for some construction work; then be assured that I shall be back in Osaka perhaps by the 6th month, or as late as the 10th day of the 7th month. I have received hostages from Iki and Tsushima and their submission. I have sent fast ships in order to urge Korea to pay homage to the Emperor of Japan, stating that, if it does not, I shall conquer it next year. I shall take even China in hand, and have control of it during my lifetime; since [China] has become disdainful [of Japan], the work will be the more exhausting.

After the last battle I feel older than I am; more and more white hairs have grown and I cannot pluck them out. I am very ashamed to be seen by anyone; only you will be tolerant of this, but I still complain.

[Letter to his wife's lady-in-waiting, for communicating to his wife, in 1590.]

We have surrounded Odawara with two or three rings and have constructed a pair of moats and walls, and we do not intend to let a single enemy out. People from the eight provinces in Kanto are entrenching themselves there, and so if we succeed in starving Odawara into surrender, the way to Oshu is so wide open that I cannot but be satisfied. Since [Kanto] is one-third of Japan, I would like to give firm orders now that we must maintain this situation even after the end of the year. From now on I intend to see to the welfare of the country. This time I will achieve as many great and meritorious deeds as possible, keep a long encampment using either the provisions or gold and silver coins, until my name shall remain for posterity, and then I shall make a triumphant return. Keep the above in mind and tell it to everybody....

I repeat: because I have shut the enemy up in a birdcage, there is no danger, so please do not worry. I am longing for the young prince [his son], but because I am looking to the future and especially since I intend to order my men to pacify the whole country, I have put these personal feelings aside....

[Letter to his wife's lady-in-waiting, to be read to his wife, in 1592 from Nagoya, his headquarters for the invasion of Korea.]

By now we have taken various castles in Korea and I have sent my men to besiege the capital there. I shall take even China around the 9th month, so I shall receive [from you] the costumes for the [next] festival of the 9th month in the capital of China. Do not worry, as I find myself more and more in good health and have a good appetite. When I capture China, I'll send someone to you in order to welcome you there.

[Letter to his mother, written at the same time as the previous letter.]

You have sent me a *katebira* [a summer robe made of hemp] for the season's festival, together with several other things. I put them on and rejoiced, wishing you a long and happy life. I intend to receive [such gifts] in China at the time off the 9th month festival. We have already captured a great number of castles in Korea. I have heard that it takes about twenty days to reach the capital of Korea from the harbor that we have taken [Pusan, on the south coast], and I have sent my men toward that capital. I expect to besiege the capital in a short time. When I have assembled the ships, I shall have my men cross over. As I expect to take China, too, I look forward to sending men [from there] to welcome you.

[Letters to his son Hideyori, then three or four years old, in the last year of his life, 1598.]

You kindly sent me the wonderful present, and I gaze at it in rapture. Within three or five days, I will give orders for some construction work here, and then I will visit you to talk about a lot of matters. This is a sort of vase which I am presenting you. When I eventually visit you in person, I shall offer you various gifts.

* * * * *

You sent me a letter quickly, and I was very glad to receive it. Now I have understood that Kitsu, Kame, Yasu, and Tsushi have acted against your wishes. As this is something extremely inexcusable, ask your Mother, and then bind these four persons with a straw rope and keep them like that until your Father comes to your side. When I arrive, I shall beat them all to death; don't let them free....

I repeat ... should anyone try to thwart the will of Lord Chunagon [Hideyori's title], he must beat and beat such a man to death, and then nobody will be against him....

[Two months before his death, ill and lonely, Hideyoshi wrote to an unknown person, named Gomoji.]

As I am ill and feel lonely, I have taken up the brush. I have not eaten for fifteen days and am in distress. Since I went out for amusement yesterday to a place where some construction work is going on, my illness has become worse and worse, and I feel I am gradually weakening. You must take care of yourself, and if you get a little better, please come to me. I look forward to seeing you....

[Although he had made his vassals swear allegiance to his son in 1595 and again in 1596, Hideyoshi repeated the request from his deathbed, as follows:]

Until Hideyori reaches adulthood, I am asking for the help of the people whose names are listed in this document. This is the only request I want to make.
   Sincerely,

               Hideyoshi
8th month, 5th day [1598]

I repeat: concerning the business of Hideyori, I am begging and begging you five [regents]. The details have been conveyed to the five men. I am loath to part. I end here.

[In his last poem, written shortly before his death, Hideyoshi may have had a premonition that his arrangements for his son would not hold, just as he himself had betrayed his oath of allegiance to Oda's grandson. Osaka Castle is his strongly fortified headquarters.]

         I am as
         The dew which falls,
         The dew which disappears.
         Even Osaka Castle
         Is only a dream.

Boscaro, Adriana, ed. and trans. *101 Letters of Hideyoshi: The Private Correspondence of Toyotomi Hideyoshi*. Tokyo: Sophia University, 1975. Pp. 30-31, 37-38, 45-46, 73, 76-78.

WILLIAM AND MARY AND THE "GLORIOUS REVOLUTION" OF 1688

England's Glorious Revolution in 1688 was the culmination of two long-standing, intertwined conflicts: the Protestant Church versus Roman Catholicism, and royal absolutism versus parliamentary supremacy. These struggles had climaxed in a civil war in the mid-seventeenth century, which pitted parliament against the king. The defeated King Charles I (r. 1625-1649) was executed, and monarchy was briefly abolished. In 1660, the monarchy was restored with the coronation of Charles II (r. 1660-1685), son of the executed king. Charles II avoided confrontations over crucial issues by keeping secret his profession of Catholicism and by accepting covert subsidies from Louis XIV of France rather than seeking funds from Parliament; in return, he pursued a pro-French foreign policy.

Matters came to a head in 1685, when the childless Charles was succeeded by his brother the Duke of York (for whom New York is named), now James II (r. 1685-1688). James alienated most of his English subjects by openly professing and favoring Catholicism, and by raising taxes without Parliament's consent. When James had a son by his Catholic wife, leaders of both the Whig and Tory parties invited James's nephew, William, stadtholder [chief magistrate] of the Netherlands, and his wife Mary, James's elder daughter, both staunch Protestants, jointly to ascend the English throne. James II fled to France. William and Mary landed in England at the head of 15,000 troops and were proclaimed king and queen.

The expulsion of James II and installation of William and Mary in 1688 is known as the Glorious Revolution. In a Declaration of Rights, which the monarchs acceded to, Parliament sealed the victory of constitutional government by asserting control of the army, taxation, and elections, and by guaranteeing freedom of the press. Subsequent legislation banned Catholics and those married to Catholics from the throne.

James II, however, had Catholic supporters in Ireland, an English possession. To regain the English throne, James landed in Ireland at the head of troops supplied by Louis XIV. On 1 July 1690, he was soundly defeated by his son-in-law, William, at the decisive Battle of the Boyne. Except for minor uprisings in support of James's son and grandson, called the Old and Young Pretenders (the latter is better known as Bonnie Prince Charlie), Britain did not suffer civil war again.

The Glorious Revolution, the Bill of Rights, and the Battle of the Boyne secured the supremacy of the Protestant Church of England in religion and of Parliament in government. The Battle of the Boyne, in which Irish Catholics sided with James II, also resulted in the oppression of Irish Catholics for two hundred years by Britain's official Anglican Church. The eminent nineteenth-century British historian, Lord Macaulay, recorded these stirring events in his monumental *History of England*.

QUESTIONS:

1) How does Macaulay present James II?

2) What is Macaulay's opinion of the characters of William and Mary, as individuals, and as rulers?

3) How does religion figure in Macaulay's account of the Glorious Revolution?

On the afternoon of the twelfth of March, James landed in the harbour of Kinsale. By the Roman Catholic population he was received with shouts of unfeigned transport.... James learned that his cause was prospering. In the three southern provinces of Ireland the Protestants were disarmed, and were so effectually bowed down by terror that he had nothing to apprehend from them. In the North there was some show of resistance: but Hamilton was marching against the malcontents; and there was little doubt that they would easily be crushed....

When the news that James had arrived in Ireland reached London, the sorrow and alarm were general, and were mingled with serious discontent. The multitude, not making sufficient allowance for the difficulties by which William was encompassed on every side, loudly blamed his neglect....

In no long time it appeared that James would have done well to hearken to those counsellors who had told him that the acts by which he was trying to make himself popular in one of his three kingdoms would make him odious in the others. It was in some sense fortunate for England that, after he had ceased to reign here, he continued during more than a year to reign in Ireland. The Revolution had been followed by a reaction of public feeling in his favour. That reaction, if it had been suffered to proceed uninterrupted, might perhaps not have ceased till he was again King: but it was violently interrupted by himself. He would not suffer his people to forget: he would not suffer them to hope: while they were trying to find excuses for his past errors, and to persuade themselves that he would not repeat those errors, he forced upon them, in their own despite, the conviction that he was incorrigible, that the sharpest discipline of adversity had taught him nothing, and that, if they were weak enough to recall him, they would soon have to depose him again.... Every week came the news that he had passed some new Act for robbing or

murdering Protestants. Every colonist who succeeded in stealing across the sea from Leinster to Holyhead or Bristol, brought fearful reports of the tyranny under which his brethren groaned.... Meanwhile the Protestants of Ulster were defending themselves with stubborn courage against a great superiority of force.

William had been, during the whole spring, impatiently expected in Ulster. The Protestant settlements along the coast of that province had, in the course of the month of May, been repeatedly agitated by false reports of his arrival. It was not, however, till the afternoon of the fourteenth of June that he landed at Carrickfergus. The inhabitants of the town crowded the main street and greeted him with loud acclamations: but they caught only glimpse of him. As soon as he was on dry ground he mounted and set off for Belfast. He was welcomed at the North Gate by the magistrates and burgesses in their robes of office. The multitude pressed on his carriage with shouts of "God save the Protestant King." For the town was one of the strongholds of the Reformed Faith....

The night came: but the Protestant counties were awake and up. A royal salute had been fired from the castle of Belfast. It had been echoed and reechoed by guns which Schomberg had placed at wide intervals for the purpose of conveying signals from post to post. Wherever the peal was heard, it was known that King William had come. Before midnight all the heights of Antrim and Down were blazing with bonfires. The light was seen across the bays of Carlingford and Dundalk, and gave notice to the outposts of the enemy that the decisive hour was at hand. Within forty eight hours after William had landed, James set out from Dublin for the Irish camp, which was pitched near the northern frontier of Leinster....

The two rival princes meanwhile were busied in collecting their forces. Loughbrickland was the place appointed by William for the rendezvous of the scattered divisions of his army. While his troops were assembling, he exerted himself indefatigably to improve their discipline and to provide for their subsistence. He had brought from England two hundred thousand pounds in money and a great quantity of ammunition and provisions. Pillaging was prohibited under severe penalties. At the same time supplies were liberally dispensed; and all the paymasters of regiments were directed to send in their accounts without delay, in order that there might be no arrears....

William was all himself again. His spirits, depressed by eighteen months passed in dull state, amidst factions and intrigues which he but half understood, rose high as soon as he was surrounded by tents and standards.... [His men] observed with delight that, infirm as he was, he took his share of every hardship which they underwent; that he thought more of their comfort than of his own; that he sharply reprimanded some officers, who were so anxious to procure luxuries for his table as to forget the wants of the common soldiers; that he never once, from the day on which he took the field, lodged in a house, but, even in the neighbourhood of cities and palaces, slept in his small travelling hut of wood; that no solicitations could induce him, on a hot day and in a high wind, to move out of the choking cloud of dust, which overhung the line of march, and which severely tried lungs less delicate than his. Every man under his command became familiar with his looks and with his voice; for there was not a regiment which he did not inspect with minute attention. His pleasant looks and sayings were long remembered. One brave soldier has recorded in his journal the kind and courteous manner in which a basket of the first cherries of the year was accepted from him by the King, and the sprightliness with which His Majesty conversed at supper with those who stood round the table.

On the twenty fourth of June, the tenth day after William's landing, he marched southward from Loughbrickland with all his forces. He was fully determined to take the first opportunity of fighting.... When William caught sight of the valley of Boyne, he could not suppress an exclamation and gesture of delight. He had been apprehensive that the enemy would avoid a decisive action, and would protract the war till the autumnal rains should return with pestilence in their train. He was now at ease. It was plain that the contest would be sharp and short....

Each of the contending princes had some advantages over his rival. James, standing on the defensive, behind entrenchments, with a river before him, had the stronger position: but his troops were inferior both in number and in quality to those which were opposed to him. He probably had thirty thousand men. About a third part of this force consisted of excellent French infantry and excellent Irish cavalry. But the rest of his army was the scoff of all Europe. The Irish dragoons were bad; the Irish foot worse....

William had under his command near thirty six thousand men, born in many lands, and speaking many tongues. Scarcely one Protestant Church, scarcely one Protestant nation, was unrepresented in the army which a strange series of events had brought to fight for the Protestant religion in the remotest island of the west. About half the troops were natives of England....

[James] watched, from a safe distance, the beginning of the battle on which his fate and the fate of his race depended. When it became clear that the day was going against Ireland, he was seized with apprehension that his flight might be intercepted, and galloped towards Dublin.... The French auxiliaries, who had been employed the whole morning in keeping William's right wing in check, covered the flight of the beaten enemy....

The slaughter had been less than on any battle field of equal importance and celebrity. Of the Irish only about fifteen hundred had fallen: but they were almost all cavalry, the flower of the army, brave and well disciplined men, whose place could not easily be supplied. William gave strict orders that there should be no unnecessary bloodshed, and enforced those orders by an act of laudable severity. One of his soldiers, after the fight was over, butchered three defenceless Irishmen who asked for quarter. The King ordered the murderer to be hanged on the spot.... The loss of the conquerors did not exceed five hundred men ....

* * * * *

In order that the questions which had been in dispute between the Stuarts and the nation might never again be stirred, it was determined that the instrument by which the Prince and Princess of Orange were called to the throne, and by which the order of succession was settled, should set forth, in the most distinct and solemn manner, the fundamental principles of the constitution. This instrument, known by the name of the Declaration of Right, was prepared by a committee .... In a few hours the Declaration was framed and approved by the Commons. The Lords assented to it with some amendments of no great importance.

The Declaration began by recapitulating the crimes and errors which had made a revolution necessary. James had invaded the province of the legislature; had treated modest petitioning as a crime; had oppressed the Church by means of an illegal tribunal; had, without the consent of Parliament, levied taxes and maintained a standing army in time of peace; had violated the freedom of election, and perverted the course of justice. Proceedings which could lawfully be questioned only in Parliament had been made the subjects of prosecution in the King's Bench. Partial and corrupt juries had been returned: excessive bail had been required from prisoners: excessive fines had been imposed: barbarous and unusual punishments had been inflicted: the estates of accused persons had been granted away before conviction. He, by whose authority these things had been done, had abdicated the government. The Prince of Orange, whom God had made the glorious instrument of delivering the nation from superstition and tyranny, had invited the Estates of the Realm to meet and to take counsel together for the securing of religion, of law, and of freedom. The Lords and Commons, having deliberated, had resolved that they would first, after the example of their ancestors, assert the ancient rights and liberties of England. Therefore it was declared that the dispensing power, as lately assumed and exercised, had no legal existence; that, without grant of Parliament, no money could be exacted by the sovereign from the subject; that, without consent of Parliament, no standing army could be kept up in time of peace. The right of subjects to petition, the right of electors to choose representatives freely, the right of the legislature to freedom of debate, the right of the nation to a pure and merciful administration of justice

according to the spirit of our mild laws, were solemnly affirmed. All these things the Convention claimed, as the undoubted inheritance of Englishmen. Having thus vindicated the principles of the constitution, the Lords and Commons, in the entire confidence that the deliverer would hold sacred the laws and liberties which he had saved, resolved that William and Mary, Prince and Princess of Orange, should be declared King and Queen of England for their joint and separate lives, and that, during their joint lives, the administration of the government should be in the Prince alone. After them the crown was settled on the posterity of Mary, then on Anne and her posterity, and then on the posterity of William....

On the morning of Wednesday, the thirteenth of February, the court of Whitehall and all the neighboring streets were filled with gazers. The magnificent Banqueting House, the masterpiece of Inigo, embellished by masterpieces of Rubens, had been prepared for a great ceremony. The walls were lined by the yeoman of the guard. Near the northern door, on the right hand, a large number of Peers had assembled. On the left were the Commons with their Speaker, attended by the mace. The southern door opened: and the Prince and Princess of Orange, side by side, entered, and took their place under the canopy of state.

Both Houses approached bowing low. William and Mary advanced a few steps. Halifax on the right, and Powle on the left, stood forth; and Halifax spoke. The Convention, he said, had agreed to a resolution which he prayed Their Highnesses to hear. They signified their assent; and the clerk of the House of Lords read, in a loud voice, the Declaration of Right. When he had concluded, Halifax, in the name of all the Estates of the Realm, requested the Prince and Princess to accept the crown.

William, in his own name and in that of his wife, answered that the crown was, in their estimation, the more valuable because it was presented to them as a token of the confidence of the nation. "We thankfully accept," he said, "what you have offered us." Then, for himself, he assured them that the laws of England, which he had once already vindicated, should be the rules of his conduct, that it should be his study to promote the welfare of the kingdom, and that, as to the means of doing so, he should constantly recur to the advice of the Houses, and should be disposed to trust their judgment rather than his own. These words were received with a shout of joy which was heard in the streets below, and was instantly answered by huzzas from many thousands of voices. The Lords and Commons then reverently retired from the Banqueting House and went in procession to the great gate of Whitehall, where the heralds and pursuivants [attendant officers] were waiting in their gorgeous tabards [capes emblazoned with coats of arms]. All the space as far as Charing Cross was one sea of heads.

The kettle drums struck up: the trumpets pealed: and Garter King at arms, in a loud voice, proclaimed the Prince and Princess of Orange King and Queen of England, charged all Englishmen to bear, from that moment, true allegiance to the new sovereigns, and besought God, who had already wrought so signal a deliverance for our Church and nation, to bless William and Mary with a long and happy reign.

Macaulay, Lord Thomas Babington. *The History of England from the Accession of James II*. Vol. 2 [orig. 1848]. Philadelphia 1861. Pp. 140, 143-144, 179, 181, 456-459, 472-475, 477-479, 488-489, 495-496.

▶ Silver Medal of Frederick II

THE ENLIGHTENED DESPOT IN THEORY AND IN PRACTICE

The second half of the eighteenth century is known in Europe as the era of enlightened despotism, because during this period, some rulers sought to put in practice the theories of Enlightenment philosophes.

The enlightened despots made sweeping economic reforms and limited the powers and prerogatives of the aristocracy and of the church. They also tried to make their central governments more rational in structure and function. Enlightened despots typically favored religious toleration, instituted progressive legal and judicial systems, and improved education and public health facilities.

Enlightened monarchs differed from their predecessors in de-emphasizing such old absolutist notions as divine right of kings, and stressed instead their beneficent role. They trusted in their own ability to discern what was best for all segments of society. Unfortunately, enlightened despots often failed to gain the support they needed to enact what they espoused in theory.

In the first of the following passages, Frederick II of Prussia (r. 1740-1786) rebuts some of the theories of the most famous political theorist of the Italian Renaissance. Niccolò Machiavelli, in his masterpiece, *The Prince*, had explained the principles of power politics; *The Prince* is a blueprint for the seizure and maintenance of power by an unscrupulous leader guided only by concern for his own dominance rather than for the welfare of his people. Frederick II argues that this recipe for tyranny will produce neither efficient government nor security for the head of state.

The second passage consists of three letters by Joseph II of Austria (r. 1780-1790). Joseph was the most earnest of enlightened reformers, but the radical nature of his reforms provoked widespread opposition and unrest; his successor rescinded most of his innovations. The letters show Joseph's intent to curtail the disproportionate influence of leaders of the Catholic church and to extend religious toleration to all faiths. They also show Joseph as a truly enlightened despot, justifying his position by complete devotion to the well being of his people.

QUESTIONS:

1) What are the most important specific objections that Frederick makes to Machiavelli's recommendations?

2) What are the "enlightened" sentiments that come through in the letters of Joseph II?

3) What are Joseph's attitudes about the role of religion?

Machiavel maintains, that, in this wicked and degenerate world, it is certain ruin to be strictly honest: for my part, I affirm, that in order to be safe, it is necessary to be virtuous. Men are commonly neither wholly good, nor wholly bad; but both good and bad; and such as are between the two will unanimously revere a powerful Prince, who is just and virtuous. I had much rather make war upon a tyrant than upon a good king, upon a Lewis XI than upon a Lewis XII, upon a [Roman emperor] Domitian rather than upon a Trajan; for the good king will be well served, whereas the tyrant's subjects will join my troops. Let me go into Italy with ten thousand men against an Alexander VI, half Italy will side with me: but let me march with forty thousand against an Innocent XI, and all Italy will rise in his defence. No wise and good king in England was ever dethroned by great armies; all their bad kings have been ruined by competitors, who, when they began the war, could not muster four thousand regular troops. Every wise prince therefore will look upon virtue as his chief security, and as the means of gaining and preserving the attachment and fidelity of his subjects, and striking terror into his enemies....

It is with the office of a prince, as with all others; no man, whatever his employment may be, can gain the confidence of others, without justice and integrity, as well as prudence: the most vicious men always choose to deal with the most virtuous; in the same manner as those princes who have the least capacity for governing, trust to him who passes with them for having the most. And why should vice be more necessary to the office of sovereignty, than to that of the meanest magistrate? Upon the whole, a prince who would preserve his dominions, as he must gain the hearts of the people, so for that purpose he is obliged to be just, virtuous, and beneficent, and not, as Machiavel through the whole of his work endeavours to form him, unjust, cruel, ambitious, and solely intent upon aggrandizing himself, by any means whatever.

Thus have I endeavoured to unmask this politician, who passed in his own age for an extraordinary man, whom several ministers of state have thought a dangerous writer, and yet have followed his abominable maxims, and recommended the study of them to their masters, an author who yet was never expertly answered,

and whom several statesmen follow, without thinking it any reproach to them. Happy would be the man who were able to banish such doctrines out of the world. I have here endeavoured to show the inconsistency of them; and it is incumbent on those who rule over others, to shew it by their example, and to set the public right, with regard to the false notion they entertain of politics, which should only be a system of wisdom, but commonly passes for a breviary of fraud and imposture: it is incumbent on them to banish subtleties and insincerity, which are so common in treaties; to revive honesty and candour, which, in truth, are very rare among sovereigns, and to shew themselves as indifferent about conquering the provinces of their neighbors, as jealous of preserving their own. The prince who would possess every thing, is not less absurd than the man who would devour every thing, and expects he could digest as much as he devours. Whereas he who is content to govern wisely what he justly possesses, is like the man who loads his stomach with nothing more than it is able to digest.

* * * * *

To Cardinal Herzan, Imperial Royal Minister in Rome:

Monsieur le Cardinal,--Since I have ascended the throne, and wear the first diadem in the world, I have made philosophy the legislator of my empire.

In consequence of its logic, Austria will assume another form, the authority of the Ulemas [religious leaders] will be restricted, and the rights of majesty will be restored to their primitive extent. It is necessary I should remove certain things out of the domain of religion which never did belong to it.

As I myself detest superstition and the Sadducean doctrines, I will free my people of them; with this view, I will dismiss the monks, I will suppress their monasteries, and will subject them to the bishops of the diocese.

In Rome they will declare this an infringement on the rights of God; I know they will cry aloud, "the greatness of Israel is fallen"; they will complain, that I take away from the people their tribunes, and that I draw a line of separation between dogma and philosophy; but they will be still more enraged when I undertake all this without the approbation of the servant of the servants of God.

To these things we owe the degradation of the human mind. A servant of the altar will never admit that the state is putting him into his proper place, when it leaves him to no other occupation than the gospel, and when by laws it prevents the children of Levi from carrying on a monopoly with the human understanding.

The principles of monachism, from Pachomius up to our time, have been directly opposed to the light of reason; respect for their founders ultimately became adoration itself, so that we behold again the Israelites going up to Bethel, in order to adore golden calves.

These false conceptions of religion were transmitted to the common people; they no longer knew God, and expected every thing from their saints.

The rights of the bishops, which I will re-establish, must assist in reforming the ideas of the people; instead of the monk, I will have the priest to preach, not the romances of the canonised, but the holy gospel and morality.

I shall take care that the edifice, which I have erected for posterity, be durable. The general seminaries are nurseries for my priests; whence, on going out into the world, they will take with them a purified mind, and communicate it to the people by wise instruction.

Thus, after the lapse of centuries, we shall have Christians; thus, when I shall have executed my plan, the people of my empire will better know the duties they owe to God, to the country, and to their fellow-creatures; thus shall we yet be blessed by our posterity, for having delivered them from the overgrown power of Rome; for having brought back the priests within the limits of their duties; and for having subjected their future life to the Lord, and their present life to the country alone.
Vienna, October, 1781   Joseph

To -----:

My friend,--Because there have been Neroes, and a Dionysius [tyrant of Syracuse], who exceeded the limits of their authority; because there have been tyrants, who abused the power which destiny confided to them;--is it for that reason just, that, under the pretext of fear lest the rights of a nation might suffer, a people should throw all possible obstacles in the way of a prince, in his arrangements of government, which have not other aim than the welfare of his subjects?

Since my accession to the throne, I have ever been anxious to conquer the prejudices against my station, and have taken pains to gain the confidence of my people; I have several times since given proof, that the welfare of my subjects is my passion; that to satisfy it, I shun neither labor, nor trouble, nor even vexations, and reflect well on the means which are likely to promote my views; and yet in my reforms, I everywhere find opposition from people, of whom I least expected it.

As a monarch, I do not deserve the distrust of my subjects; as the Regent of a great empire, I must have the whole extent of my state before my eyes, and embrace the whole in one view; I cannot always listen to the voices of single provinces, which consider only their own narrow sphere.

Private advantage is a chimera, and while on the one hand I lose it in order to make a sacrifice to my country, I may on the other hand share in the common welfare.--But how few think of this!

If I were unacquainted with the duties of my station--if I were not morally convinced, that I am destined by Providence to wear my diadem, together with all the load of obligations which it imposes upon me--melancholy, discontent, and the wish not to exist, would fill my bosom. But I know my heart; I am internally convinced of the honesty of my intentions, and hope that when I am no more, posterity will examine, and judge more equitably, more justly, and more impartially, all that I have done for my people.
Vienna, October, 1787.   Joseph

To van Swieten:

Sir,--Till now the Protestant religion has been opposed in my states; its adherents have been treated like foreigners; civil rights, possession of estates, title, and appointments, all were refused them.

I determined from the very commencement of my reign to adorn my diadem with the love of my people, to act in the administration of affairs according to just, impartial, and liberal principles; consequently, I granted toleration, and removed the yoke which had oppressed the protestants for centuries.

Fanaticism shall in future be known in my states only by the contempt I have for it; nobody shall any longer be exposed to hardships on account of his creed; no man shall be compelled in future to profess the religion of the state, if it be contrary to his persuasion, and if he have other ideas of the right way of insuring blessedness.

In future my Empire shall not be the scene of abominable intolerance. Fortunately no sacrifices like those of Calas and Sirven have ever disgraced any reign in this country.

If, in former times, the will of the monarch furnished opportunities for injustice, if the limits of executive power were exceeded, and private hatred acted her part, I can only pity those monarchs who were nothing but kings.

Tolerance is an effect of that beneficent increase of knowledge which now enlightens Europe, and which is owing to philosophy and the efforts of great men; it is a convincing proof of the improvement of the human mind, which has boldly reopened a road through the dominions of superstition, which was trodden centuries ago by Zoroaster and Confucius, and which, fortunately for mankind, has now become the highway of monarchs. Adieu!

Vienna, December, 1787.   Joseph.

Frederick II. *Anti-Machiavel: or, an Examination of Machiavel's Prince, with Notes Historical and Political.* Trans.: London 1741. Pp. 168-169, 294-295. "Letters of Joseph. Written to Distinguished Princes and Statesmen, on Various Interesting Subjects. Now First Translated from the German." *The Pamphleteer* (London) 19.38 (1822) 274-275, 288-291.

VIEWS ON GOD AND JUSTICE IN THE ENLIGHTENMENT ERA

The Enlightenment era in eighteenth-century Europe and North America shaped the growth of modern social, economic, and political thought. Enlightenment thinkers were strongly influenced by classical thought, the discoveries of the age of exploration, and the scientific revolution. They opposed the religious intolerance that typified the Reformation era and favored secular values and the scientific method in solving society's problems. Enlightenment writers known as *philosophes* critically analyzed traditional institutions and exposed the injustices and weaknesses of contemporary society.

France was in the forefront of the Enlightenment. François Marie Arouet, better known as Voltaire (1694-1778), and Denis Diderot (1713-1784), both Frenchmen, were among the most influential philosophes. Voltaire wrote prolifically in the areas of history, philosophical fiction, drama, poetry, popular science, and essays on social questions. He aimed to free society from religious tyranny and advocated peaceful change through enlightened thinking: "the more enlightened men are, the more they will be free." Denis Diderot edited the famous *Encyclopedia*, a massive work to which most of the philosophes contributed. Diderot suffered condemnation and imprisonment on charges of sedition and immorality, because of the highly critical tone of the *Encyclopedia*.

Many Enlightenment writers were deists in their religious thought. Deists believed in a rational God who had created the world the scientists studied and thereafter ceased to intervene in human affairs. They believed that not only Christians, but also Muslims, Buddhists, and others all had access to God.

The Baron de la Brède et de Montesquieu (1689-1755) and the Englishman John Locke (1632-1704) formulated persuasive new political and legal doctrines. Locke claimed that all people are born with certain natural rights and are entitled to enjoy freedom, equality, and ownership of private property. He maintained that legitimate governments must be based on a "social contract" or constitution supported by the people. Montesquieu contended that governmental power should be divided among executive, legislative, and judicial branches to ensure checks and balances and to prevent tyranny--ideals incorporated into the U.S. Constitution.

The first of the following passages is Diderot's definition of the true philosopher and of the philosophic spirit. The second describes a short-lived attempt by the French revolutionary leader Pierre Gaspard Chaumette (1763-1794) to replace Catholicism with the worship of deified Reason in France. The third is from the influential book on *Crimes and Punishments* (1764) by the Italian philosophe, Cesare Beccaria (1735-1794).

QUESTIONS:

1) What are the distinguishing traits of a philosopher, by Diderot's definition?

2) From the description in the second selection of the attempts to establish the worship of Reason, does the whole effort seem doomed from the start?

3) What are the "enlightened" aspects of Beccaria's views of crime and punishment?

Here is the character which we give [the philosopher]:

Other men make up their minds to act without thinking, nor are they conscious of the causes which move them, not even knowing that such exist. The philosopher, on the contrary, distinguishes the causes to what extent he may, and often anticipates them, and knowingly surrenders himself to them. In this manner he avoids objects that may cause him sensations that are not conducive to his well being or his rational existence, and seeks those which may excite in him affections agreeable with the state in which he finds himself. Reason is in the estimation of the philosopher what grace is to the Christian. Grace determines the Christian's action; reason the philosopher's.

Other men are carried away by their passions, so that the acts which they produce do not proceed from reflection. These are the men who move in darkness; while the philosopher, even in his passions, moves only after reflection. He marches at night, but a torch goes on ahead.

The philosopher forms his principles upon an infinity of individual observations. The people adopt the principle without a thought of the observations which have produced it, believing that the maxim exists, so to speak, of itself; but the philosopher takes the maxim at its source, he examines its origin, he knows its real value, and only makes use of it, if it seems to him satisfactory.

Truth is not for the philosopher a mistress who vitiates his imagination, and whom he believes to find everywhere. He contents himself with being able to discover it wherever he may chance to find it. He does not confound it with its semblance; but takes for true that which is true, for false that which is false, for doubtful that which is doubtful, and for probable that which is only probable. He does more--and this is the great perfection of philosophy; that when

he has not real grounds for passing judgment, he knows how to remain undetermined.

The world is full of persons of understanding, even of much understanding, who always pass judgment. They are guessing always, because it is guessing to pass judgment without knowing when one has proper grounds for judgment. They misjudge of the capacity of the human mind; they believe it is possible to know everything, and so they are ashamed not to be prepared to pass judgment, and they imagine that understanding consists in passing judgment. The philosopher believes that it consists in judging well: he is better pleased with himself when he has suspended the faculty of determining, than if he had determined before having acquired proper grounds for his decision....

The philosophic spirit is then the spirit of observation and of exactness, which refers everything to its true principles; but it is not the understanding alone which the philosopher cultivates; he carries further his attention and his labors....

Our philosopher does not believe himself an exile in the world; he does not believe himself in the enemy's country; he wishes to enjoy, like a wise economist, the goods that nature offers him; he wishes to find his pleasure with others; and in order to find it, it is necessary to assist in producing it; so he seeks to harmonize with those with whom chance of his choice has determined he shall live; and he finds at the same time that which suits him: he is an honest man who wishes to please and render himself useful...

The philosopher is then an honest man, actuated in everything by reason, one who joins to the spirit of reflection and accuracy the manners and qualities of society....

The philosophic spirit is a gift of nature, perfected by effort, art and usage, for judging sanely of all things. When one possesses in an exceptional degree this spirit, it produces a marvelous intelligence, a force of reasoning, an accurate and reflective taste in that which there is of good and bad in the world; it is the criterion of the true and beautiful. There is nothing estimable in the various works that issue from the hands of man that is not animated with this spirit. On it depends, in an especial measure, the glory of literature; but since it is the portion of very few among the learned, and it is neither possible nor necessary for the success of letters that a talent so rare should be found in all those who cultivate this art, it is sufficient for a nation that certain great spirits shall possess it to an eminent degree, and that the superiority of their judgment shall render them arbiters of taste, oracles of criticism, dispensers of literary glory.

* * * * *

It was resolved that the Metropolitan church of Notre-Dame should be converted into a republican edifice, called "The Temple of Reason." A festival was instituted for all the Décadis [tenth days of the ten-day periods of the republican calendar], to supersede the Catholic ceremonies of Sunday. The mayor, the municipal officers, the public functionaries, repaired to the Temple of Reason, where they read the declaration of the rights of man and the constitutional act, analyzed the news from the armies, and related the brilliant actions which had been performed during the décade [ten-day period]. A "mouth of truth" [suggestion box], resembling the mouths of denunciation which formerly existed at Venice, was placed in the Temple of Reason, to receive opinions, censures, advice, that might be useful to the public. These letters were examined and read every Décadi; a moral discourse was delivered, after which pieces of music were performed, and the ceremonies concluded with the singing of republican hymns. There were in the temple two tribunes, one for aged men, the other for pregnant women, with these inscriptions: "Respect for old age--Respect and attention for pregnant women."

The first festival of Reason was held with pomp on the 20th of Brumaire (the 10th of November). It was attended by all the sections, together with the constituted authorities. A young woman represented the goddess of Reason. She was the wife of Momoro, the printer .... She was dressed in a white drapery; a mantle of azure blue hung from her shoulders; her flowing hair was covered with the cap of liberty. She sat upon an antique seat, intwined with ivy and borne by four citizens. Young girls dressed in white, and crowned with roses, preceded and followed the goddess. Then came the busts of Lepelletier and [Jean Paul] Marat [1743-1793, a radical revolutionary journalist later assassinated], musicians, troops, and all the armed sections. Speeches were delivered, and hymns sung in the Temple of Reason; they then proceeded to the Convention, and Chaumette spoke in these terms:

"Legislators! Fanaticism has given way to reason. Its bleared eyes could not endure the brilliancy of the light. This day an immense concourse has assembled beneath those Gothic vaults, which, for the first time, re-echoed the truth. There the French have celebrated the only true worship, that of liberty, that of reason. There we have formed wishes for the prosperity of the arms of the republic. There we have abandoned inanimate idols for reason, for that animated image, the master-piece of nature." As he uttered these words, Chaumette pointed to the living goddess of Reason. The young and beautiful woman descended from her seat and went up to the president, who gave her the fraternal kiss, amidst universal bravoes and shouts of "The Republic for ever! Reason for ever! Down with fanaticism!" The Convention [a branch of the revolutionary government], which had not yet taken any part in these representations, was hurried away, and obliged to follow the procession, which returned to the Temple of Reason, and there sang a patriotic hymn....

Of Torture

The torture of a criminal during the course of his trial is a cruelty consecrated by custom in most nations. It is used with an intent either to make his confess his crime, or to explain some contradictions into which he had been led during his examination, or discover his accomplices, or for some kind of metaphysical and incomprehensible purgation of infamy, or, finally, in order to discover other crimes of which he is not accused, but of which he may be guilty.

No man can be judged a criminal until he be found guilty; nor can society take from him the public protection until it have been proved that he has violated the conditions on which it was granted. What right, then, but that of power, can authorise the punishment of a citizen so long as there remains any doubt of his guilt? This dilemma is frequent. Either he is guilty, or not guilty. If guilty, he should only suffer the punishment ordained by the laws, and torture becomes useless, as his confession is unnecessary. If he be not guilty, you torture the innocent; for, in the eye of the law, every man is innocent whose crime has not been proved. Besides, it is confounding all relations to expect that a man should be both the accuser and the accused; and that pain should be the test of truth, as if truth resided in the muscles and fibers of a wretch in torture. By this method the robust will escape, and the feeble be condemned. These are the inconveniences of this pretended test of truth, worthy only of a cannibal, and which the Romans, in many respects barbarous, and whose savage virtue has been too much admired, reserved for the slaves alone.

What is the political intention of punishments? To terrify and be an example to others. Is this intention answered by thus privately torturing the guilty and the innocent? It is doubtless of importance that no crime should remain unpunished; but it is useless to make a public example of the author of a crime hid in darkness. A crime already committed, and for which there can be no remedy, can only be punished by a political society with an intention that no hopes of impunity should induce others to commit the same. If it be true, that the number of those who from fear or virtue respect the laws is greater than those by whom they are violated, the risk of torturing an innocent person is greater, as there is a greater possibility that, *caeteris paribus* [all else being equal], an individual has observed, than that he has infringed the laws.

There is another ridiculous motive for torture, namely, to purge a man from infamy. Ought such an abuse to be tolerated in the eighteenth century? Can pain, which is a sensation, have any connection with a moral sentiment, a matter of opinion? Perhaps the rack may be considered as the refiner's furnace.

It is not difficult to trace this senseless law to its origin; for an absurdity, adopted by a whole nation, must have some affinity with other ideas established and respected by the same nation. This custom seems to be the offspring of religion, by which mankind, in all nations and in all ages, are so generally influenced. We are taught by our infallible church, that those stains of sin contracted through human frailty, and which have not deserved the eternal anger of the Almighty, are to be purged away in another life by an incomprehensible fire. Now infamy is a stain, and if the punishments and fire of purgatory can take away all spiritual stains, why should not the pain of torture take away those of a civil nature? I imagine, that the confession of a criminal, which in some tribunals is required as being essential to his condemnation, has a similar origin, and has been taken from the mysterious tribunal of penitence, where the confession of sins is a necessary part of the sacrament. Thus have men abused the unerring light of revelation; and, in the times of tractable ignorance, having no other, they naturally had recourse to it on every occasion, making the most remote and absurd applications. Moreover, infamy is a sentiment regulated neither by the laws nor by reason, but entirely by opinion; but torture renders the victim infamous, and therefore cannot take infamy away....

This infamous test of truth [i.e., torture] is a remaining monument of that ancient and savage legislation in which trials by fire, by boiling water, or the uncertainty of combats, were called "judgments of God"; as if the links of that eternal chain, which beginning is in the breast of the first cause of all things, could ever be disunited by the institutions of men. The only difference between torture and trials by fire and boiling water is, that the event of the first depends on the will of the accused, and of the second on a fact entirely physical an external: but this difference is apparent only, not real. A man on the rack, in the convulsions of torture, has it as little in his power to declare the truth, as, in former times, to prevent without fraud the effects of fire or boiling water....

A confession made during torture is null, if it be not afterwards confirmed by an oath, which if the criminal refuses, he is tortured again. Some civilians and some nations permit this ... to be only three times repeated, and others leave it to the discretion of the judge; therefore, of two men equally innocent, or equally guilty, the most robust and resolute will be acquitted, and the weakest and most pusillanimous will be condemned, in consequence of the following excellent mode of reasoning: "I, the judge, must find some one guilty. Thou, who art a strong fellow, hast been able to resist the force of torment; therefore I acquit thee. Thou, being weaker, hast yielded to it; I therefore condemn thee. I am sensible that the confession which was extorted from thee has no weight; but if thou dost not confirm by oath what thou hast already confessed, I will have thee tortured again."

Diderot, Denis. "The Philosopher" [from the *Encyclopédie*]. In Merrick Whitcomb, ed. *French Philosophers of the Eighteenth Century*. 1899. Pp. 21-23. Thiers, Louis Adolphe. *The History of the French Revolution* [1823-1827]. Ed. Frederick Shoberl. New York: Appleton, 1854. Vol. 2. Pp. 370-371. Bonesana, Cesare, Marchese di Beccaria. *An Essay on Crimes and Punishments* [1764]. Trans. Edward D. Ingraham. 2nd ed. Philadelphia: Nicklin, 1819. Pp. 59-63, 66.

BENJAMIN FRANKLIN, AN AMERICAN MAN OF REASON

Benjamin Franklin (1706-1790) was one of the most distinguished and influential figures of the American colonial and revolutionary war eras. He was born in Boston and apprenticed as a printer at the age of thirteen. Franklin moved to Philadelphia in 1723, established his own printing house, purchased a newspaper, the *Philadelphia Gazette*, and quickly became a successful businessman and prominent member of local intellectual circles. In 1748, Franklin sold his printing business and began an active political, serving as a member of the Pennsylvania Assembly, deputy postmaster general, colonial representative in England. After the war for independence, he was a member of the Second Continental Congress, postmaster general, ambassador to France, president of the Pennsylvania executive council, and delegate to the U.S. constitutional convention (1787).

Benjamin Franklin is equally famous as a man of letters, and as a philosopher and scientist. He was instrumental in founding the first public library in America in 1731 and his *Proposals Relating to the Education of Youth in Pennsylvania* helped to launch the Philadelphia Academy (later University of Pennsylvania) in 1751. As a man of reason, Franklin believed in the scientific method and conducted experiments with electricity. His scientific work won him wide recognition, many honors, and membership in the prestigious Royal Society of London for Improving Natural Knowledge. He was also an inventor: the "Franklin stove" produced heat in a more efficient manner than existing stoves.

Franklin's enlightened outlook is best exemplified in his philosophy of life, embodied in his *Poor Richard's Almanack* (1732), and in his unfinished *Autobiography*. In these, he propounds a pragmatic system of ethics and the possibility of moral improvement through self-control, conscientious work habits, and a sense of duty. His writings show Franklin's homespun wisdom, common sense, and belief in reason as guide to proper behavior.

In the following passage from his *Autobiography*, Franklin describes his part in the founding of the public library. He also explains his dissatisfaction with organized religion, specifically the Presbyterian church he had been raised in, and prescribes his own rules for living a healthy and productive life.

QUESTIONS:

1) What in this selection from Franklin's *Autobiography* justifies his reputation as "an American man of reason"?
2) What is Franklin's view of the religious upbringing he received?
3) Does Franklin's list of moral precepts seem based purely on reason?

[I will now give] and account ... of the means I used to establish the Philadelphia public library, which from a small beginning is now become so considerable ....

At the time I established myself in Pennsylvania, there was not a good bookseller's shop in any of the colonies to the southward of Boston. In New York and Philadelphia the printers were indeed stationers, they sold only paper, etc., almanacs, ballads, and a few common school books. Those who loved reading were obliged to send for their books from England. The members of the Junto [a society of individuals who met for dinner and discussions of philosophy and other topics; the forerunner of the American Philosophical Society] had each a few. We had left the alehouse where we first met, and hired a room to hold our club in. I proposed that we should all of us bring our books to that room, where they would not only be ready to consult in our conferences, but become a common benefit, each of us being at liberty to borrow such as he wished to read at home. This was accordingly done, and for some time contented us. Finding the advantage of this little collection, I proposed to render the benefit from books more common by commencing a public subscription library. I drew a sketch of the plan and rules that would be necessary, and got a skillful conveyancer Mr. Charles Brockden to put the whole in form of articles of agreement to be subscribed, by which each subscriber engaged to pay a certain sum down for the first purchase of books and an annual contribution for increasing them. So few were the readers at that time in Philadelphia, and the majority of us so poor, that I was not able with great industry to find more than fifty persons, mostly young tradesmen, willing to pay down for this purpose forty shillings each, and ten shillings per annum. On this little fund we began. The books were imported. The library was open one day in the week for lending them to the subscribers, on their promissory notes to pay double the value if not duly returned. The institution soon manifested its utility, was imitated by other towns and in other provinces, the libraries were augmented by donations, reading became fashionable, and our people having no public amusements to divert their attention from study became better acquainted with books, and in a few years were observed by strangers to be better instructed and more intelligent than people of the same rank generally are in other countries....

This library afforded me the means of improvement by study, for which I set apart and hour or two each day; and thus repaired in some degree the loss of the learned education my father once intended for me. Reading was the only amusement I allowed myself. I spent no time in taverns, games, or frolics of any kind. And my industry in my business continued as indefatigable as it was necessary. I was in debt for my printing-house, I had a young family coming on to be educated, and I had to contend with for business two printers who were established in the place before me. My circumstances however grew daily easier: my original habits of frugality continuing. And my father having among his instructions to me when a boy, frequently repeated a proverb of Solomon, "Seest thou a man diligent in his calling, he shall stand before Kings, he shall not stand before mean men." I from thence considered industry as a means of obtaining wealth and distinction, which encouraged me; though I did not think that I should ever literally stand before kings, which however has since happened, for I have stood before five, and even had the honour of sitting down with one, the king of Denmark, to dinner.

We have an English proverb that says,

He that would thrive Must ask his wife.

It was lucky for me that I had one as much disposed to industry and frugality as myself. She assisted me cheerfully in my business, folding and stitching pamphlets, tending shop, purchasing old linen rags for the paper-makers, etc. We kept no idle servants, our table was plain and simple, our furniture of the cheapest. For instance my breakfast was a long time bread and milk (no tea), and I ate out of a twopenny earthen porringer [a small bowl with a handle] with a pewter spoon. But mark how luxury will enter families, and make a progress, in spite of principle. Being called one morning to breakfast, I found it in a china bowl with a spoon of silver. They had been bought for me without my knowledge by my wife, and had cost her the enormous sum of three and twenty shillings, for which she had no other excuse or apology to make, but that she thought her husband deserved a silver spoon and china bowl as well as any of his neighbors. This was the first appearance of plate and china in our house, which afterwards in a course of years as our wealth increased, augmented gradually to several hundred pounds in value.

I had been religiously educated as a Presbyterian; and though some of the dogmas of that persuasion, such as the eternal decrees of God, election, reprobation, etc. appeared to me unintelligible, others doubtful, and I early absented myself from the public assemblies of the sect, Sunday being my studying-day. I never was without some religious principles; I never doubted, for instance, the existence of the Deity, that he made the world, and governed it by his providence; that the most acceptable service of God was the doing good to man; that our souls are immortal; and that all crime will be punished and virtue rewarded either here or hereafter; these I esteemed the essentials of every religion, and being to be found in all the religions we had in our country I respected them all, though with different degrees of respect as I found them more or less mixed with other articles which without any tendency to inspire, promote or confirm morality, served principally to divide us and make us unfriendly to one another. This respect to all, with an opinion that the worst had some good effects, induced me to avoid all discourse that might tend to lessen the good opinion another might have of his own religion; and as our province increased in people and new places of worship were continually wanted, and generally erected by voluntary contribution, my mite for such purpose, whatever might be the sect, was never refused.

Though I seldom attended any public worship, I had still an opinion of its propriety, and of its utility when rightly conducted, and I regularly paid my annual subscription for the support of the only Presbyterian minister or meeting we had in Philadelphia. He used to visit us sometimes as a friend, and admonish me to attend his administrations, and I was now and then prevailed upon to do so, once for five Sundays successively. Had he been, in my opinion, a good preacher perhaps I might have continued, notwithstanding the occasion I had for the Sunday's leisure in my course of study: but his discourses were chiefly either polemic arguments, or explications of the peculiar doctrines of our sect, and were all to me very dry, uninteresting and unedifying, since not a single moral principle was inculcated or enforced. At length he took for his text that verse of the 4th chapter of Philippians, "Finally, brethren, whatsoever things are true, honest, just, pure, lovely, or of good report, if there be any virtue, or any praise, think on these things," and I imagined in a sermon on such a text, we could not miss of having some morality. But he confined himself to five points only as meant by the apostle, viz. 1. keeping holy the Sabbath day. 2. Being diligent in reading the Holy Scripture. 3. Attending duly the public worship. 4. Partaking of the sacrament. 5. Paying a due respect to God's ministers. These might be all good things, but as they were not the kind of good things that I expected from that text, I despaired of ever meeting with them from any other, was disgusted, and attended his preaching no more. I had some years before composed a little liturgy or form of prayer for my own private use ... in 1728, entitled, *Articles of Belief and Acts of Religion*. I returned to the use of this, and went no more to the public assemblies. My conduct might be blameable, but I leave it without attempting farther to excuse it, my present purpose being to relate facts, and not to make apologies for them.

It was about this time that I conceived the bold and arduous project of arriving at moral perfection. I wished to live without committing any fault at any time; I would conquer all that either natural inclination, custom, or company might lead me into. As I knew, or thought I knew, what was right and wrong, I did not see why I might not *always* do the one and avoid the other. But I soon found that I had undertaken a task of more difficulty than I had imagined: while my care was employed in guarding against one fault, I was often surprised by another. Habit took the advantage of inattention. Inclination was sometimes too strong for reason. I concluded at length, that the mere speculative conviction that it was our interest to be completely virtuous, was not sufficient to prevent our slipping, and that the contrary habits must be broken and good ones acquired and established, before we can have any dependance on a steady uniform rectitude of conduct. For this purpose I therefore contrived the following method:

In the various enumerations of the moral virtues I had met with in my reading, I found the catalogue more or less numerous, as different writers included more or fewer ideas under the same name. Temperance, for example, was by some confined to eating and drinking, while by others it was extended to mean the moderating every other pleasure, appetite, inclination or passion, bodily or mental, even to our avarice and ambition. I proposed to myself, for the sake of clearness, to use rather more names with fewer ideas annexed to each, than a few names with more ideas; and I included under thirteen names of virtues all that at that time occurred to me as necessary or desirable, and annexed to each a sort of precept, which fully expressed the extent I gave to its meaning.

These names of virtues with their precepts were

1. Temperance.
   Eat not to dulness.
   Drink not to elevation.
2. Silence.
   Speak not but what may benefit others or yourself. Avoid trifling conversation.
3. Order.
   Let all your things have their places. Let each part of your business have its time.
4. Resolution.
   Resolve to perform what you ought. Perform without fail what you resolve.
5. Frugality.
   Make no expense but to do good to others or yourself: i.e., Waste nothing.
6. Industry.
   Lose no time. Be always employed in something useful. Cut off all unnecessary actions.
7. Sincerity.
   Use no hurtful deceit. Think innocently and justly; and, if you speak, speak accordingly.
8. Justice.
   Wrong none, by doing injuries or omitting the benefits that are your duty.
9. Moderation.
   Avoid extremes. Forbear resenting injuries so much as you think they deserve.
10. Cleanliness.
    Tolerate no uncleanness in body, clothes, or habitation.
11. Tranquility.
    Be not disturbed at trifles, or at accidents common or unavoidable.
12. Chastity.
    Rarely use venery [sexual activity] but for health or offspring, never to dulness, weakness, or the injury of your own or another's peace or reputation.
13. Humility.
    Imitate Jesus and Socrates.

… On the whole, though I never arrived at the perfection I had been so ambitious of obtaining, but fell far short of it, yet I was by the endeavour made a better and happier man than I otherwise should have been, if I had not attempted it ….

It will be remarked that, though my scheme was not wholly without religion there was in it no mark of any of the distinguishing tenets of any particular sect. I had purposely avoided them; for being fully persuaded of the utility and excellency of my method, and that it might be serviceable to people in all religions, and intending some time or other to publish it, I would not have anything in it that should prejudice anyone of any sect against it.

Franklin, Benjamin. *The Autobiography of Benjamin Franklin*. Ed. John Bigelow. New York: Putnam, 1889. Pp. 139-140, 142-149, 160-162.

"GIVE US THE BLOOD OF FOULON!"--MOB VIOLENCE IN REVOLUTIONARY PARIS

► Guillotine

While aristocrats enjoyed both wealth and high social status under the Ancien Regime in eighteenth-century France, poor citizens sank ever deeper into grinding poverty. The French Revolution began in 1789 with the convening of the Estates General to deal with the government's fiscal crisis. The pervasive and extreme violence that wracked the country during the early years of the Revolution stemmed in part from the cruel and inequitable difference in living conditions between the opulent few and the deprived masses. The storming of the Bastille, an old prison in Paris, in the summer of 1789 heralded a long phase of mob violence directed against the aristocratic "enemies of the people."

In the following episode from *A Tale of Two Cities*, novelist Charles Dickens presents portrays the brutal justice meted out in the streets of the Paris, in a district called Saint Antoine. He recreates the execution of a minor government functionary, "old Foulon," who had been particularly corrupt and vicious in his dealings with the common people. Foulon had once advised the poor to "eat grass"--a remark that dogged him to his death. Even an attempt to evade justice by staging his own death, complete with a mock-funeral, failed to save him from the wrath of the revolutionaries.

Old Foulon was an actual historical figure, who indeed died in the way Dickens recounts. The other principals in Dickens novel, the Defarges, The Vengeance, and others, are fictional. Dickens' vivid descriptions capture the atmosphere of mass hysteria that pervaded the early stages of the French Revolution. The passage begins with a personification of the Saint Antoine district, where the Defarges' wine shop is located.

QUESTIONS:

1) Dickens' account of the execution of Foulon stresses the outrage of the poor; what about Foulon's behavior triggered that outrage?

2) Does Dickens appear to side with either the victim or the mob in his recreation of the death of Foulon?

3) How successful in this passage is Dickens in fashioning a kind of metaphor or allegory for certain aspects of the French Revolution?

Haggard Saint Antoine had had only one exultant week [since the fall of the Bastille] in which to soften his modicum of hard and bitter bread to such extent as he could, with the relish of fraternal embraces and congratulations, when Madame Defarge sat at her counter, as usual, presiding over the customers. Madame Defarge wore no rose in her head, for the great brotherhood of Spies had become, even in one short week, extremely chary of trusting themselves to the saint's mercies. The lamps across the streets had a portentously elastic swing with them.

Madame Defarge, with her arms folded, sat in the morning light and heat, contemplating the wine-shop and the street. In both, there were several knots of loungers, squalid and miserable, but now with a manifest sense of power enthroned on their distress. The raggedest night-cap, awry on the wretchedest head, had this crooked significance in it: "I know how hard it has grown for me, the wearer of this, to support life in myself; but do you know how easy it has grown for me, the wearer of this, to destroy life in you?" Every lean bare arm, that had been without work before, had this work always ready for it now that it could strike. The fingers of the knitting women were vicious, with the experience that they could tear. There was a change in the appearance of Saint Antoine; the image had been hammering into this for hundreds of years, and the last finishing blows had told mightily on the expression.

Madame Defarge sat observing it, with such suppressed approval as was to be desired in the leader of the Saint Antoine women. One of her sisterhood knitted beside her. The short, rather plump wife of a starved grocer, and the mother of two children withal, this lieutenant had already earned the complimentary name of The Vengeance.

"Hark!" said The Vengeance. "Listen, then! Who comes?"

As if a train of powder laid from the outermost bound of the Saint Antoine Quarter to the wine-shop door, had been suddenly fired, a fast-spreading murmur came rushing along.

"It is Defarge," said Madame. "Silence, patriots!"

Defarge came in breathless, pulled off a red cap he wore, and looked around him. "Listen, everywhere!" said madame again. "Listen to him!" Defarge stood, panting, against a background of eager eyes and open mouths,

formed outside the door; all those within the wine-shop had sprung to their feet.

"Say then, my husband. What is it?

"News from the other world!"

How, then?" cried madame, contemptuously. "The other world?"

"Does everybody here recall old Foulon, who told the famished people that they might eat grass, and who died, and went to Hell?"

"Everybody!" from all throats.

"The news is of him. He is among us!"

"Among us!" from the universal throat again. "And dead?"

"Not dead! He feared us so much--and with reason--that he caused himself to be represented as dead, and had a grand mock-funeral. But they have found him alive, hiding in the country, and have brought him in. I have seen him but now, on his way to the Hôtel de Ville, a prisoner. I have said that he had reason to fear us. Say all! *Had* he reason?"

Wretched old sinner of more than threescore years and ten, if he had never known it yet, he would have known it in his heart of hearts if he could have heard the answering cry.

A moment of profound silence followed. Defarge and his wife looked steadfastly at one another. The Vengeance stooped, and the jar of a drum was heard as she moved it at her feet behind the counter.

"Patriots!" said Defarge, in a determined voice, "are we ready?"

Instantly Madame Defarge's knife was in her girdle; the drum was beating in the streets, as if it and a drummer had flown together by magic; and The Vengeance, uttering terrific shrieks, and flinging her arms about her head like all the forty Furies at once, was tearing from house to house, rousing the women.

The men were terrible, in the bloody-minded anger with which they looked from windows, caught up what arms they had, and came pouring down into the streets; but, the women were a sight to chill the boldest. From such household occupations as their bare poverty yielded, from their children, from their aged and their sick crouching on the bare ground famished and naked, they ran out with streaming hair, urging one another, and themselves, to madness with the wildest cries and actions. Villain Foulon taken, my sister! Old Foulon taken, my mother!

Miscreant Foulon taken, my daughter! Then, a score of others ran into the midst of these, beating their breasts, tearing their hair, and screaming, Foulon alive! Foulon who told the starving people they might eat grass! Foulon who told my old father that he might eat grass, when I had no bread to give him! Foulon who told my baby it might suck grass, when these breasts were dry with want! O mother of God, this Foulon! O Heaven, our suffering! Hear me, my dead baby and my withered father: I swear on my knees, on these stones, to avenge you on Foulon! Husbands, and brothers, and young men, Give us the blood of Foulon, Give us the head of Foulon, Give us the heart of Foulon, Give us the body and soul of Foulon, Rend Foulon to pieces, and dig him into the ground, that grass may grow from him! With these cries, numbers of the women, lashed into blind frenzy, whirled about, striking and tearing at their own friends until they dropped into a passionate swoon, and were only saved by the men belonging to them from being trampled under foot.

Nevertheless, not a moment was lost; not a moment! This Foulon was at the Hôtel de Ville, and might be loosed. Never, if Saint Antoine knew his own sufferings, insults, and wrongs! Armed men and women flocked out of the Quarter so fast, and drew even these last dregs after them with such a force of suction, that within a quarter of an hour there was not a human creature in Saint Antoine's bosom but a few old crones and the wailing children.

No. They were all by that time choking the Hall of Examination where this old man, ugly and wicked, was, and overflowing into the adjacent open space and streets. The Defarges, husband and wife, The Vengeance, and Jacques Three were in the first press, and at no great distance from him in the Hall.

"See!" cried madame, pointing with her knife. "See the old villain bound with ropes. That was well done to tie a bunch of grass upon his back. Ha, ha! That was well done. Let him eat it now!" Madame put her knife under her arm, and clapped her hands as at a play.

The people immediately behind Madame Defarge, explaining the cause of her satisfaction to those behind them, and those again explaining to others, and those to others, the neighboring streets resounded with the clapping of hands. Similarly, during two or three hours of drawl, and the winnowing of many bushels of words, Madame Defarge's frequent expressions of impatience were taken up, with marvelous quickness, at a distance: the more readily, because certain men who had by some wonderful exercise of agility climbed up the external architecture to look in from the windows, knew Madame Defarge well, and acted as a telegraph between her and the crowd outside the building.

At length the sun rose so high that it struck a kindly ray as of hope or protection, directly down upon the old prisoner's head. The favour was too much to bear; in an instant the barrier of dust and chaff, that had stood surprisingly long, went to the winds, and Saint Antoine got him!

It was known directly, to the furthest confines of the crowd. Defarge had but sprung over a railing and a table, and folded the miserable wretch in a deadly embrace--Madame Defarge had but followed and turned her hand in one of the ropes with which he was tied--The Vengeance and Jacques Three were not yet up with them, and the men at the windows had not yet swooped into the Hall, like birds of prey from their high perches--when the cry seemed to go up, all over the city, "Bring him out! Bring him to the lamp!"

Down, and up, and head foremost on the steps of the building; now, on his knees; now, on his feet; now, on his back; dragged, and struck at, and stifled by the bunches of grass and straw that were thrust into his face by hundreds of hands; torn, bruised, panting, bleeding, yet always entreating and beseeching for mercy; now full of vehement agony of action, with a small clear space about him as the people drew one another back that they might see; now, a log of dead wood drawn through a forest of legs; he was hauled to the nearest street corner where one of the fatal lamps swung, and there Madame Defarge let him go--as a cat might have done to a mouse--and silently and composedly looked at him while they made ready, and while he besought her: the women passionately screeching at him all the time, and the men sternly calling out to have him killed with grass in his mouth. Once, he went aloft, and the rope broke, and they caught him shrieking; twice, he went aloft, and the rope broke, and they caught him shrieking; then, the rope was merciful, and held him, and his head was soon on a pike, with grass enough in the mouth for all Saint Antoine to dance at the sight of.

Nor was this the end of the day's bad work, for Saint Antoine so shouted and dance his angry blood up, that it boiled again, on hearing when the day closed in that the son-in-law of the despatched, another of the people's enemies and insulters, was coming into Paris under a guard five hundred strong, in cavalry alone. Saint Antoine wrote his crimes on flaring sheets of paper, seized him--would have torn him out of the breast of an army to bear Foulon company--set his head and heart on pikes, and carried the three spoils of the day, in wolf-procession, through the streets.

Not before dark did the men and women come back to the children, wailing and breadless. Then, the miserable bakers' shops were beset by long files of them, patiently waiting to buy bad bread; and while they waited with stomachs faint and empty, they beguiled the time by embracing one another on the triumphs of the day, and achieving them again in gossip. Gradually, these strings of ragged people shortened and frayed away; and then poor lights began to shine in high windows, and slender fires were made in the streets, at which neighbors cooked in common, afterwards supping at their doors.

Scanty and insufficient suppers those, and innocent of meat, as of most other sauce to wretched bread. Yet, human fellowship infused some nourishment into the flinty viands, and struck some sparks of cheerfulness out of them. Fathers and mothers who had had their full share in the worst of the day played gently with their meager children; and lovers, with such a world around them and before them, loved and hoped.

It was almost morning, when Defarge's wine-shop parted with its last knot of customers, and Monsieur Defarge said to madame his wife, in husky tones, while fastening the door:

"At last it is come, my dear!"

"Eh well!" returned madame. "Almost."

Saint Antoine slept, the Defarges slept: even The Vengeance slept with her starved grocer, and the drum was at rest. The drum's was the only voice in Saint Antoine that blood and hurry had not changed. The Vengeance, as custodian of the drum, could have wakened him up and had the same speech out of him as before the Bastille fell, or old Foulon was seized; not so with the hoarse tones of the men and women in Saint Antoine's bosom.

Dickens, Charles. *A Tale of Two Cities*. London 1859. Book 2: chap. 22.

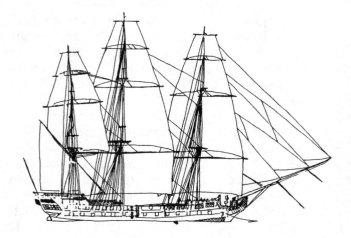

"ENGLAND EXPECTS EVERY MAN WILL DO HIS DUTY!"--THE BATTLE OF TRAFALGAR

► British Ship of the Line

In 1805, Great Britain won a momentous naval victory at the Battle of Trafalgar, one of the most famous naval engagements in history. It prevented Napoleon's threatened invasion of Great Britain. The Nelson Monument in London's Trafalgar Square commemorates the hero and the victory that saved Britain from Napoleon.

Since 1803, Napoleon had been preparing to invade England with a joint Franco-Spanish fleet based at Cádiz, on the Atlantic coast of Spain, near Gibraltar. Lord Horatio Nelson, admiral of the British navy, had been stationed with a squadron of British ships off Cádiz to blockade the joint French/Spanish fleet, commanded by Admiral Pierre Charles de Villeneuve, and if possible to draw it into a decisive battle. On 21 October 1805, the French and Spanish forces set out for the Straits of Gibraltar and were quickly intercepted by Nelson's ships. The British admiral's brilliant two-pronged attack successfully cut through the enemy's fleet and inflicted heavy losses. Twenty French and Spanish vessels were captured or destroyed, while the British lost not a single ship, though they sustained some 1500 casualties, including Lord Nelson.

In the first of the following passages, an officer of the *Victory*, Lord Nelson's flagship, recounts the great admiral's exhortation of his men before battle and his fatal wounding and death during it. The second passage, by an officer aboard the *Bellerophon*, provides a log of the course of the battle and an account of the officer's perilous experience as a member of the boarding party sent to secure the badly disabled Spanish ship *Monarca*.

QUESTIONS:

1) What about Nelson's behavior strikes the author of the first passage as especially glorious or noteworthy?

2) Do the accounts in these selections seem biased or impartial?

3) Does the account of in the second selection seem realistic?

Aboard the *Victory*.

Previously to the commencement of the battle of Trafalgar, Lord Nelson went over the different decks of the Victory, saw and spoke to the different classes of seamen, encouraged them with his usual affability, and was much pleased at the manner in which the seamen had barricaded the hawse holes of the ship. All was perfect death-like silence, till just before the action began. Three cheers were given his Lordship as he ascended the quarter-deck ladder. He had been particular in recommending cool, steady firing, in preference to a hurrying fire, without aim or precision, and the event justified his Lordship's advice, as the masts of his opponents came tumbling down on their decks, and over their sides. Within half an hour after, the battle began to rage in its full fury; the royal marines on the poop soon felt the effect (as well as the officers, seamen, and royal marines on the quarter-deck) of the system of sharp-shooting from the tops of the Bucentaure, or 84 guns, Admiral Villeneuve. The men began to drop fast; and poor Captain Adair, of the royal marines, was struck with a rifle ball, which so irritated him, that he asked Lord Nelson leave to take up in the tops and place some of his royal marine party, with an officer, to counteract the destructive fire of those sharp-shooters of the enemy. The men went up to the shrouds, and as Captain Adair was ascending, he fell quite dead on the poop, perforated through with nearly 20 balls from those marksmen. The action then became very hot, and Lord Nelson was advised not to appear so conspicuously, in full uniform, to the mark of the topmen of the enemy. His answer ought to be recorded in the heart of every Briton, and engraven on his monument--"No," said his Lordship, "whatever may be the consequence, the insignia of the honours I now wear I gained by the exertions of British seamen, under my command in various parts of the world; and in the hour of danger, I am proud to show them and the enemies of old England, I will never part with them; if it please God I am to fall, I will expire with these trophies entwined round my heart." About a quarter before two the fatal bullet struck his Lordship above the star on the left side, and his Secretary, Mr. Scott, fell quite dead on the deck, with many seamen and marines.

Lord Nelson was conveyed below, and perfectly sure that the wound was fatal. A Master's Mate, one of his signal officers, and a protégé of his Lordship, was with him to his last moment--he was to have been promoted to a Lieutenancy by his Lordship, for his great merit. The Surgeon came and probed the wound; the ball was extracted, but his Lordship, though apparently exhausting, told the Surgeon he was sure his wound was fatal, and begged, when he had dressed it, he would attend the other poor fellows, equal sufferers with himself.--Frequent messages passed from Lord Nelson to Captain Hardy, respecting the fate of the battle. His countenance brightened as the number of ships that had struck [lowered their flags to signify surrender] were related; but when the number of nineteen sail was mentioned, an hectic flush of joy appeared on his wan face, and he seemed to revive a little. It was the hectic of a moment.-- Before and after he was wounded, several kind messages and inquiries came from Lord Collingwood, and it appeared to soothe the last hour and moments of this great Hero to find himself so ably seconded. About a quarter before four, the battle ceased to rage with its pristine fury, and word being brought below that the defeat of the enemy was complete, the dying Nelson pronounced the word Victory; but upon attempting to repeat it, he convulsively grasped the hand of Captain Hardy--the blood rushed from the lungs into the throat, and he expired calmly, and without a groan. Thus died the greatest Hero that England ever produced.

Aboard the *Bellerophon*.

A few moments before the action commenced, Lord Nelson conveyed the following sentence by telegraph, to the fleet--"England expects every man will do his duty!" The loud and repeated cheering with which this was received, was a convincing proof that such an injunction was needless.

At noon precisely the action commenced by the Fongeux and Monarca opening fire on the Royal Sovereign. Now follows an extract from our log:--"12:10 Royal Sovereign opened fire on the enemy's centre.--12:13 answered 16 general.--12:20 Royal Sovereign, at the head of the larboard division, broke the enemy's line astern of a Spanish three-decker, and engaged her to leeward, being followed by the Mars, Belleisle, and Tonnant, who engaged their respective opponents.--12:25 opened our fire on the enemy.--12:28 Victory, at the head of the starboard division, opened her fire on the enemy.--12:30 engaging both sides in passing through the enemy's line, astern of a Spanish two-decker (El Monarca)--12:35 fell on board the

French two-deck ship l'Aigle, whilst hauling to the wind, our fore-yard locking with her main one, kept up a brisk fire both on her, on our starboard bow, and a Spanish two-decker (El Monarca) on the larboard bow, at the same time receiving and returning fire with a Spanish two-decker (Bahama) on the larboard quarter, and receiving the fire of a Spanish two-decker (St. Juan Nepomuceno) athwart our stern, and a French two-decker (la Swiftsure) on the starboard quarter: the action soon after became general. At one the main and mizzen-top-masts fell over the starboard side, main-top-sail and top-gallant-sail caught fire.--1:05 the Master, and 1:11 the Captain fell, still afoul of l'Aigle, and keeping up a brisk fire from the main and lower decks; quarter-deck, poop, and forecastle being nearly cleared by the enemy's musketry, chiefly from troops on board l'Aigle.--1:20 the jib-boom was shot away.--1:40 l'Aigle dropt astern under a raking fire from us as she fell off, our ship at this time quite unmanageable from braces, bowlines, &c. shot away.--1:45 l'Aigle was engaged by the Defiance.--2:05 she struck.--On the smoke clearing up, observed several of the enemy's ships had struck.--Fired several shot at El Monarca, our first opponent, when she struck.-- 3:00 sent an officer and party of men to take possession of her.--3:06 the ship being ungovernable, and in danger of falling on board of Tonnant, Temeraire, and prizes, made 318 to Sirius, out-boats and sent them a-head to tow, towed and swept the ship clear of them; received prisoners from our prizes.--4:05 answered 101.-- 4:10 opened out fire on five French ships making off to windward, the sternmost of which was cut off, and struck to the Minotaur.--5:07 the firing ceased, thirteen sail of the enemy's ships making off to leeward, four of their line to windward.-- 5:20 answered 99 general.--5:30 took possession of El Bahama, Spanish 74.--Sunset, one of the prizes sunk, another blew up." Thus far our log; but it will not be amiss to mention, that whilst engaged with the five ships in this situation, l'Aigle twice attempted to board us, and hove several grenades into our lower deck, which burst and wounded several of our people most dreadfully, she likewise set fire to our fore chains; our fire was so hot, that we soon drove them from the lower deck, after which our people took the coins out, and elevated their

guns, so as to tear her decks and sides to pieces: when she got clear of us, she did not return a single shot whilst we raked her, her starboard quarter was entirely beaten in, and, as we afterwards learnt, 400 men *hors de combat* [out of action], so that she was an easy conquest for the Defiance, a fresh ship: we were well matched, she being the best manned ship in the Combined, and we in the British fleet. Unfortunately situated as we were, I have no doubt she would have struck, had we been able to follow and engage her for a quarter of an hour longer; but had we been fairly alongside of her, half an hour would have decided the contest; for I must say I was astonished at the coolness and undaunted bravery displayed by our gallant and veteran crew, when surrounded by five enemy's ships, and for a length of time unassisted by any of ours. Our loss, as might be expected, was considerable, and fell chiefly on our prime seamen, who were foremost in distinguishing themselves; twenty-eight, including the Captain, Master, and a Midshipman, were killed outright; and 127, including a Captain of Marines, who had eight balls in his body, and his right arm shot off, before her quitted the deck; Boatswain, and five Midshipmen, were badly wounded, and about forty more slightly, so as not to be incapable of duty; nineteen of the wounded had already died before we left Gibraltar. I consider myself as very fortunate in having escaped unhurt, as our class suffered so severely. Our second Lieutenant, myself, and eight men, formed the party that took possession of the Monarca: we remained till morning without further assistance, or we should most probably have saved her, though she had suffered much more than ourselves; we kept possession of her however for four days, in the most dreadful weather, when having rolled away all our masts, and being in danger of immediately sinking or running on shore, we were fortunately saved by the Leviathan, with all but about 150 prisoners, who were afraid of getting into the boats. I can assure you I felt not the least fear of death during the action, which I attribute to the general confidence of victory which I saw all around me; but in the prize, when I was in danger of, and had time to reflect upon the approach of death, either from the rising of the Spaniards upon so small a number as we were composed of, or what latterly appeared inevitable from the violence of the storm, I was most certainly afraid; and at one time, when the ship made three feet water in ten minutes, when our people were almost all lying drunk upon deck, when the Spaniards, completely worn out with fatigue, would no longer work at the only chain pump left serviceable; when I saw the fear of death so strongly depicted on the countenances of all around me, I wrapped myself up in a union jack, and lay down upon deck for a short time, quietly awaiting the approach of death; but the love of life soon after again roused me, and after great exertions on the part of the British and Spanish officers, who had joined together for the mutual preservation of their lives, we got the ship before the wind, determined to run her on shore: this was at midnight, but at day-light in the morning, the weather being more moderate, and having again gained upon the water, we hauled our wind, perceiving a three-decker (El Rayo) dismasted, but with Spanish colours up, close to leeward of us: the Leviathan, the first British ship we had seen for the last thirty hours, seeing this, bore down, and firing a shot a-head of us, the Rayo struck without returning a gun.

Naval Chronicle 14 (1805) 13-15; 15 (1806) 205-208.

READING 8.10

"HERE YOU WILL FIND ONLY ASHES"--THE BURNING OF MOSCOW, 1812

Napoleon Bonaparte (1769-1821), the son of a minor nobleman in Corsica, was educated at a military academy in France. The wars between revolutionary France and most other European nations gave him the chance to demonstrate his military genius. Following a meteoric rise to power, he proclaimed himself Emperor of the French in 1804 and had defeated every continental enemy by 1807. Great Britain, however, remained outside his reach and destroyed his fleet at the Battle of Trafalgar. Hoping to bring Britain to its knees through economic strangulation, Napoleon compelled his subjects and allies in Europe to join in the Continental System, a blockade against British trade. When economic hardships forced Tsar Alexander I of Russia to defy the system, Napoleon decided to enforce compliance by invading Russia. The ill-fated Russian campaign of 1812 was Napoleon's undoing. In June of 1812, Napoleon led his grand army of 600,000 French conscripts and levies from subject allies into Russia. He expected to defeat the Russians decisively and quickly and to dictate a favorable peace treaty. Russian forces, however, avoided battle and drew the French troops deep into their country. They practiced a scorched earth policy in order to deprive the French of provisions and shelter.

The French were able to win a costly victory on 7 September at the battle of Borodino, opening the way to the Russian capital, Moscow. Napoleon expected to quarter his army in Moscow for the winter and to induce the Tsar to sue for peace. These plans were thwarted when a devastating fire swept through the city. Napoleon was forced to retreat via the same route by which he had entered the country. The French Grand Army suffered immense losses during this withdrawal, because of a lack of food and supplies, harassment by the Russian army, and an extraordinarily harsh and early winter. The route of the retreat was littered with abandoned loot and dead bodies. Napoleon escaped from Russia with only some 50,000 starving, bedraggled survivors, the remnants of a half million men who had died, deserted, or been captured by the Russians.

The Russian debacle was the beginning of Napoleon's downfall, and the burning of Moscow was its signal. The following description of the fire is by, Armand Augustin Louis de Caulaincourt, a French diplomat and Napoleon's foreign minister. Caulaincourt's memoirs are a fascinating and important source for the Napoleonic era.

QUESTIONS:

1) What made the fire so difficult for the French to cope with?
2) Why does Caulaincourt include a transcription of the notice that Rostopchin posted on his house?

3) What sort of picture of Napoleon emerges from Caulaincourt's account of his actions (or inaction) during the burning of Moscow?

At eight o'clock in the evening flames broke out in one, of the suburbs. Assistance was sent, without more attention being paid to the matter, for it was still attributed to the carelessness of the troops.

The Emperor retired early; everyone was fatigued and as anxious to rest as he was. At half-past ten my valet, an energetic fellow who had been in my service during my embassy to Petersburg, woke me up with the news that for three-quarters of an hour the city had been in flames. I had only to open my eyes to realize that this was so, for the fire was giving off so much light that it was bright enough to read in the middle of my room. I sprang from bed and sent by valet to wake the Grand Marshal [Duroc], while I dressed. As the fire was spreading in the quarters farthest away from the Kremlin, we decided to send word to Mortier, to put the Guard under arms, and to let the Emperor sleep a little longer, as he had been extremely tired during the past few days.

I mounted my horse hurriedly to go and see what was happening, to gather what assistance I could muster, and to make sure that everyone connected with my own department, scattered throughout the city as they were, were running no unnecessary hazards. A stiff wind was blowing from the north, from the direction of the two points of conflagration that we could see, and was driving the flames toward the centre, which made the blaze extraordinarily powerful: About half-past twelve [16 September] a third fire broke out a little to the west, and shortly afterwards a fourth, in another quarter--in each case in the direction of the wind, which had veered slightly towards the west. About four o'clock in the morning the conflagration was so widespread that we judged it necessary to wake the Emperor, who at once sent more officers to find out how things really stood and discover whence these fires could be staring.

The troops were under arms; the few remaining inhabitants were fleeing their houses and gathering in the churches; there was nothing to be heard but lamentation. Search had been made for the fire-engines since the previous day,

but some of them had been taken away and the rest put out of action. From different houses officers and soldiers brought *boutechnicks* [policemen on point duty] and *moujiks* [peasants], who had been taken in the act of setting fire to inflammable material which had been laid in houses for the purpose of burning them down. The Poles reported that they had already caught some incendiaries and shot them; and they added, moreover, that from these men and from other inhabitants they had extracted the information that orders had been given by the Governor of the city and the police that the whole city should be burned during the night. These reports seemed incredible. The arrested men were put under guard, and fresh search and increased watchfulness were enforced. Pickets had already been sent to those quarters of the town which were not already in flames; and the further particulars which continued to arrive confirmed our gravest suspicions.

The Emperor was deeply concerned. Towards half-past nine he left the courtyard of the Kremlin on foot, just when two more incendiaries, caught in the act, were being brought in. They were in police uniform. When interrogated in the presence of the Emperor they repeated their declarations: their commanding officer had ordered them to burn everything. Houses had been designated to this end. In the different quarters everything had been prepared for starting the fire--in accordance with orders from Governor Rostopchin, so they had been told. The police officers had spread their men in small detachments in various quarters, and the order to carry out their instructions had been given in the evening of the previous day and confirmed by one of their officers on the following morning. They were reluctant to tell the name of this official, but one of them did so at last: he was a mere underling. They could not or would not indicate where he was at the moment, nor how he might be found. Their replies were translated to the Emperor in the presence of his suite. Many other depositions confirmed unmistakably what they said. All the incendiaries were kept under observation; some were brought to judgment and eight or ten executed.

The conflagration continued to spread from the borders of the boroughs where it had started. It had already reached the houses around the Kremlin. The wind, which had veered slightly to the west, fanned the flames to a terrifying extent and carried enormous sparks to a distance, where they fell like a fiery deluge hundreds of yards away, setting fire to more houses and preventing the most intrepid from remaining in the neighbourhood with safety. The air was so hot, and the pine-wood sparks were so numerous, that the beams supporting the iron plates which formed the roof of the arsenal all caught fire. The roof of the Kremlin kitchen was only saved by men being placed their with brooms and buckets to gather up the glowing fragments and moisten the beams. Only by superhuman efforts was the fire in the arsenal extinguished. The Emperor was there himself; his presence inspired the Guard to every exertion.

I hastened to the Court stables, where some of the Emperor's horses were stabled and the coronation coaches of the Tsar were kept. The utmost zeal, and, I may add, the greatest courage on the part of the coachmen and grooms, were necessary to save the place; they clambered on to the roof and knocked off the cinders that fell there, whilst others worked two fire-engines which I had had put in order during the night. (They had been totally dismantled.) I may say without exaggeration that we were working beneath a vault of fire. With these men's help I was able to save the beautiful Galitzin Palace and the two adjoining houses, which were already in flames. The Emperor's men were ably assisted by Prince Galitzin's servants, who displayed the utmost devotion to their master's interests. Everyone did his best to further the measures we took to check this devouring torrent of flame, but the air was charged with fire; we breathed nothing but smoke, and the stoutest lungs felt the strain after a time. The bridge to the south of the Kremlin was so heated by the fire and the sparks falling on it that it kept bursting into flames, although the Guard, and the sappers in particular, made it a point of honour to preserve it. I stayed with some generals of the Guard and aides-de-camp of the Emperor, and we were forced to lend a hand and remain in the midst of this

deluge of fire in order to spur on these half-roasted men. It was impossible to stand more than a moment in one spot; the fur on the grenadiers' caps was singed.

The fire made such progress that the whole of the northern and the greater part of the western quarter, by which we had entered, was burned, together with the splendid playhouse and all the larger buildings. One drew breath in a sea of fire--and the westerly wind continued to blow. The flames spread continuously; it was impossible to predict where or when they would stop, as there was no means of staying them. The conflagration passed beyond the Kremlin; it seemed that the river would surely save all the district lying to the east.

About four o'clock in the afternoon, while the fire was still raging, the Emperor began to think that this great catastrophe might be connected with some movement of the enemy, even though frequent reports from the King of Naples assured him that the Russians were still retreating along the Kazan road. The Emperor therefore gave orders to leave the city, and forbade anything to be left within its walls.

Headquarters were established at the Petrowskoïe Palace, on the Petersburg road, a country mansion where the Tsars were accustomed to take up residence before making their solemn entries into Moscow for their coronations. It was impossible to proceed thither by the direct road on account of the fire and the wind; one had to cross the western part of the town as best one could, through ruins, cinders, flames even, if one wanted to reach the outskirts. Night had already fallen when we got there; and we spent the following day in the palace. Meanwhile the fire continued with renewed violence, but a part of the quarter between the Kremlin and Petrowskoïe, where headquarters and the Guard were billeted, was saved. The Emperor was deep in thought; he spoke to no one....

With the exception of the King of Naples's corps, the entire army was in the town or quartered close at hand. Fugitives from the fire had sought shelter in churches, cemeteries, or wherever they felt secure from annoyance by the troops. The churches, which for the most part stood in the clear on public squares, had offered also greater security from the ravages of the flames. Many of these unfortunate refugees had made their way out to Petrowskoïe. We did what we could for them. I housed some two dozen of them in the Galitzin mansion, and among the number was M. Zagriaski, Master of Horse to the Tsar, who had hoped, by remaining in Moscow, to save his house, the object of his lifelong care. There was also a major-general, German by birth, who had gone into retirement in Moscow after long service with the Empress Catherine. These unhappy men had lost everything; nothing remained to them but the greatcoats which they wore.

Our return to Moscow was no less gloomy than our departure. I cannot relate all that I had suffered since the death of my brother. The sense of these recent events was the last straw; the horror of all that was going on around us added to my grief at his loss. True, one cannot nurse one's personal troubles exclusively in the midst of so many public disasters--but one is only the more wretched on that account. I was overwhelmed. Happy are they who never saw that dire spectacle, that picture of destruction!

A greater portion of the city was reduced to ashes; the northern district, nearest the Kremlin, had been saved by the wind shifting to the west; some isolated districts to windward had not suffered at all. The splendid mansions all round the city had escaped the plans for their destruction; only that of M. Rostopchin, the Governor, had been burned to the ground by its proprietor. He had posted up a notice of his intention, unquestionably very patriotic in his eyes, on the signpost that marked the road into his estate at Wornzowo, a short distance from Moscow. This notice was brought to the Emperor, who turned the whole thing to ridicule. He joked a lot about it and sent it to Paris, where doubtless it produced, as it had in the army, an impression quite contrary to what His Majesty expected. It had a profound effect on every thinking man, and won the Governor more admirers than critics--though only, of course, for the patriotism he had shown in sacrificing his house. This is how the notice was worded:

For eight years I have improved this land, and I have lived happily here in the bosom of my family. To the number of one thousand seven hundred and twenty the dwellers on my estate are leaving it at your approach, while, for my part, I am setting fire to my mansion rather than let it be sullied by your presence. Frenchmen!--in Moscow I have abandoned to you my two residences, with furniture worth half-a-million roubles. Here you will find only ashes.

Libaire, George, ed. *With Napoleon in Russia: The Memoirs of General de Caulaincourt, Duke of Vicenza.* New York: Morrow, 1935. Pp. 116-121, 125-127.

MAZZINI, GARIBALDI, CAVOUR, AND THE UNIFICATION OF ITALY

► **Count Camilio di Cavour**

Italy in the mid-nineteenth century was a collection of small states, a mere geographical expression. Austria ruled Venetia and Lombardy in the north and dominated the duchies in central Italy and the Kingdom of the Two Sicilies in the south, while the Papal States straddled the central peninsula. Only the kingdom of Piedmont and Sardinia, ruled by the House of Savoy, was truly independent.

The unification of Italy, completed in 1870, was led by the House of Savoy and its great prime minister, Count Camilio di Cavour (1810-1861). Two other men made indispensable contributions. One was Giuseppe Mazzini (1805-1872), an intellectual and inspirational writer who organized a nationalist group known as Young Italy. His call for a united Italy inspired Italian patriots and won widespread support for Italian unification in Britain and France. Another was Giuseppe Garibaldi (1807-1882), dubbed "The Liberator," whose redshirt volunteers conquered Sicily and southern Italy for the Italian Kingdom.

Using Sardinia as a base, Cavour led the campaign for unification. His reforms made Sardinia a model state, and won the admiration of Italians and many western Europeans. Because Sardinia was militarily weak, Cavour made an alliance with the Emperor Napoleon III of France. He next provoked Austria to declare war against Sardinia in 1859. His ally France defeated the Austrians in two bloody battles and drove them out of Lombardy. Sardinia gained Lombardy and duchies in central Italy, which had previously been controlled by Austrian authorities.

Garibaldi, the firebrand nationalist, now entered the picture. With Cavour's secret backing, he led an expedition to conquer the south, where a revolution had broken out against the reactionary government of the Kingdom of the Two Sicilies. Garibaldi and 1000 untrained redshirt volunteers landed in Sicily in May 1860. Gathering men as he campaigned, he was master of the island within a few weeks. Next he crossed to the mainland and advanced almost unopposed on Naples, which he entered amid the wild acclamation of a joyful populace.

Garibaldi planned to follow up his swift success with a march on Rome, the capital of the Papal States. This was bound to lead to intervention by Napoleon III, who had stationed French soldiers in Rome to protect the pope. To forestall a clash with France, Victor Emmanuel led a Sardinian force south to intercept Garibaldi; en route, it seized all papal territories except Rome. Confronted by Victor Emmanuel's army, Garibaldi yielded gracefully and went back to his humble farm on Caprera.

In a series of plebiscites, the people of the Two Sicilies and the papal provinces voted overwhelmingly for union with Sardinia. On 17 March 1861, the Kingdom of Italy was proclaimed with Victor Emmanuel as king (r. 1861-1878). All Italy except Venetia and Rome had been united. In

1866, Italy allied itself with Prussia against Austria in the Austro-Prussian or "Six Weeks" War. Although the Italians were defeated by Austrian forces in Venetia, the Prussians won decisively and Austria ceded Venetia to Italy as part of the peace settlement. When the Franco-Prussian War broke out in 1870 and Napoleon III withdrew his troops from Rome, Italian troops took possession of the city, except for the Vatican. The Romans voted to join Italy, and Rome became capital of the completely unified Italy.

The triumph of Italian nationalism was largely the result of the life work of three men: Mazzini the dreamer, Cavour the architect, and Garibaldi the liberator. The first of the following selections is a biographical sketch of Giuseppe Mazzini, the founder of the radical Young Italy movement. In the second passage, a British naval officer describes one of the battles in Garibaldi's lightning campaign through Sicily that so enthralled his contemporaries and made him the military hero of the unification movement. The third passage is a portrait of the shrewd political engineer of Italian unity, Count Cavour by an admiring contemporary biographer.

QUESTIONS:

1) What were the ideals of the Young Italy organization as Mazzini conceived of them?

2) According to the author of the second selection, what were Garibaldi's leadership qualities? Why was he so popular with his troops?

3) What does Cavour's biographer find notable and admirable about the great man?

MAZZINI

Born in Genoa in 1805, Joseph Mazzini was brought up not only in love of country, but also in the "worship of equality" through the democratic principles of his parents, "whose bearing towards high or low was ever the same." He tells us that while walking one Sunday in April 1821 with his mother and a friend of the family in the streets of Genoa, they were addressed by "a tall black-bearded man, with a severe and energetic countenance, and a fiery glance that I have never since forgotten. He held out a white handkerchief towards us, merely saying, 'For the refugees of Italy.' My mother and friend dropped some money into the handkerchief, and he turned from us to put the same request to others." The man was one Rini, a captain in the national guard instituted by the Piedmontese in their insurrection against Austria in March 1821. The insurrection was crushed, and many of the revolutionists had flocked to Genoa, there to await another opportunity. From this incident dates the spiritual new birth of Mazzini; the fruitful idea of struggle for the right, for Italy, for mankind, falling on fertile soil and bearing during the following half century the rich harvest of a sorrowful but inexpressibly precious life....

Mazzini ... turned resolutely to the political problem--how to gain freedom and unity for Italy--and forthwith joined the secret society of the Carbonari. He was sent by the leaders of this body to Tuscany to plant the order there. Entrapped by an *agent provocateur*, Mazzini was arrested ... [and] sent to the fortress of Savona, overlooking the sea on the Western Riviera. Here he remained for some time, the Bible, Tacitus, and Byron being the companions of his solitude. He was acquitted by a committee of senators at Turin; but not before he had conceived in his solitary cell the design of a new association of Young Italy--a society of young men bound together by a common faith and zeal--for the emancipation of the country. A journey to Switzerland and France followed; and at Marseilles, whither great numbers of Italian exiles had flocked, Mazzini sketched out the design and rules of the new society. About this very time (April 1831) Charles Albert, who had been numbered in the ranks of the Carbonari, ascended the Sardinian throne, and many believed that he would achieve the liberty and unity of Italy. Mazzini did not share these views. He did, indeed, in a memorable letter, urge the Sardinian king to put himself at the head of the movement for Italian independence, telling him that he had the choice of being judged by posterity as the greatest of men or the last of Italian tyrants. But no man ever believed so firmly in the divine right of the Republic as did Mazzini. The salvation of Italy, he held, could never be achieved by any monarch, but only through the republican association of the Italian people....

Mazzini's republican idea was, however, no mere political mechanism, but an organic union, the life of which was a religious faith.... He was filled with hope that Italy might not only achieve her own unity, but might once more accomplish, as she had in the Rome of the Caesars and the Rome of the Church, the unity of the Western world.... The Italians were to be convinced that their "sole path to victory was through sacrifice --constancy in sacrifice." Instead, therefore, of the old wire-pulling mechanism of Carbonarism, we have as the exponent of these ideas, the association of Young Italy, filled with the breath of new life. In the general instructions for the members of Young Italy Mazzini gives the reasons for his republican creed. Young Italy is republican, he says, because every nation should form a free and equal community of brothers; because all true sovereignty resides in the nation; because privilege tends to undermine the equality of the citizens, and therefore to endanger the liberty of the country."

GARIBALDI

These red-shirted, ragged-looking scarecrows, under this far from prepossessing exterior, were endowed with many of those sterling qualities which have often enabled impromptu levies to triumph over more elaborate organizations. A musket or rifle, sixty rounds of ammunition, a water-bottle, and, for the most part, an empty haversack, and you have the *impedimenta* [baggage] of a Garibaldian.

Of commissaries in gorgeous uniform there are none, yet of beef and bread there is an occasional supply--of discipline there is the mere shadow; all, however, are animated with unbounded confidence in their chiefs, and especially Garibaldi, who may be said to exercise an individual power over his followers wholly without parallel amongst modern commanders, who are too apt to lay influence on one side, and place their trust in fear. With this imaginative race, their faith in their chief almost amounts to a superstition: whatever he says, is--wherever he appears, victory follows as a matter of course. This feeling, combined with an utter contempt, and, with the Sicilians, an implacable hatred, for Neapolitans, has been the keystone of Garibaldi's successes, and of victories won in utter defiance of all martial tactics ....

Garibaldi in person, as usual, was ever in the thickest of the fray, cigarette *en bouche* [in his mouth], and walking-stick in hand, cheering his guides and Genoese carbineers [riflemen], his calm and benevolent features bearing their usual happy expression, as if he were on a day's excursion, rather than leading a death struggle on which the fate of his country depended.

Strongly but symmetrically built, and of middle stature, this paladin [knight] of Italy is chiefly distinguished from his followers by his unassuming manner and aspect. Though dressed somewhat in sailor fashion, with a red shirt, grey trousers, wideawake [soft felt wide-brimmed hat], and loose bandana flowing over his shoulders, his appearance is scrupulously clean and neat, and his manner gentlemanly though genial. There is something most winning and honest in his address, and you are at once impressed with the conviction that you are face to face with a man whose word would be his bond, and upon whose guidance, either by sea or land, you would implicitly rely. No wonder, then, that his men advance again with such confidence where perhaps routine troops would have hesitated.

But it is hot work: Medici's horse has been killed under him; Cosenz has been hit in the neck; still the General leads his guides under Missori, and the Genoese carbineers, who ever behave admirably. Suddenly a three-gun battery opens on them with "mitraille" [grape-shot] at twenty paces. In this murderous discharge Garibaldi was slightly hurt, Missori's horse killed, Major Breda killed, Statella alone left standing on foot with a few men... Garibaldi now gathered himself up for a fresh attack; and the reserve consisting of the English regiment having arrived, 150 men, with Major Wyndham, were sent to try and break through the line toward S. Marina; and Dunne, with the remainder, about 200 strong, was ordered by the General to advance and endeavor to carry the battery in flank; whilst Missori, Statella, and the remnant of their men, attempted the same movement in the opposite direction....

Dividing themselves on either side of the road, the Garibaldians placed their backs to the wall and prickly-pear bushes, and opened fire on the cavalry from either side. This was the struggle of the day, and very nearly cost Garibaldi his life, and with it the life of Italy. Afraid of advancing too far, and finding himself between two fires, the Neapolitan commander halted, and endeavored to return; but Garibaldi, Missori, Statella, and a handful of guides, barred the way. Summoned by the Neapolitan officer to surrender, [Garibaldi] ... merely replied by springing at his horse's bridle and cutting down the owner. Three or four troopers seconded their officer; one of them Garibaldi wounded; Missori killed two others, and shot the horse of a third; Statella killed another; and this murderous struggle was concluded by Missori, who killed a third with the fourth barrel of his revolver. The remnant of the cavalry now charged back and escaped, leaving the guns in the hands of Garibaldi....

But the Neapolitans fought like beaten troops, and were evidently bent on gradually retiring to the castle, their retreat being covered by a heavy fire of shot and shell from that fortress, in spite of which the heroic Garibaldians gradually advanced from position to position, driving back the troops, until, about four o'clock, they worked their way up to the entrance of the castle.... Barricades were thrown up in all the immediate approaches toward the town, in readiness to repel any sortie; and officers and men, alike worn out and weary, lay down on their posts for the night--Garibaldi, with his head on a saddle, under the portico of a church near the centre of the Marina. Their successes, however, had been dearly bought; no less than 750 Garibaldians were *hors de combat* [out of action].

Garibaldi, when asked to write a bulletin after the battle by one of his generals, made a very characteristic reply: "No; if I write an account, I shall be compelled to say that some did better than others. You may write if you please; and the best thing you can say is, that the action commenced at daylight, and in the evening we had possession of the town...."

There is a sort of intimate communion of mind between Garibaldi and the masses which is perfectly electrifying. They look up to him as a sort of link between themselves and the Deity.

CAVOUR

The real cause of Cavour's superiority and authority in parliament, as well as at the head of affairs, was the quality of the man--the attractive originality of his marvellously well-balanced nature. Cavour had nothing in common with the mediocre statesman, ambitious of power and yet encumbered with it; full of his own importance, exhausting subtleties and complications, and, with much labour, achieving infinitesimal results. In him there was no arrogance, no strain, no uncertainty. He was the most natural and straightforward of politicians, carrying out his innumerable engagements with the greatest ease; doing the most engrossing work without effort or fatigue; holding cheaply all etiquette and regulations; cordial and pleasant in all his relations with men. He shrank instinctively from whatever savoured of affectation or display; and when, after having been hard at work ever since daybreak in sending off despatches or receiving visits, he went on his way along the colonnade of the Via di Po to the Office of Foreign Affairs, or that of Finance, he seemed only a worthy citizen of Turin, bowing to an acquaintance here, or talking to one there, affable with everyone. In the midst of the most important affairs he had the gift of a cheerful animation, the wholesome brightness of an elastic temperament and a well-regulated mind; a cheerfulness which manifested itself in a hearty laugh, or in a way of rubbing his hands in a certain manner which has become traditional.

Thus endowed with a happy spirit, a ready intelligence, and a great enjoyment of life, he never knew what *ennui* was, any more than rancour or bitterness. He used to say that rancour was absurd, and that nothing need ever be wearisome. Thus he would pass with perfect equanimity from the study of some profound political problem to the reading of a novel or a newspaper article; from conferring with an ambassador to conversing with some humble peasant or modest applicant for office; from the most complicated state affairs to mere parish matters....

He could indeed find time for everything, because he took an interest in everything, and he could find good in everything. He despised neither men nor things, and he used to say wittily that many card-players only lose because they have no regard for the small cards; as for him, he knew the value of the small cards--of insignificant people, even of counsels and remarks which he would call forth and listen to and make his own. But under this apparent facility and good humour, Cavour possessed the highest qualities of a statesman; clearness and precision of ideas, and a strength of will which at times could make all give way before it. Neither peril nor difficulty proved an obstacle to his will. Only, this iron will was clad in graciousness, the sharp outline of his ideas was veiled in the garb of amiability; his practical good sense, so unerring and fully developed, was combined with great and broad conceptions; and thus this gifted nature--hearty, liberal, impetuous, and fascinating--became irresistible: friends, adversaries, dissentients, all were attracted and carried along by it.

The innumerable speeches by which Cavour defended his policy, and which subsist as a monument of the parliamentary *régime*, represent faithfully his character and tone of mind. Cavour was not a born orator, and at the beginning of his career he obtained a hearing with some difficulty. His voice was rather harsh; there was a certain sharpness in his tones, not abated by the wear and tear of conflict; and he never lost a slight cough, which at times interfered with his well-rounded periods [complex sentences], and which, indeed, he knew how to turn to account when necessary. Besides this, he had to acquire the habit of speaking Italian, and he rather piqued himself upon his literary inability; he used sometimes to pretend to consult his friends as to the correctness of some sentence; but he rapidly became the first debater in the Piedmontese parliament, riveting attention by the reliableness of his views and the substantial soundness of his elucidations; fascinating his hearers by the subtlety of his reasoning, and making himself formidable by the brilliant sarcasm of his repartees.

Clarke, William. "Mazzini." In *Essays: Selected from the Writings, Literary, Political, and Religious, of Joseph Mazzini*. London: Walter Scott, n.d. Pp. viii, ix-xi. Forbes, Charles. *The Campaign of Garibaldi in the Two Sicilies*. London 1861. Pp. 92-101, 118. Mazade-Percin, M. Charles de. *The Life of Count Cavour*. London: Chapman & Hall, 1877. Pp. 118-121.

SECTION 9

GLOBAL POLITICS IN THE LATE NINETEENTH AND EARLY TWENTIETH CENTURIES

Nationalism and imperialism are two dominant themes in history since 1800. Two prominent twentieth-century phenomena were the rise and fall of Marxism, which began as an economic theory but was hijacked to serve nationalist and imperialist causes, and Nazism, which was a perversion of nationalism. These four "isms" provided the ideological fuel that ignited most major and minor wars from late nineteenth century to the present.

Anglo-French imperial rivalries caused many conflicts; one, the Fashoda Incident, nearly led to war in 1898. Most non-Western nations became colonies of major European powers and the United States; although China did not formally become a colony, it was nevertheless the victim of imperialism. Among Africans, only Ethiopia escaped European domination by defeating Italy, while in Asia, Japan alone rose from victim to become an imperialistic nation. In Europe, there were subject nationalities in the Russian, German, Austro-Hungarian, and British empires, while in South Africa, the Boers (Dutch descended settlers) were unwilling British subjects who sought to break free.

Resistance to imperialism took the form of national revival under Sun Yat-sen in China and under Arab leaders in Muslim areas, in Gandhi's development of non-violent resistance in India, and in Serbian terrorism against the Austro-Hungarian Empire. Serbian terrorism provided the fuse that ignited World War I. At the end of that war, representatives of the victorious "Big Four" countries sought to redress nationalist grievances. But it proved impossible to satisfy conflicting demands among rival national groups. Throughout the 1920s and 1930s, all over Europe and in Japan, people abandoned democratic institutions and pinned their hopes and aspirations on new authoritarian regimes. By the 1930s, Nazis Germany and Japanese militarists joined forces in an attempt to dominate the world and started World War II. Accounts of China's resistance to Japanese aggression and of the bombing of Pearl Harbor foretell the doom of the aggressors' cause. Meanwhile Marxism found fertile ground in a revolutionary Russia devastated by World War I; the triumph of communism and the rise of Joseph Stalin in the U.S.S.R. created of one of the most brutally repressive totalitarian states in history.

The readings in this section speak to the major geopolitical forces that have shaped our world.

ETHIOPIA REPELS ITALIAN INVADERS IN 1896

Starting in the 1880s, European powers began a furious race to partition Africa into colonies. By World War I, only two African states retained their independence: Liberia in west Africa, which had been settled by former slaves from the United States, and Ethiopia in the interior of east Africa.

Ethiopia was an ancient kingdom with a history that dated to biblical times. Most Ethiopians were Coptic Christians, a minority were Muslims, and there was a small community of Jews. Starting in the 1880s, Ethiopia became embroiled in international diplomacy between Great Britain (which developed an interest in Egypt and the Sudan along the river Nile, and established a protectorate over part of Somaliland on the coast of the Horn of Africa), France (which also established a protectorate over parts of Somaliland and had an interest in the Sudan until 1896), and Italy (which took over Eritrea and sections of Somaliland on the Horn of Africa). Italy sought to expand its empire into the interior and to that end signed the Treaty of Ucciali with emperor Menelik of Ethiopia in 1889. Italy interpreted some ambiguous language in the treaty to mean that it had established a protectorate over Ethiopia. War broke out when Emperor Menelik disagreed and renounced the treaty. The over-confident and ill-prepared Italians were resoundingly defeated in the Battle of Adowa in 1896. In the resulting Treaty of Addis Ababa, Italy recognized Ethiopian independence. This was the only instance during the Scramble for Africa in which an African nation repelled European aggression and retained its independence. Emperor Menelik, who accomplished that feat, also began the modernization of Ethiopia.

QUESTIONS:

1) What qualities made Menelik a good ruler?
2) Why did Italy covet Ethiopia and what was its excuse for war?
3) Give the reasons for Italy's loss and Ethiopia's victory at the Battle of Adowa.

Menelik, who reigned as King of Shoa from 1865 and as Emperor of Ethiopia from 1889 to 1913, was perhaps the greatest of Ethiopia's rulers. His reign was of considerable importance in that it witnessed the reunification and modernization of his country, as well as a great increase in its position in world affairs....

Menelik's personality, his innate intelligence and ability, his grasp of world affairs and his interest in modernization, impressed all observers. "During the many interviews I had with him," recalls the British diplomat, Rennell Rodd, "I formed a high opinion both of his intelligence and his character.... His energy was astonishing. By rising before dawn and beginning his day with prayers in chapel at 6 a.m. he made time to attend personally to every detail of the administration in a country constituted of many heterogeneous elements. Accessible to all his subjects from the highest to the lowest, he had succeeded in winning universal regard and affection." ... The sovereign's physician, Dr. Merab, confirms this picture, adding that Menelik embodied law and order in his person and guaranteed justice to all, being called the "father of his people" by all his country's numerous tribes, Amharas, Gallas, Gurages and Shankellas, etc. ....

The British envoy, Hohler, relates that Menelik often assisted in such varied work as church building and grass cutting. It was not therefore surprising that the Emperor should have issued a decree castigating his people for their traditional dislike of manual work, and declaring the farmer more important than the king. "All mankind," it added, "is descended from Adam and Eve; there was no other ancestor. Discrimination is the result of ignorance...."

Menelik was also greatly interested in the import of fire-arms and was much more successful in obtaining them than any previous Ethiopian ruler. Possessing fairly convenient access to the coast through the ports of the French Somali colony and the Italian port of Assab, which were being improved in this period, he had the additional advantage that the French and Italian governments were both for reasons of their own strongly in favour of his obtaining arms. The French hoped that by supplying him with arms they would win his friendship which would be useful to them in their rivalry with the British, while the Italians were no less anxious to win his co-operation or at least neutrality in their conflict with his nominal overlord the Emperor Yohannes, the ruler of the north....

On the death of the Emperor Yohannes in March 1889, Menelik succeeded him as Emperor and was crowned on November 3. The first years of his reign were clouded by difficulties with the Italians who had seized the Red Sea port of Masawa in February 1885, and began to advance on to the Eritrean plateau not long after the death of his predecessor. This was the period of the Scramble for Africa, which had become particularly fierce in 1885....

Notwithstanding growing Italian interest in East Africa, Menelik had been on friendly terms with Italy until his accession as Emperor. On May 2, 1889--less than two months after the death of Yohannes--he signed a Treaty of Perpetual Peace and Friendship with Italy. This treaty, which was destined to be of crucial significance in the history of Ethiopian relations with the European Powers, contained articles of benefit to both signatory Powers. Menelik recognized Italian sovereignty over the Eritrean plateau including Asmara, while the Italian Government recognized Menelik as Emperor of Ethiopia and agreed in Article VI that he was entitled to import arms and munitions through Italian territory. The most important article, however, was Article XVII which was soon the basis of a dispute between the two signatories. The quarrel arose from the fact that the treaty had two texts, one in the Ethiopian language, Amharic, and the other in Italian.... The Italian text, however, made it obligatory for the Emperor to conduct all his transactions with the other Powers through the Italian Government.... The Italian formula was soon used by the Italian Government to claim that it had established a Protectorate over Ethiopia....

The Italian Government, which was by now in control of the Eritrean plateau, now [1889] felt that it was in a position to proclaim to the world that Italy had obtained a Protectorate over Ethiopia. This was done on October 11, over five months after the signing of the Ucciali Treaty....

The Emperor, however, refused to accept this interpretation of the Ucciali treaty. On September 27, 1890--eleven months after the announcement of the Italian claim--he wrote to King Umberto I of Italy:.... "When I made the treaty of friendship with Italy, in order that our secrets be guarded and that our understanding should not be spoiled, I said that because of our friendship, our affairs in Europe might be carried on with the aid of the Sovereign of Italy, but I have not made any treaty which obliges me to do so. I am not the man to employ the aid of another to carry on my affairs...."

After a delay of over two years, which he turned to good advantage by importing very large quantities of fire-arms especially from France and Russia, Menelik at length denounced the Treaty of Ucciali on February 12, 1893; a week or so later, on February 27, he informed the European Powers of his decision, declaring: "Ethiopia had need of no one; she stretches out her hands unto God."

Fighting began in January 1895. The invaders were at first victorious and succeeded in occupying a large stretch of territory including Adigrat, Makalle and Amba Alagi. Later in the year, however, Menelik moved north with a large and moderately well armed force and, himself commanding operations, won significant victories over the Italians at Amba Alagi in December and at Makalle at the turn of the year. The Italians were obliged to fall back on Adowa.

The first weeks of 1896 witnessed a period of inaction on either side, neither the Italian nor the Ethiopian army desiring to take the initiative. Finally on February 25, Crispi [premier of Italy], exasperated by the delay, telegraphed to General Baratieri [commander of the Italian expeditionary force]: "It is clear to me that there is no fundamental plan in this campaign, and I should like one to be formulated. We are ready for any sacrifice in order to save the honour of the army and the prestige of the Monarchy."

Baratieri's reaction to this telegram was to order his army to attack; accordingly the battle of Adowa opened in the early morning of March 1.

The Emperor from the outset was in a relatively good position. He had the wholehearted support of the local population, whose patriotism was intensified by the fact that the Italians had been expropriating a sizeable amount of land in an attempt to settle Italian colonists. The inhabitants of the area in which the battle was fought were therefore most willing to show Menelik's troops the best paths and to bring news of enemy movements. The Italians, on the other hand, had to face the enmity of the local people and had no accurate maps to help them. Their army therefore moved in the greatest possible confusion.

The Ethiopian army moreover was much larger than that of the Italians. Not counting soldiers with spears he had well over 100,000 men with modern rifles. The Italians for their part had somewhat more cannon--56 as against Menelik's 40--but only about 17,000 men, of whom 10,596 were Italian and the rest Eritrean levies.

The result of the battle was the complete defeat and rout of the invaders. Official Italian figures record that 261 European officers, 2,918 non-commissioned officers and men, and about 2,000 *askaris*, or native troops, were killed, and that a further 954 Italian soldiers were permanently missing and had therefore to be presumed killed. Total Italian casualties thus amounted to over 7,560, or nearly 43 per cent. of the original fighting force of 10,596 Italian and about 7.100 native troops. The Italians also abandoned all their cannons, as well as about 11,000 out of 14,519 rifles with which they started the battle.

As a result of this battle Menelik gained enormous local and international prestige. On October 26 the Italians agreed to the Peace Treaty of Addis Ababa, whereby they accepted the annulment of the Treaty of Ucciali and recognized the absolute and complete independence of Ethiopia. Menelik, on the other hand, did not consider himself in a position to insist on an Italian withdrawal from Eritrea though he had often expressed a desire of obtaining access to the sea. In the months which followed, the French and British governments sent diplomatic missions to sign treaties of friendship with Menelik; other missions came from the Sudanese Mahdists, the Sultan of the Ottoman Empire and the Tsar of Russia. Addis Ababa thus emerged as a regular diplomatic centre where several important foreign powers had legations.

Pankhurst, Richard. "Emperor Menelik II of Ethiopia." *Tarikh* 1 (1965) 1-3, 6-11.

ANGLO-FRENCH RIVALRY AND THE FASHODA INCIDENT

▶ **European Astride Africa**

Egypt, which had been a possession of the Ottoman Empire since the fifteenth century, became important to Europe in 1798 when Napoleon Bonaparte (1769-1821) landed an expeditionary force in Alexandria, defeated the local garrison and then entered Cairo. Napoleon dreamt of using Egypt as staging ground to conquer Syria, and then to march overland to oust the British from India. Although the British destruction of the French fleet at the Battle of the Nile ended Napoleon's unrealistic dream, Egypt remained pivotal in Anglo-French rivalry throughout the nineteenth century. Egypt became vital to Great Britain's imperial strategy when the Suez Canal was opened in 1869, because the canal shortened voyages between Europe and Asia by two weeks, and Britain had the largest empire in Asia and dominated world trade.

During the nineteenth century, the khedives or hereditary governors of Egypt incurred huge debts to European banks to finance their modernizing projects and because of their profligacy. Unable to repay his debts, Khedive Ismail (r. 1863-1879) put his shares in the Suez Canal Company up for sale in 1875. The British government snatched them up and as a result became the largest shareholder in the Suez Canal Company. In 1882, nationalistic Egyptian army officers revolted against their weak khedive over the issue of European interference in Egyptian affairs. When France refused to join Britain in protecting their interests, the British moved alone to suppress the revolt. After restoring order, Britain reorganized the Egyptian government and established a de facto protectorate over the land. A British Resident oversaw the Egyptian government and British advisors supervised every branch of the Egyptian administration.

Meanwhile the Egyptian claim of overlordship of the Sudan was challenged by Mohammed Ahmed, a religious fanatic who claimed to be the Mahdi or "rightly guided one" of Islam. His forces defeated the Egyptian army in 1883, and trapped the small garrison of General Charles Gordon, who had been sent to the Sudan to evacuate the Egyptian troops, in Khartoum. They captured Khartoum in 1885 and massacred Gordon and his contingent. Even though the Mahdi died later in 1885, his successor, the Khalifa Abdullah, and his dervish supporters continued to control the Sudan.

Revenge, the need to control the water supply of the Nile River for Egypt's rising agricultural needs, and the quest to forestall French or other European ambitions in the region propelled Britain to reconquer the Sudan. In 1896, General Herbert Kitchener (1850-192) was appointed Sirdar (commander-in-chief) of the Egyptian Army and commander of the Anglo-Egyptian forces of the Sudanese campaign. Kitchener proceeded with the greatest caution, building a Desert Railway as he advanced. On 2 September 1898, he defeated the Khalifa decisively at the Battle of Omdurman, and took Khartoum, the capital of the Sudan.

Kitchener heard that a French expedition had reached the upper Nile to lay claim to the land. It was no secret that France hoped to establish an African empire that stretched from the Atlantic to the Indian Ocean. Kitchener immediately set sail southward from Khartoum in search of the French party. On 19 September he reached Fashoda and found a small French force under Major Marchand. Marchand, who had begun his journey in 1896 from Niger in west Africa, had arrived at Fashoda on 10 July, 1898. He refused to evacuate his outpost without orders from his government.

The Fashoda Incident was the greatest crisis between Britain and France before World War I. Britain which claimed the Sudan on behalf of Egypt, and by right of conquest prevailed; Marchand received his orders to evacuate on November 3. France agreed to renounce its claims in the Nile Valley in return for control over the Sahara. The episode illustrates imperialist rivalry in the vital Middle East and Africa.

Winston Churchill (1874-1965) was a young subaltern in the British army during the River War for the reconquest of the Sudan. He was also war correspondent for an English newspaper. The following is from a book he wrote about the war and the Fashoda Incident.

QUESTIONS:

1) How did the members of the English and French expeditions regard one another when they met at Fashoda?

2) How did the English public react to news that France had ambitions over the Sudan?

3) How did the Africans in the Sudan react to the presence of the Europeans?

Toward the end of 1896 a French expedition was despatched from the Atlantic into the heart of Africa under the command of Major Marchand....

[By early 1898] The advance [of Anglo-Egyptian forces] into Khartoum and the reconquest of the lost provinces [Sudan] had been irrevocably undertaken. An Anglo-Egyptian force was already concentrating at Berber. Lastly, the Marchand Mission was known to be moving towards the Upper Nile, and it was a probable contingency that they would arrive at their destination within a few months. It was therefore evident that the line of advance of the powerful army moving south from the Mediterranean, and of the tiny expedition moving east from the Atlantic must intersect before the end of the year, and that intersection would involve a collision between the Powers of Great Britain and France....

On the 7th of September, five days after the battle and capture of Omdurman, the *Tewfikia*, a small Dervish steamer ... came drifting and paddling down the river. Her Arab crew ... soon found themselves surrounded by the white gunboats of the 'Turks,' and so incontinently surrendered. The story they told their captors was a strange one. They had left Omdurman a

month earlier ... with the Khalifa's orders to go up the White Nile and collect grain. For some time all had been well, but on approaching the old Government station of Fashoda they had been fired on by black troops commanded by white officers under a strange flag--and fired on with such effect that they had lost some forty men killed and wounded. Doubting who these formidable enemies might be, the foraging expedition had turned back.... The story was carried to the Sirdar [General Herbert Kitchener], and ran like wildfire through the camp. Many officers made their way to the river, where the steamer lay, to test for themselves the truth of the report. The woodwork of the hull was marked with many newly made holes, and cutting into these with their penknives the officers extracted bullets ... [and found they were] the conical nickel-covered bullets of small-bore rifles such as are fired by civilized forces alone. Here was positive proof. A European Power was on the Upper Nile: which? Some said it was the Belgians from the Congo; some that an Italian expedition had arrived; others thought that the strangers were French.... The Arab crew were cross-examined as to the flag they had seen. Their replies were inconclusive. It had bright colours, they declared; but what those colours were and what their arrangement might be they could not tell; they were poor men, and God was very great....

On the 8th the Sirdar started up the White Nile for Fashoda with five steamers.... The *sudd* which was met with two days' journey south of Khartoum did not in this part of the Nile offer any obstacle to navigation, as the strong current of the river clears the waterway; but on either side of the channel a belt of the tangled weed, varying from twelve to twelve hundred yards in breadth, very often prevented the steamers from approaching the bank to tie up. The banks themselves depressed the explorers by their melancholy inhospitality. At times the river flowed past miles of long grey grass and swamp-land, inhabited and inhabitable only by hippopotami. At times a vast expanse of dreary mud flats stretched as far as the eye could see. At others the forest, dense with an impenetrable undergrowth of thorn-bushes, approached the water, and the active forms of monkeys and even of leopards darted among the trees. But the country--whether forest, mud-flat, or prairie--was always damp and feverish: a wet land steaming under a burning sun and humming with mosquitoes and all kinds of insect life.

Onward and southward toiled the flotilla, splashing the brown water into foam and startling the strange creatures on the banks, until on the 18th of September they approached Fashoda. The gunboats waited, moored to the bank for some hours of the afternoon, to allow a message which had been sent by the Sirdar to the mysterious Europeans, to precede his arrival, and early in the morning of the 19th a small steel rowing-boat was observed coming down stream to meet the expedition. It contained a Senegalese sergeant and two men with a letter from Major Marchand announcing the arrival of the French troops and their formal occupation of the Soudan. It, moreover, congratulated the Sirdar on his victory, and welcomed him to Fashoda in the name of France.

A few miles' further progress brought the gunboats to their destination, and they made fast to the bank near the old Government buildings of the town. Major Marchand's party consisted of eight French officers or non-commissioned officers, and 120 black soldiers drawn from the Niger district.... They had six months' supplies of provisions for the French officers, and about three months' rations for the men; but they had no artillery, and were in great want of small-arms of any sort, and with no means of either withstanding an attack or of making a retreat....

Their joy and relief at the arrival of a European force was undisguised. The Sirdar and his officers on their part were thrilled with admiration at the wonderful achievements of this small band of heroic men. Two years had passed since they left the Atlantic coast. For six months they had been absolutely lost from human ken. They had fought with savages; they had struggled with fever.... Five days and five nights they had stood up to their necks in swamp and water. A fifth of their number had perished; yet at last they had carried out their mission, and arriving at Fashoda on the 10th of July, had planted the tricolour upon the Upper Nile. Happy the nation that can produce such men!...

Moved by such reflections the British officers disembarked. Major Marchand, with a guard of honour, came to meet the General. They shook hands warmly. 'I congratulate you,' said the Sirdar, 'on all you have accomplished.' 'No,' replied the Frenchman, pointing to his troops; 'it is not I, but these soldiers who have done it.' And Kitchener, telling the story afterwards, remarked, 'Then I knew he was a gentleman.'...

The Sirdar politely ignored the French flag, and, without interfering with the Marchand Expedition and the fort they occupied, hoisted the British and Egyptian colours with all due ceremony, amid musical honours and the salutes of the gunboats. A garrison was established at Fashoda ... under the command of Colonel Jackson, who was appointed military and civil commandant of the Fashoda district.

At three o'clock on the same afternoon the Sirdar and the gunboats resumed their journey to the south, and the next day reached the mouth of the Sobat, sixty-two miles from Fashoda. Here other flags were hoisted and another post formed with a garrison....

[News of the French claim of the Sudan] found England united. The determination of the Government was approved by the loyalty of the Opposition, supported by the calm resolve of the people, and armed with the efficiency of the fleet.... There is no Power in Europe which the average Englishman regards with less animosity than France. Nevertheless, on this matter all were agreed. They should go. They should evacuate Fashoda, or else all the might, majesty, dominion, and power of everything that could by any stretch of the imagination be called 'British' should be employed to make them go.

Those who found it difficult to account for the hot, almost petulant, flush of resolve that stirred the nation must look back over the long history of the Soudan drama. It had always been a duty to reconquer the abandoned territory....

First of all, the country was determined to have Fashoda or fight; and as soon as this was made clear, the French were willing to give way. Fashoda was a miserable swamp, of no particular value to them.... The Abyssinians had held aloof. The negro tribes gazed with wonder on the strangers, but had no intention of fighting for them. The pride and barbarism of the Khalifa rejected all overtures and disdained to discriminate between the various breeds of the accursed 'Turks.' Finally, the victory of Omdurman and its forerunner--the Desert Railway--had revolutionized the whole situation in the Nile valley. After some weeks of tension, the French Government consented to withdraw their expedition from the region of the Upper Nile....

[Until diplomats resolved the crisis] On this dismal island, far from civilization, health, or comfort, the Marchand Mission and the Egyptian garrison lived in polite antagonism for nearly three months. The French fort stood at the northern end. The Egyptian camp lay outside the ruins of the town. Civilities were constantly exchanged between the forces, and the British officers repaid the welcome gifts of fresh vegetables [the French grew] by newspapers and other conveniences. The Senegalese riflemen were smart and well-conducted soldiers, and the blacks of the Soudanese battalion soon imitated their officers in reciprocating courtesies. A feeling of friendship sprang up between Colonel Jackson and Major Marchand.... Realizing the difficulties, he appreciated the magnificence of the achievements; and as he spoke excellent French a good and almost cordial understanding was established, and no serious disagreement occurred. But not withstanding the polite relations, the greatest vigilance was exercised by

both sides, and whatever civilities were exchanged were of a formal nature.

The Dinkas and Shillooks had on the first arrival of the French made submission, and had supplied them with provisions. They knew that white men were said to be coming, and they did not realize that there were different races among the whites. Marchand was regarded as the advance guard of the Sirdar's army. But when the negroes gradually perceived that these bands of white men were at enmity with each other-- were, in fact, of rival tribes--they immediately transferred their allegiance to the stronger force, and, although their dread of the Egyptian flag was at first very marked, boycotted the French entirely....

Then it became known that the French Government had ordered the evacuation of Fashoda. Some weeks were spent in making preparations for the journey, but at length the day of departure arrived. At 8.20 on the morning of the 11th of December the French lowered their flag with salute and flourish of bugle. The British officers, who remained in their own camp and did not obtrude themselves, were distant but interested spectators....

Once again the eight Frenchmen, who had come so far and accomplished so much, set out upon their travels, to make a safe though tedious journey through Abyssinia to the coast, and thence home to the country they had served faithfully and well....

Colonel Jackson remained at Fashoda until, after several months, his health was so broken by constant fever that he was invalided home for a short period of recuperation....

The disputes between France and England about the valley of the Upper Nile were terminated, as far as material cause was concerned, by an Agreement, signed at London on the 21st of March, 1899, by Lord Salisbury and M. Cambon. The Declaration limiting the respective Spheres of Influence of the two Powers took the form of an addition to the IVth Article of the Niger Convention concluded in the precious year.... Its practical effect is to reserve the whole drainage system of the Nile to England and Egypt, and to engage that France shall have a free hand, so far as those Powers are concerned, in the rest of Northern Africa not yet occupied by Europeans west of the Nile Valley. This stupendous partition of half a continent by two European Powers could scarcely be expected to excite the enthusiasm of the rest. Germany was, however, soothed by the promise of the observance of the 'Open Door' policy upon the Upper Nile. Italy, protesting meekly, followed Germany. Russia had no interest in this quarter. France and England were agreed. The rest were not consulted: and the Declaration may thus be said to have been recognized by the world in general.... Great Britain and Egypt, upon the other hand, have secured a territory which, though smaller, is nevertheless of enormous extent, more fertile, comparatively easy of access, practically conquered, and containing the waterway of the Nile....

It only remained to discuss the settlement made between the conquerors of the Soudan. Great Britain and Egypt had moved hand in hand up the great river, sharing, though unequally, the cost of the war in men and money. The prize belonged to both. The direct annexation of the Soudan by Great Britain would have been an injustice to Egypt. Moreover, the claim of the conquerors to Fashoda and other territories rested solely on the former rights of Egypt.... [In] the Soudan Agreement by Great Britain and Egypt, published on 7th of March, 1899 ... Great Britain and Egypt [agreed to] rule the country together. The allied conquerors have become the joint-possessors.

Churchill, Winston S. *The River War: An Historical Account of the Reconquest of the Sudan*. Vol. 2. London: Longmans, 1900. Pp. 302-312, 314-321.

AFRIKANER NATIONALISM AND THE BOER WAR

▶ **Boer Commando**

The Boers or Afrikaners are Europeans of Dutch descent in South Africa. Afrikaner nationalism has been a major shaping force in African developments since the nineteenth century.

The Netherlands acquired the Cape of Good Hope from Portugal in 1652, and settled *boers* or farmers there to grow food to supply their passing ships. Great Britain seized the Cape from the Netherlands during the Napoleonic wars to prevent the French from establishing a base there, and gained permanent possession of the Cape Colony in 1815 from the Dutch for six million pounds. English settlers then began to settle in southern Africa.

The relationship between the British authorities and the Boers was strained throughout the nineteenth century, because the British emancipated the Boers' slaves in 1834 and Britain's more liberal policy towards Africans. Between 1835 and 1837, about 10,000 Boers embarked on a Great Trek to free themselves from British control. They walked out of British-controlled territories to settle in lands beyond the Vaal and Orange Rivers. Britain however maintained that Boers continued to be British subjects and refused to recognize the independence of the two Boer republics, Orange Free State and Transvaal. The discovery of diamonds in the region between the Vaal and Orange Rivers in 1867 and gold a little later in southern Transvaal exacerbated the Anglo-Boer rivalry. A gold rush brought over 100,000 *Uitlanders* or foreigners, mainly Britons, to the gold fields in southern Transvaal, who provided most of the capital and technology for gold mining. Over 1.2 million ounces of gold was mined in the Transvaal in 1892.

The Transvaal government raised most of its revenue through heavy taxes imposed on gold mining, but refused to provide essential services to the Uitlanders in the mining towns, and denied them citizenship until they had established residence in that state for ten years. Paul Kruger (1825-1904), president of the Transvaal since 1883, also refused to join a customs union with self-governing but English dominated Cape Colony and Natal. By 1899, the British government was convinced that Kruger was planning to drive the British out of South Africa. Kruger confirmed British fears by joining with the Orange Free State and declaring war on Britain.

The South African or Boer War lasted from 1899 to 1902. The 25,000 British forces at the start were outnumbered by over 60,000 Boer troops, called commandos, and suffered humiliating defeats. The situation was quickly reversed with the arrival of General Frederick Roberts (1832-1914), his chief-of-staff General Herbert Kitchener (conqueror of the Sudan), and over a quarter million reinforcements from Britain, Canada, Australia, India, and many colonies. Although British forces conquered both Transvaal and Orange Free State by the end of 1900, Boer guerrillas continued to resist. After Kitchener built blockhouses, burned farms, and herded 120,000 Boer non-combatants into concentration camps, they finally submitted in 1902.

By the Treaty of Vereeniging, the Boers accepted British sovereignty, but were promised elections, self government and money to rebuild farms. In 1909, the two former republics and two British colonies formed the Union of South Africa, a self-governing dominion of the British Empire. Afrikaans (Dutch with local modifications) and English were declared equal official languages, and the franchise was granted to all adult white males. Black South Africans, Asians, and people of mixed descent were denied the vote.

Deneys Reitz, the son of a prominent Boer family, joined a commando unit as soon as war broke out. After the war, he went into exile, returning after self government had been restored. His war memoirs, quoted below in part, paint a vivid picture of the simple and self reliant lives of the Boers, the tragedy of their struggle, and the inevitable outcome.

QUESTIONS:

1) What sort of man and leader was President Paul Kruger?
2) How did local support help the Boer commandos?
3) What led the Boers to surrender in the end?

[When the Boer War broke out in 1899] I was seventeen years old and thus too young to be enrolled as a burgher. President Kruger himself solved this difficulty for me. One morning when I was at the government buildings, I met him and my father in the corridor and I told the President that the Field-Cornet's office had refused to enroll me for active service. The old man looked me up and down for a moment and growled, "Piet Joubert says the English are three to one-- Will you stand me good for three of them?" I answered boldly, "President, if I get close enough I'm good for three with one shot." He gave a hoarse chuckle at my youthful conceit and, turning to my father, asked how old I was. When he heard my age he said, "Well then, Mr. State Secretary, the boy must go--I started fighting earlier than that," and he took me straight to the Commandant-General's room nearby, where Piet Joubert in person handed me a new Mauser carbine and a bandolier of ammunition, with which I returned home pleased and proud.

I saw a good deal of the President in these days as I used to go with my father to his house on the outskirts of the town, where they discussed state matters while I sat listening. The president had an uncouth, surly manner, and he was the ugliest man I have ever seen, but he had a strong rugged personality which impressed all with whom he came in contact. He was religious

to a degree, and on Sundays he preached in the queer little Dopper church he had built across the street, where I sometimes heard him.

There was Mrs. Kruger too, whom I often saw with her pails in the yard, for she kept dairy cows and sold milk to the neighbours. Once she brought us coffee while we were looking at a picture of the statue of her husband that was being set up on Church Square. The President was shown dressed like an elder of the church in a top hat, and the old lady suggested that the hat should be hollowed out and filled with water to serve as a drinking fountain for the birds. My father and I laughed heartily on our way home at her simplicity, but we agreed that it was decent of her to have thought of such a thing....

[More than two years later, in 1901, Reitz was serving with a unit under general Smuts and en route to attack a British position in Cape Colony.] Our road took us through rough country, and he [Smuts] ordered every man to go on foot to spare the horses. The English made no attempt to come after us, their orders apparently being to hold the roads and exits, so we trekked all day, seeking to turn their extreme right flank. Throughout the expedition into the Cape we had no difficulty in getting local sympathizers to act as guides, and on this occasion a young farmhand volunteered to lead us. He picked his way so unerringly that towards nightfall we had not only succeeded in finding the end of the British line, but had even got round behind them, and we could see the town of Dordrecht in the distance. We must have covered nearly thirty miles since setting out that morning, but as we were not yet out of danger of being headed back, we trudged all through the night, with only an occasional halt, mostly along steep mountain paths, wet and slippery from the rains.

When daybreak came our young guide had done his work with such skill that we were well beyond the cordon, and there now lay before us the long mountain chain of the Stormbergen, stretching east to west as far as the eye could see. He told us that we could cross almost anywhere so he was allowed to return home, and we made for a large farm lying at the foot of the range, where we turned our horses into the fields, and set about preparing a meal, once again hoping to spend the rest of the forenoon in sleep, for we had been on the move for twenty-four hours. But we had scarcely slaughtered a few sheep and broken our fast, when the well-known cry of "Opsaal! Opsaal!" sent us scurrying to fetch our unfortunate animals, for coming down the slopes was a long column of English horses making our way. Nearby ran a pass up the mountains, and as it seemed clear of troops, we made for it, and in an hour stood on the top of the Stormbergen, with the enemy force slewed round and following us....

[Though the following days saw many skirmishes with the pursuing British forces, the Boers escaped capture.] We rode out of the mountain country into the open plains of the Karroo. In the face of great odds we had broken across the successive barriers placed in our way, and although we had still many troubles to meet, the English had failed to turn us back. We now slowly marauded southwards. At the village of Maraisburg a large number of troops was waiting for us, but General Smuts skillfully led the commando through at night without firing a shot, and we continued unmolested.

During this time the Rijk Section [Reitz's unit] came into its own. Our share in the attack on the [British] 17th Lancers had enhanced our reputation, and in this open country our services as scouts were in great demand, so we ranged far ahead, hospitably entertained by the Dutch-speaking population, and philosophically tolerated by the English farmers with whom we came in contact....

On the surface [in early 1902] things looked prosperous. Five months ago we had come into this western country hunted like outlaws, and today we practically held the whole area from the Olifants to the Orange River four hundred miles away, save for small garrison towns here and there, whose occupants could not show themselves beyond the range of their forts without the risk of instant capture at the hands of the rebel patrols told off to watch them, while we roamed all the territory at will. We enjoyed a number of successes which the British probably regarded as minor incidents, but which our men looked upon as important victories....

Unfortunately, while matters stood thus well with us, the situation in the two Republics up north was far otherwise. Lord Kitchener's relentless policy of attrition was slowly breaking the hearts of the commandos. We had been out of touch with them for so long that we did not realize the desperate straits to which they had come, and our men judged the position from our own more favourable circumstances. Personally, I was not quite so sanguine, for, from such English newspapers as had come my way, I had learned something of the true state of affairs....

Towards the end of April [1902] I rode out one afternoon with Dunker and Nicolas Swart to snipe at the English posts on the other side of O'Okiep, and, as we were returning to our horses, we saw a cart coming along the road from the south with a white flag waving over the hood. Galloping up, we found two British officers inside, who said they were the bearers of a dispatch from Lord Kitchener [now commander-in-chief of British forces]. We took them to Concordia....

When we reached Concordia, General Smuts took them inside his house and remained closeted with them for some time, after which he came out and walked away into the veld by himself deep in thought. We knew then that there was grave news.

That evening he showed me the dispatch. It was a communication from Lord Kitchener to say that a meeting between the English and Boer leaders was to be held at Vereeniging, on the banks of the Vaal River, with a view to discussing peace terms, and he was summoned to attend....

General Smuts set to work at once. Next morning a messenger was sent into O'Okiep, to advise the garrison that both sides were to refrain from active military operations while the Congress lasted....

The day after that the commandos came in from the outlying posts to say good-bye to their leader. The men paraded before the court house, each man sitting his horse, rifle at thigh, while General Smuts addressed them. He briefly told them of the object of his going, and asked them to be prepared for disappointment if need be, but there were only cheers and shouts of courage, as they pressed from all sides to wish him well....

It took us the better part of a week to reach Kroonstad in the northern Free State, where Lord Kitchener was to meet us. Soon after our arrival he rode up to the station on a magnificent black charger, followed by a numerous suite, including turbaned Pathans in Eastern costume with gold-mounted scimitars.

His retinue waited outside whilst he came into our compartment to talk. He was anxious to bring the war to a close, for he referred again and again to the hopelessness of our struggle, telling us that he had four hundred thousand troops in South Africa against our eighteen thousand. He said he was prepared to let the burghers retain their horses and saddles in recognition of the fight that they had made, and that the British government would help to rebuild the destroyed farmhouses, the burning of which he defended on military grounds....

Before going he told us that we were to proceed to the eastern Transvaal, to find General Botha, and that the conference at Vereeniging would only take place after that.... [After several days' travel under British escort] we reached a point where a party of horsemen sent by General Botha was awaiting us. They had brought spare horses, so we left the cart with the troopers, and, striking across the country, travelled for two days over bare and deserted plains, to the place where the Commandant-General was expecting us. Here about three hundred men were assembled. They were delegates from every commando in the eastern Transvaal, come to elect representatives to the Peace Congress to be held at Vereeniging, and nothing could have proved

more clearly how nearly the Boer cause was spent than these starving, ragged men, clad in skins or sacking, their bodies covered with sores, from lack of salt and food, and their appearance was a great shock to us, who came from the better-conditioned forces in the Cape. Their spirit was undaunted, but they had reached the limit of physical endurance, and we realized that, if these haggard, emaciated men were the pick of the Transvaal Commandos, then the war must be irretrievably lost.

Food was so scarce that General Botha himself had only a few strips of leathery biltong [dried meat] to offer us, and he said that, but for the lucky chance of having raided a small herd of cattle from the British a fortnight before, he would have been unable to hold the meeting at all....

Next day the elections were held ... [and] by evening the complicated balloting was finished, and some thirty delegates elected.

Next morning the gathering dispersed, the men riding off on their hungry-looking horses to rejoin their distant units, while General Botha and the successful deputies started back for the English block-house line.

We arrived here by the following evening. The troops supplied us with food, for we were famished, and we now returned along the block-houses to Standerton, the soldiers everywhere standing respectfully to attention as our tattered cavalcade went by....

The British had prepared a large tented camp for our reception, and almost the first man I saw as we entered was my father, shaggy and unkempt, but strong and well, and our greeting after so long a parting was deep and heartfelt.

And now the delegates came in from the rest of the Transvaal and from the Free State. Every leader of note was there....

I know little of the actual Peace Conference as I was not a delegate, but the outcome was a foregone conclusion. Every representative had the same disastrous tale to tell of starvation, lack of ammunition, horses, and clothing, and of how the great blockhouse system was strangling their efforts to carry on the war. Added to this was the heavy death-toll among the women and children, of whom twenty-five thousand had already died in the concentration camps, and the universal ruin that had overtaken the country.

Every homestead was burned, all crops and livestock destroyed, and there was nothing left but to bow to the inevitable.

After prolonged debates the conference suspended its sittings for a day, whilst General Botha, my father, General de la Rey and others went to Pretoria to conclude the final treaty with Lord Kitchener and Lord Milner. On their return peace was an accomplished fact.

Of the sting of defeat I shall not speak, but there was no whining or irresponsible talk. All present accepted the verdict stoically, and the delegates returned quietly to their respective commandos, to make known the terms of surrender.

Reitz, Deneys. *Boer Commando: An Afrikaner Journal of the Boer War*. New York: Sarpedon, 1993. Pp. 15-16, 188-189, 203, 272-274, 276-279.

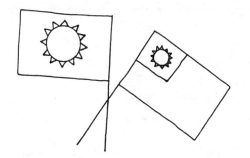

CHINA: VICTIM OF IMPERIALISM

▶ **Flags of Sun Yat-sen's Chinese Republic**

For a century between 1842 and 1943 China suffered the humiliation of unequal treaties dictated by Western nations. When China attempted to stop British merchants from bringing in opium Great Britain defeated China in the First Opium War, 1839-1842. Subsequent defeats by Britain, France, and Japan forced the Chinese to accept opium, cede territories, open ports, and exempt Westerners in China from Chinese laws. By 1900, Western powers and Japan had divided China into their respective spheres of influence.

In 1900 Peking and parts of northern China was convulsed by the Boxer Rebellion, instigated by frustrated and ignorant peasants and vagrants who believed that their shadow boxing and magic made them invulnerable to Western guns. They to end foreign imperialism by killing Westerners and Chinese Christians. Tragically, the power-crazed and xenophobic Dowager Empress Tz'u-hsi, believed in the Boxers' claims. She declared war on the whole Western world, and allowed the Boxers to besiege the Western diplomatic compounds and terrorize Peking and nearby regions. Chinese diplomats abroad declared her orders illegal and maintained friendly international relations and most provincial officials protected foreigners. However it took an joint expeditionary force of six European nations, the United States, and Japan to relieve the siege of the diplomatic quarters in Peking. The lifting of the siege was accompanied by massacres, looting, and destruction by the soldiers of the relieving powers.

The first section of this reading is an eye-witness account by an English officer who participated in the relief expedition. He describes the carnage Western soldiers inflicted in China, and the humiliation and crushing financial burden imposed on the defeated Chinese. He predicted that: "Once [they] have raised their army to anything like the proportions of those of European countries, they will then for the first time, but finally, be able to hold "China for the Chinese" against the rest of the world, as the Japanese have succeeded in doing with Japan."

Sun Yat-sen (1866-1925) was a Western educated Chinese who dedicated his life to overthrowing the moribund Ch'ing dynasty and making China into a modern democratic nation. He enunciated the Three People's Principles of nationalism, democracy, and livelihood in place of the outdated monarchial ideals. He also founded the Kuomintang or Nationalist party. In 1911 Sun's followers began a revolution that overthrew the Ch'ing dynasty and established Asia's first republic. Parts of Sun's lectures on the Principle of Nationalism, in which he analyses China's abysmal position, forms the remainder of this reading. Sun, however, admired the West for its advances. He dreamed of China accepting the best from the West and envisioned a powerful modern China that would play a positive role in the world and help to uplift other oppressed peoples.

QUESTIONS:

1) How had troops of the Western powers marching on Peking treated the Chinese?
2) How had the unequal treaties damaged China's economy?
3) What did Sun Yat-sen tell the Chinese people to do to save themselves?

The country between Tonku and Tientsin was a dead level swampy plain.... It was a track of graves and desolation. All the houses on the way lay in ruins. There were no signs of human life along the route, except where Russian pickets were guarding the railway.

Here one got the first touch of that feeling which intensified as we advanced--a palpable breath of blasting desolation that seemed to have passed over the land. It was a strange feeling passing through what had evidently been a densely populated country, but what was now the scene of tenantless houses, often roofless, frequently with charred walls, empty doors and windows, that gave them a skull-like appearance to the imagination.... The hoofs of our horses sounded loud in the profound death-like stillness of the empty streets.... We traversed miles of those empty streets without seeing anybody until we neared the outskirts of the town, where here and there a few decrepit and very old men and women were to be seen peeping timorously from the houses....

As we went along, we passed the bodies of many Chinese lying on the wayside, or on the fringe of the fields of high *kowliang* or millet on either side. The first soldiers that we came across were some French stragglers in the rear of their forces. As we came upon them they had just espied a Chinaman with a bag on his back in a field close by. They shouted to him, and beckoned to him to come to them. He was evidently afraid to do so, and one of the soldiers ran towards him and pulled him by the pigtail, when he was loaded up and made to carry some of the Frenchman's baggage. He was an old man and protested volubly. But the prick of a bayonet made him quickly realize that his protestations would be of no avail....

Our whole intercourse with the Chinese has been neither honest, serious, nor reputable. It is only the slang word "rot" that epitomises our Pharisaical conduct....

Now to my mind, the events of the past year have fittingly climaxed the history of our contact. The Viceroy of Canton in 1847 said that "if a mutual tranquility is to subsist between the Chinese and the foreigners, the common feelings of mankind as well as the just principles of Heaven must be considered and conformed with". As far as sustaining a mutual tranquility is concerned between China and the foreign Powers, we have now reached a point in which we have outraged every "common feeling of mankind". We have fired on their forts, captured them without any declaration of war; we have (and I speak of the common action of the Allies) initiated a campaign by massacring a shipload of helpless coolies; from that we have progressed through their country up to its capital, disregarding all the rules and customs of civilized warfare as laid down in the regulations of the Hague Conference. We have violated their temples and their shrines, we have outraged their women, driving them to such a pitch of exasperation and despair that they have committed suicide in thousands. We have sent marauding excursions throughout the land encircling Pekin, and, finally, we have imposed the overpowering burden of indemnity, not alone on the actual offenders, but on the whole of the law-abiding population of China, who had nothing whatever to do with the outrages on foreigners and on the people of those provinces whose viceroys were most friendly to us. And thus the climax is reached of this awful history of the vulgar aggression of the West against the East.

* * * * *

China has become the colony of all the Powers, but we Chinese still think of ourselves as the "semi-colony" of the Powers. Chinese use the term "semi-colony" to comfort ourselves. In fact the economic oppression the Powers have imposed on China is greater than the oppression suffered by their respective colonies. For example Korea is a Japanese colony and Annam [Vietnam] is a French colony. This makes the Koreans slaves of Japan and the Annamese slaves of France.... But what is the position of us Chinese? Most of us do not know that we are actually worse off than the Koreans and Annamese ... because China is a semi-colony we are the slaves of all nations that have treaties with China.... By comparison it is better to be slaves of one nation, because in that position, when you suffer from flood or other natural disasters, the colonizing nation will regard it as a duty of masters to bring relief to the stricken colony.... However when China suffers from natural disasters, no nation regards it a duty to relieve its suffering.... Thus China is in worse position than Korea or Annam. Therefore it is better to be slave to one nation than to be slave to all.... I have coined a term from chemistry for China's position, it is that of a "hyper-colony," that is, it is even lowlier than a colony....

Now the Powers use economic means to oppress China, using control of the maritime customs as weapon.... Before China was opened to international commerce, its handicraft industries supplied its needs and it was largely self-sufficient. According to our ancient custom, men farmed the land and women wove cloths.... Then western textiles entered China and because of low customs duties [imposed by the Powers], western machine made cloths could sell for lower prices than Chinese handloomed cloths. Thus China's handicraft textile industry was destroyed and many people became unemployed....

Since China was opened to international commerce, the amount of her imports has exceeded her exports, increasing inexorably. According to statistics, ten years ago imports into China exceeded exports by two hundred million dollars; however the most recent report said that in 1921 imports exceeded exports by 500 million dollars. This is an increase of two and half times in ten years.... In addition to low customs duties the Powers oppress China through their banks in China ... which take business from Chinese banks, and they also print and circulate currency in China....

Chinese goods are carried overseas mainly in foreign owned ships. Foreign ships have moreover largely taken over the carrying trade along China's coast and rivers....

China's economy is further damaged from lands it lost through cessions and concessions, for example Hong Kong, Taiwan [ceded to Britain and Japan respectively], Shanghaim Tientsin, Dalien, and Hankow [cities where Western nations had concessions]. The Powers annually collect at least 200 million dollars in taxes from Chinese who live under their control....

Nationals of Western Powers also take advantage of the unequal treaties between their countries and China in unfair economic competition with Chinese. The monetary value of their gains is difficult to calculate. Take the [Japanese owned] South Manchurian Railroad Company for example. Its annual profit is over 50 million dollars. One can deduce from this company alone that the total annual profit of all foreign companies in China is at least in the hundreds of millions of dollars....

In future we Chinese must find means to revive our national spirit. Only if we revive our national spirit can we successfully resist foreign political and economic oppression, avoid enslavement and survive into future millennia.... Heaven has not in past destroyed our 400 million Chinese people. If the Chinese nation does not survive in future, we will only have ourselves to blame....

Our present problem is how to revive our national spirit.... We have seen that China's decline is because of the decline of our national spirit.... That is why our race was conquered and ruled for over two hundred years [by the Manchus]. We became slaves of the Manchus, now we are the slaves of the Powers, an even worse fate.... Thus if we want to save China, we must revive Chinese nationalism....

Foreigners often refer to the Chinese nation as a bowl of loose sand. [They say] Chinese have no concept of nationalism, no cohesion, and are just like loose sand.... But as I had said before we Chinese have very deep commitment to family and clan.... When two Chinese strangers meet and establish that they are of the same surname or from the same clan they become very warm towards each other. We need to expand these concepts from clan to nation. To revive nationalism we must expand our small group loyalty to a very large group and forge a unity among this group.... Once we realize our strength through unity, we four hundred million [Chinese] must unite and strive together to revitalize our nation. United we can succeed whatever the obstacles....

We must learn from foreign nations and strive to catch up rather than just follow. In the sciences we can vault over two hundred years of others' achievements.... We now know we must follow the flow of the world, learn where others are better and strive to outdo them.... Japan is a good example. The Japanese were much behind the Chinese in the past and learned from China. Recently Japan began to learn from Europe and the United States. In only a few decades she has become one of the world's great powers. I believe that Chinese are not inferior to Japanese in talent and ability. We should be able to learn from Europe and the United States with more success than the Japanese have.... Then China can become a leading world power....

If China succeeds, we will not just recover our national greatness, we will also discharge a great responsibility to the world community ... by not behaving as the great Powers have done towards us ... but by aiding other weak nations to resist ... and overcome imperialism. Only then can China and the world be at peace. But first we need to revive our national spirit and reestablish the rightful place of our nation. We must establish morality as the base of the new world order ... this is our mission, the mission of 400 million Chinese. Every Chinese must shoulder a share of this responsibility. This is the spirit of our nationalism.

Lynch, George. *The War of the Civilizations, Being the Record of a "Foreign Devil's" Experiences with the Allies in China*. London: Longman, 1901. Pp. 19-20, 24-26, 299-300. Sun, Yat-sen. *Tsung-li chuan ch'i*. Ed. Hu Han-min. Vol. 1.1: *San-min Chu-i, Min-chu chi-i* [Lectures on Nationalism]. Shanghai: Min-chi Publishing, n.d. Pp. 21-24, 27-28, 43, 57, 64, 69, 82. Edited and translated by Jiu-Hwa Lo Upshur.

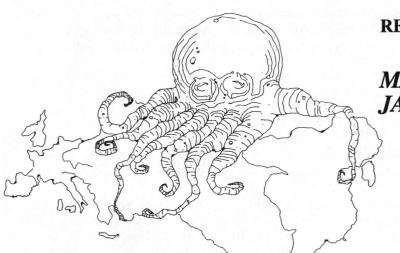

MAKERS OF MODERN JAPAN

▶ **Japanese Propaganda Image of Russian Imperialism**

Between 1603 and 1868, a dynasty of military commanders called the Tokugawa Shogunate ruled Japan. Fearing European influences, the Tokugawa shoguns closed Japan to the Western world, except for two Dutch ships that could dock at Nagasaki annually. Thus while the Western world made amazing advances in the sciences and technology, isolated Japan stood still. The Tokugawa shogunate maintained an outdated feudal political order, and a rigidly stratified social system with the samurai on top and the despised though prosperous merchants at the bottom.

In 1853, the United States forced Japan to open its doors by a show of naval force. The discredited shogunal government was overthrown in a coup d'état in 1868, engineered by dissatisfied young samurai from feudal domains hostile to the Tokugawas. It was called the Meiji Restoration because the new leaders "restored" the imperial dynasty to power in the person of a young emperor, who took the reign name of Meiji (r. 1868-1911), which means enlightened rule.

The dedicated Meiji-era leaders came from the samurai class. They inspired the disciplined Japanese citizens to toil and sacrifice for emperor and state. Under Meiji, Japan strove diligently to learn from the advanced Western nations in the areas of science, technology, government and legal systems, and above all military organization and methods. Thus modern Japan combines ancient traditions with Western institutions and ideas. Because of this, Japan alone in Asia was successfully evolved from a traditional feudal state to a great modern power.

This reading consists of vignettes from the lives of three Meiji-era leaders. Each played a major role in forging a new Japan and making it a great military power, successful in war and respected internationally. Although they initially intended chiefly to give Japan a place in the modern world, their successes inspired others to continue militarist and imperialist policies for Japan in the twentieth century.

Nogi Maresuke (1846-1911) was a distinguished general who fought in the Sino-Japanese War (1894-1895) and the Russo-Japanese War (1904-1905). He was also Governor-General of Taiwan, Japan's first colony, wrested from China in the Sino-Japanese War. In the tradition of the samurai he committed suicide in 1911 after Emperor Meiji's death.

Yamagata Arimoto (1838-1922) organized the Japanese army on the German model and made the military directly responsible only to the emperor. He was called the Wellington of Japan (after the English general who defeated Napoleon at the Battle of Waterloo). Like Wellington, Yamagata also served as prime minister.

Togo Heihachiro (1847-1934) was called the Nelson of Japan (after the British admiral who destroyed Napoleon's fleet at the Battle of Trafalgar) because he annihilated the Russian Baltic fleet at the Battle of Tsushima in 1905.

QUESTIONS:

1) Give examples of Nogi's love and care of men under his command.
2) How did Yamamoto's grandmother inspire patriotism in him?
3) What did Togo and his men achieve for Japan?

When Maresuke was only five or six years old, his father took him monthly to Sengaku Temple, the sacred burial-ground, where the famous fifty seven loyalists had disemboweled themselves, and thus perpetuated their names in the history of Japan. As the child toddled on, the father would tell him their loyal stories once every month. He was by nature a strict samurai, and was specially strict with diet. If the child said that he disliked a certain food, the father would let him take only that food for ten or twenty consecutive days. One day a raw egg was placed on a small dining table, and the child left it untouched.

"Look here!" exclaimed the father, in a temper: "a samurai should show neither liking nor disliking for any food. I'll soon make thee like it."

Instantly the father broke the egg, opened the child's mouth, and let him gulp it down. Ever since the child had shown no sign of disliking of any food....

[During the Satsuma Rebellion in 1877, a subordinate officer in major Nogi's regiment died in battle while carrying the regimental colors, causing its loss.] Since then Major Nogi had fought desperately and achieved wonders. When his leg was seriously wounded, he moved in a mat earth-carrier, and commanded his men with a drawn sword. In the midst of the Rebellion, he was promoted to the rank of lieutenant-colonel. Nevertheless he felt his great responsibility for the loss of the regimental colours; and, therefore, made an inquiry as to whether he should hand in his resignation; but the reply was, "It is unnecessary."

In the twenty seventh year of the Meiji era [1894], Maresuke, Commander of the First Brigade, left Tokyo for the front in China. When he attacked Kinshujo, he always stood at the head of his army, and directed it with vigour

and strength. The morale of his troops was thus stirred up; and after terrible struggles, he and his men eventually occupied Kinshujo. It was the end of November. The vast field of Manchuria was entirely covered with snow; and yet the commander himself never wore any special material for protection against cold.

Shortly after the occupation, a staff-officer received material for protection against cold from the father land. He at once brought one of them to the commander.

"What is it?" enquired the commander, looking at him.

"A material for protection against cold," replied the staff-officer, respectfully. "Pray put it on first. I'm intending to distribute them among the other officers."

"What about soldiers?" demanded Maresuke, anxiously.

"There is none for them, sir," replied the subordinate officer.

"How could the officers wear them, when the men have none to put on?"...

Maresuke left it untouched. All the other officers under him followed his noble example. The men soon heard of this.
Some were moved to tears....

[Under Nogi's command the Japanese defeated the Russians at the Battle of Port Arthur during the Russo-Japanese War after heavy casualties. He also lost both his sons during the campaign.] Hardly had Maresuke arrived at Shimbashi Station, when he proceeded straight to the Imperial Palace, where he was received in audience by the Emperor Meiji [who] thanked him for his long suffering and hardships, and graciously bestowed upon him a gold watch emblazoned with the Imperial crest and a large sum in a sealed paper-parcel. He received them and withdrew in a most reverential manner. He then handed the paper- parcel over to his aide-de-camp without examining its contents.

"It is wrong to receive the money only for myself," said Maresuke. "Distribute it among all the officers and men...."

[The aide-de-camp] hit upon a plan. Presently he called on the general.

"A gold watch to each officer?" he said to the victor respectfully.

"What about the non-commissioned officers and men?" inquired the conqueror, at once.

"Cash to every one of them?"

"All Right."

His Imperial bounty was thus distributed among them, and yet there was some left.

"The surplus money for the festival [for the souls] of your two sons?" suggested the aide-de-camp, considerately.

"Yes, Colonel," was the reply....

While the Emperor Meiji had been seriously ill, he had gone to the Imperial Court one hundred and thirty times in fifty six days to inquire after His Majesty's illness. On the thirtieth of July in the forty-fifth year of the Meiji era, the demise of the Emperor was at last announced.

On the thirteenth of September, the grand and sublime Imperial funeral procession began to proceed from the Imperial Palace, when Maresuke laid a table down in the direction of the Imperial Palace, set up the late Emperor's photograph upon it, and placed an offering in front of it. He then laid his and her [his wife's] death odes and his testament beside it, and immolated himself at the funeral of Meiji the Great. His wife, Shizuko, soon followed his example, and thus both the general and his wife followed the great Emperor to the other world.

According to his testament, he had always felt a deep sense of responsibility for the loss of his regimental colours during the Satsuma Rebellion; and ever since he had always been thinking of fulfilling it by killing himself; but Meiji the Great never allowed it; and his military achievements always prevented him from fulfilling it. Now that the Emperor Meiji had died, he at last discharged his ever haunted duty for the loss of the regimental colours.

* * * * *

Aritomo Yamagata was the son of a foot-soldier under the feudal lord of Choshu. During his childhood he lost his parents, and was then brought up by his grand-mother, who was a model of old samurai women....

Of all the Choshu young men, Arimoto, Hirobumi, and three other young men were sent to Kyoto as the students supported by the clan-government [of Choshu]. During his stay there, he constantly thought of his grand-mother, and took every opportunity to send a letter to her. On one occasion he bought a piece of silk-cloth, and forwarded it to her, as he thought that it might please her. Contrary to his expectations, however, he received a scolding letter, which ran as follows:

My dearest grandson,
In the busiest time of your study, if you constantly think of an old woman like me, your future will be utterly hopeless. I know that your present is a very considerate one; but I am not at all pleased with it. As I am praying every day that you may soon distinguish yourself and render great services to your feudal lord, you shall not think of me any more.

Aritomo read the letter carefully and felt ashamed.... After the lapse of over a year, he returned home, when his grand-mother talked with him cheerfully all night.

On the following day, she plunged into the river, which runs near his house, and died at the age of seventy seven. She left a brief note behind her: "If an old woman like me leans upon you, your resolution will become enervated. I, therefore, go to the other world, so that you may concentrate your mind and devote your life to the clan-services."

Haunted by her tragic death, Aritomo's loyal resolutions became much firmer than that of anyone else....

On the first of August in the twenty seventh year of Meiji [1894], Aritomo, President of the Privy Council, was appointed to the Commandership of the First Japanese Army. Since the beginning of the Chino-Japanese War, his army won every battle, and occupation followed occupation. After the occupation of Port Arthur, his army was rapidly advancing towards Peking, when he began to suffer from his chronic catarrh of the stomach and bowels [and became bedridden]....

Suddenly Arimoto descried a body of horsemen, who were escorting some personages and approaching the quarters. He ordered his attendant to bring his military uniform, then put it on, and fastened the Grand Cordon of the Rising Sun on his chest. He then sat erect on his bed. They were the three Imperial messengers, who were despatched by the Emperor to inquire after his illness. After cordial greetings, the chief Imperial messenger said solemnly:--

"His Imperial Majesty the Emperor is exceedingly anxious for your safety, and you are, therefore, commanded to leave the quarters and to return home."

At this Aritomo was moved to tears.

"Is it not the momentous time," exclaimed Aritomo, resolutely, "when even the Emperor himself repaired to the head-quarters at Hiroshima, and by night and by day is personally controlling the military affairs? It is, therefore, a matter of course that I should die for the Emperor and the country to requite his exceptional kindness. I am firmly resolved to die in battle. Let me, therefore, die in the Manchurian field. Pray report for me to the Emperor, sirs, that my innermost desire is never to return home, unless and until we have captured the city of Peking."

"Should you ever happen to die," said the chief Imperial messenger, "your will not only offend the Emperor, but may also dishearten the spirit of the whole army. I should, therefore, suggest that you should shift your sick-bed to inside of a warship."

"A thousand pities!" exclaimed Aritomo, facing his subordinate officers [as he yielded to the Emperor's wishes].

* * * * *

Impelled by her vital interests, Japan had at last declared war against Russia [in 1904]. Since then, Japan, contrary to the world's expectations, won victories on land and on sea. Driven to despair, the giant Russia at last despatched her Baltic fleet of 37 warships for the invasion of little Japan. The final and decisive naval battle was expected in either the Sea of Japan or the Pacific Ocean.

Heihachiro [Togo] was then a Vice-Admiral and the Commander-in-chief of the Combined Japanese Squadrons. The taciturn sailor firmly resolved a plan in his mind and was wistfully waiting for the advent of the so called invincible fleet. He despatched the lookout ship "Shinano-maru" to let her watch their movements.

At four o'clock in the morning of the twenty seventh day of May in the thirty eighth year of Meiji [1905], the lookout ship descried black smoke on the horizon; and at once reported them to the flag-ship "Mikasa." Heihachiro stood mute with his staff-officers on board the flagship, and peered through his marine-glass, but nothing could be seen. He stood speechless, and was deep in thought. Suddenly he called to the signal man, and sternly ordered him to signal the following message to all the Japanese war-ships:- "The rise of fall of the Empire depends entirely upon this battle. Do your utmost, every one of you!"

Deeply impressed with this important message, every officer began to take his allotted post with full vigour and strength.

"Remember!" cried one of the officers: "the fate of our Empire depends upon this battle."

"For the Emperor," responded another officer, "and for our beloved country, we must fight to the end of our lives."

At two o'clock in the afternoon, the Japanese main squadron began to move south-westwards from Okinoshima; and the other squadrons also appeared to fight with the mighty Baltic fleet. At the distance of 6,000 meters, the signalman of the flagship signalled to all the Japanese warships:

"All of you shall begin fighting!"

Instantly began the unprecedentedly great naval battle in the Sea of Japan. In three-quarters of an hour's time the Baltic fleet were fatally damaged. Some were sent to the bottom, some caught fires; and the others began to flee. At night the Japanese torpedo boats began their activities and sent their rival warships to the bottom. Early the next morning the silent but dauntless Heihachiro at last caused the Commander-in-chief of the Baltic fleet and his staff-officers to surrender.

As the outcome of this unprecedented naval victory, the thorough-going Togo and his sailors destroyed twenty Russian warships, and captured five of them. Meanwhile the Russian casualty numbered no less than 3,500 killed and wounded and 6,114 captured; whereas Japan lost only three torpedo-boats and sustained the casualty of a little more than 800 killed and wounded.

After the war, Heihachiro, the idol of the nation, was promoted to the rank of Admiral and created a Count.... He is now known as the Nelson of Japan.

Matsumoto, Tadashige. *Stories of Fifty Japanese Heroes*. Tokyo: Koseikaku, 1929. Pp. 349, 351-352, 357-358, 393-394, 397, 406-407, 410-411.

THEODORE ROOSEVELT AND AMERICAN IMPERIALISM

Theodore Roosevelt's colorful life (1858-1919) was dedicated to public service of the United States. As assistant secretary of the Navy in 1898, when the Spanish-American War broke out, he raised and commanded the "Roosevelt's Rough Riders" and campaigned in Cuba. He became Republican vice-president in 1901 and succeeded to the presidency in the same year upon the assassination of President McKinley. He was elected president in his own right in 1904.

In an era when European empire building reached its apogee, and when Japan had also enthusiastically joined the imperial race, Roosevelt advocated a strong navy, so that the United States, too, could play a global role. This was also an era in which Darwin's theory of "the survival of the fittest" was applied to competition among cultures, peoples, and nations. Called Social Darwinism, it explained why some nations became stronger while others declined. Going one step further, some claimed it justified strong, or "superior" nations controlling and dominating weak or "inferior" ones.

Roosevelt subscribed to the Social Darwinist theory and became the embodiment of American imperialism. He exemplified his beliefs: a fanatic for "manly" activities, he was an active sportsman and hunter, rode to battle in Cuba, and participated in the digging of the Panama Canal. He believed that the United States should play an active role in global affairs and in 1905 mediated the peace treaty that ended the Russo-Japanese War. He received the Nobel Peace Prize for his peace-making efforts. Convinced that the United States had a mission to spread the benefits of its civilization to other shores, Roosevelt advocated the annexation of the Philippines as an American duty. Similarly he praised British rule as beneficial to India and Egypt. Rudyard Kipling, a contemporary British poet and journalist, was a kindred spirit: he cheered on the United States to assume the "white man's burden" and annex the Philippines. In domestic policy Roosevelt introduced laws that regulated trusts and monopolies, and established the first national parks to preserve and manage wild life. The "teddy" bear was named after him.

The following is from a famous speech Roosevelt gave in Chicago in 1899, titled "The Strenuous Life." He called on Americans to live up to his ideal of a manly life and fulfill their imperial responsibility of uplifting less fortunate peoples. He also warned that if Americans failed, others more virile would take place, while the United States would sink to the ignominy of have-been empires like China and Spain.

QUESTIONS:

1) Why is it bad for individuals and nations to be idle and slothful?

2) Why is an active and strenuous life good?
3) What are the international duties of the United States?

I wish to preach, not the doctrine of ignoble ease, but the doctrine of the strenuous life, the life of toil and effort, of labor and strife; to preach that highest form of success which comes, not to the man who desires merely easy peace, but to the man who does not shrink from danger, from hardship, or from bitter toil, and who out of these wins the splendid ultimate triumph.

A life of slothful ease, a life of that peace which springs merely from lack either of desire or of power to strive after great things, is as little worthy of a nation as of an individual. I only ask that what every self-respecting American demands from himself and from his sons shall be demanded of the American nation as a whole....

We ... cannot, if we would, play the part of China, and be content to rot by inches in ignoble ease within our borders, taking no interest in what goes on beyond them ... heedless of the higher life, the life of aspiration, of toil and risk, busying ourselves only with the wants of our bodies for the day, until suddenly we should find, beyond a shadow of question, what China has already found, that in this world the nation that has trained itself to a career of unwarlike and isolated ease is bound, in the end, to go down before other nations which have not lost the manly and adventurous qualities. If we are to be a really great people, we must strive in good faith to play a great part in the world. We cannot avoid meeting great issues. All that we can determine for ourselves is whether we shall meet them well or ill. In 1898 we could not help being brought face to face with the problem of war with Spain. All we could decide was whether we should shrink like cowards from the contest, or enter into it as beseemed a brave and high-spirited people; and, once in, whether failure or success should crown our banners. So it is now. We cannot avoid the responsibilities that confront us in Hawaii, Cuba, Porto [sic] Rico, and the Philippines. All we can decide is whether we shall meet them in a way that will redound to the national credit, or whether we shall make of our dealings with these new problems a dark and shameful page in our

history. To refuse to deal with them at all merely amounts to dealing with them badly....

We cannot sit huddled within our own borders and avow ourselves merely an assemblage of well-to-do hucksters who care nothing for what happened beyond. Such a policy would defeat even its own end; for as the nations grow to have ever wider and wider interests, and are brought into closer and closer contact, if we are to hold our own in the struggle for naval and commercial supremacy, we must build up our power without our own borders. We must build the isthmian [Panama] canal, and we must grasp the points of vantage which will enable us to have our say in deciding the destiny of the oceans of the East and the West.

So much for the commercial side. From the standpoint of international honor the argument is even stronger. The guns that thundered off Manila and Santiago left us echoes of glory, but they also left us a legacy of duty. If we drove out a medieval tyranny only to make room for savage anarchy, we had better not have begun the task at all. It is worse than idle to say that we have no duty to perform, and can leave to their fates the islands we have conquered. Such a course would be the course of infamy. It would be followed at once by utter chaos in the wretched islands themselves. Some stronger, manlier power would have to step in and do the work, and we would have shown ourselves weaklings, unable to carry to successful completion the labors that great and high-spirited nations are eager to undertake....

The army and the navy are the sword and the shield which this nation must carry if she is to do her duty among the nations of the earth--if she is not to stand merely as the China of the western hemisphere. Our proper conduct toward the tropic islands we have wrested from Spain is merely the form which our duty has taken at the moment....

In the West Indies and the Philippines alike we are confronted by most difficult problems. It is cowardly to shrink from solving them in the proper way; for solved they must be, if not by us, then by some stronger and more manful race....

The problems are different for the different islands. Porto Rico is not large enough to stand alone. We must govern it wisely and well, primarily in the interests of its own people. Cuba is, in my judgement, entitled ultimately to settle for itself whether it shall be an independent state or an integral portion of the mightiest republic. But until order and stable liberty are secured, we must remain in the island to insure them, and infinite tact, judgement, moderation, and courage must be shown by our military and civil representatives in keeping the island pacified, in relentlessly stamping out brigandage, in protecting all alike, and yet in showing proper recognition to the men who have fought for Cuban liberty. The Philippines offer a yet graver problem. Their population includes half-caste and native Christians, war-like Moslems, and wild pagans. Many of their people are utterly unfit for self-government, and show no signs of becoming fit. Others may in time become fit, but at present can only take part in self-government under a wise supervision, at once firm and beneficent. We have driven Spanish tyranny from the islands. If we now let it be replaced by savage anarchy, our work has been for harm and not for good. I have scant patience with those who fear to undertake the task of governing the Philippines, and who openly avow that they do fear to undertake it, or that they shrink from it because of the expense and trouble; but I have even scanter patience with those who make a pretence of humanitarianism to hide and cover their timidity, and who cant about "liberty" and the "consent of the governed," in order to excuse themselves for their unwillingness to play the part of men....

England's rule in India and Egypt has been of great benefit to England, for it has trained up generations of men accustomed to look at the larger and loftier side of public life. It has been of even greater benefit to India and Egypt. And finally, and most of all, it has advanced the cause of civilization. So, if we do our duty aright in the Philippines, we will add to that national renown which is the highest and finest part of national life, will greatly benefit the people of the Philippine Islands, and, above all, we will play our part well in the great work of uplifting mankind. But to do this work, keep ever in mind that we must show in a very high degree the qualities of courage, of honesty and of good judgement. Resistance must be stamped out. The first and all-important work to be done is to establish the supremacy of our flag....

When once we have put down armed resistance, when once our rule is acknowledged, then an even more difficult task will begin, for then we must see to it that the islands are administered with absolute honesty and with good judgement. If we let the public service of the islands be turned into the prey of the spoils politician, we shall have begun to tread the path which Spain trod to her own destruction. We must send out there only good and able men, chosen for their fitness, and not because of their partizan service, and those men must not only administer impartial justice to the natives and serve their own government with honesty and fidelity, but must show the utmost tact and firmness, remembering that, with such people as those with whom we are to deal with, weakness is the greatest of crimes, and that next to weakness comes lack of consideration for their principles and prejudices....

The twentieth century looms before us big with the fate of many nations. If we stand idly by ... then the bolder and stronger people will pass us by and will win for themselves the dominion of the world. Let us therefore boldly face the life of strife, resolute to do our duty well and manfully; resolute to uphold righteousness by deed and by word; resolute to be both honest and brave, to serve high ideals, yet to use practical methods. Above all, let us shrink from no strife, moral and physical, within or without the nation, provided we are certain that the strife is justified, for it is only through strife, through hard and dangerous endeavor, that we shall ultimately win the goal of true national greatness.

Roosevelt, Theodore. *The Strenuous Life, Essays and Addresses*. London: Alexander Mooring, 1910. Pp. 1, 6-7, 9-10, 15-20.

THE ASSASSINATION OF THE ARCHDUKE FRANZ FERDINAND, 28 JUNE 1914

World War I was ignited by the assassination of Archduke Franz Ferdinand, heir to the throne of the Austro-Hungarian empire, in Sarajevo, Bosnia, then a province of the empire. The assassin, Gavrilo Princip, belonged to the secret Serbian terrorist organization popularly known as the "Black Hand," which advocated the union of all southern Slavs under Serbia's leadership and resorted to assassinations to attain its goals. Many southern Slavs were subjects of the Austro-Hungarian Empire, and it was widely believed that Franz Ferdinand would grant them equality with Magyars and Germans when he became emperor. This would have dampened the south Slavs' desire to secede from the Austro-Hungarian Empire and join Serbia.

The plot to assassinate the Archduke was devised by Colonel Dragutin Dimitrijevic, who headed the intelligence service of the Serbian army, and was a principal figure in the Black Hand. Though there is no evidence that the Serbian government actively abetted the conspiracy, several high officials of the government, including the prime minister, were aware of the plot and took no measures to forestall it.

Austria-Hungary seized the opportunity offered by the assassination to punish Serbia, long a thorn in its side. After obtaining a "blank check" of unconditional support from its ally Germany, Vienna issued an ultimatum to Serbia demanding punishment of the guilty and assurances that the Serbs would not engage in future hostile actions. Parts of the ultimatum were so worded as to make its rejection inevitable. Thus Austria declared war on Serbia on 28 July 1914. Russia vacillated and then mobilized its forces along its border with both Austria-Hungary and Germany to back its ally Serbia and to preserve its influence in the Balkans. Germany, France, and Great Britain soon mobilized their forces as well to back their respective allies. By early August, the Great War was underway.

In the passage that follows, Borijove Jevtic, one of Princip's co-conspirators, writing for a New York newspaper a decade later, recalls the sequence of events on the fateful day in late June 1914 that ignited Word War I.

QUESTIONS:

1) What is the tone of this specifically Serbian account of the assassination?
2) Does the narrator seem to be a patriot?
3) How did circumstances play into the hands of the conspirators?

A tiny clipping from a newspaper mailed without comment from a secret band of terrorists in Zagreb, a capital of Croatia, to their comrades in Belgrade, was the torch which set the world afire with war in 1914. That bit of paper wrecked old proud empires. It gave birth to new, free nations.

I was one of the members of the terrorist band in Belgrade which received it and, in those days, I and my companions were regarded as desperate criminals. A price was on our heads. Today my little band is seen in a different light, as pioneer patriots. It is recognized that our secret plans hatched in an obscure café in the capital of old Serbia, have led to the independence of the new Yugoslavia, the united nation set free from Austrian domination.

The little clipping was from the *Srobobran*, a Croatian journal of limited circulation, and consisted of a short telegram from Vienna. This telegram declared that the Austrian Archduke Franz Ferdinand would visit Sarajevo, the capital of Bosnia, 28 June, to direct army manoeuvers in the neighboring mountains.

It reached our meeting place, the café called Zeatna Moruana, one night the latter part of April, 1914 .... We sat and read it. There was no advice nor admonition sent with it. Only four letters and two numerals were sufficient to make us unanimous, without discussion, as to what we should do about it. They were contained in that fateful date, 28 June.

How dared Franz Ferdinand, not only the representative of the oppressor but in his own person an arrogant tyrant, enter Sarajevo on that day? Such an entry was a studied insult.

28 June is a date engraved deeply in the heart of every Serb, so that the day has a name of its own. It is called *vidovnan*. It is the day on which the old Serbian kingdom was conquered by the Turks at the battle of Amselfelde in 1389. It is also the day on which in the second Balkan War [1913] the Serbian arms took glorious vengeance on the Turk for his old victory and for the years of enslavement.

That was no day for Franz Ferdinand, the new oppressor, to venture to the very doors of Serbia for a display of the force of arms which kept us beneath his heel.

Our decision was taken almost immediately. Death to the tyrant!

Then came the matter of arranging it. To make his death certain twenty-two members of the organization were selected to carry out the sentence. At first we thought we would choose the men by lot. But here Gavrilo Princip intervened. Princip is destined to go down in Serbian history as one of her greatest heroes. From the moment Ferdinand's death was decided upon he took an active leadership in its planning. Upon his advice we left the deed to members of our band who were in an around Sarajevo under his direction and that of Gabrinovic, a linotype operator on a Serbian newspaper. Both were regarded as capable of anything in the cause.

The fateful morning dawned. Two hours before Franz Ferdinand arrived in Sarajevo all the twenty-two conspirators were in their allotted positions, armed, and ready. They were distributed 500 yards apart over the whole route along which the Archduke must travel from the railroad station to the town hall.

When Franz Ferdinand and his retinue drove from the station they were allowed to pass the first two conspirators. The motor cars were driving too fast to make an attempt feasible and in the crowd were Serbians: throwing a grenade would have killed many innocent people.

When the car passed Gabrinovic, the compositor, he threw his grenade. It hit the side of the car, but Franz Ferdinand with presence of mind threw himself back and was uninjured. Several officers riding in his attendance were injured.

The cars sped to the Town Hall and the rest of the conspirators did not interfere with them. After the reception in the Town Hall General Potiorek, the Austrian Commander, pleaded with Franz Ferdinand to leave the city, as it was seething with rebellion. The Archduke was persuaded to drive the shortest way out of the city and to go quickly.

The road to the manoeuvres was shaped like the letter V, making a sharp turn at the bridge over the River Nilgacka. Franz Ferdinand's car could go fast enough until it reached this spot but here it was forced to slow down for the turn. Here Princip had taken his stand.

As the car came abreast he stepped forward from the curb, drew his automatic pistol from his coat and fired two shots. The first struck the wife of the Archduke, the Archduchess Sofia, in the abdomen. She was an expectant mother. She died instantly.

The second bullet struck the Archduke close to the heart.

He uttered only one work: "Sofia"--a call to his stricken wife. Then his head fell back and he collapsed. He died almost instantly.

The officers seized Princip. They beat him over the head with the flat of their swords. They knocked him down, they kicked him, scraped the skin from his neck with the edges of their swords, tortured him, all but killed him.

Then he was taken to the Sarajevo gaol. The next day he was transferred to the military prison and the round-up of his fellow conspirators proceeded, although he denied that he had worked with anyone.

He was confronted with Gabrinovic, who had thrown the bomb. Princip denied he knew him.

Others were brought in, but Princip denied the most obvious things.

The next day they put chains on Princip's feet, which he wore till his death.

His only sign of regret was the statement that he was sorry he had killed the wife of the Archduke. He had aimed only at her husband and would have preferred that any other bullet should have struck General Potiorek.

The Austrians arrested every known revolutionary in Sarajevo and among them, naturally, I was one. But they had no proof of my connection with the crime. I was placed in the cell next to Princip's, and when Princip was taken out to walk in the prison yard I was taken along as his companion.

Jevtic, Borijove. "The Murder of the Archduke Franz Ferdinand at Sarajevo, 28 June 1914." *New York World* (29 June 1924).

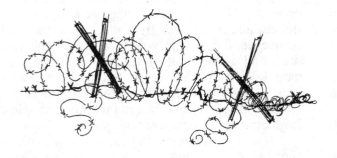

A "BLOODY PICNIC" ON THE WESTERN FRONT, 1916

When World War I began in August 1914, the European powers involved in it thought that the conflict would be a short one, won in decisive battles. In all countries, the general population greeted the outbreak of hostilities with patriotic enthusiasm and optimism about a quick victory. However, the war became a protracted struggle, with many battles and thousands of indecisive skirmishes.

Revolutionary changes in military technology since the late nineteenth century produced an array of new weapons, such as machine-guns, poison gas, tanks, and bombs dropped from airplanes and dirigibles. These weapons transformed military tactics and strategies; those belligerents who failed to take them into account paid a high price in lives lost. The machine-gun, for example, allowed defending armies to decimate the enemies' charging infantry. To avoid sustaining large casualties in futile charges both sides along the Western front dug vast underground trenches for their soldiers in the stalemated war.

The passage that follows, from the memoirs of Ernest Parker, a British infantryman, is a first-hand account of the terrors of modern warfare. Parker describes the First Battle of the Somme during July-November 1916. British and French forces were pitted against the German army along the Somme River in France. Both sides sustained huge casualties. The Allies won and considered it a turning point of the war.

QUESTIONS:

1) Is this account typical of what you know about combat during World War I?
2) Does anything about Ernest Parker's conduct seem heroic?
3) What part did chance play in Parker's survival?

The order came to advance and, passing from the communication trench into Delville Wood, we were surprised by the security of our transit. That morning the enemy had at last been compelled to retreat beyond the ridge and could no longer fire point-blank at the khaki figures scurrying between the trees. As we jumped over the old front line we saw inside it a number of light field guns which overnight had been emplaced to fire at the retreating Germans on the morning of the attack.

Getting through Delville Wood for the first time without casualties, we were swept by a tornado of angry explosions as we defiled into the open; but in spite of falling figures around us, we kept moving forward, choked by the acrid columns of smoke that climbed high into the air and from within a few yards of our feet. The shells arrived so suddenly that we had scarcely time to flinch, and without ducking pushed onwards to the ridge, where we scattered ourselves along a line of shell craters. Here we waited, looking back towards our former trenches in the Wood and noting the ease with which the Germans had been able to scourge it with machine-gun fire.

Under our eyes a R.H.A. [Royal Horse Artillery] gun team galloped through the wood, coming into action on the fringes of its leafless, shell-torn tree stumps. The German observers had seen it, too, for immediately the first round was fired, a covey of high explosives whirred over our heads, alighting accurately in the form of a cross with the squealing horses in the middle. Two of them were on their backs, hooves lashing the air, and immediately the surviving drivers dismounted to put them out of their pain. Cutting the traces, they galloped home with the remains of their team, leaving the gunners to blaze off over our heads.

The German artillery became irritated and, firing short, found our shell holes repeatedly, so that in a few minutes we lost our Captain and Company Sargeant-Major, as well as many men. We remained in this position, however, until nightfall, when we went forward to relieve the Rifle Brigade in their new line of trenches. We were surprised to find that their attack had taken so much ground, and we marched a long way before we reached a shallow trench in which the survivors were still hurriedly digging. When they had handed over, and were disappearing rearwards, hundreds of skilfully handled miners' shovels were already hard at work, fast tearing chunks of soil from the trench bottom. The Durhams secretly enjoyed digging, and although I laboriously did my share, it was always a source of satisfaction to my miner comrades that they could work more than twice as fast as a mere Southerner. After a while I was sent forward with my section to form a listening post, and a hundred yards in front of our new line I selected a large crater over the rim of which we took turns to keep watch in case the enemy should attempt to regain his lost ground under cover of the night....

As the dawn broke on 16 September the order to "Fix bayonets" was passed down the trench, and in the wan light we grimly took stock of one another. One young fellow of the recent draft had given a lot of trouble and was already well known for his sharp tongue, but now his face was green with fear so that in noticing him my spirits rose, and when the moment came I leapt among the first over the parapet.

For some minutes we ran onwards without a shot being fired, but gradually a machine-gun or two got to work, making some gaps in the line of running men. By the time our breath grew short the signal came to lie down. Then at the end of a brief pause we raced on, drawing a blizzard of bullets from numbers of fresh machine-guns. Now the fire began to increase in volume, tearing more and more gaps in our line. Our rushes became shorter and faster. We literally dived head downwards to finish each run forward, and, once down, remained motionless, offering as small a target as possible.

After a longer breathing space, completely deafened by the continuous roaring of the machine-guns, I began to look cautiously around, and discovered that my right-hand neighbor, Lieutenant James, was now trying to attract my attention. Even at a distance of three yards, his voice was inaudible and I therefore crept over to take his message. He bawled into my ear "Pass the word along: are we in touch on the left flank?" and I crawled over with the message to my left-hand neighbor. Before I reached him a bullet went through the brim of my shrapnel helmet giving me the sensation of being hit. Finding no traces of blood, I crept still more carefully to the man on my left, and passed on the message.

Still we advanced, even though our flanks were still in the air, until after a final rush I found myself lying head downwards on the forward slope of a small ridge. Ahead of me, the ground, after dipping for twenty yards, rose abruptly towards a position where I suspected the enemy to be lurking. Beyond this, the ground ascended gradually for half a mile, forming against the skyline a slight eminence on which was the village of Gueudecourt, crowned by the church spire, the aiming point of the attack.

The only man near me was one of our last draft, recognizable by his new khaki uniform.

After waiting longer than usual without any sign of fresh activity, I began to take stock of the situation. During the last rush that had brought us to this hilltop I noticed how alarmingly few we had become, and now, fearing we might be alone, I badly wanted to talk to my neighbour. When I hailed him he turned his head sharply rearwards, and to my horror, before he could speak, blood spouted through his hair, and his head sank limply downwards. This example of marksmanship warned me to take care. All around, bullets were angrily whipping into the grass and I wondered how long they could take to reach their small target. Moving so gradually that no observer could notice it, I allowed my head to sink downwards, while, through the bullet hole in my helmet I could see very little immediately to my front.

Every now and then the firing died down, blazing up into an angry continuous roar as succeeding waves attempted to reach the ridge on which I was lying, for following us were other divisions bent on breaking through the enemy's defences. After a time I prayed and fell into a peaceful reverie, thinking of the beautiful years of peace, and the happiness of my old home. What would it matter if this life were ended and I could escape being hunted like an animal, harassed by a perpetual torment of physical fatigue and hardship?...

One day, if I am spared, I will revisit that little undulation in the fields between Gueudecourt and Delville Wood on an early morning in mid-September. There I will give thanks for being spared another fifty years of happy and fruitful life to add to the twenty that seemed so likely to end on 16 September 1916.

When after a foretaste of eternity I came out of this daydream, the firing had died down into the desultory snap shooting of snipers with only an occasional burst from the machine-guns. The long rest had brought me not only a wonderful sense of well-being but new courage, and, choosing the moment, I dived head first down the slope into a crater in the valley bottom. As I hurled myself towards it I caught sight of the glittering steel blade of an upturned bayonet, and with my forearm struck it aside as I landed on the unsuspecting occupant of the shell hole. Several bullets zipped into the earth a moment too late, for I was already safely under cover....

Henry, the C.O.'s [Commanding Officer's] runner, popped into our shell hole before continuing his journey rearwards. "The battalion is scuppered [defeated]," he said.

In the afternoon a whole company of Jägers [sharpshooters] rushed forward about one or two hundred yards to our right front. I ... began firing rapidly over the top of the crater.... The dark green figures were drawing level with our position and now they began to falter, falling fast under our enfilading [raking] fire. As they worked steadily behind us, each shot winged its man and we kept up the fire until all movement ceased and our ammunition was exhausted. When we looked at the bottom of the shell hole, there were two or three hundred empty cartridge cases under our feet. Not a shot from the German trenches had come in reply, showing plainly that the enemy had retreated from his position of the morning. After we had watched closely for signs of any survivors we began to realize that we had wiped out the whole company. It seemed strange that no one on the British side had joined in. Clearly we were alone.

Before nightfall a tremendous bombardment was opened up by our own artillery and we soon realized that we were in the thick of it. Shells exploded with terrific concussion quite close to our little crater, throwing up black columns of smoke and chunks of earth. The debris sometimes fell on top of us, sounding more dangerous than it was, as it clanged on our helmets and bounced harmlessly aside. During a terrible hour we buried ourselves into the sides of the crater, not expecting to survive, yet when the gunfire suddenly ceased, we were still uninjured. We then noticed with gratitude that the long day was closing.

As soon as we could move safely into the open we went back to the ridge and selected a good place to dig in. Our new position overlooked the front on three sides, and presently we were joined by two or three other survivors who began to help us in digging our strongpoint. We next collected ammunition, bombs, rations and food from the dead bodies, which lay in long lines across the crest of the ridge. Some of the still forms were not quite dead, and through agonized eyes watched our movements as if they knew they were beyond our help. There were so many of them that the task was hopeless, even if we had abandoned our attempt to form a strongpoint before daylight.

Our little band seemed to be the sole survivors of the Battalion. We knew that on both sides the line fell back considerably, leaving us at the apex of a salient, marking the furthest point reached by the attack. Not one of us thought of going back. On the contrary, we collected rations, bombs and thousands of rounds of ammunition and prepared to give the counter-attack of tomorrow a rough time. We had dug our trench nearly waist-deep when approaching footsteps warned us of danger, and with pointed bayonets we waited while two tall figures emerged from the darkness. On challenging them, we discovered the Colonel and Adjutant, who had been searching for the body of the Adjutant's brother, though to be lying among the attackers on the hillside....

I found that the thought of so many helplessly wounded men lying in front and doomed to lie there all the next day was becoming an obsession, so, seeing no officers about, I called for volunteers. Four men accompanied me back to the fatal hillcrest, where we soon discovered by their feeble moaning a number of still-living bodies. Carrying our first man on his waterproof sheet was stiff work, for the sheet sagged in the middle, so that the corners were gradually dragged out of the grip of our fingers. On our return, four more volunteers joined our party, and we were able to collect fresh casualties, selecting them from the long swathes of khaki figures, mown down by the machine-gunners as the succession of waves reached the crest and melted away. Not all were of our own Battalion, and several of us noticed the badges of other divisions. In addition to those we had placed on waterproof sheets, I attempted to carry on my back a very badly injured man. One leg had been shot away and his cries were too pitiful for me to pass him by. Unhappily the effort caused him such terrible agony that he asked me to put him down and, gently lowering his body to the ground, I promised to fetch assistance to carry him back. Setting off alone, however, I soon realized that I was lost, and instinct warned me that I had walked into the German lines. Suddenly the mist lifted and through the haze of the foreground the church tower of Flers stood out clearly etched in the silvery light of dawn. Turning my back on that light I made off swiftly in the opposite direction until, against the skyline, I caught sight of a line of men walking in single file. Who were they? I went forward with great caution until I could distinguish British shrapnel helmets and then, drawing closer, I discovered my own Battalion, now the size of a platoon, withdrawing from the unfinished trench....

As we looked around us, a stretcher party with its burden was blown to fragments, not ten yards from the head of our tiny column. Pressing forward as fast as we could, we hurried out of this fiendish place, and on leaving it behind, noticed a complete absence of disturbing sound, due no doubt to the withdrawal of the enemy's artillery against the possibility of a further attack.

We halted once more ... and at roll call only fifty men were present. These could render an account of but few of their comrades, and the remainder were therefore reported missing. The survivors drew the rations for five hundred men, and for once had more food that they could eat. Everyone had a tin of butter, and as many tins of beans as he liked.

In my bomb bandolier I discovered a bent detonator intended for my liquid-fire grenade, and counted this yet another escape. Very few of us were without marks to show, and most tunics and equipments were ripped by passing bullets. When I heard of the fate of one of our bombing corporals I shuddered, for he, too, had carried a liquid-fire bomb and was burnt to death in sight of his comrades.

As the battalion marched back to Mericourt we passed fresh divisions, with shining buttons and smart uniforms, marching in the opposite direction to take their turn for the first time in the fighting. When these laughing men turned their eyes towards us, their smiles froze on their faces. "What a bloody battalion!" their expressions seemed to say and they shouted, "What is it like up there, chum?" We replied grimly "A bloody picnic," and had a vision of those smart N.C.O.s [non-commissioned officers] and officers abandoning their parade manners after a short acquaintance with Brother Bosch.

Parker, Ernest. *Into Battle: 1914-1918.* London: Longmans, 1964. Pp. 52-60.

THE "BIG FOUR" AT THE PARIS PEACE CONFERENCE OF 1919

In January 1919, delegates of the Allied and Associated nations, victors in World War I, gathered in Paris to attend peace conferences. The "Big Four" leaders--President Wilson of the United States, Premier Georges Clemenceau of France, and Prime Ministers David Lloyd George of Great Britain, and to a lesser degree Premier Vittorio Orlando of Italy--drew up the peace treaties. (Although Japan was also a major victorious power, its interests lay in Asia and the Pacific. Japanese delegates therefore did not actively participate in the general discussions.)

While all the leaders wanted to bring about a lasting peace, they differed on its specific terms. Wilson hoped to base the peace treaties on his Fourteen Points, which he had proclaimed in 1918. Wilson's pet project was the establishment of a League of Nations, and he was willing to compromise on other issues in order to realize it. Clemenceau despised Wilson's idealism and did his best to punish and cripple Germany. Lloyd George concentrated on averting the emergence of one dominating power in Europe and on expanding British influence in the Middle East. Orlando was only interested in realizing Italy's territorial claims. The peace negotiations, which lasted from January to May 1919, resulted in many compromises that left few parties happy and sowed the seeds of future conflict.

On 11 November 1918, the victorious allies and Germany had signed an armistice ending World War I. Germany, having accepted that armistice in the expectation of a peace based on Wilson's Fourteen Points, felt betrayed by the terms of the Treaty of Versailles. However, its only alternative was to face renewed war. On 28 June 1919, the fifth anniversary of the assassination of Archduke Franz Ferdinand of Austria-Hungary, Germany and the victorious allies signed the Treaty at Versailles.

During the following months, the victors also concluded peace treaties with the other Central Powers--Austria, Hungary, the Ottoman Empire, and Bulgaria. The treaties that concluded World War I with all the Central Powers are collectively called the Paris Peace Treaties. The Soviet Union, which had made a separate peace with Germany, was not invited to participate. The U.S. Senate did not ratify the Treaty of Versailles because of disagreements with Wilson over the League of Nations and his acquiescence in Japan's gains in China. Although the United States did sign a separate treaty with Germany, it did not join the League of Nations.

Robert Lansing was U.S. Secretary of State and the second delegate on the U.S. team. He was an able diplomat and a shrewd observer. The following biographical sketches of the Big Four leaders are from his memoir of the Paris Peace Conference.

QUESTIONS:

1) Which of the four leaders sketched below appear to have entered the treaty negotiations in a true spirit of fair play?

2) Which of the four leaders appears to have had the most influence at the peace talks?

3) Why were Wilson's Fourteen Points not adopted by the assembled leaders?

CLEMENCEAU

Of the four heads of states M. Clemenceau, the president of the Peace Conference, was, in my judgment, the dominant figure and the strongest man of the many strong men who participated in the negotiations at Paris. Possibly his age, which in no way impaired his keenness of wit or vigor of address, his long and turbulent political career, and the courage and firmness which he had shown during the perils of the German offensive in May, June, and July, 1918, had much to do with the impression which he made upon me. But without the background of accomplishment M. Clemenceau possessed a strength of character and a forcefulness which would have raised him above his colleagues. Persistent though patient, he was always ready, when the moment arrived, to use all his skill and cleverness in debate to obtain a decision which would be in the interest of his country. Every question was viewed by him in the light of how it would affect France....

I cannot better describe M. Clemenceau's personal appearance than to say that he suggested in face and figure a Chinese mandarin of the old empire.... He had the sallow complexion, the prominent high cheek-bones, the massive forehead with protuberant brows, the slant of the dark eyes, the long, down-curving gray mustache, the short neck, the broad, rounded shoulders, and the bulky body. As he sat in the council chamber with his clenched gloved hands resting on the arms of his chair, his eyes with their raised brows and heavy, drooping lids, and his features immobile and expressionless, he might have been the model for a bronze Chinese statue of Buddha. He was a striking type, indicative of intellectual force, of self-mastery, and of cold, merciless will power....

He showed, in what he sought and in what he accomplished rather than in what he said, that he believed that selfishness was the supreme impulse with nations as with individuals, and that it was the only real factor to be reckoned with.

Altruism was well enough to talk about because it was pleasing to some people, but to construct international society on such a foundation was to deny human nature. He was in no sense a visionary.

The League of Nations to M. Clemenceau--if I read his mind correctly--was a utopian dream of impractical theorists, until a concert of the Great Powers was incorporated in the covenant and the United States and Great Britain agreed to enter into treaties to come to the aid of France in the event that German should again attack her. From the time that these treaties of protection were arranged, and his country had no longer to depend for its security upon the uncertain guaranty of the covenant, M. Clemenceau supported, or rather did not oppose, the League of Nations. He probably thought that it might have some practical uses in carrying out the terms of the treaty. If the authors and sponsors wished to try out their theory, he had no objections, provided there was nothing in the covenant which weakened or lessened the material advantages gained for France in the terms of the peace.

He watched calmly and with little comment the formulation of the League by the Commission on the League of Nations, over which President Wilson presided, but I imagine that he did so with a scornful cynicism for the work of those who, he doubtless thought, were wasting their time on a dream. Had the authors of the covenant attempted, however, to modify his purposes, there can be little doubt that there would have been and explosion and the covenant would have had a difficult road to travel before it was accepted.

WILSON

There can be little doubt that President Wilson expected to find in the principal statesmen of Europe, at least in a measure, the same philanthropic and altruistic motives which he possessed to so high a degree.... Entertaining idealistic motives and unfortunately lacking practical experience in international negotiations, the President did not appear to appreciate at the first that the aims of his foreign colleagues were essentially material or to realize that their expressions of high principle were merely an assent to a moral standard which they thought basicly right, but at present impracticable. The result was that he assented to certain arrangements before he became aware of the selfishness, if not the greed, which was so evidently a frequent impulse of many of the European delegates in formulating their demands or supporting those of others. Having once passed his word in regard to a decision, his high sense of honor or possibly an unwillingness to admit his error prevented him from withdrawing it.

Obsessed with the idea that the organization of a league of nations was the supreme object to be attained at the Paris Conference, the President devoted his time, his effort, and his influence to drafting its charter and removing or neutralizing the objections which stood in the way of its acceptance.... It was very apparent that he did not desire counsel and criticism, but approval and commendation of the covenant. It was unfortunate for the President and for the League that he took this attitude, as subsequent events proved.

As the leaders of the Allied Powers, with their practical ideas, came to a realization of the situation and saw that the President was willing to concede much in exchange for support of the covenant, they utilized his supreme desire to obtain by barter material advantages for their own nations. From the results of the negotiations it may be deduced that by clever representations they gained concession after concession. The apparent support of the idealism of the President by these statesmen was in my opinion chiefly for a purpose and not out of conviction. They loudly applauded the President's declarations of principle as the just bases of peace, but they never once attempted to apply them unless their own national interests were advanced. They praised the covenant as a wonderful document, as the Magna Charta of the world, as an eternal memorial to its author, and they subtly flattered the President by confiding to the League every

question which could not be immediately solved, ostensibly to show their faith in the proposed organization, but really to postpone the settlement of dangerous disputes....

If the President had inflexibly demanded that no terms should be written into the treaty which were not wholly just, he would have gone far toward accomplishing the purpose of his mission to Europe. And if he had also advocated a plan for a league of nations which was not open to the charge of establishing a supernational authority, vested to all intents in an oligarchy of the Great Powers, he would have been acclaimed the greatest statesman on earth. Unfortunately for the present generation and for the future peace of the world, he did not pursue this course, but distorted his declared purpose to silence opposition to his ambitious conception of a dominant international organization. The natural conclusion is that he convinced himself that the covenant as drafted could not be obtained if he insisted on complete justice in all the settlements. He chose the covenant and won support to it by compromise with those who demanded the material rewards of conquest.

The courtesy of President Wilson in greeting the members of the Council of Ten and in his intercourse with them during the sessions was unvarying. He never, so far as I can recall, showed anger or impatience. I know, however, that beneath this outward calm the President often seethed with indignation at the way matters progressed, but never by word, gesture, or change of countenance did he permit his displeasure or irritation to find open expression. He listened with greater attention to a speaker than did any other man present, and whenever opportunity offered he smiled or told an anecdote which some turn in the debate suggested. He was invariably considerate of the expressed opinions of others, and manifested an open mind in valuing those opinions.

While these qualities are as a general rule useful and admirable in a negotiator, there come times when firmness and frankness are necessary. The failure to insist in certain cases when the conditions of a debate required insistence lost the President an advantage which I am sure he would have otherwise had. Prone to postpone a decision to the last possible moment, he puzzled his colleagues in the Council, who could not understand how so alert a mind needed more time to form an opinion after listening to three hours of discussion. This peculiarity of the President's mental make-up was frequently commented upon by his foreign associates in terms by no means complimentary.

LLOYD GEORGE

While Mr. Lloyd George was vague as to general principles, which accounted largely for the fluid state of his judgments, he had made certain promises during the parliamentary elections of December, 1918, which he considered binding upon him in the negotiations at Paris. Of these Germany's payment of the costs of the war and the public trial of the Kaiser by an international tribunal of justice attracted the most attention. He was very insistent that the treaty should make these promises good, although he must have known that the first was impossible and the second unwise as well as in defiance of all legal precepts.   In   addition   to   his   political commitments, he was determined to obtain the cession of the principal German colonies in Africa and the German islands in the Pacific south of the equator, control of Mesopotamia, a protectorate over Egypt, a practical protectorate over Persia in the event that Persian affairs came before the Conference, the destruction of the German naval power and the elimination of the German merchant marine as a rival of Great Britain in the carrying trade of the world. To these well-defined national policies, which were essentially selfish and material, the British Prime Minister clung tenaciously and was able to obtain nearly all of them by skillful maneuvering. His idea seemed to be that, if these objects were attained, the decisions as to other matters were of relatively little importance unless British interests were directly affected, and that to study them thoroughly was a needless expenditure of time and energy. It was very evident to any one who was familiar with the subjects that he counted on his skill as a ready debater and on the promptings of   his   experts   to   handle   the   questions satisfactorily when they were presented to the Council of Four or Council of Ten.

Mr. Lloyd George had a pleasing personality and a hearty manner of address, which won him friends even among those who were disposed to charge him with vacillation. Of him it may be said that he possessed personal magnetism. He was short in stature, and rather thickset. His complexion, which was ruddy and almost as clear as a child's, was set off by an abundance of silvery-white hair brushed back from his broad forehead, and by a short white mustache which curved over his lips. His eyes were keen and twinkling, and when he smiled the wrinkles at the corners were very marked. He would enter the council chamber at the Ministry of Foreign Affairs, generally late, with a quick step, which on account of its length made it a bit swaggering, and greet his colleagues with a genial smile and a bluff heartiness which were attractive....

Mr. Lloyd George possessed a wonderfully alert mind which fairly bubbled over with restless energy.... He, in my opinion, had the quickest mind of the Big Four, but it seemed to lack stability. He gave the impression of a man who through   force   of   circumstances   had   been compelled to jump at conclusions instead of reaching them through the surer but slower processes of reason....

Vivacious, good-tempered, and possessing a strong sense of humor, Mr. Lloyd George was socially an attractive person, while in debate his cleverness in finding the weak spots in an opponent's armor and his utter indifference to his own errors made him a dangerous antagonist. He attacked with vigor and he defended by attacking. But this unusual man possessed none of the arts of diplomacy. He was not by nature a negotiator. His successes at Paris--and they were not a few--were largely due to the excellent advice which was given him, and which he wisely received.

ORLANDO

Signor Orlando possessed physical and mental characteristics which have left pleasant memories of intercourse with him. Short and rotund in person, with thick white hair worn pompadour and a white mustache partially covering his rather full lips, he was not in personal appearance typical of Italy. His shortness of stature, which was about that of Mr. Lloyd George, was emphasized by his usual custom of wearing a close-fitting sack coat, which he generally kept tightly buttoned. With a friendly eye and a smile which dimpled his cheeks, one knew at a glance that he was of a kindly nature and not disposed to quarrel without a sufficient provocation. His clear complexion and unwrinkled face indicated good health and a capacity to enjoy life.

The mentality of Signor Orlando was moulded on different lines from those of any other member of the Council of the Heads of States. It had been trained and developed in the field of jurisprudence, and possessed the precision of thought and clearness of expression which are the attributes of a mind accustomed to the exactness of legal expressions....

Though Signor Orlando possessed admirable traits of character and exhibited a skill in debate which none of his confrères excelled, he was nevertheless the least influential of the Big Four and had the least to do with formulating the terms of peace with Germany. This was doubtless due in large measure to the relative military, naval, and financial strength of the Great Powers represented in the Council of Four. Comparison by this standard--which, it is to be regretted, was the principal standard in weighing influence at the Peace Conference--tended to place Italy in the background and to subordinate the views of her statesmen. I know also that some felt the Italian Government had driven too sharp a bargain with the Entente in 1915, and was now demanding more than its pound of flesh, in spite of the small part, which the more critical in Europe asserted, Italy had taken in the later months of the struggle. There seemed to be a disposition to repudiate the Italian claims or at least to reject many of them. It was with evident reluctance that France and Great Britain conceded their treaty obligations. Neither of them vigorously supported Italy when her claims were urged. The attitude seemed to be that of tolerance for a nation which had not won by arms a right to a voice in the decisions, but was by agreement entitled to it. It was therefore especially fortunate for the Italian people that they had in Signor Orlando so well-trained a statesman, so talented an advocate, and so keen a logician to represent them at the Conference. He could not be and was not ignored. Another representative less able might have been.

Lansing, Robert. *The Big Four, and Others of the Peace Conference*. Boston: Houghton Mifflin, 1921. Rpt. Freeport, NY: Books for Libraries, 1972. Pp. 10, 32-35, 48-51, 54-56, 79-81, 102-105, 125-126.

MAHATMA GANDHI, APOSTLE OF NON-VIOLENT REFORM

► Gandhi's Spinning Wheel

Mohandas K. Gandhi (1869-1947) was called Mahatma (Great Soul or Holy One) by Indians. His father was prime minister of a small Indian princely state, his mother was a pious and respected lady, and he was their youngest child. He was married at thirteen in an arranged marriage, continued his schooling in England at eighteen after graduating from high school, while his wife and baby stayed with his family. He returned to India upon earning his law degree. He later took his family to South Africa to represent some Indian clients. There he championed Indian rights against the dominant white South Africans by non-violent protests and demonstrations, calling his movement against injustice *satyagraha* (truth force).

Gandhi returned to India in 1915 and joined the Indian National Congress in its battles to gain self-government from the British. He also plunged into campaigns for social reform. His own unhappy experience with early marriage led him to crusade against child marriages, which he thought especially cruel and unjust for girls. He also championed the rights of laborers against poverty and bad working conditions; he decried discrimination against untouchables by caste Hindus, and other injustices in Hindu society. He also taught the dignity of labor and self sufficiency and made spinning and weaving cloth for his own simple clothing a hallmark of the Congress and a symbol of India's struggle for independence.

Gandhi was deeply religious and set high moral standards for himself. He had a vision of a united, self-reliant India true to its traditions. Because he abhorred violence, he advocated letting Indian Muslims have a separate nation in Pakistan rather than put millions of Hindus and Muslims through a bloody civil war. Soon after predominantly Hindu India and Muslim Pakistan won independence from Great Britain, a Hindu fanatic assassinated Gandhi for having been too lenient on Muslims. Since independence, Indian governments have striven to industrialize and modernize, forgetting the Gandhian dream. Nevertheless Indians revere Gandhi as a saintly man, and his techniques of non-violent protest for just causes have made him the patron saint of all who seek justice by peaceful struggle.

The following excerpts come from Gandhi's *Autobiography*.

QUESTIONS:

1) Why did Gandhi marry at thirteen and why did he turn against child marriages?
2) What were the ideals of Gandhi's ashram and how were they threatened?
3) How did Gandhi deal with the issue of strikes by workers?

Much as I wish that I had not to write this chapter, I know that I shall have to swallow many such bitter draughts in the course of this narrative. And I cannot do otherwise, if I claim to be a worshipper of Truth. It is my painful duty to have to record here my marriage at the age of thirteen. As I see youngsters of the same age about me who are under my care, and think of my own marriage, I am inclined to pity myself and to congratulate them on having escaped my lot. I can see no moral argument in support of such a preposterously early marriage.

Let the reader make no mistake. I was married, not betrothed.... It appears that I was betrothed thrice, though without my knowledge. I was told that two girls chosen for me had died in turn, and therefore I infer that I was betrothed three times. I have a faint recollection however, that the third betrothal took place in my seventh year. But I do not recollect having been informed about it....

It will be remembered that we were three brothers. The first was already married. The elders decided to marry my second brother, who was two or three years my senior, a cousin, possibly a year older, and me, all at the same time. In doing so there was no thought of our welfare, much less our wishes. It was purely a question of their own convenience and economy.

Marriage among Hindus is no simple matter. The parents of the bride and the bridegroom often bring themselves to ruin over it. They waste their substance, they waste their time. Months are taken up over the preparations--in making clothes and ornaments and preparing budgets for dinners. Each tries to outdo the other in the number and variety of courses to be prepared....

It would be better, thought my elders, to have all this bother over at one and the same time. Less expense and greater *éclat*.... My father and my uncle were both old, and we were the last children they had to marry. It is likely that they wanted to have the last best time of their lives....

It was only through these preparations that we got warning of the coming event. I do not think it meant to me anything more than the prospect of good clothes to wear, drum beating, marriage processions, rich dinners and a strange girl to play with....

I was learning at the high school when I was married. We three brothers were learning at the same school. The eldest brother was in a much higher class, and the brother who was married at the same time as I was, only one class ahead of me. Marriage resulted in both of us wasting a year. Indeed the result was even worse for my brother, for he gave up studies altogether. Heaven knows how many youths are in the same plight as he. Only in our present Hindu society do studies and marriage go thus hand in hand.

My studies were continued.... I wanted to make my wife an ideal wife. My ambition was to make her live a pure life, learn what I learnt, and identify her life and thought with mine.

I do not know whether Kasturbai [Mrs. Gandhi] had any such ambition. She was illiterate. By nature she was simple, independent, persevering and, with me at least, reticent. She was not impatient of her ignorance and I do not recollect my studies having ever spurred her to go in for a similar adventure. I fancy, therefore, that my ambition was all one-sided....

[In 1915 Gandhi decided to establish and live in an *Ashram* in Ahmedabad, where all would share in communal living and practice manual labor.] The question of untouchability was naturally among the subjects discussed with the Ahmedabad friends. I made it clear to them that I should take the first opportunity of admitting an untouchable candidate to the Ashram if he was otherwise worthy.

The Ashram had been in existence only a few months when we were put to a test such as I had scarcely expected. I received a letter from Amritlal Thakkar to this effect: "A humble and honest untouchable family is desirous of joining your Ashram. Will you accept them?"

I was perturbed. I had never expected that a untouchable family with an introduction from no less a man than Thakkar Bapa ["Bapa" means father, a respectful term of address] would so soon be seeking admission to the Ashram. I shared my letter with my companions. They welcomed it.

I wrote to Amritlal Thakkar expressing our willingness to accept the family, provided all the members were ready to abide by the rules of the Ashram.

The family consisted of Dudabhai, his wife Danibehn and their daughter Lakshmi, then a mere toddling babe. Dudabhai had been a teacher in Bombay. They all agreed to abide by the rules and were accepted.

But their admission created a flutter amongst the friends who had been helping the Ashram. The very first difficulty was found with regard to the use of the well, which was partly controlled by the owner of the bungalow. The man in charge of the water-lift objected that drops of water from our bucket would pollute him. So he took to swearing at us and molesting Dudabhai. I told everyone to put up with the abuse and continue drawing water at any cost. When he saw that we did not return his abuse, the man became ashamed and ceased to bother us.

All monetary help, however, was stopped. The friend who had asked that question about an untouchable being able to follow the rules of the Ashram had never expected that any such would be forthcoming.

With the stopping of monetary help came rumours of proposed social boycott. We were prepared for all this. I had told my companions that, if we were boycotted and denied the usual facilities, we would not leave Ahmedabad. We would rather go and stay in the untouchables' quarters and live on whatever we could get by manual labour....

Just as there was a storm outside, so was there a storm in the Ashram itself ... my wife and other women did not seem quite to relish the admission into the Ashram of the untouchable friends. My eyes and ears easily detected their indifference, if not their dislike, towards Danibhen. The monetary difficulty had caused me no anxiety; but this internal storm was more than I could bear....

The admission of this family proved a valuable lesson to the Ashram. In the very beginning we proclaimed to the world that the Ashram would not countenance untouchability. Those who wanted to help the Ashram were thus put on their guard, and the work of the Ashram in this direction was considerably simplified. The fact that it is mostly the real orthodox Hindus who have met the daily growing expenses of the Ashram is perhaps a clear indication that untouchability is shaken to its foundations. There are indeed many other proofs of this, but

the fact that good Hindus do not scruple to help an Ashram where we go the length of dining with the untouchables is no small proof....

[Workers in the cotton mills of Ahmedabad came to Gandhi to complain of low wages and poor working conditions.] I had therefore to advise the labourers to go on strike. Before I did so, I came in very close contact with them and their leaders, and explained to them the conditions of a successful strike:

1. never to resort to violence,

2. never to molest blacklegs [strike-breakers or "scabs"],

3. never to depend upon alms, and,

4. to remain firm, no matter how long the strike continued, and to earn bread, during the strike, by any other honest means.

The leaders of the strike understood and accepted the conditions and the labourers pledged themselves at a general meeting not to resume work until either their terms were accepted or the mill-owners agreed to refer the dispute to arbitration....

For the first two weeks the mill-hands exhibited great courage and self-restraint and daily held monster meetings.... But at last they began to show signs of flagging.... Finally the information was brought to me that the strikers had begun to totter. I felt deeply troubled and set to thinking furiously as to what my duty was in the circumstances....

One morning--it was at a mill-hands' meeting while I was still groping and unable to see my way clearly, the light came to me. Unbidden and all by themselves the words came to my lips: "Unless the strikers rally," I declared to the meeting, "and continue the strike till a settlement is reached, or till they leave the mills altogether, I will not touch any food."

The labourers were thunderstruck.... The labourers broke out, "Not you but we shall fast. It would be monstrous if you were to fast. Please forgive us for our lapse, we will now remain faithful to our pledge to the end."

"There is no need for you to fast," I replied. "It would be enough if you could remain true to your pledge. As you know we are without funds, and we do not want to continue our strike by living on public charity. You should therefore try to eke out a bare existence by some kind of labour, so that you may be able to remain unconcerned, no matter how long the strike may continue. As for my fast, it will be broken only after the strike is settled."...

My fast was not free from a grave defect. For...I enjoyed very close and cordial relations with the mill-owners, and my fast could not but affect their decision. As a Satyagrahi [one who practices satyagraha or truth force] I knew that I might not fast against them, but ought to leave them free to be influenced by the mill-hands' strike alone. My fast was undertaken not on account of lapse of the mill-owners, but on account of that of the labourers in which, as their representative, I felt I had a share. With the mill-owners I could only plead: to fast against them would amount to coercion. Yet in spite of my knowledge that my fast was bound to put pressure upon them, as in fact it did, I felt I could not help it. The duty to undertake it seemed to me to be clear....

The net result of it was that an atmosphere of good-will was created all round. The hearts of the mill-owners were touched, and they set about discovering some means for a settlement ... [a mutual friend] was in the end appointed arbitrator, and the strike was called off after I had fasted only for three days. The mill-owners commemorated the event by distributing sweets among the labourers, and thus a settlement was reached after 21 days' strike....

[Gandhi decided to adopt spinning and weaving to promote several goals: to promote the dignity of labor, to revive rural industries, and to add to the income of poor families.] I do not remember to have seen a handloom or spinning wheel when in 1908 I described it in *Hind Swaraj* as the panacea for the growing pauperism of India. In that book I took it as understood that anything that helped India to get rid of the grinding poverty of her masses would in the same process also establish Swaraj [self-rule].... When the Satyagraha Ashram was founded at Sabarmati, we introduced a few handlooms. But no sooner had we done this than we found ourselves up against a difficulty. All of us belonged either to the liberal professions or to business: not one of us was an artisan. We needed a weaving expert to teach us to weave before we could work the looms....

The object that we set before ourselves was to be able to clothe ourselves entirely in cloth manufactured by our own hands. We therefore forthwith discarded the use of mill-woven cloth, and all the members of the Ashram resolved to wear hand-woven cloth made from Indian yarn solely. The adoption of this practice brought us a world of experience. It enabled us to know, from direct contact, the conditions of life among the weavers, the extent of their production, the handicaps in the way of their obtaining their yarn supply, the way in which they were being made victims of fraud, and, lastly, their ever growing indebtedness.

Gandhi, M.K. *The Story of My Experiments with Truth*. Trans. Mahadev Desai. Ahmedabad, India: Navajivan Press, 1945. Pp. 18-19, 23, 26, 482, 485-487, 521-522, 526-529, 599-600.

ISLAMIC FUNDAMENTALISM AND ARAB NATIONALISM

▸ **Egyptian Village Mosque**

Beginning in the fifteenth century, most Arab peoples were subjects of the Ottoman Empire, dominated by Muslim Turks. By the early 1900s, with the Empire in steep decline, all Arab north Africa had fallen under French, British, Spanish, and Italian control. After World War I and the collapse of the Ottoman Empire, France and Great Britain gained control of most of the Middle East also, governing them as mandates under the authority of the League of Nations.

Successive foreign imperial domination led to an Arab wakening that began in the nineteenth century. Harkening back to the golden age of Islam, to their common Islamic and Arabic culture and religion, Arab nationalists sought to overthrow Turkish and Western domination. While some nationalists envisioned independent, secular Arab states modeled on Western industrial societies and espoused economic and political theories such as Marxism, others were inspired by traditional models.

The Muslim Brotherhood originated in Egypt in 1928, and became influential elsewhere in the Muslim world as well. It insisted that all Muslim states adhere to Islamic principles and eschew both Marxism and liberal Western secularism. This brand of Muslim fundamentalism appealed to poor Muslims in many lands. The first section of the reading below is by Hassan Al-Banna (1906-1948), founder of the Muslim Brotherhood.

"Arabism," another powerful force in Arab nationalism, emphasized Arab ethnicity and culture despite geographic and national boundaries. This is the gist of the second reading that follows, by Makram Ebeid (1889-1961), an Egyptian intellectual and politician.

The last passage is by Munah Al-Sulh (b. 1926), a historian from Lebanon. He champions the force of populist-radical Islam against Western cultural imperialism.

QUESTIONS:

1) What are the basic teachings of the Muslim Brotherhood?
2) Why is it important that Egyptians stress their unity with all Arabs?
3) How can Islamic traditions combat Western cultural imperialism?

The Credo of the "Muslim Brotherhood"

1. I believe that all things must be rendered unto God, that our master Muhammad--God's blessing be upon Him--was the last of the prophets sent amongst men, that the Qur'an is the book of God, that Islam is a general law regulating the order of this world and the next. I

promise to apply the noble Qur'an's teachings in my own life, to adhere to the purifying *Sunnah* [Islamic custom] and to study the life of the Prophet and the history of his noble disciples.

2. I believe that rectitude, virtue and science are part of the foundations of Islam. I promise to be upright, to carry out the rites, to shun what is forbidden, to be virtuous, to cultivate good habits and avoid bad ones, to accomplish the rituals of Islam as far as I am able, to prefer love and affection over disputes and contention ... to be proud of Islam's rites and its language, and to spread science and useful knowledge amongst the various classes of the *Umma* [Muslim community].

3. I believe that a Muslim must work and earn money, and that any needy person who asks for charity has a right to part of the money I earn. I promise ... to encourage any useful economic project, to give preference to the products of my own country and those of other Muslim countries....

4. I believe that a Muslim is responsible for his family.... I promise ... to propagate the teachings of Islam amongst my family, not to place my sons in any school where their faith and their morality would not be strengthened, to boycott any newspaper, publication, book, organization, group or club which opposes the teachings of Islam.

5. I believe that a Muslim has a duty to revive the glory of Islam by promoting the renaissance of its peoples and by restoring its legislation. I believe that the flag of Islam should dominate all mankind, and that it is the duty of every Muslim to educate the world in the rules of Islam....

6. I believe that all Muslims form a single nation, united by the Islamic faith, and that Islam commands its sons to work for the good of all. I promise to bend my efforts to reinforce the ties of fraternity between all Muslims....

7. I believe that the secret of the Muslims' backwardness is their estrangement from the religion, and that the basis of reform should be a return to the precepts and judgements of Islam; I believe that this is possible if the Muslims work towards this goal and if the doctrine of the Muslim Brotherhood is implemented....

A. The law of the Muslim Brotherhood is inspired by the rules established by Muhammad himself.... There is not a single word in the credo of the Muslim Brothers which is not based on the Book of God, the *Sunnah* of his Prophet and the spirit of true Islam....

B.... The religion which satisfies man's spiritual hunger and offers him the necessary tranquility of conscience and happiness is Islam.... Islam reinforces general understanding between peoples and confidently leads the world towards a general unity, the highest aspiration of reformers and sages and the basis of human welfare....

There is a lesson here for those Oriental rulers who in the past have sought or in the future will seek to find some other path than Islam in order to lead their people towards renaissance and to reconstitute the religion, the *Umma* and the state.

C. The Muslims of today will only succeed by following the same path as their Master, Muhammad.... In fact, ever since the Oriental nations forsook the teachings of Islam and attempted to substitute others which they believed would help solve their problems, they have been caught in a morass of uncertainty and have suffered bitter defeats; the price of deviation has been high, in dignity, morality, self-respect and administrative efficiency.

The great strength of the Orient is its morality and its faith.... Let the leaders of the Orient, then, take pains to fortify its soul and to restore its lost morality, for such is the only means whereby to bring about a genuine renaissance....

D. As for the application of this method to the situation faced by present day Muslims ... it will take considerable time. The gulf that political and social events have opened up between the Muslims and their faith is wide, and the subjective methods used by the enemies of Islam to draw Muslims away from the religion during the modern area have been effective. Indeed, the Muslims themselves are at war with their faith; they break their own sword and freely hand a dagger to those who would bring them down, by co-operating with those who seek to demolish the religion which is the very foundation of their regimes and the source of their strength....

O Muslim Brothers, victory will come if we are patient; our salvation lies in firmness. Those who love God will surely be rewarded.

The Egyptians are Arabs

We are brothers in the struggle to save our homelands and win our freedom. Catastrophes reinforce the bonds uniting their victims, and we are talking of nations united by a shared language, a common tradition and the same fundamental sociological characteristics.

The history of Arabism is made up of continuous links, forming a closely knit chain. The ties of language and culture are more pronounced in the Arab countries than in any other area of the world. Religious tolerance was born, prospered and still exists between members of different religions in the fraternal neighbouring countries. Who then can doubt that my phrase "the Egyptians are Arabs" encompasses affinities and ties that have never been broken by geographical boundaries or political ambition, despite all the efforts that have been made to divide the Arab countries, kill their inhabitants' Arab spirit and disunite and persecute those who work towards Arab unity. That unity undoubtedly constitutes one of the major foundations of the modern renaissance of the Arab East, which so needs unity and solidarity in the face of the European wave which has submerged it.

The Arabs need to believe in their Arabism and in all its constructive features which, in the past, helped them to build a flourishing civilization and subjugate the European countries for so long....

We are Arabs in this open struggle, which is developing in all of Arabism's territories, to win complete freedom and revive the glory of Arab civilization, to improve our public affairs, to guide our youth towards high ideals, to educate our people soundly so as to shake them out of the inertia of the past years, encourage them to look after their own interests, awaken them from their slumbers and light up the path before them. They will then see contemporary life in its true colours and will be able to distinguish between that which serves their cause and that which is harmful to it; they will choose that which will enable them to build a new life based on the glories of the past, with all that that means in

terms of spiritual strength and celestial faith, yet solidly attached to the best of what the era has to offer in the way of scientific progress and industrial production.

Yes, we are Arabs, both in this way and in terms of the history of the Arab civilization in Egypt and the closeness of our ancestral stock to that of the Semitic tribes who emigrated to our country from the Arabian Peninsula long ago....

Arab unity is an effective unity, but it requires an organization whose task it will be to constitute a front against imperialism, preserve national specificity, ensure prosperity, develop economic resources, encourage local production, intensify exchange and mutual interests, and co-ordinate relations.... Our destiny will lead us to rally round a common ideal and purpose, to unite in a single bloc, joining our countries together in a single national league or in a great homeland made up of several territories, each with its own personality but all with the same general national characteristics, all solidly linked to the great homeland.

Islamicity and Arabism

When the Arab masses refer to their being Muslims in the context of a political situation or of a civilization, they usually mean to underline that they refuse to be vassals of the West and that they feel themselves part of an historical and geographical whole, with their own values, roots and inheritance. In a word, these masses share the same principles as the vanguards of Arabism and the Arab liberation movement....

Sometimes, by proclaiming their Muslim faith, the popular masses seek to signal their positive commitment to this dimension, thereby telling the intellectuals and the Westernized pseudo-vanguards: "I belong to one world and you belong to another: we are different." The popular masses, by clinging to their Islamicity, proclaim that they are in tune with the personality of the nation, not that they lag behind it.

It may even be that through their Muslim faith the popular masses experience a level of harmony with Arab aims and a willingness to serve those aims greater than the most sincere of nationalist intellectuals....

A huge portion of imperialism's efforts goes into building up a certain vision of Islam, both in the eyes of the Arab citizen and in those of the world at large.... How does cultural imperialism wish us to see Islam? ... [It] casts Islam either as the cause of the backwardness of the Arabs, and perhaps even of international life in general, or as a religion just like any other religion, with a role in Arab life identical to the role of other religions in other countries.... Imperialism has succeeded in its efforts to convince certain revolutionary intellectuals that a revolution in Arab life would have to begin with a revolution against the rites and prescriptions of Islam....

[However] from the point of view of the Arab liberation movement, we notice that, on the contrary, now that Islam has been liberated from the relative oppression it suffered under imperialism and reaction, it has become a natural and powerful support to the Arab liberation movement, as its essence requires. Islam has become the property of the masses.

Abdel-Malek, Anouar, ed. *Contemporary Arab Political Thought*. Rev. ed. London: Zed Books, 1983. Pp. 45-47, 141-142, 151-153.

STALIN: THE MAKING OF A DICTATOR

▶ Lenin Sweeps Away His Enemies

Joseph Stalin (1879-1953) was born Joseph Djugashvili, son of a shoemaker, near Tiflis, capital of Georgia. His mother took in sewing and washing to supplement the family income. Georgia, in the Caucasus Mountains, was independent until it was annexed by Russia in the eighteenth century. Georgians had their own language and church, closely related to the Russian Orthodox church.

Joseph's mother wished him to be a priest. While studying in a seminary, he became involved with the Social Democrats, Marxist revolutionaries, for which he was expelled in 1899. Like other revolutionaries, Joseph had many aliases. One was Koba, after a legendary Georgian hero; but finally he settled on Stalin which means "man of steel."

Stalin played relatively minor roles in the Bolshevik party led by Vladimir Lenin, and suffered periods of exile and imprisonment under the Tsars. He was freed from internal exile as a result of the February Revolution in 1917, and soon became a rising star among the Bolsheviks. Stalin successively served as editor of *Pravda*, the Bolsheviks' official newspaper, Commissar of Nationalities in charge of forging a new union between the dominant Russians and the minority nationalities, and finally as general secretary of the Communist Party in 1922. In this last post, he engineered the elimination of his rivals and his own rise to supreme power. Lenin had misgivings about Stalin during his last years, denouncing him as "too rude," and thought that he should be replaced by someone "more patient, more loyal, more courteous and more considerate of his comrades."

For several years after Lenin's death in 1924, Stalin, Leon Trotsky, father of the Red (Soviet) Army, and others were engaged in a fierce power struggle. Stalin used his position of party general secretary to destroy his rivals. Trotsky was expelled from the Soviet Communist party in 1927; two years later he fled the Soviet Union, eventually settling near Mexico City, where he used his powerful pen to continue his battle against Stalin's totalitarian rule and cult of personality. He was assassinated in 1940 at Stalin's order. He was writing a biography of Stalin when he died; Charles Malamuth, his translator and editor, finished the last chapters of the book from Trotsky's notes. Although Trotsky's enormous hatred of Stalin is apparent, the biography is valuable because of Trotsky's unique personal knowledge of Stalin and other Soviet leaders.

In this reading, Trotsky portrays young Stalin as a mediocrity, but already possessing the characteristics of a murderous tyrants. Trotsky condemns Stalin's brutal policy as Commissar of Nationalities in Georgia, which set the pattern for forced integration of other ethnic groups into the Union of Soviet Socialist Republics.

QUESTIONS:

1) What was Stalin's role as a young revolutionary?

2) How did Stalin's ethnic background prepare him to become Commissar of Nationalities?
3) How did Stalin deal with ethnic minorities in the Soviet Union?

His intellect always remained immeasurably inferior to his will. In a complex situation, when confronted with new considerations, Koba prefers to bide his time, to keep his peace, or to retreat. In all those instances when it is necessary for him to choose between the idea and the political machine, he invariably inclines toward the machine.... At the same time he invariably is inclined to favour the most resolute action in solving the problems he has mastered. Under all conditions well-organized violence seems to him the shortest distance between two points. Here an analogy begs to be drawn. The Russian terrorists were in essence petty bourgeois democrats, yet they were extremely resolute and audacious. Marxists were wont to refer to them as "liberals with a bomb." Stalin has always been what he remains to this day--a politician of the golden mean who does not hesitate to resort to the most extreme measures. Strategically he is an opportunist; tactically he is a "revolutionist." He is a kind of opportunist with a bomb.

Soon after his departure from the seminary Koba became something in the nature of a bookkeeper at the Tiflis Observatory. Despite its "miserly salary," he liked his job. "He was least of all concerned with his personal welfare. He made no demands on life, regarding them as incompatible with Socialist principles. He had sufficient integrity to make sacrifices for his ideal." Koba was true to that vow of poverty which was taken unostentatiously and without any ado by the young people who went into the revolutionary underground....

Joseph Djugashvili was a member of that order [professional revolutionary] and shared many of its traits; many but not all. He saw the purpose of his life in overthrowing the powers that be. Hatred of them was immeasurably more active in his soul than love for the oppressed. Prison, exile, sacrifices, privations did not frighten him. He knew how to look danger straight in the eye. At the same time he was keenly sensitive about such of his traits as his slowness of intellect, lack of talent, the general colorlessness of his physical and moral countenance. His overweening ambition was tinged with envy and ill will. His pertinacity marched hand in hand with vindictiveness.... the Caucasian environment proved most favorable for nurturing these basic attributes of his nature. Without being swept off his feet while in the midst of enthusiasts, without catching fire while in the midst of those who were easily inflamed yet quick to cool down, he learned early in life to prize the advantages of icy grit, of circumspection and especially of astuteness, which in his case became subtly transformed into wiliness. Special historical circumstances were to invest these essentially secondary attributes with primary significance.

[After the failure of the 1905 Revolution] ... Lenin got him interested in working on the problem of minor nationalities--an arrangement thoroughly in the spirit of Lenin!

A native of the Caucasus, with its scores of semi-cultured and primitive yet rapidly awakening nationalities, he did not have to have proved to him the importance of the nationalities problem. The tradition of national independence continued to flourish in Georgia. It was from that that Koba himself had received his first revolutionary impulse. His very pseudonym harked back to his own nationality's struggle for national independence.... The one thing beyond is that, having become a Bolshevik, Koba forsook the nationalistic romanticism that continued to live in peace and harmony with the nerveless socialism of the Georgian Mensheviks. But after repudiating the idea of Georgian independence, Koba could not, like many Great-Russians, remain wholly indifferent to the nationalities problem, because relations between Georgians, Armenians, Tatars, Russians and others constantly complicated revolutionary activities in the Caucasus....

"Marxism And The National Problem" is undoubtedly Stalin's most important--rather, his one and only--theoretical work. On the basis of that single article, which was forty printed pages long, its author is entitled to recognition as an outstanding theoretician. What is rather mystifying is why he did not write anything else of even remotely comparable quality either before or after. The key to the mystery is hidden away in this, that Stalin's work was wholly inspired by Lenin, written under his unremitting supervision and edited by him line by line....

No less significant was Stalin's article, "On the Abolition of National Limitations" [*Pravda*, 7 April (25 March) 1917.] His basic idea, acquired from propagandist pamphlets as far back as Tiflis Seminary days, was that national oppression was a relic of medievalism. "The social basis of national oppression," he wrote, "the force that inspires it, is the degenerating landed aristocracy.... In England, where the landed aristocracy shares its power with the bourgeoisie ... national oppression is softer, less inhuman, provided of course we do not take into consideration the special consideration that during the war, when the power passed into the hands of the landlords, national oppression increased considerably (persecution of the Irish, the Hindus)."...

"To the extent that the Russian Revolution has won," the article concluded. "it has already created conditions [for national freedom] by having overthrown the sovereignty of feudalism and serfdom...."

[After the Bolshevik Revolution of October 1917] The People's Commissariat of Nationalities was created to organize all the formerly oppressed nations of Russia through national commissariats--such as the Armenians, the Byelo-Russian, the Jewish, the Latvian, the Mussulman (which was later renamed the Tataro-Bashkir), the Polish--and the departments of the Mountaineers of the Caucasus, the German, the Kirghiz, the Ukrainian, the Chuvash, the Estonian, the Kalmyk, the Southern Slavs, the Czechoslovaks (for serving the Czech military prisoners), the Votyak and the Komi. The Commissariat tried to organize the education of the nationalities on a Soviet basis. it published a weekly newspaper, *The Life of the Nationalities*, in Russian and a number of publications in various national languages. But it devoted itself chiefly to organizing national republics and regions, to find the necessary cadres of leaders from among the nationals themselves, to general guidance of the newly-organized territorial entities, as well as to caring for the national minorities living outside of their own segregated territory. In the eyes of the backward

nationalities which were for the first time called upon by the Revolution to lead an independent national existence the Commissariat of Nationalities had an undoubted authority. It opened to them the doors leading to an independent existence within the framework of the Soviet regime. In that sphere Stalin was an irreplaceable assistant to Lenin. Stalin knew the life of the aboriginal people of the Caucasus intimately--as only a native could. That aboriginality was in his very blood.... Lenin valued these attributes of Stalin's, which were not shared by others, and in every way tried to bolster Stalin's authority in the eyes of all sorts of national delegations. "Talk it over with Stalin. He knows that question well. He knows the conditions. Discuss the question with him." Such recommendations were repeated by him scores and hundreds of times. On all those occasions when Stalin had serious conflicts with the national delegates, or in his own collegium, the question was referred to the Politburo, where all the decisions were invariably brought out in favor of Stalin. This should have reinforced his authority even more in the eyes of the ruling circles of the backward nationalities; in the Caucasus, on the Volga, and in Asia. The new bureaucracy of the national minorities later became a not an unimportant bulwark of Stalin's power....

Stalin was People's Commissar of Nationalities from the moment of the Revolution until the liquidation of the Commissariat in 1923 in connection with the creation of the Soviet Union and the Council of Nationalities of the Central Executive Committee of the U.S.S.R....

In 1923 he was to place on the same plane with Great-Russian nationalism, which had behind it age-old traditions and the oppression of weak nations, the defensive nationalism of these latter nations. These crude errors, Stalinist errors, taken together are explicable, as has already been pointed out, by the fact that not on a single question does he rise to a systematic conception. He utilizes disjointed propositions of Marxism as he needs them at the moment, selecting them just as shoes are selected according to size in a shoe store. That is why at each turn of events he so easily contradicts himself. Thus, even in the field of the national problem, which became his special sphere, Stalin could not rise to an integrated conception.

"Recognition of the right to secede does not mean the recommendation to secede," he wrote in *Pravda* of October 10, 1920. "The secession of the borderlands would have undermined the revolutionary might of Central Russia, which stimulated the liberation movement of the West and the East. The seceded borderlands would have inevitably fallen into slavery to international imperialism, It is enough to take a look at Georgia, Armenia, Poland, Finland, etc., which have separated from Russia, and which have preserved merely the appearance of independence, while actually having become transformed into unconditional vassals of the Entente [Britain, France, and the United States]. It is sufficient to recall the recent history of the Ukraine and of Azerbaijan, the former ravished by German capitalism and the latter by the Entente, in order to understand fully the counter-revolutionism of the demand for the secession of a borderland under contemporary international conditions."

"The revolutionary wave from the north," wrote Stalin on the first anniversary of the October Revolution, "has spread over all of Russia, pouring over one borderland after another, But at this point it met with a dam in the form of the "national councils" and territorial "governments" (Don, Kuban, Siberia) which had been formed even before October. Bourgeois by nature, they did not at all desire to destroy the old bourgeois world. On the contrary, they deemed it their duty to preserve and fortify it with all their strength.... They naturally became the hearths of reaction, drawing around themselves all that was counter-revolutionary in Russia.... But the struggle of the "national" and territorial "governments" (against the Soviet Center) proved to be an unequal struggle. Attacked from both sides, from the outside by the Soviet Government and on the inside by their own workers and peasants, the "national governments" had to retreat after the first battle.... Completely routed, the "national governments" were obliged to turn for help against their own workers and peasants to the imperialists of the West."

Thus began the wave of foreign intervention and the occupation of the borderlands, populated predominantly by non-Russian nationalities, which could not help hating Kolchak, Denikin, Wrangle [anti-Bolshevik or White Russian leaders in the Civil War], or their imperialistic and Russifying policy. In a report Stalin made at Baku on the 8th of November, 1920, under the title, "Three Years of the Proletarian Revolution," we find the following concluding words: "There is no doubt that our road is not one of the easiest but there is equally no doubt that we are not afraid of difficulties.... "

[The Red Army invaded Georgia in 1921 to annex it to the Soviet Union.] The military intervention passed quite successfully and did not provoke any international complications, if one does not take into account the frantic campaign of the bourgeoisie and the Second International. And yet, the method of the sovietization of Georgia had tremendous significance during the next few years. In regions where the toiling masses prior to the Revolution had managed in most cases to go over to Bolshevism, they accepted subsequent difficulties and sufferings as connected with their own cause. This was not so in the more backward regions, where the sovietization was carried out by the Army. There the toiling masses considered further deprivations a result of the regime imposed from the outside. In Georgia, premature sovietization strengthened the Mensheviks for a certain period and led to the broad mass insurrection in 1924, when, according to Stalin's own admission, Georgia had to be "replowed anew."

Trotsky, Leon. *Stalin: An Appraisal of the Man and His Influence.* Ed. and trans. Charles Malamuth. London: Hollis and Carter, 1947. Pp. 51, 54, 56-57, 189, 257-258, 261-262, 268.

TERROR IN STALIN'S SOVIET UNION

► Soviet Propaganda

Elena Bonner was born in 1923 into an intellectual family that had been well to do in the pre-revolutionary days and was prominent in the Communist government. She grew up amidst comfortable surroundings with many relatives, was looked after by nannies, and attended schools reserved for the children of the elite. Her grandmother introduced her to literature and her father read poetry to her. They frequented concerts and theatrical performances in Moscow and spent summers in a comfortable dasha [cottage] in the countryside. Their neighbors were other prominent Communists from the Soviet Union and other countries.

Her world fell apart in 1936 when her father, along with countless others, became a victim in Stalin's great purge. Men from state security agencies became familiar sights in her family's apartment building. When the head of a family was arrested, his family was bundled off too and their apartment doors was sealed. When the NKVD (secret service) summoned her father, the family never saw him again. Nor did it find out how he died. Later her mother was also arrested and would spend eight years in a labor camp because she was "wife of a traitor." Other relatives suffered similar fate, as indeed did millions of other victims of Stalin's paranoia. Elena and her younger brother would endure years of privation because of these purges.

Elena Bonner volunteered for army duty in 1941, served at the front and was seriously injured. After the war she entered university, first to study philosophy, later switched to medicine. She practiced as a pediatrician. She joined the Soviet Communist Party in 1965. Disillusionment with Communism led her to join the dissident movement. She met prominent physicist Andrei Sakharov in 1970 at the trial of a fellow dissident. They were married in the following year. Because of her Sakharov joined the Soviet human rights movement, and as a result became the most prominent victim of Soviet persecution. They spent six years between 1980 and 1986 in internal exile in Gorky and were only allowed to return to Moscow after Mikhail Gorbachev came to power and began his reform movement. They continued to work for democratization and human rights in the Soviet Union; after his death in 1989 she has carried on alone. Both Sakharov and Bonner are respected throughout the world for their commitment to democracy and human dignity.

The following are excerpts from Elena's second book, *Mothers and Daughters*, published in 1992.

QUESTIONS:

1) How did the elite members of the Communist party live?
2) Describe the questioning of a victim in a purge.
3) What happened to families of the purge victims?

I'm ashamed to admit it, but I don't remember anything about the rationing of those years [early 1930s]. Apparently our living conditions were such that it didn't affect my memory--that is, the question of hunger did not come up....

I do remember the food parcels. Papa's was delivered to the house, twice a month or more, but I don't know whether we paid for it. It had butter, cheese, candies, and canned goods. There were also special parcels for the holidays, with caviar, smoked and cured fish, chocolate, and also cheese and butter. You had to pick up Mama's parcels--not far away, on Petrovka. The dining room of the Moscow Party Committee was on the corner of Takhamanovsky Alley, and once a week they gave out the parcels. I often went for ours, and you had to pay. It contained butter and other items, but it was much less fancy that Papa's.

Mama never took part at all in running the household. Nura [housekeeper] was given expense money and she made the decisions on how to spend it. Mama gave the other nannies money once a week (I think), and grew angry when they tried to account for their expense to her.... I remember that on one of her visits, Batanya [Elena's maternal grandmother] scolded Mama and said that neither she nor Papa knew how much bread or sugar cost. She gave them a quiz. They failed.

[The family lived in Moscow in a large apartment building called the Luxe which was reserved for the elite.] The population of the Luxe was unofficially divided into Soviets and foreigners, but they were all tied to the Comintern.... There was a Pioneer room at the Luxe--a club for children, set up not so much for ideological reasons as to keep the kids out of the hallways. Of course, I spent some time there, but it wasn't interesting. Our main life took place in the corridors and lobbies. We played hide-and-seek, cossacks and robbers, and other group games there.

The children divided into groups according to both age and class, the latter based on the parents' positions.... There was also a language barrier for the foreign children, but that broke down quickly. All the children soon learned Russian, with their parents lagging behind.... One of the boys, a close friend was Zharko Walter, Tito's nephew [after World War II Tito became leader of Communist Yugoslavia] (Tito was also called Walter then). Zharko lived almost without supervision at the Luxe; his uncle didn't have time for him....

On the second floor of the Luxe to the left of the main lobby was the so-called Little Red Corner. "Some little corner," I thought the first time I looked in. It was big and high-ceilinged, a full two stories high, perhaps a restaurant or even a concert hall previously.... The Little Red Corner was used for meetings and movies. When Dimitrov, Tanev, and Popov came after the Reichstag Fire trial at Leipzig, the children in our building and many other "strangers" met with them and made them "honorary Pioneers" with speeches and red ties....

And in that room they conducted the purges --I don't remember when, but I'm sure it wasn't the winter that I ate a piece of metal and I had the operation, in January, 1934, but before that. The purging took place in the evening right after the adults finished work and went on a rather long time--maybe two weeks, maybe a month. The first few days it was interesting and many of the children hid behind the drapes of the Little Red Corner, to be part of it. But after just a few days most of the kids got sick and tired of it. I lasted the longest. Probably, it was my love of eavesdropping and spying. They purged only the Soviet Cominterners, but not all of them: the ones in the apparat, and the members of the Executive Committee, and the ones who worked in the dining room, and the motor pool, and the commandant's office (that is, for the superintendent of the building). His name was Brant. He seemed to love our family, especially Egorka [Elena's brother] and me. Of course, once Papa was arrested, the love died, and after that Brant was arrested too.

This is how the purging went. Several people sat at the table on stage. They called on someone who stood at the side of the stage but still in front of them and replied to questions facing the audience, with his side to the table. The questions came from the table and from the audience. And before the questions the person spoke about himself. Sometimes at length, sometimes briefly. You could see that they were nervous and some spoke very badly. There were a lot of words like "I mean" and "So to say," and coughing--they were like schoolchildren who had not learned their lessons....

They asked about people's wives and sometimes about their children. It turned out that some people beat their wives and drank a lot of vodka.... Sometimes the one being purged said that he wouldn't beat his wife anymore or drink anymore. And a lot of them said about their work that they "wouldn't do it anymore" and that "they understood everything."...

I went a few evenings in a row, but then I stopped. I'd look in as I walked past and see that the purges were still on and I'd keep walking. Once I saw my father on the stage.... Apparently, I was very late. Papa wasn't talking about himself, he was being asked about Leningrad and Zinoviev. Papa explained that he had had a fight with him and had returned to Leningrad with Kirov. Then someone at the table said that Papa had written something incorrect in Leningrad. Papa immediately agreed and said he hadn't understood right away. Another man at the table mentioned a name and said that Papa had insulted that man and had been crude and that he had to correct himself. Papa agreed again....

I didn't go to the purges anymore. It was very unpleasant--watching and listening to a group of adults being examined and behaving that way. Papa too....

[The family's real troubles began with Kirov's assassination in 1934. Elena's father had worked with Kirov. No the night they heard the news] my parents and their visitors weren't only saddened, they seemed extinguished somehow ... haunted. A cloud of smoke floated over the table. Only one lamp, over the telephone, was lit. Mama had not turned on the overhead light, a large old-fashioned candelabrum when she'd called Papa to eat, though in retrospect it seemed simply that no one thought to turn it on. They looked like conspirators to me....

[After the purge began in earnest] Every night at the Luxe bands of soldiers made arrests and we could hear their loud masterful steps. The faces of the residents reflected doom. Papa's too. The father of my friend from the fifth floor, Lusya Chermina, was arrested. I tried to console her. I told her it happened to everyone. And she said, "Not at your house." I answered with a convinced "It will." Hiding my wild secret hope that maybe, just maybe, it wouldn't. Lusya Chermina's mother later shared a room with my mother in the lower floor of the Luxe's outbuilding in the courtyard, which was called the "Nepman" building--temporarily, until the wives were arrested. Mama was taken a few days before Lusya Chernina's mother. They later met at the Akmolinsky Camp for Wives of Traitors of the Homeland, the acronym of which ALXHIR, sounded like Algiers.

Almost every day Seva [a friend] gave me news about neighbors and friends. Among others, the father of Yura Selivansky. Among others, the father of Sofa Bespalova....

I replied in kind. Among others, the mother of Elka. Among others, the father of Nadya Suvorova....

I don't remember my parents' attitude toward the families of their friends who were arrested before Papa, or who was arrested when. They seemed to go all at once.

[After the occupant of an apartment was arrested, his apartment was sealed. Elena remembered going to a store with her friend Seva.] When we got back, Mama had come home for lunch. Seva declined to join us, and so I saw him to the stairs. On the right-hand side of the corridor, there was a big reddish brown seal on the third door from the lobby. A weight hung from a tiny string embedded in the wax. Seva stared at me. "The people who lived here became among others last night," I replied to his unspoken question.

Those seals that jumped into your eyes appeared on many doors on every floor of our building over the winter of 1936-37, and especially in the spring of 1937. The seals were broken in a few days. Under the supervision of Commandant Brant, two or three suitcases and bundles of books were removed. The furniture and things that had the Comintern tags were cleaned. The floor polishers showed up, and in a few days a smiling Brant welcomed the new tenant and helped him with his things or called a porter. And right away, that same evening one of the kids would knock at the door and ask the standard question posed by all Muscovite children: "Do you have stamps?" The one who got there first would tell the other collectors to keep away.

The change in residents in our building kept pace with the arrests so that the population remained about the same. And the taking away of people became an ordinary, commonplace event. Quietly, at night, in the first half. So that the steps, cries, and occasional weeping were heard before three.... The number of children at the Luxe did not diminish as quickly as the number of adults taken away. The families were moved into the "Nepman" building in the courtyard. After some time the mother was usually arrested, and then the child was taken to an orphanage. Or by relatives. The ones who were older--like me--usually went off on their own. Sometimes the adolescents whispered questions like, "Do you know where---went off to?" The name was sometimes Russian, more often foreign....

The Pioneer room at the Luxe stopped functioning, and the corridor became deserted and quiet. No longer did hordes of "cossacks and robbers" gallop through them. The children who had been "resettled" from the fancy floors to the "Nepman" building sidled through the halls. When I became "resettled," I spoke very loudly. When I ran into Stella Blagoeva, the future Bulgarian Minister of Foreign Affairs, and saw she was trying to pretend I wasn't there, I barked a "Hello!" at her. That prompted her to tell me I was brazen and obnoxious. She had a good command of Russian.

Even the children who had not been resettled were subdued. Sometimes I had the feeling that everyone in the beautiful Luxe was hidden away like mice. Perhaps that's why the world revolution never came?

[Coming home from school one day] I pulled at our door, but it was locked. [After being let in by the housekeeper] I went in. And ... and I came down to earth. A soldier was with the Nun [the housekeeper] and I could see another one through the open door of the dining room. He was at Papa's chess table. The Nun said nothing, but I didn't need an explanation. It was clear. It was our turn, that's all.... But who? Papa or Mama?.... I sat down on the chair near my desk and did not move. Mama's look at me was, in farewell. That meant it was she. That was better than Papa, because Papa would save her. No. No one could save anyone. Otherwise they would have saved their friends....

[Elena was sent to Leningrad, but returned to Moscow to see her mother just before the latter was sent to prison.] I entered the room with them [soldiers]. Mama said in a resounding voice, "Well, that's it." She was still wearing Papa's purple-blue shirt. She quickly pulled a sweater over it and took her suitcase, packed long ago, from beneath the bed. As she threw her leather coat from Torgsin onto her shoulders, she turned to me. I was astonished by the radiance of her face and by the smile she gave me. She embraced me and kissed me several times and whispered barely audibly, "I have only you, only a daughter, no son. Never mention Egorka; they will take him away."

She smiled and gently pushed me aside. She went out the door, and one soldier immediately followed her. The other looked around the room and then said, "Tomorrow we'll come back for your brother." He left without closing the door. The corridor was very quiet. I shut the door and saw the chocolate bar on the table. I put it in my pocket. I took the tiny case that I had brought from Leningrad. I tiptoed down the corridor to the backstairs and out into the courtyard. I never set foot in the Luxe again.

Bonner, Elena. *Mothers and Daughters*. Trans. Antonia W. Bouis. New York: Knopf, 1992. Pp. 126-129, 146-150, 188, 261-262, 264-266, 287-288, 298, 322.

HOW TO BE A GOOD NAZI

▶ *Ein Volk, ein Reich, ein Führer* ("One People, One Empire, One Leader")

After World War I, totalitarian regimes of both the left and right emerged in Europe. They exerted absolute control over the political and social lives of their peoples and also tried to mold their minds. Germany became one of the most vicious and rigid totalitarian states under Adolf Hitler (1889-1945).

Hitler, an Austrian by birth, had been wounded and decorated during the First World War and became an ardent German nationalist. He joined the newly formed National Socialist (Nazi) Party, which opposed the Weimar government. Convicted for his part in a failed coup in 1923, Hitler served a short jail term, during which he wrote *Mein Kampf* [*My Struggle*], a book that detailed his plans and views.

Hitler imitated the violent tactics pioneered by Benito Mussolini and his totalitarian right-wing Fascist Party in Italy. He used a uniformed paramilitary force of "Brownshirts," and mobilized public support through party rallies and the mass media. He exploited nationalism, hatred for communism, and virulent anti-Semitism to win the support of some big businessmen, the lower middle classes, and all who felt victimized by the Treat of Versailles and the massive economic problems caused by the Great Depression. To alleviate divisiveness among the major political parties in the German legislature, the elderly President Paul von Hindenburg appointed Hitler chancellor (prime minister) in 1933. Hitler and the Nazis quickly swept all opposition aside through political maneuvering and the terror tactics of storm troopers and secret police. After Hindenburg's death in 1934, Hitler combined the powers of the president with those of the chancellorship in himself as *Der Führer* (The Leader). Hitler banned all other political parties, making membership in the Nazi Party the only avenue to advancement and power.

The following selection is from a Nazi Party Handbook. It outlines requirements for admission to the Party and instructs members on proper behavior and correct attitudes.

QUESTIONS:

1) While much of the Nazi Party Handbook seems innocuous, almost like a boy-scout code, threads of very sinister ideas and attitudes run through it. What are some of these ideas?

2) How does the notion of a Führer as a supreme model appear in the handbook?

3) What do Nazi party officials seem to be looking for in particular in prospective party members?

GENERAL BEARING OF THE NATIONAL SOCIALIST

The National Socialist must regard himself as a servant of the movement and of the people. This applies especially to the political leaders, the leaders of all party formations, and the administrative officers and members of the associated organizations.

To keep alive the idea of the people's community and constantly to strengthen it is the highest mission of National Socialism. It is incompatible with this mission for any individual to separate himself from his party comrades and his fellow Germans, to regard himself as better than they, and to open up those chasms which it has cost the heart's blood of the best German men to bridge over. In assuming a higher office, a National Socialist undertakes higher duties. His increased powers are lent to him only so that he will be able to fulfil these higher duties. They do not give him the right to become high and mighty, arrogant, and mysterious. He will never win the confidence and the willing obedience of his followers through threats and aggravating words. On duty he should be a leader and promoter; off duty he should be a good comrade and helper to his sub-leaders, party comrades, and fellow Germans. The more his deeds are in harmony with his words, the more willingly will his party comrades and his fellow Germans follow him.

Every National Socialist should be simple and modest in his bearing as was customary during National Socialism's struggle for power.... A leading party comrade must never be vain or supersensitive, and he must always prefer the honest and candid words of a proved fighter to the honeyed words of those creatures who seek to flatter by agreeing with him. He should always remain in touch with the humblest members of our people and have a willing ear for their needs and their troubles. They will come to him gladly if he is still the same person and if he moves in the same company and the same environment as during the years of struggle.

The political leaders and administrators and the leaders of the organizations should not take part in elaborate banquets nor express their favor by awarding gifts and honors, nor frequent the most expensive places, but on and off duty they should always so act as is to be expected of a representative of the German freedom movement and a participator in the unspeakably hard work of constructing a better Germany. Above all, the excessive indulgence in alcohol should be avoided in a time when many German families still do not have the barest necessities of life and will lose their painfully restored faith if the men of the movement engage in drinking bouts which last beyond the legal hour whenever possible and if they damage the prestige of the movement by appearing publicly in a drunken condition.

A true National Socialist does not boast of his deeds and he demands no thanks. His highest rewards are the consciousness of having fulfilled his duty, the success of his work, and the confidence of his followers. A National Socialist will always act rightly if he daily examines himself and asks himself whether his work and his attitude could stand inspection by the Führer.

THE PARTY MEMBER

Admission:

Any member of the German people who has a clean record, who is of pure German blood, who does not belong to a Freemason's lodge or any related organization, and who has completed his twenty-first (in some cases his eighteenth) year can become a member of the NSDAP by filling out the admission form and paying the regular admission fee. The party leadership can decree a ban on new admissions at any time or can limit the admissions to certain groups of people. Announcements regarding these matters may only be made by the national treasurer of the NSDAP.

Refusal of membership is made without any explanation of reasons by the local group leader in agreement with the party court for that district. Against this refusal there is no legal redress.

Membership is finally confirmed by the issuance of a membership card or a membership book. Anyone who becomes a party member does not merely join an organization but he becomes a soldier in the German freedom movement and that means much more than just paying his dues and attending the members' meetings. He obligates himself to subordinate his own ego and to place everything he has in the service of the people's cause. Only he who is capable of doing this should become a party member.   A selection must be made in accordance with this idea.

Readiness to fight, readiness to sacrifice, and strength of character are the requirements for a good National Socialist. Small blemishes, such as a false step which someone has made in his youth, should be overlooked; the contribution in the struggle for Germany should alone be decisive. The healthy will naturally prevail over the bad if the will to health finds sufficient support in leadership and achievement. Admission to the party should not be controlled by the old bourgeois point of view. The party must always represent the elite of the people. Therefore, care should be taken in the admission of members and all narrow-minded or self-important types who are self-seeking or lacking in true character should be denied admission or cast out....

Procedure for the Admission of a New Member:

No individual member of the people has a legal claim to admission into the NSDAP--not even if he fulfils the conditions prescribed for admission. In admitting people into the party, it must be the first principle of all offices which are concerned with admissions that the Führer wishes to be able to count upon the party as a community pledged to a political fighting spirit.

In accordance with the will expressed by the Führer only the best National Socialists should be admitted to membership in the party. The persons in authority should therefore propose such persons for admission as are ready and willing to work and to fight for the Führer and his movement. In admitting new members, the persons in authority are expected always to remain fully conscious of their great obligation to the Führer and the movement. In the selection of new party members, they bear responsibility for the smooth running and the success of our work not only for the next period but also for the more distant future. The admission of new members is of the greatest importance not only for the local spheres of the individual party authorities but also for the party throughout the whole Reich and for the future formation of the political destiny of the German people....

As a matter of principle younger applicants for admission are to be shown preference. In general only persons who have already completed their twenty-first year may be admitted.

Male applicants under 25 years of age must show proof that they have completed their military service before they can be admitted. Persons who have been found unsuited for military service can only be admitted to the party if they are capable and qualified to wear the party uniform--that is, if they are not afflicted with any serious physical or mental incapacity. The party offices which are concerned with admissions are obligated to ascertain the presence of all the necessary qualifications and to confirm them in a report to the national leadership of the party....

Only those racial comrades are eligible for admission who possess German citizenship.

In the selection of prospective members the greatest care must be taken to prevent the infusion of religious disagreements into the party. Clergymen and other persons who have strong denominational connections cannot be admitted. Here must also be included professors on the theological faculties of the philosophical and theological universities and similar educational institutions for clergymen and theological students. Likewise excluded from admission to the NSDAP are former members of the disbanded Theosophic Society as well as members of the Anthroposophic Society. Former members of the French Foreign Legion also cannot be admitted....

All the party comrades who participate in refusal proceedings should in every case secure for themselves a complete picture of the entire personality of the applicant and should decide on the basis of this investigation whether he can be counted among the best National Socialists who, according to the will of the Führer, should become party members. The correct filling out of the questionnaire will curtail and alleviate the work of the offices of the party jurisdiction and administration.

The application must be refused in all cases where:

a) The marriage partner of the applicant is not free from Jewish or colored racial admixture;

b) Such a marriage has been dissolved by divorce or by the death of the partner, but there remain children from this marriage;

c) The applicant has belonged to a Freemason's lodge or similar organization

(Odd Fellows, Druid Order, etc.) or to any secret society;

d) The applicant has been convicted of defamatory actions--however, undue harshness is to be avoided if special merits are present;

e) The applicant has not been honorably discharged from the armed forces;

f) The applicant suffers from a hereditary illness, as defined by the law of July 14, 1933 for the prevention of the procreation of congenitally unhealthy elements....

Pledging:

Upon receipt of his membership card the member takes a solemn pledge. This pledge must be taken by all new party comrades, regardless of whether or not they are members of the SA or the SS.

The pledge is administered by the *Ortsgruppenleiter* [local group leader] in a meeting of the members. In a short address he explains the duties of the party member and he points out the significance of the pledge of allegiance. Then he pronounces the pledge of allegiance sentence by sentence. Those who are to be pledged, while facing him, repeat it after him with their right arms raised in the German greeting. The pledge of loyalty is as follows: "I pledge allegiance to my Führer, Adolf Hitler. I promise at all times to respect and obey him and the leaders whom he appoints over me."

The solemn presentation of the membership book is made at the same meeting by the *Ortsgruppenleiter*, with the words: "In the name of the Führer I present to you your membership book. Remain true to the party as you have been in the past."...

Duties of the Party Comrade:

The National Socialist commandments:

The Führer is always right!

Never go against discipline!

Don't waste your time in idle chatter or in self-satisfying criticism, but take hold and do your work!

Be proud but not arrogant!

Let the program be your dogma. It demands of you the greatest devotion to the movement.

You are a representative of the party; control your bearing and your manner accordingly!

Let loyalty and unselfishness be your highest precepts!

Practice true comradeship and you will be a true socialist!

Treat your racial comrades as you wish to be treated by them!

In battle be hard and silent!

Spirit is not unruliness!

That which promotes the movement, Germany, and your people, is right!

If you act according to these commandments, you are a true soldier of your Führer.

Guiding Principles for Members of the *Ortsgruppen* [local groups]:

The following guiding principles are to be made known to all members, and all men and women of the party should impress them upon themselves:

Lighten the work of the political leaders by the punctual performance of your duties.

Women of the party should participate in the activities of the NS Association of Women; there they will find work to do.

Don't buy from Jews!

Spare the health of the part comrades and speakers and refrain voluntarily from smoking at the meetings.

Don't make yourself a mouthpiece for our political opponents by spreading false reports.

To be a National Socialist is to set an example.

The Wearing of Insignia and Uniforms by Party Comrades:

1) It is the duty of every party comrade, whether political leader, member of a party formation or an associated organization, to wear his party button at all times.

2) After two years of membership the member is entitled to wear the brown shirt with his civilian dress.

3) The wearing of the service dress or parts of the service dress of the political leaders of the SA, the SS, the NSKK, or the HJ, with or without the party button, is only permitted to those who officially belong to the formation in question and who are in possession of the proper identification card.

4) Party members who are employed in Jewish enterprises may not wear uniforms or insignia of the party or of any of its

formations or associated organizations
while they are at work.

5) The wearing of service dress (but not of the
brown shirt alone, without any insignia) is
forbidden when appearing before the courts
(including the labor courts). Witnesses
may appear in service dress.

U.S. Department of State, Division of European Affairs.
*National Socialism: Basic Principles, Their Application by
the Nazi Party's Foreign Organization, and the Use of
Germans Abroad for Nazi Aims*. Washington: Government
Printing Office, 1943. Pp. 186-195.

BLUEPRINT OF
JAPANESE IMPERIALISM

▶ **Flags of Imperial Japan**

Japan, Italy, and Germany formed an alliance called the Axis in 1938 in their quest to conquer the world. The Axis was the logical culmination of each nation's militaristic, racist, and imperialistic policies. Their policy of world domination led to World War II.

Unique among Asian nations in successfully modernizing and industrializing, Japan began an imperialistic policy in late nineteenth century. After acquiring Taiwan and Korea, it obtained special economic privileges in northeastern China (called Manchuria in the West). A special branch of the Japanese Army, called the Kwantung Army, guarded Japanese interests in Manchuria and spearheaded Japanese aggression. A hotbed of ultranationalism, Kwantung Army officers formed the Black Dragon Society and the Imperial Way Faction, bent on "direct action" including assassinations, dirty tricks, pre-emptive attacks, and threatened coups to achieve their goals.

In 1927, Prime Minister Tanaka Giichi called a conference on East Asian affairs for high-ranking military and civil officials. They drafted a policy document, the Tanaka Memorial, which became the blueprint for Japanese aggression against China during the next decade. Part of the Memorial forms the first part of this reading.

Because China had no effective central government until 1927, Japan had relied on the compliance of Marshal Chang Tso-lin, warlord of Manchuria, to maintain and expand its privileges in that resource-rich region. In 1927, officers of the Kwantung Army murdered Chang Tso-lin in hopes of seizing Manchuria in the ensuing chaos. However, they bungled this attempt, and when Chang's son and successor resisted Japanese domination, Doihara Kenji, head of the intelligence section of the Kwantung Army, masterminded a plot to seize Manchuria.

On 18 September 1931, ostensibly in reaction to a small explosion on a Japanese controlled railway in Manchuria, units of the Kwantung Army swung into action, quickly seizing over a dozen cities across Manchuria. This event is called the Manchurian or Mukden (after the administrative capital of Manchuria) Incident.

Too weak to resist on its own, China appealed to the League of Nations which called on Japan to cease its aggression. Unable to restrain the army, the Japanese cabinet fell. Reinforced by the Japanese army in Korea, the Kwantung Army conquered Manchuria by 1932. Before that, Doihara had lured the last Ch'ing emperor to Manchuria where he was "restored" as emperor of a Japanese-sponsored puppet state. When the League of Nations Report condemned Japanese aggression, Japan resigned in protest. This defiance doomed the League and later encouraged Mussolini to conquer Ethiopia, and Hitler to scrap the Treaty of Versailles.

The second and third segments of this reading are from the Judgement of the International Military Tribunal for the Far East that tried Japanese war criminals after World War II, and from the statement of the crimes committed by Doihara Kenji. He was found guilty of plotting aggression and other crimes against China crimes and hanged.

QUESTIONS:

1) Why, according to the Tanaka Memorial, must Japan control Manchuria and Mongolia?
2) Why did the Japanese engineer the murder of Chang Tso-lin?
3) How did Doihara entice Pu-Yi to become a Japanese puppet?

The Tanaka Memorial

The Three Eastern Provinces [Manchuria] are situated in a region of East Asia where political developments have not been stable. If we Japanese wish to preserve and advance our interests in East Asia, we must be willing to implement a policy of blood and iron, and begin by using blood and iron to secure the Three Eastern Provinces. We must understand that China is anxious to use the United States against us in pursuing its policy of "using barbarians to control barbarians." Since the United States will be swayed by China's claims, we will not be able to avoid a confrontation with the United States in the future. Going one step further ... unless we pursue a forward policy in East Asia, our country will have no hope for expansion in the years to come and will not be able to face the inevitable war with Russia in the future. Thus in order to conquer China, we must first neutralize the power of the United States ... then we must conquer Manchuria and Mongolia as a first step toward conquering China, and we must first conquer China before we can realize our goal of world domination....

If we are to implement the new Showa [reign title of Emperor Hirohito] Era, we must aggressively seize political advantages in Manchuria and Mongolia and use them to advance our economic interests. Only thus can we prevent China from building its own industries and forestall further European advances in the East.... If we succeed in seizing Manchuria and Mongolia and use them as our forward command posts, we can gain control of all the resources of China. With China's resources at our command, we can then conquer India and Southeast Asia, and further expand to Central Asia and Asia Minor, and beyond to Europe. Thus the securing of Manchuria and Mongolia are crucial to the conquest of the Asian mainland by our race.

Murder of Marshal Chang Tso-lin

Marshal Chang Tso-lin [Chinese ruler of Manchuria] had not only disregarded the advice of Premier Tanaka in attempting to extend his authority south of the Great Wall, but had shown increasing unwillingness to allow Japan to exploit China by privileges she derived from various treaties and agreements. This attitude of the Marshal had caused a group of officers in the Kwantung Army to advocate that force should be used to promote the interests of Japan in Manchuria and to maintain that nothing was to be gained by negotiating with the Marshal.... This resentment of the Marshal by certain officers of the Kwantung Army became so intense that a senior staff officer of the army, Colonel Kawamoto, planned to murder the Marshal. The purpose of the murder was to remove him as the obstacle to the creation of a new state in Manchuria, dominated by Japan, with the Marshal's son, Chang Hsueh-liang, as its nominal head.

In the latter part of April 1928, the Marshal was defeated by the nationalist armies of Generalissimo Chiang Kai-shek. Premier Tanaka advised him to withdraw into Manchuria behind the Japanese lines before it was too late. The Marshal resented this advice, but was forced to follow it. The Kwantung Army, in accordance with Tanaka's declaration, that Japan would prevent defeated troops from entering Manchuria, was engaged in disarming Chinese troops retreating toward Mukden from Peking. The Marshal, with his bodyguard, boarded a train for Mukden. The Japanese 20th Engineer Regiment, which had arrived at Mukden from Korea, mined the railroad with dynamite and a Japanese Captain placed his soldiers in position around the mine. On June 4, 1928, when the Marshal's train reached the mine ... there was an explosion. The Marshal's train was wrecked and Japanese soldiers began firing upon the Marshal's bodyguard. The Marshal was killed as planned. An attempt was made to obtain an order to muster the entire Kwantung Army into action and exploit the incident and attain its original purpose, but the effort was thwarted by a staff officer who apparently did not understand the real purpose of those desiring the issuance of the order.

The Tanaka Cabinet was taken by surprise and greatly embarrassed as it saw its program endangered by this murder of the Marshal. Premier Tanaka made a full report to the Emperor and obtained his permission to court-martial those responsible.... [However the Minister of War thwarted the court martial by citing] the opposition of the Army General Staff based ... on the idea that to court-martial those responsible would force the Army to make public some of its military secrets. This was the first time ... that the Army had projected itself into the formulation of government policy.

It was at this time that DOIHARA appeared upon a scene in which he was to play an important part. He had spent approximately eighteen years in China prior to the murder of Marshal Chang Tso-lin ... and was present in Manchuria when the Marshal was killed.

The Young Marshal, Chang Hsueh-liang, succeeded his father; but he proved to be a disappointment to the Kwantung Army. He joined the Kuomintang Party in December 1928; and anti-Japanese movements began to be promoted on an organized scale and gained greatly in intensity. The movement for the recovery of Chinese national rights gained strength. There was a demand for the recovery of the South Manchurian Railway and for the limitation of the Japanese influence in Manchuria.... Japanese-Chinese relations in Manchuria became extremely aggravated.

Indictment against Doihara, Kenji
Facts found:

DOIHARA became acquainted with former accused OKAWA [an ultra-nationalist writer associated with Japanese imperialist causes] who advocated the incorporation of Manchuria into the Japanese Empire in order to make Japan economically self-sufficient and capable of waging a protracted war with the United States. For over two years prior to the Manchurian Incident, OKAWA hada been agitating for positive action in collaboration with the Army. DOIHARA and others in the Army made it possible for OKAWA to lecture openly at the General Staff. OKAWA also lectured throughout Japan. He urged the unification of public opinion on foreign policy and claimed that the solution of the Manchurian problem was an absolute condition of the very existence of Japan. He advocated world supremacy for Japan; urged Japan to prepare for war with America; and attacked the *status quo*. DOIHARA was implicated with OKAWA in the drafting of a plan to set up a Cabinet centering around the Army with a more positive policy towards Manchuria.

In August 1931, DOIHARA was appointed the Chief of the Special Service Organ of the Kwantung Army at Mukden and arrived there on 18th August 1931....

Early in September 1931, reports reached Tokyo that ITAGAKI and other staff officers of the Kwantung Army ... were scheming to start military action in Manchuria. DOIHARA was summoned to Tokyo to report. Despite the wish of General Chang Hsueh-liang for a peaceful settlement, DOIHARA was quoted by the Tokyo press as an advocate of the solution of all pending issues in Manchuria by force, if necessary, and as soon as possible.

Although DOIHARA was not in Mukden on the night of the 18th September 1931, the office of his Special Service Organ was the centre of invasion operations. This organ served as a link in the chain of communications between the outposts and the Headquarters of the Kwantung Army.

On the morning of 19th September 1931, Mukden was occupied by Japanese troops after the Japanese had created an "incident" for the purpose. The Kwantung Army moved into Mukden on the same morning. Following his return from Tokyo, DOIHARA was appointed on 21st September Mayor of Mukden assisted by an Emergency Committee with a majority of Japanese members. All the important positions in his administration were occupied by Japanese.

In the latter part of September 1931, when the Self-Government guidance Board was set up in Mukden to foster the so-called independence movement, DOIHARA was in charge of the Special Service or Espionage Division....

In November 1931, DOIHARA in Tientsin was planning to take Pu-Yi [last emperor of the Ch'ing dynasty in China, abdicated in 1912] to Mukden, but the latter refused and was being threatened....

DOIHARA had been previously told by his Government ... that the creation of an independent state in Manchuria at that time would raise the question of its being contrary to Section 1, Article 1 of the Nine Power Treaty [1922, signed by Japan and eight other nations to guarantee the independence and territorial integrity of China]. But he insisted upon carrying out the plan ... [saying] that it would be possible to pretend that Japan had nothing to do with it by landing the ex-Emperor at Yinkow [a port in Manchuria]. On the same day, DOIHARA pointed out ... that in case the enthronement of the Emperor became indispensable in order to save the situation, it would be outrageous for the Japanese Government to take action to prevent it. He added that in case of interference by the Government, the Kwantung Army might separate from the Government and accidents graver than assassination might occur in Japan.

Doihara then had an interview with Pu-Yi and insisted upon the latter's return to Manchuria by all means before November 16th. In the meantime DOIHARA associated himself with various factions and subversive organizations to cause a riot to occur on 8th November, and carried out the ex-Emperor's passage to Manchuria amid confusion following the riot. Consul Arakawa [Japanese consul in Tientsin] reported on 13th November that DOIHARA headed the plot for the escape of the ex-Emperor from Tientsin under armed guard. Pu-Yi was at first placed under the "protective custody" of the Japanese army at Yinkow....

After Pu-Yi's departure from Tientsin, DOIHARA remained there until the end of November, and caused a second riot on 26th November. In the evening, a terrific explosion was heard, immediately followed by firing of cannon, machine guns and rifles, while plain-clothes men emerged from the Japanese concession to attack the police station in the vicinity. Using this as a pretext, the Kwantung Army sent troops across the Liao River on 27th November and bombed Chinchow [last Chinese controlled outpost in Manchuria].

As Chinchow was situated between the areas occupied by Japanese troops and the Tientsin-Peiping area, the disturbances in the latter area, where there were some Japanese, gave the Kwantung Army a pretext to push towards the Great Wall and thereby dislodge the Chinese troops from Chinchow....

DOIHARA was promoted to major general on 11th April 1932.

After 18th September 1931, many opium shops were opened in Mukden by the Japanese. DOIHARA was mayor when the Municipal Administrative Office planned the monopolization of opium and the issuing of lottery tickets for the purpose of raising funds.

Prior to the setting up of the Opium Control Board in 1935, the Mukden Special Service Organ headed by DOIHARA was in control of opium traffic in southern Manchuria.

Lu-hai-k'ung chun tsung shih ling pu, Jih-pen Tien-chung nei-ko chin-lioh Man-Men shih-chih cheng-cheh tsu chang [The Tanaka Cabinet's Memorial on the Implementing of an Aggressive Policy toward Manchuria and Mongolia]. Pp. 7-8. Translation by Jiu-Hwa Lo Upshur. *Judgement of the International Military Tribunal for the Far East*. Part B. Chapter V: *Japanese Aggression against China*. Sections 1-7. Pp. 527-529. Webb's Judgement. Part 6. In *Individual Cases Before the International Military Tribunal for the Far East*. Pp. 292-299.

JAPANESE AGGRESSION AGAINST CHINA

▶ **Chinese Soldier Bids Farewell to Wife and Child**

Japan alone among Asian countries succeeded in transforming itself from a feudal agrarian to a powerful modern industrial nation. In late nineteenth century, Japanese leaders initiated an imperialistic foreign policy to acquire an overseas empire. China and Korea were its first victims. Defeating China in the Sino-Japanese war of 1894-1895, Japan annexed its first colony, China's Taiwan province; China was also forced to end its centuries-long overlordship over Korea. After defeating Russia decisively in 1905, Japan moved to annex Korea in 1910. After World War I, Japan acquired former German possessions in the Pacific called the Micronesian Islands, and replaced Germany in its sphere of influence in China's Shantung province. Its appetite whetted by repeated successes, Japan began to covet other regions in China.

In 1928, the Kuomintang or Nationalist party under general Chiang Kai-shek (1887-1975) defeated the many warlords who had ruled China since 1912, and established China's first modern government. During the next decade the Nationalist government strove to unify and modernize the country, while Japan accelerated the pace of its of aggression in China to forestall the completion of Chinese programs. Thus in 1931 Japanese forces staged an "incident" in China's rich northeast (Manchuria) as pretext to conquer a territory larger than France and Germany combined. China appealed to the League of Nations, which called on Japan to cease its aggression, which the Japanese army ignored. The League-appointed Commission reported that Japan been the aggressor, that the puppet government it established in Manchuria had no public support, and recommended that Manchuria be restored to China. Japan promptly resigned from the League. Impotent to do anything else, the League was doomed. The United States, in a Doctrine of Non-recognition, stated that it would not recognize the illegally established Manchukuo regime of the Japanese in Manchuria. No other international actions were taken against Japan.

Japan continued to advance against China, detaching regions in north China and forming puppet regimes, destabilizing the Chinese currency by armed smuggling, and harassing the Chinese government in other ways. Faced with a communist rebellion, a backward economy, and numerous other problems, the Chinese government made concessions to Japan, trading space for time, while it hurried desperately to build up its armed forces. Its appeals to the international community were all in vain, because the western nations were struggling to recover from the Depression and because of the prevailing sentiment that aggressors could be appeased by concessions.

In Japan, a military uprising in 1936 solidified military control of the government, thus ensuring accelerated aggression against China. Events in China in 1936 led to negotiations between the Kuomintang and the Chinese Communists to end their civil war and form a united front government to resist Japan. Thus the fate of both China and Japan were sealed.

On 7 July 1937 Japanese troops provoked an incident at Lukouchiao (known in the west as Marco Polo Bridge) near Peking that led to Japan's invasion of north China, and quickly to an all out war against China. The Chinese were agreed that the time for a last ditch stand had arrived. The Sino-Japanese War, which later expanded to World War II in Asia, lasted from 1937 to 1945.

The first part of this reading is a statement by Chiang Kai-shek, chairman of the Military Affairs Commission of China and leader of the Kuomintang, made on 17 July 1937. Here he clarified the position of the Chinese government and set down the terms that China could accept. He also made clear that, if compelled, China would fight an all out war of resistance. The second selection is an appeal Chiang made to the reporter of the *Paris Evening News* for international support. He prophetically pointed out that it was in the West's self interest to stop Japanese aggression, because Japan's imperial agenda also included the expulsion of western empires from their Asian colonial possessions.

QUESTIONS:

1) What were Japan's goals in instigating the Lukouchiao Incident?
2) Why must China resist Japan?
3) Why was it in Western interest to help China stop Japan?

Gentlemen: The "Lukouchiao Incident" happened as China is engaged in the pursuit of international peace and domestic unity. The incident has caused great indignation at home and shocked the international community. This is because both China's continued existence as a nation and the well-being of humanity are tied to the development and resolution of the incident. You who are concerned about the fate of our nation are especially interested in this matter. Therefore I shall frankly state several important points that pertain to this issue.

First: the Chinese people are deeply peace loving. The foreign policy of the National Government is based on the maintaining of national independence and peaceful co-existence with all nations.... We have consistently followed this aim in our policy toward Japan during the past two years. We hoped to end the incidents that have plagued our past relations and to use diplomacy to solve our problems in the future. Our records are open for all to see. I have always felt that we need to recognize our nation's position as we seek to meet our national emergency. We are a weak nation ... and because we want to build up our nation, we absolutely need peace. That is why we have swallowed our pride and submitted to humiliations during past years in order to maintain peace. As I stated in the foreign policy report to the Fifth Party Congress two years ago:

"We will not abandon our quest for peace until there is absolutely no hope for peace; nor will we speak lightly of sacrifice until we have reached the last ditch when sacrifice cannot be avoided."... [But] when we reach the last ditch, our whole race must be ready to make the final sacrifice for the survival of our country ... because only through a resolution to sacrifice to the end can we win final victory. If we waver, our race will face annihilation.

Second: Some people have suggested that the "Lukouchiao Incident" was unpremeditated [on Japan's part]. But we feel [otherwise because] ... for over a month prior to the incident, the other side [Japan] has orchestrated a diplomatic offensive [against China]. It demanded [that China agree to] the expansion of the Tangku Agreement, an increase in the territory controlled by the East Hopei Bogus Regime [agreement and concessions Japan had earlier wrested from China], the expulsion of the 29th Army from its garrison territory, etc., etc. .... We know from these demands that they have expanded their aggressive designs, that peace has become more elusive. If we want peace now, it can only be purchased at the price of allowing their military forces unlimited access to our land, while our own armed forces must submit to severe limitations in their right to garrison parts of our own country. It means that we may not return fire while their military can attack us at will....

We have been required to submit to indignities that no self-respecting people in the world can be expected to submit to. It is six years since we lost the four northeastern provinces [Manchuria].... We are now threatened at Lukouchiao, almost at the gate of Peiping [Peking]. If we lose Lukouchiao, then strategic Peiping, also China's cultural city and capital for five hundred years, will become a second Shenyang [capital of Manchuria].... If Peiping can become a second Shenyang, what will prevent Nanking [China's capital] from becoming a second Peiping? Thus the resolution of the Lukouchiao Incident will affect the future of our entire nation. Thus we are faced with a last ditch.

Third: If we are confronted with an unavoidable last ditch, we will of course be resolved to sacrifice ourselves in a war of resistance. We do not wish war, but we will resist.... Although weak, we must resist to preserve our nation. This is a historic responsibility bequeathed to us by our ancestors.... We must understand that once war begins all possibility of negotiation ends. We must fight to the end to preserve our territory and sovereignty, or we will forever be condemned as traitors to our race. Then we must be prepared to sacrifice all for final victory.

Fourth: Whether the Lukouchiao Incident will expand to an all out war between China and Japan will entirely depend on the Japanese government's attitude. Whether peace can be restored will depend solely on the actions of the Japanese military. We will persevere in our quest for peace down to the last second before all hope for a peaceful diplomatic solution is lost. But there are four points we must insist on in a peaceful solution: (1) No compromise to China's sovereignty or territorial integrity. (2) No unlawful changes in the administration of Hopei and Chahar provinces [which Japan hoped to detach from Chinese control]. (3) Officials appointed by the Chinese central government in Hopei and Chahar ... cannot be removed on demand [Japan had demanded the right to veto Chinese government appointments in Hopei and Chahar]. (4) The 29th Army cannot be restricted in its garrison area [Japan had demanded that Chinese garrisons be removed from Hopei and Chahar provinces, leaving them open to Japanese

occupation]. The above four points are the minimum a weak nation like China must insist on [to preserve its independence].... We hope the other side realizes that the future of our two nations is at a crucial turning point, and that it does not pursue a policy that will make China and Japan everlasting enemies. We therefore sincerely hope that it will not treat our minimum demands lightly.

In conclusion, the government has determined its policy principles on the resolution of the Lukouchiao Incident and will not deviate from them. We hope for peace, but not at any price. We are preparing to resist but do not wish war. We know that once war begins, we can only sacrifice to the end, and will not sue for peace. Once war begins there will be no distinction between north and south, between old and young, everyone will equally be responsible for defending our nation, and everyone must be prepared to sacrifice all....

* * * * *

The present war between China and Japan is the result of Japanese aggression against China. China has been compelled to resist to defend its existence. In deploying a huge military force to carry out aggressions against China, Japan's goal is the annihilation of the Chinese nation. Our policy in meeting this aggression is to preserve the existence of the Chinese nation. Shanghai and north China [two areas Japanese forces were attacking China] are equally parts of China.... China will not cease to resist as long as Japan pursues its aggression anywhere in China. We will continue to resist to the last gun and bullet.... I fervently hope that the international community will insist on discharging its responsibility under the League of Nations Covenant, and force Japan from continuing its aggression. Only firm actions will preserve world peace, human civilization, the sanctity of treaties, and the enforcement of international law. For six years since 1931, Japan's brutal aggressions against China have proved that its ambition is to dominate all East Asia. If the Powers do not act in time to halt Japan's aggressions, not only will they lose their existing commercial rights in China, their possessions in East Asia will also come under jeopardy. Thus the halting of Japanese aggression will not only help China, but will preserve the rights and interests of members of the League of Nations, and non-members with interest in the region [U.S.].   I am convinced that far-sighted statesmen from many nations understand the stakes and will do their duty to stop Japan.

Chiang, Kai-shek. *K'ang chan erh nien chien, Chiang chung ts'ai yen lun chi*. 1939. Pp.1-4, 10. Translation by Jiu-Hwa Lo Upshur.

ADOLF HITLER'S PLANS TO DOMINATE EUROPE

Adolf Hitler came to power in Germany in 1933. By 1934, he had transformed Germany into a totalitarian state ruled by the National Socialist or Nazi Party he headed. In foreign policy, Hitler demanded that territories of German-speaking peoples should be incorporated into the Third Reich (empire). He inaugurated programs to rearm Germany and rebuild German armament industries. In 1936, Hitler sent the German army into the Rhineland, demilitarized under the Treaty of Versailles as a buffer zone between Germany and France. Although France had the strength to stop the Germans and enforce the treaty, it failed to do so. Hitler won his gamble and his prestige soared.

Early in 1938, Hitler again violated the Treat of Versailles by absorbing German-speaking Austria in a bloodless *Anschluss* (annexation). A few months later, he turned his attention to Czechoslovakia, where three million ethnic Germans lived in the Sudeten mountain region bordering Germany. When Hitler demanded the incorporation of this region into the German Reich, British prime minister Neville Chamberlain, joined by the French premier Edouard Daladier, and the leader of Fascist Italy, Benito Mussolini, met with Hitler at Munich in September 1938, to address this issue. The Czech representative was not admitted to the discussions. Britain and France decided to appease Hitler. By the terms of the Munich Agreement, they allowed Hitler to annex the Sudetenland in return for his assurances that the rest of Czechoslovakia would remain free. As a result, Czechoslovakia lost a third of its population, much of its heavy industry, and important defensive fortifications. By March 1939, Hitler and the governments of Hungary and Poland had divided the remainder of Czechoslovakia.

Hitler then seized Memel, a Baltic port with a large German population, from Lithuania, and demanded Danzig, which also had a German-speaking population, and other concessions from Poland. British and French leaders finally realized that Hitler's word was worthless and announced that they would fight if Poland were attacked. Hitler, reflecting on past experience, naturally doubted their resolve.

To secure Germany from a two-front war if the British and French attack the Reich, Hitler had signed a non-aggression pact with Joseph Stalin in August 1939. Germany and the Soviet Union agreed not to attack each other and to remain neutral should either be attacked by a third nation. Stalin signed in order to gain time to build up the Soviet military for an eventual reckoning with Hitler. In an appended secret protocol, the Soviet Union and Germany agreed to partition Poland. Thus protected, Germany invaded Poland on 1 September 1939 and ushered Europe into World War II.

The following reading is from Hitler's address to his top military commanders in November 1939. It reviews his aggressions since becoming *Führer* and outlines his plans for an assault on western Europe.

QUESTIONS:

1) Hitler liked to emphasize the heroism of the struggle he undertook in order to rise the political prominence and then dominance; how does this address reflect such a self-image?

2) Why does Hitler see himself as irreplaceable in the war just beginning in November 1939?

3) Does this address attempt to rationalize an action that critics saw as too hasty and ill-conceived? If so, is it convincing?

Nov. 23, 1939, 1200 hours. Conference with the Führer, to which all Supreme Commanders are ordered. The Führer gives the following speech:

The purpose of this conference is to give you an idea of the world of my thoughts, which governs me in the face of future events, and to tell you my decisions. The building up of our armed forces was only possible in connection with the ideological education of the German people by the Party. When I started my political task in 1919, my strong belief in final success was based on a thorough observation of the events of the day and the study of the reasons for their occurrence. Therefore, I never lost my belief in the midst of set-backs which were not spared me during my period of struggle. Providence has had the last word and brought me success. On top of that, I had a clear recognition of the probable course of historical events, and the firm will to make brutal decisions. The first decision was in 1919 when I after long internal conflict became a politician and took up the struggle against my enemies. That was the hardest of all decisions. I had, however, the firm belief that I would arrive at my goal.... When I came to power in 1933 ... I had to reorganize everything beginning with the mass of the people and extending it to the armed forces. First reorganization of the interior, abolishment of appearances of decay and defeatist ideas, education to heroism. While reorganizing the interior, I undertook the second task: to release Germany from its international ties. Two particular characteristics are to be pointed out: secession from the League of Nations and denunciation of the disarmament conference. It was a hard decision. The number of prophets who predicted that it would lead to the occupation of the Rhineland was large, the number of believers was very small. I was supported by the nation, which stood firmly behind me, when I carried out my intentions.

After that the order for rearmament. Here again there were numerous prophets who predicted misfortunes, and only a few believers. In 1935 the introduction of compulsory armed service. After that militarization of the Rhineland, again a process believed to be impossible at that time. The number of people who put trust in me was very small. Then the beginning of the fortification of the whole country especially in the west.

One year later, Austria came, this step also was considered doubtful. It brought about a considerable reinforcement of the Reich. The next step was Bohemia, Moravia and Poland. This step also was not possible to accomplish in one campaign. First of all, the western fortifications had to be finished. It was not possible to reach the goal in one effort. It was clear to me from the first moment that I could not be satisfied with the Sudeten-German territory. That was only a partial solution. The decision to march into Bohemia was made. Then followed the erection of the Protectorate and with that the basis for the action against Poland was laid, but I wasn't quite clear at that time whether I should start first against the east and then in the west or vice-versa.... Under pressure the decision came to fight with Poland first. One might accuse me of wanting to fight and fight again. In struggle I see the fate of all beings. Nobody can avoid a struggle if he does not want to lose out. The increasing number of people requires a larger living space. My goal was to create a logical relation between the number of people and the space for them to live in. The struggle must start here. No people can get away from the solution of this task or else it must yield and gradually die out. That is taught by history....

In our case 82 millions of people were concerned. That means the greatest responsibility. He who does not want to assume this responsibility is not worthy of belonging to the mass of the people. That gave me the strength to fight. It is one eternal problem to bring the number of Germans to a proper relationship to the available space.... No calculated cleverness is of any help; [the] solution [comes] only with the sword. A people unable to produce the strength to fight must withdraw. Struggles are different than those of 100 years ago. Today we speak of a racial fight. Today we fight for oilfields, rubber, treasures of the earth, etc.....

In 1914 there came the war on several fronts. It did not bring the solution of these problems. Today the second act of this drama is being written. For the first time in 67 years it must be made clear that we do not have a two-front war to wage.... But no one can know how long that will remain so. I have doubted for a long time whether I should strike in the east and then in the west. Basically I did not organize the armed forces in order not to strike. The decision to strike was always in me. Earlier or later I wanted to solve the problem. Under pressure it was decided that the east was to be attacked first. If the Polish war was won so quickly, it was due to the superiority of our armed forces....

Now the situation is as follows: The opponent in the west lies behind his fortifications. There is no possibility of coming to grips with him. The decisive question is: how long can we endure this situation? Russia is at present not dangerous.... Moreover, we have a pact with Russia. Pacts, however, are only held as long as they serve the purpose. Russia will hold herself to it only so long as Russia considers it to be to her benefit.... At the present moment [Russia] has retired from internationalism. In case she renounces this, she will proceed to Pan-Slavism. It is difficult to see into the future.... At the present time the Russian army is of little worth. For the next one or two years the present situation will remain.

Much depends on Italy, above all on Mussolini, whose death could alter everything. Italy has a great goal for the consolidation of her empire. Those who carry this idea are fascism and the Duce, personally.... As long as the Duce lives, then it can be calculated that Italy will seize every opportunity to reach her imperialistic goal. However, it is too much to ask of Italy, that it should join in the battle before Germany has seized the offensive in the west: Just so Russia did not attack until we had marched into Poland. Otherwise Italy will think that France has only to deal with Italy, since Germany is sitting behind its West Wall. Italy will not attack until Germany has taken the offensive against France. Just as the death of Stalin, so the death of the Duce can bring danger to us. Just how easily the death of a statesman can come I myself have experienced recently. The time must be used to the full, otherwise one will suddenly find himself faced with a new situation. As long as Italy maintains this position then no danger from Jugoslavia is to be feared. Just so is the neutrality of Rumania achieved by the position of Russia. Scandinavia is hostile to us because of Marxist influences, but is neutral now. America is still not dangerous to us because of its neutrality laws. The strengthening of our opponents by America is still not important. The position of Japan is still uncertain, it is not yet certain whether she will join against England.

Everything is determined by the fact that the moment is favorable now: in 6 months it might not be so anymore.

As the last factor I must name my own person in all modesty: irreplaceable. Neither a military nor a civil person could replace me. Assassination attempts may be repeated. I am convinced of the powers of my intellect and of decision. Wars are always ended only by the destruction of the opponent. Everyone who believes differently is irresponsible. Time is working for our adversary. Now there is a relationship of forces which can never be more propitious, but can only deteriorate for us. The enemy will not make peace when the relationship of forces is unfavorable for us. No compromise. Sternness against ourselves. I shall strike and not capitulate. The fate of the Reich depends only on me. I shall deal accordingly. Today we have a superiority such as we have never had before....

In summary:

1. The number of active organizations in Germany is greatest.
2. Superiority of the Luftwaffe.
3. Anti-aircraft beyond all competition.
4. Tank corps.
5. Large number of anti-tank guns, five times as many as 1914 machine guns.

6. German artillery has great superiority because of the 10.5 gun.

7. French superiority in howitzers and mortars does not exist.

There is no doubt that our armed forces are the best. Every German infantryman is better than the French. Not the exhilaration of patriotism but tough determination. I am told that the troops will only advance if the officers lead the way. In 1914 that was also the case. I am told that we were better trained then. In reality we were only better trained on the drill field, but not for the war. I must pay the present leadership the compliment that it is better than it was in 1914....

Five million Germans have been called to the colors. Of what importance if a few of them collapse? Daring in the army, navy and Luftwaffe. I can not bear it when one says the army is not in good shape. Everything lies in the hands of the military leader. I can do anything with the German soldier if he is well led....

We have an Achilles heel: The Ruhr. The progress of the war depends on the possession of the Ruhr. If England and France push through Belgium and Holland into the Ruhr, we shall be in the greatest danger. That could lead to the paralyzing of the German power of resistance. Every hope of compromise is childish: Victory or defeat! The question is not the fate of a national-socialistic Germany, but who is to dominate Europe in the future. The question is worthy of the greatest efforts. Certainly England and France will assume the offensive against Germany when they are armed. England and France have means of pressure to bring Belgium and Holland to request English and French help. In Belgium and Holland the sympathies are all for France and England....

If the French army marches into Belgium in order to attack us, it will be too late for us. We must anticipate them. One more thing. U-boats, mines, and Luftwaffe (also for mines) can strike England effectively, if we have a better starting point. Now a flight to England demands so much fuel that sufficient bomb loads cannot be carried. The invention of a new type mine is of the greatest importance for the Navy.

Aircraft will be the chief mine layers now. We shall sow the English coast with mines which cannot be cleared. This mine warfare with the Luftwaffe demands a different starting point. England cannot live without its imports. We can feed ourselves. The permanent sowing of mines on the English coast will bring England to her knees. However, this can only occur if we have occupied Belgium and Holland. It is a difficult decision for me. None has ever achieved what I have achieved. My life is of no importance in all this. I have led the German people to a great height, even if the world does hate us now. I am setting this work on a gamble. I have to choose between victory or destruction. I choose victory.... I shall attack France and England at the most favorable and quickest moment. Breach of the neutrality of Belgium and Holland is meaningless. No one will question that when we have won....

I ask you to pass on the spirit of determination to the lower echelons.

1. The decision is irrevocable.

2. The only prospect for success [is] if the whole armed forces are determined.

The spirit of the great men of our history must hearten us all. Fate demands from us no more than from the great men of German history. As long as I shall live I shall think only of the victory of my people. I shall shrink from nothing and shall destroy everyone who is opposed to me. I have decided to live my life so that I can stand unashamed if I have to die. I want to destroy the enemy. Behind me stands the German people ....

If we come through this struggle victoriously--and we shall come through victoriously--our time will enter into the history of our people. I shall stand or fall in this struggle. I shall never survive the defeat of my people. [There can be] no capitulation to the outside forces, no revolution from the interior forces.

Office of United States Chief of Counsel for Prosecution of Axis Criminality. *Nazi Conspiracy and Aggression*. Washington: U.S. Government Printing Office, 1946. Vol. 3. Pp. 572-580.

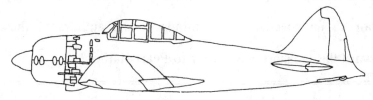

READING 9.18

"AIR RAID--PEARL HARBOR--THIS IS NO DRILL!"

▶ Japanese "Zero"

Pearl Harbor is located on the island of Oahu, Hawaii, roughly six miles from Honolulu. The United States gained exclusive rights to use the harbor in 1887 and upgraded the facilities after annexing the Hawaiian Islands in 1898; it became the base for the U.S. Pacific Fleet. In 1936, Japan joined the anti-Comintern Pact with Germany and Italy, becoming one of the Axis powers. When General Tojo Hideki became prime minister in 1941, Japan had been at war with China for four years, and Japan's Axis partners had been waging aggressive war in Europe for two years. Unable to reduce China to its New Order in East Asia, Japanese planners turned south to form a "Greater East Asia Co-Prosperity Sphere," embracing Japan, China, Korea, the Pacific islands, southeast Asia, Australia, and New Zealand. Such an empire would make Japan economically self-sufficient. The mission of the Japanese military was to eliminate British, American, and Dutch influence in the region. (French Indochina was already under Japanese control.) Since the United States had not yet entered World War II, Japanese leaders correctly viewed U.S. resistance to its plans as most dangerous. Negotiators went to Washington hoping to persuade the U.S. government to acquiesce in Japanese designs. Instead, the United States demanded that Japan cease its aggression against China and restore already conquered territories. With talks stalling and its strategic petroleum reserves dwindling, the Japanese government decided to stage a simultaneous surprise attack on all western possessions in southeast Asia and on the U.S. naval base at Pearl Harbor. If the American Pacific fleet could be knocked out, Japanese plans for conquest would stand a better chance of success.

On 7 December, a day that, in Franklin Roosevelt's words, would live in infamy, Japanese submarines and carrier-based planes launched a surprise attack on the unsuspecting U.S. fleet at Pearl Harbor. Five battleships and three cruisers were sunk or severely damaged. Three other battleships were less seriously crippled and many smaller vessels were sunk. American aircraft losses totaled 177. Casualties stood at 2343 dead, 1272 injured, and another 876 missing. A congressional investigation after the war determined that negligence or "errors of judgment" by the army and navy commanders in Hawaii had contributed to the horrific losses sustained in the attack.

In the first of the following passages, we have an account of the attack by a teenage sailor aboard the USS *Maryland*. The second passage is by a twenty-four-year-old South Carolina native, one of only 289 survivors of the USS *Arizona*; 1104 other members of the ship's crew were killed or missing in action.

QUESTIONS:

1) What was the state of readiness (or unreadiness) in the U.S. fleet at Pearl Harbor on 7 December 1941?

2) Why was the attack on Pearl Harbor so unexpected in the minds of the authors of these accounts?

3) What was the attitude of navy men toward the Japanese navy prior to Pearl Harbor?

Carl Whitaker (USS *Maryland*).

A week prior to 7 December, the fleet had been at sea on maneuvers. It was an unforgettable sight to see the ships of the line with battle flags flying and foamy seas breaking over their forecastle. However, this was an illusion of strength. Against enemy capital ships, their large main battery could have been most effective, but against enemy aircraft they were pitifully unprepared. The *Maryland* had slow-firing five-inch anti-aircraft guns that found it difficult to hit a sleeve towed by [at] slow speeds--let alone a dive bomber or torpedo bomber. We also had several tubs of automatic weapons, but they were largely experimental in nature. So at this time the ships returned to Pearl Harbor, several of them having put to sea for the last time. Although negotiations with Japan were breaking down, the commanders (both army and navy) in the Hawaiian area were never fully informed or advised to put their forces on a wartime-alert status. Lieutenant General Short deducted from communiqués from Washington that his greatest danger was subversion by the Japanese elements in Hawaii. Therefore, he prepared for sabotage by grouping his air-force units closely together so that they would be more easily guarded. No attempt had been made to implement the Joint Army-Navy Hawaiian Defense Plan, which had been widely acclaimed by Admiral Stark, chief of naval operations.

So dawned 7 December. At 6:00 A.M., Admiral Nagumo, the commander of the Pearl Harbor strike force, launched forty torpedo planes, fifty-one dive bombers, and forty-nine high-level bombers from the decks of his six carriers. At this point, they were 250 miles from Pearl Harbor and completely unexpected. Of all the military planes in the area, only seven navy PBYs were on patrol and were many miles to the southwest. Of the 780 anti-aircraft guns on ships in Pearl, only a fourth were manned, and, of the army's 31 anti-aircraft batteries, only 4 were in position, having no ammunition. They had been returned to depot to avoid getting rusty. The Japanese plan was simple but effective. Their first strikes were the navy bases at Kaneohe and Ford Island; the army bases, Wheeler, Bellows and Hickam, and the marine base at Ewa were almost completely wiped out. The planes, closely grouped for security against sabotage, were perfect targets. Three minutes later, at 7:58, the message heard around the world was "Air raid--Pearl Harbor--this is no drill."

A battleship is much like a modern city, providing its own electricity, water converted from sea water, its own hospital facility, laundry, machine shop, and all of the facilities to support the activities of fourteen hundred men. We were observing a typical Sunday routine. Breakfast had been served at 7:00. I was writing a letter to a friend in Long Beach when I happened to look out of one of the portholes and saw several airplanes. My first reaction was "Damn the army"--practicing on Sunday, and they have even gone to the trouble of painting the rising sun on the wings. Just then general quarters sounded, and all hands went to their battle stations. I immediately reported to main engine control, which was the nerve center for the engineering department. This was located twenty-five feet below the waterline. Almost immediately, the news from the bridge was unbelievable. Within one minute after the attack, the *Oklahoma*, which had come alongside and moored the previous morning, was hit with four torpedoes and almost immediately listed to port and turned over, trapping four hundred of her ship's company inside. Seven battleships were tied up in Battleship Row--first was the *California*, next the *Maryland* and the *Oklahoma*, the *Tennessee*, and *West Virginia*, then the *Arizona*. The *Arizona* was hit by a torpedo, and a moment later she was attacked by high-level bombers. Five bombs were dropped, some going through the forecastle and starting a fire, which quickly spread to 1,600 pounds of black powder. This is the most dangerous of all explosives and should have been stored in magazines below the armor-plated deck. As soon as the powder exploded, the ship literally leaped out of the water amidst a blast of smoke and debris; then the 32,600-pound ship broke in two and quickly settled to the bottom. This murdered over eleven hundred men, and *no* war had yet been declared.

Ironically, many of the company I originally started with in boot camp, were shipped to the *Arizona*, and only the fact that I contacted "cat fever" and was held back a month kept me from being on this ill-fated ship. In fact, a friend of mine from Lindsay, California, is still down there. He and some other musicians were playing in a combo ashore just the night before--a friend I will always remember.

Next in line was the *Nevada*, which sustained a torpedo and a bomb hit, but succeeded in getting underway. However, as she headed out of the harbor she became the target of planes from a second raid--eighty dive bombers, fifty-four high-level bombers, and thirty-six fighters. She was immediately hit by six bombs and was forced to run aground to keep from blocking the entrance to the channel. The other battleship in the harbor was the *Pennsylvania*, which was in dry dock. She was also damaged, as was the target ship *Utah*. She was sunk when the Japs mistook her for an aircraft carrier.

As suddenly as it started, the attack ended. The state of shock on the *Maryland* was unbelievable. This was particularly true of the older officers and chiefs who had been raised in the navy on the legend of our superiority over the Japanese and of the indestructibility of the battleship. I believe the results would have been even more catastrophic if we had had sufficient warning to put to sea. Our land-based planes might have been destroyed, and the only two aircraft carriers in operation were more than five hundred miles from Pearl. I feel sure that, without air support, the entire fleet would have been sunk, as were the *Prince of Wales* and the battle cruiser *Repulse*--sunk off the coast of Malaya when they were left to defend themselves against enemy aircraft. Many of the battleships at Pearl returned to the war--the *Maryland*,

Tennessee, *West Virginia*, *Nevada* and *Pennsylvania*--and served for bombardment purposes in the long journey through the island chain that led to Tokyo Bay on surrender day.

John Rampey (USS *Arizona*).

On 7 December, a beautiful, clear, typical island day dawned. Being Sunday, the entire ship would be on "holiday routine." Sunrise over the harbor on Sunday was in itself a religious experience. With the stillness and quietness which surrounded the water, it was as if every Sunday was an Easter sunrise service. Certainly, this Sunday was to be no exception.

I was a gunner's mate third class on the main battery of the number-three turret, part of the third division. Morning chow was over, and we were just loafing around in our living quarters, down in the base of the turret. Some of the men went topside to enjoy a bit of fresh air after breakfast. Without a doubt, loafing and lounging around were the most popular Sunday activities aboard the battleship. It was almost 8:00 A.M., nearly time for colors, when the men in the turret were notified that something unusual was going on. A seaman from the deck unit rushed into our quarters to inform us that ships in the dry dock were being bombed. We thought he was kidding because he was a character, but the strange expression on his face convinced us he might be serious.

At this point, I think a bit of explanation is in order. A few days prior, the *Arizona* had been in dry dock for repairs and was probably in that location during the final Japanese photo recording of the fleet positions in Pearl Harbor. Between that time and the time of the attack, the USS *Pennsylvania*, identical sister ship of the *Arizona*, changed places with the *Arizona*. The *Pennsylvania* was the flagship of the U.S. Pacific Fleet, so this might explain the force of the attack on the *Arizona*.

Within moments, general quarters were sounded. "This is no drill. I repeat, this is no drill," echoed down the steel corridors of the ship. The words sent a cold, shuttering chill down my spine. At our battle stations on the fourteen-inch guns, there was little to do but pray. In the space of a few seconds, some men made up for twenty and more years of tardy prayers. Inside the turret, there was an eerie silence. Everyone seemed afraid to breathe, much less speak, as if that would somehow give away our position to the enemy or attract the attention of one of the bombs. We waited anxiously for some word from topside. Even though we were protected by the heavy plating of the turret, we felt helpless and defenseless, not being able to take any kind of action to defend ourselves and our fellow sailors. We could hear the thunder and feel the ship shudder as the bombs fell upon her. At one point in time, we felt a tremendous jolt, as if the ship had been lifted up in the air and slammed back down. Little did we realize that this was the fatal blow for the *Arizona*. Rivets popped from the steel walls and flew about the place. It wasn't until sometime later that we realized the number-three turret was the only one spared from the bombs. The number-four turret had a hit, but damage was minor. Being shut away at battle stations within the turret, little did we know the extent of damage to our ship and the chaos taking place on the decks around us.

After what seemed like an eternity, the order came over the speakers, "All hands abandon ship." I looked around for some comfort, but all my shipmates seemed to have the same awareness as myself. Our life together aboard the old *Arizona* was over. I climbed down the ladder on the outside of the turret. Everywhere I touched or grabbed onto the ship, I felt the effects of the fires and explosions. The ship had become a piece of molten steel, a kind of giant tea kettle, where heat was being transferred to all metal and steel parts. The deck was covered with oil, and my first impulse was to return to the turret. I can't explain why, but I did not want to step in the oil. Perhaps it was because I thought the oil would be boiling hot. Finally being outside the turret, it looked as if the rest of the ship was a blazing inferno, encircled by a wall of fire which was quickly closing in. I remember looking around the deck and seeing my shipmates from the deck division with their bodies burned black or lying on the deck bleeding from open wounds. Some men were screaming and jumping over the side of the ship. Others were spread about the deck in various positions, crying and moaning in agony. Charred and mutilated bodies were scattered everywhere in the wreckage of the ship. They lay crumpled like broken dolls who had

been picked up in the air by some giant hand and slammed against the structures of the ship. With all the smoke and fire on the decks, it seemed difficult to catch one's breath. I don't know if it was from the elements, or just the excitement. All around, the air was filled with the smell of burning oil and burning flesh. It was a smell which lingered in the air like a heavy fog, saturating one's clothes and body.

I walked, then crawled, very calmly and carefully to the side of the ship and looked down into the water. The water was partially covered with oil, most of which was burning. There was a raft directly below, and men were climbing aboard frantically. From where I stood, all I could see forward was a crumbling mass of twisted metal that had only minutes before been the proud superstructure. The command to abandon ship was being repeated over and over again. Enemy planes were still strafing the ship when I made the decision to jump. The warm water was certainly a refresher. When I came to the surface, I was hoping that the whole thing was a bad dream, some sort of hellish nightmare. I swam a few strokes over to the raft and grabbed hold. The raft was too slow and seemed to take forever to move. I decided to take my chances alone in the water, so I began swimming toward Ford Island. The swim wasn't far, but it was very exhausting swimming an obstacle course filled with oil, debris, and bodies. I reached the island in relatively good shape, considering the ordeal which I had been through. After a short rest and a couple of mouthfuls of water, I got my second wind and was ready to help whenever needed.

It wasn't until many hours later that I learned so many of my shipmates were dead. Of the fifteen from my boot platoon that I went aboard with, I was the only one who survived. This is one thing that has stayed with me to this day, and I think about it often. After a short period on Ford Island, we were taken ashore to the main base at Pearl Harbor. It was here that I learned that all of our turret crew had survived without any injuries. We were without a doubt the most luckiest men on the face of the earth for this one day.

Travers, Paul Joseph. *Eyewitness to Infamy: An Oral History of Pearl Harbor.* Lanham, MD: Madison Books, 1991. Pp. 117-120, 139-142.

SECTION 10

THE CONTEMPORARY ERA

The contemporary era refers here to the period since World War II. The readings in this section begin with the trial of Nazi war criminals at Nuremberg. The Cold War that divided the Communist and the Western world began immediately after the defeat of the Axis powers in World War II and persisted till the fall of the Communist government of the U.S.S.R. in 1991. Therefore most of the readings in this section deal with some aspect of the Cold War. They include British prime minister Winston Churchill's speech describing the division of the world into two armed camps separated by an ideological Iron Curtain, and an account of the building of the Berlin Wall that symbolized that division. Other readings deal with the spread of the Cold War to the Western Hemisphere, evidenced in the Cuban Missile Crisis and Marxist revolutionary insurgencies in Latin America, and with Egypt's role in the Cold War as well as its relations with Israel. Life in Communist China, described here, had parallels in other Communist countries.

Another major theme in the history of the contemporary world is the triumph of nationalism in Asia and Africa. The memoir of Jawaharlal Nehru, India's first post-independence prime minister, recounts the struggle for independence in that important country. The graphic statement of a Kenyan independence fighter typifies the struggle for independence in many regions of Africa.

While the rise of Communism as an ideology of government marked the first half of the twentieth century, the decline and fall of Marxist governments in the Soviet Union and Eastern Europe signaled the bankruptcy of that ideology in the latter part of the century. In the last two readings in this section, Russian President Boris Yeltsin tells of the corruption of the Communist party and state in the U.S.S.R., while political scientist and National Security Advisor to President Jimmy Carter Zbigniew Brzezinski analyzes the deep-seated reasons for the failure of Marxism.

Across the world from former Communist countries to newly independent ones, citizens seek economic well-being and human dignity through the right to participate in their government. Their quest is well exemplified by the Burmese leader an Nobel Peace Prize winner Aung San Ssu Kyi in the last selection.

DEFENSE AND JUDGMENT AT NUREMBERG

The trials held in Nuremberg, Germany, after World War II set an important precedent in the history of international law. Twenty-two major figures of the Nazi regime were charged on one or more of four counts: (1) conspiracy to commit crimes alleged in other counts, (2) crimes against peace, (3) war crimes, (4) crimes against humanity. The dramatic evidence regarding the mass killings of European Jews highlighted the trial. One of the purposes of the trial was to ensure that acts of genocide would not be tolerated and that those who perpetrated them would be held accountable before the community of civilized nations. The claim to have been following orders carried no weight.

Of the twenty-two war criminals indicted before the International Military Tribunal (a twenty-third, Martin Bormann, who had escaped capture, was tried in absentia), eleven (twelve, including Bormann) were sentenced to death by hanging, seven received prison terms ranging from ten years to life, three were acquitted, and one committed suicide before judgment.

The following passages are selected from the final pleas of Julius Streicher and Albert Speer and the verdicts against them. Streicher was a rabid anti-Semite who published a weekly newspaper titled *Der Stürmer* ("The Militant" or, more literally, "The Stormer"); Streicher, like many of the other defendants at Nuremberg tried to exonerate himself by claiming he had no knowledge of the atrocities against Jews and by attributing the entire responsibility for crimes against Jews to Adolf Hitler.

Albert Speer, as Hitler's Reichsminister for armaments and war production had possessed extraordinary powers in the direction and coordination of munitions manufacturing throughout the Third Reich. As the historian Alan Bullock put it, "without Speer Hitler would have lacked the power to stage his fight to the finish." Speer was convicted on charges of deportation and forced labor of prisoners of war and citizens of occupied countries in factories under his jurisdiction.

QUESTIONS:

1) What (if any) differences in moral outlook and attitudes are perceptible in the final statements of Streicher and Speer?

2) Many of the defendants at Nuremberg adopted the "just following orders" defense strategy. Does either Streicher or Speer seem to rely on that tactic?

3) Why do you think Streicher was sentenced to death and Speer not?

Julius Streicher (Defendant):
Your Honors:

At the beginning of this Trial I was asked by the President whether I pleaded guilty in the sense of the Indictment. I answered that question in the negative.

The completed proceedings and the evidence presented have confirmed the correctness of the statement I gave at that time.

It has been established that:

(1) Mass killings were carried out exclusively upon orders by the Head of the State, Adolf Hitler, without other influence.

(2) The mass killings were carried out without the knowledge of the German people and in complete secrecy by the Reichsführer SS, Heinrich Himmler.

The Prosecution had asserted that mass killings would not have been possible without Streicher and his *Stürmer*. The Prosecution neither offered nor submitted any proof of this assertion.

It is clearly established that on the occasion of the Anti-Jewish Boycott Day in 1933, which I was ordered to lead, and on the occasion of the demonstration of 1938 ordered by Reich Minister Dr. Goebbels, I, in my capacity as Gauleiter [district leader], neither ordered, demanded, nor participated in any acts of violence against Jews.

It is further established that in many articles in my weekly paper, the *Stürmer*, I advocated the Zionist demand for the creation of a Jewish state as the natural solution of the Jewish problem.

These facts prove that I did not want the Jewish problem to be solved by violence....

These actions of the leader of the State against the Jews can be explained by his attitude toward the Jewish question, which was thoroughly different from mine. Hitler wanted to punish the Jews because he held them responsible for unleashing the war and for the bombing of the German civilian population.

It is deeply regrettable that the mass killings, which can be traced back to the personal decision of the leader of the State, Adolf Hitler, have led to a treatment of the German people which must also be considered as not humane. I repudiate the mass killings which were carried out, in the same way as they are repudiated by every decent German.

Your Honors! Neither in my capacity as Gauleiter nor as political author have I committed a crime, and I therefore look forward to your judgment with a good conscience.

I have no request to make for myself. I have one for the German people from whom I come. Your Honors, fate has given you the power to pronounce any judgment. Do not pronounce a judgment, Your Honors, which would imprint the stamp of dishonor upon the forehead of an entire nation.

The President [of the Tribunal]:

Streicher is indicted on Counts One and Four. One of the earliest members of the Nazi Party, joining in 1921, he took part in the Munich Putsch. From 1925 to 1940 he was Gauleiter of Franconia. Elected to the Reichstag in 1933, he was an honorary general in the SA. His persecution of the Jews was notorious. He was the publisher of *Der Stürmer*, an anti-Semitic weekly newspaper, from 1923 to 1945 and was its editor until 1933.

Crimes against Peace

Streicher was a staunch Nazi and supporter of Hitler's main policies. There is no evidence to show that he was ever within Hitler's inner circle of advisers; nor during his career was he closely connected with the formulation of the policies which led to war. He was never present, for example, at any of the conferences when Hitler explained his decisions to his leaders. Although he was a Gauleiter there is no evidence to prove that he had knowledge of these policies. In the opinion of the Tribunal, the evidence fails to establish his connection with the conspiracy or common plan to wage aggressive war as that conspiracy has been elsewhere defined in this Judgment.

Crimes against Humanity

For his 25 years of speaking, writing, and preaching hatred of the Jews, Streicher was widely known as "Jew-Baiter Number One." In his speeches and articles, week after week, month after month, he infected the German mind with the virus of anti-Semitism and incited the German people to active persecution. Each issue of *Der Stürmer*, which reached a circulation of

600,000 in 1935, was filled with such articles, often lewd and disgusting.

Streicher had charge of the Jewish boycott of 1 April 1933. He advocated the Nuremberg Decrees of 1935. He was responsible for the demolition on 10 August 1935 of the synagogue in Nuremberg. And on 10 November 1938, he spoke publicly in support of the Jewish pogrom which was taking place at that time.

But it was not only in Germany that this defendant advocated his doctrines. As early as 1938 he began to call for the annihilation of the Jewish race. 23 different articles of *Der Stürmer* between 1938 and 1941 were produced in evidence, in which extermination "root and branch" was preached. Typical of his teachings was a leading article in September 1938 which termed the Jew a germ and a pest, not a human being, but "a parasite, an enemy, an evil-doer, a disseminator of diseases who must be destroyed in the interest of mankind." Other articles urged that only when world Jewry had been annihilated would the Jewish problem have been solved, and predicted that 50 hence the Jewish graves "will proclaim that this people of murderers and criminals has after all met its deserved fate."...

As the war in the early stages proved successful in acquiring more and more territory for the Reich, Streicher intensified his efforts to incite the Germans against the Jews.... With knowledge of the extermination of the Jews in the Occupied Eastern Territories, this defendant continued to write and publish his propaganda of death. Testifying in this Trial, he vehemently denied any knowledge of mass executions of Jews. But the evidence makes it clear that he continually received current information on the progress of the "final solution." His press photographer was sent to visit the ghettos of the East in the spring of 1943, the time of the destruction of the Warsaw ghetto. The Jewish newspaper, *Israelitisches Wochenblatt* [*Israelite Weekly*], which Streicher received and read, carried in each issue accounts of Jewish atrocities in the East, and gave figures on the number of Jews who had been deported and killed.... In November 1943 Streicher quoted verbatim an article from the *Israelitisches Wochenblatt* which stated that the Jews had virtually disappeared from Europe, and commented: "This is not a Jewish lie."... In January 1943 he wrote ... that

it was wonderful to know that Hitler was freeing the world of its Jewish tormentors.

Streicher's incitement to murder and extermination at the time when Jews in the East were being killed under the most horrible conditions clearly constitutes persecution on political and racial grounds in connection with War Crimes, as defined by the Charter, and constitutes a Crime against Humanity.

Conclusion

The Tribunal finds that Streicher is not guilty on Count One, but that he is guilty on Count Four.

[Streicher received the death sentence and was hanged on 16 October 1946; a rank anti-Semite to the very end, he shouted from the scaffold "Purim Fest 1946!" alluding to the Jewish holiday that commemorates the defeat and hanging of Haman, an ancient Persian persecutor of the Jews, c. 475 B.C.E.]

Albert Speer (Defendant):

Mr. President, may it please the Tribunal: Hitler and the collapse of his system have brought a time of tremendous suffering upon the German people. The useless continuation of this war and the unnecessary destruction make the work of reconstruction more difficult. Privation and misery have come to the German people. After this Trial, the German people will despise and condemn Hitler as the proven author of its misfortune. But the world will learn from these happenings not only to hate dictatorship as a form of government, but to fear it.

Hitler's dictatorship differed in one fundamental point from all its predecessors in history. His was the first dictatorship in the present period of modern technical development, a dictatorship which made complete use of all technical means in a perfect manner for the domination of its own nation.

Through technical devices such as radio and loudspeaker 80 million people were deprived of independent thought. It was thereby possible to subject them to the will of one man. The telephone, teletype, and radio made it possible, for instance, for orders from the highest sources to be transmitted directly to the lowest-ranking units, where, because of the high authority, they were carried out without criticism. Another result was that numerous offices and headquarters were directly attached to the supreme leadership, from which they received their sinister orders directly. Also, one of the results was a far-reaching supervision of the citizen of the state and the maintenance of a high degree of secrecy of criminal events....

This war ended with remote-controlled rockets, aircraft traveling at the speed of sound, new types of submarines, torpedoes which find their own target, with atom bombs, and with the prospect of a horrible kind of chemical warfare.

Of necessity the next war will be overshadowed by these new destructive inventions of the human mind.

In 5 or 10 years the technique of warfare will make it possible to fire rockets from continent to continent with uncanny precision. By atomic power, it can destroy one million people in the center of New York in a matter of seconds with a rocket operated, perhaps, by only 10 men, invisible, without previous warning, faster than sound, by day and by night. Science is able to spread pestilence among human beings and animals and to destroy crops by insect warfare. Chemistry has developed terrible weapons with which it can inflict unspeakable suffering upon helpless human beings.

Will there ever again be a nation which will use the technical discoveries of this war for the preparation of a new war, while the rest of the world is employing the technical progress of this war for the benefit of humanity, thus attempting to create a slight compensation for its horrors? As a former minister of a highly developed armament system, it is my last duty to say the following:

A new large-scale war will end with the destruction of human culture and civilization. Nothing can prevent unconfined engineering and science from completing the work of destroying human beings, which it has begun in so dreadful a way in this war.

Therefore this Trial must contribute towards preventing such degenerate wars in the future, and towards establishing rules whereby human beings can live together.

Of what importance is my own fate, after everything that has happened, in comparison with this high goal?...

Mr. Biddle [one of the Justices]:

Speer is indicted under all four Counts. Speer joined the Nazi Party in 1932. In 1934 he was made Hitler's architect and became a close personal confidant. Shortly thereafter he was made a department head in the German Labor Front and the official in charge of capital construction on the staff of the Deputy to the Führer, positions which he held through 1941. On 15 February 1942, after the death of Fritz Todt, Speer was appointed Chief of the Organization Todt and Reich Minister for Armaments and Munitions (after 2 September 1943, for Armaments and War Production). The positions were supplemented by his appointments in March and April 1942 as Plenipotentiary General for Armaments and as a member of the Central Planning Board, both within the Four Year Plan. Speer was a member of the Reichstag from 1941 until the end of the war.

Crimes against Peace

The Tribunal is of opinion that Speer's activities do not amount to initiating, planning, or preparing wars of aggression, or of conspiring to that end. He became the head of the armament industry well after all of the wars had been commenced and were under way. His activities in charge of German armament production were in aid of the war effort in the same way that other productive enterprises aid in the waging of war, but the Tribunal is not prepared to find that such activities involve engaging in the common plan to wage aggressive war as charged under Count Two.

War Crimes and Crimes against Humanity

The evidence introduced against Speer under Counts Three and Four relates entirely to his participation in the slave labor program. Speer himself had no direct administrative responsibility for this program. Although he had advocated the appointment of a Plenipotentiary General for the Utilization of Labor because he wanted one central authority with whom he could deal on labor matters, he did not obtain administrative control over [Plenipotentiary General, Fritz] Sauckel. Sauckel was appointed directly by Hitler, under the decree of 21 March 1942, which provided that he should be directly responsible to Göring, as Plenipotentiary for the Four Year Plan....

As the dominant member of the Central Planning Board ... Speer took the position that the board had authority to instruct Sauckel to provide laborers for industries under its control and succeeded in sustaining this position over the objection of Sauckel. The practice was developed under which Speer transmitted to Sauckel an estimate of the total number of workers needed; Sauckel obtained the labor and allocated it to the various industries in accordance with instructions supplied by Speer.

Speer knew when he made his demands on Sauckel that they would be supplied by foreign laborers serving under compulsion. He participated in conferences involving the extension of the slave labor program for the purpose of satisfying his demands....

Speer was also directly involved in the utilization of forced labor as chief of the Organization Todt. The Organization Todt functioned principally in the occupied areas on such projects as the Atlantic Wall and the construction of military highways, and Speer has admitted that he relied on compulsory service to keep it adequately staffed. He also used concentration camp labor in the industries under his control. He originally arranged to tap this source of labor for use in small out-of-the-way factories; and later, fearful of Himmler's jurisdictional ambitions, attempted to use as few concentration camp workers as possible.

Speer was also involved in the use of prisoners of war in armament industries, but contends that he only utilized Soviet prisoners of war in industries covered by the Geneva Convention.

Speer's position was such that he was not directly concerned with the cruelty in the administration of the slave labor program, although he was aware of its existence. For example, at meetings of the Central Planning Board he was informed that his demands for labor were so large as to necessitate violent methods in recruiting. At a meeting of the Central Planning Board on 30 October 1942, Speer voiced his opinion that many slave laborers who claimed to be sick were malingerers and stated: "There is nothing to be said against SS and Police taking drastic steps and putting those known as slackers into concentration camps." Speer, however, insisted that the slave laborers be given adequate food and working conditions so that they could work efficiently.

In mitigation it must be recognized that Speer's establishment of blocked industries did keep many laborers in their homes and that in the closing stages of the war he was one of the few men who had the courage to tell Hitler that the war was lost and to take steps to prevent the senseless destruction of production facilities, both in occupied territories and in Germany. He carried out his opposition to Hitler's scorched earth program in some of the Western countries and in Germany by deliberately sabotaging it at considerable personal risk.

Conclusion

The Tribunal finds that Speer is not guilty on Counts One and Two, but is guilty under Counts Three and Four.

[Speer was sentenced to twenty years imprisonment and served the entire term at Spandau prison in Berlin. He died of a cerebral hemorrhage on 1 September 1981, almost fifteen years after his release.]

International Military Tribunal. *Trial of the Major War Criminals before the International Military Tribunal, Nuremberg, 14 November 1945 – 1 October 1946.* Nuremberg: Secretariat of the Tribunal, 1948. Vol. 22. Pp. 385-387, 405-407, 547-549, 576-579.

WINSTON CHURCHILL'S IRON CURTAIN SPEECH

Although the United States, Great Britain, and the Soviet Union formed a grand alliance to fight Nazi Germany in Europe, each had an agenda to protect its own interests. The Soviet Union, which suffered terrible devastation and 26 million wartime dead, sought security from future invasions by controlling eastern Europe. The Soviet dictator, Joseph Stalin, also wanted to expand the areas of Communist domination.

Soviet policies conflicted with the plans of the United States and Great Britain to rebuild postwar Germany as a potential trading partner, and to prevent the spread of communism in Europe by supporting democratic elections and self-determination in liberated areas.

By war's end, the Soviet army was in control of much of eastern Europe and parts of the Balkan Peninsula. Stalin intended to keep a strong military presence in these occupied areas to bolster the Soviet Union's security and strategic position. Thus eastern Europe was the main arena of East-West contention immediately after the war. The Soviet Union did not bow to pressure from the west to permit free elections in occupied regions and restricted trade with the west.

Winston Churchill (1874-1965) was an early opponent of Adolf Hitler and vigorously but vainly opposed the appeasement policy of the pre-World War II British Prime Minister, Neville Chamberlain. As World War II neared its end, Prime Minister Churchill foresaw a dangerous threat in Stalin's Soviet Union. Without much success, he resisted concessions to the Soviets at wartime allied summit meetings held at Yalta and Potsdam.

After Churchill's conservative party was defeated at the polls in 1945, he saw his wartime forebodings about Soviet intentions in eastern Europe become reality. Fearful that a war-weary western world would countenance further incursions into Europe by an aggressive Soviet Union, Churchill used the occasion of an address at Westminster College in Fulton, Missouri, on 5 March 1946 to issue a warning about the division of Europe; he coined the phrase "Iron Curtain" to characterize the Soviet isolation of eastern Europe from the west. This Iron Curtain remained in place till the end of Soviet domination in 1989.

QUESTIONS:

1) How prophetic does Churchill's Iron Curtain speech seem in light of the Cold War years that followed? What in particular strikes you as most perceptive?

2) What is most convincing (or unconvincing) about Churchill's characterization of the state of world affairs in 1946?

3) What role does Churchill see for the United States in the post-World War II era?

I spoke earlier of the Temple of Peace. Workmen from all countries must build that temple. If two of the workmen know each other particularly well and are old friends, if their families are intermingled, and if they have "faith in each other's purpose, hope in each other's future and charity toward each other's shortcomings"--to quote some good words I read here the other day--why cannot they work together at the common task as friends and partners? Why cannot they share their tools and thus increase each other's working powers? Indeed they must do so or else the temple may not be built, or, being built, it may collapse, and we shall see all be proved again unteachable and have to go and try to learn again for a third time in a school of war, incomparably more rigorous than that from which we have just been released? The dark ages may return, the Stone Age may return on the gleaming wings of science, and what may now shower immeasurable material blessings upon mankind, may even bring about its total destruction. Beware, I say; time may be short. Do not let us take the course of allowing events to drift along until it is too late. If there is to be a fraternal association of the kind I have described, with all the extra strength and security which both our countries can derive from it, let us make sure that that great fact is known to the world, and that it plays its part in steadying and stabilizing the foundations of peace. There is the path of wisdom. Prevention is better than cure.

A shadow has fallen upon the scenes so lately lighted by the Allied victory. Nobody knows what Soviet Russia and its Communist international organization intends to do in the immediate future, or what are the limits, if any, to their expansive and proselytizing tendencies. I have a strong admiration and regard for the valiant Russian people and for my wartime comrade, Marshal Stalin. There is deep sympathy and goodwill in Britain--and I doubt not here also--towards the peoples of all the Russias and a resolve to persevere through many differences and rebuffs in establishing lasting friendships. We understand the Russian need to be secure on her western frontiers by the removal of all possibility of German aggression. We welcome Russia to her rightful place among the leading nations of the world. We welcome her flag upon the seas. Above all, we welcome constant, frequent and growing contacts between the Russian people and our own people on both sides of the Atlantic. It is my duty, however, for I am sure you would wish me to state the facts as I see them to you, to place before you certain facts about the present position in Europe.

From Stettin in the Baltic to Trieste in the Adriatic, an iron curtain has descended across the Continent. Behind that line lie all the ancient capitals of the ancient states of Central and Eastern Europe. Warsaw, Berlin, Prague, Vienna, Budapest, Belgrade, Bucharest and Sofia, all these famous cities and the populations around them lie in what I must call the Soviet sphere, and all are subject in one form or another, not only to Soviet influence but to a very high and, in many cases, increasing measure of control from Moscow. Athens alone--Greece with its immortal glories--is free to decide its future at an election under British, American and French observation. The Russian-dominated Polish Government has been encouraged to make enormous and wrongful inroads upon Germany, and mass expulsions of millions of Germans on a scale grievous and undreamed-of are now taking place. The Communist parties, which were very small in all these Eastern States of Europe, have been raised to pre-eminence and power far beyond their numbers and are seeking everywhere to obtain totalitarian control. Police governments are prevailing in nearly every case, and so far, except in Czechoslovakia, there is no true democracy.

Turkey and Persia [Iran] are both profoundly alarmed and disturbed at the claims which are being made upon them and at the pressure being exerted by the Moscow government. An attempt is being made by the Russians in Berlin to build up a quasi-Communist party in their zone of Occupied Germany by showing special favours to groups of left-wing German leaders. At the end of the fighting last June, the American and British armies withdrew westwards, in accordance with an earlier agreement, to a depth at some points of 150 miles upon a front of nearly four hundred miles, in order to allow our Russian allies to occupy this vast expanse of territory which the Western Democracies had conquered.

If now the Soviet Government tries, by separate action, to build up a pro-Communist

Germany in their areas, this will cause new serious difficulties in the British and American zones, and will give the defeated Germans the power of putting themselves up to auction between the Soviets and the Western Democracies. Whatever conclusions may be drawn from these facts--and facts they are--this is certainly not the Liberated Europe we fought to build up. Nor is it one which contains the essentials of permanent peace.

The safety of the world requires a new unity in Europe, from which no nation should be permanently outcast. It is from the quarrels of the strong parent races in Europe that the world wars we have witnessed, or which occurred in former times have sprung. Twice in our own lifetime we have seen the United States, against their wishes and their traditions, against arguments, the force of which it is impossible not to comprehend, drawn by irresistible forces, into these wars in time to secure the victory of the good cause, but only after frightful slaughter and devastation had occurred. Twice the United States has had to send several millions of its young men across the Atlantic to find the war; but now war can find any nation, wherever it may dwell between dusk and dawn. Surely we should work with conscious purpose for a grand pacification of Europe, within the structure of the United Nations and in accordance with its Charter. That I feel is an open cause of policy of very great importance.

In front of the iron curtain which lies across Europe are other causes for anxiety. In Italy the Communist Party is seriously hampered by having to support the Communist-trained Marshal Tito's claims to former Italian territory at the head of the Adriatic. Nevertheless, the future of Italy hangs in the balance. Again one cannot imagine a regenerated Europe without a strong France. All my public life I have worked for a strong France and I never lost faith in her destiny, even in the darkest hours. I will not lose faith now. However, in a great number of countries, far from the Russian frontiers and throughout the world, Communist fifth columns are established and work in complete unity and absolute obedience to the directions they receive from the Communist centre. Except in the British Commonwealth and in the United States where Communism is in its infancy, the Communist parties or fifth columns constitute a growing challenge and peril to Christian civilization. These are sombre facts for anyone to have to recite on the morrow of a victory gained by so much splendid comradeship in arms and in the cause of freedom and democracy; but we should be most unwise not to face them squarely while time remains.

The outlook is also anxious in the Far East and especially in Manchuria. The Agreement which was made at Yalta, to which I was a party, was extremely favourable to Soviet Russia, but it was made at a time when no one could say that the German war might not extend all through the summer and autumn of 1945 and when the Japanese war was expected to last for a further eighteen months from the end of the German war. In this country you are all so well informed about the Far East, and such devoted friends of China, that I do not need to expatiate on the situation there.

I have felt bound to portray the shadow which, alike in the west and in the east, falls upon the world. I was a high minister at the time of the Versailles Treaty [1919] and a close friend of Mr Lloyd George, who was the head of the British delegation at Versailles. I did not myself agree with many things that were done, but I have a very strong impression in my mind of that situation, and I find it painful to contrast it with that which prevails now. In those days there were high hopes and unbounded confidence that the wars were over, and that the League of Nations would become all-powerful. I do not see or feel that same confidence or even the same hopes in the haggard world at the present time.

On the other hand I repulse the idea that a new war is inevitable; still more that it is imminent. It is because I am sure that our fortunes are still in our own hands and that we hold the power to save the future, that I feel the duty to speak out now that I have the occasion and the opportunity to do so. I do not believe that Soviet Russia desires war. What they desire is the fruits of war and the indefinite expansion of their power and doctrines. But what we have to consider here today while time remains, is the permanent prevention of war and the establishment of conditions of freedom and democracy as rapidly as possible in all countries. Our difficulties and dangers will not be removed by closing our eyes to them. They will not be removed by mere waiting to see what happens; nor will they be removed by a policy of appeasement. What is needed is a settlement, and the longer this is delayed, the more difficult it will be and the greater our dangers will become.

From what I have seen of our Russian friends and Allies during the war, I am convinced that there is nothing they admire so much as strength, and there is nothing for which they have less respect than for weakness, especially military weakness. For that reason the old doctrine of a balance of power is unsound. We cannot afford, if we can help it, to work on narrow margins, offering temptations to a trial of strength. If the Western Democracies stand together in strict adherence to the principles of the United Nations Charter, their influence for furthering those principles will be immense and no one is likely to molest them. If, however, they become divided or falter in their duty and if these all-important years are allowed to slip away then indeed catastrophe may overwhelm us all.

Last time I saw it all coming and cried aloud to my fellow-countrymen and to the world, but no one paid any attention. Up till the year 1933 or even 1935, Germany might have been saved from the awful fate which has overtaken her and we might all have been spared the miseries Hitler let loose upon mankind. There never was a war in all history easier to prevent by timely action than the one which has just desolated such great areas of the globe. It could have been prevented in my belief without the firing of a single shot, and Germany might be powerful, prosperous and honoured today; but no one would listen and one by one we were all sucked into the whirlpool. We surely must not let that happen again. This can only be achieved by reaching now, in 1946, a good understanding on all points with Russia under the general authority of the United Nations Organization and by the maintenance of that good

understanding through many peaceful years, by the world instrument, supported by the whole strength of the English-speaking world and all its connections. There is the solution which I respectfully offer to you in this Address to which I have given the title "The Sinews of Peace."

Let no man underrate the abiding power of the British Empire and Commonwealth. Because you see the forty-six millions in our island harassed about their food supply, of which they only grow one-half, even in wartime, or because we have difficulty in restarting our industries and export trade after six years of passionate war effort, do not suppose that we shall not come through these dark years of privation as we have come through the glorious years of agony, or that half a century from now, you will not see seventy or eighty millions of Britons spread about the world and united in defence of our traditions, our way of life, and of the world cause which you and we espouse. If the population of the English-speaking Commonwealths be added to that of the United States with all that such co-operation implies in the air, on the sea, all over the globe and in science and in industry, and in moral force, there will be no quivering, precarious balance of power to offer its temptation to ambition or adventure. On the contrary, there will be an overwhelming assurance of security. If we adhere faithfully to the Charter of the United Nations and walk forward in sedate and sober strength seeking no one's land or treasure, seeking to lay no arbitrary control upon the thoughts of men; if all British moral and material forces and convictions are joined with your own in fraternal association, the highroads of the future will be clear, not only for us but for all, not only for our time, but for a century to come.

Cannadine, David, ed. *Blood, Toil, Tears and Sweat: The Speeches of Winston Churchill*. Boston: Houghton Mifflin, 1989. Pp. 302-308.

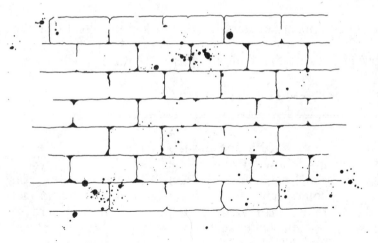

DIVIDED BERLIN: SYMBOL OF THE COLD WAR

The Cold War began after World War II in Europe and involved economic and military competition between adversary blocs of nations led by the United States and the Soviet Union. It spread to embrace Asia, Africa, and Latin America, ending only with the dissolution of the Soviet Union in 1991.

Germany was a principal area of friction between the Soviet Union and the western Allies. After World War II, Germany was partitioned into four occupation zones controlled by Britain, France, the United States, and the U.S.S.R. Likewise, Berlin was divided into four sectors. Fearful of western intentions, the Soviets in 1948 closed "for repairs" the railroads and highways leading through their eastern sector of Germany to Berlin. The United States and Britain responded by airlifting food, clothing, coal, and other supplies to some two million people in West Berlin. The Berlin Blockade and "Operation Vittles" airlift dragged on for almost a year before the Soviets caved in and reopened the highways and railroads in May 1949. Berlin, however, remained a trouble spot in the Cold War.

The western allies combined their three occupation zones in into the Federal Republic of Germany, or "West Germany." The Soviet Union reacted by setting up a communist puppet state known as the German Democratic Republic, or "East Germany." This East-West split of Germany lasted till 1990.

In 1949, President Truman's administration joined its anti-communist European allies and Canada in the North Atlantic Treaty Organization (NATO); the joint military forces of the alliance were under U.S. leadership. An effective military umbrella protected the NATO nations in western Europe against the threat of Soviet attack.

In 1955, the Soviet Union formed its own military alliance, called the Warsaw Pact, which integrated the armed forces of its eastern European satellite states into a unified force under Soviet command. Soviet armed forces were stationed in all Warsaw Pact countries not only to counter NATO, but also to ensure their obedience to the U.S.S.R.

Another Berlin crisis occurred in 1961. Embarrassed by the flight of tens of thousands of east Germans who voted with their feet every year by fleeing from East to West Berlin, the Soviet Union authorized East Germany to build a wall to seal off East Berlin. For nearly thirty years the Wall symbolized the Cold War and communist repression, until it was dismantled to great jubilation in 1990, as part of the reunification of Germany.

In the passage that follows, the distinguished German politician and statesman, Willy Brandt (b. 1913), who was mayor of West Berlin in 1961 (and later chancellor of West Germany), recalls West Berliners' reaction to the sudden splitting of their city during the Cold War.

QUESTIONS:

1) How did the "Four-Power" status of Berlin complicate matters for Brandt and the West German government during the crisis he describes?

2) Brandt stresses the direct personal consequences of the Wall for German citizens; what were some of these consequences?

3) Brandt was forced to play the role of the level-headed pragmatist. Why?

13 August 1961, the day on which the building of the "Wall" was decreed, was a hot summer Sunday. Unable to spend their holidays outside the city, many of my fellow-citizens had been looking forward to a carefree swim in one of the lakes on the city's outskirts--perhaps to a few hours' reading. They were startled to hear the early morning news: Berlin had been divided and sealed off. 13 August 1961 became a day of horror, alarm and bewilderment.

News of the closure--the physical wall was not actually erected until three days later, under the supervision of armed contingents--reached me as I was travelling by train from Nuremberg to Kiel. I had addressed a big party gathering at Nuremberg the day before and planned to launch the election campaign proper at Kiel that Sunday. Just five weeks separated us from the Bundestag elections, in which my political associates had nominated me as their candidate for the Chancellorship.

It was dawn when a railway official knocked at the door of my compartment. He informed me that a complete closure of the Eastern Sector had begun, and that I was requested to return to Berlin by the fastest possible route. Accompanied by a small party of colleagues, I left the train at Hanover at about 5 a.m., caught the early morning flight to Berlin and drove at once from Tempelhof Airport to the sector boundary, first Potsdamer Platz and then the Brandenburg Gate. I surveyed the barriers that had been hauled into place in the past few hours and were now being reinforced with a truly German attention to detail. Concrete posts had been sunk in the streets and were being draped with barbed wire. I saw some of the strong military units--East German, not Russian--whose instructions were to seal the border. I looked into the vacant eyes of uniformed compatriots doing their duty on the other side. Above all, I

saw concern and despair written on the faces of my fellow-citizens of West Berlin.

Like any responsible person in an emergency, I felt it incumbent on me to act rather than look on helplessly. It was hard to remain calm and composed. We had been obliged to keep our heads in many an earlier Berlin crisis. Though not a direct military threat, this was the gravest challenge since the Blockade of 1948. Then, it had been we who were segregated from the outside world by force; this time, a régime was segregating itself and its citizens from us. Even so, the feverish work on the barricades and the heavily armed border guards presented a menacing picture. According to our interpretation of the city's "Four-Power status," East German forces had no business in the territory of East Berlin. Were we to swallow this crude violation of the law governing and pertaining to Germany? Were we to tolerate what was being done to our compatriots, the citizens of East Berlin and the "Zone"? Would the Allies sit back and accept this new development? Would we again be "fobbed off"-- as more than one person phrased it that Sunday morning--with feeble protests?

At the Rathaus--Berlin's city hall--I conducted a special session of the Senate, as our municipal government was called .... Later that morning I drove to the Allied Kommandantura [Headquarters] building for the first and only time in my years as Mayor, my normal practice being to meet the Western Commandants at their residences, at my office in the Rathaus or in a private setting....

The three Western Allies--or, as we used to call them in Berlin, our Protecting Powers--were confronted by grave problems on this 13 August. The Russians had transferred all essential areas of control over East Berlin to the government of the GDR [German Democratic Republic]. The latter sent in troops, assumed unilateral control of internal means of communication and controlled passenger traffic. Such inhabitants of West Berlin as were, in the usual arbitrary manner, termed "peace-loving" received permission to cross the border for a further ten-day period. Thereafter, and until the signing of the passes agreement at the end of 1963, border traffic was abruptly and totally suspended for Berliners-- though not for West Germans, who could still visit the GDR provided they paid the stipulated toll.

The Interior Minister of the GDR issued regulations affecting the Allies themselves. Though not in principle denied access to the eastern part of the city--provocation was not carried to those lengths--the Americans, British and French were restricted to specific crossing- points. Within a few days, the only one left available to them was the Friedrichstrasse access which gained worldwide notoriety as "Checkpoint Charlie." The truly novel and dramatic feature of the situation--a development of fundamental importance--was that the Western Powers were complying not with Russian but with "East German" orders. To put it more bluntly, the mighty United States was letting itself be pushed around, in contemporary parlance, by a "satellite" of the other super- power.

The Allied Commandants and their civilian deputies, who were foreign office personnel, felt just as disconcerted and disoriented that 13 August as did we, their German partners in Berlin. They gave us an attentive hearing but could not so much as lodge a protest with the Soviet Commandant at Karlshorst in default of instructions from their various capitals--it was Sunday! Scanning the troubled faces of my American friends, I could imagine what had happened. They had alerted the Pentagon, the State Department and the White House, only to be told that ungovernable reactions must be avoided at all costs. Besides, West Berlin was under no immediate threat.... The Russians kept order in their German domain, as one US Senator put it. They employed brutal methods, to be sure, but one could understand their desire to halt the unceasing flow of refugees that threatened to bleed the "Zone" to death, economically and intellectually.

The Commandants did not, of course, disguise their sympathy for our citizens. They had grown close to "their" Berliners and had come to identify themselves with the city's problems, but they were expressly advised that "trouble" was undesirable and strictly forbidden to act on their own initiative. Negotiations would have to be preceded by consultations between Washington, London and Paris. If any reference was made to Bonn in this context, it could only have been peripheral.

The President of the United States was on his yacht, but his day of rest did not go undisturbed. He must have been primarily interested in knowing whether any Allied Rights in West Berlin had been directly infringed. This was not the case. On the other hand, allied rights pertaining to Berlin as a whole had been almost contemptuously brushed aside.

We were later able to glean from the memoirs of Kennedy's associates that Khrushchev's ultimatum and the possibility of a nuclear crisis preyed more heavily on the President than any other problem because events in Berlin seemed to threaten a war capable of destroying civilization--"and he thought about little else that summer" (Arthur Schlesinger Jr). At the beginning of August, the President remarked to one of his aides that Khrushchev would probably have to undertake some action (in the GDR) in order to regain control of the situation. He went on: "I can set the alliance in motion if he (Khrushchev) does something against West Berlin, but not if he starts something in East Berlin." Since a few crossing- points still remained open, the tendency in Washington on that grim August Sunday was to believe that the Russians and their East German allies meant to curb the flow of refugees rather than stem it altogether--in retrospect, an incomprehensible miscalculation. This, to quote one witness, "would scarcely have been a reason for marching into the Eastern Sector, thereby provoking a counter-blow and risking war."

I was equally destitute of proposals for any real counter-measures at the morning meeting on 13 August in the Allied Kommandantura, but I did urge that a protest be lodged, not only in Moscow but in the capitals of the other Warsaw Pact countries in whose name a statement justifying the closure had just been issued. (The central organ of the SED [Socialist Unity Party, the East German ruling party] announced on Sunday morning that the closure of East Berlin accorded with a decision reached some days earlier by the Warsaw Pact governments, though this official "blessing" did not necessarily imply that the operation had been unopposed.) "At least send some patrols to the sector border immediately," I said, "to combat the sense of insecurity and show the West Berliners that they are not in jeopardy."

Twenty hours elapsed before the military patrols I had requested appeared on the city's internal border.

Forty hours elapsed before a legal protest was dispatched to the Soviet Commandant.

Seventy-two hours elapsed before a protest--couched in terms that were little more than routine--was lodged in Moscow.

On the evening of 13 August our Berlin Chamber of Deputies met in special session. My task was to voice the outrage of our fellow-citizens but restrain them and counsel prudence. It was not the first or last time this duty fell to me, and I did not always find it easy to perform. Seldom if ever during my mayoral term had the meaning of impotent fury been more gallingly apparent to me. Separation from those across the Wall was not just a political problem to be dismissed as a remote abstraction --it affected millions of people. Ties were being sundered between countless individuals who loved, needed and depended on each other, between us and many friends on the other side, fellow social democrats who had boldly stood their ground. (Our party was not banned in East Berlin and led a legal but shadowy existence there, as opposed to the "Zone," where its amalgamation with the communist KPD [German Communist Party] into the SED, or German Socialist Unity Party, had been universally enforced in 1946.) I did not pay many visits to East Berlin during the years between the Blockade and the Wall but had occasionally called upon my political associates there. They, in turn, had still been able to participate regularly in our discussions in West Berlin.

World War II had reduced Berlin to a sea of rubble. Rebuilding had proceeded considerably faster in the western sectors than in the eastern part of the city. West Berlin, with its two-and-a-quarter million inhabitants, had again become Germany's largest industrial city after weathering a period of severe unemployment. It was also making strides as a scientific and cultural center, and its artistic achievements enjoyed widespread esteem. One noticeable concomitant of all these things was a certain insularity bred by the absence of a territorial hinterland and restricted communication with West Germany. Doubts about the future were offset by a substantial does of local pride. Irrespective of social status, the Berliners were touchingly devoted to their little homeland.

How, I wondered, would the people of Berlin withstand the shock and strain? We had assured them, repeatedly and in good faith, that we would not allow access to be barred. Now the bar had fallen and we were helpless. It must have seemed painfully obvious to many people, just as it did to me, that Berlin's claim to be the German capital-in-retirement had been shaken. The rupture was a deep one indeed, and not for me alone, and it prompted consideration of how our people (and a divided Europe) would fare against such a background.

To the people of Berlin, the Wall itself was more than a mere stimulus-word, more than the symbol of a latent material and moral crisis threatening the GDR's existence: they regarded it as a provocation and an acute threat. We had extreme difficulty in controlling the angry demonstrations that marked the first anniversary of 13 August. A few days later, on 17 August 1962, an eighteen-year-old building worker named Peter Fechter bled to death near Checkpoint Charlie while a crowd looked on, unable and forbidden to help. He had tried to scale the Wall with a companion (who succeeded) and was shot several times. Many had suffered a similar fate before him, but not within sight of so many West Berliners. The [East German] People's Police took their time about removing his body, and angry spectators on our side of the Wall refused to accept a US lieutenant's statement to the effect that it was not his problem. This incident hit the Berliners hard and exacerbated their sense of outrage. Many voiced their disillusionment at the Americans' inability to help a young man who was bleeding to death. Righteous indignation was commingled with disorder and demagogy. Young people talked of blasting holes in the Wall. One cheap rag accused us of treachery on the grounds that we were employing the police to protect it. I was summoned to the Rathaus by phone one evening because an impromptu demonstration was expected. Addressing the youngsters over the loud-hailer of a police car, I told them that the Wall was harder than the heads that wanted to batter it down, and that indulging in escapades would not help our compatriots on the other side. We had to convince students and other young people that the problem of the Wall could not be solved with plastic explosives. By dint of much talking in factories and offices, my colleagues and I strove to show the people of Berlin what was possible and what was not.

Brandt, Willy. *People and Politics: The Years 1960-1975.* Trans. J.M. Brownjohn. New York: Little, Brown and Co., 1978. Pp. 13-17, 37.

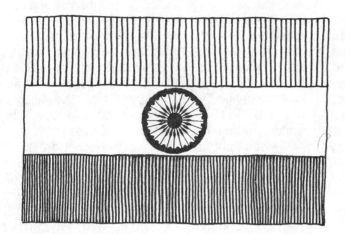

► **Republic of India**

THE MAKING OF AN INDIAN NATIONALIST

Jawaharlal Nehru (1889-1964) was a leader of the Indian National Congress and the first Prime Minister of independent India. He came from a distinguished Brahman family and was the only son of a wealthy and successful lawyer. Nehru was educated in England, graduating from Oxford University, where he was president of the Union Club, a prestigious debating society that was the training ground for future politicians. Following his father Motilal Nehru's footsteps, he became active in the Indian National Congress, eventually as its president for many years. Like other Congress leaders who emulated Mohandas Gandhi's civil disobedience against the continuation of British rule, Nehru served several stints in jail.

After 1909, in response to Indian demands, the British government granted greater self-government to Indians. When Congress candidates won a majority of seats in the federal legislature elections held in 1936, the British authorities appointed Nehru and his colleagues to cabinet positions in the government. Congress politicians objected vehemently when Great Britain declared war against Nazi Germany in 1939, bringing India and other members of the British Empire and Commonwealth automatically into World War II. Nehru and his colleagues argued that an India that was not itself free could not join the Allies in the fight for freedom against Nazi aggression. They demanded that the British government immediately grant full freedom to India. They they promised to fight for the Allied cause. Faced with the urgent demands of war, the British government promised to give India full independence after the war, declared emergency powers and sent Nehru and other leaders of the Congress to jail for non-cooperation. Nehru wrote *The Discovery of India* in 1944 while incarcerated in an old castle. The book attests to his pride in India's past, his shame at its degradation under foreign rule, and above all, his patriotism. He also argues here for a united India based on a common heritage despite the rich diversity of the subcontinent.

Nehru served as India's first prime minister from independence in 1947 until his death in 1964. However, Indian unity ended with British withdrawal. Two nations emerged: predominantly Hindu India, and Muslim Pakistan.

QUESTIONS:

1) Who are some of the diverse peoples of India?
3) Why did Indians fall behind the West?
3) What did Nehru hope for the India of the future?

During these years of thought and activity my mind has been full of India, trying to understand her and to analyze my own reactions toward heree.... It produced a sensation of pride in me as well as that of shame, for I was ashamed of much that I saw around me, of superstitious practices, of outworn ideas, and above all, our subject and poverty-stricken state....

The search for the source of India's strength and for her deterioration and decay is long and intricate. Yet the recent causes of that decay are obvious enough. She fell behind in the march of techniques, and Europe, which had long been backward in many matters, took the lead in technical progress. Behind this technical progress was the spirit of science and a bubbling life and spirit which displayed itself in many activities and adventurous voyages of discovery. New techniques gave military strength to the countries of western Europe and it was easy for them to spread out and dominate the East. That is the story not of India only but of almost the whole of Asia....

Behind the past quarter of a century's struggle for India's independence, and all our conflicts with British authority, lay in my mind and that of many others the desire to revitalize India. We felt that through voluntarily facing risk and suffering and sacrifice, through refusal to submit to what we considered evil and wrong, we would recharge the battery of India's spirit and waken her from her long slumber. Though we came into conflict continually with the British government in India, our eyes were always turned toward our own people.... We aimed high and looked far ... but in no time did we forget that our main purpose was to raise the whole level of the Indian people, psychologically and spiritually and also, of course, politically and economically. It was the building up of that real inner strength of the people that we were after, knowing that the rest would inevitably follow. We had to wipe out the evil aftermath from some generations of shameful subservience and timid submission to an arrogant alien authority.

[Modern Indian nationalism was initially a Westernized upper middle class movement, later] New forces arose that drove us to the masses in the villages, and for the first time, a new and different India rose up before the young intellectuals who had almost forgotten its existence, or attached little importance to it. It was a disturbing sight, not only because of its stark misery and the magnitude of its problems, but because it began to upset some of our values and conclusions. So began for us the discovery of India as it was, and it produced both understanding and conflict within us....

I do not idealize the conception of the masses, and as far as possible I try to avoid thinking of them as a theoretical abstraction. The people of India are very real to me in their great variety ... [in the 1920s, on behalf of the Indian National Congress, he travelled widely in north India to organize the people for elections granted by the British government] I grew to know the sturdy Jat of the northern and western district, the typical son of the soil, brave and independent-looking, relatively prosperous; the Rajput peasant and petty landholder, still proud of his race and ancestry, even though he might have changed his faith and adopted Islam; the deft and skillful artisans and cottage workers, both Hindu and Moslem; the poorer peasantry and tenants in their vast numbers, especially in Oudh and the eastern districts, crushed and ground down by generations of oppression and poverty, hardly daring to hope that a change would come to better their lot, and yet hoping and full of faith....

The diversity of India is tremendous; it is obvious; it lies on the surface.... It concerns itself with physical appearances as well as with certain mental habits and traits. There is little in common, to outward seeming, between the Pathan of the northwest and the Tamil in the far south. Their racial stock are not the same, though there may be common strands running through them; they differ in face and figure, food and clothing, and of course, language. In the North-West Frontier Province there is already the breath of Central Asia, and many a custom there, as in Kashmir, reminds one of the countries on the other side of the Himalayas. Pathan popular dances are singularly like Russian Cossack dancing. Yet with all these differences, there is no mistaking the impress of India on the Pathan, as this is obvious on the Tamil. It is not surprising, for these border lands, and indeed Afghanistan also, were united with India for thousands of years.... The frontier area was one of the principal centers of old Indian culture, and it abounds still with ruins of monuments and monasteries and especially of the great university of Taxila, which was at the height of its fame two thousand years ago, attracting students from all over India as well as different parts of Asia. Changes of religion made a difference but could not change entirely the mental backgrounds which the people of those areas had developed.

The Pathan and the Tamil are two extreme examples; the others lie somewhere in between. All of them have their distinctive features, all of them have still more the distinguishing marks of India....

All of us, I suppose, have varying pictures of our native land and no two persons will think exactly alike. When I think of India, I think of many things: of broad fields dotted with innumerable small villages; of towns and cities I have visited; of the magic of the rainy season which pours life into the dry, parched-up land and converts it suddenly into a glistening expanse of beauty and greenery, of great rivers and flowing water; of the Khyber Pass in all its bleak surroundings; of the southern tip of India; of people individually and in the mass; and above all, of the Himalayas, snow-capped, or some mountain valley in Kashmir in the spring, covered with new flowers, and with a brook bubbling and gurgling through it. We make and preserve the pictures of our choice, and so I have chosen this mountain background rather than the more normal picture of a hot, subtropical country. Both pictures would be correct, for India stretches from the tropics right up to the temperate regions, from near the equator to the cold heart of Asia....

* * * * *

[Nehru concluded his "discovery" of India in these words.]

India will find herself again when freedom opens out new horizons and the future will fascinate her far more than the immediate past of frustration and humiliation. She will go forward with confidence, rooted in herself and yet eager to learn from others and co-operate with them. Today she swings between a blind adherence to her old customs and a slavish imitation of foreign ways. In neither of these can she find relief or life or growth. It is obvious that she has to come out of her shell and take full part in the life and activities of the modern age....

We are citizens of no mean country and we are proud of the land of our birth, of our people, our culture and traditions. That pride must not be for a romanticized past to which we want to cling; nor should it encourage exclusiveness or a want of appreciation of other ways than ours. It must never allow us to forget our many weaknesses and failings or blunt our longing to be rid of them. We have a long way to go and much leeway to make up before we can take our proper station with others in the van of human civilization and progress. And we have to hurry, for the time at our disposal is limited and the pace of the world grows ever swifter....

My generation has been a troubled one in India and the world. We may carry on for a little while longer, but our day will be over and we shall give place to others, and they will live their lives and carry their burdens to the next stage of the journey. How have we played our part in this brief interlude that draws to a close? I do not know. Others of a later age will judge. By what standards do we measure success or failure? That too I do not know. We can make no complaint that life has treated us harshly, for ours has been a willing choice, and perhaps life has not been so bad to us after all. For only those can sense life who stand often on the verge of it, only those whose lives are not governed by the fear of death. In spite of all the mistakes that we might have made, we have saved ourselves from triviality and an inner shame and cowardice. That, for our individual selves has been some achievement.

Nehru, Jawaharlal. *The Discovery of India*. Ed. Robert J. Crane. Garden City, NY: Doubleday, 1946. Pp. 21-22, 24-26, 30, 32, 414, 416-417.

KENYANS STRUGGLE FOR INDEPENDENCE

Decolonization in Africa proceeded quickly after World War II, as European colonies became independent states. This was the result both of African struggles for independence and the loss of will on the part of the imperial powers to maintain control. The winning of independence varied from peaceful transfers of power as in French ruled Morocco and Tunisia and British ruled Uganda, to United Nations supervised transitions as in the former Italian colony Libya, to guerrilla wars or "wars of liberation" as in French Algeria, Portuguese Angola or British Kenya. The last generally resulted from the unwillingness of European settlers to give up privileged positions in favor of African majority rule.

In Kenya, white settlers, mainly farmers in the highlands, obstructed Great Britain's program of gradual self-government based on multiracial cooperation between European and Indian settlers, and Africans. The Kikuyus, the largest ethnic group among indigenous Africans in Kenya, opposed concessions to the non-African minorities. In 1952, under the leadership of British educated Jomo Kenyatta, the Kenya African Union began guerrilla warfare against continued British rule. Commonly called the Mau Mau, these guerrilla fighters assassinated and assaulted British officials, white settlers, and uncooperative Kenyans. Britain finally granted independence to Kenya in 1963 and Kenyatta became its leader under a single-party system.

Waruhiu Itote, known as "General China," was the first major Mau Mau leader to write an autobiography. He described his transformation from a soldier fighting for the British Empire in World War II to Mau Mau leader.

QUESTIONS:

1) How did fighting in the British army in World War II make Itote into a Kenyan nationalist?
2) How did the Kenyan guerrilla forces fight?
3) How did the oath taking ceremony bind the guerrillas?

The first time I ever thought of myself as a Kenyan was in 1943, in the Kalewa trenches on the Burma Front [against Japan in World War II]. I'd spent several evenings talking to a British soldier, and thought we had become friends. But I was rather surprised one evening when, after we had been talking for a while, he said, "You know, sometimes I don't understand you Africans who are out here fighting. What do you think you are fighting for?"

I didn't have to reflect much on that question--we had all had it drilled into our heads many times.

"I'm fighting for the same thing as you are, of course," I told him.

"In a funny way," he said, "I think you're right--and I'm not sure that's such a good idea."

I asked him to explain this.

"Look," he began, I'm fighting for England, to preserve my country, my culture, all those things which we Englishmen have built up over the centuries of our history as a nation; it's really my 'national independence' that I'm fighting to preserve. And, I suppose, all that goes with it, including the British Empire. Does it seem right to you, that you should be fighting for the same things as I?"

I did not know how to answer this, so I said, "I doubt it, I don't think so."

"You'd better not think so," he replied. "Naturally we're all fighting to protect not only our own countries but the whole world against Fascism and dictatorship; we know that. But I can't see why you Africans should fight to protect the Empire instead of fighting to free yourselves. Years from now, maybe, your children will fight a war to preserve the national independence of your country, but before that it's up to you to see that they get an independence in the first place, so they can preserve it later!"...

[In 1952, back in Kenya, Jomo] Kenyatta told us of other countries where men had fought and died for freedom....

"They succeeded--but they suffered," he said. "We too, after suffering, will get what we want. But we must be courageous and determined, and have faith in our ultimate victory...."

While we were at Gatundu, I blessed the circumstance which had made me join the army. Although at times I regretted having fought for our Colonial masters, on that day I was glad, for I was now going to use the knowledge they had given me, against them....

A few days after this meeting with Kenyatta, the moment for which I had been waiting arrived. I received instructions from the (Nyeri) Nairobi Committee to report to Karatina, an important market town on the slopes of Mount Kenya. At Karatina I was to meet forty young men, untrained and unarmed, but inspired with patriotism and ready to fight. These men were to join me in the Mount Kenya Forest and to become the nucleus of an Army of Liberation. I was also told that Nairobi would send us money, guns, ammunition and medical supplies, while the District Committee would provide us with food, and would control the supply lines. It turned out that we had to find our own arms and ammunition....

[At the base] we held a massive oath-taking ceremony in which two hundred people ... participated. Afterwards we explained what was expected of them: the British had taken our land, we said, and we had dedicated ourselves to the fight for our liberty--those who had taken the oath must now help us in every way possible way. This continued as the basic theme of our ceremonies: the oath-giving, an explanation of our people's fate under British colonialism, and a clarification of the new obligations to which the oath bound its takers....

In the evening, members of the local committee called us and administered the second oath, the forest or *mbatuni* oath, to us. After four of us had taken this oath we were introduced to the forty young men who were to form the core of our army.... I was requested to teach them all that I knew about fighting, and particularly to show them the "jungle" methods used by the Japanese in Burma. Gaitho said that the local committee would help us with money, clothes and communications, but that it was up to us to find weapons....

As it became more difficult to acquire weapons accidentally or by theft, we decided to try our hands at making our own guns.... Car type tube rubber, water pipes and roughhewn wood stocks were combined to make a manageable, though not always reliable, rifle, The stock itself was fashioned from the wood of the *Muthiti* or *Thirikwa* tree, which never cracks under any weather conditions. The barrel, generally made from water pipes, was fastened to this, and a smaller pipe or piece of iron, one which would fit smoothly within the barrel, was used as a hammer. The hammer was released by a mechanism built out of a barbed wire spring and a piece of car or bicycle tube. Eventually we progressed from single-shot to "repeating" rifles, using magazines made from the iron of drums, and springs made from the metal bands which sealed boxes shipped overseas. Better triggers were fashioned later as well, using springs from chicken weighing machines. With all the proper materials, and enough time, there is no telling the limits our imaginations would have reached....

Aside from guns, we used and manufactured our own arrows ... but we didn't find this method of warfare very satisfactory, for arrows required considerable work and were rarely retrievable. At first we poisoned them with certain herbs, such as *Mung'athu*, and later we discovered a virulent poison which, to the best of my knowledge, had no antidote. Even a scratch from an arrow tipped with the poison produced a speedy death. I soon banned the use of this poison entirely, for just as the armies in European wars had banned poison gas and germ warfare, we too knew that this terrible weapon could be turned against us, and against the innocent people of the reserves. As our gun manufacturing flourished, in fact, we ceased entirely to make arrows....

The word "oath" in connection with the "Mau Mau" movement has somehow been associated in the minds of many people with "savagery".... Rather than try to figure out why so many western writers have been able to see nothing but blood, sex and bestiality in our rituals, I would prefer to describe some of our oaths, how they were administered, and what purposes they served....

From the point of view of our fighting forces, the most important oath was the Action Oath, which was given before a man joined the army. Those who had taken the oath were identified by means of an armband of animal skin....

While the potential Forest Fighter waited nearby, but out of sight, a he-goat all of one colour was slaughtered. Kikuyu custom was followed, and the goat was strangled quickly by pressure on its windpipe. As soon as the animal was dead, it was stabbed in the breast next to the heart, and the blood which ran out was allowed nearly to fill a gourd. Typical Kikuyu food, such as milk and millet, were then mixed in with the blood, and bile added to give a bitter taste. The goat's carcass was dismembered and placed on a flaming fire but the head was put to one side and the fluid from its eyes added to the gourd. Special slaughter knives were used throughout this procedure. Finally the goat's skin was cut into small pieces to be made into armbands for the new recruits. One long strip of hide was cut to tie around the stone of sacrifice....

A place was cleared for the ceremony itself ... well decorated with banana plants, sugar-cane stems and other plants, placed in a wide circle around the stone. On the stone itself were placed the *mugere* stick and seven black plants, within which rested a bunch of bananas, the full gourd and the meat of the goat. The men about to take the oath were brought naked into the circle of sacrifice in such numbers as the oath administrator decreed; the latter wore ceremonial dress but no shoes.

When the men entered the circle, they first walked round it seven times and then stood still, while the administrator took the gourd and the goat's meat and passed them round each man-- again seven times. The men were then given a small ball of soil or clay, which they had to hold in their hands. The jaw of the goat, which had been placed in the gourd, was removed by a piece of string tied round it. Each man in turn took the jaw bone, tied it round his neck with the string, and held a *mugere* stick in his hand as he repeated the oath:

If I reveal our secrets, let this oath turn against me;

If I spy falsely, let this oath turn against me;

If my father, my mother or my child betray the nation and I refuse to kill him or her, let this oath turn against me;

If I leave any comrade in danger, let this oath turn against me;

If I kill a leader to gain promotion or a higher post, let this oath turn against me;

If I surrender before we have gained our Independence, let this oath turn against me;

If I see a weapon of the enemy and fear to take it, let this oath turn against me;

If I hand over my gun or our books to the enemy, let this oath turn against me;

If I kill a fellow soldier out of enmity, let this oath turn against me;

If I betray our country or our nationalists, let this oath turn against me.

While repeating these words, the man would strike the jawbone with the stick, and when he had finished he would pass them to the man next in line. When they had finished, the administrator took the meat and went to the first man, who was told to repeat the following words:

I swear in truth before God and this Council that I will obey the laws of the Council and will be a steadfast soldier who will obey the Council and the commander's orders. If I disobey or fail to fulfil any commission, let this meat turn against me and let my legs be fractured.

I swear that if I become a commander I will judge all cases fairly, without fear or favour to any person, whether a friend or relative.... [There are five more oaths.]

At the end of each statement, the man would bite a small piece of the goat's meat and swallow it whole.... [All initiates took the oaths.] Then the troop commander held the point of a sharpened panga against the back of the first man. The administrator held the gourd to the initiate's lips, dipped a knife into it and drew a cross on the man's forehead, saying: "I mark you with the mark of Gikuyu and Mumbi, who were granted this country by God for themselves and their generations. Be brave and firm, knowing that if you die in the fight to liberate your land, God will preserve you in heaven...." While these words were being spoken, the panga rested on the man's neck and at the conclusion of the speech he sipped the blood from the gourd....

Each man then sipped from the gourd, and was given an armband of skin.... He then took a hammer and a goat's leg and said: "If I fail to fulfil my oath, let me be smashed like this leg," and he hit the leg with the hammer. When all of the men had completed this, they put on their clothes and turned to face Mount Kenya, saying: "God bless this sacrifice." The men were then registered as soldiers in our official books, and the Action Oath was over.

A similar but slightly modified oath was taken by women scouts who worked with and for us. They, however, did not remove their clothes during the oath.

Itote, Waruhiu. *"Mau Mau" General*. Nairobi: East African Publishing House, 1967. Pp. 9-10, 45-47, 49-50, 103-104, 107-108, 273-278.

FROM NASSER TO SADAT: EGYPT'S SHIFTING STANCE IN THE COLD WAR

Egypt played an important role in the Cold War because of its pivotal location in the Middle East and the presence of the Suez Canal. Egypt is also the most populous Arab nation. Egyptian leaders attempted to manipulate both super-powers to Egypt's benefit; but because Egypt is a weak and poor nation, both power blocs used Egypt as a pawn.

In 1947, a United Nations resolution partitioned Palestine into an Arab and a Jewish state (Israel). Israel's Arab neighbors immediately challenged its right to exist; four wars have been fought between the protagonists. Although the Soviet Union and Western nations had supported the UN resolution that created Israel, the Middle East became a theater of the Cold War between the superpowers: the United States supported Israel, while the Soviet Union aided opposing Arab states.

In 1952, a coup by nationalist officers overthrew the corrupt Egyptian monarchy and brought Colonel Gamal Abdel Nasser (1913-1970) to power. Because Egypt had resented Western (British) domination, Nasser established good relations with the Soviet Union and China. Thus Egypt joined neutral and newly independent nations in the Non-Aligned bloc of Third World countries in 1956. The Non-Aligned nations were consistently critical of the United States, NATO, and other U.S. led alliances throughout the Cold War. When the United States refused to help Egypt build the Aswan High Dam in 1956, the Soviet Union offered technical and financial aid, in return for which Egypt allowed the Soviet navy to use Alexandria's port facilities.

Nasser died in 1971 and was succeeded by his fellow army officer Anwar Sadat (1918-1981). After three humiliating defeats by Israel, Sadat launched a surprise attack in 1973, scoring initial successes. The United States led the major powers to contain the conflict and bring about a cease-fire. U.S. Secretary of State Henry Kissinger then began a shuttle diplomacy among Middle Eastern capitals to defuse tensions. Eager to achieve peace so he could address Egypt's massive economic problems, and seeing greater advantage in cooperation with the United States, President Sadat cooled relations with the Soviet Union.

In 1977, Sadat astounded the world by announcing that he would go to Jerusalem to work for peace. This historic initiative led to peace talks between Egypt and Israel, mediated by the United States and culminating in the Camp David Agreement in 1979. Israel returned oil-rich conquered territory in the Sinai Peninsula, and in return Egypt recognized Israel and guaranteed their mutual border. The United States pledged generous economic aid to both nations. Although peace did not immediately become contagious throughout the Middle East, as President Jimmy Carter had hoped,

Egypt's new stance has prevented other Arab nations from instigating another Arab-Israeli war. The Camp David Agreement brought Egypt into the Western camp in the Cold War and strengthened the United States' position in the Middle East.

The first part of this reading, from President Nasser's speeches, shows his pro-Soviet and pro-Chinese foreign policy. The second is from parts of President Sadat's historic speech before the Israeli parliament, and Israeli Prime Minister Menachem Begin's response.

QUESTIONS:

1) Why was the Aswan High Dam important to Egypt and what was the Soviet Union's role in building it?
2) What was Sadat offering to Israel?
3) On what terms was Israel seeking peace with Egypt?

President Nasser on 9 January 1963, at a rally at the High Dam:

We were living in only 5 percent of our territory and the other 95 percent will now have to be explored and exploited to the maximum. We are working in the New Valley. While we are working on the High Dam we are gaining new land to exploit the New Valley. We are continuously drilling water wells and reclaiming land. As more water is made available, land in Upper Egypt and the Delta will widen.

Moreover, we are discovering minerals and oil. Our production of oil and minerals is increasing....

We have an excess population.... The only solution we have is work.... You can feel proud of having given the example. You are building one of the world's greatest enterprises--the High Dam--under difficult conditions.... I think it is our duty to express our thanks to the U.S.S.R. for the great aid which it gave us in this work. The Soviet Minister of Electric Power is right here with us.... We thank the Soviet people for their great aid and for their help in the construction of the High Dam after the long battle which we fought.

We thank Mr. Nikita Khrushchev for his response and for extending to us the loan to construct the High Dam. It is a very generous loan. We also thank him for the machinery we obtained from the U.S.S.R. as part of the loan....

We also express our thanks to the U.S.S.R. for another loan granted to us. This second loan, which amounted to 100 million [Egyptian] pounds, was for the construction of the second

stage of the High Dam scheduled to start next year, 1964. This second stage will complete the Dam....

We also greet the Soviet technicians and workers who are working here in this country the weather of which is so much different from their country.... We appreciate their ability and endurance, and we appreciate the spirit they have shown, as well as their fortitude and the aid and assistance in the construction of the High Dam. We also tell them that the construction of the High Dam will always stand as a symbol of Arab-Soviet friendship.

President Nasser on 14 December 1963, at a banquet for Premier Chou En-lai of China:

Dear Friend,

I returned to Cairo from the meeting of Bandung [Indonesia, 1956, in which both Chou and Nasser participated, establishing the bloc of Non-Aligned Nations. China joined despite its alliance with the Soviet Union.] to face a war that had been already started against the attempt to force us to join military pacts, which were being imposed on the peoples of the Arab nation. The last means of pressure was the arms monopoly which aimed at exposing us to imperialist aggression through Israel--established as a [base to menace] the unity and security of the Arab land....

It pleases me to pay tribute and express appreciation to the great people of China who were the first of all those nations in standing by us and upholding the ideals of mankind. The aggression [1956 Anglo-French invasion of the Suez Canal] fell back and the aggressors suffered a crushing defeat in Port Said--a defeat which pursued them after Port Said into the heart of the African Continent, spurring its peoples to continue their efforts. Today the fight is still in progress and the flags of independence are rising one after the other every day, heralding the birth of a new African State.

President Sadat's address to the Israeli Knesset [parliament] on 20 November 1977:

In the Name of God, the Merciful, the Compassionate.
Mr. Speaker,
Ladies and Gentlemen,

God's peace and mercy be upon you; Peace for all of us, God willing.

Peace for all of us in the Arab lands, in Israel and everywhere in our big globe, beset by its sanguinary conflicts, confused by its sharp contradictions, jeopardized from time to time by destructive wars, these wars unleashed by man to annihilate his fellowmen. However ultimately, from among the debris of what man has constructed, from among the remnants of his fellowmen, neither victor nor vanquished will emerge. The vanquished will also always be man, the paragon of God's creation. Man whom God has created as Gandhi, the saint of peace, has put it, "to trudge on earth, building life and worshipping God."

Today, I have come to you with firm steps, to build a new life and to establish peace. We all on this earth, Moslems, Christians and Jews alike, worship God and nobody but Him....

I declared that I will go anywhere in the world, I will go to Israel, because I want to lay down all the facts before the Israeli people....

When I say that I wanted to spare the Arab people the horrors of another holocaust, I want to declare before you quite sincerely that I bear the same feeling and responsibility toward every one in the world, and certainly toward the Israeli people....

I have born--and I still bear--the exigencies of a historic responsibility. For this purpose I declared some years back, on February 4, 1971 to be exact, that I was ready to sign a peace agreement with Israel. It was the first declaration--ever to be made by an Arab responsible official since the onset of the Arab-Israeli conflict.

Moved by all these motivations ... I called on October 16, 1973, before the Egyptian People's Assembly, for the convening of an international conference to decide upon a just and durable peace....

Moved by all these reasons, I have decided to come to you with an open mind and heart, and with a conscious free will, to establish a durable peace based on justice....

You want to co-exist with us in this part of the world, and I tell you quite sincerely: We welcome you among us in all peace and security.

This, in itself, constitutes a sharp turning point, a landmark in a historic and decisive change.

In the past we rejected you and we had our reasons and claims.

Yes, we refused to meet you--in any place.

Yes, we used to describe you as so-called Israel.

Yes, we attended the same international conferences or organizations. Our representatives never--and still do not--exchange greetings....

But, I tell you today, and declare to the whole world, that we accept to live with you in durable and just peace. We do not want to encircle each other with rockets ready to destroy or with missiles of feuds and hatred.

I have declared more than once that Israel has become an established fact recognized by the entire world. The two super-powers have committed themselves to security and the safe-guarding of its existence.

And since we really and sincerely want peace, we welcome you to live among us in real peace and security....

Let me tell you truthfully: Today we have a good chance for peace, an opportunity that cannot be repeated, if we are really serious in the quest for peace....

What is peace for Israel? ... The answer will be, that Israel should live within its borders in peace and security with its Arab neighbours, within the framework of all the guarantees it may want, and which are given to the other party.

But how can this be achieved?...

There are Arab territories which Israel occupied, and still occupies, by armed force. We insist on complete withdrawal from these territories, including Arab Jerusalem....

Jerusalem must be a free city, open to all the faithful....

I have chosen to depart from all precedents and traditions practised by belligerent countries, although the Arab territories are still occupied. My announcement about my readiness to come to Israel was a major surprise and stirred many feelings, astounded many minds.... I chose this difficult course, which in the view of many is the most difficult ... [to] battle for a just and lasting peace.

Prime Minister Menachem Begin's speech to the Israeli Knesset on 20 November 1977:

Mr. Speaker, President of the State of Israel, President of the Arab Republic of Egypt, Worthy and learned men, members of the Knesset, I greet and welcome the President of Egypt on the occasion of his visit to our country and his participation at this Knesset session. The time of the flight from Cairo to Jerusalem is short, but the distance between Cairo and Jerusalem was, until last night, almost indefinite.

But President Sadat crossed the distance courageously. We, the Jews, know how to appreciate such courage, and we shall know how to appreciate it when we see it in our distinguished guest, because with courage we are here and this is how we continue to exist and we shall continue to exist....

And we do believe that if we make peace, if we make a real peace, we can help one another in all the walks of life, and a new period for the Middle East can be ushered in, a period of growth and blossoming of developments....

Let us not be bogged down by the memories of the past. All these bitter memories. Let us overcome them and look into the future, for our nation and for our children ... for our common future, because we shall all have to live here in this area forever and ever--the great Arab Nation in its various states and countries and the Jewish people in its country, the land of Israel....

Let us sign a peace treaty. Let us lay down this situation forever and ever both in Jerusalem and in Cairo....

You will have an ambassador in Jerusalem-- you will have our Ambassador, and we will have yours. Even if there is a divergence of opinions, we will be able to clear it up. We are civilized people, and through the good offices of our Ambassadors, we could do that....

Anybody who says that--in the relationship between the Arab peoples around us and the State of Israel--there are things which must be removed from the realm of negotiations is mistaken. Everything must be negotiated and can be negotiated. No side will present preliminary conditions. We will conduct our negotiations with respect. If there is a divergence of opinion between us, it is not unusual. He who studied the history of wars and that which happened to peace treaties knows that all negotiations concerning a peace treaty began with a difference of opinion, disagreement, and that within the negotiations they reached agreement and consent, consensus which brought about the signing of peace treaties. This is the way that we suggest that we follow.

We shall conduct these negotiations as equals. There are no victors and no vanquished. All the people in this area, in the region, are equal and let everybody treat his neighbour with due respect in the spirit of openness, of readiness to listen one to the other, to hear facts, explanations, reasons. With all the experience of convincing each other, that which is accepted, let us conduct negotiations as I requested and suggested, to open negotiations, to continue negotiations until we reach a treaty for peace.

Nasser, Gamal Abdel. *President Gamal Abdel Nasser's Speeches and Press Interviews, January-December, 1963* [n.p.: n.p., n.d.]. Pp. 8-10, 287-288. Egypt, Arab Republic of [Ministry of Foreign Affairs]. *White Paper on the Peace Initiatives undertaken by President Anwar Al-Sadat (1971-1977)* [n.p.: n.p., n.d.]. Pp. 167, 169-170, 173, 175-176, 181, 185-188, 192.

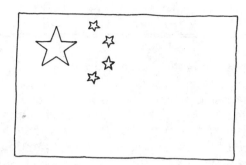

READING 10.7

GROWING UP IN COMMUNIST CHINA

▸ **People's Republic of China**

Just as the Communist party grabbed power in exhausted Russia toward the end of World War I, it likewise seized power in victorious but war-wrecked China soon after World War II. In both countries, the Communist Party established a totalitarian state. Three factors dominated life under Communism. First was a monopoly of power, with the party dictating every aspect of citizens' lives from cradle to grave, including education, job, marriage and housing; it even sought to control thinking. Second was pervasive fear of a party and state apparatus that could summarily throw citizens in jail or labor camps and ruin careers and families. Third was shortages and deprivation. In China as in the USSR, the central government formulated Five Year Plans and dictated the quantity, quality, and price of all products without concern for the needs of the citizens. The economic planners emphasized heavy industry, such as iron, steel, cement, etc., and ignored light industry and consumer needs. Such policies resulted in shoddy and useless products, and perennial shortages of everything from food to clothing to housing.

Liang Heng was born in Changsha, a city in central China, in 1954. His father was a newspaper reporter and his mother worked in a government office; both were enthusiastic supporters of the Communist party and hoped to join it. The family's troubles began in 1958 when the government ordered citizens to offer criticisms for its shortcomings. Mrs. Liang, who was ordered to criticize her boss, was doomed because of it. Divorcing her did not save her husband and children from guilt by association. In *Son of the Revolution*, Liang Heng chronicles his harrowing experiences growing up and his family's vain attempts to prove that he and the children were loyal citizens; he also tells about the hunger and terrible hardships his family lived through.

In *Eighth Moon: The True Story of a Young Girl's Life in Communist China* by Sansan as told to Bette Lord, the author describes a dreary life of shortages and her pain at being thwarted from following a career interest because of the dictates of the state. In 1946, Sansan's mother took her elder sisters to the United States to join her husband who was working there. The infant Sansan was left in the care of her aunt and uncle. Her parents had expected to return to China when her father's assignment finished, but stayed in the U.S. when the Communists took over China in 1949. Sansan's uncle and aunt, who were lower level professionals with no interest in politics adopted her to save her from the stigma of having parents in the U.S.

QUESTIONS:

1) How did one become guilty by association in Communist China?
2) Give examples of how the Communist Party determined people's lives.

3) How was it dangerous to speak the truth in a Communist state? Give examples.

[At three or four years old Liang Heng had run away from his day-care center to his grandmother's home nearby. After he had been returned to the center he recalls that the nurses] locked me up in a room with two other offenders, saying, "You are not Chairman Mao's good little boy; you haven't upheld Revolutionary discipline. You can stay here until you think things over."...

The nurses' words had another kind of sting for me, since I had been taught Chairman Mao was like the sun itself. At home, "Mao" had been my first word after "Mama," "Baba," and "Nai Nai," (Grandma).... Later I had learned how to say "I love Chairman Mao" and "Long Live Chairman Mao." ... When the nurses told me the next day that Chairman Mao had forgiven me, I was the happiest child in the world.

During the next year ... I learned how to write my first characters. The first word was made up of the four strokes in the Chairman's name. Next I learned to write the characters in my own name....

[In 1958 Heng's mother fell into deep trouble after she had been encouraged to make criticisms about her boss.] It was disastrous. When she was allowed to see her file in 1978, she found out that she had been given a Rightist's "cap" solely because of those three criticisms she had made.... At the time she had no idea what the verdict was based on, she only knew that a terrible wrong had been done. But there was no court of appeal. Mother was sent away to the suburb of Yuan Jia ing for labor reform. She lost her cadre's rank and her salary was cut from fifty-five to fifteen *yuan* per month....

Father's traditional Confucian sense of family obligation told him to support Mother while his political allegiance told him to condemn her. In the end, his commitment to the Party won out, and he denounced her. He believed that was the only course that could save the family from ruin....

In fact Father had been much too optimistic, and the divorce did nothing to rid us of having a Rightist in the family. He even forbade our having the slightest contact with Mother, thinking that if we drew a clear line of separation, things

might be better. But there wasn't the slightest change in our status: in the eyes of the Party, my sisters and I were the children of a Rightist and Father had a Rightist wife. Liang Fang [Heng's oldest sister] still had to say she had a Rightist mother on her application to go to middle school, Liang Wei-ping [his second sister] still found "Rightist's child' written on her desk in chalk when she went to class, and I was still turned down when I asked to be allowed to join the Young Pioneers....

But as I got older, more and more stress was placed on the three stages of Revolutionary glory: the Young Pioneers, the Communist Youth League, and the Party itself. It is because success in the political arena was a prerequisite for success in anything else, and if I had the slightest ambition for myself I had to achieve these basic signs of social recognition. [Applying for membership in the Young Pioneers] was no use. I was rejected year after year, until I found myself in a tiny minority of outsiders. [At school the other students] would slap me, or kick me when I wasn't looking, and then pretend not to have done anything. Sometimes I would get into real fights, and then there were reprimands from Father and the teachers. The other Rightist's son was as lonely as I, but we never spoke much, for that might have made things even worse.

[In 1958 the Chinese government forced peasants into communes, deprived them of all incentives and exhausted them with labor and political indoctrination. These and other disastrous economic policies resulted in a massive famine. Liang recalls his family's brush with long bouts of semi-starvation.] It was in 1960, just around the time of the divorce, that all China fell on hard times. I was about seven. Rice, cooking oil, and soybean products were severely rationed, and meat, eggs, flour, and sugar gradually disappeared from the market completely. The cost of fresh vegetables went out of sight, and the *mantou* (steamed buns) we bought in the dining hall became rough and dark because the good flour was all gone. We were always hungry....

The situation dragged on and got worse, month after month, until a whole year had passed. I grew accustomed to going with my sisters to the Martyrs' Park to pull up a kind of edible grass that could be made into a paste with broken grains of rice and steamed and eaten as "bittercakes." Gradually even this became scarce and we had to walk miles to distant suburbs to find any.

Many of the old people and almost all the children I knew had the "water swelling disease," dropsy. Our bodies puffed up and wouldn't recede, and we walked listlessly to school and arrived exhausted. When acquaintances met, they squeezed each others' legs to see how swollen they were and examined each others' skin to see if they were yellow. It was a game for me to poke Nai Nai's [Grandma] cheek and leave a hole that would fill up again only very slowly, like dough....

By the second year Nai Nai's condition was very bad, because she often gave away the small share that was hers.... We were too ignorant and hungry to refuse.

Then one day, when my sisters got up Nai Nai stayed in bed. She slept so long that at last they went to rouse her. Finally they called in Father. When he too failed to awaken her he threw himself on her body weeping, cursing himself for having been a bad son.... I wished he would stop, but he cried for a long time.

[During another politically caused time of great hardships in the late 1960s, now living in a boarding school for boys, Lianga Heng and his friends steal food at the farmers' market, and forage in the fields.] We had our techniques down to perfection. A group of us would approach some poor vendor and someone would haggle with him about prices until he was blind with fury and had lost his usual vigilance. Then the rest of us went into action. Preserved eggs disappeared into eager pockets and peanuts vanished in greedy fistfuls. We were never caught; we were much too experienced for that. To us, stealing wasn't a moral question, but a question of survival.

It was too easy, and we were too hungry. So we started to go out at night as well. After the dormitory was quiet, the twelve of us picked our way through the complicated structure of intersecting beds where our forty classmates lay near-naked and snoring. Headed for the sweet potato fields, we ran silently into the night, trained now to use the moon shining in the rice paddies as our torchlight. We went farther each time, to fresher and safer territory, recognizing the potato plants by the dew glittering on their tangled leaves.

Even today, I want to cry when I think about that life, how I wriggled down between the rows, nearly burying myself, and scrabbled in the earth with my fingers until I felt a hard tuber. Fear and barking dogs made me greedy: I wiped off as much dirt as I could and devoured the potatoes raw, right then, as I lay there on my stomach with the clinging earth grinding like metal in my teeth, the pulp tough, juicy, and bittersweet, creating revolutions in my belly. It wasn't until we were nearly sick that we filled up the extra pair of pants we had made into a sack by tying the ankles with string, always urging each other "That's enough, that's enough," in our terror of being discovered....

[After returning to school] We still had to hide our plunder in the back of the deserted storeroom, where it would stay until we pretended to have bought it in the next market day. And we had to wash ourselves in the pond, our splashing setting off all the dogs in the town. It was often near dawn by the time we lay back in our beds, our swollen bellies already aching and cramping with their strange burden. I was grateful many times over for the precious mosquito netting that had hidden my absence.

* * * * *

[Sansan enters eighth grade after having spent much time during the previous year in labor chores assigned by the school] My hopes for a labor-free school year ended as soon as I learned of my class schedule for the semester. We were to be more involved in political campaigns than ever; along with my courses in zoology and botany, physics, chemistry, geometry and algebra, physical education, music, Chinese literature and grammar, there was a new class called "political discussion." Beginning in 1957, all students in all schools were assigned to weekly political-discussion groups. At my school, we were allotted to specific groups of approximately fifteen students with one student group leader, and we met for two class periods or more each Wednesday afternoon.... At first we were all puzzled as to exactly what was expected of us, but soon we all learned and tried to find a way to fulfill our obligations without making a mistake.

It was at a meeting to discuss the violation of classmate Han that I learned a genuine opinion was not appreciated even though you had to speak. At this meeting we were asked our views of Han's violating the rule against social dancing for students. A teacher had discovered music scores for dance tunes in Han's desk, and after scolding him severely, asked that he be reprimanded by his own classmates. I knew Han and knew that he could not dance, but only liked to hum dance tunes. I announced this to my group and argued that Han really did not violate the rule against dancing.

"We as students are not allowed to dance, but it is perfectly proper for adults. So there is nothing really bad about dancing, is there? When Han grows older, he will be allowed to dance. Besides, in this case, Han didn't even dance. He merely hums the tunes, and what can be serious about that?"

I had hardly finished when all hands went up and each person in turn reprimanded me. After that experience, I knew better than to speak my convictions. I realized that while it was not smart to keep quiet and thus arouse suspicions, I was expected to express only opinions that echoed the ones suggested by the group leader. Sometimes it was very hard to find a new way of saying the same thing, and I often spoke up early in the discussion so that no one else could steal my ideas. Later, I discovered an even better method: I would volunteer to take minutes of the meetings, knowing that the recorder was always the last one asked for an opinion. Usually time ran out before the group leader could call on me

[Bad things happened to students whose critical remarks were reported, as happened to a schoolmate, a boy of] about fourteen, who had an excellent chance of going on to high school and whose remarks were reported. He had been very discouraged with *lao dung* (mandatory labor) and he asked his classmates to explain to him the difference between their work on the farms and the drafted labor gangs of previous emperors. He claimed there was no difference; it

meant forced labor whether the government was a dynastic reign or Communist....

Nothing happened to him immediately. But a few months later, at graduation, he was assigned to work instead of further education.

[Ration coupons were needed for buying most items, but still one had to wait in long lines, sometimes not knowing the outcome.] Because of this tight ration system, every day except Sunday began for me at three in the morning. When my alarm rang.... I would stumble out of bed and grope in the dark for my shoes and jacket and the food basket. I tried to leave them within easy reach the night before because I didn't want to turn on the overhead bulb and really be awakened. Then I sought my way down the dark stairs by leaning my shoulder against the wall. The outside air was brisk, but I was still more or less sleepwalking as I made my way down the block to fin d the queue of empty baskets. I then left my basket in line, anchored down by a huge rock to discourage anyone from stealing it.... With the skies still dark, I returned to bed for another two and half hours.

At about six, the huge iron cart with our daily vegetable ration normally appeared on our block. Sometimes I would time it just right and run to help the man pull his load in return for first turn at the market. But usually I waited in line behind my neighbors. It was not a pleasant group of people--everyone still grouchy from sleep, anxious to get their share and hurry home for breakfast and work. Also as the food supply grew smaller and smaller, and as our diet consisted inevitably of dried beans or sweet potatoes, we all suffered from stomach growls and other involuntary body sounds....

We all spent many hours a day just waiting in queues. Whenever we spotted a line of people in the street, we would automatically get on it. No matter what was being sold, we could use it. Only once did I learn of an exception to this rule. My neighbor down the block got on the tail of a very long queue one day and waited almost three hours before reaching her turn. The salesman then asked, "What measurements?"

Bewildered, she replied, "What measurements do you need?"

"Comrade, don't you even know what you have been waiting to buy?"

"No, but it doesn't matter. Whatever it is, I am sure I need it."

The man smiled. "OK, OK, but I will still have to have somebody's measurements for the coffin."

Liang, Heng, and Judith Shapiro. *Son of Revolution*. New York: Knopf, 1983.   Pp. 6-7, 9, 15-18, 192-193. Sansan. *Eighth Moon: The True Story of a Young Girl's Life in Communist China* [as told to Bette Lord].   New York: Harper and Row, 1964. Pp. 47-49, 75-77.

AT THE BRINK OF NUCLEAR WAR: THE CUBAN MISSILE CRISIS

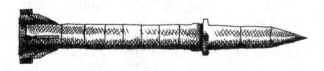

▶ **Surface-to-Surface Missile**

In 1959, revolutionary forces led by Fidel Castro succeeded in expelling Fulgencio Batista from power in Cuba. Castro then instituted political and social changes based on Marxist principles. His intent was to make Cuba a model communist state in the western hemisphere.

Because of the Cold War, the presence of a communist state close to its shores embarrassed the United States. Therefore, it sought to overthrow the Castro regime. In 1961, President John Kennedy authorized an invasion that was badly managed and ended in failure. Nikita Khrushchev and the Soviet Union interpreted the Bay of Pigs fiasco as a sign of weakness in President Kennedy's leadership, and decided to increase Soviet military strength in Cuba; the Castro regime, fearing U.S. intentions, welcomed the Soviet presence.

The Soviet Union began to build bases for medium-range ballistic missiles in Cuba, both to defend Castro and to pose a threat to the United States in retaliation for the placement of U.S. missile bases in Europe and Turkey near the Soviet Union.

In October 1962, U.S. spy planes took photographs of Soviet missile sites under construction in Cuba. The Kennedy administration acted promptly to demand the removal of Soviet missiles and bombers from Cuba, threatening military intervention if the Soviets failed to comply. A naval "quarantine" or blockade was imposed on Cuba and Strategic Air Command bombers were placed on alert. For almost a week, the world stood at the brink of war between the two superpowers. Fearing U.S. military superiority, Khrushchev "blinked" and ordered Soviet ships carrying missiles to turn back from Cuba. He also agreed to remove all missiles and bombers already in Cuba. In return, the United States gave assurances that it would not invade Cuba and agreed to remove missiles from Turkey.

At the time of the missile crisis, Raymond L. Garthoff was an adviser in the U.S. State Department, specializing in intelligence analysis, Soviet affairs, and political/military affairs. In the memoranda he wrote during the crisis, Garthoff assessed the possible results of various courses of action. His appraisals show the intense concern with carefully calculated power shifts that influenced policy decisions during the cold war era. Portions of these memoranda follow.

QUESTIONS:

1) How does the first memorandum assess the strengths and weaknesses of the Soviet position vis-à-vis the United States.

2) Does the Soviet Union seem to have used Cuba as a pawn to counteract U.S. influence in, for example, Turkey?

3) According to the evaluation in the third memorandum, who seems to have been the "winner" in terms of the short-run effects of the missile crisis? Who in terms of the long-run effects?

TOP SECRET [Declassified November 20, 1981]
MEMORANDUM   October 23, 1962
....
FROM: G/PM--Raymond L. Garthoff
SUBJECT: Reflections on the Confrontation over Cuba

The Soviets have doubtless had a number of motives in establishing missile bases in Cuba. They have probably been tempted by the first opportunity to establish a counterpart to American bases encircling the Soviet Union. There can be little doubt that they have recognized that such an action is provocative to Washington, though they may have underestimated the compulsion to react vigorously.

The Soviet leaders probably calculate that the new period of tension (which, incidentally, they had sought in advance to moderate by their relatively quiescent stand of late on Berlin, Laos, and the like) can be exploited to their advantage. While there are several ways in which the United States could have reacted, and may still react, each would offer certain opportunities for Soviet maneuver.

From a period of exuberant confidence following the first Soviet *sputnik* and first ICBM [intercontinental ballistic missile] test in late 1957, the Soviets have thrice marched up the hill on Berlin and down again. From a period of publicly anticipated and acknowledged Soviet superiority in over-all military power in 1960, the military balance has by late 1961 and since swung more and more against them, and above all this is publicly accepted. It may appear in Moscow that missile bases in Cuba represent both the first, and probably the last, opportunity to place a lever under the US positions of strength on the Eurasian periphery.

At the extreme, the United States might militarily neutralize Cuba, at a cost to the American posture of peace, but also at the price of impairing the image of the USSR as a global power. Since the United States has chosen to act in the first instance resolutely, but not drastically, both sides will have the opportunity of assessing world reactions to the limited measures undertaken.

The chief Soviet "strategic" assets are: an intercontinental capability which works to restrain the United States from sharp escalation; a powerful nuclear missile force poised against Western Europe; a quantitative advantage in conventional strength in Europe, and especially on the access routes to Berlin; a highly vulnerable situation in Laos; and now, the missile bases in Cuba. "Tactically" the Soviets have the advantages of: ability to match a selective blockade of Cuba by a comparable selective "filter" on Allied weapons allowed to go to Berlin; doubtless some sympathy for the view that "defensive" long-range missiles in Cuba are not essentially different from "defensive" long-range missiles in Turkey; the ability to trade off their Cuban bases for some inroads into the US overseas base system; and the "opportunity" to make the United States fire the first shot if they wish to precipitate an incident in the blockade.

The chief weaknesses in the Soviet position are: a basic military inferiority in the event of general war, compounded by Western alert and possible Western preemption in some cases; ineffective sea power either to challenge the American naval blockade, or to institute strictly reciprocal measures; and the inability to interpose their own power between that of the United States and Cuba at any acceptable risk.

These remarks are an incomplete draft of thoughts stemming from your request of this morning; being now fully engaged on more immediate aspects of the problem I am passing this on now without waiting for the chance to complete it, though I may return to it later.

SECRET [Declassified November 20, 1981]
MEMORANDUM   October 27, 1962
SUBJECT: The Khrushchev Proposal for a Turkey-Cuba Tradeoff

Khrushchev now recognizes that his position is weak. The whole Soviet ploy with Cuban missile sites was probably based on a three-level course of action.

First, the Soviets hoped for, and probably expected, US acquiescence in the buildup of a Soviet missile complex in Cuba which would substantially augment Soviet strength in negotiations over Berlin, and in general. The appreciable military gain, while not seriously affecting the strategic military balance, could have been converted into a high card at the negotiation table.

Second, as a firstline fallback position, the Soviets could react to a US blockade or similar pressure short of direct military invasion or attack on the bases by proposing a trade of Turkish, Italian, and UK IRBMs [intermediate range ballistic missiles] for those in Cuba. It is the lower end of this range of action to which the Soviets have now fallen back.

Third, at worst, the Soviets would react to US military action against the bases by whatever forms of political protest were warranted by world reactions--even up to breaking diplomatic relations. The Khrushchev message of October 27 strengthens the conclusion that the USSR would not resort to direct military confrontation or reprisal--on the seas, in Cuba, or in Turkey. To date, the world reactions have not been what Moscow had hoped for; in particular, the unanimous OAS [Organization of American States] action must have been a severe disappointment.

The third course is still the remaining Soviet recourse if we reject their offer at the second level. The Soviet statement clearly evades any commitment to military action if the US should decline its offer and eliminate the missile site by unilateral military action. It states that the missiles in Cuba are in Soviet hands and would be used only if there were (a) an invasion of Cuba, or (b) an attack on the Soviet Union or any of her allies. It can scarcely be an oversight that the contingency of a strike to neutralize the missiles is not included in this commitment. The Soviets can probably still be compelled to withdraw the missile bases if they see the only alternative will be our destruction of them. However, even that outcome would almost certainly not provoke even limited Soviet military escalation.

The Turks have already made abundantly clear that they do not want to be compared with the Cubans, used as a pawn, or shorn of the Jupiters [missiles] which have always been to them a proud symbol of their ability to strike back if they are hit. Hasty surfacing of long-held US military evaluations of the obsolescence of the Jupiters would be ineffective in meeting these strongly held views. The Jupiters are not important as a military-strategic asset--but, then, neither is Berlin. Yet both have elemental significance as symbols of the integrity of the Alliance and especially of our commitment to stand by the interests of each of its members.

The United States can, while solving the Cuban base question with determination, forcefully reaffirm its readiness to reach agreements on arms control and disarmament. We could thus indicate our pursuit of peace at the same time that we disposed of the latest Soviet disruption of the peace.

The United States has a unique opportunity to deal a major setback to the Soviet leaders, and once and for all to disabuse them--and others--of any illusion that the alternative to any Soviet gamble for high stakes will not be fallback advantages, but a defeat. Precisely such an outcome is the way to discourage such ventures in the future.

SECRET [Declassified June 10, 1977]
MEMORANDUM   October 29, 1962
SUBJECT: Significance of the Soviet Backdown for Future US Policy
1. *Short-Run Effects*
    Political--The short-run effects should be very favorable to the US. Unquestionably the US will emerge from this confrontation with increased prestige world-wide. The Soviet action should demonstrate once again the offensive nature of Soviet motivations more clearly than anything we could say. It should also demonstrate that the Soviets are not prepared to risk a decisive military showdown with the US over issues involving the extension of Soviet power. (We should be clear however that this is not to be confused with Soviet lack of willingness to "go to the mat" over an interest vital to Soviet security.) More specifically, short-run political effects should include the following:
    a. Soviet ability to penetrate Latin America should suffer a reversal, though a base for future penetration may remain in Cuba for some time. Soviet intentions have been unmasked, and Soviet

inability to force its will clearly demonstrated. Our problems in assisting Latin America to achieve a higher state of political and economic development will still require all of our best efforts. However, our efforts should be focused on the fundamental nature of the problem, and it is important that we continue to pursue our Latin American country internal programs, along with our broader development programs.

b. NATO should be strengthened. The firmness of the US stand, and perhaps even more importantly the categorical refusal to barter NATO assets for immediate US security interests, should provide assurance of US commitment to the Alliance.

c. Our position on Berlin should be greatly strengthened. Our resolute willingness to act in Cuba should result in a complete reassessment by the Soviets as to how far they can safely push US will in general, including Berlin. Similarly it should provide our Allies with fortitude for meeting Soviet threats.

d. The effect upon the neutrals is more difficult to estimate, but in general is favorable. It must raise in the minds of many of the neutrals who may have a pro-Communist leaning questions as to how far they may safely "get in bed" with the Soviets and still protect their own national interests.

e. While there is probably very little immediate effect on Soviet-Satellite relations, it cannot help but plant the seed of doubt as to Soviet omnipotence. This could have important implications for the future.

f. The effect on the USSR can be beneficial, but this will depend on how we further use our present strong position. It is conceivable that within the Soviet leadership the events of the past several days may be considered so serious a setback that changes may occur in the current Soviet leadership.

Military--The military benefits secured as a result of the Soviet backdown are similarly immense. Agreement not to proceed with additional missiles, and to dismantle existing missiles and launch facilities, cancels out the temporary increase in capability vis-à-vis the continental United States, which the Soviets achieved in their shortlived attempt to offset the current US nuclear strategic advantage.

2. *Long-Run Effects*

Political--An analysis of long-run effects is of course more uncertain. Unquestionably the Soviet defeat will have its impact on Soviet thinking and policymaking. Over the long run, one effect may be to make the Soviets far more responsive to our efforts at finding peaceful solutions to the whole range of world problems. However, and this is an important qualification, this effect is certain to take a considerable period of time. We should not delude ourselves into believing that great and rapid changes will result in Soviet policy. People and governments simply do not and cannot change that quickly, even assuming the stimulus for doing so. Thus while it is useful to explore all avenues of solutions to world problems, such as disarmament, we must not expect quick or easy solutions. We would expect that the US will meet with the usual Soviet criticism, resistance, and negotiatory pressure. In short, we must not slip into euphoria over the successful course of events, assuming it continues to develop favorably.

Military--Viewed in its long-run perspective, the Soviet backdown does not affect the Soviet military position in any important essential other than, of course, the important removal of the missiles from Cuba and awareness in Moscow of US refusal to permit *any* such venture. It is possible that the effect of these events might be to set in motion a redoubled Soviet effort to close the gap to development by the Soviets of a secure second strike capability.

3. *General Conclusion*

Our over-all preliminary conclusion may be summarized as follows:

a. We have in the recent situation gained broad political and military assets, on which we should attempt to capitalize. We have probably gained important, but less definitive, long-range benefits.

b. In these circumstances, it is vitally important that the US take the initiative in offering to negotiate on major issues between East and West. Without being bellicose in the basis of our new-found strength, nor on the other hand making concessions which would adversely affect our position of strength, we should press for fair but safeguarded solutions to outstanding problems.

If we have learned anything from this experience, it is that weakness, even only apparent weakness, invites Soviet transgression. At the same time, firmness in the last analysis will force the Soviets to back away from rash initiatives. We cannot now, nor can we in the future, accept Soviet protestations of "peaceful" coexistence at face value. The words may sound the same, but the meaning is different. Their willingness to cooperate in common endeavors can only be judged by performance.

The difficult task for US policy in the future is to strike the correct fine balance between seeking cooperation from a forthcoming posture, while retaining the necessary strength and skepticism to insure ourselves and our friends against future duplicity.

Garthoff, Raymond L. *Reflections on the Cuban Missile Crisis*. Rev. ed. Washington: Brookings Institution, 1989. Pp. 195-196, 200-201, 214-216.

CHÉ GUEVARA-- REVOLUTIONARY AND MARXIST MARTYR

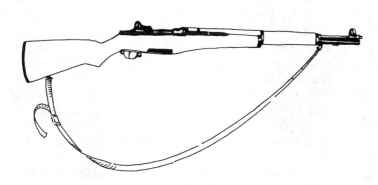

Ernesto Guevara (1928-1967), better known as Ché Guevara, was born in Argentina. After studying medicine for a time, he devoted his life to Marxist revolution to right social injustices in Latin America. In 1954, he joined Cuban exiles led by Fidel Castro and participated in the guerrilla campaign to overthrow the Cuban dictator Fulgencio Batista. He then served in Castro's Marxist, Soviet-supported government as minister of industry from 1961 to 1965.

With the encouragement of Castro and the Soviets, Guevara left Cuba for Bolivia in 1966 to instigate a revolutionary movement among the oppressed peasants. Guevara and his Marxist sponsors meant to thwart U.S. influence in Latin America. His guerrilla insurgency in Bolivia ended in failure, as his dream of an upsurge of peasant support for his cause never materialized. He was killed by the Bolivian army in 1967. However, his name came to symbolize Marxist martyrdom for revolutionaries and leftist radicals around the world.

The following are excerpts from Ché Guevara's diaries during the final months before his death in October 1967.

QUESTIONS:

1) Do the entries in Ché Guevara's diary paint a "romantic" picture of "freedom fighting" in the Marxist cause?

2) How does Guevara portray his own role in the guerrilla activity he recounts?

3) What are the limitations that Guevara is trying to cope with in his guerrilla operations?

July 27 [1967]

We had everything ready to leave and the people in ambush had received instructions to carry it out promptly at 11, when a few minutes before that time Willy arrived saying that the Army was there, Willy, Ricardo, Inti, Chino, Leon and Eustaquio went there, and together with Antonio, Arturo and Chaparo, took action, which developed as follows: 8 soldiers appeared on the hill, walked toward the south following a blind road and returning lifting some mortars, making signals with a rag. At one point we heard one Melgar being called. He could be the one from Florida. After resting for a while the 8 soldiers began walking toward the ambush. Only four fell in it because the others were proceeding apart. Three were surely killed and the fourth one if not killed was at least wounded. We withdrew without taking their weapons and equipment because it became difficult to take them, and we left down stream. Where the stream met another little canyon, we laid a new ambush; the horses went as far as the road.

My asthma hit me hard and the supply of sedatives is getting low.

Altitude 800 meters

July 28

I sent Coco with Pombo, Raul and Aniceto to cover the mouth of the river which we believe is the Suspiro. We walked a little, opening the path through a rather narrow canyon. We camped apart from the vanguard because Miguel had gone too fast for the horses whose legs sank in the sand or were hurt by rocks.

July 29

We kept on walking through a canyon which goes down toward the south with good shelter along the sides in an area with plenty of water. At approximately 16 hours we met Pablito who told us that we were at the mouth of the Suspiro; for a moment I thought that canyon could not be the Suspiro because of its southernly direction, but on the last bend it turned westward and led to the Rosita. The rearguard arrived at approximately 16:30 and I decided to continue the journey to get away from the mouth of the Suspiro River. At night I let Chino have the floor so that he could talk about the independence of his country (28 July) and after that I explained why the camp was poorly located, giving instructions to rise at 5 and leave to follow Paulino's clearing.

Radio Havana reported an ambush in which the army suffered some casualties which were rescued by helicopter, but radio reception was not good.

July 30

My asthma kept me awake all night. At 4:30 as Moro was making coffee he reported seeing a lantern across the river. Miguel, who was awake because he had just changed guards, and Loro went to detain the wanderers. From the kitchen I heard:

"Who goes there?"

Trinidad Detachment. Right then the shooting began. Miguel was bringing an M-1 and a cartridge-belt from one of the wounded and the news that there were 21 men on the way to

Abapo and 150 in Moroco. We caused them more casualties but were unable to determine these because of the confusion that ensued. It took long to load the horses and Negro was lost with the hatchet and a mortar that had been captured from the enemy. It was almost 6 o'clock and more time was lost because some bundles fell. The result was that in the last crossings we were under fire by the soldiers who had become very bold. Paulino's sister was in the clearing. Quite calmly she told us that all the men in Moroco had been arrested and were in La Paz.

I hurried the men and went with Pombo, again under fire, to the river canyon where the road ends and where the resistance could be organized. I sent Miguel to take the lead with Coco and Julio while I led the men on horseback. Covering the retreat, there remained 7 men of the vanguard, 4 of the rearguard and Ricardo, who fell back to reinforce the defense.... The developments were as follows: Ricardo and Aniceto foolishly crossed an open space, the former got hit, Antonio organized a line of fire and between Arturo, Raúl, Aniceto, and Pacho rescued them, but Pacho was wounded and Raúl was killed by a bullet through his mouth. The withdrawal was very difficult. The two wounded men had to be dragged and there was little collaboration from Willy and Chapero, especially the latter. Later they were joined by Urbano and his group with the horses and by Benigno with his men, leaving the other wing unprotected, for which reason Miguel was overtaken. After an arduous march through the woods they came out on the river and joined us. Pacho came on horseback but Ricardo was unable to ride and he had to be carried in a hammock. I sent Miguel with Pablito, Dario, Coco and Aniceto to follow the outlet of the first brook on the right side, while we treated the wounded. Pacho has a superficial wound through his buttocks and the skin of his testicles, but Ricardo was gravely wounded and the last plasma has been lost in Willy's knapsack. At 22:00 Ricardo died and we buried him near the river in a hidden spot, so that the police will not find him.

July 31

At 4, we left by way of the river and after crossing a shortcut, we went downstream without leaving tracks, arriving in the morning at the brook where Miguel, who had not understood instructions, lay in ambush and had left tracks. We walked some 4 kilometers upstream and went into the forest, erasing our tracks and camping near a tributary of the brook. At night I explained the mistakes of the action: 1) poor location of the camp; 2) poor timing which permitted them to shoot at us; 3) overconfidence which resulted in the loss of Ricardo and later Raúl in rescuing him; 4) lack of determination to salvage all the impedimenta. We lost 11 knapsacks containing medicines, binoculars and equipment such as the tape recorder used for copying the messages from Manila, Debray's book with my notations, a book by Trotsky, not to mention the political significance that the capture of these items has for the government and the confidence it gives the soldiers. We calculate their casualties were approximately 2 killed and 5 wounded, but there are two contradictory reports: one from the Army reporting 4 dead and 4 wounded on the 28th. Another report from Chile mentions 6 wounded and 3 killed on the 30th. The Army later put out another report saying they had picked up their dead and that a sub-lieutenant was out of danger. Of our dead, Raúl hardly needs to be counted. He was an introvert, not much of a fighter or worker; however, he was continually interested in the political problems though he did not ask questions. Ricardo was the most undisciplined one of the Cuban group and the one that had the least determination in facing daily sacrifices, but was an extraordinary fighter and an old comrade in adventure during Segundo's first failure in the Congo and now here. With this loss there are only 22 of us left including two wounded men, Pacho, Pombo, and I with my asthma going at full speed.

Analysis of the Month

The negative aspects of last month prevail, including the failure to make contact with Joaquín and the outside, and the loss of men; we are now 22 men, three of whom are disabled, including myself. Thus our mobility has decreased. We have had three clashes including the capture of Samaipata inflicting Army casualties of 7 killed and 10 wounded, approximate figures in accordance with confirmed reports. Our losses were 2 men killed and one wounded. The most important features are:

1) We are still completely out of contact.

2) The peasantry still is not joining us, although there were some encouraging signs from some peasants we know.

3) The legend of the guerrillas is acquiring continental dimensions; [General Juan Carlos] Ongañía [President-dictator of Argentina] closes the border [of Argentina]; Peru is taking precautions,

4) The attempt to make contact through Paulino failed.

5) The morale and fighting spirit of the guerrilla increases after each clash; Camba and Chapaco are still lazy.

6) The Army is still ineffective but some units appear to be more combative.

7) The political crisis in the government is getting worse but U.S.A. is giving small loans which on the Bolivian level are a great help and temper discontent.

The most urgent tasks are: To establish contacts, increase the capabilities of the combatants, obtain medicines.

James, Daniel, ed. *The Complete Bolivian Diaries of Ché Guevara*. New York: Stein and Day, 1968. Pp. 187-191.

THE FALL OF COMMUNISM

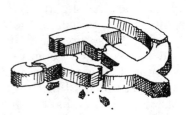

The most important event of 1991 was undoubtedly the fall of communism and the disintegration of the Soviet Union, the land of its inception. Boris Yeltsin, the first elected president of the Russian Republic, said at a town meeting hosted by Peter Jennings of ABC News that although Marxism embodied worthy ideals, its implementation in Russia had been a great disaster, causing untold miseries.

The collapse of communism in the Soviet Union began when Mikhail Gorbachev became First Secretary of the Communist Party of the U.S.S.R. in 1985. In retrospect, the Leonid Brezhnev era, 1964-1982, was one of stagnation and decline, of repression of domestic dissent, and of a continued arms race with the United States. Brezhnev could barely function after suffering a stroke in 1976, and he was succeeded by two sick old men who died in rapid succession. Thus the world was much relieved that Gorbachev walked unassisted and spoke coherently.

Gorbachev understood that internal rot of the communist system had rendered the Soviet Union a hollow shell, and that its inefficient planned economy was on the verge of collapse. To save the Soviet Union, Gorbachev inaugurated *glasnost*, or the "opening" of Soviet society to the outside world and freedom of speech for its citizens; and *perestroika*, or the "restructuring" of the economy. These changes further discredited communism.

Like Gorbachev, Boris Yeltsin had peasant roots; both rose to power through the communist system until each ruled a province. Unlike their predecessors, both were well educated. Gorbachev brought Yeltsin to head the Communist Party in Moscow. But Yeltsin demanded faster, systemic change. The two men broke ranks, and while Gorbachev vacillated, Yeltsin quit the Communist Party and joined the democratic forces. When Gorbachev's cronies attempted to reverse the course of reform in the August 1991 coup, Yeltsin led and won the fight to save democracy. The Soviet Union collapsed in December 1991.

In *Boris Yeltsin, A Political Biography*, co-authors Vladimir Solovyov and Elena Klepikova, émigrés from the Soviet Union, recount the suffering, corruption, and iniquities that made the Soviet system a mockery, and the dynamic Yeltsin's guidance of Russia toward democracy. The following selection contrasts Yeltsin with his former mentor and nemesis Mikhail Gorbachev.

QUESTIONS:

1) What was life like for the Yeltsin family when he was a boy and who determined their lives?
2) How did Yeltsin govern his province?
3) Describe the privileged life a top Soviet official enjoyed.

Born in 1931 in a Russian village is not a sign of good fortune. That year saw the peak of forced collectivization of peasant households and the apogee of mass terror against those who resisted the New Agricultural Policy. Since the better off peasants resisted the enslavement the most, it was decided to annihilate them as a social class.

Almost all of Yeltsin's ancestors ... lived and died in the village of Butka.... The year of his birth coincided with catastrophe for his entire numerous family. All nine of them--three generations--lived in the same hut, sleeping on the floor; their relative security--they were hardly well off--came from backbreaking labor. Still, the head of the family, Boris Yeltsin's grandfather, the village blacksmith and church elder, was classified as a *kulak* (as the new rulers pejoratively called well-off peasants); his house, his mill, and his possessions of any value were confiscated. The family patriarch, by then almost seventy, and his wife, along with a dozen other *kulak* families, were exiled north to remote taiga forests. The old couple lived in an unheated barrack in a place where thirty below Centigrade was a normal winter temperature. Four months later Yeltsin's grandfather died.

Those remaining in the village after the punitive campaign were forced to join the kolkhoz [collective farm]. The new kolkhoz members' horses were taken away, and died that winter in the collectivized stable. Then the harvest, reaped with so much toil, was confiscated by the State, down to the last grain, the Yeltsins ... along with their fellow villagers, faced death by starvation. But the kolkhoz chairman took a chance--the Party would not have spared him had they known--and allowed the villagers to leave for the town for the winter, to earn a living....

In Berezniki, Yeltsin senior found a job as a construction worker. The entire family settled in a barrack--a drafty, long wooden barn. On one side was a communal corridor; on the other, up to twenty tiny rooms, with one--sometimes large--family per room. The barrack was a child of early five-year plans; a temporary shelter, hastily hammered together near a huge industrial project under construction....

Again, Soviet fate struck the Yeltsins; this time it was a direct hit. In 1937 Yeltsin's father, Nikolai Ignatyevich, was arrested and spent several months in jail. After his release he was unemployed for a long time.... Yeltsin's mother worked as a seamstress. Boris's only memory of domestic cheer was the nightly buzzing of her sewing machine in the corner of their tiny room. The family tried to survive and had no plans beyond that.... Yeltsin's eighty-four-year-old mother remembers Boris as a mother's little helper: he took care of his little brother and later his baby sister, cooked dinner, fetched water from the well, washed dishes, and hoed the vegetable patch. During the war he stood long nights in lines for a loaf of bread.... Every summer mother and son went to do seasonal work out of town. They mowed grass and dried and sold hay to buy bread in town....

The barrack would dominate Yeltsin's life for another ten years, till he left for Sverdlovsk to enter college. It would surface thirty-odd years later, when, as the Party Boss, he would attempt to eliminate barracks, to erase them from his memory, by moving all of the Sverdlovsk barrack-dwellers to new apartments in just one year. Barracks are a motif in his life worth emphasizing, for they hold some clues to the Yeltsin phenomenon, his so-called populism, and his unprecedented popularity....

From the Party standpoint ... despite a superficial resemblance ... [Yeltsin and Gorbachev] were complete opposites. Gorbachev was of course a Party prodigy--few people joined so early, at twenty-one, and while still in college. Yeltsin, on the other hand, was joining too late; at thirty, from a career standpoint he was overripe.

The Parties that Gorbachev and Yeltsin joined were identical in name only. The Party Gorbachev joined in 1952 was Stalinist; while the Party Yeltsin joined in 1961, the heyday of reform and liberalization was a Khrushchev one. By then both men were formed professionally: Gorbachev an *apparatchik* [member of the party hierarchy], Yeltsin an industrial manager--a Partocrat and a technocrat. Finally a long-waited point of convergence: both Gorbachev and Yeltsin were made Party Bosses of their respective native regions. Gorbachev made the grade six years earlier: he became the Party Secretary of the Stavropol Territory in 1970, at thirty-nine, while the forty-five-year-old Yeltsin took a similar job in Sverdlovsk only in 1976....

For the nine years he spent as the First Secretary of the Sverdlovsk Region, he remained a manager, master of a huge estate, an area of 80,000 square miles. His inspection trips across his domain demonstrate his managerial fervor. Every year he visited the towns and larger villages of the region--all sixty-three of them. Those were no junkets; they were working trips, tests of endurance. Yeltsin met with experts and made spot decisions. Staying on top of problems, examining them in detail, was the only way he could confidently rule his domain....

Even when he visited Moscow to see the Central Committee or Brezhnev personally, Yeltsin went with an economic agenda; he avoided court intrigues and claimed no Kremlin patron. Perhaps he did a bit of scheming, but it was for the cause, for Sverdlovsk--never for himself. Once, he managed to outmaneuver Brezhnev, by now senile, and cajole him into signing, without looking at, the authorization to build a subway in Sverdlovsk.

While still in Sverdlovsk, Yeltsin closed down the special stores and canceled all special rations. He let the special hospital alone for a while, but its doors were now opened to retirees and old Party members....

While his method of running the Party machinery was far from democratic, Yeltsin insisted on democratic forms of communication with various groups of the population. This dialogue was his personal innovation....

Andrei Goryun [a Sverdlovsk citizen], first met Boris Yeltsin in November, 1981 at the meeting of social scientists, organized by the regional Party Committee. Such meetings were routine, and Goryun had expected to hear the standard ideological dogmas, Party formulas, and bureaucratic Newspeak. What actually happened left the audience wide-eyed.

"A tall, snowy-haired man stepped up to the podium," Goryun recalls, "dressed in a well-cut suit that showed off his athletic build. He began to speak. With the very first phrases, people held their breath. Many grabbed their note pads, trying to write down every word. What was he saying.... This meeting was the first time I learned the truth about this country. Perhaps not the entire truth, perhaps a minuscule part of it-- but it was a revelation to me."

In Sverdlovsk, Yeltsin is remembered not merely as a "good Tsar" who took care of his people. As far back as the early '80s, the masses throughout the entire region, i.e., throughout his Party domain, perceived him as a charismatic leader. His popularity was immense....

It is worth recalling that through the six years of so-called glasnost, not once did Gorbachev risk running as a candidate anywhere in the Soviet Union--not even in his native Stavropol, where he had left behind mixed memories. Unlike Yeltsin, who, as First Secretary of the Sverdlovsk Region, took his job as a creative challenge, constantly searching for new forms of management within a dying system the First Secretary of the Stavropol Region ruled his domain in a passive, undistinguished manner.... In Khrushchev's day Gorbachev would have been kicked out for poor economic performance, lack of initiative, and bureaucratic complacency. But by then Brezhnev had given up on reform and on agriculture; he decided it was more profitable and less troublesome to spend hundreds of millions of dollars on importing grain rather than invest this money at home.

[In 1985, Gorbachev called Yeltsin to Moscow and appointed him Moscow's First Party Secretary. He set out to reform the city's problems.] Boris Yeltsin's name was quickly on everyone's lips. Stories circulated of his incognito voyages by bus and subway, of his sudden appearances in stores and cafeterias, of his standing in a long line for pastries that ran out just as his turn came. He mentions some of these stories in his memoirs:

At a store, Yeltsin discovers bags with delicacies in the manager's office. "Who are these for?"

"These are pre-ordered."

"Can anyone pre-order?"

Silence.

He finds out that "pre-orders" are distributed hierarchically: District Soviet, Foreign Ministry, Party District Committee, other city authorities. The bags vary in size, in assortment, and in quality. Just what Marx predicted: from each according to his ability, to each according to his need. And as one moves up the career ladder, the needs rise accordingly....

According to Yeltsin, the [top party leaders] had already built themselves a shining Communist future: its benefits were spread out among two dozen or so people: Politburo members and Central Committee Secretaries. This mini-Communist society was run by the KGB's Section Nine, which specialized in perks: food packages with exotic items at half-price, junkets across the country in personal planes, imported drugs, and the inanely luxurious dachas. After Gorbachev had one built especially for himself, he passed his old one on to Yeltsin. As Russians say, a fur coat off the master's back.

On his visit to his new dacha, Yeltsin recalls, he was greeted by the senior guard, who introduced the help: three chefs, three waitresses, chambermaids, more guards, and a gardener with his own staff. Then a tour of the house.

On the first floor: a huge marble lobby, beautiful rugs, a fireplace, and elegant furniture. A number of rooms, each with a color TV. A giant glassed-in terrace. A full-sized dining hall with a table long enough to feed a soccer team. In the back, a restaurant-sized kitchen with an underground freezer. A screening room and a pool room. Bathrooms? Yeltsin, used to an ascetic lifestyle, lost count.

He was led up a wide marble staircase to the second floor. Another hall, another fireplace, and a door leading to the greenhouse. Further, a study, bedrooms, cut glass chandelier antique and modern, precious rugs, oak parquet floors, more bathrooms. It looked more like a hotel for nobility than a house for one family. The Yeltsins, unused to such luxury, did not know what to do with themselves; they felt out of place. Eventually they refused the dacha.

Besides the dachas near the capital, there were ones in the Crimea, in the Caucasus--all over the country, all of them plush. In one, the owners and guests were driven by car to the beach--the whole two hundred yards, noted Yeltsin.

None of this was personal property; it all came with the job; when an unfortunate person lost his Kremlin position, he lost all his privileges and was reduced to the status of an ordinary mortal. Imagine how hard one must strive to get to the top, and how one must fight to stay there.

Here, too, Yeltsin was an exception: he did not value the privileges bestowed upon him, and this freed him from depending on them. On the contrary, he perceived them as chains he had to shake off as soon as possible; they galled him not just for reasons of style or personal taste, but for what they stood for. He was the only Soviet ruler who had ever made it to the top of the mountain, then hurried down back to the valley-- of his own free will....

According to Yeltsin, he did not adopt egalitarianism out of belief in some sort of ideal, primitive form of equality or in search of cheap popularity, but: "As long as our lives are so poor and miserable, I cannot eat sturgeon and caviar; I cannot speed away in a limo, ignoring traffic lights and people leaping out of my way; I cannot take imported miracle drugs, knowing that my next-door neighbor has no aspirin for her child. I would simply be ashamed to do that."

It was this feeling of shame that distinguished Yeltsin from his Kremlin colleagues. As he exposed the Kremlin's dolce vita existence, he did not exaggerate anything-- more likely, through his lack of information, he seriously underestimated its extent....

Special dachas, sanatoriums, hotels, schools, restaurants, the Sunny Kindergarten, famous all over Moscow--even its own furniture factory that provided furnishings for the apartments of the elite--we could go on and on. No wonder Yeltsin's crusade against privilege was so popular.

As his popularity soared, so did the Kremlin's displeasure....

Solovyov, Vladimir, and Elena Klepikova. *Boris Yeltsin: A Political Biography*. Trans. David Gurevich. New York: Putnam, 1992. Pp. 41-44, 117-119, 140-141, 153-154.

THE COLLAPSING MARXIST ORDER

World War I brought the communists to power in Russia, World War II resulted in the spread of communism to China and Eastern Europe, and decolonization spread it to some of the newly independent states in Asia and Africa. Despite these spectacular victories, Marxism as an ideology, and communism as an economic and political system has become the "grand failure" of the twentieth century.

Zbigniew Brzezinski, Assistant to the President for National Security Affairs, and Director of the National Security Council to President Jimmy Carter between 1976 and 1980, is a political scientist with special expertise in Marxism and the Soviet Union. His *The Grand Failure, The Birth and Death of Communism in the Twentieth Century* caused a sensation when it was published in 1989 because at the time, Mikhail Gorbachev, General Secretary of the Communist Party of the Soviet Union, was engaged in a seemingly successful restructuring of that party to give it a new lease of life.

As he traced the history of the Marxist movement and the rise of the Soviet Union in the twentieth century, Brzezinski concluded that Marxist theory was deeply flawed; its application was warped, making failure inevitable. He predicted that the Soviet Union was doomed because the enormity of its internal crisis was beyond restructuring, and stated that communism was no longer a practical model for other nations to emulate. For Brzezinski communism was a mammoth tragedy because of its brutal rule for a third of the human race in the twentieth century. He forecasted its demise in the Soviet Union and Eastern Europe, and asserted that as a failed ideology in China its continued survival in name was due to the manipulations of the small clique in power. Several years later, most of his predictions had been realized.

The post World War II world order was built on competition between the United States-led democratic and capitalist Western bloc and the Soviet-led Marxist Eastern bloc. The collapse of the Soviet empire in Eastern Europe and the breakup of the Soviet Union in 1991 has caused world-wide instability. The repercussions from these changes will continue into the twenty-first century.

The following passage is from *The Grand Failure*.

QUESTIONS:

1) In what ways was Marxism an attractive ideology for the newly independent underdeveloped countries?

2) What differences developed between the ideology and the practice of Communism in the Soviet Union?

3) How and why did Communism fail in the developing world?

Fermenting in the Soviet Union, repudiated in Eastern Europe, and more and more commercialized in China, communism has become a globally discredited ideology. Marxist-Leninist "praxis"--the unity of theory and action-- no longer commands respect even among party members....

Around the world, people now equate Soviet-style communism with arrested development. This perception is dominant in both halves of Europe, in the Far East, in Southeast Asia, and in North America. It is also beginning to permeate the perspectives of the opinion leaders in Latin America and Africa. In the more developed parts of the world, including the so-called newly industrializing countries, few see in communism a relevant program for the future.... Even China's improving performance cannot compensate for this perception of communist failure because the more recent Chinese economic successes have been accomplished largely by very evident diversions from past communist "praxis."

The new global consensus represents an epochal change and carries devastating political consequences for world communism.... The notion that communism, once in power, means stagnation and waste is a dramatic reversal of the views preponderant as recently as a mere two decades ago. It involves a massive alteration in political attitudes regarding the critical question of the proper relationship of the individual to society and of society to the state. Ultimately, therefore, the shift in the global perception is one of fundamental philosophy and of basic outlook-- and not just of political style or allegiance. It is historic in nature....

In theory, communism should have been most successful in the developed world. According to classical Marxist doctrine, the socialist revolution should have taken place in developed countries as the historically inevitable consequence of the crisis of capitalism within industrialized society....

Not only was this diagnosis wrong, but by the late twentieth century an even more stark proposition stood out: the more advanced the society, the less politically relevant its communist party. This is the central surprise of communism's confrontation with history....

The twentieth century thus did not become the century of communism. Its grand oversimplification could not encompass all the complexities of the advanced society's social structure. This structure did not correspond to Marx's antiquated view of the centrality of the industrial proletariat. Nor could the doctrine provide any meaningful guide for social policies that had to assimilate the creative innovations of ultra-science and high-tech. Moreover, the perversion of Marxism by the contributions of Lenin and Stalin reduced the doctrine to a sterile justification for arbitrary and dictatorial power, thereby further inhibiting its capacity to adapt to changing circumstances. In the democratic West, where choices were made on the basis of open debate, communism could not withstand the exposure of its manifest irrelevance to modernity....

Though communism has been more successful in gaining political power in several underdeveloped countries, it has proven to be a systemic failure in all of them. Socioeconomic policies modeled on the Soviet Union have not produced the desired development and modernization. Over the last decade, such repeated failures have fostered a wider disillusionment in the Third World, not only with the Soviet example but with the communist doctrine itself.

Initially, it appeared that the post-World War II and anti-colonial wave might be dominated by the Marxist praxis, creating an irresistible dynamic in the Third World in the direction of Soviet-led communism.... The Soviet Union seemed to be on the historic march, expecting soon to leapfrog the United States in the economic competition....

During this phase of communism's historical optimism, the Soviet leaders also revised their traditional notion of the world divided into two hostile camps, the encircled socialist camp--led by the Soviet Union--and the aggressive imperialist camp--led by the United States.... Accepting decolonization as an important and new historical development, and claiming that the major impetus for it came from the Leninist doctrine and from the support provided by the Soviet Union, Khrushchev propounded the argument that the newly liberated countries ... could make a relatively rapid transition to socialism. The Soviet Union would aid the process by grants of military and economic assistance, by friendly ideological guidance based on the Soviet experience, and by deterring the imperialists from obstructing the inevitable progression toward full-blown socialism. The eventual result would be an encircled capitalist camp....

In different ways, the new governments of such major countries as India or Indonesia and of the new African states adopted some form of state socialism as the norm, though in every case insisting that they were blending it with their own specific national cultures....

Nevertheless, the new leaders did find the Soviet support helpful and were inclined to flirt with Soviet-propagated doctrines, especially for political reasons. They were particularly attracted by Leninist techniques for the seizure and maintenance of power, and the concept of a disciplined and hierarchical ruling party was especially appealing to the new generation of rulers interested in perpetuating their personal authority....

For a while, Africa and Latin America looked more promising for the adopting of Communist programs. In Africa, radical tendencies were naturally intensified by the inherent racism of the colonial experience, and in southern Africa by the reality of institutionalized racism in South Africa itself.... The appeal of Marxist grand oversimplification was inevitably stronger in countries which badly wanted to leapfrog into modernity but which lacked strong intellectual and cultural traditions for formulating their own historical visions....

In the 1970s, several African countries thus embraced Marxism as their doctrine and proclaimed themselves to be engaged in the task of building socialism.... Reality proved unkind, however, both to the native, and somewhat naive, socialist hopes and to Soviet expectations. The levels of Soviet economic aid were inadequate to influence decisively internal economic development. Local mismanagement, corruption, and the dislocations caused by the abrupt rupture of economic relations with the former colonial powers produced in most of these countries large-scale economic failures.... In brief, the Communist record in Africa involved limited political success, marred by demonstrable systemic failures....

More generally, by the 1980s the very notion of socialist development, an idea with which the Soviet Union could identify and thereby benefit politically, was increasingly discredited in much of the Third World. Asia led the way in economic development, but in a demonstrably nonsocialist fashion. Those countries that took the Communist path--Vietnam, Laos, and Cambodia--represented spectacular examples of socioeconomic failure....

The cumulative consequence of communism's loss of revolutionary élan, of its manifest irrelevance to the politics of the advanced world, and of its failure to capitalize on the socioeconomic dilemmas of the Third World, as well as of its difficulties in creating functioning and united communist systems in conditions as diverse as those of Eastern Europe, the Soviet Union, and China, has been a deep ideological crisis.... Marxist historical expectations and Leninist political tactics have proven to be either anachronistic or erroneous. The impoverishment of the working class under capitalism did not occur, the anti-colonial wave did not turn into a Marxist-Leninist revolution, while the attempt to maintain Soviet political and doctrinal leadership in the Communist movement produced isolation and rebellion. Last but not least, the failure of the Soviet model discredited the notion of any universally valid doctrinal guidelines for socialist construction....

A historical watershed had thus been crossed. Having failed as a united movement in both the developed and the developing worlds, the era of a monolithic Communist movement built around a shared dogma was now irrevocably a thing of the past. The mid-1980s witnessed not only the end of the unity of communist theory and practice but also the end among Communist parties of unified doctrine and of united action.

Brzezinski, Zbigniew. *The Grand Failure: The Birth and Death of Communism in the Twentieth Century*. New York: Scribner's, 1989. Pp. 189-190, 200-201, 210-214, 225, 228.

THE QUEST FOR HUMAN RIGHTS AND DEMOCRACY

Citizens of the United States, Canada, Western European countries, Japan, and India enjoy democratically elected governments and basic freedoms guaranteed under the law. Beginning in 1989, Eastern European countries and the republics of the Soviet Union have shaken off Communist governments that kept them in bondage through terror, and begun building democratic societies. The peoples of China, Vietnam, North Korea and Cuba continued to live under monolithic Communist regimes. Many Asian, Middle Eastern, Latin American, and African countries are ruled by authoritarian regimes that deny citizens rights and liberties. Burma's government is among the most violently oppressive of these.

Burma gained independence from Great Britain in 1947. In 1962, a coup by general Ne Win overthrew the unstable civilian government and installed a military regime. The Burmese economy has plummeted under the corrupt military's mismanagement, and all peaceful protests have been bloodily suppressed.

Aung San Suu Kyi (b. 1945) is the daughter of one of the heroes of Burma's struggle for independence. She lived in exile in Britain because of her opposition to the military regime, but received permission to return to Burma in 1988 to tend to her gravely ill mother. Soon after her return, General Ne Win resigned from office. When the officers who succeeded him rejected to popular demands for a referendum to decide Burma's future, Suu Kyi took up the cause of democracy and human rights in Burma. When she toured the country calling for peaceful reform and democracy, the military put her under house arrest. Although the political party she founded won a huge victory in elections in 1990, the military junta has refused either to hand over power to the elected representatives or to release Suu Kyi from house arrest.

Aung San Suu Kyi was awarded the Nobel Peace Prize in 1991. She was nominated by Vaclav Havel, who had led Czechoslovakia out of Communist rule and Soviet dominance a year earlier. The announcement of her award said in part: "Suu Kyi's struggle is one of the most extraordinary examples of civil courage in Asia in recent decades. She has become an important symbol in the struggle against oppression. In awarding the Nobel Peace Prize for 1991 to Aung San Suu Kyi, the Norwegian Nobel Committee wishes to honor this woman for her unflagging efforts and to show its support for the many people throughout the world who are striving to attain democracy, human rights and ethnic conciliation by peaceful means." Suu Kyi was not allowed to travel to Norway to receive the prize and remains under detention.

This reading is from an essay titled "In Quest for Democracy" which Suu Kyi was writing at the time of her arrest. Her crusade for democracy and human rights in Burma spoke eloquently to all who live under oppression.

QUESTIONS:

1) Why is the charge that democracy is unsuitable for Burma invalid?
2) Why is the Burmese economy stagnant?
3) What sort of government do the Burmese people want?

Opponents of the movement for democracy in Burma have sought to undermine it by on the one hand casting aspersions on the competence of the people to judge what was best for the nation and on the other condemning the basic tenets of democracy as un-Burmese. There is nothing new in Third World governments seeking to justify and perpetuate authoritarian rule by denouncing liberal democratic principles as alien. By implication they claim for themselves the official and sole right to decide what does or does not conform to indigenous cultural norms. Such conventional propaganda aimed at consolidating the powers of the establishment has been studied, analysed and disproved by political scientists, jurists and sociologists. But in Burma, distanced by several decades of isolationism from political and intellectual developments in the outside world, the people have had to draw on their own resources to explode the twin myths of their unfitness for political responsibility and the unsuitability of democracy for their society. As soon as the movement for democracy spread out across Burma there was a surge of intense interest in the meaning of the word "democracy," in its history and its practical implications. More than a quarter-century of narrow authoritarianism under which they had been fed a pabulum of shallow, negative dogma had not blunted the perceptiveness or political alertness of the Burmese. On the contrary, perhaps not all that surprisingly, their appetite for discussion and debate, for uncensored information and objective analysis, seemed to have been sharpened. Not only was there an eagerness to study and to absorb standard theories on modern politics and political institutions, there was also widespread and intelligent speculation on the nature of democracy as a social system of which they had little experience but which appealed to their common-sense notions of what was due to a civilized society. There was a spontaneous interpretative response to such basic ideas as representative government, human rights and the rule of law. The privileges and freedoms which would be guaranteed by democratic institutions were commemorated with understandable enthusiasm.... It was natural that a people who have suffered much from the consequences of bad government should be preoccupied with theories of good government....

Why has Burma with its abundant natural and human resources failed to live up to its early promise as one of the most energetic and fastest-developing nations in South-east Asia?.... [The answer is] when democratic rights had been lost to military dictatorship sufficient efforts had not been made to regain them, moral and political values had been allowed to deteriorate without concerted attempts to save the situation, the economy had been badly managed, and the country had been ruled by men without integrity or wisdom....

Under totalitarian socialism, official policies with little relevance to actual needs had placed Burma in an economic and administrative limbo where government bribery and evasion of regulations were the indispensable lubricant to keep the wheels of everyday life turning. But through the years of moral decay and material decline there has survived a vision of a society in which the people and the leadership could unite in principled efforts to achieve prosperity and security. In 1988 the movement for democracy gave rise to the hope that the vision might become reality. At its most basic and immediate level, liberal democracy would mean in institutional terms a representative government appointed for a constitutionally limited term through free and fair elections. By exercising responsibly their right to choose their own leaders the Burmese hope to make an effective start at reversing the process of decline....

The people of Burma view democracy not merely as a form of government but as an integral social and ideological system based on respect for the individual. When asked why they feel so strong a need for democracy, the least political will answer: "We just want to be able to go about our own business freely and peacefully, not doing anybody any harm, just earning a decent living without anxiety and fear." In other words they want the basic human rights which would guarantee a tranquil, dignified existence free from want and fear....

It was predictable that as soon as the issue of human rights became an integral part of the movement for democracy the official media should start ridiculing and condemning the whole concept of human rights, dubbing it a western artefact alien to traditional values. It was also ironic--Buddhism, the foundation of traditional Burmese culture, places the greatest value on man, who alone of all beings can achieve the supreme state of Buddhahood. Each man has in him the potential to realize the truth through his own will and endeavour and to help others to realize it. Human life therefore is infinitely precious....

But despotic governments do not recognize the precious human components of the state, seeing its citizens only a faceless, mindless--and helpless--mass to be manipulated at will. It is as though people were incidental to a nation rather than its very life-blood. Patriotism, which should be the vital love and care of a people for their land, is debased into a smokescreen of hysteria to hide the injustices of authoritarian rulers who define the interests of the state in terms of their own limited interests. The official creed is required to be accepted with an unquestioning faith more in keeping with orthodox tenets of the biblical religions which have held sway in the West than with the more liberal Buddhist attitude....

The proposition that the Burmese are not fit to enjoy as many rights and privileges as the citizens of democratic countries is insulting. It also makes questionable the logic of a Burmese government considering itself fit to enjoy more rights and privileges than the governments of those same countries. The inconsistency can be explained--but not justified--only by assuming so wide a gulf between the government and the people that they have to be judged by different norms. Such an assumption in turn casts doubt on the doctrine of government as a comprehensive spirit and medium of national values.

Weak logic, inconsistencies and alienation from the people are common features of authoritarianism. The relentless attempts of totalitarian regimes to prevent free thought and new ideas and the persistent assertion of their own rightness bring on them an intellectual stasis which they project on to the nation at large. Intimidation and propaganda work in a duet of oppression, while the people, lapped in fear and distrust, learn to dissemble and keep silent. And all the time the desire grows for a system which will lift them from the position of "rice-eating robots" to the status of human beings who can think and speak freely and hold their heads high in the security of their rights.

From the beginning Burma's struggle for democracy has been fraught with danger. A movement which seeks the just and equitable distribution of powers and prerogatives that have long been held by a small elite determined to preserve its privileges at all costs is likely to be prolonged and difficult. Hope and optimism are irrepressible but there is a deep underlying premonition that the opposition to change is likely to be vicious....

Revolutions generally reflect the irrepressible impulse for necessary changes which have been held back by official policies or retarded by social apathy. The initiations and practices of democracy provide ways and means by which such changes could be effected without recourse to violence. But change is anathema to authoritarianism, which will tolerate no deviation from rigid policies. Democracy acknowledges the right to differ as well as the duty to settle differences peacefully. Authoritarian governments see criticism of their actions and doctrines as a challenge to combat. Opposition is equalled with "confrontation," which is interpreted as violent conflict.... The insecurity of power based on coercion translates into a need to crush all dissent....

The words "law and order" have so frequently been misused as an excuse for oppression that the very phrase has become suspect in countries which have known authoritarian rule.... There is no intrinsic virtue to law and order unless "law" is equated with justice and "order" with the discipline of a people satisfied that justice has been done. Law as an instrument of state oppression is a familiar feature of totalitarianism. Without a popularly elected legislature and an independent judiciary to ensure due process, the authorities can enforce as "law" arbitrary decrees that are in flagrant negation of all acceptable norms of justice. There can be no security for citizens in a state where new "laws" can be made and old ones changed to suit the convenience of the powers that be. The iniquity of such practices is traditionally recognized by the precept that existing laws should not be set aside at will. The Buddhist concept of law is based on *dharma*, righteousness or virtue, not on the power to impose harsh and inflexible rules on a defenceless people. The true measure of the justice of a system is the amount of protection it guarantees to the weakest.

Where there is no justice there can be no secure peace. The Universal Declaration of Human Rights recognizes that "if man is not to be compelled to have recourse, as a last resort, to rebellion against tyranny and oppression," human rights should be protected by the rule of law.

That just laws which uphold human rights are the necessary foundation of peace and security would be denied only by closed minds which interpret peace as the silence of all opposition and security as the assurance of their own power....

The people of Burma want not just a change of government but a change in political values. The unhappy legacies of authoritarianism can be removed only if the concept of absolute power as the basis of government is replaced by the concept of confidence as the mainspring of political authority: the confidence of the people in their right and ability to decide the destiny of their nation, the mutual confidence in the principle of justice, liberty and human rights....

In their quest for democracy the people of Burma explore not only the political theories and practices of the world outside their country but also the spiritual and intellectual values that have given shape to their own environment....

The quest for democracy in Burma is the struggle of a people to live whole, meaningful lives as free and equal members of the world community. It is part of the unceasing human endeavour to prove that the spirit of man can transcend the flaws of his own nature.

Aung San Suu Kyi. "In Quest for Democracy." In *Freedom from Fear and Other Writings*. New York: Viking, 1991. Pp. 167-169, 173-179.

SECTION 11

SOCIAL CONDITIONS, SCIENCE, AND TECHNOLOGY FROM THE EIGHTEENTH CENTURY TO THE PRESENT

Diverse readings in this section illustrate the evolution of societies across the world from traditional to contemporary during the past two centuries. Three readings recreate the manners and mores of traditional societies--for the upper class in eighteenth-century China, for the working class in early nineteenth-century England, and for African descended slaves in the United States. Examples of Romantic poetry portray the sensibilities of the educated upper class in early nineteenth-century England and the United States. Two readings testify to the misery of the factory workers, victims of the early Industrial Revolution, and address the demand for improvements. Nineteenth-century ideologies, including Marxism, took form partly in response to abuses and wretched conditions during the early Industrial Revolution

Most of the readings demonstrate the rapidity of change in the modern era. Changing attitudes towards women are exemplified in the works of the late eighteenth-century English champion for female emancipation Mary Wollstonecraft and in the pioneering struggles of a twentieth-century Chinese woman Mao Yen-wen. Profound shifts in our understanding of the world are shown by the works of naturalist Charles Darwin, explorer David Livingstone, and scientist Marie Curie. Changes in the method of production are featured in a reading on industrialist Henry Ford, a pioneer in the automobile industry and inventor of the assembly-line. Increased industrial productivity ultimately enabled workers to demand and attain improved living standards. Uncertainties in human lives produced by downturns in the economy are vividly embodied in poignant letters from dispossessed Americans during the Great Depression.

The world remains a harsh and merciless place for millions living in poor countries, and for some unfortunate people in rich societies also. Among the many humanitarians who dedicate their lives to helping the sick and destitute, none is more noble than the Albanian-born Catholic nun the world knows as Mother Teresa, founder of the Order of the Sisters of Charity. Her saintly life and message are an inspiration to the world and to each person's better self.

FESTIVALS AND CELEBRATIONS IN EIGHTEENTH-CENTURY CHINA

► **Woodblock Illustration from *Dream of the Red Chamber***

Ts'ao Hsueh-ch'in (c. 1723-1763) was the author of an autobiographical novel titled *Hung Lou Meng* (*Dream of the Red Chamber*). Considered the greatest Chinese novel, it has been much loved and widely read for over two centuries. Born into a powerful and cultured family with close connections to the court, Ts'ao was raised amid wealth during the height of the Ch'ing dynasty, when traditional Chinese culture enjoyed its last flowering before dynastic decline and Western invasion changed China irrevocably.

This novel depicted life in the extended aristocratic Chia family. Although over two hundred individuals young and old ranging from aristocrats to servants are portrayed over several years' period, the main characters are two adolescent cousins, Pao-yu and Tai-yu. The chief plot deals with their tragic love story. Because well-intended but bumbling elders failed to recognize their love for one another and arranged another bride for Pao-yu, Tai-yu died of a broken heart. As he had promised her, Pao-yu left home after her death and became a wandering monk. Some interpret this sad story as a protest against the tyranny of arranged marriages.

The one hundred and twenty chapters of this novel with their many subplots of realistic characters are a rich repertoire of life in eighteenth century China. The passages selected below show how people in China celebrated special occasions like the lunar new year, which falls towards the end of January. Schools and workplaces close for at least two weeks of fun and festivities that begin with formal family ceremonies to honor ancestors. New Year holidays end with the lantern festival that celebrates the first full moon. Fancy lanterns are lit on that night and good food and drinks are again in order. Children make up and guess each other's riddles for prizes.

There are many other holidays; the two mentioned below are in late spring to honor the fairies of the flowers, and the mid-autumn festival during the full moon sometime in September which is a harvest celebration. A birthday celebration for some young people is also included. In China as in other cultures birthdays are special occasions. While birthdays of old people are solemnly and formally celebrated, those of young people are festive events. Because of the Chia family's wealth and position, their celebrations were obviously on a grander scale than those of ordinary people, but the occasions themselves were universal.

QUESTIONS:

1) How did Chinese pay respect to their ancestors and senior family members at New Year's celebrations?

2) What are some of the other traditional holidays celebrated by the Chinese?

3) What similarities are there between modern birthday celebrations and those for young people in eighteenth-century China?

On the twenty-ninth of the twelfth month, everything had been prepared for the new year: new paintings of the door guardians had been pasted on front gates, festive couplets and hangings were in place, and two rows of large red candles had been placed along a path from the front gate, all the way to the main reception hall. When they were lit the rows of shining lights resembled two golden dragons. On the thirtieth, all members of the family with court ranks, from the Dowager Duchess down, donned their court robes, and were carried to the palace in procession in their sedan chairs to offer felicitations. After attending a banquet in the palace, they returned home to be greeted by younger members of the family who had no official rank and therefore did not attend the palace reception....

All members of the Chia family then stood in order according to their generation ... men and women in separate ranks .... Led by the Dowager Duchess they proceeded to the main ceremonial hall where portraits of the two founding dukes of the clan dominated, flanked by those of other ancestors, set amidst rich tapestry, carpets and formal ritual objects. Candles shone and incense burned.... Course after course of offerings from wine, meats, vegetables, and tea were passed up to the Dowager Duchess who reverently placed them on the offering table.... When all were in place the Dowager Duchess lit incense and knelt down, followed by everyone in attendance. All was quiet except for the gong that signalled the procedure as all performed kowtows [obeisance to the ancestors]. When the ceremony ended ... [all male members of the family] withdrew to the main reception chamber of the Yung-kuo Mansion to await the arrival of the Dowager Duchess ... [then all family members] rendered her homage and offered one another felicitations....

[After the formal congratulations were over the Dowager distributed] packets of New Year money, purses, and gold and silver coins to all. A festive meal was served with appropriate auspicious dishes, male members of the family were seated in the eastern wing, and females in the western wing of the great dining hall. When the Dowager rose and the meal came to an end, all dispersed to their quarters. That night incense and other offerings were placed before all Buddhist altars and other shrines throughout the mansions.... The gardens and halls were brightly lit with candles and lanterns. Everyone down to the servants was dressed in his or her best clothes, as all enjoyed themselves through the night, laughing, talking, and setting off rockets and firecrackers. At dawn the next morning the Dowager Duchess and the others with court ranks once again donned their formal court regalia and went to the palace to wish Cardinal Spring [her eldest grand-daughter and consort to the emperor] happy new year. After taking part in a banquet in the palace, they returned, and again made offerings to the ancestors. After that [the Dowager Duchess] received no more visitors, spending her time chatting with relatives, and playing cards, go, and other games with Pao-yu [her favorite young grandson] and her granddaughters. Meanwhile Lady Wang [the dowager's daughter-in-law] and Hsi-feng [her granddaughter-in-law] were busy everyday with entertaining [female] guests and relatives, as were male members of the family [with male guests and relatives].

So the festivities went on for another seven or eight days. By then it was time to prepare for the Lantern Festival [first full moon of the New Year]. Beautifully decorated lanterns were hung throughout the mansions. On the evening of the fifteenth the Dowager Duchess hosted a party for all members of her family in the main dining hall, which was festooned with many different kinds of floral lanterns. She also ordered a troupe of youthful operatic performers to entertain…. Ten tables were set up to accommodate all junior members of the family she had invited…. [At the end of the entertainment] the Dowager praised the child singers and said "we must reward them." At which [her grandsons], who had prepared a large tray of money, ordered the servants to spill it on the stage for the children to pick up…. The sound of falling money clattering on the stage made her very happy….

[Another year at Lantern Festival time as Pao-yu, Tai-yu, and two other cousins were playing] Suddenly a servant came to announce that Her Highness [Cardinal Spring] had sent a "riddles lantern" from the palace and that they should all go and see it. All four hurried over to the Dowager Duchess's sitting room. A young eunuch was already in the room, holding a specially made square lantern of white silk, each of whose four corners was hung with a riddle. Everyone rushed to guess the riddles. But the eunuch said: "Young ladies and gentlemen, please do not reveal your solutions. Her Highness has asked that you write down your answers for her to judge." … Pao-yu, Tai-yu [and all others] thus wrote down their solutions, then each made up a riddle also, which they hung on the lantern.

The eunuch took the lantern back to the palace. Around evening time he returned with the message: "Her Highness's riddles were correctly guessed by all except two [one of Pao-yu's cousins and his younger half-brother]. She has also written down her solutions to all your riddles and wants to know whether they are correct…. The eunuch also took out the prizes, items made in the palace workshops [that Her Highness] had prepared for all who had guessed correctly….

Happy at the good cheer, the Dowager Duchess then added to the joyous occasion by ordering a special revolving lantern made. She had it placed in her reception room and had her grandchildren make up riddles and write them out on slips of paper which were then attached to the lantern. Then she had special snacks and condiments prepared, and various prizes for those who made the correct guesses. When Chia Cheng [the dowager's son and father of the Imperial Consort] returned from his office in the evening and saw his mother so happy, he also joined in the festivities….

The twenty-sixth of the fourth month [early June] was the date for the Grain in Ear Festival. According to ancient custom presents were set out on this day to bid farewell to all the flower fairies, who, having blossomed, and with the onset of summer, took their leave for another year. This festival was special to maidens. Thus all the young ladies and servant girls of … [the Chia mansions] got up early that morning, and festooned every tree branch with the horses and carriages they had woven with willow twigs and flowers, and pennants and hangings that they made with silks and satins. Every tree in the garden was swaying with these beautiful decorations, secured with silken chords. All the girls were dressed especially beautifully for this festive occasion, as they played in the garden, outshining even the flowers and birds in their finery….

[The fifteenth of the eighth month is the mid-autumn festival] After dinner Chia Tseng [a grand nephew of the dowager, who also had rank of duke and who lived in the adjoining mansion] and his wife came over to the Yung-kuo Mansion. They found the Dowager Duchess, her sons and grandsons chatting together in her drawing room…. The Dowager said: "The moon cakes you sent over yesterday were very good; the water melons looked good but did not taste special." Chia Tseng replied smiling: "The moon cakes were made by a new pastry chef, and when I tasted them and found them good, I decided to present them to you. The water melons were good in previous years, but I don't know what happened this year." … The Dowager then said with a smile: "The moon has risen, let's go and offer incense." So saying, she leaned on Pao-yu and led everyone into the garden. The main gate to the garden had been opened and the garden itself was lit with lanterns with opaque horn shades. Candles and incense had been set on the altar to the moon, as were melons, fruits, and moon cakes…. The floor before the altar was covered with carpets and cushions. The Dowager cleaned her hands and offered incense, then kowtowed, followed by the others. She then said: "The best place to enjoy the moon is on top of a hill." So she led everyone to the pavillion on top of the hill in the garden.... [After all were seated around a big table in the pavillion] the Dowager had a branch of flowering laurel brought over. Then she ordered a maid to begin beating a drum as the branch was passed from hand to hand around the table. When the drum stopped, the person holding the branch first drank a glass of wine, and then told a joke as penalty....

[After rounds of story telling, eating and drinking] the Dowager looked up, saw that the moon had risen high in the sky and the scenery looked lovelier than ever. She said: "The moon is so good, we must also have some music." ... She added: "Too many instruments will detract, only the flute will do." So a young flutist was ordered to play from a distance.... As everyone chatted, sipped warm wine and enjoyed the laurel blossoms, the lonely sound of the flute drifted in from the laurel tree grove. Everyone quieted down, looked at the moon in the cloudless sky, listened, sipped tea, and enjoyed the cool breeze.... When it ended everyone was full of praise. More warm wine was served.... The Dowager then said: "A slower tune would have been even better." She then ordered a large goblet of wine to be given to the musician, asking that she play another tune, a truly slow one, after she had finished drinking her wine....

It was Pao-yu's birthday ... but because Lady Wang [his mother] was not at home, it was not as festive as in previous years. However, he received four gifts, all auspicious items, from the Taoist monk Chang [and from others].... From his maternal uncle Wang there was the usual suit of clothing, a pair of socks and shoes, one hundred longevity peaches [a pastry made in the shape of peaches] and a hundred packets of noodles [also for good luck]. His aunt Hsieh gave fifty each of longevity peaches and noodles. From other family members, he received a pair of shoes from Lady Yu [a cousin's wife] and Hsi-feng [another cousin's wife] gave him a finely embroidered four-sided purse made in the palace workshop, with a gold statuette of the god of longevity inside, plus an ornament from Persia.... Pao-chin's [a visiting distant cousin] birthday happened to fall on the same day also. She too received a number of presents. Among the siblings and cousins presents exchanged on such occasions usually consisted of items of needle work, a few line of poetry, a painting, some calligraphy, always the handiwork of the giver....

Tan-chun [Pao-yu's younger sister who took charge] then said: "It so happens that we did not order meals from the kitchen today. We will therefore order noodles [equivalent to birthday cake, a must at all Chinese birthday parties] and other special dishes from the outside. We will take up contributions and Matron Liu will take our orders and later set out our dinner in our inside dining room." Everyone agreed that it was a good idea. Tan-chun then sent maids to invite all the cousins for dinner, and also spoke to Matron Liu to order enough special dishes for two banquet tables of guests....

Ts'ao, Hsueh-ch'in. *Hung Lou Meng*. Rpt. Taipei: Chih-yang Publishing, 1989. Pp. 186-188, 229, 458-463, 536-538, 668-669. Translation by Jiu-Hwa Lo Upshur.

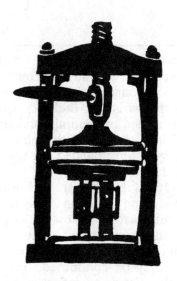

THE TEXTURE OF LIFE IN EARLY NINETEENTH-CENTURY CORNWALL

Since the early seventeenth-century, newspapers have kept their readers abreast of current events. They also provide the historian with an invaluable records of past eras. In addition to distinguished major papers like the *Times* of London, the *Journal de Genève*, and the *New York Times*, which devote much space to national and international news, smaller regional news publications give precious insights into local events of concern to common people. The following passages appeared between 1810 and 1833 in *The West Briton*, a local newspaper of Cornwall, a region in the extreme southwest part of England.

Economic life in Cornwall centered on mining, farming, and shipping. The majority of the inhabitants were hard-working members of the rural underclass. Here as elsewhere, a minority of wealthy, propertied, aristocrats thrived from their ownership land and other investments. *The West Briton* provides a rich tapestry of the life of the time. The reader today is struck by the extreme hardships that most people had to endure and by the violent tenor of life in general. The following selections show how similar life was then in many respects to the present. Readers then as now relied on local newspapers for national and local news, for advertisements and public service announcements, and for interesting and sometimes bizarre stories.

QUESTIONS:

1) Do any of the reports included here seem comparable to what might be read in newspapers today?

2) Does the tenor of life in nineteenth-century Cornwall seem especially violent?

3) Does the newspaper from which these selections are excerpted perform a worthwhile social function? In more than one way?

WORLD AFFAIRS

-- [2 November 1810] Caution to owners of boats, etc. The escapes of French prisoners of war in this county, and especially those on parole, having of late become exceedingly frequent, and such prisoners being in the practice of proceeding to the points of the sea coast nearest to the places from whence they abscond, and there seizing upon any boat or other vessel which they may not find properly guarded. A caution is hereby given to all owners of boats, etc. to be upon their guard against any such seizure; and they are recommended particularly to be careful not to leave any masts, sails, or oars in their boats, excepting when actually in use.

-- [22 May 1818] On Wednesday morning, sailed from the port of Charlestown, the *Charlestown*, Williams, master, with about 50 persons on board, as passengers for America; amongst whom are some whole families, including infants at the breast. In the number of those who have thus bid adieu to the land of their nativity, in pursuit of better fortune on a distant shore, is a woman of 70 years of age, whose husband emigrated seven months since.

-- [3 February 1826] The French slave vessel, which was forced into St. Ives, by stress of weather, was taken possession of by Lieut. G.H. Rye, and his party of seamen belonging to the coastguard service. She is pierced for 20 guns, has six on board; her main booms are fitted with boarding spikes, and her cabin with cutlasses and loaded fire arms; she has also an implement for turning red-hot shot from the furnace into her guns (which are 12 pounders). She had made 14 slave voyages in the last eight years since she was built. Lieut. Rye gave a poor negro child his freedom, by taking him from his cruel master's grasp, and carrying him home to his own five motherless young children. The master of the vessel, as may well be imagined, is described as one of the most brutal hardhearted monsters on the face of the earth. The vessel still lies at St. Ives under detention.

CRIME AND PUNISHMENT

-- [18 October 1811] At the Sessions, or Law Court, held at Launceston, on Wednesday last, Jonathan Barnes was found guilty of stealing oats, and sentenced to be publicly whipped on Saturday next.

-- [22 November 1811] Ran away from her master, Mark Richards, of St. Agnes, Innkeeper, Jane Snell, his apprentice, about 15 years of age, fair complexion, light hair, and about 4½ feet high; wore away a green stuff skirt, a blue coat, a buff-colour bed-gown, and a black silk bonnet. Whoever harbours or employs the apprentice after this public notice will be prosecuted.

-- [30 April 1813] Catherine Mitchell being found guilty of keeping a house of ill-fame in Falmouth, was sentenced to be imprisoned for two months and to pay a fine of ten pounds; and to be farther imprisoned until it was paid. Elizabeth Tresidder, for committing a similar offence in the parish of Budock, was sentenced to be imprisoned a fortnight, and fined one shilling. Ann Lampshire, who surrendered in discharge of her bail, was found guilty of keeping a disorderly house in the parish of Budock, and was ordered to be imprisoned one month, and fined a shilling. Matilda Lisle, charged with frequenting houses of ill-fame, was reprimanded by the chairman and discharged.

-- [16 July 1813] Cornwall Quarter Sessions. Ann Holman was found guilty of stealing milk from a cow belonging to James Grey, and sentenced to two months imprisonment. The ease with which this species of felony may be committed, and its frequency, induced the Bench to inflict a punishment, that might otherwise be considered as rather severe.

-- [9 December 1814] A tall stout woman of a tolerably decent appearance who has something of the Irish accent, in company with a stout set made man about five feet nine or ten inches high with a dark beard and sallow complexion, has lately been travelling through the county and, especially at fairs, circulating base silver, mostly shillings. In doing this their chief instrument is a little girl, who is supposed to be about ten or eleven years of age.

-- [22 November 1822] On Tuesday last was committed to the House of Correction, at Bodmin, for six months to hard labour, by J.F. Devonshire, Esq. and the Rev. T. Carlyon, magistrates for this county, James Taylor, for removing his furniture by night, with intent to defraud his landlord of the rent.

-- [23 March 1827] This practice [the stealing of corpses], so very distressing to the feelings of surviving relatives, has, it seems, commenced in Cornwall. On the night of Monday last, the body of a person named Abraham, which had been interred on the preceding evening, in the parish of St. Veep, near Fowey, was abstracted from the grave. It appears that the interment took place late in the evening, and that the sexton [gravedigger], having partly filled up the grave, intended to complete the operation the next morning. On coming to the spot, however, he found that the grave had been disturbed, and in consequence the coffin was uncovered and examined, when it was found that the body had been carried off.

ACCIDENTS AND HUMAN MISFORTUNES

-- [7 September 1810] On Monday last Thomas Hunkin of Mevagissey hung himself in a small room in which he had been confined for some time, in consequence of his evidencing symptoms of derangement. He has left a wife and five children.

-- [20 August 1813] On Sunday last, the body of a young woman was buried at a place where four roads meet, in the parish of Morvah, near Land's End. This unfortunate creature having become pregnant in consequence of an illicit intercourse, resolved to put a period to her existence. She purchased a quantity of arsenic under the pretence of a purpose to poison rats.

-- [2 September 1814] The charitable feelings of the public are called upon on behalf of Grace, the truly distressed widow of Joseph Burnett, who was unfortunately shot in the public street of Lostwithiel, on Sunday the 21st of this present August, and is thereby left a widow with nine children, six of whom are wholly unable to get their bread, viz. Mary, aged 11 years, Jane 9, Grace 7, Helena 5, Joseph 3 and Hannah, only 10 weeks old.

-- [27 October 1815] A child two years old, belonging to a person who lives at Higher-town, near Truro, was last week scalded to death by drinking boiling water out of a tea-kettle which was just taken from the fire. The infant lived two days in great agony. This, with many circumstances of a like nature, should operate as a caution to those who have the care of children to place boiling water and dangerous liquids out of their reach. A practice too common among the poor, of giving young children drink from a tea-pot, should be carefully avoided.

-- [28 February 1817] About 12 o'clock on the night of Saturday last, a range of houses occupied by the poor of the parish of St. Buryan, about 6 miles from Penzance, was discovered to be on fire, and as no engine could be procured, the flames spread with such rapidity as to bid defiance to every effort to arrest their progress, until the whole was reduced to a heap of ruins. There were 27 paupers in the houses at the time of the accident; 21 of these saved themselves by jumping out of the windows, but two men and four women were unable to escape, and unhappily perished, one of these was a poor girl, 19 years of age, who being subject to fits and occasional derangement, was lately removed to the poor-house, because the overseers thought two shillings a week too much for her maintenance; her father is an industrious fisherman, with a large family; her mother is blind. The unfortunate girl became violent on being separated from her friends, and was secured by a chain. She was seen struggling in the flames but could not free herself from the fetters, and no assistance could be afforded her.

-- [6 March 1818] Since the wreck of three vessels at St. Minver, near Padstow ... the shore near the place where these disasters occurred, has been visited by numbers of the peasantry, who have picked up quantities of bacon, etc. these vessels being laden with provisions from Ireland. On Friday last, two men who had ventured too far into the sea, in endeavoring to secure a bale of bacon, were overwhelmed by the waves, and unfortunately drowned. They were both married and have left, the one four, the other three children.

-- [5 March 1819] The town of Bodmin having been lately much infested by vagrants, the Mayor issued a notice Saturday last, that any wanderers who should after that day be found within the precincts of the borough should be dealt with according to law. This intimation not being attended to, some of the offenders were seized on Monday, and being convicted of begging in the borough, were sentenced to be flogged through the fore-street, which is of considerable length. The sentence was forthwith carried into execution, though rather leniently, and the delinquents dismissed with an intimation that if they again offended, they would be treated more severely. How are these unhappy creatures to avoid beggary, or where are they to obtain employment? Are they to be whipped from parish to parish until they perish under the lash, or expire from want, in a ditch?

-- [28 April 1820] On Saturday a boy named Hosking, being in one of the levels of Dolcoath mine, where a person was preparing to blast a hole in a damp part of the rock, he took up part of a tin tube used as a fuse in such cases, and not observing that it contained powder, attempted to look at the candle through it, when approaching too near, the powder exploded, and the tube being driven through his eye into his head, he was killed on the spot.

-- [6 May 1825] On Monday night, at St. Austell, a miner, in a state of intoxication, to prove the strength of some gunpowder of which he had a considerable quantity in a bag, enclosed a little in paper, and held it to a candle, leaving the open bag close at hand. As might have been expected, the smaller quantity ignited the larger; which exploding, burst out the window of the room, shattered and threw down a partition which separated that apartment from the next, and otherwise damaged the premises. The man, his wife, and child are dreadfully burnt, but their lives are not considered to be in danger.

-- [12 July 1833] On Wednesday evening a lad about 15 years of age, called Jas. Oliver, who worked at the Consolidated Mines, in Gwennap, fell from the ladder on which he was ascending to the surface, to a depth of 200 fathoms [1200 feet], and was literally dashed to atoms. The pieces of his body when collected amounted to at least one hundred.

ANNOUNCEMENTS, ADVISORIES, AND ADVERTISEMENTS

-- [31 August 1810] Married on Monday last, at Kingston-Lacy, Edward Viscount Falmouth, to Miss Bankes, daughter of Henry Bankes, Esq. of Kingston-Hall, Dorsetshire. His Lordship with his usual benevolence has ordered a suit of clothes to be given to every poor person in the parish of St. Michael Penkevil.

-- [8 February 1811] Mr. and Mrs. Boardman, dentists, at the house of Miss Parkyn, St. Nicholas Street, Truro, beg leave to inform the ladies and gentlemen of Truro and its neighborhood that they render the teeth white and beautiful, though ever so tarnished, without impairing the enamel; such as are loose they fasten. They also fix real and artificial teeth, from one to a whole set, and human teeth in artificial gums. They engraft teeth also on old stumps, with gold pivots; the same in gold gums, and transplant them with the greatest safety. N.B. The most dangerous stumps drawn, without the use of a surgeon's implement.

-- [24 May 1811] The celebrated Windsor Fairy, better known by the title of Lady Morgan (a title which his present Majesty [George III] was pleased to confer upon her) is now travelling through this county, and we understand will be at Truro Fair, the Wednesday in Whitsun-week

[Pentecost week]. This unparalleled woman is in the 54th year of her age, and only 18 lb. weight. She was introduced to their Majesties at the Queen's Lodge, Windsor on the 4th of August 1781, by the recommendation of the late Dr. Hunter, when they were pleased to pronounce her the finest display of human nature in miniature they ever saw. We shall say no more of this wonder of nature, let those who honor her with a visit judge for themselves.

-- [25 October 1811] Sleeman, druggist, Truro, has received the following valuable medicines from their respective proprietors, viz.: --Cephalic snuff; Ching's worm lozenges; Charcoal tooth powder; Dalby's carminative [flatulence medication]; Daffy's elixir; Ford's balsam of horehound; German corn plaster; odontalgic, a specific for the tooth-ache; Pomade divine; Roche's embrocation [liniment] for hooping cough; Roseate powder for superfluous hairs; Taylor's remedy for deafness; Trotter's Asiatic tooth powder; Tolu [aromatic resin] lozenges.

-- [2 January 1824] Whereas I, James Skinner, of the parish of Camborne, in the county of Cornwall, was separated from my wife Jane Skinner, on the 5th day of September, 1822, by the means of Captain William Michell, and his wife Jane Michell, my said wife's parents. My said wife leaving behind her, at the time she went from my house, two infant children, the one eighteen months old, and the other, who was at the time suckled by her, five months. Now, I do hereby give notice that I will not be answerable for any debts my said wife may contract, in my name, she being wholly separated from me, without my consent. Treswithen, near Camborne.

-- [13 August 1824] The most afflicting accounts every day reach us, through the public papers, of the lamentable consequences which have attended the bite of dogs, during the present summer. Numbers in various parts of the country, have lost their lives under all the horrors attendant on that most deplorable of all maladies, hydrophobia [rabies]. Precautions have been taken by the magistrates in different towns, to prevent disasters from rabid animals, and directions have been given that, after public notice, all dogs found at large, unmuzzled, should be killed by persons appointed for that purpose. But we have not as yet heard that the magistrates in any of the towns of Cornwall have judged it necessary to bestir themselves, in order to guard the public against this most direful of human calamities. The Mayor of Truro, we know, cannot be blamed, for he is absent, but we suppose he has delegated his authority and the superintendence of the police of the town to some suitable person, during his absence; who, we should suppose, cannot fail to observe the great number of dogs, which have no legal owners, that roam through the streets by day, to the no small alarm of the inhabitants, whose rest is frequently disturbed by their howls and contests during the night.

-- [3 October 1828] A tradesman, aged 43 years, of the first respectability, in a certain town in Cornwall, whereof he is a native, and now carrying on a long-established trade, which is most respectable, the advertiser is a remarkably temperate, sober, steady man, who would study domestic comfort, and is in every way qualified to render the marriage state desirable. Any middle aged, agreeable lady, who can command £1000, who feels desirous of meeting with a sociable, tender and kind companion, will find this advertisement worthy of notice. Not any part of the above sum is wanted in trade, that being entirely independent. The advertiser having a great taste for building, the money would be laid out in that way, and the wife to have the sole property settled on her for life. The advertiser will have a personal interview anywhere in the county. Honour and the greatest secrecy may be depended on. As a security against mere curiosity, letters, post-paid, with real name and address, will meet with most respectful attention. Direct to A.B. to be left at the Post-office, Falmouth until called for.

-- [3 June 1831] In a public house at Truro, on Tuesday last, a man actually ate two eels and a plaice [edible marine flatfish], undressed, for a trifling wager. The eels were alive at the time he commenced this brutal feat, and he devoured them, bones, etc. just as they were brought from the market.

Selected from *The West Briton* (1810-1833).

TWO ACCOUNTS OF SLAVE LIFE IN THE OLD SOUTH

During the nineteenth century, beginning with Great Britain in 1833, one western nation after another emancipated slaves in their lands. In the United States, slavery persisted in the southern states till 1863. The reasons for its prolongation were chiefly economic: the agricultural economy of the southern states, especially in the cotton industry, depended on cheap slave labor. The debate over the morality of slavery and the divergent economic interests of the farming South and the industrial North led to the American Civil War of 1861-1865.

Slavery in the southern states consigned some four million people of African origin to lives of grinding, unpaid labor. It ensured a high margin of profit and a luxurious style of life for southern white slave-masters. Wealthy plantation owners exerted great political influence in their states and in the U.S. Congress to stymie the demands of abolitionists for an end to slavery. They maintained the issue was one of states' rights.

Abraham Lincoln's election to the presidency in 1860 brought matters to a head. His Republican Party favored abolition without compensation to slave owners. Eleven southern states seceded from the Union and founded the Confederate States of America. Lincoln mobilized the armed forces with the intent of protecting the territory of the United States and preserving the Union. The resulting Civil War was the most costly war in U.S. history, with over 600,000 combatants killed. In 1863, President Lincoln issued the Emancipation Proclamation, which freed slaves in areas held by the southern confederacy. In 1865, the Thirteenth Amendment to the Constitution abolished slavery in the United States.

In the 1930s, the Federal Writers' Project, a Depression-era work project for unemployed authors and researchers, began a program to interview ex-slaves. Over two thousand elderly individuals told their stories to the interviewers. A massive, 10,000-page repository of oral history, known as *Slave Narratives*, now housed in the Library of Congress, was the outcome. The following are two of the personal accounts in that collection.

QUESTIONS:

1) Were male and female slaves treated differently? Were females made to work less than males?
2) Did emancipation bring immediate benefits for the former slaves?
3) What methods of control did slave masters adopt?

Mattie Curtis, age 98 when interviewed at Route #4, Raleigh, N.C., by Mary A Hicks:

I was born on the plantation of Mr. John Hayes in Orange County ninety-eight years ago. Several of the chilluns had been sold before the speculator come and buyed Mammy, Pappy and we three chilluns. The speculator was named Bebus, and he lived in Henderson, but he meant to sell us in the tobacco country.

We come through Raleigh, and the first thing that I remembers good was going through the paper mill on Crabtree. We traveled on to Granville County on the Granville Tobacco Path till a preacher named Whitfield buyed us. We lived near the Granville and Franklin County line, on the Granville side.

Preacher Whitfield, being a preacher, was supposed to be good, but he ain't half fed nor clothed his slaves, and he whipped them bad. I seen him whip my mammy with all the clothes off her back. He'd buck her down on a barrel and beat the blood out of her. There was some difference in his beating from the neighbors. The folks round there would whip in the back yard, but Marse Whitfield would have the barrel carried in his parlor for the beating.

Speaking about clothes, I went as naked as your hand till I was fourteen years old. I was naked like that when my nature come to me. Marse Whitfield ain't caring, but after that, Mammy told him that I had to have clothes.

We ain't had no sociables, but we went to church on Sunday, and they preached to us that we'd go to hell alive if we sassed our white folks.

Marse Whitfield ain't never pay for us, so finally we was sold to Miz Fanny Long in Franklin County. That woman was a devil if there ever was one. When I was little, I had picked up the fruit, fanned flies off the table with a peafowl fan and nursed the little slave chilluns. The last two or three years I had worked in the field, but at Miz Long's I worked in the tobacco factory. Yes ma'am, she had a tobacco factory where tobacco was stemmed, rolled, and packed in cases for selling. They said that she had got rich on selling chewing tobacco.

We was at Miz Long's when war was declared. Before that she had been pretty good, but she was a devil now. Her son was called to the war, and he won't go. They come and arrest

him; then his mammy try to pay him out, but that ain't no good. The officers says that he was yeller, and that they was going to shoot his head off and use it for a soap gourd. The Yankees did shoot him down here at Bentonville, and Miz Long went after the body. The Confederates has got the body but they won't let her have it for love nor money. They laugh and tell her how yeller he was, and they buried him in a ditch like a dog.

I don't know how come it, but just before the end of the war, we come to Moses Mordicia's place, right up the hill from here. He was mean too, he'd get drunk and whip niggers all day, off and on. He'd keep them tied down that long too, sometimes from sunrise till dark.

Mr. Mordicia had his yeller gals in one quarter to theirselves, and these gals belong to the Mordicia men, their friends, and the overseers. When a baby was born in that quarter, they'd send it over to the black quarter at birth. They do say that some of these gal babies got grown, and after going back to the yeller quarter, had more chilluns for her own daddy or brother. The Thompsons sprung from that set, and they say that a heap of them is halfwits for the reason that I just told you. Them yeller women was highfalutin' too; they thought they was better than the black ones. Have you ever wondered why the yeller women these days are meaner than black ones about the men? Well, that's the reason for it, their mammies raised them to think about the white men.

When the Yankees come, they come and freed us. The woods was full of Rebs what had deserted, but the Yankees killed some of them.

Right after the war, northern preachers come around with a little book a-marrying slaves, and I seed one of them marry my pappy and mammy. After this, they tried to find their fourteen oldest chilluns what was sold away, but they never did find but three of them.

Some sort of corporation cut the land up, but the slaves ain't got none of it that I ever heard about. I got married before the war to Joshua Curtis. Josh ain't really care about no home, but through this land corporation I buyed these fifteen acres on time. I cut down the big trees that was all over these fields, and I mauled out the wood and sold it, then I plowed up the fields and planted them. Josh did help to build the house, and he worked out some.

I done a heap of work at night too, all of my sewing and such, and the piece of land near the house over there ain't never got no work except at night. I finally paid for the land. Some of my chilluns was born in the field, too. When I was to the house, we had a granny, and I blowed in a bottle to make the labor quick and easy. All of this time I had nineteen chilluns, and Josh died, but I kept on, and the fifteen what is dead lived to be near about grown, every one of them.

I'll never forget my first bale of cotton and how I got it sold. I was some proud of that bale of cotton, and after I had it ginned, I set out with it on my steer cart for Raleigh. The white folks hated the nigger then, specially the nigger that was making something, so I dasn't ask nobody where the market was. I thought that I could find the place by myself, but I rid all day and had to take my cotton home with me that night, 'cause I can't find no place to sell it at. But that night I think it over, and the next day I go back and ask a policeman about the market. Lo and behold, child, I found it on Blount Street, and I had pass by it several times the day before.

This young generation ain't worth shucks. Fifteen years ago I hired a big buck nigger to help me shrub, and before eleven o'clock he passes out on me. You know about eleven o'clock in July it gets in a bloom. The young generation with their schools and their divorcing ain't going to get nothing out of life. It was better when folks just lived together. Their loafing gets them into trouble, and their novels makes them bad husbands and wives too.

Jacob Manson, age 86 when interviewed at 317 N. Haywood Street, Raleigh, N.C., by T. Pat Matthews:

I belonged to Colonel Bun Eden. His plantation was in Warren County, and he owned about fifty slaves or more. There was so many of them there he did not know all his own slaves.

Our cabins was built of poles and had stick-and-dirt chimneys, one door, and one little window at the back end of the cabin. Some of the houses had dirt floors. Our clothing was poor and homemade.

Many of the slaves went bareheaded and barefooted. Some wore rags around their heads, and some wore bonnets. We had poor food, and the young slaves was fed out of troughs. The food was put in a trough, and the little niggers gathered around and et. The chillun was looked after by the old slave women who were unable to work in the fields, while the mothers of the babies worked. The women plowed and done other work as the men did. No books or learning of any kind was allowed. No prayer meetings was allowed, but we sometimes went to the white folks' church. They told us to obey our marsters and be obedient at all times.

When bad storms come, they let us rest, but they kept us in the fields so long sometimes that the storm caught us before we could get to the cabins. Niggers watched the weather in slavery time, and the old ones was good at prophesying the weather.

Marster lived in the great house. He did not do any work but drank a lot of whiskey, went dressed up all the time, and had niggers to wash his feet and comb his hair. He made me scratch his head when he lay down, so he could go to sleep. When he got to sleep, I would slip out. If he waked up when I started to leave, I would have to go back and scratch his head till he went to sleep again. Sometimes I had to fan the flies away from him while he slept.

Marster would not have any white overseers. He had nigger foremen. Ha! Ha! He liked some of the nigger womens too good to have any other white man playing around with them. He had his sweethearts among his slave women. I ain't no man for telling false stories. I tells the truth, and that is the truth. At that time, it was a hard job to find a marster that didn't have women among his slaves. That was a general thing among the slave owners. One of the slave girls on a plantation near us went to her missus and told her about her marster forcing her to let him have something to do with her, and her missus told her, "Well, go on, you belong to him."

A lot of the slave owners had certain strong, healthy slave men to serve the slave women. Generally they give one man four women, and that man better not have nothing to do with the other women, and the women better not have nothing to do with other men.

We worked all day and some of the night, and a slave who made a week, even after doing that, was lucky if he got off without getting a beating. We got mighty bad treatment, and I just want to tell you, a nigger didn't stand as much show there as a dog did. They whipped for most any little trifle. They whipped me, so they said, just to help me get a quicker gait.

The pattyrollers come sneaking around often and whipped niggers on Marster's place. They nearly killed my uncle. They broke his collarbone when they was beating him, and Marster made them pay for it 'cause Uncle never did get over it.

One morning the dogs begun to bark, and in a few minutes the plantation was covered with Yankees. They told us we was free. They asked me where Marster's things was hid. I told them I could not give up Marster's things. They told me I had no marster, that they had fighted four years to free us and that Marster would not whip me no more. Marster sent to the fields and had all the slaves to come home. He told me to tell them not to run but to fly to the house at once.

All plowhands and women come running home. The Yankees told all of them they was free.

Marster offered some of the Yankees something to eat in his house, but they would not eat cooked food, they said they wanted to cook their own food.

After the war, I farmed around, one plantation to another. I have never owned a home of my own. When I got too old to work, I come and lived with my married daughter in Raleigh. I been here four years.

I think slavery was a mighty bad thing, though it's been no bed of roses since, but then no one could whip me no more.

Hurmence, Belinda, ed. *My Folks Don't Want Me to Talk about Slavery: Twenty-One Oral Histories of Former North Carolina Slaves*. Winston-Salem, NC: John F. Blair, 1984. Pp. 35-43.

MARY WOLLSTONECRAFT ON THE EARLY EDUCATION OF DAUGHTERS

Mary Wollstonecraft (1759-1797), an early feminist, wrote several important works on women's rights. The product of an unhappy marriage, in which her mother suffered at the hands of her abusive father, Wollstonecraft wrote with a special fervor about the problems women faced in a society based on unfair notions of gender roles.

Mary Wollstonecraft drew on the ideas of equality of sexes discussed by French philosophes of the Age of Reason and by reformers of the French revolutionary era (1789-1799). She especially stressed the crucial part that proper education must play in the improvement of women's lives. In the passage quoted below, she argues that female children if they are denied the educational opportunities of males will be doomed forever to play the part of the "lesser sex," placed on earth for the advantage and amusement of males. In particular, she deplored the notion that women's chief role was sexual and reproductive. Women of her day were married young and were expected to devote all of their energies to making themselves physically attractive to a prospective husband.

Mary Wollstonecraft died shortly after giving birth to a daughter, Mary, later the wife of the English Romantic poet, Percy Bysshe Shelley. Her principal political writings were *A Vindication of the Rights of Men* (1790) and *A Vindication of the Rights of Women* (1792). The following passages are taken from the latter and from an earlier book of *Thoughts on the Education of Daughters* (1787).

QUESTIONS:

1) In what ways does Mary Wollstonecraft seem "enlightened" in her outlook?
2) Does Mary Wollstonecraft anticipate major elements of twentieth-century feminist writings? For example?
3) What is the author's view of the value of education?

I ... venture to assert, that till women are more rationally educated, the progress of human virtue and improvement in knowledge must receive continual checks. And if it be granted that woman was not created merely to gratify the appetite of man, or to be the upper servant, who provides his meals and takes care of his linen, it must follow, that the first care of those mothers and fathers, who really attend to the education of females, should be, if not to strengthen the body, at least, not to destroy the constitution by mistaken notions of beauty and female excellence; not should girls ever be allowed to imbibe the pernicious notion that a defect can ... become an excellence....

But should it be proved that woman is naturally weaker than man, whence does it follow that it is natural for her to labour to become still weaker than nature intended her to be? Arguments of this cast are a insult to common sense .... The *divine right* of husbands, like the divine right of kings, may, it is to be hoped, in this enlightened age, be contested without danger ....

Pursuing these reflections, the fondness for dress, conspicuous in women, may be easily accounted for, without supposing it the result of a desire to please the sex on which they are dependent. The absurdity, in short, of supposing that a girl is naturally a coquette, and that a desire connected with the impulse of nature to propagate the species, should appear even before an improper education has ... called it forth prematurely is ... unphilosophical.

* * * * *

Early marriages are, in my opinion, a stop to improvement. If we were born only "to draw nutrition, propagate and rot," the sooner the end of creation was answered the better; but as women are here allowed to have souls, the soul ought to be attended to. In youth a woman endeavours to please the other sex, in order, generally speaking, to get married, and this endeavour calls forth all her powers. If she has had a tolerable education, the foundation only is laid, for the mind does not soon arrive at maturity, and should not be engrossed by domestic cares before any habits are fixed. The passions also have too much influence over the judgment to suffer it to direct her in this important affair; and many women, I am persuaded, marry a man before they are twenty, whom they would have rejected some years after. Very frequently, when the education has been neglected, the mind improves itself, if it has leisure for reflection, and experience to reflect on; but how can this happen when they are forced to act before they have had time to think, or find that they are unhappily married? Nay, should they be so fortunate as to get a good

husband, they will not set a proper value on him; he will be found much inferior to the lovers described in novels, and their want of knowledge makes them frequently disgusted with the man, when the fault is in human nature.

When a woman's mind has gained some strength, she will in all probability pay more attention to her actions than a girl can be expected to do; and if she thinks seriously, she will choose for a companion a man of principle; and this perhaps young people do not sufficiently attend to, or see the necessity of doing. A woman of feeling must be very much hurt if she is obliged to keep her children out of their father's company, that their morals may not be injured by his conversation; and besides, the whole arduous task of education devolves on her, and in such a case it is not very practicable. Attention to the education of children must be irksome, when life appears to have so many charms, and its pleasures are not found fallacious. Many are but just returned from a boarding-school, when they are placed at the head of a family, and how fit they are to manage it, I leave the judicious to judge. Can they improve a child's understanding, when they are scarcely out of the state of childhood themselves?

Dignity of manners, too, and proper reserve are often wanting. The constant attendant on too much familiarity is contempt. Women are often before marriage prudish, and afterwards they think they may innocently give way to fondness, and overwhelm the poor man with it. They think they have a legal right to his affections, and grow remiss in their endeavours to please. There are a thousand nameless decencies which good sense gives rise to, and artless proofs of regard which flow from the heart, and will reach it, if it is not depraved. It has ever occurred to me, that it was sufficient for a woman to receive caresses, and not bestow them. She ought to distinguish between fondness and tenderness. The latter is the sweetest cordial of life; but, like all other cordials, should be reserved for particular occasions; to exhilarate the spirits, when depressed by sickness, or lost in sorrow. Sensibility will best instruct. Some delicacies can never be pointed out or described, though they sink deep into the heart, and render the hours of distress supportable.

A woman should have so proper a pride, as not easily to forget a deliberate affront; though she must not too hastily resent any little coolness. We cannot always feel alike, and all are subject to changes of temper without an adequate cause.

Reason must often be called in to fill up the vacuums of life; but too many of our sex suffer theirs to lie dormant. A little ridicule and smart turn of expression, often confutes without convincing; and tricks are played off to raise tenderness, even while they are forfeiting esteem.

Women are said to be the weaker vessel, and many are the miseries which their weakness brings on them. Men have in some respects very much the advantage. If they have a tolerable understanding, it has a chance to be cultivated. They are forced to see human nature as it is, and are not left to dwell on the pictures of their own imaginations. Nothing, I am sure, calls forth the faculties so much as being obliged to struggle with the world; and this is not a woman's province in a married state. Her sphere of action is not large, and if she is not taught to look into her own heart, how trivial are her occupations and pursuits! What little arts engross and narrow her mind! "Cunning fills up the mighty void of sense;" and cares, which do not improve the heart or understanding, take up her attention. Of course, she falls prey to childish anger, and silly capricious humors, which render her rather insignificant than vicious.

In a comfortable situation, a cultivated mind is necessary to render a woman contented; and in a miserable one, it is her only consolation. A sensible, delicate woman, who by some strange accident, or mistake, is joined to a fool or a brute, must be wretched beyond all names of wretchedness, if her views are confined to the present scene. Of what importance, then, is intellectual improvement, when our comfort here, and happiness hereafter, depends on it.

Principles of religion should be fixed, and the mind not left to fluctuate in the time of distress, when it can receive succour from no other quarter. The conviction that everything is working for our good will scarcely produce resignation, when we are deprived of our dearest hopes. How they can be satisfied, who have not this conviction, I cannot conceive; I rather think they will turn to some worldly support, and fall into folly, if not vice. For a little refinement only leads a woman into the wilds of romance, if she is not religious; nay, more, there is no true sentiment without it, nor perhaps any other effectual check to the passions....

Wollstonecraft, Mary. *A Vindication of the Rights of Women*. London 1792. Rpt. Toronto: Univ. of Toronto Press, 1993. Pp. 113-114, 116. *Thoughts on the Education of Daughters*. London 1787. Facs. ed.: Clifton, NJ: A.M. Kelley, 1972. Pp. 93-103.

TESTIMONY OF A CHILD WORKER IN EARLY INDUSTRIAL ENGLAND

Beginning in the late eighteenth century, the industrial revolution has brought enormous changes to the world. It began in Britain in the textile industry because of the availability of raw materials and the technological ingenuity of British inventors, who transformed a handicraft industry to one driven by water-powered and later steam-powered looms. Because the industrial revolution began in Britain, its attendant problems and abuses first surfaced there as well. Lacking precedents for dealing with such problems, Britain had to devise solutions by conducting investigations and passing legislation to regulate industrial practices. Countries that followed Britain in industrializing benefitted from its experience in problem solving.

The vast economic changes brought by industry also triggered profound social transformations. Large cities grew up as factories attracted workers from the countryside, who soon became an exploited urban underclass. The unrestrained profit motive and vagaries in economic cycles led employers to demand long hours at low wages from their workers. Labor conditions in the factories were appalling. Reforms came about only gradually, as enlightened members of the government tried to limit the abuses of laissez-faire capitalism and to regulate industries.

In Britain, beginning in the 1820s, reform movements focused debate on the issue of child labor. Michael Sadler, a member of parliament, was a prominent leader in the struggle against the abuses of child labor. He headed a committee which investigated the problem and got a Factories Regulations Act passed in 1833. This set standards that today seem quite inhumane, but improved on existing conditions. It forbad children under age nine in textile mills, and limited the working day to nine hours for children 9-12 years old and to twelve hours for children 13-17 years old.

The following passage is taken from Sadler's questioning of a seventeen-year-old boy, Joseph Hebergam, who began working in a textile mill at age seven. The boy's quite matter-of-fact report of the brutality of the factory owners and supervisors speaks volumes about the exploitation of workers during the early stage of the industrial era.

QUESTIONS:

1) What sort of work was Joseph Hebergam engaged in?
2) Why was the work so dangerous?
3) Could working conditions have been made safer for the employees? Could child workers have worked safely in such a factory in any case?

Sadler [S]: Where do you reside?

Hebergam [H]: At North Great Huddersfield, in Yorkshire.

S: What age are you?

H: I was seventeen on the twenty-first of April.

S: Are your father and mother living?

H: No; I have been without a father six years on the eighth of August.

S: Your mother survives?

H: Yes.

S: Have you worked in factories?

H: Yes.

S: At what age did you commence?

H: Seven years of age.

S: At whose mill?

H: George Addison's, Bradley Mill, near Huddersfield.

S: What was the employment?

H: Worsted-spinning.

S: What were your hours of labour at that mill?

H: From five in the morning till eight at night.

S: What intervals had you for refreshment and rest?

H: Thirty minutes at noon.

S: Had you time for breakfast or refreshment in the afternoon?

H: No; not one minute; we had to eat our meals as we could; standing or otherwise.

S: You had fourteen and a half hours of actual labour at seven years of age?

H: Yes.

S: What wages had you at that time?

H: Two shillings and sixpence a week.

S: What means were taken to keep you at your work so long?

H: There were three overlookers; there was a head overlooker, and then there was one man kept to grease the machines, and then there was one kept on purpose to strap.

S: Was the main business of one of the overlookers that of strapping the children up to this excessive labour?

H: Yes, the same as strapping an old restive horse that has fallen down and will not get up.

S: Was that the common practice?

H: Yes, day by day.

S: Were there straps regularly provided for that purpose?

H: Yes, he is continually walking up and down with it in his hand.

S: Where is your brother John working now?

H: He died three years ago.

S: What age was he when he died?

H: Sixteen years and eight months.

S: To what was his death attributed by your mother and the medical attendants?

H: It was attributed to this, that he died from working such long hours, and that it had been brought on by the factory. They have to stop the flies [fly shuttles] with their knees, because they go so swift they cannot stop them with their hands; he got a bruise on the shin by a spindle board, and it went on to the degree that it burst; the surgeon cured that, then he was better; then he went to work again; but when he had worked about two months more his spine became affected, and he died.

S: What effect had this labour upon your own health?

H: It had a great deal; I have had to drop it several times in the year.

S: How long was it before the labour took effect on your health?

H: Half a year.

S: And did it at length begin to affect your limbs?

H: When I had worked about half a year, a weakness fell into my knees and ankles; it continued, and it has got worse and worse.

S: How far did you live from the mill?

H: A good mile.

S: Was it very painful for you to move?

H: Yes, in the morning I could scarcely walk, and my brother and sister used out of kindness to take me under each arm, and run with me to the mill, and my legs dragged on the ground in consequence of the pain; I could not walk.

S: Were you sometimes too late?

H: Yes; and if we were five minutes too late, the overlooker would take a strap, and beat us till we were black and blue.

S: The overlooker nevertheless knew the occasion of your being a little too late?

H: Yes.

S: Did you state to him the reason?

H: Yes, he never minded that; and he used to watch us out of the windows.

S: Did the pain and weakness in your legs increase?

H: Yes.

S: Just show the Committee the situation in which your limbs are now--

[The witness accordingly stood up, and showed his limbs.]

S: Were you originally a straight and healthy boy?

H: Yes, I was straight and healthful as any one when I was seven years and a quarter old.

S: How long have you been in the Leeds Infirmary?

H: A week last Saturday night; if I had been this week at Leeds I should have been a fortnight next Saturday.

S: Have any cases of accidents in mills or factories been brought into the Infirmary since you were there?

H: Yes, last Tuesday but one there was a boy brought in about five or six o'clock in the evening from a mill; he had got catched with the shaft, and he had both his thighs broke, and from his knee to his hip the flesh was ripped up the same as if it had been cut by a knife, his head was bruised, his eyes were nearly torn out, and his arms broken. His sister, who ran to pull him off, got both her arms broke and her head bruised, and she is bruised all over her body. The boy died last Thursday night but one, about eight o'clock; I do not know whether the girl is dead, but she was not expected to live.

S: Something has been said about the fear of giving evidence regarding this factory question; do you know whether any threats have ever been used on that account?

H: Yes; Dr. Walker ordered me to wear irons from the ankle to the thigh; my mother was not able to get them, and he said he would write a note, and she might go to some gentlemen in the town, and give them that note, and see if they would not give her something towards them; and so she did, and I have got the bare irons made; and I was coming into the yard where I live; and there was a man who worked at the same place that I did, asked me to let him look at them; I told him I could not get money to line them with, and he said, "I will tell you where there is a gentleman who will give you the money"; he told me of Mr. Oastler, and he said, "I will go and see if he is at home, that you may not lose your trouble." Mr. Oastler was at home, and said I was to be there at eight o'clock in the morning, because he wanted to go off on a journey; I got there about half-past eight. Mr. Wood of Bradford gave me a sovereign, and Mr. Oastler gave me three shillings sixpence, and so I had them made. He asked me questions what my lameness came on with, and I told him, and he happened to mention it at the County Meeting at York; my master saw it in the newspaper; I think it was in Mr. Baines's newspaper, of Leeds; he is an enemy to the Ten Hours' Bill, and he happened to see it in the paper, and he sent the foreman on to our house where I lived; he had not the patience to read it, and he said to my mother, "I suppose it is owing to our place that your Joseph got the use of his limbs taken away?" and my mother said he was informed wrong, that he had it before he went to that factory; but he said, "If he has said anything about our factory, we shall certainly turn him off, and both his brothers." I have two little brothers working at the same place.

S: Did the foreman say this to you?

H: To my mother and me; he said he did not know exactly how it was, but he would go back and see the paper himself, and if he found out that we said anything about the factory system, that we should be turned off.

S: Have you been turned off?

H: I have not, but my master will not speak to me or look at me: I do not know whether he will let me start again or not.

S: You stated that you found it your duty to go to those mills, in order to maintain your mother, who is a widow, and very poor?

H: Yes.

"Report of the Select Committee on the Factories Bill." *Industrial Revolution: Children's Employment*. Vol. 2. Pp. 157-159, 163-164. In *British Parliamentary Papers*. Shannon: Irish University Press, 1968-1972.

"SOCIAL MURDER" IN THE NEW INDUSTRIAL WORLD

The rapid industrialization of Western Europe and North America in the nineteenth century brought profound social and economic changes. The industrial revolution transformed the skilled artisans of cottage industries into workers who spent long days toiling in new factories that sprang up in fast-growing cities. At the same time, improvements in agriculture increased the food supply and medical advances extended life spans, both bringing rapid population growth. The population of Britain, for example, increased from about 5 million in 1700 to 32 million in 1900. Workers, men, women, and children, filled tenements in sprawling slums made hellish by pollution, poor sanitation, disease, grinding poverty, and high crime rates.

The deplorable working and living conditions of people in the new industrial cities led political and social theorists to formulate new ideologies and stress the need for radical, systemic change. The most influential of these theorists, Karl Marx (1818-1883) and his long-time associate Friedrich Engels (1820-1895), analyzed the economic ills of the capitalist system in books like *Das Kapital* (1867-1894). Marxist theory emphasizes the role of economics and class struggle as driving forces in history. Marx and Engels' famous propaganda tract, *The Communist Manifesto* (1848), proclaimed, "Communists everywhere support every revolutionary movement against the existing social and political order of things.... Working men of all countries, unite!" Marx and Engels discounted the possibility of improvement through reform and foresaw a worldwide revolution in which the working class would triumph over the upper and middle classes (bourgeoisie). With the victory of communism, a dictatorship of the proletariat (industrial wage-earners) would secure the means of production for all, and class struggle would cease.

The following passage is from Friedrich Engels' classic study, *The Condition of the Working Class in England in 1844*. It vividly portrays the economic and social afflictions of the urban poor in the new industrial world.

QUESTIONS:

1) What aspects of urban life does Engels identify as the worst effects of industrialization?

2) What social and psychological consequences does Engels attribute to living in industrial cities?

3) Are Marxist revolutionary principles inherent in Engels' analysis of social ills in industrial cities?

A town, such as London, where a man may wander for hours together without reaching the beginning of the end, without meeting the slightest hint which could lead to the inference that there is open country within reach, is a strange thing. This colossal centralization, this heaping together of two and a half millions human beings at one point, had multiplied the power of this two and a half millions a hundredfold; has raised London to the commercial capital of the world, created the giant docks and assembled the thousand vessels that continually cover the Thames. I know nothing more imposing than the view which the Thames offers during the ascent from the sea to London Bridge. The masses of buildings, the wharves on both sides, especially from Woolwich upwards, the countless ships along both shores, crowding ever closer and closer together, until, at last, only a narrow passage remains in the middle of the river, a passage through which hundreds of steamers shoot by one another; all this is so vast, so impressive, that a man cannot collect himself, but is lost in the marvel of England's greatness before he sets foot upon English soil.

But the sacrifices which all this has cost become apparent later. After roaming the streets of the capital a day or two, making headway with difficulty through the human turmoil and endless lines of vehicles after visiting the slums of the metropolis, one realizes for the first time that these Londoners have been forced to sacrifice the best qualities of their human nature, to bring to pass all the marvels of civilisation which crowd their city; that a hundred powers which slumbered within them have remained inactive, have been suppressed in order that a few might be developed more fully and multiply through union with those of others. The very turmoil of the streets has something repulsive, something against which human nature rebels. The hundreds of thousands of all classes and ranks crowding past each other, are they not all human beings with the same qualities and powers, and with the same interest in being happy? And have they not, in the end, to seek happiness in the same way, by the same means? And still they crowd by one another as though they had nothing in common, nothing to do with one another, and their only agreement is the tacit one, that each keep to his own side of the pavement, so as not to delay the opposing streams of the crowd, while it occurs to no man to honour another with so much as a glance. The brutal indifference, the unfeeling isolation of each in his private interest becomes the more repellent and offensive, the more these individuals are crowded together, within a limited space. And, however much one may be aware that this isolation of the individual, this narrow self-seeking is the fundamental principle of our society everywhere, it is nowhere so shamelessly barefaced, so self-conscious as just here in the crowding of the great city. The dissolution of mankind into monads, of which each one has a separate principle, the world of atoms, is here carried out to its utmost extreme.

Hence it comes, too, that the social war, the war of each against all, is here openly declared.... People regard each other only as useful objects; each exploits the other, and the end of it all is, that the stronger treads the weaker under foot, and that the powerful few, the capitalists, seize everything for themselves, while to the weak many, the poor, scarcely a bare existence remains.

What is true of London, is true of Manchester, Birmingham, Leeds, is true of all great towns. Everywhere barbarous indifference, hard egotism on one hand, and nameless misery on the other, everywhere social warfare, every man's house in a state of siege, everywhere reciprocal plundering under the protection of the law, and all so shameless, so openly avowed that one shrinks before the consequences of our social state as they manifest themselves here undisguised, and can only wonder that the whole crazy fabric still hangs together.

Since capital, the direct or indirect control of the means of subsistence and production, is the weapon with which this social warfare is carried on, it is clear that all the disadvantages of such a state must fall upon the poor. For him no man has the slightest concern. Cast into the whirlpool, he must struggle through as well as he can. If he is so happy as to find work, i.e., if the bourgeoisie does him the favour to enrich itself by means of him, wages await him which scarcely suffice to keep body and soul together; if he can get no work he may steal, if he is not afraid of the police, or starve, in which case the police will take care that he does so in a quiet and inoffensive manner. During my residence in England, at least twenty or thirty persons have died of simple starvation under the most revolting circumstances, and a jury has rarely been found possessed of the courage to speak the plain truth in the matter. Let the testimony of the witnesses be never so clear and unequivocal, the bourgeoisie, from which the jury is selected, always find some backdoor through which to escape the fruitful verdict, death from starvation. The bourgeoisie dare not speak the truth in these cases, for it would speak its own condemnation. But indirectly, far more than directly, many have died of starvation, where long continued want of proper nourishment has called forth fatal illness and death. The English working-men call this "social murder," and accuse our whole society of perpetrating this crime perpetually. Are they wrong?

True, it is only individuals who starve, but what security has the working-man that it may not be his turn to-morrow? Who assures him employment, who vouches for it that, if for any or no reason his lord and master discharges him to-morrow, he can struggle along with those dependent upon him, until he may find someone else "to give him bread"? Who guarantees that willingness to work shall suffice to obtain work, that uprightness, industry, thrift, and the rest of the virtues recommended by the bourgeoisie, are really his road to happiness? No one. He knows that he has something to-day, and that it does not depend upon himself whether he shall have something to-morrow. He knows that every breeze that blows, every whim of his employer, every bad turn of trade may hurl him back into the fierce whirlpool from which he has temporarily saved himself, and in which it is hard and often impossible to keep his head above water. He knows that, though he may have the means of living to-day, it is very uncertain whether he shall to-morrow.

Meanwhile, let us proceed to a more detailed investigation of the position, in which the social war had placed the non-possessing class. Let us see what pay for his work society does give the working-man in the form of dwelling, clothing, food, what sort of subsistence it grants those who contribute most to the maintenance of society; and, first, let us consider the dwellings.

Every great city has one or more slums, where the working-class is crowded together. True, poverty often dwells in hidden alleys close to the palaces of the rich; but, in general, a separate territory has been assigned to it, where, removed from the sight of the happier classes, it, may struggle along as it can. These slums are pretty equally arranged in all the great towns of England, the worst houses in the worst quarters of the towns; usually one or two-storied cottages in long rows, perhaps with cellars used as dwellings, almost always irregularly built. These houses of three or four rooms and a kitchen form, throughout England, some parts of London excepted, the general dwellings of the working-class. The streets are generally unpaved, rough, dirty, filled with vegetable and animal refuse, without sewers or gutters, but supplied with foul, stagnant pools instead. Moreover, ventilation is impeded by the bad, confused method of building of the whole quarter, and since many human beings live here crowded into a small space, the atmosphere that prevails in these working-men's quarters may readily be imagined. Further, the streets serve as drying grounds in fine weather; lines are stretched across from house to house, and hung with wet clothing.

Let us investigate some of the slums in their order. London comes first, and in London the famous rookery of St. Giles which is now, at last, about to be penetrated by a couple of broad streets. St. Giles is in the midst of the most populous part of the town, surrounded by broad, splendid avenues in which the gay world of London idles about, in the immediate neighbourhood of Oxford Street, Regent Street, or Trafalgar Square and the Strand. It is a disorderly collection of tall, three or four-storied houses, with narrow, crooked, filthy streets, in which there is quite as much life as in the great thoroughfares of the town, except that, here, people of the working-class only are to be seen. A vegetable market is held in the street, baskets with vegetables and fruits, naturally all bad and hardly fit to use, obstruct the sidewalk still further, and from these, as well as from the fish-dealers' stalls, arises a horrible smell. The houses are occupied from cellar to garret, filthy within and without, and their appearance is such that no human being could possibly wish to live in them. But all this is nothing in comparison with the dwellings in the narrow courts and alleys between the streets, entered by covered passages between the houses, in which the filth and tottering ruin surpass all description. Scarcely a whole window-pane can be found, the walls are crumbling, doorposts and window frames loose and broken, doors of old boards nailed together, or altogether wanting in this thieves' quarter, where no doors are needed, there being nothing to steal. Heaps of garbage and ashes lie in all directions, and the foul liquids emptied before the doors gather in stinking pools. Here live the poorest of the poor, the worst paid workers with thieves and the victims of prostitution indiscriminately huddled together, the majority Irish, or of Irish extraction, and those who have not yet sunk in the whirlpool of moral ruin which surrounds them, sinking daily deeper, losing daily more and more or their power to resist the demoralising influence of want, filth, and evil surroundings.

Engels, Friedrick. *The Condition of the Working Class in England in 1844*. Trans. Florence K. Wischenewetzky. London: Swan Sonnenschein, 1892. Pp. 284-89.

FOUR POETS OF THE ROMANTIC MOVEMENT

Romanticism was a reaction against the earlier classical and neoclassical canons of taste and art. From the late eighteenth century till around 1870, the Romantic movement affected art, music, and poetry.

Jean Jacques Rousseau (1712-1778) in France anticipated the Romantic ideal of the freedom of the human spirit by his stress on the individual. Johann Wolfgang von Goethe (1749-1832) in Germany was a major figure in the *Sturm und Drang* (storm and stress) movement that inaugurated German Romanticism. His short novel, *The Sorrows of the Young Werther*, in which the sensitive hero commits suicide over his unrequited love for a beautiful young woman, set the pattern of the Romantic style of life and writing.

In Britain, the most famous Romantic writers William Blake (1757-1827), William Wordsworth (1770-1850), Samuel Taylor Colderige (1772-1834), George Gordon, Lord Byron (1788-1824), John Keats (1795-1821), and Percy Bysshe Shelley (1792-1822). They stressed feeling, imagination, and inspiration over reason, logical analysis, and mere craftsmanship in the creation of great poetry. Their poems and prose works reflect this outlook.

Romantic authors and artists were concerned with several major themes. One was the primacy of nature. They delighted in the wonders of their natural surroundings, and their works vividly evoke images of the beauty and fragility of the countryside. The Romantics also loved the exotic, often choosing settings in the Gothic past of the Middle Ages or distant eastern lands.

Also featured in Romanticism is the lure of the supernatural. This was in large measure a reaction against the preceding enlightenment period's preoccupation with the rational and scientific. Romantic writers often drew on folk traditions of demonic visitations, of spirits and ghosts.

The most crucial element of the Romantic philosophy, however, was its iconoclasm. Romantic artists and writers sought to free the human spirit from the trappings of conventional wisdom, laws, and customs; they strove to open their own and their audience's eyes to a fuller appreciation of the mysteries and beauties of the universe.

The following selections are from the work of three English Romantic writers--Blake, Wordsworth, Shelley--and one American--Edgar Allan Poe (1809-1849).

QUESTIONS:

1) What is the importance of nature in the poets quoted here?
2) What is the attitude toward supernatural powers in the poets quoted here?
3) Which of the poets quoted here strikes you as the most iconoclastic?

William Blake,
"Proverbs of Hell" [1793]
in *The Marriage of Heaven and Hell*

In seed time learn, in harvest teach, in winter enjoy.
Drive your cart and your plow over the bones of the dead.
The road of excess leads to the palace of wisdom.
Prudence is a rich, ugly old maid courted by Incapacity.
He who desires but acts not, breeds pestilence.
The cut worm forgives the plow.
Dip him in the river who loves water.
A fool sees not the same tree that a wise man sees.
He whose face gives no light, shall never become a star.
Eternity is in love with the productions of time.
The busy bee has no time for sorrow....
No bird soars too high, if he soars with his own wings.
A dead body revenges not injuries.
The most sublime act is to set another before you.
If the fool would persist in his folly he would become wise....
Prisons are built with the stones of Law, Brothels with bricks of Religion.
The pride of the peacock is the glory of God.
The lust of the goat is the bounty of God.
The wrath of the lion is the wisdom of God.
The nakedness of woman is the work of God.
Excess of sorrow laughs. Excess of joy weeps....
Joys impregnate. Sorrows bring forth....
The rat, the mouse, the fox, the rabbet watch the roots; the lion, the tyger, the horse, the
    elephant watch the fruits.
The cistern contains: the fountain overflows.
One thought fills immensity....
The eagle never lost so much time as when he submitted to learn of the crow....
Think in the morning. Act in the noon. Eat in the evening. Sleep in the night....
The tygers of wrath are wiser than the horses of instruction.
Expect poison from the standing water.
You never know what is enough unless you know what is more than enough....
The thankful receiver bears a plentiful harvest.
If others had not been foolish, we should be so....
As the catterpiller chooses the fairest leaves to lay her eggs on, so the priest lays his curse on
    the fairest joys.
To create a little flower is the labour of ages.
Damn braces: bless relaxes....
The head Sublime, the heart Pathos, the genital Beauty, the hands and feet Proportion....
Exuberance is Beauty....
Sooner murder an infant in its cradle than nurse unacted desires.

William Wordsworth,
from Preface to the Second Edition of
Lyrical Ballads [1800]

I have said that poetry is the spontaneous overflow of powerful feelings: it takes its origin from
emotion recollected in tranquillity: the emotion is contemplated till, by a species of re-action, the

tranquillity gradually disappears, and an emotion, kindred to that which was before the subject of contemplation, is gradually produced, and does itself actually exist in the mind.   In this mood successful composition generally begins, and in a mood similar to this it is carried on; but the emotion, of whatever kind, and in whatever degree, from various causes, is qualified by various pleasures, so that in describing any passions whatsoever, which are voluntarily described, the mind will, upon the whole, be in a state of enjoyment.   If Nature be thus cautious to preserve in a state of enjoyment a being so employed, the Poet ought to profit by the lesson held forth to him, and ought especially to take care, that, whatever passions he communicates to his Reader, those passions, if his Reader's mind be sound and vigorous, should always be accompanied with an overbalance of pleasure.   Now the music of harmonious metrical language, the sense of difficulty overcome, and the blind association of pleasure which has been previously received from works of rhyme or metre of the same or similar construction, an indistinct perception perpetually renewed of language closely resembling that of real life, and yet, in the circumstance of metre, differing from it so widely--all these imperceptibly make up a complex feeling of delight, which is of the most important use in tempering the painful feelings always found intermingled with powerful descriptions of the deeper passions.   The effect is always produced in pathetic and impassioned poetry; while, in lighter compositions, the ease and gracefulness with which the Poet manages his numbers are themselves confessedly a principal source of the gratification of the Reader.   All that it is necessary to say, however, upon this subject, may be effected by affirming, what few persons will deny, that, of two descriptions, either of passions, manners, or characters, each of them equally well executed, the one in prose and the other in verse, the verse will be read a hundred times where the prose is read once.

From Wordsworth,
"Intimations of Immortality from Recollections of Early Childhood" [1807]

Ye blessed Creatures, I have heard the call
        Ye to each other make; I see
The heavens laugh with you in your jubilee;
        My heart is at your festival,
        My head hath its coronal,
The fulness of your bliss, I feel--I feel it all.
        Oh evil day! if I were sullen
        While Earth herself is adorning,
            This sweet May-morning,
        And the children are culling
            On every side,
        In a thousand valleys far and wide,
        Fresh flowers; while the sun shines warm,
And the Babe leaps up on his Mother's arm:--
        I hear, I hear, with joy I hear!
        --But there's a Tree, of many, one,
A single Field which I have looked upon,
Both of them speak of something that is gone:
        The Pansy at my feet
        Doth the same tale repeat:
Whither is fled the visionary gleam?
Where is it now, the glory and the dream?

Our birth is but a sleep and a forgetting:
The Soul that rises with us, our life's Star,
        Hath had elsewhere its setting,
        And cometh from afar:

Not in entire forgetfulness,
And not in utter nakedness,
But trailing clouds of glory do we come
From God, who is our home:
Heaven lies about us in our infancy!
Shades of the prison-house begin to close
    Upon the growing Boy,
But He beholds the light, and whence it flows,
    He sees it in his joy;
The Youth, who daily farther from the east
    Must travel, still is Nature's Priest,
    And by the vision splendid
    Is on his way attended;
At length the Man perceives it die away,
And fade into the light of common day....

And O, ye Fountains, Meadows, Hills, and Groves,
Forebode not any severings of our loves!
Yet in my heart of hearts I feel your might;
I only have relinquished one delight
To live beneath your more habitual sway.
I love the Brooks which down their channels fret,
Even more than when I tripped lightly as they;
The innocent brightness of a new-born Day
            Is lovely yet;
The Clouds that gather round the setting sun
Do take a sober colouring from an eye
That hath kept watch o'er man's mortality;
Another race hath been, and other palms are won.
Thanks to the human heart by which we live,
Thanks to its tenderness, its joys, and fears,
To me the meanest flower that blows can give
Thoughts that do often lie too deep for tears.

Percy Bysshe Shelley,
from *A Defense of Poetry* [1821]

Poetry is indeed something divine. It is at once the center and circumference of knowledge; it is that which comprehends all science, and that to which all science must be referred. It is at the same time the root and blossom of all other systems of thought; it is that from which all spring, and that which adorns all; and that which, if blighted, denies the fruit and the seed, and withholds from the barren world the nourishment and the succession of the scions of the tree of life. It is the perfect and consummate surface and bloom of all things; it is as the odor and the color of the rose to the texture of the elements which compose it, as the form and splendor of unfaded beauty to the secrets of anatomy and corruption. What were virtue, love, patriotism, friendship--what were the scenery of this beautiful universe which we inhabit; what were our consolations on this side of the grave, and what were our aspirations beyond it--if poetry did not ascend to bring light and fire from those eternal regions where the owl-winged faculty of calculation dare not ever soar?...

Poetry is the record of the best and happiest moments of the happiest and best minds. We are aware of evanescent visitations of thought and feeling, sometimes associated with place or person, sometimes regarding our own mind alone, and always arising unforeseen and departing unbidden, but elevating and delightful beyond all expression; so that even in the desire and the regret they leave, there cannot but be pleasure, participating as it does in the nature of its object. It is as it were the interpenetration of a diviner nature through our own; but its footsteps are like those of a wind over the sea, which the morning calm erases, and whose traces remain only as on the wrinkled sand which paves it....

Poetry turns all things to loveliness; it exalts the beauty of that which is most beautiful, and it adds beauty to that which is most deformed; it marries exultation and horror, grief and pleasure, eternity and change; it subdues to union under its light yoke all irreconcilable things. It transmutes all that it touches, and every form moving within the radiance of its presence is changed by wondrous sympathy to an incarnation of the spirit which it breathes; its secret alchemy turns to potable gold the poisonous waters which flow from death through life; it strips the veil of familiarity from the world, and lays bare the naked and sleeping beauty which is the spirit of its forms.

Shelley,
"Ozymandias" [1818]

I met a traveler from an antique land
Who said: Two vast and trunkless legs of stone
Stand in the desert .... Near them, on the sand,
Half sunk, a shattered visage lies, whose frown,
And wrinkled lip, and sneer of cold command,
Tell that its sculptor well those passions read
Which yet survive, stamped on these lifeless things,
The hand that mocked them, and the heart that fed:
And on the pedestal these words appear:
"My name is Ozymandias, king of kings:
Look on my works, ye Mighty, and despair!"
Nothing beside remains. Round the decay
Of that colossal wreck, boundless and bare
The lone and level sand stretches far away.

Edgar Allan Poe,
The Poetic Principle [1848]

We shall reach ... more immediately a distinct conception of what true poetry is, by mere reference to a few of the simple elements which induce in the poet himself the true poetical effect. He recognizes the ambrosia which nourishes his soul, in the bright orbs that shine in heaven--in the volutes of the flower--in the clustering of low shrubberies--in the waving of the grain fields --in the slanting of tall, eastern trees--in the blue distance of mountains--in the grouping of clouds--in the twinkling of half-hidden brooks--in the gleaming of silver rivers--in the repose of sequestered lakes --in the star-mirroring depths of lonely wells. He perceives it in the songs of birds--in the harp of Aeolus [a kind of wind-chime]--in the sighing of the night wind--in the repining voice of the forest--in the surf that complains to the shore--in the fresh breath of the woods--in the scent of the violet--in the voluptuous perfume of the hyacinth--in the suggestive odor that comes to him, at eventide, from far-distant undiscovered islands, over dim oceans, illimitable and unexplored. He owns it in all noble thoughts--in all unworldly motives--in all holy impulses--in all chivalrous, generous, and self-sacrificing deeds. He feels it in the beauty of woman--in the grace of her step--in the luster of her eye --in the melody of her voice--in her soft laughter--in her sigh--in the harmony of the rustling of her robes. He deeply feels it in her winning endearments--in her burning enthusiasms--in her gentle charities--in her meek and devotional endurances--but above all--ah, far above all--he kneels to it--he worships it in the faith, in the purity, in the strength, in the altogether divine majesty--of her *love*.

Poe,
"The Lake: To -----" [1845]

In the spring of youth it was my lot
To haunt of the wide world a spot
The which I could not love the less--
So lovely was the loneliness
Of a wild lake, with black rock bound,
And the tall pines that towered around.

But when the Night had thrown her pall
Upon that spot, as upon all,
And the mystic wind went by
Murmuring in melody--
Then--ah then I would awake
To the terror of the lone lake.

Yet the terror was not fright,
But a tremulous delight--
A feeling not the jewelled mine
Could teach or bribe me to define--
Nor Love--although the Love were thine.

Death was in that poisonous wave,
And in its gulf a fitting grave
For him who thence could solace bring
To his lone imagining--
Whose solitary soul could make
An Eden of that dim lake.

Keynes, Geoffrey, ed. *The Complete Writings of William Blake*. London: Oxford Univ. Press, 1966. Pp. 150-152. Wordsworth, William. *Selected Poems and Prefaces*. Ed. Jack Stillinger. Boston: Houghton Mifflin, 1965. Pp. 460-461, 187-188, 190-191. Allen, Gay Wilson, and Harry H. Clark, eds. *Literary Criticism: Pope to Croce*. 1941; rpt. Detroit: Wayne State Univ. Press, 1962. Pp. 311-313, 366. Abrams, M.H., et al., eds. *The Norton Anthology of English Literature*. Vol. 2. New York: Norton, 1962. Pp. 417-418. Mabbott, T.O., ed. *The Selected Poetry and Prose of Edgar Allan Poe*. New York: Random House, 1951. Pp. 11-12.

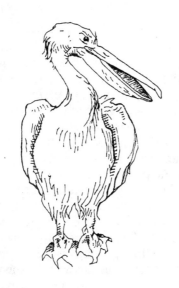

VIGNETTES FROM THE LIFE OF CHARLES DARWIN

Charles Darwin (1809-1882) was the most important natural scientist of modern times. His theories of natural selection and of the evolution of life have permanently altered the fields of botany and zoology and have profoundly influenced intellectual history to the present.

Darwin was born into a wealthy and highly cultured British family. He briefly studied medicine at the University of Edinburgh and later attended Cambridge University to study theology. However, in 1831, soon after graduating, he signed on as naturalist aboard the *HMS Beagle* for a five-year, round-the-world scientific expedition. In retrospect, Darwin called this journey "by far the most important event of my life, [one that] has determined my whole career." It gave him a golden opportunity to study at first hand a tremendous range of natural phenomena and plant and animal life in such remote places as Tierra del Fuego at the southern tip of South America, and the Galapagos Islands off the coast of Ecuador. His painstaking observations not only provided a factual basis for much of his later theoretical work, but also fixed procedural methods essential to his success as a scientist and writer.

Darwin's famous book *On the Origin of the Species* (1859) revolutionized scientific opinion regarding the mutability of species and the logic of possible connections among similar species. Drawing on the demographic theories that the British economist Thomas Malthus expounded in *An Essay on the Principle of Population* (1798), Darwin devised his pioneering theory of evolution through natural selection. He showed members of a given species compete in a the never-ending struggle for survival. The stronger, successful individuals live to procreate and pass on their traits through heredity to their progeny. Darwin's book titled *The Descent of Man* (1871) discussed the descent of modern humans from primates; it caused a furor among theologians and religious leaders, by seeming to disprove the doctrine of divine creation.

In the passages that follow, from his memoir written near the end of his life, Darwin describes the circumstances of his voyage on the *Beagle* and assesses the intellectual traits that shaped his career.

QUESTIONS:

1) What aspects of his personality does Darwin identify as contributing to his success as a scientist?
2) Why does Darwin call the voyage of the *Beagle* "the most important event of my life"?
3) What motives did Darwin have in undertaking scientific work?

On returning home from my short geological tour in North Wales, I found a letter from [naturalist, John Stevens] Henslow, informing me that Captain Fitz-Roy was willing to give up part of his own cabin to any young man who would volunteer to go with him without pay as naturalist to the Voyage of the *Beagle*.... I was instantly eager to accept the offer, but my father strongly objected, adding the words, fortunate for me, "If you can find any man of common sense who advises you to go I will give my consent." So I wrote that evening and refused the offer. On the next morning I went to Maer to be ready for September 1st, and, while out shooting, my uncle sent for me, offering to drive me over to Shrewsbury and talk with my father, as my uncle thought it would be wise in me to accept the offer. My father always maintained that he was one of the most sensible men in the world, and he at once consented in the kindest manner. I had been rather extravagant at Cambridge, and to console my father, said, "that I should be deuced clever to spend more than my allowance whilst on board the *Beagle*"; but he answered with a smile, "But they tell me you are very clever."

Next day I started for Cambridge to see Henslow, and thence to London to see Fitz-Roy, and all was soon arranged. Afterwards, on becoming very intimate with Fitz-Roy, I heard that I had run a very narrow risk of being rejected, on account of the shape of my nose! He was an ardent disciple of Lavater, and was convinced that he could judge of a man's character by the outline of his features; and he doubted whether any one with my nose could possess sufficient energy and determination for the voyage. But I think he was afterwards well satisfied that my nose had spoken falsely.

Fitz-Roy's character was a singular one, with very man noble features: he was devoted to his duty, generous to a fault, bold, determined, and indomitably energetic, and an ardent friend to all under his sway. He would undertake any sort of trouble to assist those whom he thought deserved assistance. He was a handsome man, strikingly like a gentleman, with highly courteous manners, which resembled those of his maternal uncle, the famous Lord Castlereagh, as I was told by the Minister at Rio....

Fitz-Roy's temper was a most unfortunate one. It was usually worst in the early morning, and with his eagle eye he could usually detect something amiss about the ship, and was then unsparing in his blame. He was very kind to me, but was a man very difficult to live with on the intimate terms which necessarily followed from our messing by ourselves in the same cabin. We had several quarrels; for instance, early in the voyage at Bahia, in Brazil, he defended and praised slavery, which I abominated, and told me that he had just visited a great slave-owner, who had called up many of his slaves and asked them whether they were happy, and whether they wished to be free, and all answered "No." I then asked him, perhaps with a sneer, whether he thought that the answer of slaves in the presence of their master was worth anything? This made him excessively angry, and he said that as I doubted his word we could not live any longer together. I thought that I should have been compelled to leave the ship; but as soon as the news spread, which it did quickly, as the captain sent for the first lieutenant to assuage his anger by abusing me, I was deeply gratified by receiving an invitation from all the gun-room officers to mess with them. But after a few hours Fitz-Roy showed his usual magnanimity by sending an officer to me with an apology and a request that I would continue to live with him. His character was in several respects one of the most noble which I have ever known.

The voyage of the *Beagle* has been by far the most important event of my life, and has determined my whole career; yet it depended on so small a circumstance as my uncle offering to drive me thirty miles to Shrewsbury, which few uncles would have done, and on such a trifle as the shape of my nose. I have always felt that I owe to the voyage the first real training or education of my mind; I was led to attend closely to several branches of natural history, and thus my powers of observation were improved, though they were always fairly developed.

The investigation of the geology of all the places visited was far more important, as reasoning here comes into play. On first examining a new district nothing can appear more hopeless than the chaos of rocks; but by recording the stratification and nature of the rocks and fossils at many points, always reasoning and predicting what will be found elsewhere, light soon begins to dawn on the district, and the structure of the whole becomes more or less intelligible.... .

Another of my occupations was collecting animals of all classes, briefly describing and roughly dissecting many of the marine ones; but from not being able to draw, and from not having sufficient anatomical knowledge, a great pile of [manuscripts] which I made during the voyage has proved almost useless. I thus lost much time, with the exception of that spent in acquiring some knowledge of the Crustaceans, as this was of service when in after years I undertook a monograph of the Cirripedia [barnacles and like organisms].

During some part of the day I wrote my Journal, and took much pains in describing carefully and vividly all that I had seen; and this was good practice. My Journal served also, in part, as letters to my home, and portions were sent to England whenever there was an opportunity.

The above various special studies were, however, of no importance compared with the habit of energetic industry and of concentrated attention to whatever I was engaged in, which I then acquired. Everything about which I thought or read was made to bear directly on what I had seen or was likely to see; and this habit of mind was continued during the five years of the voyage. I feel sure that it was this training which has enabled me to do whatever I have done in science.

Looking backwards, I can now perceive how my love for science gradually preponderated over every other taste. During the first two years my old passion for shooting survived in nearly full force, and I shoot myself all the birds and animals for my collection; but gradually I gave up my gun more and more, and finally altogether, to my servant, as shooting interfered with my work, more especially with making out the geological structure of a country. I discovered, though unconsciously and insensibly, that the pleasure of observing and reasoning was a much higher one than that of skill and sport. That my mind became developed through my pursuits during the voyage is rendered probable by a remark made by my father, who was the most acute observer whom I ever saw, of a sceptical disposition, and far from being a believer in phrenology; for on first seeing me

after the voyage, he turned round to my sisters, and exclaimed, "Why, the shape of his head is quite altered."

To return to the voyage. On September 11th (1831), I paid a flying visit with Fitz-Roy to the *Beagle* at Plymouth. Thence to Shrewsbury to wish my father and sisters a long farewell. On October 24th I took up my residence at Plymouth, and remained there until December 27th, when the *Beagle* finally left the shores of England for her circumnavigation of the world. We made two earlier attempts to sail, but were driven back each time by heavy gales. These two months at Plymouth were the most miserable which I ever spent, though I exerted myself in various ways. I was out of spirits at the thought of leaving all my family and friends for so long a time, and the weather seemed to me inexpressibly gloomy. I was also troubled with palpitation and pain about the heart, and like many a young man, especially one with a smattering of medical knowledge, was convinced that I had heart disease. I did not consult any doctor, as I fully expected to hear the verdict that I was not fit for the voyage, and I resolved to go at all hazards....

The glories of the vegetation of the Tropics rise before my mind at the present time more vividly than anything else; though the sense of sublimity, which the great deserts of Patagonia and the forest-clad mountains of Tierra del Fuego excited in me, has left an indelible impression on my mind. The sight of a naked savage in his native land is an event which can never be forgotten. Many of my excursions on horseback through wild countries, or in the boats, some of which lasted several weeks, were deeply interesting: their discomfort and some degree of danger were at that time hardly a drawback, and none at all afterwards. I also reflect with high satisfaction on some of my scientific work, such as solving the problem of coral islands, and making out the geological structure of certain islands, for instance, St. Helena. Nor must I pass over the discovery of the singular relations of the animals and plants inhabiting the several islands of the Galapagos archipelago, and of all of them to the inhabitants of South America.

As far as I can judge of myself, I worked to the utmost during the voyage from the mere pleasure of investigation, and from my strong desire to add a few facts to the great mass of facts in Natural Science. But I was also ambitious to take a fair place among scientific men,--whether more ambitious or less so than most of my fellow-workers, I can form no opinion.

The geology of St. Jago is very striking, yet simple: a stream of lava formerly flowed over the bed of the sea, formed of triturated [pulverized] recent shells and corals, which it has baked into a hard white rock. Since then the whole island has been upheaved. But the line of white rock revealed to me a new and important fact, namely, that there had been afterwards subsidence round the craters, which had since been in action, and had poured forth lava. It then first dawned on me that I might perhaps write a book on the geology of the various countries visited, and this made me thrill with delight. That was a memorable hour to me, and how distinctly I can call to mind the low cliff of lava beneath which I rested, with the sun glaring hot, a few strange desert plants growing near, and with living corals in the tidal pools at my feet. Later in the voyage, Fitz-Roy asked me to read some of my Journal, and declared it would be worth publishing; so here was a second book in prospect!

Towards the close of our voyage I received a letter whilst at Ascension, in which my sisters told me that [geologist, Adam] Sedgwick had called on my father, and said that I should take a place among the leading scientific men. I could not at the time understand how he could have learnt anything of my proceedings, but I heard (I believe afterwards) that Henslow had read some of the letters which I wrote to him before the Philosophical Society of Cambridge, and had printed them for private distribution. My collection of fossil bones, which had been sent to Henslow, also excited considerable attention among palaeontologists. After reading this letter, I clambered over the mountains of Ascension with a bounding step, and made the volcanic rocks resound under my geological hammer. All this shows how ambitious I was; but I think that I can say with truth that in after years, though I cared in the highest degree for the approbation of such men as [geologist, Sir Charles] Lyell and [Joseph] Hooker, who were my friends, I did not care much about the general public. I do not mean to say that a favorable review or a large sale of my books did not please me greatly, but the pleasure was a fleeting one, and I am sure that I have never turned one inch out of my course to gain fame....

My books have sold largely in England, have been translated into many languages, and passed through several editions in foreign countries. I have heard it said that the success of a work abroad is the best test of its enduring value. I doubt whether this is at all trustworthy; but judge by this standard my name ought to last for a few years. Therefore it may be worthwhile to try to analyze the mental qualities and the conditions on which my success has depended; though I am aware that no man can do this correctly.

I have no great quickness of apprehension or wit which is so remarkable in some clever men, for instance, [biologist, Thomas Henry] Huxley. I am therefore a poor critic: a paper or book, when first read, generally excites my admiration, and it is only after considerable reflection that I perceive the weak points. My power to follow a long and purely abstract train of thought is very limited; and therefore I could never have succeeded with metaphysics or mathematics. My memory is extensive, yet hazy: it suffices to make me cautious by vaguely telling me that I have observed or read something opposed to the conclusion which I am drawing, or on the other hand in favor of it; and after a time I can generally recollect where to search for my authority. So poor in one sense is my memory, that I have never been able to remember for more than a few days a single date or a line of poetry.

Some of my critics have said, "Oh, he is a good observer, but he has no power of reasoning!" I do not think that this can be true, for the *Origin of the Species* is one long argument from the beginning to the end, and it has convinced not a few able men. No one could have written it without having some power of reasoning. I have a fair share of invention, and of common sense or judgment, such as every fairly successful lawyer or doctor must have, but not, I believe, in any higher degree.

On the more favourable side of the balance, I think that I am superior to the common run of men in noticing things which easily escape attention, and in observing them carefully. My industry has been nearly as great as it could have been in the observation and collection of facts.

What is far more important, my love of natural science has been steady and ardent....

My habits are methodical, and this has been of not a little use for my particular line of work. Lastly, I have had ample leisure from not having to earn my own bread. Even ill-health, though it has annihilated several years of my life, has saved me from the distractions of society and amusement.

Therefore my success as a man of science, whatever this may have amounted to, has been determined, as far as I can judge, by complex and diversified mental qualities and conditions. Of these, the most important have been--the love of science--unbounded patience in long reflecting over any subject--industry in observing and collecting facts--and a fair share of invention as well as of common sense. With such moderate abilities as I possess, it is truly surprising that I should have influenced to a considerable extent the belief of scientific men on some important points.

Darwin, Francis, ed. *The Life and Letters of Charles Darwin*. New York: Appleton, 1887. Vol. 1. Pp. 49-55, 82-83, 85-86.

DAVID LIVINGSTONE: MISSIONARY AND AFRICAN EXPLORER

▶ **19th-Century African Wood Sculpture of a Christian Missionary**

Although Europeans had been trading along the coast of Africa for many centuries, little was known about the continent's interior until mid-nineteenth century. David Livingstone (1813-1873), an Englishman, was the best known and one of the most intrepid explorers of Africa. From age ten to twenty-four he worked in a cotton mill in Lancashire, England. Then he studied medicine and became a doctor, was ordained a minister, and in 1841 sailed for southern Africa as a missionary. However, it was as an explorer that Livingstone made his mark in the world. Between 1853 and 1856 he explored the interior of southern Africa between the Atlantic and Indian Oceans, mapping the Zambezi River and discovering Victoria Falls. His *African Journal* published after his return to Britain in 1857, received wide recognition because of its vast and accurate information about the geography, products, and peoples of the lands Livingstone had explored. His maps were recognized as great contributions to cartography. Livingstone later made other journeys, to Lake Nyasa, up the Congo River, among other destinations. In 1871, while exploring the possible source of the Nile River, he was "found" by Henry Stanley, who had been sent to look for him by the *New York Herald*. Stanley's question: "Dr. Livingstone, I presume?" has immortalized their encounter.

Livingstone's interests in exploration were scientific, religious, commercial, and humanitarian. He gathered information on continued slaving in Africa by Arabs and Portuguese so as to end its depredations. Great Britain had led the world in abolishing slave trade in 1807 and slavery in the British Empire in 1837. Since the British fleet ruled the seas, Britain's abolition of slave trade in effect ended it in all western nations. Livingstone's discoveries not only added significantly to knowledge about Africa but also spurred European nations to imperialistic expansion there. As a result, most of Africa was partitioned by European powers during the last quarter of the nineteenth century.

The reading that follows shows Livingstone's interest in furthering all four of his goals. The section on slavery is taken from a letter written in 1854 to his brother Charles, then living in Boston; the remainder comes from his *African Journal*.

QUESTIONS:

1) What caused the price of slaves to drop, with what results for slaves?
2) What did the Africans sell to Europeans and what European products did they value?
3) What were some of the dangers and problems Livingstone faced? How did he get along with Africans he met?

Indeed in 1837, or just before the treaty for slave trade suppression with Portugal came into operation, Mr. Gabriel counted 39 ships in Loanda harbour, all waiting for cargoes of slaves. At present no ship dare appear on the coast with slave fittings except to make a dash into some one or two harbours, load hastily by night, and put to sea the next morning.

But to return to the slaves of the time when there were no British cruizers on the coast. All that came down were sold and exported, and as they cannot now export them neither can they buy them....

Again, before the English squadron began its operations the prices of good young slaves throughout the country near the coast, or say within 200 miles of the coast line, varied from 70 to 80 dollars per head (as they say). Now the very best may be had for from 10 to 20. If the reason is asked, it invariably is, "Because we cannot not export them." ... Slaves are very cheap now in Angola, and that is clearly the effect of the intervention of an armed force. They are said to be dear in proportion in Cuba and Brazil. As soon as a trader gets his ten dollars a head cargo clear off the African coast, does he value them at that, or at the 150 or 200 dollars he expects to get in Cuba? Clearly to my mind ... the most powerful motive he knows comes into play to make him lessen the horrors of the middle passage. Though he regards them as beasts, it is well known all over the world that the most brutal being alive will be more likely to treat well a horse worth 200 pounds than if it were worth ten pounds only.

* * * * *

Tuesday 27th Decr. '53.... The water of the Leeba is black, coming by the Kabompo or main stream is discoloured brownish-yellow. It contains sand the grains of which can be distinguished in it easily, and when a cupful of it stands a few minutes a considerable quantity of sand is deposited at the bottom. The banks are constantly falling in, large portions being detached constantly as we pass. The Leeambye seems to be wearing for itself a deeper and wider channel in this quarter, and will probably at some future time send all its water down the Borotse valley, the Bashukulompo river being left dry. The current of the Leeambye is very rapid. The

Leeba flows placidly here {all are tributaries of the Zambezi River}....

Friday 30th Decr. 1853. The river Leeba is very beautiful. It winds placidly through most lovely meadows, each of which has either a sedgy soft bottom or large pond or trickling rill in its centre. The trees, covered with a profusion of the freshest foliage, are planted in groups of such pleasant graceful outline art could add no additional charm. The grass at present is short and green, and the scenery is that of a carefully-tended gentleman's park, but there is so much of it one is reminded of being in uncultivated regions. The parts covered with trees are of every variety of shape and size, and I suspect the beautiful meadows are at certain seasons flooded by the river, for shells are seen scattered on the ground. The tree covered parts, too, are raised about four feet above the level of the meadows, and are generally of soft sandy soil, while the lower grounds are of black alluvial ground. Miles of forest are common, and the trees are so thickly planted one can with difficulty proceed in anything like a straight line. The rays of the sun do not reach the ground except in the form of mild diffused light, yet there is quite a crop of young trees springing up in order to fill the places of any of their predecessors which may decay....

Shot a motbolo or smaller waterbuck ... yet [it] ran off ... took to the river and swam nearly across, when an alligator got on its hind quarters, and though my boatman called out, "O, don't take our meat, O, don't take our meat," as it reached the shore pulled it under water....

Sat. 31st. The party of Sekilenke ferried themselves over and defiled past our camp, bearing large quantities of dried elephant's flesh. They were 94 in number, and most of them came and visited us....

All the men who have visited us are strongly built and black. All are of the Borotse family, but have very large masses of hair on their heads and are excessively found of butter for their heads. A pot of fat if from the meat or milk of cattle is an acceptable present to a chief. All were armed with large bows and arrows headed with iron. They kill much game, and have many dogs with which to kill elephants. The tusks are carefully kept for the traders who come up the Makondo.

How wonderful is commerce. The prints [of cotton cloth] of Manchester are by means of it brought to the centre of Africa, and seem so wonderful it is with difficulty I can persuade the people they are indeed the works of mortal hands. The Mambari told the Makololo, when questioned as to the origins of the prints so curiously written upon, that they came out of the sea. Beads are believed collected on its shore. It is now the same with these Africans and the fairy fabrications of cotton mills as it was with our ancestors and the silken robes of the East.... I hope commerce will do something more for this degraded land than she has hitherto done. God grant that the slave trade may cease. The internal evils of Africa can be remedied by the gospel alone. May the privilege be granted to me to plant it in this region....

Sunday 1st January 1854.... One of the Balonda hunted a motloba yesterday, and chased it through the river close to our encampment.... He is a rather talkative person, and brought his wives to see us. One apparently the mother of one, anxiously enquired after her daughter, who had been taken captive by a party of Makololo last year. We could give no information.

Unless these forays are put an end to, it seems impossible that the Basutu can prosper. The chief is wanting in energy, and destroys himself by smoking wild hemp. All his companions follow his example.... I have never seen a wild-hemp smoker attain old age. The principal men of the Makololo fear each other, and some are feared by the chief.

10th June '55.... A most eligible site for a commercial and missionary settlement would be the right bank of the Leeba near the confluence with the Leeambye, or, more easterly, the confluence of the Kabompo with the Leeambye as it comes from the north. It is a considerable river on the eastern side of Mataimvo, and as it flows south receives the river of the Babiza, then parts with the large branch Loenge or Bashukulompo, which again joins it near Tete. There would [be] water carriage over extensive territories, and ultimately the result would be glorious for Africa. I pray God that the good men and true of our benevolent England may be inclined to look to this desirable point. It surely is of as great importance as any in the Niger. There is fever, it is true, and I find it fatal even among natives, but there are few other diseases....

The fever generally puts on an intermittent, or the safest, form. I have had [it] 27 times, and I attribute the frequency in my attacks to the hardships it was necessary to undergo in exploration. Few could remain month after month sleeping on the ground and fed only on the manioc roots or meal nearly pure starch, which affects the eyesight if no animal food can be obtained, or a meal made from fine bird-seed, which is better than the other but cannot be compared to wheaten or oaten meal. In some part of the country we could get nothing but the manioc and ground nuts. Few could bear this and frequent wettings without suffering in health. My experience is therefore no criterion by which to judge of what others, better provided, might suffer or bear....

{On discovering Victoria Falls} 21st November 1855.... On the day following we went down to see the falls of Mosioatunya or, as it was called anciently, Shungue. After 20 minutes sail we viewed for the first time the vapour or, as it is appropriately called, "smoke," arising exactly as when large tracts of grass are burned off. Five columns rose and bended in the direction of the wind against a low ridge covered with trees, and seemed at this distance (about 6 miles) to mingle with the clouds. They were coloured white below and higher up became dark, probably as the vapour condensed and returned in showers.

Having got small and very light canoes farther down, we went in the care of persons well acquainted with the rapids, and sailed swiftly down to an island situated at the middle and on the northern verge of the precipice over which the water roars. At one time we seemed to be going right to the gulph, but though I felt a little tremour I said nothing, believing I could face a difficulty as well as my guides.

The falls are singularly formed. They are simply the whole mass of the Zambesi waters rushing into a fissure or rent made right across the bed of the river. In other falls we have usually a great change of level both in the bed of the river and adjacent country, and after the leap the river is not much different from what it was above the falls; but here the river, flowing rapidly among numerous islands and from 800 to

1,000 yards wide, meets a rent in its bed at least 100 feet deep and at right angles with its course, or nearly due east and west, leaps into it, and becomes a boiling white mass at the bottom ten or twelve yards broad. Its course is changed also. It runs, or rather rolls and wriggles, from east to west until it reaches what above was its left bank then turns a corner, and follows or rather is guided by the fissure away in its usual route of S.E. and by E....

Returning with Sekeletu on the following day, I planted a lot of peach and apricot stones and coffee seeds on the island, which being already covered with trees seemed well adapted to be a nursery. The spot selected for experiment was one which is visited with a fine sprinkling of the condensed vapour many times daily.... We gave directions for the construction of a fence to prevent the hippopotami from treading down our seedlings, and as this climate requires tender plants to be frequently moistened I have no doubt but Mosioatunya will prove a more careful nurseryman than any of the Makololo would be.

The chiefs Sekote, Mokuine, and Licuane, appropriated the three larger falls as places at which they prayed to the gods or departed spirits. The roar of the waters were well fitted to inspire feelings of awe. Sekote was a Batonga chief, and he and Licuane enjoyed despotic sway over the fords of the river. On Kalai, as Sekote's island was called, we saw the grave of his father surrounded by 70 large elephants' tusks stuck in the ground, the points turned inwards. About 30 others were placed as sort of grave stones over the members of his family. They think, in cases of sickness, that the departed are angry with them for not offering food etc etc. There were fifteen skulls placed on poles, of persons who had been executed, and a pot which when opened they believed would inflict death on those they hated....

2d February 1856. We came a few hours on foot to Mosusa's village at Chowe R., which is a brackish stream affording salt to the inhabitants in its sand. It is about 100 yards broad, and only occasionally flows. We were detained all the rest of the day by continuous rains, which now curiously enough come from the west.... The rich reddish-brown soil is so clammy it is very difficult to walk, but my riding oxen are all dead, and we have no canoe. New shoes don't improve matters.

The people cultivate amazing quantities of corn {grain} and maize, earth nuts and pumpkins, also cucumbers. When the plants fail in one spot they transplant others into it. {They} Build high stages with huts on them as watch houses in the gardens. This is necessary both on account of the spotted hyaena, which is here very fierce, but also as a protection against elephants. Mozinkua had his upper lip bitten off by a hyaena, so his teeth are bare.

I must express my admiration of the great liberality of these people to mine. They go into their villages and rarely return without some corn or maize. Some dance, and one, a natural bard, sings and jingles his bells, and never in vain. The real politeness with which presents of food are given through nearly all the tribes makes it easy to accept the gifts. Suppose an ox is presented: "Here is a little bread" is the phrase employed, or it is whispered to my principal man to say for them. When meal is given, an apology is invariably made about its smallness, or regret expressed that they had not notice of our approach in time to grind more. And so all the way down the river. All readily accept of our excuse of coming from a land where there are no goods for sale, saying they are perfectly aware of the fact.

I always give a good present when I have it in my power, something really useful and its usefulness known, for the honour of old England....

It is as much the law from time immemorial for the chief to feed all strangers as it is among the Arabs. It is one of the arguments for polygamy they employ. A man with one wife only could not feed strangers. The present given is by way of compensation.... But for this aboriginal law I could never have come thus far. I intend, if spared and able, to repay all my friends abundantly. Although I have now nothing to give, I never pass a chief knowingly. He is gratified by my politeness, and so are my people by his generosity.

Livingstone, David. *Family Letters, 1841-1856.* Vol. 2: 1849-1856. Ed. I. Schapera. London: Chatto and Windus, 1959. Pp. 252-254. Livingstone, David. *African Journal: 1853-1856.* Ed. I. Schapera. London:

Chatto and Windus, 1963. Vol. 1: pp. 27-29, 32, 34.
Vol. 2: pp. 256-257, 328, 386-387.

N.b. [...] indicates insertion by I. Schapera; {...} indicates
insertion by Jiu-Hwa Lo Upshur.

CHINESE WOMEN SEEK EQUALITY

Modernization is a difficult and complex process. China's attempts to modernize in the nineteenth and twentieth centuries typifies that of many Asian and African societies. China's military defeats by Great Britain and other Western nations from 1840 onward, and the resultant territorial losses and forced opening to Western trade on unequal terms awakened its leaders to the need to change ancient traditions and institutions in order to survive as an independent nation.

Political and institutional change came in stages, and its advocates met determined resistance at every step. Thus in the nineteenth century, China sought to adopt Western military technology and industries, and made piecemeal changes in its government, but with limited success. At the beginning of the twentieth century a Western educated doctor, Sun Yat-sen, advocated the replacement of the two-thousand year old imperial government by a democratic and republican one in which citizens had political rights and responsibilities similar to those enjoyed by citizens in Western nations. He also proposed social and economic reforms. China became Asia's first republic as a result of a revolution Sun led in 1911.

Contact with the West also spread a grass roots demand for change by the people. By the late nineteenth century, young Chinese were going to study in Europe, the United States, and Japan and schools were opening in China modeled on those in Western nations. An important part of modernization was a drive for the emancipation of women, symbolized by the "natural foot movement." Beginning about the eleventh century young upper class girls had their feet bound to ensure small size, a sign of beauty. Later, footbinding spread to middle-class girls (peasant girls rarely had their feet bound, for obvious reasons) and the smallness of a woman's feet became a status symbol also. In the seventeenth century, the newly established Ch'ing government had sought in vain to stop footbinding. Beginning in late nineteenth century, in large part because of Western influence, many Chinese began to deplore the practice of footbinding and other practices that restricted the role of women.

Educational and professional opportunities for women were another goal of the women's movement. Although daughters of educated families were frequently well educated and China produced many women writers and artists, girls did not attend schools, and their education was mainly intended to make them good wives and mothers. While many boys too had to fight hard for permission to enter modern schools, girls had a still harder struggle. As the following reading shows, many men and boys helped girls obtain an education.

The first girls' schools were opened in mid-nineteenth century by American missionaries and initially they met with opposition. Christian missionaries advocated a higher position for women and also spoke out against footbinding. By the late nineteenth century many Chinese men and women were also convinced of the need to end footbinding and of the need for social and educational reforms to give women greater independence and more significant role in life.

Other goals of the women's emancipation movement included the ending of concubinage (the taking of secondary wives by wealthy men), equal inheritance rights of sons and daughters, and equal political and legal rights for men and women. In the twentieth century, most of the goals were implemented in legislation. Young men and women also fought for the right to determine their own lives and destinies. They rebelled against the traditional marriages which well-intentioned parents arranged, but generally without consulting the young people concerned.

This reading is taken from the autobiography of a pioneering modern woman, Mao Yen-wen (b. 1898) and deals with her rebellion against both foot-binding and an arranged marriage. She went on to receive an advanced education, including graduate studies at the University of Michigan. She has enjoyed a long and distinguished career as an educator, philanthropist, and public servant.

QUESTIONS:

1) In what three areas did the author rebel against tradition?
2) How was education spread to girls in early twentieth century China?
3) What is an arranged marriage and why did Mao Yen-wen rebel against it?

When the Revolution that overthrew the Manchus and established the Republic began in 1911, all schools across the country were closed. Male students from Chiangshan [the author's home town] who were studying in Hangchow, Peking, and other cities thus returned home.... These young men with their new knowledge and ideas learned from the large cities were concerned that our county had no girls' school and began to consult about opening one. But they had no money, buildings or facilities. Fortunately our clan, the Maos, which was wealthy locally, owned a number of buildings and other property in Chiangsan, the county capital. Thus Mao Chien [one of the returning male students] led a delegation of his peers and negotiated with the elders of the Mao clan who agreed to loan some vacant clan buildings and gave other assistance to open a girls' school. It was named the Hsiho Girls School. All the male students became its teachers and Mao Chien was named principal. Twenty-odd girls enrolled, I was one. Early in the second year of the Republic [1913] all schools reopened, and our male teachers returned to resume their own studies, but our school continued to operate with Mrs. Chu (an aunt) as principal.

This was neither an elementary nor a secondary school, and had no accreditation; we were taught whatever our teachers could teach

us. The subjects we studied were Chinese literature, arithmetic, geography, history, physical education, singing, needlework, etc. Most of us students had previously studied at home under tutors ... and had some foundation in Chinese classical literature. For this reason the school emphasized Chinese literature, and we studied the *Analects* [of Confucius], *Mencius*, *Book of Poetry*, etc....

A major goal of the Republican government was to increase literacy among the people; thus all county governments hurried to open elementary schools. Provincial departments of education worked to provide needed teachers. In our province (Chekiang) the Department of Education ordered the Hangchow Girls Normal School [school to train teachers] to add two special classes, each lasting two years, to train additional teachers. Each county was ordered to select a girl student, aged between 20 and 25, to attend the training class on full scholarship. Upon graduation they would return to their home counties and pursue an elementary teaching career. I was lucky to be chosen, falsifying my age as twenty, although I was not yet sixteen.

Two factors account for my being chosen: one was my adequate educational background. The other was my participation in the "natural foot movement." In the spring of the second year of the Republic [1913] the natural foot movement gained momentum in our county, and a public meeting was planned to take place at the Temple of the City God to publicize it. Mr Hsu Kuang-kuo ... had written a speech and coached me to deliver it at the meeting. I spent several days memorizing the speech until both Mr. Hsu and I were satisfied that I could do it credit. When the day came the Temple was crammed full of people; County Magistrate Yao Yin-t'ai, other members of the government and local leaders filled the stage seated in a row. I was so frightened by the size of the crowd that when my turn came to ascend the stage and give my speech I could not remember a word of what I had memorized. All I could do was make a bow to each the assembled dignitaries and the audience and say "Today we are at the meeting to promote the Natural Foot Movement." Then I remembered that I had prepared to make a donation of one silver dollar [the Chinese dollar was called a *yuan*] to the Natural Foot Movement Foundation. So I quickly got out my money from a pocket, put it on the podium, and concluded by saying: "I thereby open the fund drive by donating one dollar." I then bowed and walked off the stage. Magistrate Yao asked the man seated next to him: "Whose daughter is this little girl? Even though she forgot her speech she didn't burst into tears and had enough sense to make a graceful exit. She is an intelligent girl." Thus Magistrate Yao formed a good impression of me.... So when it came time for him to make a recommendation of a scholarship student for the Normal School, I was chosen.

My winning a scholarship to the Girls Normal School in Hangchow was a big event in those days. Huichowfu found no qualified student, nor did several other counties, and everybody thought those places lost face to Chiangsan.... From now on all counties competed to find qualified girls to send to Hangchow to receive an education; many from my county were to be sent in the following years. This was a good trend in women's education....

The special classes we attended were established expressly to prepare elementary teachers, so all subjects of study were chosen to fulfill this goal. Upon graduation the students were only able to teach elementary grades; they were not adequately prepared to enter universities. My goal was to go to university, so

I did not return to Chiangsan to teach in an elementary school when I graduated. Instead I taught for a year at the county school at Yunkan. I then went to Wuhsing and entered the Wuchun Girls School [which taught a college preparatory curriculum].

* * * * *

My father became good friends with a business associate Mr. Fang Yao-t'ang of Huichow. When I was eight or nine, Mr. Fang stayed with my family on a visit and liked me very much. Fang had two sons, both slightly older than I, so he broached the subject of marriage with father. Father stalled him for a while citing my youth, but broke down at Mr. Fang's persistent entreaties. He chose one of the boys, named Fang Kuo-tung. My mother opposed the match, because the Fangs lived too far away, she did not know much about the family, and, she had not met the boy. Father and Mother had a big fight over the proposed match, but Mother had to give in when Father asserted his prerogative as head of the family. So the marriage was fixed. I was too young to understand that the engagement affected me and thought it was something concerning my parents.

At Hsiho Girls School I learned a lot of new ideas from my young teachers. One of them was not to accept a marriage arranged by parents....

[Later] At the end of the first term of my second year [at the Hangchow Girls Normal School], Father came from Chiangsan especially to Hangchow to take me home. [the trip took two weeks, longer than anticipated because they were traveling up river when water level was very low].... As we entered our front door Mother burst into tears. I then learned why Father had come to school to fetch me; it was because the Fangs were anxious over my going to school in Hangchow and demanded that the marriage take place immediately. Unknown to me, they had fixed the wedding date and Father had intended to deliver me to my husband's family for the wedding. However because the boat was delayed we had missed the wedding date, which had to be rescheduled.... Father used threats and persuasion to gain my consent.... Mother just cried, and the family was in an uproar. On the rescheduled wedding date, my family provided a feast and our house was crowded with guests. The wedding sedan chair sent by the groom's family arrived at the city gate at about ten o'clock in the morning. Mother had sent people to meet them, and to tell the groom's party: "Please wait here because the Mao family are trying to fix a lucky hour for your arrival at their house."

Being young and willful I paid no attention to the wedding festivities; in fact I felt proud of myself as I prepared to fight Father to the end, and foresaw victory in my revolution against my traditional family. After the wedding luncheon Father retired to take his customary nap. Mother then called me, uncle [her brother], and cousin Ping-chuan to her room. [They decided that the only solution to the impasse was for the bride to flee].... So Mother gave me twelve silver dollars, and I slipped out with Ping-chia [another cousin, to a pre-arranged refuge and then to stay with her mother's relatives].

Father was furious when he woke up and found out that I was gone; Mother on the other hand cried and raised a big fuss, blaming Father for my probable suicide. Father sent a messenger to Magistrate Yao to request that he order the closing of the city gates and that he mobilize the police to search for me. When the groom's party heard that the bride had fled they nevertheless carried the wedding sedan chair into my house in protest. All Father's efforts to find me failed and pandemonium prevailed at home. News that a bride had fled at her wedding spread far and wide, causing a major sensation for that era!...

Magistrate Yao [who had formed a good impression of the author several years earlier at the Natural Foot Movement meeting] came to my help over this. [Earlier] Mao Chang, a community leader, had already informed Magistrate Yao about how he and

several young people intended to help me oppose my arranged marriage, and had also sought his help in this matter. Thus Magistrate Yao never complied with Father's request to close the city gates [for the search]. Later when father went to consult him [over a settlement with the groom's family] he had advised Father to negotiate the abrogation of the marriage contract with the groom's family, and offered his good offices as mediator. Father had no option but to accept Yao's suggestions....

Although the marriage contract was nullified, most people in Chiangsan regarded this affair as setting a bad precedent. Rumours abounded. Most people argued that girls should not be sent to foreign schools (new style schools were commonly called foreign schools).... People pointed at me when I went out, which was very embarrassing. Soon news of this affair spread throughout the province, and a novel was even written about it, titled *Miss Mao Flees Her Wedding*.... At the end of the summer I wanted to return to school, but was afraid to return home to face Father, who was still angry with me. Luckily, Uncle [with whose family she had been staying] agreed to accompany me home. Upon entering the house I called out "Daddy"; although he refused to answer, still he did not scold me. Mother on the other hand burst into tears, saying: "Yueh-hsien [author's pet name], we have lost such face, and its all on your account." Thus ended the unfortunate episode of my arranged marriage. Everything returned to normal, as a sunny day after a storm. Father and Mother loved me and cared for me as before.... I returned to school without a hitch. This was my second and last year at the Girls Normal School.

Mao, Yen-wen. *Wang Shih*. Taipei: Yun Yu Publishing [privately printed], 1989. Pp. 4-12. Translation by Jiu-Hwa Lo Upshur.

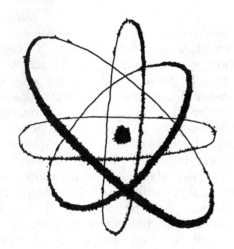

MADAME CURIE, ON AN EVENING OF "GLOWWORMS AND MAGIC"

Marja Sklodowska (better known as Marie Curie) was born in Warsaw, Poland in 1867. Her father, a high school physics teacher, gave her lessons in science. The family moved to Paris, and Marie took her degree at the Sorbonne in 1893, placing first in the physics examination. In 1894, she met Pierre Curie, a professor of physics and chemistry, and they married in 1895.

Madame Curie's professional career was devoted to the study of radiation. The Curies' research focused on the radiations emitted by . Observing that the radiation from pitchblend, a uranium-containing ore, was much greater than that of pure uranium, Pierre and Marie Curie postulated the existence of two new elements--polonium (named for her native Poland) and radium. After four years of tedious work, Madame Curie isolated a tenth of a gram of pure radium. In 1903, she and her husband won the Nobel Prize for physics for the discovery of radioactivity. Madame Curie was the first woman to receive the prize.

After her husband's death in 1906, Marie Curie her work on radioactivity, and in 1911 became the first to receive a second Nobel Prize, this time in chemistry, for her discovery and study of radium. She later headed the Institute of Radium and founded the Curie Institute. She died in 1934 of an anemia caused by excessive exposure to radiation.

Madame Curie was a giant of modern science and a pioneer for her sex. In 1921, President Warren Harding, on behalf of the women of the United States, honored her for outstanding scientific achievements. Madame Curie also raised two daughters: Irène followed in her mother's footsteps and received the Nobel Prize for chemistry in 1935; Eve wrote the memoir from which the following passage is taken.

QUESTIONS:

1) How did the personal character of Marie Curie lead to success when her husband Pierre was ready to give up?

2) How were Marie and Pierre a good team, both as scientists and as husband and wife?

3) Can Marie be seen as a prototype of the modern working woman, attempting to balance the demands of two occupations?

During the first year they busied themselves with the chemical separation of radium and polonium and they studied the radiation of the products (more and more active) thus obtained. Before long they considered it more practical to separate their efforts. Pierre Curie tried to determine the properties of radium, and to know the new metal better. Marie continued those chemical treatments which would permit her to obtain salts of pure radium.

In this division of labor Marie had chosen the "man's job." She accomplished the toil of a day laborer. Inside the shed her husband was absorbed by delicate experiments. In the courtyard, dressed in her old dust-covered and acid-stained smock, her hair blown by the wind, surrounded by smoke which stung her eyes and throat, Marie was a sort of factory all by herself.

> I came to treat as many as twenty kilograms of matter at a time [she writes], which had the effect of filling the shed with great jars full of precipitates and liquids. It was killing work to carry the receivers, to pour off the liquids and to stir, for hours at a stretch, the boiling matter in a smelting basin.

Radium showed no intention of allowing itself to be known by human creatures. Where were the days when Marie naïvely expected the radium content of pitchblend to be *one per cent*? The radiation of the new substance was so powerful that a tiny quantity of radium, disseminated through the ore, was the source of striking phenomena which could be easily observed and measured. The difficult, the impossible thing, was to isolate this minute quantity, to separate it from the gangue [worthless rock or matter] in which it was so intimately mixed.

The days of work became months and years: Pierre and Marie were not discouraged. This material which resisted them, which defended its secrets, fascinated them. United by their tenderness, united by their intellectual passions, they had, in a wooden shack, the "anti-natural" existence for which they had both been made, she as well as he....

Marie continued to treat, kilogram by kilogram, the tons of pitchblend residue which were sent her on several occasions from St. Joachimsthal. With her terrible patience, she was able to be, every day for four years, a physicist,

a chemist, a specialized worker, an engineer and a laboring man all at once. Thanks to her brain and muscle, the old tables in the shed held more and more concentrated products--products more and more rich in radium. Mme. Curie was approaching the end: she no longer stood in the courtyard, enveloped in bitter smoke, to watch the heavy basins of material in fusion. She was now at the stage of purification and of the "fractional crystallization" of strongly radioactive solutions. But the poverty of her haphazard equipment hindered her work more than ever. It was now that she needed a spotlessly clean workroom and apparatus perfectly protected against cold, heat and dirt. In this shed, open to every wind, iron and coal dust was afloat which, to Marie's despair, mixed itself into the products purified with so much care. Her heart sometimes constricted before these little daily accidents, which took so much of her time and her strength.

Pierre was so tired of the interminable struggle that he would have been quite ready to abandon it. Of course, he did not dream of dropping the study of radium and of radioactivity. But he would willingly have renounced, for the time being, the special operation of preparing pure radium. The obstacles seemed insurmountable. Could they not resume this work later on, under better conditions? More attached to the meaning of natural phenomena than to their material reality, Pierre Curie was exasperated to see the paltry results to which Marie's exhausting effort had led. He advised an armistice.

He counted without his wife's character. Marie wanted to isolate radium and she would isolate it. She scorned fatigue and difficulties, and even the gaps in her own knowledge which complicated her task. After all, she was only a very young scientist: she still had not the certainty and great culture Pierre had acquired by twenty years' work, and sometimes she stumbled across phenomena or methods of calculation which she knew very little, and for which she had to make hasty studies.

So much the worse! With stubborn eyes under her great brow, she clung to her apparatus and her test tubes.

In 1902, forty-five months after the day on which the Curies announced the probable existence of radium, Marie finally carried off the victory in this war of attrition: she succeeded in preparing a decigram of pure radium, and made a first determination of the atomic weight of the new substance, which was 225.

The incredulous chemists--of whom there were still a few--could only bow before the facts, before the superhuman obstinacy of a woman.

Radium officially existed.

It was nine o'clock at night. Pierre and Marie Curie were in their little house at 108 Boulevard Kellermann, where they had been living since 1900. The house suited them well. From the boulevard, where three rows of trees half hid the fortifications, could be seen only a dull wall and a tiny door. But behind the one-story house, hidden from all eyes, there was a narrow provincial garden, rather pretty and very quiet. And from the "barrier" of Gentilly they could escape on their bicycles toward the suburbs and the woods....

Old Dr. Curie [Pierre's father], who lived with the couple, had retired to his room. Marie had bathed her child and put it to bed, and had stayed for a long time beside the cot. This was a rite. When Irène did not feel her mother near her at night she would call out for her incessantly, with that "Mé!" which was to be our substitute for "Mamma" always. And Marie, yielding to the implacability of the four-year-old baby, climbed the stairs, seated herself beside the child and stayed there in the darkness until the young voice gave way to light, regular breathing. Only then would she go down to Pierre, who was growing impatient. In spite of his kindness, he was the most possessive and jealous of husbands. He was so used to the constant presence of his wife that her least eclipse kept him from thinking freely. If Marie delayed too long near her daughter, he received her on her return with a reproach so unjust as to be comic: "You never think of anything but that child!"

Pierre walked slowly about the room. Marie sat down and made some stitches on the hem of Irène's new apron. One of her principles was never to buy ready-made clothes for the child: she thought them too fancy and impractical....

But this evening she could not fix her attention. Nervous, she got up; then, suddenly:

"Suppose we go down there for a moment?"

There was a note of supplication in her voice--altogether superfluous, for Pierre, like herself, longed to go back to the shed they had left two hours before. Radium, fanciful as a living creature, endearing as a love, called them back to its dwelling, to the wretched laboratory.

The day's work had been hard, and it would have been more reasonable for the couple to rest. But Pierre and Marie were not always reasonable. As soon as they had put on their coats and told Dr. Curie of their flight, they were in the street. They went on foot, arm in arm, exchanging few words. After the crowded streets of this queer district, with its factory buildings, wastelands and poor tenements, they arrived in the Rue Lhomond and crossed the little courtyard. Pierre put the key in the lock. The door squeaked, as it had squeaked thousands of times, and admitted them to their realm, to their dream.

"Don't light the lamps!" Marie said in the darkness. Then she added with a little laugh:

"Don't you remember the day when you said to me 'I should like radium to have a beautiful color'?"

The reality was more entrancing than the simple wish of long ago. Radium had something better than "a beautiful color": it was spontaneously luminous. And in the somber shed where, in the absence of cupboards, the precious particles in their tiny glass receivers were placed on tables or on shelves nailed to the wall, their phosphorescent bluish outlines gleamed, suspended in the night.

"Look ... Look!" the young woman murmured. She went forward cautiously, looked forward and found a straw-bottomed chair. She sat down in the darkness and silence. Their two faces turned toward the pale glimmering, the mysterious sources of radiation, toward radium-- their radium. Her body leaning forward, her head eager, Marie took up again the attitude which had been hers an hour earlier at the bedside of her sleeping child.

Her companion's hand lightly touched her hair. She was to remember forever this evening of glowworms, this magic.

Curie, Eve. *Madame Curie, A Biography*. Trans. V. Sheean. Garden City, NY: Doubleday, 1937. Pp. 169-170, 174-177.

HENRY FORD, THE FIVE-DOLLAR DAY, AND THE AUTOMOTIVE REVOLUTION

▶ 1909 Ford "Touring Car"

No change brought by the industrializing of the modern world has been so momentous as the mass production of motor vehicles. The economies of all developed countries are built on a transportation system that relies on trucks to carry raw materials and finished products along networks of highways that link suppliers, manufacturers, distributors, and consumers. What the steam engine was to the nineteenth century, the internal combustion engine has been to the twentieth.

Personal lives, too, have changed dramatically with the advent of mass produced, relatively cheap automobiles. The ability to move quickly over considerable distances has led to the expansion of suburban life, since employees no longer need to live within walking or riding distance of their work places. Shopping malls, industrial parks, and entertainment facilities now often lie far from city-centers, along the routes of major highways.

Henry Ford was the man most responsible for the mass production of automobiles and the social and economic transformations it caused. Ford was not, strictly speaking, a great inventor or innovator. He was not the first to design an automobile, and others had developed many of the elements of the high-efficiency factory before him. But he was the first to streamline the delivery and assembly of parts in a large-scale assembly-line system of production. Capitalizing on his engineering know-how, the availability of cheap electric power, and improvements in machine technology, Ford built and organized the first truly modern factories based on assembly-line production. He coordinated workers and machines more effectively than any previous industrialist. His methods were soon widely adopted throughout the industrialized world.

The success of Henry Ford's assembly-line production made it possible to sell millions of automobiles at prices that the average citizen could afford. The great middle class benefited as never before by the growth of high-paying factory jobs and by the affordability of manufactured goods.

The following selections describe the early stages of Henry Ford's experiments with the internal combustion and his subsequent large-scale development of a new, more efficient type of factory.

QUESTIONS:

1) Is Henry Ford a good example of ingenuity and determination leading from small beginnings to major achievements?

2) What problems did the assembly line system solve?

3) How did the emergence of a mechanized industrial society change the demands placed on skilled and unskilled laborers?

When [engineer and friend of Henry Ford, Charles B.] King attended the Chicago World's Fair in 1893, he was struck by the lack of automobile exhibits. It was twenty-five years since Siegfried Marcus, a German Jew, had begun experimenting in Vienna with carriages propelled by gas-combustion engines. It was eight years since a German engineer, Gottlieb Daimler, had mounted a one-cylinder internal combustion engine on a bicycle, and another German, Karl Benz, had mated an engine to a tricycle. By the early 1890's, two Frenchmen, Armand Peugeot and Emile Levassor, were the leading automobile developers in the world. (Levassor, who placed a vertical engine in the front of the vehicle so as to counterbalance the weight of the passengers, evolved the basic design of the modern automobile.)...

In the United States, on the other hand, where the emphasis was still on railroad construction, there was little public interest.... Obtaining the American rights to Daimler, William Steinway was unable to strike a responsive chord with any of the financiers he approached for support, and went back to making pianos.

It was left to a number of the readers of *The Scientific American*, which carried extensive articles on the European development of motor carriages, to become excited about building automobiles. On September 21, 1893, two young bicycle mechanics, Charles and Frank Duryea, took to the streets of Springfield, Massachusetts, in a vehicle modeled on Benz's.

Returning from the fair, King was stimulated by the feat of the Duryeas. Assisted by Oliver Barthel, he set to work building an automobile.

[Henry] Ford, who had previously given no indication of an inventive mind, caught the fever. In December, 1893, he was promoted to chief engineer--at a salary of one hundred dollars a month--at the main Edison plant on Washington Street. On the fifteenth of the month he moved his wife and his newborn son, Edsel, into one half of a small two-story brownstone duplex three blocks from the plant. It was an important move. For the house was one of fewer than four thousand in the city wired for electricity.

Late in the evening of the ninth day in his new home, Ford brought a primitive, toylike engine into the kitchen. Its cylinder consisted of a one-inch diameter gas pipe fitted with a piston and connected to a flywheel made from an old lathe. It was Christmas Eve, and as [his wife] Clara bustled about preparing dinner for a host of relatives expected the next day, Henry clamped the engine to the sink. Since the house was on direct current, he was able to split the electric wire and use it to provide a spark. Beckoning to Clara, he had her drip gasoline into the cylinder from a can. As he spun the flywheel, the engine exploded into life. Spurting flame, popping wildly, filling the house with smoke and fumes, it shook the sink and brought coughing protestations from Clara.

Henry was elated. It was a beginning.

* * * * * *

Not until March 6, 1896, did King, with Ford following behind on his bicycle, take to the streets at eight miles per hour in his motorized carriage....

Close on the heels of King came Ford. His $1,900-a-year salary gave him a comfortable surplus over his living expenses. (His rent was $16 a month.) He drew freely on the expertise of King, Barthel, and a number of others. Between 2 A.M. and 4 A.M. on June 4 he tightened the last nut on the quadricycle, with its two-cylinder engine. As he looked about, ready to wheel the vehicle from the shed, he was struck by a minor problem.

The shed's single door was too narrow for the vehicle.

So Ford broke out one side of the shed. In the predawn drizzle, he was soon pop-popping down the street. In front of the Cadillac Hotel a group of night owls gaped as his explosive apparition loomed out of the mist.

Technically, Ford's vehicle was inferior to those of the French automobiles pioneers and of the Duryea brothers. But, capable of attaining a speed of twenty miles per hour, it was an improvement over King's.

Proudly Ford, with King accompanying him, drove the quadricycle the nine miles to Dearborn. As he brought it to a halt in front of the open kitchen door, neighbors came running across the fields. William Ford, tall, dignified, justice of the peace and church warden, stepped out to look at the pony-sized, five-hundred-pound machine. He shook his head. How could a grown man waste his time building toys? Laughing and ridiculing the quadricycle, the neighbors sympathized with him.

Crushed, Henry turned to King. "Come on, Charlie," he said. "Let's get out of here."

* * * * * *

Constructed of steel, concrete, and glass, the "crystal palace" in Highland Park was occupied by Ford on New Year's Day, 1910. The main building contained 260,000 square feet of floor space spread over four stories. A sixth of a mile long, it was paralleled by the saw-tooth-roofed machine shop. A 57-foot-wide covered craneway occupied the space between the buildings. Facing the craneway were galleries where the huge, traveling cranes picked up and delivered goods and materials. The vast, uncluttered expanse of the interiors emphasized mobility and flexibility, and facilitated experimentation in the arranging and rearranging of production. Openings in the floors permitted vertical movement. The five-stacked power plant (to which Ford's office was connected by an overhead walkway), the 40,000-square-foot foundry, the metallurgical laboratory--all emphasized self-sufficiency and the smooth flow of production....

Grappling with a continuing shortage of skilled workers, and an on-and-off shortage of unskilled workers, executives gave increasing attention to "Taylorizing" the plant. Frederick Winslow Taylor, the prototype of the efficiency expert, was urging industrialists to adopt his measures of "scientific management." To increase productivity, Taylor planned every task for every workman, the manner in which he was to do it, and the time it was to take him. The old-style foremen, with their close and personal relationship to the men, were replaced by eight efficiency experts--an inspector, a gang boss, a speed boss, a repair boss, a time clerk, a route clerk, and a disciplinarian. Since an unskilled worker was "too stupid to properly train himself," Taylor declared, he must be given an overseer who, like a drill sergeant, would control his every motion from dawn to dusk, and curse him at every misstep....

In 1909, Taylor spoke to a group of Packard executives. His theories rapidly gained credence in Detroit. At Ford the thinking went a step further. If efficiency depended upon transforming men into robots, even greater efficiency should be achieved by then mating the robots to machines.

The turn-of-the-century development of high-speed tool steel made possible a whole new generation of machine tools. By 1914, the company had fifteen thousand machines, more than one for every worker. The machines' sophistication increased as rapidly as their numbers. One automatic multi-directional steel drill was able to bore forty-five holes simultaneously in four directions in a cylinder block.

But the machining of parts did not cut through the swamp of confusion that existed in the main assembly plant. Gangs of workers moved from chassis to stationary chassis. Runners taking parts to and from the depots on the floor dodged and twisted through the maze. Foreign workmen unable to follow instructions or read labels lost their way and did not return for hours. Parts were directed to the wrong stations. Tools vanished. Despite Taylorization, lack of coordination resulted in periods of frenzied activity followed by periods in which workers sat on their machines.

If the solution to the shortage of skilled workers was to transfer the skills to the machines, then evidently the solution to the problem of the delivery of parts was also mechanization. Overhead delivery belts had been used in the Cincinnati meat packing industry since shortly after the Civil War. If a moving hook could be used to carry a carcass, there was no reason why it could not be rigged to deliver an engine block.

In fact, there was little novel about the individual components going into the new mode of production at the Ford plant. Johann Bodmer had invented the traveling crane for a Manchester factory in 1853. Ford during his boyhood had watched railroad cars rolled from point to point in the production shed of the Michigan Car Company. What was unprecedented was the application of such principles and devices to heavy industry and a product as complex as an automobile. What was unique was the coordination between scores of diverse productions, operations, and feeder and assembly lines.

What made the new mode of production possible, first, was the standardization that Ford had built into the Model T. If each part were not like every other equivalent part, and each assembly not like every other equivalent assembly, the dehumanization and coordination of production could never have been achieved.

What made it possible, second, was the layout of the factory. Technological developments in steel and reinforced concrete had brought into being a plant offering unprecedented mobility and flexibility. Never before had there been a production line a sixth of a mile long.

What made it possible, third, was electricity, and the concept ... of applying electric power to the driving of machinery. At the Piquette plant, Ford had benefited from the low-rate "energy contract" Dow had devised to induce manufacturers to switch from steam to electric power, and thus increase the usage of electricity during daylight hours. By 1909, the seventy automotive manufacturers were using 10 percent of the system's capacity, a capacity that had increased some tenfold in five years. But the Highland Park complex was unique in having an in-plant system capable of generating enough electricity to light most of the cities of the world. It was a system that made feasible the operation of a virtually unlimited number of machines, and their arranging and rearranging to the best advantage.

The devising of feeder lines to carry parts for the assembly of components like magnetos and axles was relatively simple. But to have dozens of feeder lines converging on numerous stationary assembly points was a practical impossibility. The assembly itself would have to be placed in motion. There would have to be parallel feeder lines reticulating the assembly line.

The first assembly line to go into operation was the one for the magnetos. By December, 1913, after months of experimentation, the final assembly line--on which the engines, wheels, and body were to be mounted on the chassis--was being readied for production.

As the company's executives met for a year-end assessment, they could congratulate themselves on the great strides--strides that would show up in 1914 when the company sold an almost unbelievable 19.2 cars for each worker it employed. But the problem of the labor supply, and its quality, remained unsolved....

It was imperative to upgrade the work force and reduce turnover. Since 1909, Ford had had "profit sharing" in the form of Christmas bonuses for steady employees. At the end of 1913, the company distributed $60,000 in bonuses to 640 employees, an average of less than $100 each. Yet profits for 1913 were $27 million. Dividends, of which more than half went to Ford, were $11.2 million. Evidently the company could afford to be more generous....

At 54 cents an hour, skilled workers were earning $4.86 a day. But in a factory that had more machines than it had workers, the difference between skilled and unskilled was being blurred. By learning to operate a machine, a man could move from an unskilled to a skilled position in a matter of weeks. It appeared that unskilled labor would be less and less of a factor in the company's operations. Why not, then, pay everyone a wage on which he could live and support his family decently? A wage that would enable the company, which needed to add five thousand men for its new, three-shift operation, to attract and choose from the most desirable of the labor force? Why not pay everyone $4.86, or, in effect, $5 a day?...

[On] January 5, 1914, Ford ... announced "the greatest revolution in the matter of rewards for its workers ever known to the industrial world"--the eight-hour, $5, profit-sharing day....

The Five-Dollar Day ... drew men from the mines, the forests, and the railroads. But it wanted only the best of those men. It did not want, it could not use, it would not keep the sluggards, the illiterates, the unintelligent. It was a warning of new standards. A warning that the new, ultramechanized industrial society would have decreasing use for the large number of people who continued to be procreated on the farms.

Conot, Robert. *American Odyssey*. New York: Morrow, 1974. Rpt. New York: Bantam, 1975. Pp. 145-146, 153-154, 211-216.

AMERICAN VOICES FROM THE TIME OF THE GREAT DEPRESSION

The global economic depression that began in 1929 and persisted into the 1930s resulted from the fundamental financial weaknesses of the post-World War I world: falling agricultural prices, overproduction, international debt, and unsound stock and bond investments owing to inadequate legal controls in stock exchanges and banking institutions. The Depression brought a steep drop in the demand for goods worldwide; this led many overstocked factories to close, putting millions of workers out of jobs. As nations erected protective tariff barriers, international trade fell off sharply. By 1932, a quarter of American workers were unemployed and shantytowns, called Hoovervilles (after President Herbert Hoover), overflowed with jobless and homeless people.

In 1932, the democrat Franklin D. Roosevelt was elected president. Assisted by a team of advisers dubbed the "brain trust," and encouraged by his wife Eleanor, who was active in many social causes, President Roosevelt launched a New Deal designed to pull the country out of the Depression. New laws and government bureaus provided relief payments for the hungry, low-cost mortgages, public works jobs for some of the unemployed, and assistance for farmers. The New Deal also implemented work programs for unemployed youth and gave loans to business. New laws regulated business and finance to prevent a repetition of the stock market collapse of October 1929. The New Deal began to build a welfare state in the United States, anchored in the social security system.

The letters that follow were written by Americans struggling to cope with the economic disaster of the Great Depression. Most are pleas for assistance sent in desperation to President and Mrs. Roosevelt; the final letter, however, expresses displeasure with the government's relief programs. The homely phraseology and faulty spelling and punctuation of the letters have been left uncorrected.

QUESTIONS:

1) What do these letters reveal about the state of mind of common people during the Great Depression?

2) Do the relief efforts of the U.S. government seem to have made much difference in the lives of needy individuals?

3) What objections to government relief policies are made by the author of the last letter?

Reidsville. Ga Oct 19th 1935
Hon. Franklin D. Roosevelt
President of U.S.
Washington, D.C.

Dear Mr. President
Would you please direct the people in charge of
the releaf work in Georgia to issue the provisions
+ other supplies to our suffering colored people.
I am sorry to worrie you with this Mr. President
but hard as it is to believe the releaf officials here
are using up most every thing that you send for
them self + their friends. they give out the
releaf supplies here on Wednesday of this week
and give us black folks, each one, nothing but a
few cans of pickle meet and to white folks they
give blankets, bolts of cloth and things like that.
I dont want to take to mutch of your time Mr.
President but will give you just one example of
how the releaf is work down here   the witto
Nancy Hendrics own lands, stock holder in the
Bank in this town and she is being supplied with
Blankets cloth and gets a supply of can goods
regular this is only one case but I could tell you
many.
Please help us mr President because we cant help
our self and we know you is the president and a
good Christian man   we is praying for you.
Yours truly   cant sign my name Mr President
they will beat me up and run me away from here
and this is my home

[Anonymous]

Buncombe County Jail
Asheville N.C.
Feb. 1.19.34

President hoover Dear Sir

well you Pleas help Poor me i am a Colored
woman 34 years old have 4 Children 3 Girls 1
Boy I have work awFully hard Every Senice i 9
years old. Did not Get to Go to School But very
little--But I have all ways held my Job never Ben
turn off unless Sickness I was Born in a little
town By the name of Laurens S.C. I Came to
ashevill N C 10 years aGo and I had very good
Luck For awhile My husband wasen So well but
he work on Just the Same he Got hurt in the
world War at the Camp/wheller Makon Ga he
and I Done all that we Could to Rear our 4
Children up RiGht well he took Real Sick and

Died. Well i nely went Crazy when the Dr told
me that they Could Not Save him and BeGain to
Drink I tried to Drink it off and Got in Jail why
I Drank Every thing aney one would give me …
I was Sick and worred nely to Deth I have tried
and tried to Get a Job But they are Scarse the
City Releaf takes Care of my Children at Present
Dear President Pleas--give me a Job. and I well
Do my Best all I want is a Chance and I well
Prove to the world that I can Come up the hill in
Stead of goin Down I Relize it was wrong to
Drink and I am Sorry that I Ever tourch it But I
was Cold and hunGry a menie Day that no one
Knew But God and I is had Plenty of Friend
when my husband was--livinG and we all ways
help others as Mutch as we Could. now my
health is not So Good may hart is Bad and I
haven Got aney Job no whear harley to Stay I
had to all most give furnitur a way Because I
Could not Pay the house Rent I Pray that you
well Give Me Some thing to Do I Dont Care
what I sure well thank god and you then I well
Get me Some Clouse an Shoes an go to Church
Every Sunday I have made up in my mind to
Stop DrinkinG and if god for Give me and you
give me a Job I never.never.tourch it aGain
Pleas answer Soon i well Get out on the 18 of
Feb. and haven Got aney money an no home no
Job So I Pray you well tell Poor me what to Do
may god tourch your hart that you well
underStand Every thinG and help me I Feel Just
like the whole world is aGainst Me Sometime I
am not a Bad--woman Just worred Crazy Pleas
Give me a trial--

your truly
Mrs. M.R.
Buncombe County Jail
Ashevill N C.

Warren, Ohio
Dec. 22, 1935

Dear President Roosevelt,
    Please help us my mother is sick three year
and was in the hospital three month and she came
out but she is not better and my Father is
peralised and can not work and we are poor and
the Cumunity fun gives us six dollars an we are
six people four children three boy 15, 13, 12, an
one gril 10, and to parents. We have no one to

give us a Christmas presents. and if you want to buy a Christmas present please buy us a stove to do our cooking and to make good bread.

Please excuse me for not writing it so well because the little girl is 10 year old is writing.

Merry Christmas
[Anonymous]

[February, 1936]

Mr. and Mrs. Roosevelt.
Wash. D.C.

Dear Mr. President:

I'm a boy of 12 years. I want to tell you about my family My father hasn't worked for five months He went plenty of times to relief, he filled out application. They won't give us anything. I don't know why. Please you do something. We haven't paid 4 months rent, Everyday the landlord rings the door bell, we don't open the door for him. We are afraid that we will be put out, been put out before, and don't want to happen again. We haven't paid the gas bill, and the electric bill, haven't paid grocery bill for 3 months. My brother goes to Lane Tech. High School. he's eighteen years old, hasn't gone to school for 2 weeks because he got no carfare. I have a sister she's twenty years, she can't find work. I told him why you are crying daddy, and daddy said why shouldn't I cry when there is nothing in the house. I feel sorry for him. That night I couldn't sleep. The next morning I wrote this letter to you. in my room. Were American citizens and were born in Chicago, Ill. and I don't know why they don't help us Please answer right away because we need it. will starve Thank you.

God bless you.

[Anonymous]
Chicago, Ill.

December. 11--1935

to the President,
Executive Mansion, Washington, D.C.
Your Excellency--President of the United States,

this is to inform you to let you know how we are suffering as workers on the P.W.A. project here in Chicago. We are suppose to get $55.00 a month, and you knows at it best, $55.00 a month is too small amount for a man and his family to live on without any other help, when he have to pay just as small as $12.50 at the lowest rent, and buy coal, food, clothes, medicine or doctor bill and other expenses, on this small amount of money a month. Now I know that you are a man of a family too, and you knows the expenses of a family in this high price of living, and I knows and think that you feels our care, and means right. And you will do what is right if you knows the suffering of the people.

Now dont think that I want to live over my means, or want to live like a rich man, I only wants a common living to exist without starving and freezing to death. $55.00. a month not only too small for a family, but we are [not] even getting $55.00. a month, because we dont get two pays a month, it be three and four weeks before we get one pay, and when we do gets it we owe all of it and more besides. And the landlords and the groceryman runs us down for that, and if we continue to get paid like this. it will be that lots of us to be set out on the streets, and will have a hard way to get anywhere to stay.

If you dont believe what tell you is true, just have this investagated, and if the truth is known you will see that this is true.

Now dont think that I am a red, I am not and would not be one, I am only suffering, not only me myself, but my family, and lot others, Christmas will soon be here and we will have nothing for our family.

I am not trying to make trouble, and am not going to sign my name to this letter because it might make it harder for myself. Just investagated what I say.

[Anonymous]

Dec. 14--1937
Columbus, Ind.

Mrs. F.D. Roosevelt,
Washington, D.C.

Mrs. Roosevelt: I suppose from your point of view the work relief, old age pensions, slum clearance and all the rest seems like a perfect remedy for all the ills of this country, but I would like for you to see the results, as the other half see them.

We have always had a shiftless, never-do-well class of people whose one and only aim in life is to live without work. I have been rubbing elbows with this class for nearly sixty years and have tried to help some of the most promising and have seen others try to help them, but it can't be done. We cannot help those who will not try to help themselves and if they do try a square deal is all they need, and by the way that is all this country needs or ever has needed: a square deal for all and then, let each one paddle their own canoe, or sink....

The women and children around here have had to work at the fields to help save the crops and several women fainted while at work and at the same time we couldn't go up or down the road without stumbling over some of the reliefers, moping around carrying dirt from one side of the road to the other and back again, or else asleep. I live alone on a farm and have not raised any crops for the last two years as there was no help to be had. I am feeding the stock and have been cutting the wood to keep my home fires burning. There are several reliefers around here now who have been kicked off relief, but they refuse to work unless they can get relief hours and wages, but they are so worthless no one can afford to hire them....

As for the old people on beggars' allowances: the taxpayers have provided homes for all the old people who never liked to work, where they will be neither cold nor hungry: much better homes than most of them have ever tried to provide for themselves. They have lived many years through the most prosperous times of our country and had an opportunity to prepare for old age, but they spent their lives in idleness or worse and now they expect those who have worked like slaves, to provide a living for them and all their worthless descendants. Some of them are asking for from thirty to sixty dollars a month when I have known them to live on a dollar a week rather than go to work. There is many a little child doing without butter on its bread, so that some old sot can have his booze and tobacco: some old sot who spent his working years loafing around pool rooms and saloons, boasting that the world owed him a living.

Even the child welfare has become a racket. The parents of large families are getting divorces, so that the mothers and children can qualify for aid. The children to join the ranks of the "unemployed" as they grow up, for no child that has been raised on charity in this community has ever amounted to anything.

You people who have plenty of this worlds goods and whose money comes easy, have no idea of the heart-breaking toil and self-denial which is the lot of the working people who are trying to make an honest living, and then to have to shoulder all these unjust burdens seems like the last straw. During the worst of the depression many of the farmers had to deny their families butter, eggs, meat etc. and sell it to pay their taxes and then had to stand by and see the dead-beats carry it home to their families by the arm load, and they knew their tax money was helping pay for it. One woman saw a man carry out eight pounds of butter at one time. The crookedness, selfishness, greed and graft of the crooked politicians is making one gigantic racket out of the new deal and it is making this a nation of dead-beats and beggars and if it continues the people who will work will soon be nothing but slaves for the pampered poverty rats and I am afraid these human parasites are going to become a menace to the country unless they are disfranchised....

Is it any wonder the taxpayers are discouraged by all this penalizing of thrift and industry to reward shiftlessness, or that the whole country is on the brink of chaos?

M.A.H. [female]
Columbus, Ind.

National Archives: Federal Emergency Relief Administration Central Files [FERA], Box 88. National Archives: Civil Works Administration Administrative Correspondence, Box 55. FERA Central Files, Boxes 88, 87. FERA New Subject File 002. Franklin D. Roosevelt Library: Eleanor Roosevelt Papers, Box 2735. Rpt. in McElvaine, Robert S., ed. *Down and Out in the Great Depression: Letters from the "Forgotten Man."* Chapel Hill: Univ. of North Carolina Press, 1983. Nos. 38, 42, 73, 75, 91, 104 = pp. 83, 85-86, 116-117, 133, 145-147.

"CHICANO CHINAMAN"-- THE NEW WORLD PERSON

The course of world history can be seen as a record of migrations. North and South America came to be inhabited because of migration from Asia across the Bering Strait more than 30,000 years ago. In the past 500 years Europeans have migrated to the two continents, and quite distinctive cultures have evolved out of the mingling of different ethnic groups. The great colonizing periods of world history have come to an end and onetime colonies have become independent nations. Most of the nations of the Americas contain populations of diverse backgrounds.

The writings of the Chicano author Rudolfo Anaya reflect the interaction of several cultures. Born in 1937, Anaya has written several novels, a collection of short stories, plays, children's stories, and a travel book titled *A Chicano in China*. Though he has lived all his life in New Mexico, his work lends itself to a global, comparative analysis. One of Anaya's principal themes is the emergence of a New World identity that is not exclusively or even mainly western. While he writes about Spanish-speaking people (his *Bless Me, Ultima* is the best known Chicano novel), he sees the Hispanic culture of the American Southwest as rooted in a pre-Columbian, Amerindian culture.

In the interview that follows, Rudolfo Anaya interprets Amerindian culture in global terms, stressing distant Asian origins. The interviewer, Feroza Jussawalla, is a professor at the University of Texas, El Paso.

QUESTIONS:

1) How has Rudolfo Anaya used the awareness of a prehistoric migration of people from Asia to North America in constructing his own self-image?

2) In Anaya's view, what is distinctive about the roots of "New World" people like himself?

3) In what sense does Anaya see culture as both a potential negative?

Feroza Jussawalla: I've used *A Chicano in China* a lot in my classes because it speaks to my students, here in El Paso, about identity and crossing cultures. In a way you've made identity the central issue in the book. In what way does China speak to you? There's quite a bit of reference in *A Chicano in China* about the connection between the Chicanos and the Asians. Your grandfather, for example, puts his ear to the ground, and he says that you can hear the Chinese. You have a whole theory about Asian immigration from Asia through the Northwest coast into the Llano area, into New Mexico, establishing a connection between the Chinese people and the Chicano people. I'm interested in this partially because I'm from Asia and I'm living in New Mexico. How did China and Asia become relevant to your personal history?

Anaya: I have always been very interested in the migrations of people, especially in the Southwest. This has been a migration path since time immemorial. Basically, the migrations from the Asiatic continent took place from North to South. Those people came across the Bering Strait and then settled all of the Americas and kept going to Tierra Del Fuego. That's a very important migration. If you look at the legends of the Aztecs, they talk of that migration. We came from north of Mexico; we came from Aztlan. That was one of their stopping places in their migration. Then you get the migration of the Español going in the opposite direction, going upstream from Mexico up into Nuevo Mexico. Then finally in the last century you get a new migration of the Anglo-American coming East to West and running into this very important corridor. What happens in these corridors of migration interests me--how people treat them, how they live there, what consciousness and new awarenesses they come to and what kinds of conflict develop when different peoples mix, as we have here in the Southwest. We have the Indio, Español, Mexicano, and finally the Anglo-American. I use the metaphor of being a fish in the stream of migration--which I think blends perfectly into the golden carp and the fish people that I have always used as a theme in my work. So here I was swimming upstream of the original migration, thinking of that part of me that is native American, that is, what I call the New World man, and feeling very much at home because by going to China I had returned to part of my roots, my symbols, and the Sipapu, the homeland. Aztlan might be in China, if you push it back far enough, if you push it back to its original source. I have always traveled and tried to see what I have in common with people, how we all fit into the human salad. It was very natural for me to see myself as a Chicano Chinaman. I became a Chicano Chinaman.

F.J.: Is this a revelation that came to you upon going to China, or had you always thought about this?

Anaya: No, everything evolved naturally. I didn't preplan anything or plot anything. I went with an open mind. The allusions to my grandfather were very important because I've always used a mentor or a guide for my characters in my literature. I felt the need, especially in this trip, to have a mentor, a guide. The place was very foreign, very far away, very strange, and I really knew it only through the stereotypes that we most often have of foreign countries, especially of the East. I alluded to this in the work, to Charlie Chan movies; what else did we know about China? So I was trying to learn the truth about China, not the stereotype, and I felt someone like my grandfather, a wise old person, would be that spiritual guide that I needed, that mentor.

F.J.: Had he any connection with China or Asia?

Anaya: This man lived all his life in a little valley in New Mexico, in the Puerto de Luna valley. He was a farmer, he was born there, he was raised there. The old people didn't know a world beyond that, but they were so intuitively wise enough to know that we are connected to the world out there.

F.J.: You've said before that when you're asked about your roots, you look down at your feet, and there your roots are, and that's just New Mexico. So your roots lie in New Mexico rather than tracing any Spanish genealogy? How do you see yourself in that context?

Anaya: My roots are in New Mexico because New Mexico is one of the Indo-Hispano cultures of the New World. What I am trying to do in my work and when I talk to people, is--by having them look down at there feet and their roots, at the soil of the New World--to take a meaning and identification from it. We don't have to go to Europe or to Spain to find our roots. We have finally become New World persons. I think if we don't do that, we will never meet our authentic selves. We'll always be rushing to Spain as the mother country. Those connections are important, those roots are there, but we have evolved in the New World.

F.J.: Can you give me your definition of the New World man? What does he incorporate?

Anaya: The New World man, the New World person, takes his perspective from indigenous history and spiritual thought and mythology and relationships. The New World person is a person of synthesis, a person who is able to draw, in our case, on our Spanish roots and our native indigenous roots and become a new person, become that Mestizo with a unique perspective. That's who we are and how we define ourselves.

F.J.: That tension is played out very strongly in *Bless Me, Ultima* because you have the Lunas who identify with the Spanish colonizers and who cultivated the valley and grew things and made it green, and then you have the Marez, the vaqueros [cowboys], the people of Llano. How did you come to working that tension out?

Anaya: As I look back in my work, as I said in the essay "The New World Man," which I read at the conference in Barcelona this past summer, it seems to me that I have always been in search of this person. I have not been able to feel authentic until I found this person because I was being led to believe that I was too many other things by too many foreign, outside influences that didn't even know who I was. So how could they describe me? Looking back at *Bless Me, Ultima*, at least one way to describe Antonio is that Antonio is the beginning of my search for the New World person. He incorporates the Español and the Indio, the old world and the new.

F.J.: I've used chapter six of *Bless Me, Ultima* in my freshman classes a great deal. That's the chapter in which Antonio comes to school for the first time. The teacher looks at him and calls him Tony, and then the students make fun of him when he's eating his lunch of tacos. It's an experience that must speak out to my students because my students respond: "Oh yes, this happened to me, this happened to me," and they respond to it with a genuine gut feeling. Is that a colonization process you're depicting, a new colonization, the way in which someone like Antonio is colonized into becoming an American?

Anaya: Yes, but after all, this area that I speak about and this corridor that I belong to, this Rio Grande spiritual corridor, has always been colonized. There have been successive colonizations, successive migrations. People pass through and make this place their home. When the Anglo-American finally comes here in the mid-nineteenth century, he becomes the most recent colonizer of the indigenous peoples, and so Antonio in that chapter, and I think probably in all of the book, reflects that indigenous person. I think a lot of people have missed this in the book, but my concern is how will Antonio ever find himself, truly see himself?

F.J.: Can you tell me how he will?

Anaya: It's going to be a long process because the reality of the colonization mode or model is to destroy the roots that bind you to the authentic self. Everybody has to search, to continue searching. It happened to my generation, and you're saying your students still reflect on that; so it's still happening. I believe that history and literature and all the arts are important; they feed the person that we really are because they go to our values and our roots.

F.J.: I've talked about *Bless Me, Ultima* with [Chicano novelist] Rolando Hinojosa, and he said that most people consider *Bless Me, Ultima* as a mythical novel, but that it is really a political statement. Do you see a political statement in *Bless Me, Ultima*, and if so what would you say it is?

Anaya: I've just told you that the novel has a structure by which a boy who is very small begins to inquire into who he really is. When you find out who you really are, you become a person of incredible power.

F.J.: What I was thinking of was the scene when he finally decides he's not going to become a priest, or does he decide that?

Anaya: I would hope that he would be a shaman, but, you know, a shaman is another kind of priest. The point is not so much what he becomes. We can't dictate what people become, but what we can hope to do is to liberate people by having them become their most true selves, their authentic selves, to find their deepest potential. Then you will recognize the models of colonialism that are set over you, and you'll know how to react and how to accomplish your goals in life. So to me the important aspect of *Bless Me, Ultima* is that process of liberation.

F.J.: Antonio is essentially shucking off two levels of colonialism--one is the Spanish colonialism that comes through his mother's family, the religious colonialism of the Catholic church, and at the same time the kind of Anglo-American colonialism that's coming to him through the Anglo-American education system.

Anaya: I think that's fair to say.

F.J.: What about the people of the Golden Carp? Do they ever get set free, or do they just go around in a circle?

Anaya: I'm not sure I follow that line of thinking.

F.J.: Antonio says at one point that the Golden Carp is never set free from Narciso's mythology. He says it's never set free, it just goes around and around seasonally.

Anaya: You must know that in one sense no one is ever set free. This is the nature of our humanity. We struggle to be free, and we struggle depending on the philosophy that we follow, right? If I wish to achieve a total freedom, must I die, or must I turn to the Zen or to Nirvana or to the Buddha or become a priest for the Catholic church? I don't prescribe and tell people what will set them free, but I'm very interested in the process. There is a process by which you can get to know yourself and to be liberated in yourself. That liberation also has a very important component in the community because as you liberate yourself, you liberate others, and you get to know more of your humanity. I am interested in that process; other people will be interested in the political ends of that process.

Culture is something we create. We're creators of culture; we love it, you know. And in many ways, there is as much of a trap as in anything else. I'm interested not only in the individual, but in the communal group. I'm also interested in the fact that cultures can be as binding and enslaving as anything else. But

they can also provide the context where you explore your relationships with other people, explore the possibility of being that authentic self I talk about. So nothing is good or bad categorically; it's what we make it. I think that we have the possibility of making our culture a vehicle for the exploration of that self, for communal fulfillment. Perhaps I'm being too idealistic, but I really believe that it is possible in community because that's all we have. We look around and we only have each other, and how we relate to each other is important.

F.J.: So the "Heart of Aztlan" doesn't have any kind of particular specific locus for you. It shifts with communities and people, would you say?

Anaya: No, I think it has a definite locus. It is a Barrio which is a definition of community, set in a specific place and a specific time with specific goals.

F.J.: I don't mean the novel with that title, *Heart of Aztlan*, as much as metaphorically. Does the culture have a specific locus or can it move to communities and cultures in Northern New Mexico or Southern New Mexico or West Texas?

Anaya: Everything we write should be able to move like that. Everything we write should be able to move out into the world and be a reflection of everybody else's community.

Jussawalla, Feroza, and Reed Way Dasenbrock, eds. *Interviews with Writers of the Post-Colonial World.* Jackson and London: Univ. Press of Mississippi, 1992. Pp. 245-250.

HOLOKA

MOTHER TERESA'S MESSAGE OF LOVE

In the twentieth century, Marxism and other ideologies have sought to supplant traditional religions and philosophies through indoctrination and repression, but have failed. In fact, a resurgence of religious faith has typified the post-Marxist world. Related to this has been the continuing need for private individual actions to remedy many of the evils that persist in rich and poor nations alike.

Mother Teresa of Calcutta, founder of the Missionaries of Charity, has combined religious faith and individual endeavor to alleviate the suffering of unfortunate people. She was born Agnes Bojaxhiu in 1910 to a prosperous and devout Catholic family in Albania. She became a nun in 1937 and for twenty years taught in a girls' school in India. In 1950, Mother Teresa founded an order of nuns to do charity work amongst the poorest of the poor; it later added a Missionary Brothers of Charity. Beginning in India, the Missionaries of Charity had by 1984 spread to 63 countries on every continent with 238 orphanages, schools, leper sanctuaries, hospitals, and shelters.

Wearing a white cotton sari with a blue border that is the habit of her order (she has three, "one for wearing, one for washing, one for mending"), Mother Teresa keeps a busy schedule of administration, travel, missionary work of service, and fund raising. Mother Teresa is the recipient of the Jawaharlal Nehru Award for International Understanding given by the government of India (1969), the Vatican's Pope John XXIII Peace Prize (1971), and the Nobel Peace Prize (1979). In naming her, the Nobel Committee said: "This year, the world has turned its attention to the plight of children and refugees and these are precisely the categories for whom Mother Teresa has for many years worked so selflessly." At the award ceremony in Oslo, Norway, Chairman John Sanness of the Nobel Committee added: "The hallmark of her work has been the respect for the individual and the individual's worth and dignity. The loneliest and the most wretched, the destitute, the abandoned lepers, have been received by her and her Sisters with warm compassion devoid of condescension, based on their reverence for Christ in man."

Mother Teresa, whose faith and work have touched the lives of millions throughout the world, has written no books. This reading is comprised of excerpts from her addresses and interviews.

QUESTIONS:

1) Why is the vow of poverty important to Mother Teresa's order?
2) What does Mother Teresa mean when she says that money is a means to an end?
3) What sort of people do the Sisters of Charity help in poor countries and rich countries?

Our sisters and brothers live totally committed to the poorest of the poor. We need the vow of poverty because we must understand the poor. In order to understand the poor, we have to know what poverty is. We need to be poor. That is why in our congregation poverty is freedom for us. May it also be our strength and our joy!...

In fact, we have something special in our congregation. We have a fourth vow where we profess to offer wholehearted and free service to the poorest of the poor. We receive freely and we give freely, out of pure love for God. We don't have any income. I sometimes find myself overwhelmed by the amount of things that we receive. Money rather frightens me and it causes me to worry, especially when it comes to us in such large amounts. Still, thanks be to God! In the same way we receive it, we give of it....

I recall, for example, that for the past ten to fifteen years schoolchildren in India have been sending bread to our children in the slums. And English children have been sending milk, while German children have been sending vitamins. The result of all this love in action has been the prevention of epidemics among children in the slums. Thanks to the generosity of other children, we have not had cases of tuberculosis among our children. As you can see, it is not true that we don't need money....

I don't want people donating just to get rid of something. There are people in Calcutta who have so much money that they want to get rid of it. The government puts pressure on the wealthy. They sometimes have money to spare, money that they try to hide. In some cases they make a package, write the name of Mother Teresa on it, and then send it....

I don't like people to send me something because they want to get rid of it. Giving is something different. It is sharing.

Not so long ago a very wealthy Hindu lady came to see me. She sat down and told me. "I would like to share in your work." In India, more and more people like her are offering to help. I said, "That is fine." The poor woman had a weakness that she confessed to me. "I love elegant saris." Indeed, she had on a very expensive sari that probably cost around 800 rupies. Mine cost only eight rupies. Hers cost one hundred times more. Then I asked the Virgin Mary to help me give an adequate answer to her question of how she could share in our work. It occurred to me to say to her, "I would start with the saris. The next time you go buy one, instead of paying 800 rupies, buy one that costs five hundred. Then with the extra 300 rupies, buy saris for the poor."

The good woman now wears 100-rupie saris, and that is because I have asked her not to buy cheaper ones. She has confessed to me that this has changed her life. She now knows what it means to share. That woman assures me that she has received more than what she has given. That is the way it is with our co-workers....

Money is not an end but a means. Without money, for example, it would be impossible for us to feed more than seven thousand people daily in Calcutta. We spend around 20,000 rupies (equivalent to 1,600 U.S. dollars) a week just on food for the fifty-nine centers that we have in Calcutta, including homes for the poor who are dying, abandoned children, the elderly, and lepers. The money comes from sacrifices that people have made....

We need money, medicines, clothing, and a thousand other things for the poor we serve. If so many people weren't generous, thousands would be left unaided. Because we still have many poor, needy children and families that live in the streets--not only in Calcutta but in London, Rotterdam, Madrid, Marseilles, and Rome--the need is great. In the last city I mentioned, we have many needy. The sisters go out at night into the streets, especially around the train station, between 10 P.M. and 2 A.M. to pick up the homeless and take them to the home we have on San Gregorio al Celio.

The last time that I was in Rome, I found it unbearable to see so many homeless people living that way. So I went to see the mayor of Rome and said, "Give me a place for these people, because they refuse to come with us and would rather stay where they are." The man who listened to me was a communist. Everyone knows that the mayor of Rome is a communist. He and his staff responded wonderfully. In a few days they offered us a very nice place near the Termini Train Station. At present, all those who have nowhere else to spend the night, except in the streets, go there and sleep in beds. In the morning they leave....

In Rome alone, we have fifty-nine novices representing eighteen different nationalities. The English, Irish, Spanish, and French nationalities are represented among them. God is always drawing young people to us from all over the world.

There is something wonderful about the idealism and level of commitment among young people. We hand them a sheet of paper on which to answer this question: why do I want to become a Missionary of Charity? They all answer in more or less this way: "I am looking for a life of poverty, prayer, and sacrifice that will lead me to serve the poor." We often think that young people are attracted to a life of action. It may surprise you to know that what really attracts them is a life of poverty. They want only one thing: it is all or nothing with no compromises....

Love, to be real, must hurt. If you want to truly love the poor, you must share with them. If you want poverty to disappear, share it. A gentleman asked me, "What must we do to eliminate poverty from India?" I answered, "We need to learn to share with the poor."

That is what I want to share with you. We cannot share unless our lives are full of God's love and hearts are pure....

We have witnessed God's tender care for us in a thousand ways. In Calcutta alone we care for seven thousand people daily. If one day we don't cook, they don't eat. On Friday morning the sisters in charge of the kitchen came to me and said, "Mother, there is no food for Friday and Saturday. We should tell the people that we will have nothing to give them today or tomorrow." I was shocked. I didn't know what to tell her. But around nine o'clock in the morning, the Indian government for some unknown reason closed the public schools. Then all the bread for the schoolchildren was sent to us. Our children, as well as all our seven thousand needy ones, ate bread and even more bread for two days. They had never eaten so much bread in their lives. No one in Calcutta could find out why the schools had been closed. But I knew. I knew it was God's tender care. I knew it was his tender loving care....

The other day I went to Hyderabad to open a new center. A Hindu gentleman, whom I had never seen before, was waiting for us with a surprise. He had decided to donate his house as a free gift to the sisters. It was a beautiful house with a garden and everything else one could need. He had put it in our name without any strings attached. That is something beautiful that is beginning to happen more and more frequently.

I suppose that you know about Imperial Chemical Industries. They gave us a factory that used to manufacture all kinds of chemical products. I told them that this factory is now going to produce love, chemicals of love to help all sorts of people. And it really is producing love because so many people are becoming committed to serving the poor.

There are young people who come from all over the world to spend two weeks or a month working at the humblest of jobs out of love for others. They pick up all sorts of people off the streets for us, but they do it with a great deal of love. I feel unable to explain adequately what happens to those who lovingly serve the poor and what also happens to the people who are lovingly served. These homes of ours have become homes in which treasures of the kingdom are hidden....

The same hunger exists in India and in Europe, for example. It exists wherever the sisters find Christ under the appearance of suffering. It is possible that in Australia, in Europe, and in the United States, it isn't always hunger for a piece of bread or a garment of clothing. Everywhere there exists that same loneliness, the same deep need to be loved and cared for. Right in your midst there are those who suffer because they do not feel wanted or loved. They experience the anguish of having no one to call their own. This is real poverty without a doubt....

Some weeks ago, our sisters [in London] went out at night ... picking up abandoned people in the streets. Late that night they came across a young man alone in the street. They said to him, "You shouldn't be here. You should be with your parents."

He replied, "When I go home, my mother doesn't want me because I have long hair. Every time I go back, she kicks me out of the house."

Later when the sisters came back that way, they found that the same young man had taken an overdose of something. They had to take him to the hospital. I couldn't help but think that very possibly his mother was concerned about the hunger of our people in India, but here was her own son who was hungry for love and care. Yet she had rejected him....

In Melbourne, Australia, we have a home of compassion. We have people who have no one. We have those who roam the streets, for whom maybe jail and the road are the only places to call home....

We have picked up more than thirty-six thousand people off the streets of Calcutta. We pick them up and take them to our home for the poor who are dying. They die so peacefully. They die serenely in God's presence....

We have thousands of lepers. They are so great, so beautiful inside in spite of their physical disfigurement. Last Christmas I was with them. There are thousands of our lepers, and we always hold a Christmas party for them. I told them at the party that they are a gift from God. God has a special love for them He accepts them. What they have is not a sin. That is what I told them....

Mother Teresa. *One Heart Full of Love*. Ed. Jose Luis Gonzales-Balado. Ann Arbor: Servant Books, 1984. Pp. 36-37, 42-45, 60-64, 74, 97.

ACKNOWLEDGMENTS

A full source citation follows each of the readings included in this book. We thank the following for their permission to use previously published material in the readings indicated:

1.1: Sterling Lord Literistic, Inc. **1.2**: The University of Chicago Press. **1.4**, **1.6**: University of California Press. **1.6**: Cambridge University Press. **1.8**, **2.6**: Princeton University Press. **1.13**: Yale University Press. **1.13**: University of Washington Press. **1.15**: Stanford University Press. **1.16**: American Heritage Magazine, a Division of Forbes Inc. **2.4**: Indological Publishers and Booksellers. **2.6**: Columbia University Press. **3.6, 7.2, 7.7**: Harvard University Press **3.10**: Twayne Publishers, Inc. **3.14**: William Heinemann, Ltd. **3.15**: The Ronald Press Co. **4.3**: University of Oklahoma Press. **4.5**: Journal of English and Germanic Philology. **4.7**: University of Pennsylvania Press **4.13**: Al Saqi Books. **6.3**: Liveright Publishing Corp. **6.6**: Wayne State University Press. **9.11**: Zed Books, Ltd. **9.18**: Madison Books, Lanham, MD. **10.3**: Little, Brown and Co. **10.7**: HarperCollins. **10.8**: The Brookings Institution. **10.10**: The Putnam Publishing Group. **10.11**: Macmillan Publishing Co. **10.12**: Penguin Books. **11.3**: John F. Blair, Publisher, Winston-Salem, NC. **11.12**: William Morrow and Co., Inc. **11.13**: National Archives and Records Administration. **11.14**: University Press of Mississippi. **11.15**: Servant Publishers.

We have made every reasonable effort to identify and acknowledge the copyright owners of materials excerpted in this work. We will be grateful to anyone who can provide additional information about copyright holders and will gladly make whatever further acknowledgments might be necessary.